Driving the Soviets up the Wall

PRINCETON STUDIES IN

INTERNATIONAL HISTORY AND POLITICS

Series Editors
Jack L. Snyder,
Marc Trachtenberg,
and Fareed Zakaria

Recent Titles

Driving the Soviets up the Wall: Soviet–East German Relations, 1953–1961, by Hope M. Harrison

Legitimacy and Power Politics: The American and French Revolutions in International Political Culture, by Mlada Bukovansky

Rhetoric and Reality in Air Warfare: The Evolution of British and American Ideas about Strategic Bombing, 1914–1945, by Tami Davis Biddle

Revolutions in Sovereignty: How Ideas Shaped Modern International Relations, by Daniel Philpott

After Victory: Institutions, Strategic Restraint, and the Rebuilding of Order after Major Wars, by G. John Ikenberry

Stay the Hand of Vengeance: The Politics of War Crimes Tribunals, by Gary Jonathan Bass

War and Punishment: The Causes of War Termination and the First World War, by H. E. Goemans

In the Shadow of the Garrison State: America's Anti-Statism and Its Cold War Grand Strategy, by Aaron L. Friedberg

States and Power in Africa: Comparative Lessons in Authority and Control, by Jeffrey Herbst

The Moral Purpose of the State: Culture, Social Identity, and Institutional Rationality in International Relations, by Christian Reus-Smit

Driving the Soviets up the Wall

SOVIET–EAST GERMAN RELATIONS, 1953–1961

Hope M. Harrison

PRINCETON UNIVERSITY PRESS

PRINCETON AND OXFORD

Third printing, and first paperback printing, 2005
Paperback ISBN-13: 978-0-691-12428-5
Paperback ISBN-10: 0-691-12428-0

THE LIBRARY OF CONGRESS HAS CATALOGED THE CLOTH EDITION OF
THIS BOOK AS FOLLOWS

Harrison, Hope Millard.
    Driving the Soviets up the wall : Soviet–East German relations, 1953–1961 / Hope M.
Harrison.
        p.   cm.—(Princeton studies in international history and politics)
    Includes bibliographical references and index.
    ISBN 0-691-09678-3 (alk. paper)
        1. Germany (East)—Relations—Soviet Union.   2. Soviet Union—Relations—
Germany (East)   I. Title.   II. Series.

DD284.5.S65 H368   2003
327.43'1047'09045—dc21   2002192693

British Library Cataloging-in-Publication Data is available

This book has been composed in Sabon

Printed on acid-free paper. ∞

pup.princeton.edu

Printed in the United States of America

P

To My Parents,
and in Memory of Adam B. Ulam

Contents

List of Maps   ix

Preface   xi

Acknowledgments   xv

Abbreviations   xix

INTRODUCTION
The Dynamics of Soviet–East German Relations
in the Early Cold War   1

CHAPTER ONE
1953: Soviet–East German Relations and Power Struggles
in Moscow and Berlin   12

CHAPTER TWO
1956–1958: Soviet and East German Policy Debates
in the Wake of the Twentieth Party Congress   49

CHAPTER THREE
1958–1960: Khrushchev Takes on the West in the Berlin Crisis   96

CHAPTER FOUR
1960–1961: Ulbricht, Khrushchev, and the Berlin Wall   139

Conclusion   224

Notes   235

Note on Sources   311

Bibliography   315

Index   337

List of Maps

Map 1.   Europe during the Cold War   6
Map 2.   Divided Germany and Berlin with Western
         Access Routes   20
Map 3.   Five Places to Stop the Refugees   183

Preface

ON THE AFTERNOON of 9 November 1989, I boarded a plane on a long-planned journey to West Berlin. I was going with a group of graduate students from Harvard and Stanford for ten days on a program sponsored by the city of West Berlin. In an effort to maintain the U.S. commitment to West Berlin, the city paid for the program every year to bring "up and coming" Americans to West Berlin. At the time, I was a pre-doctoral fellow at the Center for Science and International Affairs at Harvard's Kennedy School of Government. I was working on my dissertation on the building of the Berlin Wall. I wanted to know as much about divided Berlin as possible and was eager for the trip.

Throughout the fall of 1989, East German refugees had been escaping via West German embassies in Prague and Warsaw and across the Hungarian border into Austria. They were all headed to West Germany. Bonn accepted all these refugees as West German citizens entitled to generous social welfare support. In addition, they gave each East German "welcome money" of 100 deutschmarks (worth roughly $55 at the time). Over 50,000 East Germans had fled to West Germany between May and October 1989, and by early November, this had become a crisis for the West German economic and social welfare system. The refugee numbers increased dramatically in early November. In fact, just before I left for West Berlin, 15,000 East Germans fled to West Germany via Czechoslovakia on 4–5 November,[1] and on 7 November, two hundred East Germans left East Germany each hour.[2] The question at the top of my list for all of the West Berlin and West German officials we were going to meet was, "How can you keep this up? What are you going to do about the refugees pouring into your country?"

During the night of Thursday, 9 November, our group flew to Frankfurt. When we boarded the connecting flight to West Berlin on Friday morning, everyone on the plane was reading newspapers with banner headlines declaring, "The Wall Is Open!" I looked around and thought, "Is 10 November the equivalent of April Fool's Day in Germany? What is going on?" I didn't have to wonder for long. The pilot got on the intercom system and announced, "The Wall fell in Berlin last night. We are flying into history."

I could not believe my luck at being in Berlin for this historic occasion, all the more so because of my dissertation topic. My parents, with whom I had spoken many times about the dissertation, were beside themselves with excitement at my timing. *Ich war dabei!* (*I was there!* as all the quickly manufactured T-shirts and mugs said.)

Euphoria is the only word to describe the mood on the streets of Berlin. People were selling champagne on street corners. On the afternoon of 10 November, in a jet-lagged, yet ebullient state, several of us went to Kennedy Platz (the site of Kennedy's 1963 *Ich bin ein Berliner* speech), in front of the West Berlin City Hall, Rathaus Schöneberg, to hear the West German leaders speak about the momentous opening of the Wall. Chancellor Helmut Kohl had flown back hurriedly from Warsaw that morning along with Foreign Minister Hans-Dietrich Genscher. The West Berlin mayor, Walter Momper, was also on the podium. The most popular speaker of the day, though, was Willy Brandt, who had been the mayor of West Berlin when the Wall went up in 1961 and had gone on to become the West German chancellor.[3] As a historian and as a human being, it was extraordinary to be part of the celebration at Rathaus Schöneberg—to actually be there and feel the emotion of the day, not just read about it in history books.

Back at the hotel for dinner, I befriended one of the West Berlin English teachers hosting us, Claudia Wilhelm. Claudia volunteered to drive me around in her VW Bug the next day. Claudia was and is a Berliner. She was born in the East and fled with her family to the West in 1958. When the Wall came down, she was reunited with family in the East, including some she had not even known about.

Saturday morning, 11 November, Claudia picked me up and drove me to see the celebrations at the Brandenburg Gate and the opening of the Glienecker Brücke, the famous "spy bridge" connecting West Berlin and Potsdam, East Germany. In 1962 the American U-2 pilot Francis Gary Powers had been traded for the Soviet spy Rudolf Abel in the middle of the bridge. Claudia and I stood amid crowds of cheering West Berliners as East Germans walked across the bridge and into the beautiful Grunewald section of West Berlin with its forests and lakes. People cheered. People cried. We took pictures. It was incredible.

The next morning, we drove to Potsdamer Platz, the historic center of Berlin and site of Europe's first traffic light in 1924. With the building of the Berlin Wall through the center of Potsdamer Platz, it became a barren, terrifying no-man's land of layers of wall, minefields, guard towers, anti-tank barricades, guard dogs, and guards with a shoot-to-kill order. But on this spectacular Sunday morning, we watched a bulldozer lift up and remove a section of the Wall at Potsdamer Platz. Then we stood with the thousands of people who parted to form a corridor through which East Berliners could walk or drive into West Berlin. It was the most moving experience of my ten days in Berlin. I remember watching one young couple drive through in their green Trabant, or Trabi (the tiny, cardboard-like, exhaust-emitting, popular East German car). They were alternately laughing and crying, and people were reaching through their open car windows to hand the couple money and champagne. The hood of their car was covered with red and white carnations. We were all filled with emotion.

All weekend long, it was impossible to drive a car on the main street of West Berlin, the Kürfurstendamm, due to the tens of thousands of East Berliners and East Germans strolling up and down it to get a look at West Berlin's Fifth Avenue. We wanted to take the subway to East Berlin, but it was out of the question to even enter a subway station due to the thousands of people coming in from East Berlin. Monday morning's West Berlin tabloid, *Bild*, had huge headlines in black, red, and gold, the colors of the German flag saying, "*Guten Morgen, Deutschland. Es war ein schönes Wochenende.*" "Good Morning, Germany. It was a beautiful weekend." It certainly was.

People were hammering away at the wall to take home pieces as souvenirs. In the early days, there were pieces everywhere on the ground. As Claudia and I picked up a few, I thought to myself, "Now, who is going to want to read a book about the sad story of building the Wall, when they can read an uplifting book about the fall of the Wall?"

But I also more optimistically thought, "Maybe it will be possible to tell a more complete story of how the Wall went up now that it has come down." Sure enough, once Germany united a year later and the Soviet Union collapsed in 1991, the archival doors swung open in Berlin and Moscow. This allowed me, and others, to piece together a much more complete picture of the East German and Soviet decision-making process leading to the building of the Berlin Wall in 1961. Less than a year after German unification, in the fall of 1991, I began my work in the archives.

Developments since unification have added to the importance of understanding the decision to build the Wall and the impact it had. People lost their lives trying to escape over or under the Wall. They were shot by East German border guards. The whole border system surrounding the Wall was not just something that sat passively while people stared at it in defiance. It encompassed an entire lethal response system that was activated when someone tried to cross the border without permission. Human beings were responsible for killing other human beings, Germans for killing Germans.

The "Wall trials" since unification have attempted to assign culpability for this deadly border system to the high-level East German policy makers and the border guards who implemented their superiors' directives. Some of the accused and convicted, such as former East German leader Egon Krenz, have tried to deflect the blame for the Wall and all it entailed onto the Soviets and the "cold war." The evidence presented in this book, however, demonstrates the critical responsibility of the East German leaders themselves for the building of the Berlin Wall and all that went with it.

Peter Schneider presciently forecast in his 1982 book, *Der Mauerspringer (The Wall Jumper)*, "It will take us longer to tear down the Wall in our heads than any wrecking company will need for the Wall we can see."[4] Even more than most people realized until the Wall came down, it really mattered on which side of the Wall you lived your life—the communist east or the capitalist, democratic west. Since German unification, the *Mauer im Kopf* ("the wall in the mind") has continued to divide east and west Germans.[5] The euphoria I witnessed in November 1989 faded away within months as resentments built up on both sides. The west Germans resented all the money it took to rebuild the shattered east; and the east Germans resented being "taken over," "colonized" by the west with all of the East German traditions they had developed over forty years summarily dumped on the ash heap of history along with the ubiquitous statues of Lenin. Divided by the Wall, the distance between the East and West Germans expanded. It turned out to be not so easy to bridge just by tearing down the Wall and letting East Germans drive through in their Trabis. But the next generation of Germans will surely bridge this distance.

On my final morning in Berlin in November 1989, Claudia drove me to the airport as the snow fell on pre-dawn Berlin. People were in their homes asleep after another night of celebrating the Wall's opening. As we drove through the deserted streets, past Schloss Charlottenburg, I knew that I would return many times to uncover the history of the Berlin Wall. I, too, had become a Berliner.

Acknowledgments

I AM GRATEFUL to the institutions and colleagues who have helped me over the years of work on this book. I want to thank the institutions who have generously supported my research and writing: the Harriman Institute of Columbia University, the Nuclear History Program, Harvard's Belfer Center for Science and International Affairs, the Social Science Research Council's Berlin Program for Advanced German and European Studies at the Free University of Berlin, Harvard's Davis Center, Lafayette College, the Kennan Institute, the Cold War International History Project, and the Norwegian Nobel Institute. I also benefited greatly from interacting with my colleagues at these institutions.

Since most of the key sources I used for this book were archival documents in Moscow and Berlin, I am happy to take this opportunity to thank the archivists and administrative staff who helped me: in Berlin, Herr Lange, Frau Gräfe, Frau Pardon, and Frau Rauber at SAPMO-Bundesarchiv; Herr Geyer at the (East German) Foreign Ministry archive; and Herr Förster and Frau Tschuck at the Stasi archive; in Moscow, Dr. Lebedev, Dr. Stegny, and the many archivists at the Foreign Ministry Archive; and Zoia Vodopianova, Vladimir Chernous, Yuri Malov, Rem Ussikov, Anatolii Prokopenko, and Natalia Tomilina at the post-1953 Central Committee Archive, now called the Russian State Archive of Contemporary History. Sven Holtsmark was very helpful in deciphering the filing methods of the Russian Foreign Ministry archive for me. I am grateful for the research help of Anne Kjelling and Bjørn Feen at the library of the Norwegian Nobel Institute. Olga Khomenko, Paul du Quenoy, and Justin Gibbons have been valuable research assistants at different stages of the work on this book, and Jeremy Kahn gave me helpful computer assistance with the manuscript. I was lucky to be able to supplement my archival work with interviews with former Soviet and East German officials. I want to particularly thank Karl Schirdewan (who has since passed away) and his wife Giesela, as well as Horst Brie in Berlin and Yuli Kvitsinky in Moscow for their openness.

My dear friends in Moscow and Berlin have been tremendously generous with their time and apartment space. And they made my research trips very special. Warm thanks to Lena Sorokoletovskikh and Yura

Bloshkin in Moscow; Alla Zbinovsky and Andy Braddel, formerly in Moscow, now in London; and Claudia Wilhelm, Beate Ihme-Tuchel, Johannes Tuchel, Lothar Wilker, Angelika Straub, and Hans-Hermann Hertle in Berlin. Claudia especially has been limitless in her hospitality and friendship. Thanks also to Ambassador Nikolai Gribkov in Moscow.

Several colleagues have read all or part of this work and offered valuable advice. The final product is my responsibility alone, but it has been much improved by their help. In particular, Christian Ostermann and Melvyn Leffler each read the entire manuscript at crucial points. Christian and I spent the summer of 2000 pouring over the manuscript and having very stimulating discussions about every part of it. Christian helped me think through many crucial points. I cannot thank him enough for his careful attention to my manuscript, his lively conversation, and his friendship. Mel read the manuscript in the winter of 2001–2002. He gave an extremely generous amount of his time to editing the manuscript and pressing me on key questions. His comments, advice, and encouragement were invaluable in the final stage of my work.

I appreciate the enthusiasm Jim Hershberg has shown for this project from the start and his suggestions. I also want to thank Jeff Kopstein and an anonymous reviewer for Princeton University Press for their very helpful comments. Jack Snyder, Robert Legvold, Robert Jervis, Mark von Hagen, Marc Trachtenberg, Tom Christensen, Kim Zisk, Bill Burr, John Lewis Gaddis, Tim Naftali, Geir Lundestad, and Jim Goldgeier all read parts of the manuscript in earlier stages and provided constructive comments. I also had useful discussions with many other colleagues and have benefited from their work: Hannes Adomeit, Günter Bishof, Tom Blanton, Tim Colton, Frank Costigliola, Greg Domber, Alexei Filitov, John Gearson, Beate Ihme-Tuchel, Mark Kramer, Haejong Lee, Michael Lemke, Gerry Livingston, Vojtech Mastny, Ernest May, Jim McAdams, David Murphy, Olav Njølstad, Leopoldo Nuti, Arnie Offner, Sue Peterson, Blair Ruble, Kori Schake, Doug Selvage, Dick Smyser, William Taubman, Oldrich Tuma, Matthias Uhl, Adam Ulam, Ruud van Dijk, Armin Wagner, Kathryn Weathersby, Odd Arne Westad, Gerhard Wettig, and Vlad Zubok. I am particularly grateful to Armin Wagner and Matthias Uhl, who responded from Berlin so quickly, helpfully, and thoroughly to my detailed e-mail questions in the final stage of my work on this book. A timely conversation on an airplane with Ken Reger persuaded me to add the preface.

I want to thank Lew Bateman and John Lewis Gaddis for their early support for the publication of this work. It was Marc Trachtenberg's introduction to *History and Strategy* in 1991 that sold me on the Princeton Studies in International History and Politics series. Marc made it clear that his work was at the intersection of history and political science and that scholars in the two fields had much to gain by sharing insights. I wholeheartedly agree with Marc and hope that historians and political scientists will find value in this book.

I am glad that my colleagues at the history department and the Elliott School of International Affairs at The George Washington University decided to take the risk of hiring a former political scientist and have given me a wonderful academic home. In particular, I want to thank Ron Spector, Ed Berkowitz, and Harry Harding. Ed came up with the idea for the title of this book at my job talk at George Washington. I also want to thank my dear friend Lil Fenn, formerly of George Washington's history department and now at Duke University, who made the maps for this book. The unique geography of divided Berlin and divided Germany is essential to the story here, and Lil graciously offered to portray this with maps. I am very grateful to all the people who helped me at Princeton University Press—Chuck Myers, Kevin McInturff, Gail Schmitt, Leslie Flis, Marsha Kunin, and Maria denBoer.

Loving support of friends and family is essential in my life and has sustained me over the years of writing this book. Thanks to Devin Reese, Hal Cardwell and Camilla Cardwell, Mei Zhu, Lily Marshall, Anna Kyznetsova, Rob Litwak, George Liston Seay, and to my grandmother and my aunt Mary. I am also grateful to Ray Marvin and David Longo for their special help and to my neighbor Rosemary Normand. Kevin Carroll is an angel in my life. No words can adequately express his profound influence on my life. But he knows.

I am so lucky to have my oldest and dearest friend, Beth Onufrak, in my life. She is a great source of support and happiness. Beth has cheerfully endured countless phone calls talking about Khrushchev and Ulbricht. And she is a pediatric psychologist, not a historian! We have shared many things.

I am blessed to have four wonderful parents: my mother, my father, my stepmother, and my stepfather. My stepmother, Linda Harrison, was my high school history teacher and has been a great friend and inspiration. My stepfather, Joseph Blaney, shares an interest and expertise in history with me. He has been a great support to me for over twenty years, and he and my mother (and their cat, Butterfly) graciously hosted me for a month in their home at the final stage of my work on this book. Butterfly was a great help, except when she sat on the manuscript.

I feel infinite gratitude for all my mother, Dorothy G. Blaney, and my father, Robert L. Harrison, have given me. I have inherited my father's patience and attention to detail, without which I could have never written this book. I cherish our special trips to Berlin together. My mother's love and support for me in everything, including completing this book, have been boundless. She is the rock in my life and the very definition of a mother. We have discussed most of this book, and she has read and commented on portions of it.

This book is dedicated to my parents and to the memory of Adam B. Ulam. It was Adam's examination of the Berlin Crisis—in an undergraduate class I took with him at Harvard, and in his seminal work, *Expansion and Coexistence*—that piqued my curiosity to know more. A professor can give no greater gift to a student.

Abbreviations

APRF	Archive of the President of the Russian Federation
AVPRF	Archive of the Foreign Policy of the Russian Federation
BStU	Federal Commission for Stasi Files
CDU	Christian Democratic Party
CFM	Conference of Foreign Ministers (of the Four Powers—the United States, Soviet Union, Great Britain, and France)
CM	Council of Ministers
CPSU	Communist Party of the Soviet Union
CWIHP	Cold War International History Project
FRG	Federal Republic of Germany (West Germany)
GDR	German Democratic Republic (East Germany)
GSFG	Group of Soviet Forces in Germany
GPO	Government Printing Office (U.S.)
KGB	Committee of State Security (Soviet secret police)
KPD	Communist Party of Germany
MfAA	Ministry of Foreign Affairs
MfS	Ministry for State Security (the Stasi)
MID	Ministry of Foreign Affairs
MVD	Ministry of Internal Affairs
PB	Politburo
PRC	People's Republic of China
RGANI	Rossiiskii Gosudarstvennyi Arkhiv Noveishei Istorii, Russian State Archive of Contemporary History
SAPMO-BArch, ZPA	Foundation of Archives of the Parties and Mass Organizations of the former East Germany, Federal Archive, Central Party Archive
SBZ	Soviet Zone of Occupation

SED	Socialist Unity Party of [East] Germany
SPD	Social Democratic Party of Germany
SKK	Soviet Control Commission
Stasi	State Security Service (East German secret police, MfS)
TsKhSD	Center for the Preservation of Contemporary Documentation (Archive of the Post-1953 Soviet Central Committee, now called the Russian State Archive of Contemporary History, RGANI)
WTO	Warsaw Treaty Organization (also known as the Warsaw Pact)
ZAIG	Stasi's Central Analysis and Information Group

Driving the Soviets up the Wall

The Dynamics of Soviet–East German Relations in the Early Cold War

THE TWO STATES that emerged from the defeated Germany were central to the development of the cold war. Rapidly evolving from defeated objects of Four Power policy, the two Germanys became important actors in their own right on the front line of the cold war. Both superpowers initially treated their part of Germany as war booty to be plundered and kept weak, but as the cold war developed, they would each come to see their part of Germany as an essential ally whose needs were intertwined with their own. For political, military, economic, and ideological reasons, the superpowers engaged in a competition for allies to show that their side of the cold war was the stronger, more popular, more vibrant one. They also wanted to ensure that their German ally would not unite with the other against them. Beginning in the 1950s, the superpowers invested themselves, and their reputations, increasingly in their German allies, who were adept at taking advantage of this situation.

While there have been a variety of in-depth studies of the U.S.–West German alliance,[1] there has been much less investigation of the Soviet–East German alliance.[2] This book will take advantage of the opening of former communist archives to examine the Soviet–East German side of the cold war from Josef Stalin's death in 1953 through the building of the Berlin Wall in 1961. After the profound Soviet losses of World War II, the Kremlin leaders' prime motive initially was to make sure Germany could not rise up and threaten them again. It took longer for the Soviets than for the Western Powers to shift their policy from destruction and retribution in Germany to construction and support of an ally. It was a big leap from Stalin's sanction of the raping and pillaging of the Soviet Zone of Germany[3] in the mid- to late 1940s to Soviet leader Nikita S. Khrushchev's declaration to the East Germans that "your needs are our needs" in the 1950s.[4] This book tells the story of Khrushchev's increasing commitment to a strong, socialist state in East Germany and the ways the persistent East German leader Walter Ulbricht was able to use this commitment to his advantage. It is the story of East Germany transforming its weakness into strength in its relations with the Soviet Union and the story of the East Germans' capacity to resist Soviet directives. This book will demonstrate that Soviet–East German relations from 1953–1961, particularly concerning the divided city of

Berlin, cannot be understood without studying the actions and aims of both the Kremlin and East Berlin.

An appreciation of the importance of nonsuperpower actors in the cold war is one of the primary lessons scholars have gleaned from the former Soviet bloc's new archival evidence. In response, the political scientist Tony Smith has called for a pericentric study of the cold war,[5] and the historian James G. Hershberg has urged a "retroactive debipolarization" of cold war history.[6] Both scholars point to the opportunity and need to supplement previous studies focusing on the role of the superpowers with studies that examine the contributions of other states to the dynamics and key events of the cold war. Allies mattered in the cold war both because of the importance vested in them by the superpowers and because of actions they took at times independent of their superpower patrons, especially actions that exacerbated superpower relations or dragged more powerful superpower patrons into situations and commitments they otherwise would not have chosen.[7] Only by including the actions and perceptions of key allies, such as England, France, the two Germanys, the two Koreas, the two Chinas, and the two Vietnams, in the history of the cold war can we arrive at a more nuanced and comprehensive analysis of some of the pivotal events and dynamics of that period. The roles of the two superpowers must be combined with those of important allies.

The present book is an effort to do this. This book will illustrate that the Soviet–East German relationship was more two-sided than previously understood, that in some important ways a mutual dependency existed that mattered for the evolution of the cold war. As Abraham Ben-Zvi postulates in studying U.S.-Israeli relations, "the core of numerous patron-client [relationships] is seldom characterized by pure dependence, but rather by what [Klaus] Knorr calls 'asymmetrical interdependence.'"[8] The concept of interdependence in superpower-ally relations has been well developed on the Western side of the cold war, revealing the influence of America's allies on the cold war—as persuasive allies and independent actors whose views and actions mattered to the United States for a variety of reasons. This body of literature demonstrates that it was not just U.S. preferences that were expressed in relations with its allies; the perceptions and aims of the allies were also important factors influencing U.S. policy. For example, the British played a crucial role in prodding the Americans to respond to the Soviet threat by establishing the Marshall Plan, a West German state, and NATO;[9] and the West European "invitation" for a postwar American presence was an essential part of U.S. decision making.[10] Outside of Europe, Pakistan, Taiwan, and Israel all pulled the Americans in as much as possible to assist them against their regional rivals.[11] The United States often found that its actions in these regions were guided more by the concerns of its local ally than by U.S. global strategy.[12]

American allies did not exert their influence just by being persuasive in interactions with the United States; they also at times went outside of those interactions to act independently. Thus, President Truman found that he could not control the actions of South Korean President Syngman Rhee in the armistice talks ending the Korean War;[13] and the British and French launched the Suez Crisis of 1956 without consulting with the United States.[14] Similarly, try though he did to persuade West German Chancellor Konrad Adenauer to be more flexible in handling the Berlin Crisis in the late 1950s, President Eisenhower frequently complained that Adenauer's differing views seriously constrained American options in the crisis.[15]

Scholars of the Western side of the cold war have assumed that their findings of complicated, two-sided alliance relations only applied to the West.[16] This is partly because they believed that the openness of the American democratic system to lobbying was a significant part of the reason allies were able to gain influence over American policy.[17] Thomas Risse-Kappen has argued that democratic norms and institutions enabled and even promoted "the European influence on U.S. foreign policy."[18] Given the lack of democracy in the Soviet Union and Soviet bloc, combined with the Western cold war image of the Kremlin as an autocratic master of the Warsaw Pact, most scholars have concluded that, with the exception of China, Moscow did not have to deal with troublesome allies who complicated its foreign policy making.

The treasure trove of documents made accessible since 1991, however, makes it clear that Moscow also had alliance concerns and that Soviet alliances were not as one-sided as previously surmised. This book will show that there was an important degree of mutual dependency between the Soviet Union and the German Democratic Republic (GDR). The same basic phenomenon accounts for both U.S. and Soviet vulnerabilities to alliance pressures during the cold war: the competition for allies.

As the cold war burgeoned in the 1950s, Moscow and Washington felt they needed allies not only for practical military and economic reasons, but also for reasons more connected with their reputation as leader of one of two opposing blocs. Both sides believed in the domino theory: that gaining or losing an ally would have a multiplier effect. On the Soviet side, this concern was exacerbated starting in the late 1950s when they had to worry not only about the challenge to their allies from the United States, but also from Mao's China. In Germany, Korea, Cuba, and elsewhere, the superpowers believed that if they did not defend their interests strongly, they would have no credibility as a reliable ally. As John Lewis Gaddis observes, however, "Credibility is . . . a state of mind, not an objective, independently measurable reality. [C]redibility can hardly be on the line until one has chosen to put it there. For whatever reason, the Cold War encouraged a curious fecklessness on the part of the superpowers when it came to how and where they risked their reputations. Berlin was the most dramatic example, but hardly the only one."[19]

Just as John F. Kennedy told the West Berliners in 1963, "*Ich bin ein Berliner*," so Khrushchev equated Soviet needs with those of his German ally. This book sets out to investigate both sides of the Soviet–East German relationship: how and why the Soviets saw the GDR as a crucial domino and how the East Germans responded to this. We will examine both the constraints on Soviet policy in affecting events in the GDR and the ways in which the East Germans resisted or influenced Soviet policies.[20]

Regarding relations between the Soviets and their allies, Kathryn Weathersby has argued that it is only by examining "the intersection of Moscow's and Pyongyang's aims" that one can understand what "produced the [Korean] war in June 1950";[21] and Norman Naimark has asserted that "[t]he GDR . . . was created primarily out of the interaction of Russians and Germans in the Soviet occupied zone."[22] Similarly, I will demonstrate that it is only by taking into account both the actions, urgings, and proddings of Ulbricht, and the calculations of Khrushchev, as well as the broader East-West interactions, that one can understand the climactic event of this book, the building of the Berlin Wall and the crisis surrounding it.

There are a variety of factors that can explain the influence of a smaller ally on a great power, the influence of the Kremlin's German ally on Soviet policy and on conditions in the GDR. As in any relationship between an empire's core and its periphery, the geographic distance yields significant control over local conditions to the local power. This can create a gap between the superpower's policy preferences and the actual local implementation of policy. The capacity of the local power to affect local conditions, and the implementation or nonimplementation of the superpower's declared policies, gives it the capacity to constrain these policies.[23] In spite of all the Soviet troops and advisors in the GDR, Moscow was still not able always to enforce its policies and prevent the East Germans from acting independently. The roughly 500,000 Soviet troops in the GDR may have deterred the population from repeating the uprising of 1953, but they were not able to control the actions of the East German leaders.[24] The Soviet forces could determine or protect the ultimate "fate" of the socialist regime in the GDR but could not regulate its daily "behavior."[25] Thus, through its impact on day-to-day local conditions, the smaller ally may limit the superpower's real long-term policy options.

Strategic location is central to the influence of an ally. If the country is located, for example, at the border between two military alliances, as was the case with the GDR, this gives the superpower a great stake in protecting and strengthening the ally, because the ally is a crucial part of the superpower's buffer zone. The ally is of course perfectly well aware of this situation and may be able to use it to its own advantage. It can do this by persuading the superpower that the local ally needs certain things like increased economic and military aid (or a border closure) if it is going to be able to maintain its position as a bulwark against the other bloc. Thus, while the ally is clearly dependent on the superpower for its protection in its vulnerable location on the edge of the bloc, the superpower also feels some dependence on the ally to preserve this position as bulwark or buffer.[26]

The ally may play more than just a military-strategic role for the superpower; it may have a more symbolic function, such as serving as a model for the system of its superpower patron. As Khrushchev recounted in his memoirs, he sought to use their front-line location to make the GDR and East Berlin into a "showcase of the moral, political and material achievement" of socialism for capitalists to see and so be persuaded of the superiority of socialism.[27] Khrushchev's energetic faith in the preeminence of the communist system and his determination to demonstrate this in Germany gave the GDR a means to pressure him for increased support.[28] Khrushchev testified to the importance of a strong, socialist East Germany for the Soviet Union by telling Ulbricht, "your needs are our needs." Ulbricht treated this as an invitation to elicit a Soviet response to East German "needs" even if they sometimes conflicted with broader Soviet "needs." As John Lewis Gaddis points out, the two superpowers "attached their own reputations to their respective clients . . . [and] fell into the habit of letting their German allies determine their German interests, and hence their German policies."[29]

This situation provided the GDR with opportunities to convert its weaknesses into strength in bargaining with or manipulating the Soviet Union. The lack of popular support for the East German socialist government was manifested in the hundreds of thousands of refugees who fled to the Federal Republic of Germany (FRG) each year. The leaders of East Germany's Socialist Unity Party (SED) could, with justification, use the threat of the regime's collapse to obtain more aid from Moscow.[30] In addition, as the weaker power, East Germany had more to lose, more at stake if it collapsed than the Soviet Union did and thus was more motivated and persistent in the pursuit of its narrow goals. This translated into increased bargaining strength.[31]

Glenn Snyder's concept of the "alliance security dilemma" offers a useful lens through which to view the Soviet–East German relationship, although he does not apply the concept to the Soviet side of the cold war and focuses primarily on periods of multipolarity instead of bipolar-

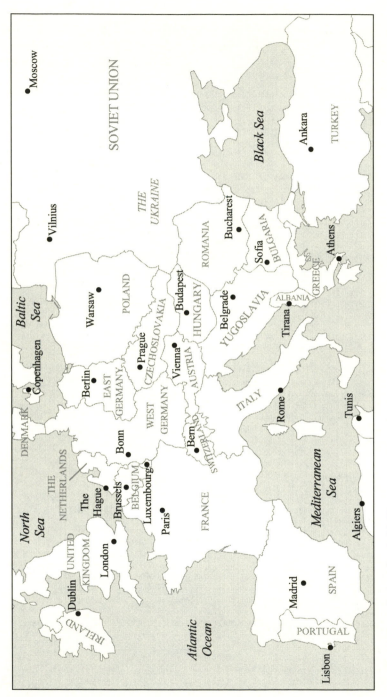

Map 1. Europe during the Cold War

ity. Snyder postulates that in an alliance, each side must find the right balance between two tendencies toward more or less active support of the other ally. On the one hand, if one ally strongly supports the other, it can risk being manipulated, or "entrapped" in Snyder's words, by that ally into adopting policies the first ally does not really support. On the other hand, if the first ally is stinting in backing the other ally, it can risk "abandonment" by the latter for a stronger supporter.[32] This entrapment-abandonment dilemma also exists in the complicated dynamics of alliance politics between a superpower and a key ally.

In the Soviet–East German case, the SED's abandonment and entrapment concerns were very similar. On the one hand, they feared the Soviets would abandon the GDR to German unification on Western terms. On the other hand, they feared being forced or entrapped by the Soviets into more liberal policies than they favored domestically and in foreign policy, which in turn might facilitate German unification on Western terms or at least the SED hard-liners' own overthrow by domestic opponents. The East German side, their fears, and their dependence on the alliance, however, have long been taken for granted and identified. It is the Soviet side that makes the story more interesting and that in fact opened up the opportunity for the East Germans to wag their tail as an ally.

The Soviets had two worries concerning East German abandonment, fears that the East Germans manipulated to serve their own interests. On the one hand, the Soviets worried that the East German regime would involuntarily abandon the alliance by collapsing and being absorbed into West Germany. This concern was made realistic by the East German popular uprising of 1953 and by the refugee exodus throughout the 1950s, which was stopped only by the building of the Berlin Wall in 1961. The other more subtle, yet mounting worry after the beginning of the Sino-Soviet rift in the mid-1950s was that the GDR regime would move closer to the Chinese. Given that the Soviets had strong security and reputational reasons for their tight connection with the East Germans, they needed to find ways to guard against the chances of these two kinds of East German abandonment. Just as Presidents Eisenhower and Kennedy perceived West Berlin and West Germany as a "superdomino," so I would like to suggest that Khrushchev treated East Germany as a "super-ally," an ally of the greatest importance to Soviet security and prestige, the loss of which was to be avoided at all costs.[33]

The extent of a small ally's bargaining power is revealed when there are policy disagreements with the superpower. There was growing discord between Ulbricht and Khrushchev from 1953 through 1961 and particularly during the Berlin Crisis. While they shared many goals, they had important differences over the relative importance of different goals and what they were willing to risk to achieve them. As this book will illustrate, Ulbricht and Khrushchev disagreed over their favored domestic and foreign policies for the GDR, how to handle the refugee exodus, the future of West Berlin, whether or not to sign a separate peace treaty, the importance of Western recognition of the GDR, the level of economic aid the Soviet Union and other socialist countries should give to the GDR, the degree of sovereignty the GDR should have, including over the access routes between the FRG and West Berlin, and the level of risk regarding confrontation with the West each was willing to adopt to achieve their ends. Differences over goals, and methods to achieve these goals, were accentuated during the Berlin Crisis, which developed into a crisis in East German–Soviet relations as much as an East-West crisis.

A superpower necessarily has broader interests and concerns than its smaller ally, especially during a crisis surrounding the status of the ally. As the crisis of the GDR regime's legitimacy mushroomed from 1953 through 1961, the East German leaders operated from an increasingly narrow and urgent frame of reference and accordingly were willing to risk more to resolve the crisis than the Soviets were.

The Soviets were under mounting pressure of their own in this period as their rift with the People's Republic of China (PRC) deepened in the late 1950s.[34] The new archival evidence indicates that the role of China and the Sino-Soviet split influenced the cold war much more than previously thought. It was a significant factor in Soviet policy in the Korean War,[35] the Berlin Crisis,[36] the Cuban Missile Crisis,[37] and the Vietnam War.[38] The Cubans, the East Germans, and the North Vietnamese, among others, sought to use the Sino-Soviet rift to their advantage, and in each case, doing so intensified the cold war.

This book examines three crucial periods in Soviet–East German relations: the six months after Stalin's death in 1953, the two years following Khrushchev's pathbreaking address to the Twentieth Congress of the Communist Party of the Soviet Union (CPSU), and the three years of the Berlin Crisis. In each period, the Soviets consciously sought to pull Ulbricht back from his hard-line domestic and foreign policies to stem the refugee exodus, stabilize the country, and improve relations with the West. To their frustration and sometimes great concern, the Soviets were not able to impose their will on the East Germans. Khrushchev wanted the GDR regime to achieve stability by virtue of its viability and legitimacy as opposed solely to the control exercised by the Soviet military presence there or by Ulbricht's "administrative measures." Yet Ulbricht's method of rule was by control, unassailable control, which he maintained was the only way given the existence of the "aggressive, revanchist, imperialistic" FRG next door. Ulbricht feared that any loosening of his tight grip on power would lead to the GDR's collapse as well as to the collapse of his own personal power, perhaps his primary concern.

To a large degree, the policies carried out in the GDR and East Berlin were formulated by the East Germans, not the Soviets, and were often implemented against Soviet wishes. The effect of these GDR hard-line policies was to deepen the division of Germany and thus intensify the cold war in Europe. Ulbricht finally put the Kremlin leaders in a position where their only realistic option to preserve a stable socialist regime in the GDR was to agree to his request to close off access to West Berlin. This outcome can only be understood by studying developments in Soviet–East German relations and in GDR policies, together with Western policies, in the years leading up to the building of the Berlin Wall.

We shall see in the portrayal of Ulbricht's background, personality, and policies, presented in chapter 1, that his tenacious, arrogant, and opportunistic personality contributed significantly to the GDR's capacity to sway the Soviets. He had the skill and audacity to convert the environmental factors conducive to the GDR's status as a key Soviet ally into influence over Soviet policy. The first two chapters of this book highlight Ulbricht's capacity to resist Soviet calls for moderation of his domestic and foreign policies and Soviet incapacity or unwillingess to insist. By the fourth chapter, the focus shifts to Ulbricht's more active efforts to change Soviet policies regarding Berlin.

After Stalin's death, his successors sought to lessen cold war tensions and alleviate the effects of Stalinism in Eastern Europe and at home. In early June 1953, the new Soviet leaders instructed the East Germans to introduce the *New Course* of liberalization of domestic and foreign policies. The combination of Ulbricht's resistance to the *New Course*, the 17 June uprising in the GDR, and the aftermath of secret police chief Lavrenty Beria's ouster led Stalin's successors to backtrack on the *New Course* in the GDR and to reverse their support for Ulbricht's more open-minded opponents. This is the subject of chapter 1.

Again in 1956, Khrushchev made efforts to diminish cold war tensions and dismantle Stalinism. Following his de-Stalinization speech at the Twentieth Congress and his support for "peaceful coexistence" and "separate paths to socialism," Khrushchev also sided with the opposition to Ulbricht that favored Khrushchev's more liberal approach in both domestic and foreign policy. Yet Ulbricht again prevailed in preventing more liberal policies from being carried out consistently and thoroughly in the GDR against the backdrop of the Soviet invasion of Hungary and was ultimately able to get Soviet support for ousting his more liberal opponents. Chapter 2 examines these developments.

In the 1958–61 Berlin Crisis, Khrushchev attempted to persuade (or coerce) the West to sign a German peace treaty and transform West

Berlin into a demilitarized "free city" in order to relieve pressure on the GDR. Although he threatened unilateral action, his goal was to achieve the stabilization of the GDR by international agreement and not by unilateral action. Ulbricht, however, favored unilateral, as opposed to multilateral means of resolving the GDR's problems, especially the refugee exodus. He doubted the West would make sufficient concessions and did not trust Khrushchev in negotiations with the West. Ulbricht's actions, combined with Western unwillingness to give in to Khrushchev's demands and Chinese pressure on Khrushchev to adopt a harder stance with the West, led to Khrushchev's reluctant agreement to build the Berlin Wall, something the Soviets had been trying to avoid since 1952. This is the subject of chapters 3 and 4.

I will not argue that East German influence was the only important influence on Soviet *Deutschlandpolitik* (policy concerning Germany) between 1953 and 1961. Based on my earlier writings, some readers have come to the erroneous conclusion that this is my belief. Of course, Soviet domestic politics, Western policy, and Chinese policy were also important in influencing Soviet foreign policy in this period. What I will argue is that the East German factor was much more important than previously recognized and indeed is an essential part of the story. The East Germans, through their own policies, narrowed Soviet options and also took advantage of tensions in U.S.-Soviet and Sino-Soviet relations, as well as tensions within the Soviet leadership. But the process of Khrushchev moving toward a decision to close the Berlin border concerned Soviet goals, East German goals and actions, as well as the policies of the West and of China. It was a complicated story with many actors, not just Ulbricht, as this book will illustrate. Nonetheless, Ulbricht was a central actor.

The opportunity to conduct research for this book was revolutionized with the end of the cold war by the opening of archives in the former communist bloc. After years of being forced to rely almost solely on Western sources and published communist sources such as newspapers,[39] since 1989–91, cold war historians have been able to examine stacks and stacks of documents from former communist regimes, including the Soviet Union and the GDR. Access to these documents, as well as the opportunity to interview former communist officials, is allowing a whole new generation of cold war historians to expand on and rewrite the history of the cold war from a broader, international, multi-archival, interdisciplinary perspective.[40] This book is part of what is called "the new cold war history."[41] The "Note on Sources" describes the East German and Russian archival and other sources that constitute the evidentiary foundation of the book.

By drawing on an extensive archival base as well as interviews, memoirs, journal articles, and other primary and secondary sources, I hope to present the reader with the most comprehensive account to date on the nature of Soviet–East German relations in this period, including the process leading to the building of the Berlin Wall. My aim is to fill in much of the missing historical detail on this period, presenting sharper portrayals of both Nikita Khrushchev and Walter Ulbricht, and to provide the reader with a new lens through which to interpret these details. I will also address the broader implications for cold war history of the dynamics of Soviet–East German relations described in this book. In addition to the traditional focus on security issues, this book will illustrate the importance of personality, ideology, reputation, and economics during the cold war.

CHAPTER ONE

1953

Soviet–East German Relations and Power Struggles in Moscow and Berlin

OUR STORY BEGINS with the pivotal six months from Stalin's death in March to the East German leaders' official visit to Moscow in August 1953. The developments in these months in Soviet policy vis-à-vis the GDR and in East German and Soviet domestic politics set the stage for much of the remainder of the GDR's existence. This chapter will introduce the key dynamics and issues in Soviet–East German relations to be examined in this book: (1) Soviet vacillations about what policy to follow regarding the GDR; (2) Ulbricht's resistance to alleviating his harsh socialist policies; (3) the East German refugee problem and conflicting views on how to resolve it; (4) East German economic difficulties and divergent views about how to handle them; (5) the precariousness of the East German regime in the face of challenges from West Germany and West Berlin; (6) Soviet policy preferences versus real policy implementation on the ground in the GDR; and (7) conflicting Soviet and East German tendencies regarding establishing legitimacy versus control in the GDR. This chapter also presents the basis for the later East German capacity to turn its domestic weakness into bargaining strength with the Soviets, the birth of a super-ally.

In 1953 and afterward, two different patterns operated in the relationship between the Soviet Union and East Germany: One followed the traditional model of a dominant patron to a subservient, dependent client; and the other showed more characteristics of the tail wagging the dog. Although on many issues between 1953 and 1961, the first pattern prevailed, there were also important instances of East Germany's independent behavior and the incapacity of the Soviets to control East German policies.

It was not clear in 1953 whether Ulbricht would maintain his hold on power in the face of Soviet and domestic criticism or whether one of his opponents would succeed him. Ulbricht's autocratic leadership style and unyielding policies were at the heart of the domestic political struggle in East Berlin and also an essential component in relations between East Berlin and Moscow.

WHO WAS WALTER ULBRICHT?

Walter Ulbricht was an essential part of the establishment of Soviet communism in Germany. Hence, following his path to power also illuminates the rise of communism there, the process of Stalinization, and the subsequent challenges of de-Stalinization. Ulbricht dominated East German politics between 1945 and 1971. His leadership style has been described by people who worked with him, and by scholars, as Stalinist, dictatorial, cold, overbearing, and rigid.[1] He was rude, had few social graces, and was hardly an inspiring speaker. He was concerned above all with his personal power and displayed indefatigable energy in propagating his own "cult of personality." Ulbricht had strong organizational skills and paid great attention to detail. He possessed an acute sense for power and how best to maintain and augment it, both domestically and in his relations with the Soviets. He was also a staunch believer in Marxism-Leninism and was quick to defend the Soviet Union as the first communist state.

The future East German leader was born on 1 July 1893 in Leipzig, Germany, the first child of Ernst and Pauline Ulbricht. Ernst was a tailor, and Pauline stayed at home taking care of Walter and then his younger brother and sister. They lived in a poor, rather unseemly area of town, Naundörfchen. Leipzig itself was an important industrial city in Germany and at the end of the nineteenth century became "the cradle of the German labor movement." Ernst and Pauline both joined the Social Democratic Party, or SPD. (The Communist Party did not then exist.) The young Walter often listened while his parents and their friends discussed socialism. He helped his father distribute leaflets and read the socialist newspaper to him while his father made clothes.

Walter Ulbricht joined the SPD in 1912 at the age of nineteen.[2] The SPD's "strong Leipzig branch soon became known for its radicalism and Marxist revolutionary zeal."[3] Ulbricht joined socialist clubs and took classes at the Leipzig Workers Educational Institute, where he wrote essays describing how the capitalists were doomed to lose out to the "youthful vigor" of the proletariat, people like himself.[4] In 1915, after World War I broke out, Ulbricht was drafted into the army and stationed in Galicia, Macedonia, Serbia, and Belgium. He managed to maintain contact with socialists in Leipzig, and they supplied him with socialist materials to distribute in the army and at the front. Ulbricht deserted the "imperialist," "Prussian" army on more than one occasion and was caught and imprisoned for several months at a time.[5]

At the end of the war, Ulbricht joined the Communist Party of Germany (KPD), which was formed in 1919. At the age of twenty-six, he began to devote himself full-time to communist activities. He wrote for the party newspaper, and then in 1921 got his first paid party job as district secretary in Jena. In 1923 he was elected to the Central Committee and became a member of the Military Council, and thus moved to Berlin. He was elected as a KPD deputy to the Reichstag in 1928 and became a full member of the KPD's ruling body, the Politburo, in 1929. Upon assuming the post of political director of the KPD in the Berlin-Brandenburg district in November 1929, Ulbricht became the top man in Berlin. He was also a member of the KPD's Organizational Buro, for which he wrote articles about the nuts and bolts of how to develop the party's base among the "proletariat" in factories.[6]

Early in his career, Ulbricht developed links to Moscow. In 1922 he was a KPD delegate to the Fourth World Congress of the Communist International (Comintern). There he met Lenin for the first and only time—a great source of pride to him, especially when others, such as Khrushchev, had never met Lenin.[7] After a communist uprising in Germany failed in 1923 and the KPD was briefly banned, Ulbricht went to Moscow to study at the Comintern's Lenin School. The Comintern sent him to Vienna in September 1924 to help organize a strike by metal workers. The Austrian authorities arrested him, discovered his counterfeit identification papers, and imprisoned him for three months. Upon his release, the Comintern sent him on to Prague as the organizational instructor of the Comintern Executive Committee.[8] He was then called back to Moscow to work in the Comintern's Organizational Division, where he earned the nickname "Comrade Cell" for his good work in organizing communist cells in factories. He specialized in very detailed work on how to start a communist factory newspaper, how to distribute it, how to conduct propaganda and agitation, and generally how to persuade people to become communists.[9] As Wolfgang Leonhard, Ulbricht's later colleague in Berlin from 1945 to 1948, observed, "His strong points were his talents as an organizer, his phenomenal memory for names, his skill in foreseeing each successive change in the Party line, and his tireless industry. He never seemed to be exhausted even after the longest day's work. . . . (A)s always when he was dealing with the practical matters of organization . . . Ulbricht seemed to be entirely in his element."[10]

In the debate raging in the KPD in the 1920s about whether or not to emulate the Soviet bolshevik methods, Ulbricht argued strongly for bolshevization. This meant tightening the organizational structure and banning any dissent from the leaders' decisions, as well as closely following Soviet policies. When Ulbricht returned from Moscow to Berlin in 1925 to work on the Central Committee's (CC) Organizational Committee, bolshevization was one of his key goals.[11] In 1925 Ulbricht became a member of the CC's Secretariat with responsibility for agitation and propaganda. In 1928, in addition to being elected to the German Reichstag, he became a member of the Comintern's political secretariat in Moscow. He was responsible for transmitting and implementing Comintern policy in Germany. As a result of his contacts in Germany and in Moscow, Ulbricht was always better connected than his opponents within the KPD and learned to use information against them.[12]

By the late 1920s and early 1930s, Ulbricht was a senior KPD and Comintern official. He was a German, yet believed that the Soviet Union was the vanguard of the communist movement. Others, even within the KPD, probably thought his loyalties were too divided between his native and communist homelands. In speeches as a Reichstag deputy, he argued for the creation of a Soviet Republic in Germany. And even as Germany was hit by the Depression, with unemployment rising dramatically, he still argued that the main German communist efforts should be directed toward supporting the Soviet Union and the Red Army.[13]

The War Years in Moscow

Ulbricht's activities during the Nazi years of 1933–45, and especially his time in Moscow, would be crucial to his emergence as the leader of the newly created communist East Germany in 1949. After Adolf Hitler came to power in January 1933 and the Reichstag fire of February was blamed on the communists, the KPD was outlawed and many members arrested. Ulbricht went into hiding and then fled to Paris, following other KPD members. Between 1933 and 1938, Ulbricht worked alternately in Paris, Prague, and Moscow to maintain connections with communists still in Germany who managed to evade arrest and detention in a concentration camp and who could thus keep fighting for communism against the Nazis.[14] In 1937, the German government deprived Ulbricht of German citizenship "because of his alleged intention to commit high treason." It is not clear whether he became a Soviet citizen or not.[15]

From 1938 through April 1945, Ulbricht lived in the Soviet Union. He was based in Moscow with other Comintern representatives at the Hotel Lux except for six months between October 1941 and March 1942 when much of Moscow was evacuated due to the Nazi advance. The Comintern leaders were sent to Ufa, farther east toward the Urals. When Hitler double-crossed Stalin by abrogating the 1939 Molotov-Ribbentrop Pact and invading the Soviet Union in June 1941, many Germans in the Soviet Union, even communist Germans, were deported or sent to the gulag. Ulbricht and several other KPD leaders, however, managed to escape this fate. They helped the Red Army to process information from German POWs about the German army and to propagandize the German POWs about the virtues of communism. For the first two years of the war between the Germans and Soviets, Ulbricht's main task was to meet with German POWs and make radio broadcasts trying to persuade German soldiers to return to Germany and fight against Hitler and for communism.[16]

Ulbricht was also one of the main organizers of the National Committee for Free Germany (NKFD), founded in July 1943 among KPD members in exile in the Soviet Union. The goals of this committee were both to train people to spread communist propaganda at the front among German soldiers and to begin training a cadre of officials who would return to a defeated Germany at the end of the war and build a new anti-fascist regime.[17] After the February 1945 Yalta Conference of Soviet, American, and British leaders Stalin, Franklin Delano Roosevelt, and Winston Churchill, planning in the NKFD accelerated for a post-Hitler, democratic, anti-fascist, parliamentary regime. According to Soviet instructions, this was *not* to be socialist; just anti-fascist.[18] Two weeks before Nazi Germany surrendered on 8–9 May, ten members of the KPD, led by Ulbricht and called the "Gruppe Ulbricht," returned to Germany. Flying in an American-made Douglas aircraft, they flew to the outskirts of Berlin to begin their task of rebuilding Germany.[19]

Back in Berlin

All of Ulbricht's organizational skills would be put to the test now, starting with getting rudimentary local administrations up and running in the wake of Germany's destruction and defeat. Ulbricht also faced a challenge from the communists who had remained in Germany, mostly in concentration camps. These communists wanted to resume where they had left off in 1933 with their plans for establishing socialism and a Soviet republic in Germany. They could not understand why Ulbricht and his Soviet bosses quashed these plans, but Ulbricht's instructions from the Soviets were clear:

> . . . to support the activities of the occupying powers in the struggle to destroy Nazism and militarism, to re-educate the German people and to carry through democratic reforms. The guarantee of victory over Hitler was the unity of the anti-Hitler coalition, maintained primarily by the U.S.A., Great Britain and the Soviet Union.
>
> Our political task was not to consist of establishing socialism in Germany or encouraging a socialist development. On the contrary, this must be condemned and resisted as a dangerous tendency.[20]

Stalin did not want to alienate the Americans and British and also did not think Germany was ready for socialism. This was reflected in the KPD manifesto, published on 11 June 1945 on the occasion of the KPD's reestablishment:

> We believe it would be wrong to force the Soviet system on Germany, because it bears no relation to Germany's present stage of development. We believe the overriding interests of the German people at present prescribe a different road—the establishment of an anti-fascist, democratic regime, a parliamentary-democratic republic, with all democratic rights and liberties for the people.[21]

The essential goal was to eradicate Nazism, not to establish socialism, and the best way to do this was for the occupiers to act together. In addition, only by maintaining cooperation with the Western Powers might the Soviet Occupation Zone of Germany gain access to the industrial resources of and reparations from the western zones of Germany.

The different approaches and backgrounds of the "Muscovite" German communists and the more radical, leftist "native" (having remained in Germany during the war) German communists, were evident in the summer of 1945[22] and would persist into the 1960s.[23] In the summer of 1945 in Berlin, Ulbricht put many "Muscovite" Germans in key positions.[24] Subsequently, in the late 1940s and early 1950s, he purged many of the German communist "natives."[25]

Ulbricht maintained a condescending, contemptuous attitude toward the "native" communists and social democrats who had remained in Germany from 1933 to 1945 and "submitted to Hitler's rule" or at least failed to stop it.[26] Ulbricht stressed that "the defeat of Hitlerlite Fascism had been achieved not by an internal rising of the German people but by the armies of the anti-Hitler coalition." He, therefore, considered "the German people . . . accomplice(s) in the crimes of Hitlerite Germany."[27]

Ulbricht resented the "native" communists' criticism of Soviet policies in Germany. Ulbricht felt that the Red Army had played the decisive role in defeating Hitler and that the German people owed the Soviets a debt of gratitude. When criticism was voiced of the behavior of the Red Army against German civilians, Ulbricht ignored it. His former colleague Wolfgang Leonhard recounts a conference in mid-May 1945 with eighty to one hundred active communists who regularly reported to Ulbricht on developments in their areas of responsibility in Berlin. They focused on the raping of German women by Russian soldiers:

> [A] Party member from the farthest corner of the hall [spoke up:] "A question has been put to us by some doctors—men with anti-Fascist background—about what course they ought to take with women who have been raped and come to them for abortions. I've promised the doctors a reply. We need a clear definition of the proper attitude to this question of abortion in such cases, from our own point of view."
>
> He was immediately supported by another voice: "The question's very urgent. It's been talked about everywhere. . . . In my view, abortion ought to be permitted officially in such cases."

Voices of assent could be heard from all over the room, but Ulbricht interrupted the discussion by saying sharply: "There can be no question of it! I
regard the discussion as closed."[28]

Faced with further protests, Ulbricht barked back in his shrill voice,
"People who get so worked up about such things today would have
done much better to get worked up when Hitler began the war."[29]

Using "his icy bolshevik discipline" to establish his regime in Germany, Ulbricht sought to establish "a centrally-led apparat of power,
the German copy of the party of a new type founded by Lenin and
formed by Stalin."[30] His plan was complicated when Stalin instructed
him in 1946 to merge the KPD and SPD into one Socialist Unity Party,
because then Ulbricht had to deal with Social Democrats more directly.[31]
But he quickly resolved this problem in his own way, by giving only a
few Social Democrats important positions and purging many others.[32]

Although Ulbricht spouted the Soviet party line that socialism would
not be established in Germany, his actions belied his words. He put his
own people in key positions and pushed ahead with the bolshevization
of the Zone.[33] While Vladimir Semenov, the political advisor to the chief
of the Soviet Military Administration in the Soviet Zone of Occupation
(SBZ), sometimes remonstrated that Ulbricht was unilaterally forging
ahead toward "the construction of socialism,"[34] instead of focusing on
unification, Ulbricht was encouraged and assisted by the uniquely influential Soviet information officer, Sergei Tiul'panov.[35] Semenov complained
to Otto Grotewohl, former SPD chief and now co-chair of the SED,
"that some of the measures introduced by T[i]ul'panov and Ulbricht go
beyond the goal of Moscow's policy and will further complicate the
present situation, which is in itself difficult already."[36] Beginning immediately after World War II and continuing for over a decade, Soviet (as
well as German) officials such as Semenov and Tiul'panov had varying
views on the best policy to be followed in the SBZ. Ulbricht, who never
wavered in his goal of establishing a socialist state under his tight control, was not afraid to take advantage of these differences to pursue this
goal.

Similarly, Ulbricht used the break between Stalin and Yugoslav leader
Josip Tito in 1948 and the subsequent Soviet move against "national
communism" in Eastern Europe to squash the campaign of his colleague
Anton Ackermann for a "separate German road to socialism" and to
insist on following the Soviet road to socialism.[37] Yet, in December
1948, Stalin still told the German communists, "No transition to people's democracy yet. . . . not direct interventions, but rather zigzag . . .
cautious policy."[38] And even after the Federal Republic of Germany was
established on 23 May 1949, Stalin moved hesitantly to establish the

German Democratic Republic on 7 October. In Stalin's final meeting with the East German leaders, in April 1952, he counseled them: "Although two states are being currently created in Germany, you should not shout about socialism at this point."[39] Ulbricht played a crucial role in pressing Stalin first to support the creation of the GDR in 1949 and then to go forward with his plan for the *Aufbau des Sozialismus (Construction of Socialism)* in July 1952.[40] By the time of Stalin's death in March 1953, Ulbricht had achieved what he ardently sought—his own socialist state. But in his pursuit of this goal, he had created enemies in Germany and in the Kremlin. These critics would seek to oust him in the months after Stalin's death.

STALIN'S SUCCESSORS GATHER INFORMATION, MARCH–MAY 1953

Following Stalin's death on 5 March 1953, the new Soviet leadership, consisting of Prime Minister Georgi Malenkov, Minister of Internal Affairs Lavrenty Beria, Central Committee Secretary Nikita S. Khrushchev, and Foreign Minister Viacheslav Molotov, began a reassessment of Stalin's domestic and foreign policies. While the new Soviet leaders were gathering information and pondering fundamental changes in policy, they made two important decisions concerning economic assistance and the border between East and West Berlin.

Unlike the border between the two parts of Germany, which had been closed in May 1952 in response to plans for the military integration of West Germany with the Western Powers, the border between East and West Berlin remained open.[41] The East German leaders wanted to close this border to prevent GDR citizens from fleeing west. The relative economic prosperity in West Berlin coupled with its political and cultural freedom lured GDR citizens away.[42] In January 1953, when Stalin was still alive, the Soviets actually had agreed to Ulbricht's request to station guards along the border between East and West Berlin so as "to end uncontrolled access to East Berlin from the Western sectors," but of course it also would have had the effect of limiting the movement of East Berliners to West Berlin.[43] Less than two weeks after Stalin's death, however, his successors backtracked and soundly rejected the East German request to take control of the inter-Berlin border. In a memorandum to Marshal V. I. Chuikov, chairman of the leading Soviet political entity in the GDR, the Soviet Control Commission (SKK), and Vladimir Sememov, political adviser to the same Commission, Foreign Minister Molotov stated:[44]

The GDR government's proposed border protection (*okhrana*) on the sectoral border of East Berlin with West Berlin and the measures connected with the

Map 2. Divided Germany and Berlin with Western Access Routes. Inset: Berlin Divided into Soviet Sector (East Berlin) and French, British, and U.S. Sectors (West Berlin).

implementation of such protection, including the regulation of transport, is politically unacceptable and grossly simplistic.

You must meet with Grotewohl and Ulbricht and tactfully explain to them the following.

a) The carrying out of such measures in Berlin with a population of several million people would certainly lead to the violation of the established order of city life, would cause the disorganization of the city's economy, and even more would negatively affect the interests of the population not only of West but also of East Berlin, [and] would call forth bitterness and dissatisfaction from the Berliners with regard to the government of the GDR and the Soviet forces in Germany, which would be used by the three Western Powers against the interests of the GDR and the USSR.

b) The carrying out of such measures with regard to West Berlin would place in doubt the sincerity of the policy of the Soviet government and the GDR government, which are actively and consistently supporting the unification of

Germany and the conclusion of a peace treaty with Germany and would seriously damage the political gains we have achieved in West Germany. . . .

c) The establishment of border protection would only complicate, to the clear disadvantage of the countries of the camp of peace and democracy, relations of the Soviet Union with the USA, England and France, which we can and must avoid.[45]

Molotov urged the GDR leadership to solve the problem in a different way than seizing control of the Berlin sectoral border. He and his Kremlin colleagues wanted the SED regime to moderate its policies and strengthen the economy so East German citizens would stay rather than flee. In fact, from 1953 to 1961, the Soviet leaders argued that "administrative measures" to close the Berlin border should be adopted "only in the extreme circumstances."[46] Similarly, some of Ulbricht's comrades, including secret police chief Wilhelm Zaisser and Rudolf Herrnstadt, the editor of the main party newspaper, *Neues Deutschland*, sought for several months in 1953 to persuade Ulbricht to alleviate his harsh style and policies to improve the domestic situation, but in vain.[47] Khrushchev later observed that "the best and most logical way to fight [Western influence] was to try to win the minds of the people by using culture and policies to create better living conditions."[48]

In addition to refusing the East German request to close the border in Berlin, the second decision the new Soviet leaders made in their initial period of information gathering and assessment was not to grant the GDR significant new economic assistance. Soviet deputy economics chief P. V. Nikitin visited East Berlin in mid-April to examine economic conditions. He reiterated what the new Soviet leaders had told Ulbricht at Stalin's funeral: The Soviets needed all their reserves to improve the living standards of their own population. The GDR, Nikitin said, should emulate this and give greater priority to light and consumer industry over heavy industry.[49] Nonetheless, the Soviets did ease the economic pressure on the GDR somewhat. They supplied the East Germans with more raw materials and semi-finished products for industry, reduced East German reparations shipments to the Soviet Union by 20–25 percent, decreased the overall cost of East German reparations obligations to the Soviet Union by 580 million marks, and extended (but did not cancel) the term for the payment of the remainder.[50]

This temporary aid to the GDR bought time for the Soviets to decide upon their long-term policy. The first sign of this policy came in May when the Soviets told Ulbricht to abandon the *Aufbau des Sozialismus* program. Ulbricht had introduced this program in the GDR rather suddenly in July 1952.[51] The *Aufbau* program called for the transformation of the GDR into a socialist state like the other people's democracies of

Eastern Europe. It prescribed the "forced," "accelerated" development of heavy industry, the collectivization of agriculture, and discriminatory measures against churches, private entrepreneurs, the intelligentsia, and East German citizens working in West Berlin. These measures exacerbated economic difficulties and drastically increased the numbers of East German refugees fleeing west.[52] The numbers of East Germans fleeing west jumped from 9,307 in April 1952 to 16,970 in December 1952, to 22,396 in January 1953, and 58,605 in March 1953.[53] Even without the problems caused by the *Aufbau* program, the East German economic situation was on shaky ground due to the massive reparations the Soviets had taken in all the years since the end of the war and also because the key German raw materials were located on West German territory. It took the post-Stalin leadership two months to gather enough information to make the connection between Ulbricht's favored *Aufbau des Sozialismus* program and the GDR's problems.

In Moscow, officials in the Third European Department of the Foreign Ministry (*Ministerstvo Inostrannykh Del*, or MID) formulated ideas on overall Germany policy. Molotov's advisors on German policy included G. Pushkin, M. Gribanov, Ya. Malik, and V. Semenov. Their job was to draft proposals for consideration by the Presidium of the Communist Party of the Soviet Union and the Presidium of the Council of Ministers (CM). Initially they reacted more to Western initiatives to integrate West Germany into the Western alliance than to the internal situation in East Germany.[54] In order to thwart the FRG's integration into the Western military alliance, they proposed an all-German provisional government. Expecting the West to reject their overtures, they also urged measures to strengthen the GDR domestically and raise its international prestige. They advised inviting an official GDR delegation to Moscow for the first time since the founding of the GDR four years earlier. At the meeting in Moscow, they suggested signing a treaty on friendship, cooperation, and mutual aid and granting amnesty for German prisoners of war. They called for upgrading Soviet relations with East Germany, transforming their diplomatic mission into an embassy, and the SKK into a Soviet Commission on German Affairs. They also recommended reducing economic demands on the GDR and granting the GDR more economic aid.[55]

On 22 April Semenov was recalled to Moscow from his position as political advisor to the SKK in Berlin. The Kremlin leaders wanted to consult on Soviet *Deutschlandpolitik* and also installed Semenov as head of MID's Third European Department.[56] On 2 May he sent Molotov a top secret "Memorandum on the German Question," summarizing the previous proposals and providing his view of what should be done. Since he did not believe the West would accept Soviet proposals for a provisional all-German government (the West objected because the GDR representatives in the government would not have been elected freely), he urged "simultaneously preparing a series of measures for the further strengthening of friendly relations between the Soviet Union and the GDR and for increasing the all-German and international prestige of the GDR."[57] He thought Soviet control in the GDR should be modulated, stating:

> Most of all it is necessary to examine the question of the desirability of the further preservation of the control of Soviet military authorities over the democratic organs of power and organization of the GDR.
>
> The Socialist Unity Party of Germany and the democratic forces in the GDR have already strengthened and matured enough to manage the leadership of the country independently. The necessary Soviet help in the future could be exercised through Soviet advisors and specialists, as occurs in other countries of people's democracy. Regarding this the stay of the Soviet troops on the territory of the GDR is a sufficient guarantee of the stability of the people's-democratic system in the Republic. Meanwhile, the further preservation of Soviet control over GDR affairs has a series of serious negative sides. It sharply emphasizes the inequality in relations between the USSR and the GDR. . . . The democratic forces in the GDR can view the further maintenance of Soviet control over the GDR as an expression of political distrust of them by the Soviet government. In addition, with the presence of the Soviet Control Commission the GDR government does not feel entire, complete responsibility for the country, which slows down the cultivation of the leading cadres of the SED.[58]

Writing this shortly before the June uprising, Semenov's view that the SED was mature enough to run the country without much Soviet supervision seems quite out of touch with the prevailing feelings of East German citizens. Indeed, Semenov had just returned to Moscow with reports from GDR officials on the alienation of the population from the SED and on the problems within the party.[59] He also knew that there were fundamental disagreements on policy and methods within the SED leadership, with Rudolf Herrnstadt, Wilhelm Zaisser, and others very critical of Ulbricht's unyielding, uncollaborative, Stalinist style of ruling. Yet Semenov and other MID officials hardly saw a crisis brewing in the GDR.

Molotov forwarded the MID proposals to Malenkov and other members of the CPSU and Council of Ministers Presidia. By late April and early May, top Soviet leaders were aware of the problems in the GDR and were discussing options for Soviet *Deutschlandpolitik*. But MID was not the only source of information on Germany. Soviet Interior Ministry (MVD) officials in the GDR also reported on the situation, but with a more critical slant. They focused on the daily domestic difficulties in the GDR and dwelled on the refugee exodus. On 6 May, Beria submitted a three-page top-secret MVD report to the CPSU Presidium containing a negative appraisal of the situation in East Germany.[60] The top MVD representative in the GDR, Colonel Ivan Fadeikin, emphasized the growing refugee exodus, including among SED members. He argued that the exodus was not simply the result of Western propaganda. He described the harsh agricultural and business policies in the GDR, the forced recruitment of youth into the military, and the inadequate supply of food and consumer goods to the GDR population. Fadeikin maintained that the GDR leaders did not know how to deal with the difficult situation. He concluded that the SED leaders "falsely assumed that as long as free circulation existed between West Berlin and the GDR, such flights were inevitable."[61]

While East German leaders believed that the remedy for the problem was to close the border, Fadeikin and Beria disagreed. Beria proposed that the SKK submit recommendations on other approaches.[62] He wanted the GDR regime to modify its policies to entice its citizens to stay in the country. Ulbricht's control-oriented, Stalinist proclivities militated against relieving his harsh socialist policies or repudiating the *Aufbau des Sozialismus*. For him, it was easier and preferable to just close the border. It would take him until 1961, however, to persuade the Soviets to agree.

On 14 May the Presidium commissioned the SKK to prepare a report on the reasons for the refugee exodus and proposals to stop it, thus adding a third group supplying information on the GDR.[63] Meanwhile, on the next day, officials in MID's Third European Department drew up a top secret report "On the Question of Stopping the Exodus of the Population from the GDR to West Germany" (which perhaps served as a draft for the SKK report three days later). On 18 May, V. Chuikov, P. Iudin, and I. Il'ichev of the SKK submitted a lengthy secret analysis that blamed the refugee exodus on the *Aufbau des Sozialismus* and set the stage for the Soviet *New Course*.

As the Kremlin was beginning to get a picture of the mounting crisis, the SED leadership took steps that exacerbated the situation. The East Germans held their Thirteenth SED CC plenum on 13–14 May. Ulbricht wanted to bolster his personal power and further the *Aufbau des Sozialismus* policy rather than relax controls. The plenum ousted Franz Dahlem, Ulbricht's main rival in the leadership, raised work norms by at least 10 percent (thereby reducing workers' pay by 10 percent), and called for "increasing vigilance against the class enemy."[64]

On the same day in Moscow, 14 May, the CPSU Presidium met and agreed to Molotov's advice to restrain Ulbricht's socialist policies in the GDR. They reproached Ulbricht for declaring that "the GDR has entered a new stage in which [it] is getting set to build the foundations of socialism."[65] Instead, they resolved to inform the East Germans "tactfully" that collectivization should be stopped for at least the rest of the year. Finally, they instructed Ulbricht to forego plans for a major public celebration of his sixtieth birthday.

The *New Course*, Mid-May through 16 June

The Soviets Formulate the New Course

By mid-May, the Soviet leaders had a broad understanding of the worsening crisis in the GDR. The 15 May MID report, "On the Issue of Stopping the Flight of the Population from the GDR to West Germany," warned that the refugee exodus had "assumed a mass character" and was "without doubt connected to a significant degree with the existing policy of constructing the bases of socialism in the Republic." Noting that many workers, farmers, engineers, technicians, scientific workers, teachers, and youth were leaving, the MID officials called for changes in SED policies, changes that would presage the Kremlin's *New Course* instructions of 2 June. "In order to stop the further exodus of the GDR population to West Germany and West Berlin," MID officials declared, "it would be expedient to" undertake a series of measures, including: a temporary stop in creating new agricultural collectives; production of more consumer goods of greater variety and quality; cessation of mass arrests; an end to the confiscation of goods from farmers who were late or incomplete in supplying their quota to the state; an amnesty to many prisoners; and a more careful and less "administrative" and "repressive" approach toward the church.[66]

While the 15 May MID document made seven concrete policy recommendations, the SKK document sent to the Presidium three days later made thirty-one recommendations broken down into economic, administrative, and political categories. In the document and its appendixes, Chuikov, Yudin, and Il'ichev itemized the social, political, and geographic backgrounds of all the GDR citizens who had fled to West Germany since 1950. Like their MID counterparts, the SKK officials blamed the GDR's problems partly on Western influences and partly on erroneous SED policies and practices. Their policy recommendations were a mixture of new and old thinking. On the one hand, they called for amnesties, the rule of law, and more lenient economic policies. On the other hand, they demanded that the East Germans fulfill their industrial production plan (without indicating where they would get the means to do this), allow East Germans to visit Berlin only with permission, and strengthen their counterpropaganda against the West, such as by building more radio stations to counter the West's Radio in the American Sector (RIAS). They criticized the "administrative approach of East German officials" and their "serious mistakes." The SKK officials declared that the East Germans introduced the *Aufbau des Sozialismus* measures "without sufficient political and economic preparations." They also were very concerned about inadequate food supplies, consumer goods, and electricity for the people, hostile policies toward the intelligentsia and the church, insufficient press and radio propaganda, numerous unjustified arrests and repressive measures, and the SED's "underestimation of the political significance of the exodus of the population." But they sympathized with the GDR as a victim of "West German and Anglo-American [efforts] aimed at disrupting the five-year plan and at discrediting the policy of the GDR government before the populace [by] enticing engineering-technical, scientific and highly-qualified workers from the enterprises and establishments of the GDR." While they identified many significant problems, they stopped short of identifying the situation in the GDR as a crisis needing urgent measures for its resolution. Nor did they recognize the significant economic aid the GDR required to "fulfill the industrial production plan" and eliminate rations, as they recommended.[67]

Before addressing the SKK's recommendations, the CPSU Presidium first approved MID's recommendation to convert the SKK into a Soviet High Commission in Germany. On 27 May, the Kremlin appointed Semenov as the High Commissioner and Yudin as his first deputy.[68] The Kremlin leaders seemed to agree with Semenov that they needed to adopt a lower profile in the GDR.

Throughout May 1953, the Kremlin leaders met regularly to discuss the broader situation in Germany and Eastern Europe. In addition to the refugee exodus from the GDR, they were also faced with strikes and riots in Bulgaria and Czechoslovakia over economic and political conditions.[69] It was clear that they needed to change their policies in Eastern Europe.

To discuss these matters, the Kremlin leaders convened sometimes under the auspices of the Presidium of the CPSU[70] and sometimes under the auspices of the Presidium of the Council of Ministers (CM),[71] both presided over by Malenkov in this period.[72] Khrushchev was the most senior member of the Central Committee Secretariat, and he and Malenkov set the agenda for CPSU Presidium meetings. While there was rivalry between Khrushchev, with his party base on the one hand, and Malenkov and Beria, with their Council of Ministers base on the other hand, all three leaders, together with Molotov, were deeply involved in the debate over *Deutschlandpolitik*. Both Presidia discussed the German question,[73] and Khrushchev often attended meetings of the CM Presidium although he was not a member.[74]

Until the 27 May CM Presidium meeting, the documentary evidence does not make it clear whether proposals for changes in Soviet *Deutsch-*

landpolitik were emanating from the CPSU and CM leaders in Moscow or from high- and middle-level officials at MID, the SKK, and the MVD. It was normal procedure for officials in MID's Third European Department, the SKK, and the MVD in Karlshorst to send regular reports, *otcheti* or *zapiski* (weekly, monthly, quarterly, and/or yearly), on political, economic, security, and other conditions in the GDR. They did not need to be asked by a top Kremlin official to do this. Within the Kremlin, Molotov and Beria were the two leaders most actively involved in considering options for *Deutschlandpolitik*. Beginning in mid-April, Molotov and members of MID's Third European Department sent a series of reports and proposals to the two Presidia. It was a MID document on proposed policy changes in the GDR that was submitted for consideration to the CM Presidium at the important 27 May meeting.[75] And Beria had called at the 6 May meeting of the CPSU Presidium for an SKK report on measures to stop the refugee exodus, measures that were then hotly debated by the leaders between 27 May and 2 June.[76]

All of the information reaching the Kremlin leadership from MID, the SKK and MVD, as well as from Bulgaria and Czechoslovakia and elsewhere in Eastern Europe, was finally assembled by the leaders in late May. Malenkov later declared that at the 27 May CM Presidium meeting, the Soviet leadership was "forced" by the refugee flight "to look at the truth soberly and recognize that without the presence of Soviet troops the existing regime in the GDR was not durable."[77]

The 27 May Meeting of the Soviet Leaders

The focus of the 27 May meeting was "to analyze the causes which had led to the mass exodus of Germans from the GDR to West Germany and to discuss measures for correcting the unfavorable political and economic situation existing in the GDR."[78] It was a stormy meeting, according to various accounts by participants afterward. At the meeting, Molotov submitted a proposal, which he had drafted with Deputy Foreign Minister Andrei Gromyko,[79] to halt the forced, accelerated rate of the *Aufbau des Sozialismus* and improve the standard of living of the people so that they would stop fleeing west and start trusting the SED regime.[80] Khrushchev and Molotov maintained afterward (and after they had arrested and ousted Beria and were looking for as many excuses as possible to justify these actions to the Central Committee and general public) that Beria called not just for slowing down the pace of the development of socialism in the GDR, but for halting it altogether.[81] They also accused Malenkov of agreeing with Beria.[82]

According to Gromyko, Beria crudely asked: "The GDR? What does it amount to, this GDR? It's not even a real state. It's only kept in being by Soviet troops, even if we do call it the 'GDR.' "[83] Beria then apparently added that it only mattered that Germany was peaceful, not whether it was socialist or not, and that it should be united, democratic, bourgeois, and neutral.[84] To this, Molotov allegedly retorted that Germany could only be peaceful if it was socialist; therefore, the question of building a socialist system in Germany was absolutely essential.[85] Khrushchev accused Beria of plotting to "put 18 million Germans under the control of American imperialists."[86] To his colleagues' relief, Beria supposedly recanted this view the next day. Between 28 May and 1 June, Molotov (with much help from Semenov), Beria, and Malenkov reworked Molotov's 27 May proposals into the document that would be accepted as the *New Course* by the CM Presidium on 2 June. This *New Course* document was entitled "On Measures for the Recovery of the Political Situation in the German Democratic Republic." Similar measures were soon applied to Hungary, Albania, and other countries, including the Soviet Union itself.[87]

The Soviets Present the New Course to the East Germans

The Soviets called the top East German leaders to Moscow from 2–4 June and presented them with their resolution on the *New Course*.[88] Politburo members Ulbricht, Grotewohl, and Fred Oelssner made the trip. The *New Course* identified the problems existing in the GDR, their causes, and measures to be taken to resolve them. The Soviets declared in point 1 that the East Germans must "recognize the course of forced construction of socialism in the GDR . . . as mistaken under current conditions" and as the main cause of the "very unsatisfactory political and economic situation in the German Democratic Republic."[89] The domestic "conditions" were not ripe because of the lack of a strong raw material base in the GDR and because not enough groundwork had been laid to attract farmers, craftsmen, entrepreneurs, intelligentsia, churchgoers, and other groups to socialism. The necessary foreign preconditions were not identified, but no doubt referred to West German hostility to the socialist system and perhaps the open border. As the resolution stated, the key proof that the *Aufbau des Sozialismus* program was incorrect was in the high numbers of East Germans fleeing to the West, including workers, middle and small farmers, craftsmen, pensioners, intelligentsia, members of the East German People's Police (VoPos), and party members of all ages.[90] Concluding that "[a]ll of this creates a serious threat to the political stability of the German Democratic Republic," the resolution listed measures necessary for "improving the political situation of the GDR and strengthening our position both in Germany itself and on the German issue in the international arena, as well as securing and broadening the bases of the mass movement for the construction of a single, democratic, peace-loving, independent Germany."[91]

The *New Course* measures, many of which had been presaged in the MID and SKK reports, were aimed to stop forced collectivization, support small and private enterprises, and give all citizens ration cards. They called for relaxing the overstrained tempo of the development of heavy industry and promoting the production of consumer goods and foodstuffs. They also aimed to reorganize the finance system, guarantee civil rights, treat the intelligentsia and churchgoers more respectfully, and strengthen the role of the other political parties and mass organizations vis-à-vis the SED. Finally, they sought to induce East Germans who had fled to return.[92]

After Oelssner translated the *New Course* for Ulbricht and Grotewohl, the Soviets and Germans discussed the resolution. The talks were extraordinarily stressful for the East Germans. Having given the GDR leaders the *New Course* document only upon their arrival in Moscow, the Soviets demanded their response the next morning. The East Germans labored into the evening, but were not convinced of the necessity of the changes demanded by the Soviets. Their "superficial and formal" written response agitated the Soviets, who rejected it as "inadequate." Beria in particular, as recounted by both Oelssner and later Khrushchev, "behaved himself particularly aggressively."[93] He castigated the East Germans for their poor attempt to respond to the *New Course* and instructed them to prepare a second response.[94] Grotewohl's handwritten notes from the 3 June meeting, on the other hand, show Beria saying, "We have all been at fault; no accusations, [but that the East Germans must] correct fast and vigorously." Presidium member Lazar Kaganovich was even more frustrated than Beria, declaring, "our document is *reversal*, yours is [merely] reform [emphasis in original]."[95]

The Soviets objected to the East German emphasis upon external conditions, specifically relations with West Germany, as the main cause for the policy change, instead of stressing the precarious East German internal situation. They insisted that the East Germans justify the *New Course* by focusing on the situation in the GDR. They tried to ease the pain, consoling the East Germans by telling them, "We don't want to put forth the question of blame; we are as guilty as you are—but you must understand, and the policy must be corrected."[96] The Kremlin wanted the East Germans to make the new policy speedily, strongly, and openly, so that it would be obvious to all of Germany and the world.[97]

The policy changes the Soviets instructed the East Germans to make were not limited to domestic policies. The references in the *New Course* to the German question as a whole, and German unification, seem to have confused the East Germans at the time, as well as Malenkov, and also scholars who have studied it. About halfway through the document, the Soviets stressed:

> At the present and in the near future it is necessary to put the tasks of the political struggle to reestablish the national unity of Germany and to conclude a peace treaty at the center of attention of the broad mass of the German people both in the GDR and in West Germany. At the same time it is crucial to correct and strengthen the political and economic situation in the GDR and to strengthen significantly the influence of the SED among the broad masses of workers and in other democratic strata of the city and the country.[98]

The final point of the *New Course* resolution stated that "at present the main task is the struggle for the unification of Germany on a democratic and peace-loving basis."[99]

These references to German unification reflected the conflicting goals of the Kremlin leaders, striving to expand their influence in a united Germany if possible, but to maintain and strengthen their position in the GDR as necessary. Malenkov himself seems to have been confused. As he said at the 31 January 1955 CPSU plenum: "We spoke then about conducting a political campaign on the question of German reunification and I believed that one should not have set the task of the development of socialism in Democratic Germany" at the same time. He apparently thought these two processes were contradictory; he did not believe that Soviet policy could focus on German unification and the development of socialism in the GDR at the same time. At the January 1955 plenum, Malenkov admitted:

> I was wrong when in April or May [1953], during the discussion of the German question I believed that in the existing international situation, when we had started a big political campaign [for peace], on the question of Germany's reunification, one should not have set the task of the development of socialism in Democratic Germany [the GDR]. . . . Today I admit that I essentially took a wrong position on the German question.[100]

The East Germans were also confused about what the Soviets wanted.[101] Perhaps the presence of rather contradictory directives in the document was a result of the Soviet leaders coming to a compromise, agreeing to put all views in the document. It may be that Beria felt that the Soviet leaders should focus more on the big picture of achieving détente with the West and coming to an agreement on Germany as part of this instead of just on building up a socialist regime in the GDR. It could also be, on the other hand, that the leaders understood that the only chance they would have of gaining influence over the FRG and perhaps gaining German unity on Soviet, socialist terms would be by building up a stable, attractive regime in the GDR. The language of the document is indicative of recurrent Soviet efforts to balance methods for influencing Germany, alternating between attempting to achieve unification on favorable terms and focusing on stabilizing or consolidating their more limited sphere of influence in the GDR.

On their last day in Moscow, the East Germans met with Grechko, Yudin, Semenov, and Chuikov. The Soviets promised to alleviate the East Germans' problems regarding reparations, foodstuffs, raw materials, agriculture, and trade. The Kremlin would also assist with the establishment of the East German armed forces.[102] Unlike previous Soviet messages to the East Germans, the Kremlin was now willing to provide direct economic aid to foster the succcess of the *New Course*.

In these Moscow meetings, the Soviets referred only fleetingly to the question of Ulbricht's excessive influence within the leadership, a subject of hot dispute in East Berlin. I. Kabin, who had replaced Semenov as head of the Third European Department at MID, told Oelssner that the Soviet Central Committee members had been filled with "consternation" when they read the SED Politburo's document planning the celebration for Ulbricht's sixtieth birthday. At first they thought that the SED Politburo members were just trying to "butter up" Ulbricht, but "they fell out of their chairs when they heard that Ulbricht himself was the author." Soviet Presidium member M. Suslov then went to persuade GDR President Wilhelm Pieck, who was recuperating from an illness near Moscow, to warn Ulbricht about his behavior.[103]

The Beria Question

There is still no convincing, contemporaneous proof that Beria, as his colleagues later charged, proposed a different policy concerning the GDR than the other leaders favored or that he was willing, even eager, to sacrifice the GDR to the West or trade it for German disarmament and neutrality.[104] Beria, Molotov, and the others seemed to be building a consensus before the 27 May meeting that they had to alleviate socialist excesses in the GDR. Only the unedited minutes or notes from the 27 May Presidium meeting would provide evidence that Beria sought to go beyond this consensus. I am not aware of anyone who has seen these, if they exist. The only direct evidence we have from Beria himself regarding Germany is a letter he wrote to Malenkov from prison (not exactly the most conducive circumstances for candor) on 1 July 1953 in which he admitted that his behavior during meetings of the Soviet leadership showed "inadmissible rudeness and insolence . . . toward comrades N. S. Khrushchev and N. A. Bulganin during the discussion on the German question" But, he asserted that

...along with all of you, I tried to introduce initiatives at the Presidium aimed at the correct solution of issues, such as the Korean, the German, the responses to Eisenhower and Churchill, the Turkish, the Iranian, etc. . . . But I must say in all sincerity that I thoroughly prepared myself and made my assistants prepare themselves for the sessions of the CC and the government, so that within the limits of strength and abilities [I tried] to assist in [finding a] correct solution of the issues under discussion. If and when I introduced initiatives, I revised them several times, together with the comrades collaborating with me, so as not to make a mistake and not to let the CC and the government down.[105]

Beria's "rude" behavior in the meetings with his colleagues and the East Germans may simply have illustrated his extreme frustration with both East German and Soviet leaders for not recognizing sooner the depth of the crisis in the GDR and for not responding with alacrity to reverse the situation.

East German Deliberations about the New Course

Following the 2–4 June meetings in Moscow, there were heated debates in the SED Politburo about the *New Course*. The Soviets sent the East Germans back to Berlin with Semenov and the instruction to publish the *New Course* resolution as their own and to set about implementing it within one week. Upon their return to East Berlin, the East German Politburo met in almost constant session from 5 to 9 June.[106] Much of the discussion focused on criticisms of Ulbricht's hard-line, uncollegial form of rule, using the *New Course* as indication that the Soviets were also opposed to that style.[107] At the Politburo session on 5 June, Ulbricht and Grotewohl presented the Soviet *New Course*, and the East Germans established commissions to handle the necessary resolutions to be made on industry, finance, agriculture, supplies, the intelligentsia and school issues, and legal matters.[108]

The next day, the sole agenda item at the Politburo meeting was discussion of the *New Course*.[109] The discussion, however, strayed far beyond this and focused on a critical analysis of the leadership situation in the GDR. The references in the Soviet resolution to the SED's "stark administrative methods" and the ways the party had distanced itself from the population struck a raw nerve in the SED leadership, which was increasingly divided about Ulbricht's heavy-handed methods.[110] Oelssner, Zaisser,[111] and others spoke of the absence of any feeling for party democracy, of the party's distance from the people, of the party's way of stifling every initiative, and of an atmosphere in which party members, including in the leadership, felt that they could not speak openly. Ulbricht's colleagues and Semenov were critical of the commanding, overbearing, incompetent work of the Secretariat, and thus Ulbricht himself who was the general secretary.[112] Semenov also told Ulbricht to cancel the official festivities planned for his sixtieth birthday on 30 June.[113]

At the end of the meeting, the East Germans resolved that "a comprehensive document must be prepared on self-criticism of the work of the Politburo and the Secretariat and be presented to the CPSU CC Presidium [and] a commission composed of comrades Ulbricht, Zaisser, Oelssner, Herrnstadt, and Jendretzky will prepare an organizational reform of the working methods of the Politburo and Secretariat."[114] Herrnstadt, in particular, had the job of formulating proposals for a new Politburo and Secretariat. It seemed that "Ulbricht was now only formally the General Secretary of the party; the leadership had already been taken away from him."[115]

Although the Soviets had asked the East Germans to focus on the internal considerations that necessitated the *New Course*, the East Germans could not help but notice the emphasis the Soviets had placed on all-German and general international considerations in justifying it. Herrnstadt thus took the opportunity to criticize the East German (i.e., Ulbricht) focus on constructing socialism while assuming that "the German question will resolve itself meanwhile somehow, or, if it does not do this, it will be resolved in the end by the bayonets of the Soviet army."[116] Now, he believed, the East Germans themselves must more actively devote themselves to the resolution of the German question, to German reunification. Ulbricht, however, resisted drawing attention away from building socialism, and his own power, in the GDR.

The criticism of Ulbricht at the 9 June Politburo meeting was even sharper than it had been three days earlier.[117] Semenov was there again and took notes throughout the session, which lasted several hours. The Soviet *New Course* document and the East German response to it were still the items for discussion. Since everyone had had the Soviet document for several days, they were far better prepared for the discussion than normally for Politburo meetings when members did not receive the materials to be discussed sufficiently in advance (giving Ulbricht his usual informational advantage over everyone else).[118]

After Grotewohl opened the meeting, Oelssner spoke first. He began with the words: "For two years I was silent; today I will speak." Once professing his agreement with the Soviet document, Oelssner then asked how the situation in the GDR could have developed in such a way that such a drastic policy change was necessary. As an answer, he gave a broad depiction of the situation in the Central Committee Secretariat, of which he had been a member since 1950. Oelssner portrayed the deplorable working style of the Secretariat, the dictatorship of Ulbricht, and the atmosphere of servility and fear. The problems, he said, had begun long before the introduction of the *Aufbau des Sozialismus* in July 1952 and were part of what later would be known as the "cult of personality." Others agreed.

Semenov and Ulbricht were surprised by this united and passionate outburst of the Politburo. At the end of the meeting, Semenov said to Ulbricht, "Well, Comrade Ulbricht, I think it is now up to you to draw serious conclusions from this very sound criticism of the Politburo." Ulbricht, however, refused to respond to the criticism.

The Politburo members decided to publish the *New Course* on 11 June as a communiqué of the 9 June Politburo meeting. Herrnstadt was in charge of drafting it. When he proposed to Semenov that it be published after two weeks of preparing the population for the *New Course* changes, Semenov sharply retorted: "In fourteen days you may not have a state anymore."[119] Thus, the East Germans published the communiqué on 11 June.[120]

Announcing such a drastic policy change from the *Aufbau des Sozialismus* with absolutely no accompanying commentary was unprecedented and caused great confusion among both the members of the party and the general population, all the more since a key sentence of the communiqué announced that the aim of the Politburo resolutions was to facilitate the "restoration of German unity by bringing the two parts of Germany closer together." In the midst of these momentous changes in a liberal direction, however, the leadership did not rescind the recent 10 percent increase in work norms. Indeed an article published the same day in the party's mouthpiece, *Neues Deutschland*, praised workers for fulfilling the higher work norms.[121] A Soviet report of 24 June would look very critically at the SED's policy toward workers and Ulbricht's role as "the initiator and primary author of the policy to increase output norms."[122] In contrast to Ulbricht, Herrnstadt published an article in *Neues Deutschland* on 14 June criticizing the increased work norms and arguing that the raised norms should not be imposed "dictatorially," but only after the workers had been convinced of their "necessity." This article was passed around among workers on 15 June. They sent a letter to Grotewohl threatening a strike if the work norms were not rescinded.[123]

Uprising in the GDR

The popular uprising of 16–17 June in the GDR exploded the closed-door deliberations on the *New Course* in Berlin and Moscow. Tens of thousands of East German strikers and protesters took the East German and Soviet leaders by surprise. Fed up with poor working conditions and few rewards to show for their work, first construction workers in

Berlin and then others stopped their work and took to the streets. Now the problem for the East German regime was not just the number of people fleeing the country, but the number of people on the streets protesting. To Soviet chagrin, their warnings about dire conditions in East Germany turned out to be all too true. The demands of the people on the streets started out as primarily economic, but grew more political as the day of 16 June wore on without a satisfactory response from the leaders. The protesters began in the morning calling for the increased work norms to be rescinded, for higher pay, and better working conditions. By the afternoon, they were also calling for Ulbricht's overthrow and German unification.[124]

When the demonstrations started, the East German Politburo was meeting in its regular Tuesday session, with Semenov in attendance. SED deputy Heinz Brandt ran to the meeting to inform Berlin party leader Hans Jendretzky of the situation. The Politburo quickly rescinded the increased work norms, but by then this was not enough for the protesters. The chief of the East Berlin police, Waldemar Schmidt, appealed to Soviet Commandant Dibrova to give him the authority to disperse the demonstrations and arrest the "ringleaders." Dibrova refused, saying that this was a "provocatory proposal" and that he did not want any bloodshed.[125]

The Politburo met throughout the night. The West Berlin station, Radio in the American Sector (RIAS), broadcast all night about the day's events. These broadcasts informed not only the Politburo, but also the rest of the GDR population about what had happened.[126] This helped spread the protests the next day.

The panicked East German leaders started negotiations with the Soviets about evacuating their families to the Soviet Union.[127] A Politburo meeting was planned for 10 A.M. on 17 June, but Semenov summoned the whole Politburo immediately to Soviet headquarters outside Berlin at Karlshorst. The uprising expanded on Wednesday 17 June and in the days after to more than 560 towns in the GDR and involved more than 500,000 people.[128] As the demonstrations became larger and more threatening, Soviet Commandant Dibrova stopped the operation of the Berlin city train (S-bahn) and metro (Ü-bahn) and proclaimed a state of emergency in East Berlin at 1 P.M. Soviet tanks began moving into East Berlin in the early morning hours of 17 June. By evening, Soviet troops had sealed off the border to West Berlin to keep out "provocateurs" from West Berlin.[129]

At the Karlshorst meeting, Semenov announced that some of the SED Politburo members would be sent to key areas in the GDR to secure order, while others would remain in Berlin, and still others at Karlshorst. Ulbricht, Grotewohl, Zaisser, and Herrnstadt stayed at Karlshorst, to be chided by Semenov. At one point, he reported to them: "RIAS is saying that there is no longer any government in the GDR." He then commented to his Soviet colleagues in the room, "Well, that is just about true."[130]

Semenov had communications with Soviet forces throughout the GDR and could thus keep the East Germans apprised of the situation as it developed. When Chief of the Soviet General Staff Marshal Sokolovsky arrived from Moscow on 17 June, he strongly reprimanded Zaisser for the Stasi's lack of forewarning of the uprising, a criticism that would become more and more significant in the next few weeks.[131] At 2 P.M., Grotewohl read a statement over the radio, blaming the uprising on "fascist and other reactionary elements from West Berlin." Grotewohl urged people to return to work and their normal life and called for the punishment of the "provocateurs."[132]

In telegrams dictated several times a day over secure, high-frequency telephones, Semenov and other officials at Karlshorst kept the Soviet leadership in Moscow well informed of the situation in Berlin and the GDR.[133] He gave an accounting of the numbers of people arrested, wounded, or killed.[134] And he reported on the activities of the demonstrators, the Soviet and East German troops, and the West Berlin "provocateurs." On 17 June Semenov and Andrei Grechko, the new commander in chief of the Group of Soviet Forces in Germany (GSFG), notified Moscow that by 6 P.M., "Groups of provocateurs were brought in from West Berlin in cargo vehicles to the border of the Soviet sector. We had to establish a guarding of the sectoral border between East and West Berlin with a prohibition of movement by Germans across the border."[135] Later, Sokolovsky and Semenov reported to Moscow that by 11 P.M. the streets in Berlin and most of the GDR were quiet:

> Our forces and the German police are controlling all main roads and the important objects in the Soviet sector of the city. We are directing special attention to guarding the sectoral border between East and West Berlin, through which several big groups of provocateurs and hooligans broke into the Soviet sector in the evening. On the streets of Brunnestrasse and Bernauerstrasse these bands began shoot-outs with the German police, which resulted in some victims.[136]

Although the situation was generally calm in Berlin and elsewhere in the GDR by the evening of 17 June,[137] the night proved to be a very difficult one for the four East German leaders who spent it at Karlshorst with the Soviets.[138] Semenov "ran around the room like a tiger in a cage, wildly gesticulating," while the East Germans sat in silence trying to prepare a report for Moscow on the uprising.[139] The next morning at breakfast with Herrnstadt, Ulbricht expressed his frustration at being made to stay in Karlshorst and being dictated to by the Soviets: "I am going into the city now, into the Central Committee—even if they want to keep me here. Our place is there. It was probably altogether wrong that we stayed here." Ulbricht told Herrnstadt that they must tell the people of the GDR that the uprising had been the fascist provocation that the West had been planning for "Day-X." He commissioned Herrnstadt to write a *Neues Deutschland* story making this point.[140]

In telegrams from Karlshorst to Moscow on 18, 19, and 20 June, Semenov and others reported that the situation was improving. The Soviets and East Germans were making arrests, enterprises were running just about normally again, food supplies were regularized, and East German party officials were holding discussions with the workers in factories. In addition, they had temporarily reopened three checkpoints for East Berliners who had been in West Berlin during the unrest to return to East Berlin.[141] Although there continued to be a few problematic incidents with "provocateurs," the Soviets and East Germans had the situation mostly under control by 20 June.

The Soviets and East Germans believed (or wanted to believe) that the West played an important part in the unrest.[142] On 19 June, Sokolovsky and Semenov told the Kremlin leadership:

> Testimony of people arrested by organs of the Ministry of Internal Affairs provides evidence of the very active organizational role of the American military in the disorders in Berlin. The people arrested testify that American officers personally selected and gathered residents of West Berlin in large groups and gave them instructions to organize disorders in East Berlin, the arson of buildings, etc. As a reward, the American officers promised money, and for the people who were the most active—a three-month vacation in a vacation home, etc. American military people personally gave instructions from cars with loudspeakers to the participants in the disorders near the home of the GDR government on the border of the Soviet sector. There is also information from the GDR provinces of American agents from West Berlin and West Germany sent there.[143]

On the other hand, the Soviets noted in a report to Moscow on the evening of 17 June that "the American radio station RIAS called upon the rebels to obey the orders of the Soviet authorities and not to allow conflicts with the Soviet forces."[144] But as they gained control of the situation and were looking back with more distance on the uprising, the Soviet portrayal of the Western role grew less balanced.

In fact, the Western Powers were very restrained in response to the uprising. And, as CIA Director Allen Dulles told President Eisenhower on 18 June, "the United States had nothing whatsoever to do with inciting these riots."[145] All the rhetoric about "rolling back" Soviet influence and "liberating . . . captive peoples" of the Soviet bloc was just that.[146]

When faced with an opportunity to help the East Germans throw off Soviet occupation, the United States felt it was too risky. Both the president and Allen Dulles feared that providing the East Berliners with arms would be "just inviting a slaughter of these people" by the Soviets. They also wanted to avoid any action that might broaden the conflict to West Berlin and West Germany and result in bloodshed there.[147] As the U.S. High Commissioner in Germany, James Conant, observed, the United States wanted to "keep the pot [of communist unrest] simmering, but not bring it to a boil."[148] The British and French were even less willing, for fear of provoking more violence and East-West tensions, to support the uprising than the Americans.[149]

The three Western commandants in Berlin wrote Dibrova on 23 June urging him to reestablish normal conditions in Berlin.[150] They wanted free movement between the sectors, normal functioning of the S-bahn, Ü-bahn, tram, and telephone, and the removal of barriers between East and West Germany.[151] Arguing against this on 24 June, Sokolovsky, Semenov, and Yudin told the Kremlin leaders that they believed

> it unwise to open the border of East Berlin with West Berlin until the commandants of West Berlin take the necessary steps to guarantee that agents and provocateurs, who carry out subversive activities against the GDR in East Berlin, are no longer sent from West Berlin.
>
> With regard to this, [we propose] to establish, in the immediate future, a system of permanent and temporary visas for permission to cross the border between East and West Berlin.[152]

Heeding their recommendation, Molotov approved a letter attacking the Western commandants for "trying to evade (their) responsibility . . . for the criminal activities of the large groups of hired provocateurs and bandits sent into East Berlin from West Berlin on 17 June."[153] On 6 July the Western commandants denied any Western role in the events of 17 June and again demanded the Soviets restore free movement in Berlin.[154] The Soviets were not ready to risk a broader conflict with the West over Four Power rights in Berlin by keeping the inter-Berlin border closed. Accordingly, on 7 July, the Soviets and East Germans restored movement across the Berlin sectoral border.[155] The East German leaders also acquiesced to complaints from the populace about the difficulty of crossing the border (especially for those who lived in East Berlin and worked in West Berlin).[156]

Developments in Berlin after the Uprising

Following the East German leaders' return from Karlshorst to East Berlin on 18 June, they held daily Politburo meetings. The Soviets, for their part, were concerned about the way the East German domestic situation had developed into an East-West conflict. Semenov, Sokolovsky, and Yudin called Ulbricht, Grotewohl, Herrnstadt, Zaisser, and Rau out to Karlshorst again after the SED Politburo meeting on 20 June. Declaring that it was "politically uncomfortable" for the Soviets to maintain the state of emergency, Semenov asked when it could be suspended. Ulbricht, Grotewohl, and Zaisser said that it was premature to end it, since the VoPos were neither completely armed nor sufficiently deployed to act against new unrest without the Soviet forces. The Soviets responded that they would focus on arming and deploying the VoPos so that the state of emergency could be lifted the following week.

At the Politburo meeting at 10 A.M. on 21 June, Herrnstadt pushed the leadership to take action, issue a statement, and overcome the "confusion and shock" of the general party members. The leaders had issued no statement since Grotewohl's 17 June radio address. Ulbricht finally agreed to call the Fourteenth Central Committee plenum for 10 P.M. that night.[157] His colleagues were gratified that at last they, not the Soviets, were seizing the initiative. The plenum's resolutions mollified the workers. Noting that "when the masses of workers do not understand the party, the party is guilty, not the worker," the resolutions contained a series of measures for improving the situation of the workers. The party members, disoriented and embittered, passed the resolutions anticipating that the Politburo would submit another self-critical statement identifying the conditions that prompted the uprising.[158]

The SED Politburo urged the Soviets to complete the economic negotiations with them that would allow them to make more specific plans for implementing the *New Course*.[159] On 24 June Molotov instructed Semenov to tell Grotewohl and Ulbricht that the Soviets would satisfy their requests for deliveries of foodstuffs and cotton.[160] These deliveries were completed on 5 August.[161] In the wake of the uprising, the Soviets were much more willing to grant the GDR economic aid. They wanted to quickly improve the standard of living in the GDR, because in the wake of the uprising U.S. authorities in West Berlin offered food aid to the East Berliners and East Germans.[162] The Kremlin ordered the East Germans, not always successfully, to refuse this aid and provided their own instead.[163]

Once the East German leaders caught their breath after 17 June, the pre-uprising criticism of Ulbricht resumed. The SED Politburo commission that had been formed on 6 June to propose organizational changes met in its first session on 25 June. Herrnstadt had been preparing his proposal for several weeks. He wanted to eliminate the Secretariat in its existing form and create a truly collective Secretariat by enlarging the number of Politburo members. He suggested that Ulbricht give up the direct leadership of the party and proposed renaming the Politburo the Presidium. A "Permanent Commission of the Presidium" would oversee the execution of the *New Course*, and the Secretariat and the functions of the General Secretary would be eliminated.[164] The Soviets seemed to support these measures. In their birthday greeting to Ulbricht on 30 June, they referred to him as one of the "most well-known organizers and leaders of the SED," not the General Secretary.[165]

Something, however, changed between the 25 June and 2 July meetings of the Politburo commission. Grotewohl told Herrnstadt of a conversation with Ulbricht and Semenov in which Semenov spoke very critically of Zaisser and very highly of Karl Schirdewan, whom he seemed to want in the Politburo.[166] The 2 July meeting was far more tense than the 25 June meeting, and Ulbricht was more combative.[167] The leaders argued about the size and composition of the Politburo and the Secretariat. Zaisser nominated Herrnstadt to replace Ulbricht as general secretary. The discussion was so heated at times that Oelssner could not translate fast enough for V. Miroshnichenko, Semenov's deputy. Miroshnichenko advised postponing the commission's discussion until Semenov and Yudin returned to Berlin from Moscow.[168] The situation, however, would be drastically different upon their return.

At Politburo meetings in early July, there was criticism of Ulbricht and also of Zaisser and Herrnstadt. Oelssner accused the latter two of proposals "directed at dividing the party leadership," especially Zaisser's proposal to replace Ulbricht with Herrnstadt. The Politburo met again on the evening of 7 July for four to five hours before Ulbricht and Grotewohl flew to Moscow on other matters in the early morning of 8 July.[169] The meeting again focused on a sharp critique of Ulbricht and the composition of a new leadership. Only Matern and Honecker supported Ulbricht remaining in the position of general secretary. Ulbricht then admitted that he must work on changing his style of leadership. The meeting ended when Ulbricht and Grotewohl had to go to the airport to fly to Moscow. Neither they nor any of the other members of the leadership knew why they had been summoned to Moscow. Nor could they foresee that Ulbricht would return from Moscow in a greatly strengthened position.

Backtracking from the *New Course*

Ulbricht and Grotewohl arrived in Moscow to learn that Beria had been arrested on 26 June and ousted from the leadership for his "criminal anti-party and anti-governmental activities." Although he was ousted because the other Soviet leaders feared his powers as head of the secret police and Minister of Internal Affairs, they felt a need to levy various and sundry charges against him. Luckily for Ulbricht, Beria was denounced as "an agent of international imperialism [who sought to] renounce the course of the construction of socialism in the German Democratic Republic and to adopt a course for the conversion of the GDR into a bourgeois government, which would have meant a direct capitulation to the imperialist forces."[170] He was also accused of playing individual party leaders off against each other to increase his own authority and of striving to raise the authority of the Ministry of Internal Affairs above that of the party. The Soviet leadership vowed to return party work to normal and work as a collective.[171]

The factions in the East German Politburo both for and against Ulbricht believed they had cause to celebrate the Soviet resolutions against Beria. Ulbricht and his supporters were relieved that "Beria's" *New Course* appeared to have been dealt a harsh blow, as had been his practice of playing the leaders off against each other. Herrnstadt, Zaisser, and their supporters, on the other hand, were heartened by criticism of Beria's heavy-handed methods and the calls for collective leadership and for a closer bond between the party and the people.

While in Moscow, Ulbricht probably received renewed backing from the Soviet leaders. This is indicated by the Soviet decision to abandon the set of proposals made by Sokolovsky, Semenov, and Yudin on 24 June. The proposals had called for drastic changes in the GDR party, government, economy, and all key organizations, including the "limitation of the functions of the SED CC Secretariat, [the] liquidation of the currently existing post of General Secretary of the SED CC [held by Ulbricht], [and the] fundamental renovation of the SED CC PB [Politburo]."[172] Unfortunately, we have no records regarding any private meetings Ulbricht may have had with the Soviets in Moscow. The rapid pace of events upon his return to Berlin, however, is strong circumstantial evidence that his trip to Moscow bolstered his determination to remove his opponents.

While we lack direct evidence of Ulbricht's conversations with the Soviet leaders and his efforts to preserve his position in the tense months of 1953, and particularly in June and July, we have a lot of evidence of his behavior with the Soviets both before and after 1953, and, given Ulbricht's strong personality, we can safely assume he behaved the same way during the important months of 1953. Ulbricht's pattern of behavior before, after, and presumably during 1953 was to go forward with the policies he wanted, even if the Soviets did not support these policies, and to maintain his leadership position at all costs. This is what "comrade cell" did in establishing a socialist state under his control, often moving further and faster than the Soviets advocated, in the mid–late 1940s and what he did in the 1950s with his resistance to the *New*

Course and later with his efforts to gain control over the borders in Berlin. Ulbricht was stubborn and tenacious in pursuing his goals, either by indirectly getting around Soviet preferences through his implementation of policies on the ground in the GDR and East Berlin or by directly persuading the Soviets in conversations and letters of his own policy preferences.

Ulbricht and Grotewohl arrived back in Berlin for an evening Politburo meeting on 9 July, having stayed in Moscow for perhaps only twenty-four hours. They reported to the meeting that representatives from all socialist countries had been called to Moscow to learn about Beria's ouster from Malenkov, Molotov, and Khrushchev. Herrnstadt and his supporters assumed that since Ulbricht acted in the same sort of autocratic way as Beria had, he would soon be removed from power.[173]

At the next Politburo meeting, however, Ulbricht attacked Herrnstadt and Zaisser. He said that the Politburo must inform the Central Committee of their "anti-party" behavior. Having moved quickly to gather support since his return from Moscow, Ulbricht now instructed Hermann Matern, the head of the Central Party Control Commission, to investigate Herrnstadt and Zaisser. Despite objections by other members of the Politburo, Ulbricht silenced them and declared that the fifteenth plenum was set for 24–26 July.

After this Politburo session, it became more and more evident that Herrnstadt and Zaisser, not Ulbricht, would be ousted from the leadership and that Soviet High Commissioner Semenov supported this. Semenov seemed to have changed his view radically from the proposals he had recently submitted with Sokolovsky and Yudin to the Foreign Ministry for fundamental changes in the SED leadership. In all likelihood, he received a directive to change his line in favor of supporting Ulbricht.

Soviet support for the ouster of Zaisser and Herrnstadt from the Politburo was obvious by the presence at the fifteenth plenum of I. Kabin, CPSU CC Secretary for Relations with Germany. Ulbricht's speech against Zaisser and Herrnstadt was much sharper than the speech he had submitted for Politburo approval the day before.[174] After speaking of Herrnstadt and Zaisser's "platform" directed against the Politburo, Ulbricht alluded to Beria's hostile activity against the party and state in the Soviet Union. He implied a connection between Beria, Herrnstadt, and Zaisser, facilitated by Beria and Zaisser's positions as secret police chiefs.[175] At the end of the fifteenth plenum, "the Central Commitee resolved unanimously to expel from the SED CC Comrades Zaisser and Herrnstadt, who behaved as a party-hostile faction with a defeatist line directed against the unity" of the party. The plenum did, however, vote to continue with the *New Course* and a self-critical examination of the conditions that triggered the June uprising.[176] But Ulbricht and his supporters clearly favored blaming the problems on "saboteurs" like Zaisser and Herrnstadt.

If the Beria episode had not intervened, Zaisser and Herrnstadt may have succeeded in their efforts to remove Ulbricht from power. The Soviets had blamed Ulbricht for most of the GDR's problems before and immediately after the uprising. They were well aware of the connection between his personality and policies and the grievances of the East German people. Thus, it was not the uprising per se that prompted Khrushchev, Malenkov, and Molotov to change track and support Ulbricht instead of his more accommodating opponents. Indeed, as Mark Kramer observes, "if Beria's arrest had come *before* rather than after the rebellion in the GDR, Soviet policy toward Germany in subsequent years might have followed a very different course. But the timing of Beria's downfall enabled his rivals . . . to blame Beria for the uprising along with a host of other purported 'crimes' (some real, many spurious)."[177] It was very bad luck for supporters of reform and liberalization in the GDR.

By early July the Soviets were focused on ousting Beria and shoring up their power at home. The attention they had devoted to the GDR in late May and early July dissipated. Accordingly, the Kremlin leaders seemingly did not feel they could sanction such a crucial change as Ulbricht's ouster. This would have necessitated much deeper involvement in GDR affairs than they were prepared for. Lacking internal Soviet records on their deliberations about Ulbricht's fate, we must content ourselves with the circumstantial evidence that the Soviets decided the safer course in the GDR was not to switch horses in midstream.

RENEWED SOVIET SUPPORT FOR ULBRICHT'S GDR

Now that the situation in the GDR leadership was stabilized, in a manner of speaking, Soviet officials at MID resumed their drafting of proposals on Germany. They generally urged a continuation of the two-track policy they had been proposing since April: trying to engage the West in talks on Germany and giving more Soviet support to the GDR. Expecting that the West would reject the former, they emphasized the latter. They urged inviting a top-level East German delegation to Moscow to raise the status of the GDR and grant the GDR more economic assistance.[178] Many of the recommendations made earlier in documents from 21, 24, 28 April; 2, 27 May; and 9 July were repeated and further developed in proposals drafted by MID officials at the end of July and in August. They urged a general activization of Soviet policy on the German question in August.[179]

The Soviet leaders adopted MID's two-track strategy. On 15 August, they sent a note to the Western Powers on the German question and invited the East German leaders to Moscow. In the note to the West, the Soviets observed that the Four Powers should be able to convene a peace conference to discuss a peace treaty with a united German government within six months. This was not the last time the Soviets would attempt to prod the West into acting on their proposals regarding Germany within six months.

MID also proposed a meeting on 10 August of the Foreign Ministers of the USSR, GDR, Poland, Czechoslovakia, Hungary, Romania, Bulgaria, and Albania in Moscow or Berlin.[180] The goals of the meeting would be to make a statement against the Bonn and Paris agreements on West German military integration with the West. The socialist leaders would also sign a treaty of friendship and of economic and cultural cooperation. MID officials declared that this treaty would be particularly useful for "raising the position of the GDR, not thus far connected with the other socialist countries by such treaties on friendship and mutual aid," and for demonstrating to the West that if the Bonn and Paris agreements were ratified, the socialist bloc would integrate the GDR into allied military relations in the bloc in a similar way. This meeting of the socialist bloc, however, did not take place until 2 December 1954 in Moscow and by that time was a prelude to the creation of the Warsaw Pact in May 1955.[181]

At the same time as they sent the note to the Western Powers, the Soviets also invited an East German governmental delegation to visit Moscow.[182] The Soviet–East German meeting to upgrade relations and consult on policy occurred in Moscow on 20–22 August. This was the first formal, public visit by an official GDR governmental delegation to Moscow since the founding of the GDR in 1949. Ulbricht probably felt that four years had been far too long to wait for this invitation, but at last the Soviets were prepared to display to the world their strong support of the GDR.

The East Germans flew to Moscow in a special Russian plane put at their disposal.[183] At the opening session in the Kremlin on 20 August, Malenkov, Molotov, Bulganin, and Mikoian told the East Germans of their intention to alleviate significantly the economic burdens upon the GDR and to transform Moscow's mission into an embassy, thus making High Commissioner Semenov the Soviet ambassador to the GDR in addition to his Four Power duties as High Commissioner.[184] Malenkov opened the meeting, discussing the Soviet note of 15 August to the Western powers and emphasizing the Soviet desire for a German peace conference to be convened within six months.

Molotov, Bulganin, and Mikoian presented the details of the economic aid they would offer the East Germans. This included ending reparations taken from the GDR by the Soviet Union and Poland as of 1 January 1954 and handing over to the GDR thirty-three Soviet joint stock companies in the GDR free of cost. They would also cancel all GDR debts with the Soviet Union and reduce the occupation costs of the Soviet troops paid by the GDR down to 5 percent of the GDR state revenue. They would transform the Soviet-owned Wismut uranium mining company in the GDR into a joint Soviet–East German stock company. Most important, they would significantly increase supplies to the GDR of foodstuffs and goods of mass consumption and would grant a large amount of credit to the GDR.[185] The Soviets informed the East Germans that even if the Western powers did not agree to end the reparations payments and cancel the debts of the FRG, they would still hold to these agreements with the GDR. The clear goal of such significant Soviet aid to the GDR was to raise the living standard of the population so as to keep people from fleeing west or taking to the streets in protest.

Judging by Grotewohl's reaction, the East Germans had not known in advance how significant the aid would be:

> What you have proposed to us here today is so surprising and overwhelming for us that we almost lack the words to say what must be said about this.
>
> You know that in the last months we suffered a period of political and economic circumstances in the GDR which was undoubtedly wrong. We took pains to come out of this cycle, but it was absolutely clear that this was entirely impossible by our own forces. We expressed our wishes to you regarding help, but the way in which you have answered this is so much more . . . [than we expected].

Ulbricht expressed his own appreciation for the sacrifices of the Soviet people to help the GDR and promised that the GDR would mobilize all of its own reserves to improve the economic situation. He declared that the aid would make it possible for the GDR "really to push forward also in West Germany and to come out of the defensive."[186]

This meeting confirmed that the Soviet leadership had decided, in light of the uprising and the developments concerning Beria, to give strong support to Ulbricht and the East German state. Both the Soviets and Ulbricht knew how close he had come to being ousted by opponents within the leadership or by a popular uprising. Ulbricht must have been been very relieved at the talks in Moscow. He had at last received a formal, public invitation to Moscow, a promise of significant Soviet economic aid, and an upgrading of Soviet–East German relations. He had weathered a very difficult several months and come out stronger, even if this was partly due to chance rather than his own actions.

Conclusion

The six turbulent months of March–August 1953 proved essential for charting the future development of Soviet–East German relations. By the end of May, Stalin's successors realized they were faced with a crisis in the GDR, manifested in the refugee exodus. They insisted, against East German leadership resistance, that the East Germans adopt the *New Course* of liberalization to escape the crisis and stabilize the situation. This proved to be too little too late in the wake of the disastrous results of the *Aufbau des Sozialismus* program pushed through by Ulbricht for almost a year. Instead of being placated, the East German people erupted in an uprising.

The SED leaders stubbornly refused to believe that their situation was dire; they were, therefore, stunned by the magnitude of the demonstrations and desperately needed Soviet help.[187] The Soviets intervened with their tanks and troops, regaining control in the GDR. In the wake of the uprising, the Soviets realized that the crisis they had identified the previous month was even greater than anticipated. At this stage, they could have adopted one of two courses: They could have decided that widespread hostility toward Ulbricht and his policies was too great to imagine a long-term improvement of the situation with him still in power; or they could have decided that they had to maintain a united front with Ulbricht in order to prevent the East German people (or the West) from detecting any signs of weakness or vacillation that could be taken advantage of regarding the East German regime. They opted for the latter, while hoping that Ulbricht would use increased Soviet aid to facilitate the *New Course* instead of just clinging to his established harsh policies.

We are still lacking some key Soviet sources, notably from the Presidential Archives, which would illuminate the process of Soviet thinking, particularly in late May, June, and July. Hence, we are left studying Soviet policy outcomes, without knowing the processes by which these policies were reached. By looking at the circumstantial evidence, we can see the great importance of Beria's ouster in leading Khrushchev, Malenkov, and Molotov to take the second course described above, that of siding with Ulbricht. After the uprising and before Beria's ouster, the Soviets had remained very critical of Ulbricht's leadership style and policies, and supportive of his opposition led by Herrnstadt and Zaisser, and were thus seemingly prepared to adopt the first course.[188] It was only with Beria's ouster and the charge that he sought to liquidate socialism in the GDR and abandon it to the imperialists that the Soviets swung back defensively to the second course.

Khrushchev himself learned some lessons from the 1953 uprising with important implications for the policies he would pursue toward the GDR and "the German question" once he rose as the leader to succeed Stalin. The uprising occurred at the beginning of Khrushchev's rise to supreme power, at a formative time for his ideas on policy making in general and for his ideas regarding Germany in particular. He learned two main lessons from the uprising: how precarious the situation was in East Germany, and how important it was to support the GDR militarily, economically, and politically. He saw the high costs of not supporting the GDR: The GDR and its socialist system could collapse, and his own political career, as Beria's, could be ruined or his life jeopardized if he appeared willing to sacrifice the GDR.

Once Khrushchev emerged as the victor of the post-Stalin succession struggle, he felt the pressure of the charges against Beria. On more than one occasion in the years to come, he would proudly, yet somewhat defensively, declare that while Beria and Malenkov had wanted to "give up the GDR," he would never do such a thing.[189] After publicly accusing Beria in 1953 of plotting to "give up" the GDR to the imperialist West, it was much less likely that Khrushchev or other Soviet officials in the future would risk policies that could be viewed in this way. Soviet policy would increasingly move away from serious consideration of German unification to a greater focus on building up the GDR.[190] Memories of the charges against Beria and Malenkov probably motivated Khrushchev's frequent assertions that the Soviet Union would never agree to the reunification of Germany "at the expense of the GDR [or] through the liquidation of the GDR and its socialist achievements." Ulbricht grasped Khrushchev's political need to separate himself from Beria and Malenkov, and the East German leader subsequently exploited this leverage.[191]

Khrushchev and his colleagues would repeatedly urge Ulbricht after 1953 to carry out the *New Course* measures, take the refugee exodus more seriously, and expand ties with "progressive circles" in West Germany, such as the SPD. Ulbricht, however, resisted these measures, since the uprising made him even more averse than he had been before to loosening his grip on power. This ultimately put the Soviets in the position of needing to agree to Ulbricht's pleas to close the border in Berlin in the summer of 1961 if they really wanted to preserve his regime and a socialist GDR.

The key factors in Soviet–East German relations, which played an important role in this chapter, will continue in the rest of this work. The Soviets remained concerned about Ulbricht's style of rule and his policies and kept urging liberalization of both. Through his capacity to control the local situation, Ulbricht resisted Soviet pressure to change, thus effectively limiting Soviet policy options in Germany. In 1953 we also see the two sides of the East German–Soviet debate over how to deal with the refugee exodus: the East German preference for closing the border and the Soviet preference for finding other ways. This debate reflected broader differences between the Soviet and GDR leaders about the character of the GDR regime, where the Soviets favored, when possible, a focus on the legitimacy of the regime in the eyes of the people, and Ulbricht favored the control of the regime over the people. The GDR's economic problems and their connection to East Germany's stability and viability were made abundantly clear in this period and would play an increasing role in Soviet–East German relations leading to the building of the Berlin Wall. The uprising made it easier for Ulbricht to claim in subsequent years that more and more Soviet economic aid was necessary to keep his citizens happy so they would not flee to the West or take to the streets in a dangerous way. The Soviets saved a socialist GDR in 1953, but in the process promoted the development of a complicated and demanding ally, as we shall see.

CHAPTER TWO

1956–1958

Soviet and East German Policy Debates in the Wake of the Twentieth Party Congress

PRIOR TO THE GDR uprising and Beria's ouster, the Soviet leadership backed a more accommodating, gradual form of socialism in the GDR, which might have led to different developments in the GDR and in Germany as a whole than in fact took place. This chain of events occurred again in 1956 in the aftermath of the CPSU Twentieth Congress and Khrushchev's secret speech denouncing Stalin. Just as the relaxation of policies in the GDR in 1953 encouraged a popular uprising, so the de-Stalinization policies of Khrushchev in 1956 opened the gates to revolts in Poland and Hungary, with the latter put down by Soviet tanks. In both 1953 and 1956, there was some chance of a mellowing of the cold war due to a liberalization of Soviet policies, but popular movements for more rapid, far-reaching change in Eastern Europe, combined with domestic politics in the Kremlin, led the Soviets to retract their more liberal policies. The dynamics of the cold war also had the effect of making its perpetuation much easier than its mellowing, and Ulbricht was particularly adept at taking advantage of this phenomenon.

In the three years after Stalin's death, while Ulbricht steadily strangled the *New Course* in the GDR, Nikita S. Khrushchev consolidated his position as primus inter pares among Stalin's successors so that by 1956 he was in a position to put his own stamp on policy. And this he would do in a dramatic way at the Twentieth Congress in February 1956. As in the previous chapter, this chapter begins with a Soviet "new course" of liberalization, which initially sets Khrushchev and Ulbricht on a collision course and redounds to the benefit of Ulbricht's opposition, but ends with Ulbricht ousting this opposition and regaining Khrushchev's support after another (although not East German) uprising. This time, however, the process lasts significantly longer, two years, and attracts more high-level opposition to Ulbricht among the East Germans and the Soviets.

The extensive debates in the SED leadership concerning the Twentieth Congress and the Hungarian revolution indicates that developments in the GDR were more fluid and contingent than previously believed. As in 1953, so in 1956 there were serious disagreements over the nature of the East German regime. Similar discussions took place in other countries of the Soviet bloc also. Even more than 1953, this was a period of opportunity to step off the Stalinist path and introduce a more liberal, open form of socialism. We pull back the iron curtain in this chapter to reveal the contentious state of affairs in the Soviet bloc three years after Stalin's death.

Many of the issues in Soviet–East German relations discussed in the previous chapter remain important in this one. Again we see Soviet vacillations about the type of leaders and policies they support in the GDR, disagreements over how to handle the refugee exodus, East German economic difficulties and need for Soviet aid, and disagreements between the Soviets and East Germans (and within the East German leadership) about policy toward West Germany and West Berlin. This chapter further demonstrates Ulbricht's capacity to disregard Khrushchev's wishes concerning East German domestic and foreign policy and thus to constrain Khrushchev's options in *Deutschlandpolitik*. The GDR's precarious strategic location, and the resulting need to take special measures to protect it, are reemphasized in the wake of the Polish and Hungarian uprisings, establishing a pattern of the East German regime gaining strength in negotiations with the Soviet Union through its vulnerability at home. This chapter also introduces us to the China factor in East German–Soviet relations as the Sino-Soviet rift begins. The similarly critical reactions of Ulbricht and Chinese leader Mao Zedong to Khrushchev's policy initiatives at the Twentieth Congress open up a whole new way for Ulbricht to put pressure on Khrushchev to support Ulbricht's aims. Finally, this chapter gives us the first chance to begin to compare the contrary and equally stubborn personalities of Khrushchev and Ulbricht.

Background: 1953–1956

East German Policies and the Continuing Refugee Exodus

Returning from the August 1953 summit in Moscow, Ulbricht declared: "There exist in fact two German states, and German unity can only come about through negotiations" between them.[1] Emboldened by Moscow's support, he decided that ousting Herrnstadt and Zaisser from their leadership positions in July had not been enough; at the seventeenth plenum on 23 January 1954, he expelled them from the SED altogether.[2] The Fourth Party Congress of the SED in April focused on collectivization and a new party statute remolding the SED closer to the Soviet model, much more reminiscent of the *Aufbau des Sozialismus* program than the *New Course*.[3] A year later Ulbricht even more clearly abandoned the *New Course*. He told the Central Committee members at the twenty-fourth plenum in June 1955:

Some of you will wonder why I haven't used the phrase "New Course." . . .
It has given a lot of people strange ideas—namely, that it is possible to con-
sume more than is produced, that wages can rise faster than productivity . . .
that it is all right to loaf on the job. . . . The ideological effects have been just
as obvious. Neutrality toward bourgeois ideology and superstition has grown.
Our call to foster a happy life for the working masses has led many functionaries to encourage a selfish, materialist outlook. What is more remarkable
about this Course is not that it is new, but that it is wrong. I must warn
people with these ideas that we never meant to, and never will, embark on
this kind of mistaken course.[4]

Not surprisingly under these conditions, refugees continued to flee the
GDR, and the Soviet concerns deepened.[5] After all, the Soviet *New
Course* given to the East German leaders in June 1953 had been motivated primarily by the refugee exodus. Now, two years later, the Soviets
still felt the East German leaders were not coping satisfactorily with the
situation. Visiting East Berlin in the summer of 1955, Khrushchev voiced
his anxiety about the refugee exodus, especially since "there are a whole
string of party members, and even party functionaries, who are joining
the march westwards. This is really indicative of a most extreme weakness. We must think of how to counter this." When Grotewohl referred
cautiously to the open borders, Khrushchev made it clear that he "did
not consider closing the border. [Instead], he demanded from us a political mastering of this problem," as the Soviets had been urging.[6]

Five months later, however, I. Tugarinov, deputy chairman of MID's
Committee of Information, wrote an alarmed memo on the refugee flow.
Gromyko forwarded it to the Soviet Politburo. Judging the refugee exo-
dus "to be one of the most serious problems for our German friends,"
Tugarinov complained:

Until recently, the party and governmental organs of the GDR have not
devoted serious attention to the issue of the exodus of GDR citizens to West
Germany, have not attached the necessary political significance to this occur-
rence. The SED CC Politburo's resolution of 15 December 1953, "On further
measures for fighting the exodus of the population from the Republic," was
not carried out, and it was practically forgotten. . . .

Only police organs are really dealing with the issue of the exodus of the
population to West Germany, and their work is practically reduced just to
registering refugees. . . .

SED organs . . . are not explaining or analyzing the reasons for the (exodus). . . .

Only very recently has the growing exodus . . . begun to upset party and
governmental organs in the GDR. Ulbricht discussed this at the SED CC
plenum in October 1955, but neither in his speech nor in the resolutions

of the plenum was there any indication of what kinds of measures should be taken.[7]

Tugarinov attributed the high numbers of refugees to a variety of factors: the better economic situation in the FRG; the draft; and the "hostile activity" in the GDR carried out by West German agents. The report concluded, as so many others did and would, that the "existing situation with the exodus of the GDR population to West Germany demands urgent preparation and implementation of serious economic and political measures which could facilitate the resolution of this difficult problem."[8] Yet, in a conversation with A. Orlov of the Soviet embassy in East Berlin in January 1956, the Berlin party leader Alfred Neumann still argued instead for restricting movement across the Berlin sectoral border.[9]

While Ulbricht did not undertake any practical measures to combat the refugee exodus or to improve relations with the East German people, he did remain worried about a repetition of the June 1953 uprising. Stasi chief Wollweber noticed that "in all conversations concerning the security of the country, (Ulbricht) had the shock of 17 June 1953 still in his bones." Especially on the first anniversary, on 17 June 1954, Ulbricht was panicked about rumors of another uprising and breathed easier only when the date passed without incident.[10]

Soviet Policies

Following Stalin's death and Beria's ouster and execution in 1953, the other Soviet leaders jockeyed for power. Khrushchev and Malenkov were the main contenders for the position of Stalin's successor. They both recognized that they needed to moderate Stalin's policies across the board. They sought to stabilize conditions in the Soviet Union and the Soviet bloc, while also reaching out to the West. Improving relations with the West would reduce the military and economic pressure on the Soviet bloc and give the Kremlin leaders more breathing space to consolidate their power.

They were also grappling with the effect of nuclear weapons on their foreign policy and international relations more generally. Malenkov made the mistake of declaring that nuclear weapons were an equalizing force between communists and capitalists, because their killing power was ideologically indiscriminate. He concluded that this danger necessitated peaceful relations between the communists and capitalists, who would have to find other nonmilitary means to carry out their competition.[11] Khrushchev seized on the opportunity to label Malenkov ideologically weak and capitulationist to the West. Khrushchev thus swung the conservative ideologues and the powerful members of the Soviet military-industrial complex over to his side in the power struggle. He succeeded in ousting Malenkov as head of state in 1955. Once Malenkov was safely out of the way, Khrushchev proceeded to adopt Malenkov's views on the necessity of improving relations with the West and the constraining effect of nuclear weapons on Soviet relations with the West.

Soon after Stalin's death, the new Kremlin leaders first signaled their interest in a more pragmatic, accommodating foreign policy with regard to the Korean War. While Stalin had dragged out the armistice negotiations inconclusively for two years, happy to keep both the Americans and Chinese preoccupied there, his successors wanted to be rid of this conflict.[12] They put an end to Stalin's stalling tactics and persuaded the North Koreans to sign an armistice in July 1953.

The Kremlin's conciliatory line in foreign policy became even more evident in 1955 under Khrushchev's lead. In April he went to Belgrade to apologize to Tito for Stalin's unfair treatment of him in 1948 and to invite him back into the Soviet bloc.[13] Khrushchev topped this unusual Soviet behavior in May by agreeing (against Molotov's opposition)[14] to withdraw Soviet forces from Austria and its capital, Vienna, in return for a united, neutral Austria as established in the Austrian State Treaty.[15] And then in July, he met Western leaders in Geneva at the first Great Power summit since 1945, contributing to a warm "spirit of Geneva" in East-West relations.[16] This Soviet leader was not afraid to travel and engage with foreign leaders. He showed a new Soviet face to the world, very different from Stalin's paranoid and brutal one.

Khrushchev's policy toward Germany reflected his broader attempt to reach out to the West while consolidating power at home. In 1953 he had not been one of the main initiators of *Deutschlandpolitik* as Molotov and Beria were, and he had very little background in foreign policy in general. He had formed part of the consensus favoring a less intense, more liberal form of socialism in the GDR in 1953, and he argued against any consideration of "putting 18 million [East] Germans under the control of American imperialists." Once Khrushchev had consolidated his power and was in a position to give serious attention to Germany in 1955, he energized both parts of Soviet *Deutschlandpolitik*: He reached out to West Germany, and he gave further direct support to East Germany.

Between 1953 and 1956, the Soviets made a big public show of granting the GDR increasing amounts of sovereignty and providing large-scale economic and diplomatic support, beginning with the negotiations in Moscow on 21–22 August 1953. Meanwhile, the Four Powers tried, in vain, to agree on the terms of a peace treaty and the reunification of Germany. After the latest attempt failed at the Conference of Foreign Ministers (CFM) in Berlin in early 1954, the Soviets announced in

March the establishment of "the same relations with the GDR as with other sovereign states and full sovereignty for the GDR in its internal and external affairs, including in its relations with the FRG."[17] On 6 August 1954, the Soviets declared all orders and instructions of the Soviet Military Administration and the Soviet Control Council regarding the political, economic and cultural life of the GDR between 1945 and 1953 null and void.[18] On 25 January 1955, the Soviets declared the end of the state of war with Germany.[19]

Nineteen fifty-five was a pivotal year in Soviet policy toward both parts of Germany. The FRG's admission to NATO in May 1955, through the Paris Agreements, reflected a failure on the part of the Soviets, since one of their major policy goals, had been preventing the alliance of any part of Germany with the West.[20] Stalin's successors responded to the new situation in three ways: They formed the Warsaw Pact (also called the Warsaw Treaty Organization, WTO);[21] they invited Adenauer to establish formal diplomatic relations; and they augmented support to the GDR. The Soviets thus continued and consolidated their two-track approach in *Deutschlandpolitik*—expanding their control in the East by forming the Warsaw Pact and strengthening their part of Germany, on the one hand, and, on the other hand, reaching out to West Germany.[22] The GDR, against Molotov's objections as we shall see, was one of the founding members of the Warsaw Pact.[23] The East German National People's Army (NVA) was created in January 1956 and then integrated into the Warsaw Pact.[24]

After six years of not recognizing the existence of the Federal Republic of Germany, its rearmament and integration into NATO in 1955 induced the Soviets to change their strategy, even without Western recognition of the GDR. Khrushchev thus adopted a "two-states policy" of relations with both Germanys. In June he invited Adenauer to Moscow. The visit took place from 9–13 September.[25] The Soviets and West Germans established diplomatic relations and expanded their trade relations. Knowing that the East Germans were worried about their talks with Adenauer, the Kremlin regularly informed East Berlin on the progress of the talks.[26] While Ulbricht certainly did not appreciate Khrushchev recognizing the FRG without Western recognition of the GDR, it was a pragmatic move on Khrushchev's part allowing him to have some direct influence on the West Germans. He hoped to moderate West German policy vis-à-vis East Germany and to pull West Germany away from its close ties with the West.

Two months earlier, Khrushchev had stopped in East Berlin for three days on the way back to Moscow from Geneva.[27] Khrushchev declared, partly to the West and partly to reassure Ulbricht, that the Soviet Union would never give up the GDR and its achievements.[28] He proclaimed that two German states existed and that the German problem would not be resolved to the detriment of the GDR's interests. He invited the East German leaders to come to Moscow immediately following Adenauer's trip.

The GDR leaders were in Moscow from 16–20 September and signed a treaty of friendship and mutual cooperation with the Soviets, in which, as Fritz Schenk has wryly observed, once again it was stated that the GDR had full sovereignty.[29] The Soviets now completely abolished the office of the high commissioner of the USSR in Germany.[30] The Soviet–East German treaty was accompanied by an important exchange of letters between Soviet Deputy Foreign Minister V. Zorin and East German Foreign Minister L. Bolz. These gave the GDR authority over the defense and control of its borders with the FRG and West Berlin, and over the transit routes between the FRG and West Berlin, except for the personnel and freight of the three Western occupying powers. The Soviets would "for the time being" oversee the movement of allied military personnel and freight between West Germany and West Berlin, but the East Germans now had control over civilian access.[31] This was an important step in Ulbricht's plans to gain control over *all* movement across GDR territory between West Germany and West Berlin.

What were Khrushchev's goals in Germany? Like most Soviets, he wanted the Soviet position in Germany to be as strong as possible. Germany was the World War II enemy; East Germany was a Soviet trophy from that war. With the wartime losses still vivid in the minds of the Kremlin leaders, they aimed to ensure Germany would not pose a threat to their country again. Military and political methods were necessary for this. Khrushchev tried to buttress his influence in East Germany as well as extend it to West Germany. The problem was that these two goals were mutually exclusive: The more the Soviets solidified socialist control in the GDR, the more suspicious West Germans were of the East Germans and Soviets, and thus the less likely that communism would gain a stronghold in West Germany.

As with the accusations against Beria in 1953, there are scattered indications that not all Kremlin leaders always favored the kind of deep and broad backing for the GDR that Khrushchev would come to support. While East Germany was an important reminder of Soviet victory in World War II, Germany as a whole was also at the heart of Soviet conflict with the West, risking war at various points. In addition, enormous Soviet resources were required to keep the GDR afloat, diverting those scarce resources from other uses. Although any one instance of Soviet reluctance to give substantial aid to the GDR may be discounted, putting together various such instances adds up to a pattern of some Soviet wavering on its commitment to East Germany (culminating with Gorbachev's decision in 1989–1990 to give it up). This wavering was partly due to a reluctance to expend the resources necessary for the GDR's upkeep and partly due to a Soviet hope that if Germany were united, the Soviets would then exert influence over *all* of Germany (although the likelihood of the latter option faded increasingly in the 1950s).

In the first case of Soviet wavering, Stalin delayed the creation of an East German state, and then he dragged his feet on giving the green light for full-scale socialist policies in that state. He may even have been willing to give up the GDR for a united, neutral Germany in 1952, although this is very unlikely.[32] A year later, if Beria's opponents are right, Beria planned to give up the GDR, thinking it was not worth the Soviet resources required to defend it or the risk of war with the West.

Then, in 1955, Molotov apparently opposed the inclusion of East Germany and Albania in the Warsaw Pact asking, "Why should we fight with the West over the GDR?" Khrushchev supposedly responded that if these countries were not included, "it [would] send a signal to our Western foes: 'You are allowed . . . to eat up Albania and the GDR.'" Khrushchev declared that this "would inflame the appetite of the revanchists and other Western powers that would like to tear from us Albania and, most importantly, the GDR." Thus, the GDR and Albania were included in the list of Warsaw Pact members.[33]

Later, as we shall see, some Kremlin leaders criticized Khrushchev's insistence on giving the GDR significant economic aid, preferring not to continue pouring Soviet resources down what they clearly believed was an East German hole. They did not place the same value that Khrushchev did on maintaining the GDR at any price. Khrushchev, however, argued in the 1950s that any other policy would mean "losing the GDR," something he was not prepared to do.

What accounted for Khrushchev's expanding commitment to the GDR in the 1950s? There were two mutually reinforcing factors, one pragmatic, the other ideological. Khrushchev did not want to follow in Beria and Malenkov's shoes. He did not want to give his colleagues ammunition to accuse him of favoring the GDR's abandonment. Khrushchev feared this even more once the Chinese started questioning his allegiance to the communist cause in the wake of his denunciation of Stalin in 1956. He also did not want a united Germany to be a part of the Western alliance, advancing the latter deeper into the Soviet bloc. Just as important, Khrushchev had great faith in communism and wanted to demonstrate to the world, at the German front line of the cold war, communism's superiority over capitalism.[34] He wanted to help the East Germans in their competition with West Germany, especially given the massive Western aid to the FRG after World War II, which was not initially matched by Soviet aid to the GDR. Khrushchev saw Germany as the main testing ground in the competition between communism and capitalism. His devotion to the communist cause explains much about his relations with Ulbricht. To understand this communist "true believer," let us examine Khrushchev's background.

WHO WAS NIKITA KHRUSHCHEV?

Khrushchev's complicated and colorful personality and policies (which led to the two most serious U.S.-Soviet crises of the cold war in Berlin and Cuba) have inspired many of his former colleagues and scholars to write about him.[35] He was earthy, emotional, irrepressible, impulsive, and sometimes over-optimistic. Khrushchev was also crude, rude, uncouth, and simply outrageous. His advisor Fedor Burlatsky describes him as bold, headstrong, daring, and at times acting from desperation to the point of adventurism.[36] Oleg Troyanovsky, another advisor to Khrushchev, writes of Khrushchev's great memory, his powers of observation, resourcefulness, humanity, and physical and moral courage. The same courage that would enable Khrushchev to denounce Stalin, however, would also lead him to take "inexcusable" risks. He had a "tendency to take his good ideas to extremes, to the point of absurdity."[37] Khrushchev's Presidium colleague Anastas Mikoian attests that Khrushchev was "prone to extremes" and that "when he had a new idea, he didn't know proportion, he didn't listen to anyone and went forward like a tank."[38] Troyanovsky similarly writes that Khrushchev did not have the "patience or . . . endurance" to wait something out; he was impulsive.[39] When things did not go his way, Khrushchev was, according to William Taubman, supersensitive to slights and likely to act in explosive and self-defeating ways.[40] In short, Khrushchev was a compelling historical figure and challenging to both colleague and adversary alike.

Khrushchev's volatile personality and often unbalanced policies made him a very unpredictable leader and contributed to his downfall. In ousting him in October 1964, Khrushchev's Presidium colleagues would speak of his proclivity for the unilateral, of his cult of personality, his adventurism, and his hare-brained schemes. The main report given by Presidium member Mikhail Suslov, on the occasion, spoke of Khrushchev's "character traits being not only extreme rudeness and disloyalty,[41] capriciousness, and touchiness. Also, administrative enthusiasm and senseless haste, prejudiced and biased opinions, animosity and talent for . . . scornfully hurling accusations, extreme boastfulness and self-assuredness."[42] Even more scathing and detailed criticisms of Khrushchev's personality and policies were contained in D. S. Polianskii's draft report (which was not used, since Khrushchev was sufficiently repentant) for Suslov's speech to the October 1964 plenum. Polianskii writes of Khrushchev regularly threatening people he did not like or who disagreed with him and calling people rude names: " 'Jerk, loafer, sluggard, stinker . . . wet hen, dung, shit, ass'—and these are just the 'printable' examples of insults he uses. The more 'popular' ones that he resorts to much more often, no paper could hold and no tongue could stand to pronounce. And these come pouring out indiscriminately even in the presence of women." Not only did he treat his colleagues this way, but he also treated the leaders of other socialist countries this way, calling Mao ("old galosh"), Ulbricht, Polish leader Wladislaw Gomulka, and others bad names in public.[43]

In his colleagues' opinions, when he was not calling someone a bad name, he was "giving away top state secrets in his improvised speeches and also in meetings with foreigners" and then accusing "the KGB of not knowing how to keep secrets." With all this talking on Khrushchev's part, he did "not listen to what people [said]. No, he himself lecture[d] without end and talk[ed] incessantly." In his behavior abroad, he "violate[d] the elementary norms of international etiquette" such as when "he took off his boot at a meeting at the UN and began banging it on the table as a sign of protest." This led people in the West to say: "If the Soviet Premier behaves this way, what can we expect of the rest of them?"[44]

Not only did Khrushchev's behavior damage the international reputation of the Soviet Union, according to Polianskii, but his foreign policy of threats and risks unnecessarily put the country at the edge of war with the West three times, in the Suez (1956), Berlin, and Cuban crises.[45] During the discussion of Khrushchev's behavior at the plenum and the need to remove him from his post as first secretary, Mikoian suggested allowing him to keep his post as chairman of the Council of Ministers. But Leonid Brezhnev, who engineered Khrushchev's ouster and would succeed him, responded that "he could perhaps accept [this suggestion] if it weren't for the character of Nikita Sergeevich." Brezhnev was "really very afraid of his determination and irrepressibility."[46]

In his emotional, colorful personality, Khrushchev could not have differed more from the other main character of this narrative, the gray, cold Ulbricht who "concealed his emotions behind a mask of inpenetrability,"[47] and of whom his former colleague Wolfgang Leonhard said: "I seldom saw him laugh, and I do not remember ever having detected any signs of personal emotion."[48] Ulbricht biographer Norbert Podewin describes a meeting of Khrushchev and Ulbricht with German POWs near Stalingrad on Christmas Eve of 1942: "By nature, there could not have been two more opposites. Khrushchev was temperamental, a lively speaker, always ready to make crude fun at the cost of others. Ulbricht did not have any of these qualities."[49] Indeed, Khrushchev remembers

making fun at Ulbricht's expense during their wartime dinners, at which they discussed Ulbricht's work at the front lines recruiting German agents. "I used to joke with him a lot: 'Well, Comrade Ulbricht, it doesn't look like you've earned your dinner today. No Germans have given themselves up.'"[50] One can just imagine how well the dour Ulbricht took Khrushchev's teasing.

While Khrushchev and Ulbricht shared little in terms of their personalities, they shared much in terms of their backgrounds. They were born a year apart, Ulbricht in July 1893 and Khrushchev in April 1894. They spent their formative years in major industrial areas, Ulbricht in Leipzig, Khrushchev in the Donbass, where they witnessed firsthand the difficult working conditions of the industrial stage of capitalism. They both turned to socialism from this experience.

Khrushchev was born to poor, illiterate peasants in Kalinovka, a small Russian village on the border of Ukraine in the Kursk province of Russia. He tended sheep and cows as a boy. In 1908, at the age of fourteen Nikita moved with his family to the Donbass industrial and mining area of southern Ukraine. As Burlatsky observes, Khrushchev was thus "typical of a certain section of the working class . . . first-generation workers who had only recently come from the countryside. . . . Men like Khrushchev had been shepherds before they became industrial workers. They hated the landowner and the capitalist equally, but they only had a vague idea of how they would topple the previous system or what they would put in its place."[51]

The move from the peasant village of Kalinovka to the industrial town of Iuzovka was a huge one, leaving the "almost medieval life of the Russian village . . . a city in the throes of Russia's industrial revolution. . . . For Khrushchev, the move to Iuzovka, with its foreign-built, foreign-owned industrial concerns, threw into sharp relief the backwardness of Russia; for the rest of his life he was driven by the desire to overcome this backwardness." After completing apprenticeships with a blacksmith and a fitter, Khrushchev "went to work as a metal fitter in a generator plant attached to a mine near Iuzovka, a move of great significant for his political development. The miners were politically the most radical element in the Donbass."[52] Working conditions were terrible in the mines, and Khrushchev was appalled by the way the bosses treated the workers.[53] As he recounts in his memoirs:

When I read Emile Zola's *Germinal*, I thought he was writing not about France, but about the mine in which my father and I worked. The worker's lot was the same both in France and in Russia. When, later on, I listened to lectures on political economy and the lecturer spoke about the wage system under capitalism, about the exploitation of the workers, it seemed to me as though Karl Marx had been at the mine where my father and I worked. It seemed as if it were from observing our life as workers that he had deduced his laws and scientifically proved why and how the workers must liberate themselves from capitalist slavery and build a Socialist society.

It is thus not surprising that Khrushchev "had some of [his] first serious political conversations at the pit in 1915."[54] He developed a passionate sense of social justice and became a labor activist, helping to organize strikes and spread communist ideas.[55]

As Khrushchev tells us, "Well before the Revolution I became an avid reader of proletarian and Social-Democrat newspapers. I read *Pravda* as soon as it started coming out regularly in 1915."[56] William Tompson notes insightfully that Khrushchev's "Marxism was more visceral than intellectual. His political views were born of life experience rather than of any real grasp of Marxist theory. Marxism described to Khrushchev the world in which he lived and offered him a path for a better life."[57] Vladislav Zubok and Constantine Pleshakov conclude that Khrushchev's "gut feelings about social justice that he had inherited from his peasant roots" and his time in the Donbass were the root of his status as "the last 'true-believer' in the mandate of the Bolshevik Revolution among the post-Stalin generation of Soviet leaders." When he was Soviet leader, these "gut feelings" were manifested in "his shoe-banging at the United Nations, and the expression on his face when he defended Soviet prestige—one of rage and fierce conviction." These actions "speak much more about his system of beliefs than his endless ideological speeches. Looking at him one could understand why the Revolution happened in Russia and what it was for."[58] Khrushchev's enthusiasm and at times unrealistic optimism for the communist cause would later facilitate Ulbricht's efforts to obtain increased Soviet support for his East German regime.

Due to Khrushchev's leadership role in the workers' strikes in the Donbass, after the February Revolution of 1917, he was elected to a workers' soviet. He continued his political work during the Civil War as a political commissar in the Red Army. When the Germans occupied the Donbass following the Brest-Litovsk Treaty of 1918, he fled and fought with the Red Army against the Whites in various areas of the country. After the Civil War, he returned to the Donbass as a miner and party cell leader. His political career took a big step forward when he attended some classes at the Don Technical College in 1921 and became the secretary of a party cell there and then secretary of a district party committee.[59]

Under the tutelage of Ukrainian party leader Lazar Kaganovich, Khrushchev rose up the ranks of the Ukrainian party organization, becoming deputy head of the Organizational Department of the Central Commitee of the Ukrainian Communist Party in Khar'kov and then head of the Organizational Department of the local government in Kiev in 1928 (following a path in organizational work similar to Ulbricht's in Germany).[60] In 1929 Khrushchev moved to Moscow for the first time. He studied at the newly founded Industrial Academy there and began his rapid ascent in the Soviet leadership. Khrushchev left the Industrial Academy sixteen months later, without having completed his diploma. But, more important, in this time he developed a reputation as the strong party secretary at the Academy. Stalin knew of Khrushchev's good work, since Stalin's wife, Nadezhda Alliluyeva, was also active in the party organization at the Academy.[61]

While Khrushchev's political career would continue to accelerate, he would always feel at a disadvantage and somewhat haunted about not being fully educated. Troyanovsky later observed that Khrushchev's "greatest weakness was the insufficiency of his education, which was especially telling in decisions on economic questions. I think he understood this and tried to make up for it by a lot of reading. But what was neglected in youth, it's hard to make up for as an adult, especially when you're busy from morning until night."[62] Khrushchev's low level of education was one of the reasons for the insecurity his advisors Troyanovsky and Burlatsky saw in him. Burlatsky relates that Khrushchev "constantly feared a reversal in his fortunes [and] that at any moment he might be thrown out and would have to return to his original occupation."[63] Troyanovsky discloses: "In my view, [Khrushchev] had a kind of insecurity complex, and not only regarding himself, but also the government which he led. So when he thought someone did not show respect to the Soviet Union or to him as the representative of the country, he could really explode and say a lot of unnecessary things."[64]

In the 1930s, however, as Khrushchev was beginning his career, he was probably much more careful. Between 1931 and 1938, he gained increasingly important positions in Moscow party politics. By 1935, at the age of forty, he was the head of both the Moscow city and Moscow province party committees. He played a crucial role in overseeing the building of the ambitious Moscow metro system and in carrying out Stalin's purges against various "enemies" in the Moscow party apparat. In 1938 he was elected as a deputy to the Supreme Soviet and a member of its Presidium, as well as a candidate member of the CPSU Politburo.[65]

Khrushchev's rapid rise in Moscow was interrupted in 1938 when Stalin sent him back to the Ukraine to run the Ukrainian party organization and carry out his purges. Although Khrushchev never assumed any responsibility for the purges, his motivation to denounce Stalin in 1956 no doubt included guilt regarding his own role in these and the Moscow purges. Khrushchev was in Kiev from 1938 to 1941 and 1944 to 1949 and served as a political officer in World War II from 1941 to 1944. As the Ukrainian leader, Khrushchev helped oversee the annexation of eastern Poland into western Ukraine in the wake of the Molotov-Ribbentrop Pact of August 1939. After the German invasion of the Soviet Union in June 1941, Khrushchev had the rank of major general and served as a political officer and member of various military councils at different fronts of the war. His jobs were to make sure the officers and soldiers were following party orders and to boost their morale, as well as to organize partisan operations behind German lines.[66] As it turned out, this was similar to the work Ulbricht was doing among German POWs in the Soviet Union during the war, and in fact, they shared a bit of it on Christmas Eve 1942. As Ulbricht remembers it:

> Prisoners of war who had fought in the Army of the fascist General Hood [*sic*—Hoth] and were wounded by Soviet troops near Kotelnikovo asked whether they could spend Holy [Christmas] Eve together. They were aviators and tank soldiers. The member of the Soviet Military Council of the Stalingrad Front, a member of the CPSU Politburo, [Khrushchev] agreed to such a gathering. He would get hold of a small Christmas tree, and there would be good food and drink. The member of the Soviet Military Council said to us that he himself would participate in this Christmas celebration.[67]

This gathering was no doubt part of Ulbricht and Khrushchev's effort to get German POWs to turn against Hitler and fascism and adopt communism, although celebrating Christmas was an unusual way (or perhaps it was a very shrewd move) to persuade German soldiers to embrace communism.

Once the Germans had been pushed out of the Ukraine, by 1944, Khrushchev's work was more focused on the task of rebuilding the Ukraine in the wake of German occupation and destruction. Until he was recalled to Moscow in 1949, Khrushchev oversaw the reconstruction of agriculture, industry, and the party, as well as the difficult task of fully integrating the new western Ukraine into the rest of the Ukraine, including collectivizing its agriculture. In December 1949 Stalin summoned Khrushchev to take over the Moscow party organization and become a Central Committee secretary for agriculture. Khrushchev believed that Stalin wanted him to act as a counterweight to Georgii Malenkov. Between 1949 and Stalin's death in March 1953, Khrushchev was a member of the dictator's inner circle.[68]

When Stalin died, Khrushchev left his post as Moscow party chief to focus on his position in the Central Committee Secretariat. He became first secretary of the CPSU in September. After having ousted Beria,[69] Khrushchev quickly turned against Foreign Minister Molotov. Although

Khrushchev had no background in foreign policy, he suddenly (and characteristically) had many ideas, all of which seemed to be different from Molotov's. As Aleksandrov-Agentov of the Foreign Ministry relates,

> [A]lmost as soon as N. S. Khrushchev came to power in 1953 . . . he began to criticize MID (that is, Molotov) more and more sharply of sluggishness, for insufficient initiatives in European, in Asian, and in disarmament matters. I . . . often happened to be a witness to such criticism by Khrushchev, as we say, in unofficial circumstances, during a lively meal between members of the leadership starting after some sort of reception when the participants (especially Khrushchev) were in a "heated up" mood.

In view of his "bitter and continous conflict with Molotov and his supporters at MID" (which was most clear over policy toward Yugoslavia and Austria, with Khrushchev winning both debates), Khrushchev quickly settled on Gromyko as a much more pliable alternative, treating him as his de facto foreign minister until appointing him as such in February 1957. Aleksandrov-Agentov, who became Gromyko's assistant in 1957, describes the relationship between Khrushchev and Gromyko: Gromyko's "independence . . . was very relative. Khrushchev was not the kind of person who allowed someone to formulate foreign policy other than him. And Gromyko wasn't the kind of person to try to put forward his own course of policy. He was ready for cooperation as a loyal executive. Khrushchev even allowed himself not very delicately to tease Gromyko about his obedience . . . including in the presence of foreigners."[70]

As Khrushchev consolidated his power vis-à-vis Molotov, Malenkov, and the others, he began to put his own stamp on foreign policy and, in his enthusiastic, excited way began making foreign trips to Belgrade, Geneva, and elsewhere. It was not only in foreign policy that Khrushchev sought to mend what Stalin had broken, but in domestic policy also. His guilt, his humanity, and his sense of right and wrong, as well as a political sense of what could help his own position, led him to make the decision to denounce Stalin and his crimes at the Twentieth Party Congress.[71]

THE TWENTIETH CONGRESS OF THE CPSU

Khrushchev laid out a broad new line in domestic and foreign policy at the Twentieth Congress of 14–25 February 1956. In his "secret speech" behind closed doors on the last night of the Congress, Khrushchev exposed and denounced Stalin's crimes. His damning portrayal of Stalin shook up the entire communist bloc. Khrushchev talked about the innocent party members Stalin had killed as "enemies of the people," Stalin's "cult of personality," and abrogation of collective leadership. He also exposed many mistakes Stalin had made in domestic and foreign policy, including ignoring precise, advance information about the German attack in June 1941 and forbidding the troops from retreating in the face of the attack.[72] Khrushchev promised to dismantle the Stalinist system and made it clear he believed this should be done in all communist countries.

Khrushchev publicly addressed foreign policy issues on the first day of the Party Congress in his General Report of the Central Committee.[73] He called for "peaceful coexistence" between countries of "different social systems" and declared that war between them was "no longer inevitable." Given the existence of nuclear weapons that could destroy mankind, Khrushchev believed that the competition between socialism and capitalism had to be carried out peacefully. He also believed that the socialist camp had grown strong enough to deter a capitalist attack, thus making war "no longer inevitable." Soviet possession of atomic and hydrogen bombs, its alliance with China, and its sphere of influence in Eastern Europe made it a force to be reckoned with. Khrushchev believed not only that Soviet relations with the West must change, but also that its relations with other socialist countries must change. In contrast to Stalin's autocratic methods with countries of the socialist bloc, Khrushchev supported "separate paths to socialism." Countries did not have to slavishly copy the Soviet model as Stalin had insisted, but could instead adapt their socialist path to the circumstances of their own "local conditions."[74]

Communists who learned of the speech were shocked and depressed at the extent of Stalin's crimes. But they had different approaches regarding a practical response. Some, such as Ulbricht, wanted to bury these problems in the past and not apply them to their own countries. Others wanted to face up to them and learn from them.

In applying his new principles to the GDR, Khrushchev seemed to have three ideas in mind, all of which Ulbricht would oppose. First, just as he believed it was necessary that the Soviet Union practice peaceful coexistence with the Western Powers, so he wanted the East German regime to practice peaceful coexistence with the West Germans, especially by expanding ties with the Social Democratic Party.[75] There were several reasons Khrushchev favored an improvement of East German relations with West Germany. He hoped such an improvement would decrease West German pressure on East Germany and thus help stabilize the situation in the GDR, including the refugee problem. By expanding East German ties with West Germany, Khrushchev also expected to increase the paths of East German influence on West Germany. He wanted this influence to induce West Germans to switch their support from Konrad Adenauer's conservative Christian Democratic Union to the more "progressive" SPD and hopefully to the SED. Khrushchev also hoped that expanded SED connections in West Germany would wean the West German regime away from the Western Powers. Days after the Twentieth Congress concluded, Soviet Deputy Foreign Minister Zorin advised telling the GDR to scale back its harsh press campaign against the FRG and to develop closer cooperation with the SPD. He also urged more SED power-sharing with other parties in the GDR.[76]

Khrushchev (as well as Ulbricht's opponents in 1953 and 1956) was much more optimistic than Ulbricht that reaching out the socialist hand of friendship to the FRG would yield good results. But Khrushchev did not consider German reunification on socialist terms to be a realistic scenario. By the late 1950s, he commented regularly that no one wanted German reunification, not the Germans, not the Western Powers, and not the Soviets.[77] In 1956 he told French Prime Minister, Guy Mollet, "We prefer 17 million Germans under our influence to 70 million in a reunited Germany, even though they may be neutralized."[78] Khrushchev's memories of fleeing the advancing Germans in the Donbass in World War I and then the Ukraine in World War II made him wary of German reunification in any form.[79] As Khrushchev told Governor Averell Harriman in 1959, "We have had German troops twice in the Soviet Union and we know what it means. This the United States does not know[,] nor has it experienced the tears that the Ukraine suffered under occupation."[80] The tightening political, economic, and military bonds between the FRG and the Western Powers in the 1950s hardly made a united socialist Germany seem likely. Khrushchev wanted East German help in exerting a positive influence on the FRG.

The second way Khrushchev believed his new principles should be applied in the GDR concerned the cult of personality. Just as Khrushchev described the detrimental effects of Stalin's cult of personality on the Soviet Union, so he was concerned with the effects of Ulbricht's cult of personality, such as on the refugee flow. The Soviet leaders had been very critical of this aspect of Ulbricht's rule in 1953, and they remained so in 1956 and afterward. Even though Khrushchev argued that socialist countries should follow their own path to socialism, he also believed that having autocratic leaders running the countries was detrimental to the long-term cause of socialism in these countries. And this definitely applied to Ulbricht.

Finally, Khrushchev believed that Ulbricht and all socialist leaders should follow his example of correcting Stalin's mistakes (or mistakes made by other Stalinist leaders), starting by openly discussing them. In the GDR this particularly meant a discussion and correction of "mistaken," harmful policies and practices that promoted the refugee exodus. Khrushchev also expected the East Germans and others to emulate his example of declaring an amnesty for people imprisoned or removed from power under false pretenses and rehabilitating them. This would include some of Ulbricht's old opposition.

THE EFFECTS OF THE TWENTIETH PARTY CONGRESS ON THE EAST GERMAN LEADERSHIP

The new path in domestic and foreign policy blazed by Khrushchev at the Twentieth Congress unleashed a deep and divisive debate within the East German leadership, as it did in Poland, Hungary, and elsewhere, including the Soviet Union itself. Officials at the highest reaches of the SED argued about the applicability of Khrushchev's new principles to the GDR. The East German debates are a window on the state of communist and Soviet rule in Eastern Europe in the mid–1950s and indicate the profound impact of Soviet policies, both good and bad, on Eastern Europe. The debates show the Soviet bloc in crisis.

In domestic politics, the East Germans debated the relevance to the GDR of Stalin's "mistakes," such as the "cult of personality," and they discussed Khrushchev's concept of "separate paths of socialism." The fundamental question regarding Khrushchev's elucidation of Stalin's crimes was the extent to which these crimes were due to Stalin personally versus the extent to which they were indicative of a core weakness of the socialist system, including the system as it was manifested in the GDR. In foreign policy, the East Germans argued about the relevance of Khrushchev's principles of peaceful coexistence and the noninevitability of war to the GDR and its relations with the FRG.

Differences of view on these issues quickly developed within the East German leadership and were quite extreme by the time of the Hungarian uprising eight months later.[81] When Ulbricht removed those officials who challenged his leadership and his policies in 1953, he promoted into the Politburo another official who would also come to challenge his leadership and policies—Karl Schirdewan. Following the events of June 1953, the Soviets had backed Schirdewan as a proponent of the *New Course*.[82] Schirdewan's championship of *New Course* policies was highlighted, however, only after the 20th Congress, by which point he occupied the second place in the SED leadership hierarchy. Ulbricht, Schirdewan, Grotewohl, and Neumann were the SED delegates to the 20th Party Congress. As all the foreign delegations, they attended only the main sessions of the Congress from 14–25 February, and not Khrushchev's secret speech on the final night. Schirdewan recounts that their delegation was awakened around 3 a.m. on 26 February and told that they should prepare to be informed of a speech Khrushchev had given the night before. The delegation chose Schirdewan to go hear the report and take notes. The CPSU Central Committee deputy who briefed Schirdewan on Khrushchev's speech spoke German so well that Schirdewan had no trouble writing down every word.[83]

While some conflicts had already arisen in Moscow within the East German delegation about how to handle the information from Khrushchev's secret speech,[84] these differences became more serious over the next few months.[85] There were differences within the East German leadership over how much to discuss the developments of the Twentieth Party Congress, what to say, and to whom. All were aware, however, of the precedent of massive criticism of the party and its leadership in June 1953 and wanted to avoid a repetition of this, although with differing ideas as to what was necessary to do so.[86]

Ulbricht sought to put off serious discussion of the Twentieth Congress as long as possible, since he feared this discussion would lead to severe criticism of him and his policies. Initially he was somewhat successful. Deputy Foreign Minister Otto Winzer complained to Ulbricht on 7 March that he and other Central Committee members had expected to hear in detail about the Twentieth Congress as soon as Ulbricht and the others returned from Moscow. By 7 March, however, they still had not been informed as they felt they should have been.[87]

Ulbricht's hand was forced after 17 March when newspapers in London and West Berlin published portions of the secret speech. Before this, specifically in a *Neues Deutschland* article of 4 March, Ulbricht had focused on the public parts of the Twentieth Congress and mentioned only in passing the problems with Stalin.[88] Part of the delay, as Ulbricht emphasized at the twenty-sixth plenum on 22 March, was also due to the fact that East German officials were waiting for receipt of an official Soviet version of what they could disseminate.[89] Once the Western media published parts of the speech on 17 March, the Politburo decided that Ulbricht would have to address some of the issues of the speech.[90]

The East German leadership finally got official Soviet permission in the form of a text of the secret speech to be distributed, and the East Germans finished translating this into German the night before the twenty-sixth plenum, on 21 March.[91] Schirdewan read the text of Khrushchev's secret speech to the CC members at the plenum. They also received other secret documents from the Twentieth Congress.[92] Once the CC members were in possession of this information, almost a full month after Khrushchev gave the secret speech on 25 February, the disagreements within the SED leadership over the Twentieth Congress could really begin.

Ulbricht's Cult of Personality

To Ulbricht, Khrushchev's secret speech was a Pandora's box of trouble that he preferred to keep closed. One of the central themes of Khrushchev's speech was Stalin's "cult of personality." By this term, Khrushchev had in mind a whole range of things from the way Stalin concentrated all power in his hands to the way he had created an atmosphere in which posters and statues of him and factories named after him were ubiquitous. As many Western and some Soviet and East German observers were quick to point out, Ulbricht had his own cult of personality. In the wake of the Twentieth Congress, Politburo member Hermann Matern reported to a Soviet official that Ulbricht was very agitated by the increased Western attacks on his cult of personality. Matern worried that the attacks were harming Ulbricht's health.[93] Some of the SED leaders also criticized Ulbricht's style of rule, as they had in 1953. Grotewohl advised him to "examine his own cult of personality and stop it."[94]

Assessing the SED's halting progess in carrying out the principles of the Twentieth Congress, Ambassador Pushkin noted in an internal MID report that

> before the 20th CPSU Congress, the cult of personality of Stalin was broadly propagandized in the GDR [and] left its mark on the SED: This is expressed in the exaggeration of the significance of certain leading officials in the SED, in the life of the party and the government. The role of W. Ulbricht, for example, was exaggerated excessively. Ulbricht's speeches are broadly propagandized in the GDR press, at party meetings and in other social organizations, and at the meetings of party organs. Even at the meetings of such an organ as the SED Central Committee, the majority of speakers consider it their duty to constantly quote W. Ulbricht. There are also times when Ulbricht himself inserts in his reports citations from his earlier published works.[95]

Pushkin cautioned, however, that the process of ridding the GDR of the cult of personality must be done very carefully so that "the enemy" would not benefit. He noted that Ulbricht was openly viewed as "Stalinist #1 in Germany" by many in the GDR and in the West. If there was an obvious curtailment in Ulbricht's power, his critics at home and in the West might seize it as an opportunity to call for his ouster and then perhaps for the downfall of the socialist system in the GDR.[96] This was precisely what had happened in June 1953. Seeking to prevent criticism and play on SED fears of a repetition of 1953, Ulbricht declared in July: "There can be no doubt that a decisive struggle against the slander of leading comrades [especially himself] must be carried out in the party and in public life."[97]

Others, however, complained about Ulbricht's efforts to deflect open discussion of problems with his leadership. At the twenty-eighth plenum in July 1956, Otto Winzer lamented that there had been little progress implementing the resolutions of the Twentieth Party Congress. He said the party was not discussing the key issues of overcoming the cult of personality and improving internal party democracy.[98] At a meeting with an advisor at the Soviet embassy, A. Orlov, Neumann also let on that "the top party organs are directing weak attention to . . . the question of the cult of personality."[99] Schirdewan had earlier told another Soviet advisor at the embassy, A. Orlov, that fear of a repetition of June 1953 was stopping serious self-critical discussion, including that regarding Ulbricht's cult of personality.[100]

At the SED twenty-ninth plenum in July, Erfurt party leader Hans Kiefert was very critical of the lack of discussion of key issues, such as the recent terse, uninformative official announcements in East Germany of the resignations of Mátyás Rakosi as the leader of Hungary and Viacheslav Molotov as Soviet foreign minister. Kiefert clearly felt that these fundamental leadership changes deserved a more detailed explanation.[101] But Ulbricht was not comfortable with the likely connection between the removal of key officials and their reluctance or incapacity to learn the lessons of the Twentieth Congress.

Rakosi had been widely seen as a Stalinist who was not interested in carrying out the de-Stalinization measures in domestic and foreign policy that the Twentieth Congress put forward.[102] At a Politburo meeting in November, Schirdewan would compare Ulbricht to Rakosi, saying that Ulbricht would perhaps share Rakosi's fate of being ousted if he continued to resist carrying out the measures of the Twentieth Congress.[103]

Discussion of Mistakes

In addition to the problem of his own cult of personality, another reason Ulbricht stonewalled on a broad discussion of the Twentieth Congress was Khrushchev's emphasis on the mistakes Stalin had made in domestic and foreign policy. Ulbricht sought to avoid a critical examination of mistakes he might have made in these areas. He also did not want to give the West any ammunition for criticism. As Ulbricht pointed out at the twenty-eighth plenum in July 1956:

> The imperialist agencies are conducting a campaign of slander against Soviet democracy and against the people's democratic order in the GDR. The radio stations of the imperialist countries and the West German reactionary press find new lies daily about any kind of mistake of the SED and the GDR. With this the enemy makes use of objective difficulties, which have resulted from the division of Germany, and difficulties which are unavoidable in the construction of a new type of society.[104]

Thus, in any discussions of the Twentieth Congress, Ulbricht wanted to keep the focus on the promising paths for the future instead of on any "discussion of mistakes" ("*Fehlerdiskussion*").[105]

Others, however, felt liberated by Khrushchev's invitation to discuss mistakes. At the first CC meeting in March to discuss the Twentieth Congress, Greta Wittkowski began by saying it had been a mistake to wait a month after the Congress to discuss Khrushchev's initiatives.[106] She was "of the view that it would have been quite possible to find the time—it would have been a few hours" to inform the CC. Now the plenum was meeting only two days before the Third Party Conference, hardly enough time to involve the CC seriously in the planning of the Conference. In addition, she complained that CC plenums generally covered too much material without enough preparation or time beforehand. She also pointed out that there were often far too many guests at the CC plenums, thus hindering CC members' willingness to speak openly. "If the [usual] hundred guests were here today, I would not be saying what I am saying right now." Asserting that there were too few CC and Politburo meetings to develop a feeling of collective work, she said they must change the working style of the CC and Politburo and promote an atmosphere in which people would speak openly.[107] Ulbricht admitted that there had been "violations of internal party democracy" in the SED.[108]

At the Third Party Conference at the end of March, the leaders formed a "Commission for Measures on the Broad Development of Democracy in the GDR."[109] Willi Bredel[110] emphasized how important this commission was: "Due to the problems which were thrown open at the 20th Party Congress of the CPSU, we are having no small and insignificant conflicts in our party and with the working class."[111]

The next plenum was not held until four months later, after being postponed twice. In the meantime, the Politburo undertook to make party life more democratic in accordance with the Twentieth Congress. The 17 April Politburo meeting heard "Proposals for Strengthening the Collectivity of Work of the Politburo and the Improvement of the Work," which included a section "against the cult of personality."[112] And the Politburo meeting of 5 June dealt with "ideological developments in the party after the 20th Congress and the Third Party Conference" and with rehabilitating people who had been expelled from the party unjustly.[113] The Politburo meeting of 19 June resolved to rehabilitate a number of these people.[114]

Throughout the summer of 1956, as the people in Poland and Hungary were inspired by the Twentieth Congress to forcefully express their economic and political grievances, the SED leadership continued to disagree over the lessons to draw from the Congress.[115] At the same time, the economic situation in the GDR worsened. This was partly because imports of key goods from Poland, most importantly coal, declined and then halted due to strikes and unrest. In July the East German leaders put off the twenty-eighth plenum and went to Moscow to seek more economic aid.

The Soviets were obliging and granted aid so as to "enable the implementation of the second five-year-plan" in the GDR. At the meetings in Moscow on 16–17 July and then at the twenty-eighth plenum afterward, Ulbricht emphasized the special challenges for East Germany:

> Since [the GDR] is the state of the socialist world system located closest to Western Europe, it is particularly exposed to the political and economic pressure of Western monopoly capital. . . . The GDR must also surpass West Germany in the economic competition, so that it reaches the world level in science and technology and achieves a higher standard of living for the workers than exists in West Germany. . . .
>
> But we cannot complete this work alone with our own power; instead we need the fraternal aid of the Soviet Union and also the other states of the socialist camp. Without international solidarity it is not possible to resolve such great problems.[116]

Ulbricht's favorite line of argument for more Soviet aid was not without justification, but the Soviets and others would tire of it, wishing that Ulbricht would do more than cry "help" all the time.

By late summer, Ulbricht may have felt supported in his efforts to say as little as possible about the Twentieth Congress by a secret CPSU report, "On the Results of the Discussion of the Resolutions of the 20th Party Congress of the CPSU and the Carrying Out of the Resolutions of the Party Congress," the German translation of which was dated 8 August 1956. This report described the difficulties of carrying out the resolutions of the Twentieth Congress and the way in which hostile groups were making use of the new opportunities presented for criticism in the Soviet Union. The report concluded that such hostile groups within the Soviet Union must be suppressed.[117] Ulbricht felt the same way about such groups and individuals in the GDR.

Speaking of mistakes that may have been caused by the cult of personality could also, very dangerously as far as Ulbricht was concerned, lead to a serious, open, and probably embarrassing discussion of the problem of the refugee exodus from East Germany.

The Refugee Problem

East Germany's refugee exodus, what the leadership called *Republikflucht* ("flight from the Republic"), was one of the biggest reasons Ulbricht opposed any discussion of his mistakes and contested Khrushchev's exortation to peaceful coexistence with the West. The fact that people were fleeing from his socialist country to the capitalist one next door was indication to him that there needed to be more, not less, distance between the two. The refugee issue also made Ulbricht very nervous about the fact that one of the main criticisms leading to Rakosi's ouster from Hungary had been his "distance from the masses." Khrushchev also criticized Stalin for this. The refugee exodus from East Germany was an obvious indication that Ulbricht's regime did not have good relations with the people. Ever since the creation of the German Democratic Republic in 1949, people had been registering their unhappiness with the life there by leaving the country permanently. According to Soviet figures, 270,440 people left in 1953; 173,279 left in 1954; 270,115 left in 1955; and 316,000 in 1956.[118] There was also increasing criticism from people within the SED leadership and from Soviet officials about the inadequate East German methods for stopping this refugee exodus. If the Twentieth Congress was going to spur the East German leaders to examine mistakes they had made, they would have to look closely at the question of why so many of their citizens were leaving the country.

In the spring and summer of 1956, the East German leadership began a concerted effort to devise methods to check the refugee exodus. Grotewohl discussed this effort at the Politburo meeting on 17 April, and the leaders then established a commission to study the problem and propose political, economic, propaganda, and border measures to correct it.[119] Interior Minister Karl Maron reported on the work of the commission at the Politburo meeting on 19 June. The commission lamented that there was "no atmosphere of a fight against flight from the Republic and no unified plan for countermeasures." It also referred to "various illegal measures and an insufficient regard for democratic legal norms" on the part of East German officials which alienated many East German citizens. Both the list of causes and the proposed remedies were almost the same as those given in 1953 and those that would be given in 1961: Little of significance really changed between 1953 and 1961 in the East German approach to the refugee exodus.[120]

The commission noted that 56 percent more East Germans had fled the country in 1955 in comparison to 1954, and the numbers leaving each month in 1956 were greater than for the same month in 1955.[121] They needed to act to stop this trend. The commission blamed some of the refugee exodus on West German policies to recruit East Germans to flee, especially skilled workers. But it also observed that West German efforts were aided by problems in the GDR, including the lack of a concerted effort to prevent the people from leaving, bureaucratic and heartless treatment of regular citizens by officials, and overly strict travel regulations for visiting West Germany. East German economic problems, especially low benefits and wages and insufficient housing were also culpable.[122] The commission suggested remedies to reverse these problems. Doctors and other members of the intelligentsia must have more places and time to vacation in the GDR and in "friendly countries," more houses must be constructed, and people must have greater financial rewards for long years on the job.[123] In addition, the East German regime should allow more people to travel to the FRG and restore movement between East Berlin and the GDR, which it had stopped in 1952. Finally, the government should eliminate the fines against East Berliners who worked in West Berlin but did not declare their status as *Grenzgänger* (border-crossers).[124]

At the twenty-eighth plenum in July, Fred Oelssner added more warnings about the problems of workers, who should have been great supporters of the socialist regime:[125]

> It is a fact, Comrades, that since 1954 the workers have been the main component of those fleeing the Republic. . . . This is . . . a decided critique of our work, a critique with feet, and this is, I think, an extraordinarily serious signal for our party, with which we must deal. . . .
>
> We have also had other serious signals recently. In recent weeks, we have had—I must say for myself at least—to an alarming degree an increase in kinds of small outbreaks of dissatisfaction of the workers. . . . We have had strikes for several hours, sitting strikes, and strike threats to a rather extensive degree.

The workers were probably influenced by the unrest in Poland and Hungary over the summer. But Oelssner did not blame foreign influences. Instead, he asserted that a primary cause of the workers' unrest was the steady increase of work norms without a corresponding increase in workers' salaries, just the kind of scenario that had led to the June 1953 workers uprising. He questioned how far in fact the SED leadership had come since the events of 1953:

> Three years ago we had to recognize that a schism had opened up in relations of the party with the masses and especially with the working class, and therefore at the 15th plenum of the Central Committee, we put the task to the party of winning over the majority of the working class, winning them over strongly for our party. We must ask ourselves today: Have we fulfilled this task? . . . We cannot answer this positively.[126]

At a time when the emerging orthodoxy in the Soviet bloc explaining the unrest in Poland and Hungary was that the party leaderships had lost touch with the masses, these comments by Oelssner with reference to 1953 in East Germany were quite pointed. At a Soviet–East German meeting in Moscow in mid-July, the Soviets pressed the SED to do everything possible to thwart the outflow of refugees. In order to help the East German economic situation, and thus hopefully the refugee problem, the Soviets agreed to halve the occupation costs paid by the GDR for Soviet troops.[127] The worrisome developments in Poland and Hungary enabled Ulbricht, in Michael Lemke's words, to "develop indirect forms of blackmail" with Khrushchev. In his 19 May letter to Khrushchev and Bulganin asking for more economic aid, he alluded to "a worsening of the supply situation compared to last year [which] would have very serious consequences for us."[128] The Soviets agreed to grant the aid. As Lemke points out, this strategy of Ulbricht's "developed into a constant of SED policy. Insufficient supplies of raw materials and consumer goods, the USSR was told 'would lead to politically very bad discussions and would facilitate . . . the work of the enemy.' The CPSU had its 17 June syndrome also," and accordingly responded positively to Ulbricht's requests.[129] By the late 1950s, Ulbricht would grow increasingly adept at playing on the Soviets' 17 June syndrome to procure more aid.

Separate Paths to Socialism

Following the Twentieth Congress, some in East Germany were excited at the prospect of no longer needing to follow the Soviet model in the development of socialism and in Germany finding its own path to socialism "given the conditions within East Germany," perhaps even finding "a third way" between socialism and capitalism, reminiscent of "the special German way" that had been advocated by Anton Ackermann in the immediate postwar period.[130] At the first SED plenum after the Twentieth Congress, Schirdewan emphasized that the Congress "gave our party many creative impulses for a more successful resolution of our tasks under full consideration of our historical and national peculiarities."[131] The latter of course meant the division of Germany and Berlin and the challenges to East Germany and its construction of socialism resulting therefrom.

Ulbricht seemed to be less sanguine at the end of March about the "creativity" East Germany could explore given its situation: "A peculiarity of the national question in Germany is that the struggle for reunification is connected with the competition between two world economic systems." Ulbricht stressed West German militaristic and hostile policies toward East Germany, the number and intensity of which had increased after the Twentieth Congress and had constrained East Germany's opportunities to "creatively" implement the resolutions of Congress.[132] Accordingly, Ulbricht and his supporters were not happy with Soviet moves toward more contacts with West Germany and West Berlin. At a July

meeting between SED Berlin Chief Neumann and an advisor at the Soviet embassy, S. Astavin, Neumann expressed concern about recent Soviet moves toward establishing normal relations with the West Berlin
authorities. Since, as Neumann said, "[East] Berlin is the capital of the
GDR," this Soviet behavior was "confusing."[133] East German–Soviet disagreements over relations with West Berlin would escalate in the years
to come. The Soviets sought to use contacts with West Berlin to wean it
away from the West. Ulbricht, however, favored the isolation of West
Berlin instead of engagement with it, fearing the latter might in fact have
negative consequences for his control over East Berlin. Thus, Ulbricht
and Neumann decided that Khrushchev's notion of separate paths to
socialism allowed them to follow a different line on relations with West
Berlin. But they also believed they must be cautious in following a separate path so as not to give "the enemy" any evidence that the East Germans were critical of the Soviets or of socialism.

In the summer of 1956, numerous party members in East Berlin admired the much more open Polish and Hungarian discussion of the need
for separate paths to socialism. At the twenty-eighth plenum, Professor
Wolfgang Steinitz and others reproached the SED's insufficient discussion of the Twentieth Congress and urged the SED leadership to emulate
the Polish example of more open discussion of the implications of this
for their own country and their past.[134]

In Poland and Hungary, the repercussions from the Twentieth Congress were in fact explosive, something Ulbricht, in particular, was anx-
ious to avoid in the GDR. Following the death of Poland's Stalinist
leader Boleslaw Bierut in March and a broadcast in June on Radio Free
Europe of Khrushchev's secret speech, the workers in Poznan, Poland,
erupted in riots. These were suppressed by tanks, but the popular desire
for political and economic reforms mounted. It became increasingly
clear that the situation would only be stabilized by returning Wladislaw
Gomulka, the former reformist leader who had been jailed by Bierut, to
power.[135] For Ulbricht, this would have been the equivalent of being
replaced by Herrnstadt, Zaisser, or Ackermann.

In Hungary the lesson of the Polish riots led to the removal of Rakosi
from power and his replacement by Ernö Gerö in July. Yet Gerö and
his associates, including Janos Kadar, were also not very interested in
reform. Liberal opposition, centered around the Petöfi Circle of dissident
intellectuals, continued to grow in number and discontent, calling for an
open discussion of the Stalinist regime. Just as many Poles wanted Gomulka to assume power, many Hungarians wanted the return to power
of the reformist Imre Nagy, who had been ousted by Rakosi in 1955.[136]

Inspired by developments in Poland and Hungary, throughout the
summer of 1956, more and more East German students and intellectuals

criticized the regime and expressed support for the democratic movements in Poland and Hungary. This was particularly the case in the departments of veterinary medicine, sociology, history, philosophy, economics, legal studies, German studies, natural science, and medicine at Humboldt and other universities and of the writers union. Some of the East German intellectuals had ties with the intellectual Petöfi Circle in Budapest.[137] Two of the leaders of the East German intellectuals critical of the SED regime were Wolfgang Harich, philosophy professor at Humboldt University and a reader for the Aufbau Press, and Walter Janka, the editor in chief of Aufbau Press in Berlin. In November, Harich wrote a "platform for a special German way to socialism" that foresaw a completely different and far more liberal path of development for the GDR.[138] Ulbricht responded to the continuing demonstrations at Humboldt University by deploying battle groups in front of the university, a move that elicited sharp criticism from other SED leaders.[139]

In light of the "contagion" the GDR was experiencing from Poland and Hungary, Ulbricht rejected calls to follow the Polish or Hungarian path. Ulbricht pointed to the "peculiar conditions prevailing in the GDR" whereby the GDR shared borders with West Germany and West Berlin. He asserted that this situation dictated that the GDR be very cautious in its policies:

> Comrade Steinitz, the Polish example, which has been recommended by various comrades, we have not imitated and we will never imitate. This must be stated clearly.
>
> Each country has its own ways, and each communist party has its own ways. But one should not come to us and recommend such steps which have led to such difficulties as there were for a time in Warsaw and Budapest. Many of our comrades underestimate this issue. In reality there was an anti–Central Committee formed. This is the fact. In the so-called Petöfi-Circle!
>
> We have some experiences in practice. We are located at the foremost place. We are the western most country of the socialist camp. We cannot allow such things. I do not mean to say by this that this cannot be done elsewhere. But we especially cannot do this.[140]

As far as Ulbricht was concerned, the Polish and Hungarian ideas of "separate paths to socialism" were dangerous and not to be imitated by the GDR.

Peaceful Coexistence and Relations with West Germany

The SED leaders differed significantly over the applicability to Germany of Khrushchev's concepts of peaceful coexistence between countries of different social systems and the non-inevitability of war between these countries. As the Central Committee noted, "On the issue of the *application of coexistence to Germany in the ideological area* there are many confusions and discussions within the party. Again and again the question is asked whether the principles of coexistence can be applied to the two German states or not. Some of the comrades are for this, some are against [emphasis in original]."[141] Ulbricht, Erich Honecker, and others would ultimately argue that these concepts could not be applied to Germany due to West German aggressive policies toward East Germany. West German subversive activities in East Germany also meant that the class struggle was still going strong in the GDR. Thus, East Germany's focus in its relations with West Germany should be "vigilance" as opposed to "peaceful coexistence." Schirdewan and others, however, were more concerned with constructing a more acceptable form of socialism in the GDR than in practicing "vigilance" with regard to West Germany.

In his opening General Report at the Twentieth Congress, Khrushchev discussed the importance of a "united front" of the working class, of socialists and communists. This had clear implications for the East German SED developing more ties with the West German SPD. Schirdewan and Ulbricht viewed the methods for doing this quite differently, as was made clear at the twenty-eighth plenum in July. For Schirdewan, the SED had to reform itself significantly and be much more democratic before the SPD would be willing to cooperate in important ways with the SED. Thus, he pointed out that within East Germany there were people who, for example, had been in the old united SPD and that these people should play more of a role in SED policy toward the West German SPD. Schirdewan was talking about policy making being less dominated by the SED and more consensus oriented, allowing people in the East German bloc parties to have more influence: "[I]t is not possible to carry out our policy in all of Germany without the leading activity of such esteemed forces."[142] For Schirdewan, peaceful coexistence, in this case with the West German SPD, had important implications for East German domestic politics.

For Ulbricht, on the other hand, the need to allow more contacts with the SPD definitely did not mean any loosening of the domestic policy reins. Nor did peaceful coexistence mean lightening up on travel procedures to West Germany, as far as Ulbricht was concerned. "A significant point of debate are vacation trips to West Germany. Several comrades express the view that they should be able to freely decide this issue and that no one should put any difficulties in their way. The members of the party leadership are not always able to persuade the comrades in discussion."[143] Given the refugee problem, Ulbricht was hardly interested in making it easier for East Germans to go on vacation in West Germany.

Finally, if anyone thought that peaceful coexistence between the two

Germanys might lead to reunification anytime soon, Ulbricht made it clear in July that they were mistaken. He cited Khrushchev's recent statement "that reunification requires a maximum of patience due to the existence of the two German states with two different social systems. 'Practicing patience, however does not mean waiting to yield to the demands of the imperialists.' "[144] Ulbricht then declared that "the fight for reunification will be a more difficult, more tense and more complicated fight" than some in East Germany seemed to believe after the Twentieth Congress.[145]

SIMILAR CHINESE AND EAST GERMAN RESPONSES TO KHRUSHCHEV'S TWENTIETH CONGRESS NEW COURSE

China's leader, Mao Zedong, criticized Khrushchev's denunciation of Stalin and his calls for reform in domestic and foreign policy. These criticisms contributed to the rift between Khrushchev and Mao and were a great aid in Ulbricht's efforts to resist Khrushchev's reforms. In the wake of Khrushchev's secret speech, relations between the GDR and People's Republic of China grew closer. There had been interaction and cooperation between German and Chinese communists since the 1920s when a German communist participated in the Long March.[146] The GDR and PRC were both founded in October 1949 and established relations then. In 1953 the Chinese followed the Soviets in upgrading their relations with the GDR, transforming their mission there into an embassy. Johannes König was the first GDR ambassador to China. While he would later complain when he was the GDR ambassador to Moscow that he was out of the information and policy-making loop, he had no such complaints when he was in Beijing.[147] The GDR ambassador and the embassy in Beijing had much more independence from Berlin than did their counterparts in Moscow, since GDR policy regarding Moscow was made by the top leaders in Berlin, not by the diplomats based at their embassy in Moscow. The GDR diplomats in Beijing had more of a chance to be involved in policy-making.[148]

The GDR and PRC had fundamental interests in common even before Khrushchev's secret speech. As an East German Ministry of Foreign Affairs (MfAA) report on East German–Chinese relations in 1954 put it: They must "strengthen their mutual support and cooperation in the struggle for . . . the resolution of burning issues of both nations—the unity of Germany [and] the liberation of Taiwan."[149] Both the East Germans and the Chinese felt that "the imperialists" had control over "their" territory in West Berlin, Taiwan, Quemoy, Matsu, and Hong Kong. They wanted to expel the imperialists from these territories, with Soviet help if necessary.[150] In December 1955 Grotewohl visited Beijing to sign a Treaty on Friendship and Cooperation. The treaty declared "the Chinese people would grant every imaginable help [to the GDR] in its struggle against German imperialism and militarism as well as for the conclusion of a peace treaty with Germany and the resolution of the West Berlin issue."[151] The two countries (and especially the GDR) were interested in expanding their cooperation, because they were both struggling for international recognition outside the communist world, and both were located on the edges of the socialist bloc, feeling pressure from the West.

For the East Germans and Chinese, their locations on the edges of the bloc raised the difficult issue of refugees fleeing from their countries to the capitalist world. The Chinese wanted to consult with the East Germans on how to stop this. In June 1957, Li, first secretary of the Chinese embassy in the GDR, requested a meeting with Stasi officials to learn about "the number of people who have fled since 1949; the reasons for the exodus; which steps the government has undertaken to hinder this; what success these measures have had; [and] how high the number of those returning is." A meeting between Shu Ming, a counselor in the Chinese embassy, and representatives of the MfAA's China Section on 5 September made it clear why the Chinese were interested in learning about the issue. Ming told the East Germans:

> [T]here is a similar issue in the PRC. In the PRC, there is an exodus of certain parts of the population to Hong Kong. It would be good if we could learn from each other on this issue. The embassy would be particularly interested to learn what causes lead to this phenomenon, which classes the refugees belong to, and when this phenomenon is strongest. In the PRC, the number of refugees to Hong Kong increased after the sharpening of the fight against the rightist elements. The refugees belong mostly to the bourgeoisie or large land-owning classes. These statements alone show that the issue of the exodus to West Germany or to Hong Kong cannot be handled in the abstract.[152]

Another important aspect of GDR-PRC relations was economic. After the 1953 uprising in East Germany, the Chinese agreed to quickly send the GDR some essential goods.[153] The MfAA's annual report on GDR-PRC relations in 1956 noted with satisfaction that "requests of the GDR government for additional deliveries of goods which we urgently need are dealt with very obligingly and are fulfilled, even when this means the PRC must make certain restrictions in its own country or in exports to other countries." The East Germans also benefited from relations with China, because "Peking (was) an extraordinarily advantageous location for the establishment of contacts with representatives of Asian countries [and] to establish contacts with embassies of capitalist countries there."[154]

The most important event of 1956 for East German–Chinese relations was the Twentieth Congress. Many of the new principles Khrushchev laid out flew in the face of the policies of both Ulbricht and Mao. Since both had their own cults of personality, both were vulnerable to and alienated by Khrushchev's sharp criticism of Stalin. Any discussion of past "mistakes" in their countries would inevitably put the blame on them personally, something they both sought to avoid. Given their animosity regarding the imperialists occupying "their" territory, they also did not support Khrushchev's notion of peaceful coexistence or the non-inevitability of war. Ulbricht and Mao both feared that Khrushchev had gone soft on the West and would not support their efforts to "unify" their national territory. Mao's aggressive foreign policy toward the West was much more in line with Ulbricht's preferences.[155] Ulbricht and Mao agreed with Khrushchev's idea of separate paths to socialism only insofar as it meant that they could follow a separate path from that laid down by Khrushchev at the Twentieth Congress. Ulbricht and Mao also asserted that their countries were at different stages of development than the Soviet Union and thus needed to have different, "separate" policies.[156]

Interestingly, for a time in 1956, although for very different reasons, the supporters of both Ulbricht and Schirdewan looked to Mao as a better role model than the Soviets. For the reasons just described, Ulbricht looked to Mao as a defender against Khrushchev's "revisionism" of traditional Marxist-Leninist(-Stalinist) thought and all that it implied in domestic and foreign policy.[157] Schirdewan and other "revisionists" in the GDR, on the other hand, were inspired by the Eighth Congress of the Chinese Communist Party (CCP), which proposed to "let hundreds of flowers bloom; let all schools of thought contend." Both Ulbricht and Schirdewan attended the Congress. Schirdewan emerged from it with the conclusion that "the Chinese had understood how to use the Twentieth CPSU Congress in a truly 'creative' fashion." Mao's change of course in early 1957 to attack "revisionist," "right deviationists" was greeted with relief by Ulbricht, who observed at the thirtieth SED plenum in February 1957: "Our main problem is not 'to tell all flowers to bloom' but rather to find the right selection of flowers, and to grow what is truly new and useful, without tolerating the growth of noxious weeds under the pretext that they are flowers."[158] Ulbricht also publicly approved of Mao's Great Leap Forward and establishment of people's communes in 1958.[159]

Ulbricht and Mao did not agree on everything, of course, and even when Ulbricht did agree with Mao, he did not always express this publicly. Ulbricht depended on Soviet military and economic support and could not afford to go too far in siding with Mao. Ulbricht also did not need to go too far, because Khrushchev felt enough pressure on his own from Mao to adopt tougher policies. As Troyanovsky later observed, by 1960, the "China dilemma was always on his mind."[160]

THE EFFECTS OF THE EVENTS IN HUNGARY ON THE GDR:
THE HUNGARIAN REVOLUTION AND THE DECLINE
OF ULBRICHT'S OPPOSITION

Calls for reform that had been building in Poland and Hungary since the summer escalated to very different results in the fall. In the case of Warsaw, the protesters were answered peacefully on 19 October with the appointment of Wladislaw Gomulka as leader of the party. This increased the demands of the protesters in Budapest. On 23 October Soviet troops put down massive demonstrations that called for Imre Nagy as leader, free elections, a multi-party system, the withdrawal of Soviet troops, and other fundamental changes in the system. On 24 October the Soviets installed Nagy as prime minister, in the hope that he could regain control over the people. This, however, was not to be. Nagy called for the withdrawal of Soviet troops and announced that Hungary would leave the Warsaw Pact and adopt neutrality.[161]

While Soviet Presidium members Mikoian and Suslov were in Budapest getting a firsthand feel for the situation and consulting the Hungarians, two top Chinese officials, Liu Shaoqui and Deng Xiaoping, were in Moscow from 23–31 October meeting with the Soviets about how to respond to events in Poland and Hungary. The Chinese told the Soviets that the problems in Poland and Hungary were the result of Soviet "great power chauvinism" and that they had to stop violating the sovereignty of other countries (clearly having previous Soviet treatment of their own country in mind). In the case of Poland, and initially in the case of Hungary, the Chinese argued strongly against intervention. Instead, they pushed the Soviets to announce on 30 October a "Declaration on Developing and Enhancing the Friendship and Cooperation between the Soviet Union and Other Socialist Countries," which promised less interference and more equality in these relations.[162] On the same day, the Soviets acceded to Nagy's request to remove Soviet troops from Hungary and end their intervention. The following day, however, the Kremlin leaders changed their minds, deciding that things had gone too far in Hungary. They believed that the "imperialists" were trying to take over Hungary just as England and France were simultaneously trying to seize the Suez Canal. Accordingly, a second massive Soviet troop intervention on 4 November crushed the Hungarian uprising for good, ousting Nagy and replacing him with Janos Kadar.

The Short-Term Reaction to the Hungarian Events in the GDR

The Hungarian revolution erupted at a crucial time for the East Berlin leaders, since they were in the midst of sharp disagreements over how to apply the resolutions of the Twentieth Congress to the GDR, still trying to cope with the refugee exodus, and frightened of a repeat of 17 June 1953. Some in the leadership saw great hope in the fact that Rakosi had been ousted in Hungary and Wladislaw Gomulka had been returned to power in Poland. They felt that East Germany too should have a leader who was honestly dedicated to realizing the goals of the Twentieth Congress. However, Ulbricht and his supporters focused on the great unrest in Poland and Hungary and wanted to prevent this from spreading to the GDR. All in the East German leadership were of course concerned when the situation in Hungary heated up to such an extent that the Soviet armed forces had to intervene twice to stop the unrest on 23–24 October and 4 November.

In the wake of the massive demonstrations in Hungary and the violent Soviet interventions in response, the immediate public reaction of the East German leadership was to bolster internal security measures. At a Politburo meeting on 8 November, four days after the massive and bloody Soviet second intervention in Hungary, the SED Politburo established a commission, chaired by Ulbricht, to formulate security measures to ensure that the unrest in Hungary could not spread to the GDR.[163] One of the commission's recommendations was for all party leaders to carry pistols and be trained in their use.[164]

Other responses to the Hungarian developments were harder to agree upon. All wanted to avoid what happened in Hungary, but there were two very contrasting views about how to do this: Ulbricht believed that the best way to avoid a repeat of Hungary and 17 June 1953 was to clamp down and bar open criticism of the regime; Schirdewan, on the other hand, believed that only by permitting open discussions within the party and among the people about problems in East Germany could these problems be resolved.

The twenty-ninth SED plenum met on 12–14 November. Schirdewan prepared the Politburo report over which there was considerable discord. He was forced to rewrite it.[165] He argued that the best strategy for East Germany to follow in light of the events in Hungary was to allow open discussion of all problems and to address them head-on. When Ulbricht and others criticized this approach, Schirdewan defended himself saying that he was trying to ensure that "Ulbricht would not go the way that Rakosi did."[166] In his criticism of Ulbricht, Schirdewan believed he had Soviet support via Ambassador Pushkin. Hermann Matern[167] later testified that Schirdewan told him on 7 November that the Soviets disagreed with Ulbricht on many issues, strongly implying that they agreed instead with Schirdewan.[168]

After being forced to change his Politburo report to the twenty-ninth plenum, Schirdewan's final report expressed both conservative and liberal responses to the events in Hungary. On the one hand, he talked about the counterrevolutionary, hostile, bourgeois revolution in Hungary, the importance of the unity of the East German party leadership, and the need to increase East German military strength and preparedness. On the other hand, he said that the events in Hungary made it an urgent necessity for every party to look seriously at its mistakes. He said that the East German leadership needed to relate to young people better, especially women, so as to learn how to persuade them not to flee the country. In addition, he spoke of the economic problems in Hungary (also found in East Germany) that contributed to the dissatisfaction of the people.[169]

CC International Relations chief Peter Florin unwittingly expressed internally contradictory views about the lessons of Hungary. Florin declared that there were "two great conclusions that can be drawn from the Hungarian events":

> One conclusion is that there is a great conflict in the world between socialism and capitalism, that one should not underestimate the imperialist forces, but must always and continuously vigilantly build up forces to fight against counterrevolutionary provocations, and that one must see the beginnings of such a development in order to nip it in the bud. . . .
>
> The second conclusion in my view is that one must recognize mistakes quickly, overcome them, and that one must proceed forward and make the construction of socialism really into an affair of the entire working class population, that one must avoid isolating the party from the masses.[170]

For guiding action, these two conclusions, or lessons, were basically incompatible. So, when forced to choose, different SED officials went in opposite directions. Alfred Neumann, on his way to replacing Schirdewan as Ulbricht's trusted second, declared: "Of course it is correct that we put the issue of security first." In particular, Neumann maintained that they must gain better control of the GDR borders to reduce opportunities for hostile infiltration:

> When for example every day 300,000–500,000 people go across the sectoral borders, one must consider how we can get better control of things. Do we have things completely under control now? No, we don't have things politically completely under control. [So the enemy uses this to put pressure on us.] I would like to assert that the enemy is better organized on issues of action directed against the GDR than we are organized in the struggle against the West. We have this impression in various places. [The enemy] appears to be very well organized.[171]

Schirdewan's initial Politburo report, as well as the speeches by Selbmann, Bruno Leuschner,[172] Paul Wandel,[173] and Fred Oelssner, while paying heed to the conservative point of view, favored a more liberal, open approach to the lessons the GDR leaders should take from Hungary. It was these speeches no doubt that had made Wollweber feel that this was the most honest, open plenum he had ever witnessed.[174] The main argument of these, for lack of a better word, "liberals" was that the Hungarian events illustrated the necessity of dealing with whatever problems (due to mistakes in leadership) there were in the country so as to resolve them and not allow them to get worse and worse, ultimately resulting in an uprising. For Selbmann, Leuschner, and Oelssner, an honest discussion of the severe economic problems of the GDR was the first necessary step. As Selbmann pointed out, unrealistic economic plans in the GDR could lead to political problems, as they had in Hungary. Khrushchev also saw, as any good Marxist would, a tight connection between economic and political strength. In Berlin and Germany, especially, Khrushchev believed that winning the economic competition was the key to the triumph of socialism over capitalism.[175] The testimony of top economic officials at the twenty-ninth plenum indicated that Khrushchev's plans were under threat.

Selbmann talked about the "mistakes that were made in the economy" in Hungary, no doubt implying that East German economic plans had followed a similar, dangerous zigzag course. He said that he was shocked on trips to Hungary to see the phenomenal amount of resources put into heavy industry for some years and that then "in a wink [these industries] were forgotten about and left to stand there." Changing economic strategies squandered scarce resources. Selbmann warned that the East Germans "must draw lessons from this."[176]

He was very critical of the "unrealistic" economic plans in the GDR, pointing out that "through an unrealistic assessment of the economic difficulties, we ourselves have prepared political difficulties which can lead to a loss of working class trust in our party."[177] As minister of industry, Selbmann was very well acquainted with the GDR's economic difficulties:

> So what is the situation here? I will say to you entirely openly: Our supply [of food and other goods] situation is extraordinarily tense. I am not saying that it is worse than it was in the past year.
>
> (Otto Grotewohl: Why do you use such words? What does this mean?)
>
> Let me finish speaking! I will say something also about the method of interjections in a minute.
>
> I repeat: our supply situation is extraordinarily tense.

Following up later on Grotewohl's attempts to interrupt Selbmann's critique, Oelssner asserted: "It is often the case with us that we cannot really put forward issues which are unpleasant. . . . It cannot continue that when unpleasant issues are put forward, they are removed quickly from the world with all authority. They should be objectively examined, discussed in a comradely way and then a decision should be made which strengthens our socialist economy and also our peasants' and workers' state."[178] Such an approach was what Oelssner thought Khrushchev had in mind at the Twentieth Congress.

Ulbricht's general response to the economic criticism was to maintain: "No one said that we must [carry out our economic plans] solely on the basis of our own power in every area." Rather Ulbricht saw the plan as a target "on which we would concentrate, but that we would achieve the world level in as many areas as possible through cooperation with the Soviet Union and above all also with the Czechoslovak Socialist Republic."[179] Thus, outside help was the main way Ulbricht saw for dealing with the economic difficulties, and this was quite apparent in his behavior in negotiations with the Soviets.

Grotewohl had a different response, which seemed to favor going full-steam ahead with confidence despite the problems. He rhetorically asked the plenum delegates:

Can we fulfill [our economic plans]? Leuschner and Oelssner spoke about this here. They proceeded from the view that all of this is so terribly difficult and that we must really think precisely about it all. Of course it is all terribly difficult. Of course we must think about it all. But is this then a basis to act as if the party is in a situation in which it will probably fail? . . . I think we can fulfill these tasks, and I think that the whole Politburo shares this view.[180]

Pessimism (or realism) was clearly not going to be tolerated.

While both conservative and liberal interpretations of "the lessons of Hungary" were expressed in detail at the twenty-ninth plenum, the fact that the key holders of power—Ulbricht, Grotewohl, Neumann, and Stoph—clearly favored the conservative interpretation, and downplayed criticism of mistakes, was an indication that it would triumph. This new dogma began to be solidified at the thirtieth plenum of 30 January–1 February 1957, and again at the thirty-third plenum of 16–18 October 1957.

One week after the twenty-ninth plenum, the Politburo decided to "remove all clearly provocative forces" from the universities and to punish "the organizers of the unrest."[181] Thus, Wolfgang Harich was arrested on 29 November 1956, and Walter Janke on 6 December.[182] The next year, Harich was condemned to ten and Janke to five years in prison for "building a conspiratorial state-hostile revolutionary group" with their criticisms of the SED regime.[183]

The Tide Turns against Ulbricht's Opposition

In an effort to make sure the situation was stable in the GDR after the unrest in Poland and Hungary in 1956, and in the spirit of "equality of

relations" and "noninterference" (in the wake of Chinese criticism of Soviet "great power chauvinism"), the Soviet leadership hosted a delegation
of East Germans in Moscow from 3–8 January 1957. The stated Soviet
goal was to discuss "open issues" in their relations, including the "temporary" stationing of Soviet troops on GDR territory, GDR control over its
air space,[184] East German economic difficulties, and the German question.[185] Ulbricht, Grotewohl, Schirdewan, Neumann, Matern, Leuschner,
Paul Verner, Rau, and Heinrich were among the key East German officials to go to Moscow.[186]

Before the meeting, several members of the East German leadership,
including Schirdewan, had told Soviet Ambassador Pushkin that there
should be an open discussion at the meeting of the conflicts within the
SED leadership. At the beginning of the East German visit, Khrushchev
said that these problems should be discussed. Mikoian, however, in private and clearly without informing Khrushchev, told members of the
East German delegation that the Soviet leadership was having its own
internal party problems and that therefore it would be better if the East
Germans did not bring up their leadership conflicts. Thus, toward the
end of the visit, when Khrushchev asked the East Germans to talk about
their party problems, Ulbricht replied that the East Germans could take
care of these themselves. According to Schirdewan, Khrushchev was
quite surprised at Ulbricht's response, but let the issue drop.[187] Ulbricht
now knew that conservatives in the Kremlin were challenging Khrushchev's domestic and foreign policy reforms, especially after the events in
Poland and Hungary.[188] Upon returning home from Moscow, as in July
1953, Ulbricht felt emboldened to move against Schirdewan and others.[189]

At the thirtieth plenum of 30 January–1 February, Ulbricht and his
supporters attacked the liberals and adopted a hard-line course against
"opportunism."[190] As Wollweber later wrote: "At the 30th plenum the
rudder was turned around. A new perspective was shown. The construction of socialism was accelerated, the security measures vis-à-vis the
West were justifiably strengthened."[191] Alfred Neumann took over Schirdewan's job as the head of the Central Committee's Department of Leading Party Organs. Schirdewan retained his position as cadre chief for the
time being, but the process of removing him from power had begun.

Erich Honecker later described the conflicts within the party on the
eve of the thirtieth plenum. He condemned "the opportunistic interpretation of the results of the 20th Party Congress of the CPSU" and accused
Schirdewan and others of underestimating the threat from "the enemy."
He also maintained, reminiscent of the accusations against Beria, Zaisser,
and Herrnstadt in 1953, that Schirdewan and his supporters had "the
illusory view of bringing about German unity at any price."[192]

Honecker delivered the Politburo report at the thirtieth plenum. As the new Hungarian government under Janos Kadar argued, Honecker maintained that the main cause of the unrest in Hungary had been "well organized counterrevolutionary forces with the support of the aggressive imperialist circles of the Western states and their secret services" and only secondarily was to be found in "the mistakes made in the political and economic areas by the leadership of the Hungary Workers' Party." Accordingly, he announced measures to enhance the GDR's security. He told the Central Committee delegates that

> [t]he arming of party and state functionaries which was decided at the 29th plenum has begun since then, as you know. According to the list of functionaries which the Politburo has confirmed, about 10,000 [male and female] comrades will be armed with a pistol. This group of people should be taught by instructors of the People's Police how to use carbines and submachine guns.

The second measure Honecker announced regarding an increase in personal responsibility for protecting the GDR was that people should become much more involved in sports. Honecker presumably wanted East Germans to be in good physical shape to do battle with the enemy, whom the events in Hungary showed was quite active and threatening. Honecker urged the delegates to help get as many of the workers as possible involved in sports.[193]

Ulbricht took up directly the lessons of Hungary in his speech and continued to focus on the conservative lessons, lessons indicating that the GDR should step up security measures and limit debate. He referred to "misunderstandings in the evaluation of the Twentieth Party Congress of the CPSU," but was clearly relieved to announce that "above all through the lessons of the Hungarian events, a realistic estimation of the situation has now taken hold." This time, he came up with a new spin on a conservative interpretation of the applicability of the Twentieth Congress to the Germans. Ulbricht declared that given that Germany had been under Nazi control for a significant part of the time Stalin was in power, and even attacked the Soviet Union, "[w]e as Germans have the least right to carry out a discussion of mistakes which occurred in the Soviet Union during the time when fascism ruled in Germany and when German fascism founded and developed its aggressive policy." The Soviet system showed how strong it was during the Nazi attack, rebuffing the attack and then destroying the fascist base in Germany. Stalin as the Soviet leader was of course in large part responsible for this. Ulbricht thus tried to end the discussion begun at the Twentieth Congress about Stalin and move forward: "Today no one will speak any more about the 'sensation of the Khrushchev speech,' instead today all forces will concentrate on the struggle against [West] German imperialism and against the reactionary ideology with which the bourgeoisie tries to penetrate the workers' movement."[194] The "lessons of Hungary" emboldened Ulbricht to end the debate about the Twentieth Congress and Stalin and to look to the future and defending the GDR from Western policies.

This was also the case with the principle of separate paths to socialism. In the Politburo report to the plenum, Honecker warned of "the danger existing now that each country will put their national peculiarities in the foreground" instead of focusing on the fact that "the main path to socialism is the same for all countries."[195] And in Ulbricht's speech ending the plenum, he reiterated: "We are not going the Polish way. . . . We are not making any Polish experiments."[196]

The Longer-Term Effects of the Hungarian Uprising in the Soviet Union and the GDR

The Hungarian events did not just have a strong and conservative effect on the East German leaders; they also proved to have that effect on the Soviet leaders. In June 1957 a group of leading party officials, the so-called anti-party group, including Molotov, Malenkov, Lazar Kaganovich, and others tried to oust Khrushchev from power.[197] They believed he was overturning too much of the old Stalinist system with explosive consequences, including the uprisings in Poland and Hungary.

Some of the debates at the June 1957 "anti-party" plenum indicate that Soviet policy concerning the GDR was one of the matters in dispute. In particular, there was strong opposition to fulfilling an East German request for 3 billion rubles in credit. The credit was to be used to produce goods for the USSR. Mikoian defended the credit and Khrushchev's policy at the plenum:

> If we don't strengthen the internal system of East Germany, where the workers support its communist government, our army will find itself under fire. And there is an army of half a million there. We cannot lose the sympathy of the population of Germany. If we lose their sympathy and trust, this will mean losing East Germany. And what would it mean to lose East Germany? We know what it would mean, and therefore we proceed from the assumption that we must keep East German industry fully occupied. Then the GDR workers will have work and produce what we need; otherwise we must give the GDR both goods and foodstuffs, not receiving equipment in exchange. I think that our policy is absolutely correct. . . .
>
> But some people say: you place orders, but can we pay for them? This question is a question of grand policy. I kept myself calm [during the discussion about this, unlike Khrushchev], although I am also an emotional person, but Nikita Sergeevich immediately understood the entire political crux of the

difficult question. He, seeing that a majority had developed against the plan, said the following phrase: "I would like to have a vote on this question and I remain in the minority." We created the socialist camp, therefore it is important to strengthen it and we cannot allow any wavering. If East Germany and Czechoslovakia remain today without orders, then the whole socialist camp will crack. Who needs that kind of camp if we cannot fulfill orders? The issue is as stands: either we feed the workers of the GDR for free, or we give them orders: or in yet another scenario we lose the GDR entirely. This is why Nikita Sergeevich exploded. I too almost blew up.[198]

Not only was there opposition to granting the GDR such a sizeable credit, but Mikoian spoke of "a majority" against it. It is quite significant that four years after the *New Course* and the uprising in East Germany, policy toward the GDR continued to be so controversial among the Kremlin leaders. Mikoian was very critical of the "wavering" of his colleagues in their support for East Germany. He and Khrushchev clearly felt that the viability of the socialist camp was riding on their economic support and that the whole thing could fall like a stack of dominoes without that support.

Lacking the argument of the critics, we can only infer that they did not place the same priority on economic aid to the GDR that Mikoian and Khrushchev did. Whether that was because they wanted to save the resources for Soviet needs, which were also great, or because they specifically did not want to help the GDR, is not clear. It is only clear that there were sharp disagreements over aid to the GDR. This evidence, combined with allegations about Beria wanting to "give up" the GDR in 1953 and about Molotov opposing East German membership in the Warsaw Pact in 1955, yields a certain pattern of high-level Soviet "wavering" regarding the GDR. The sense of fighting an uphill battle to get Ulbricht to do what the Soviets wanted and to outcompete capitalism and democracy in Germany may have inclined some in the Kremlin to be more constrained in their willingness to devote resources to the GDR.

While Mikoian did not answer his question here—"What would it mean to lose East Germany?"—he and Khrushchev would answer this in 1961. Khrushchev told the Warsaw Pact members in 1961 that if they lost the GDR, the West German army, the *Bundeswehr*, would then move up to the borders of Poland and Czechoslovakia and pose a greater threat to the communist bloc, for which they would have to pay far more than was then necessary to support the GDR. Thus, "by strengthening [East Germany's] position, we strengthen our own position."[199] In addition, Khrushchev wanted to make it "a showcase of moral, political and material achievement" to show the West how successful socialism was and to win over more adherents to socialism.[200] Similarly, Mikoian emphasized the importance of the GDR for the reputation of socialism. He told the East Germans in June 1961 that the most important proving ground for the superiority of socialism over capitalism was in Germany and that if they lost the competition in Germany, the Soviets would suffer a great loss also, a loss of reputation and credibility. Therefore, Mikoian declared that the GDR had first priority in Soviet aid.[201] Ulbricht grew increasingly adept at taking advantage of Khrushchev and Mikoian's commitment to supporting the GDR and frequently asked for more economic aid, coming under criticism from Grotewohl and Schirdewan as he did.[202]

Just as Khrushchev prevailed over his colleagues in the summer of 1957 on the question of credits to the GDR, so he prevailed over the "anti-party group." But their criticism, as well as the events in Poland and Hungary the year before, compelled Khrushchev to backtrack from the lofty principles of the Twentieth Congress. This redounded to Ulbricht's benefit in his own leadership struggle. The SED Central Committee learned of the conflict in Moscow and the demise of the "anti-party group" in mid-July.[203] Khrushchev and Mikoian then visited the GDR from 7–14 August. Khrushchev publicly reiterated that "there can be no talk of Germany's reunification at the cost of the interests of the GDR and the socialist achievements of its workers."[204] In part he hoped to influence the upcoming September West German elections. He wanted to demonstrate that Adenauer's hostile designs on the GDR were hopeless and that the West German voters should vote for a more "realistic" politician, presumably from the SPD.[205] Khrushchev supported Ulbricht personally on this trip and identified "revisionism," and thus the types of policies favored by Schirdewan, as the main danger.

The fact that a group of Soviet party leaders who had tried to oust *the* party leader were themselves ousted would not bode well for Schirdewan and others who had been challenging Ulbricht's rule. And in fact at the next SED plenum, the thirty-third plenum from 16–19 October, Ulbricht would start to move against his challengers.[206] Clearly arguing against Schirdewan, Ulbricht insisted that given the struggle with "the enemy" in the West, the SED could not afford to conduct its policies "only with means of persuasion but also [had to use] the means of state power."[207]

Schirdewan was not prepared to cave in to Ulbricht's hard line. On 11 November 1957 he discussed the situation with Wollweber. Schirdewan said that he planned to speak about internal party issues and the fact that the resolutions of the Twentieth CPSU Congress were being slowly liquidated. He would also address the refugee exodus and the need to treat it more seriously and openly. Schirdewan assured Wollweber that he had the support of many in the Secretariat and Politburo, including Grotewohl, and Ambassador Pushkin's backing. Schirdewan explained that

> he had spoke with [Pushkin], informed him in detail, that [Pushkin] knew that there were comrades who wanted a change in the sense of replacing [Walter Ulbricht] by him, Karl Schirdewan. Pushkin also found that the best thing. [Schirdewan] had spoken again with Otto Grotewohl and he [Grotewohl] had said that he would not express any political views on [Schirdewan's] ideas and would not counter his election to 1. secretary, but—if the matter went favorably—would support it.[208]

Wollweber advised against relying on Pushkin's support, because it could be easily overridden by Moscow, and on Grotewohl's support, because Grotewohl normally avoided conflict. When Schirdewan refused to give in to Ulbricht's pressure at the thirty-fourth plenum in late November, the stage was set for his ouster. The next development would indicate just how high the stakes were in the SED leadership struggle.

On 7 December 1957, Gerhart Ziller (the chief economic planner) and Fritz Selbmann, supposed allies of Schirdewan, reportedly boasted to colleagues that at the next plenum Schirdwan, Oelssner, and others would propose overturning both the political line of the party and the party leadership.[209] Upon learning of this, a majority in the Politburo quickly decided that the behavior of Ziller and Selbmann was "factional" and that this oppositional activity had probably been going on for some time. In a tragic response, Ziller killed himself on the morning of 14 December 1957.[210] Perhaps he feared that, as in Stalin's times, he would be killed for supposedly opposing the leader.

On 17 December, the Politburo told Schirdewan to examine his behavior and submit a written statement in which it was clearly hoped and probably expected that he would confess the error of his liberal views.[211] On 3 January Schirdewan submitted a statement, dated 1 January 1958.[212] The statement was rejected and Schirdewan was given the chance to write another, which he did not do.[213] In his statement, Schirdewan defended himself and condemned Ulbricht's leadership methods. He admonished Ulbricht for appealing too frequently to the Soviets for economic aid.[214] He also discussed the issue of "flight from the republic," asserting that the refugees should not be alluded to as "traitors, deserters, and pigs." Instead, he asserted that the party must reach out to the people to persuade them to stay.[215]

Schirdewan's case was discussed further at a Politburo session on 11 January 1958.[216] Ten people in the Politburo voted to remove Schirdewan from the Central Committee. Schirdewan, Oelssner, and Grotewohl voted to keep him in. They formed a delegation of Ulbricht, Grotewohl, Matern, Stoph, Ebert, and Neumann to go to Moscow to inform the Soviets of their plans to oust Schirdewan and consult with them.

The Politburo delegation met with the Soviet leaders on 29 January. As Ulbricht reported, shortly after the meeting, to Yuri Andropov, then chairman of the CPSU CC Department on Relations with Communist and Workers' Parties of Socialist Countries, the focus of the meeting was to persuade Grotewohl to support the Politburo decision to remove Schirdewan. At the meeting Grotewohl claimed that he "was just trying to avert any sort of haste in the making of a decision on the matter of Schirdewan, since he believed that the Soviet comrades viewed him as a promising figure in the SED." According to Ulbricht, the Soviets told Grotewohl that "he had been led astray by the Soviet ambassador," Pushkin, into thinking of Schirdewan in this way.[217] Grotewohl's notes of the meeting, however, indicate that Khrushchev was more even-handed in his judgment. He told the Germans: "You must resolve internal questions by yourselves." He declared that Schirdewan was "a good communist," but that "Ulbricht mistrusts Schirdewan. . . . Ulbricht cannot accustom himself to others."[218]

After the meeting, Grotewohl caved in to the pressure of his Politburo colleagues and voted with them to expel Schirdewan from the Politburo.[219] On 31 January, the Politburo suspended Schirdewan's position as Politburo and Secretariat member.[220]

At the SED's thirty-fifth plenum of 3–6 February 1958, the "opportunistic factional group" of Schirdewan, Wollweber, Ziller, Oelssner, and Selbmann was ousted. Erich Honecker, who had now effectively taken Schirdewan's place as second in the leadership, gave the Politburo report.[221] He called the opposition members "opportunistic," because they had supposedly tried to use the GDR's difficulties in constructing socialism and the increased problems in connection with the events in Hungary to bolster their own power at the expense of the party. They "opportunistically misunderstood" the decisions of the Twentieth Congress as justifying a lessening of the class struggle and a policy of German unity "at any price," the last being reminiscent of the charges against Beria, Herrnstadt, and Zaisser. Wollweber recalls in his memoirs the shock he felt at the plenum when for the first time he and others were accused of "striving for German reunification at any price."[222] He immediately asked for written or verbal proof of this charge, but received none.

Ulbricht used the same tactics against Schirdewan and other domestic opponents that he probably used against the Soviets. He argued that no changes in policy or the leadership could be made, because this might be taken advantage of by "the adversary." Kurt Hager's[223] optimistic view that the open debates in the East German leadership unleashed by the Twentieth Congress "had become a flood and could no longer be stopped" turned out to be sadly mistaken.[224] The Hungarian events had made it much easier for Ulbricht to move against liberals, since he could accuse them of supporting policies that would lead the GDR down the path that Poland and Hungary had gone in 1956. The fact that there had been no uprising in the GDR in 1956 was also a feather in Ulbricht's cap. Even though Khrushchev was frustrated with him, he also knew that Ulbricht's tight control in the GDR perhaps had prevented a repeat of 1953 in response to the Polish and Hungarian events of 1956.[225]

CONCLUSION

As we have seen, the arena of political debate in the GDR opened wide after the Twentieth Congress. Within a month, there were two strikingly different views of how its principles should be applied to the GDR. The conservatives, led by Ulbricht, wanted to get by with the minimum amount of open discussion about past mistakes and focus on socialism's bright future. The liberals, led by Schirdewan, preferred to follow the Polish path of promoting open discussion about problems within the country so that the problems would then have a better chance of being resolved instead of festering behind closed doors. While the situation heated up in Poland and Hungary during the summer and fall of 1956, the debate within East Germany also sharpened. The disagreements within the East German leadership about how much and whether the principles of the Twentieth Congress could be and should be applied to East Germany reached a climax at the twenty-ninth plenum, just as the Hungarian uprising was being crushed by Soviet tanks. Coming at this crucial time in the East German debate, the Hungarian events had a profound effect on the East German leadership.

What did Schirdewan, Wollweber, Oelssner and Zaisser and Herrnstadt before them really want? It was not to give up socialism and join the West. It was to create a more humane form of socialism instead of the harsh reality it had become under Ulbricht. They also wanted to develop better relations with West Germany, both as German patriots with an interest in the other part of their country, and as socialists who sought to spread their ideas about socialism to the rest of the country, including in cooperation with the SPD. Ulbricht always cared more about his own power than the fate of the German nation as a whole.

What did Khrushchev and the other Soviet leaders hope for in their support, albeit temporary, for Ulbricht's more open-minded opponents? They hoped, and for a time believed, that these other East Germans would find a way to rule the GDR that would be more satisfactory to

the two core Soviet interests: stabilizing and improving domestic conditions in the GDR with the effect of halting the refugee flow; and stabilizing and improving relations with the FRG so as to make West German
policies friendlier toward the GDR and the Soviet bloc.

Could Ulbricht's opponents in 1953 or 1956 have effected these changes?
What would have happened if they had? We cannot know the answers
to these questions. The events of 1989, together with those of 1953 and
1956, make it abundantly clear the Soviet communist system probably
was doomed from the start. So it is unlikely that over the long term one
of Ulbricht's more liberal, although still socialist, opponents could have
transformed East Germany into a country of happy, prosperous people.
Given that socialism and ties to the Soviets were the only things that
differentiated the East German from the West German regime, it may
have been harder than Ulbricht's opponents likely anticipated to establish a stable, more open socialist state. Ulbricht was always atuned to
this problem. Still, in the 1950s, some Soviets and East Germans wanted
to try their lot with a less Stalinist, less Ulbrichtesque regime in the
GDR. It certainly would have improved East Germans' lives and softened the cold war in Germany for as long as such a regime existed. And
it might have made the Berlin Wall unnecessary. But Ulbricht, and the
Kremlin leaders too afraid to remove him, did not take this path.

The SED leadership refused to grapple seriously with Schirdewan's
warnings about "flight from the Republic." Schirdewan maintained that
the refugee exodus had to be addressed openly instead of being treated
as a taboo subject.[226] After the events in Hungary, however, Ulbricht
sought to stifle any discussions of fundamental problems, especially a
problem as embarrassing as the refugee exodus. Thus, one of the more
long-term effects of the Hungarian events on the GDR was a decreased
willingness to confront the problem of the refugee exodus. Instead, the
entrenched leadership preferred to cut off the GDR from subversive
Western influences, leading to a situation in which ultimately a wall
would have to be built to resolve the problem.

More generally, the influence of the Hungarian events of 1956 reduced the options for the development of the GDR, as the leadership
under Ulbricht increasingly closed in on itself afraid to allow differences
of view that could destroy the leadership. This approach would ultimately destroy East Germany, but not for several decades.

Another long-term effect of the Hungarian events was to induce the
East Germans to request more economic aid to help them through their
difficult period of building socialism and prevent a Hungarian scenario
or a repeat of 17 June 1953. The Hungarian experience gave Ulbricht
more bargaining power with the Soviets on economic and other issues,
since the risks of a weak regime were now more obvious. Ulbricht could

claim that he maintained calm in the GDR during the tense period of 1956, thereby demonstrating that he was a reliable leader whom the Soviets should support with increasing amounts of economic aid. Now he could play on both the "June 1953 syndrome" and the "Hungarian syndrome" in negotiations with the Kremlin leaders.

In both this chapter and the previous chapter, we have seen a combination of Ulbricht's resistance, an uprising, and Soviet domestic conservatism leading to the end of reforms in the GDR.[227] We have also seen in both 1953 and 1956 the sharp divisions within the SED leadership and evidence that some Soviet and East German leaders saw the problems in the GDR realistically and took efforts to remedy them with reforms. The broader cold war atmosphere, however, in part contributed to making reforms harder in the GDR, since conservatives could always assert that "the enemy" would take advantage of any backtracking in the GDR and any criticism of or change in leaders. In 1953 and 1956–58, Ulbricht was able to successfully resist Soviet calls for reforms in his domestic and foreign policy.

Ulbricht was a survivor with a very clear vision of a hard-line form of socialism. He knew what he wanted in the GDR and was determined to achieve it no matter what his domestic or Soviet critics said. The uprisings of 1953 and 1956 bolstered his belief that the safest way to ensure the continued development of socialism in the GDR, and his own rule, was to maintain a tight grip on power. After his years of working underground in Germany and then seeking to influence developments in Germany from the Soviet Union, Ulbricht was used to working around formidable obstacles. He was accustomed to working in an environment where people did not agree with him and in which he had to push his ideas tenaciously. Just as he had fought to preserve and expand the KPD under the Nazis, he now acted to maintain and strengthen his vision of socialism against his domestic and Soviet foes. He was not to be deterred.

While Khrushchev would tire of Ulbricht's requests for support, which increasingly sounded like demands or threats, he admired and shared Ulbricht's commitment to the socialist cause in Germany. After two failed attempts in 1953 and 1956 to improve the situation in the GDR by altering East German domestic and foreign policies, Khrushchev changed strategies in late 1958. He would now focus on compelling the West to reduce its threats to the GDR. Maybe it would be easier to change Western policies than it had been to change Ulbricht's policies.

CHAPTER THREE

1958–1960

Khrushchev Takes on the West in the Berlin Crisis

A BOLD INITIATIVE by Khrushchev and the reaction it provoked again takes center stage in this chapter. Yet Khrushchev's initiation of the Berlin Crisis was very different from his de-Stalinization campaign and emphasis on peaceful coexistence at the Twentieth Congress described in the previous chapter. Khrushchev's accommodating style toward the West became coercive in the fall of 1958. How and why did Khrushchev change his approach, and why did he decide to focus his foreign policy on Berlin and Germany? What was the role of Ulbricht in the crisis? This chapter and the next will examine these questions. The present chapter traces the process leading to Khrushchev's 10 November speech and 27 November ultimatum, which launched the Berlin Crisis. It then follows the development of the crisis through the summer of 1960 and the aborted Four Power Paris summit, after which Khrushchev decided to wait to negotiate with the next U.S. President, John F. Kennedy. Chapter 4 examines the final year of the Berlin Crisis climaxing with the building of the Berlin Wall.

Between 1953 and 1958, the Soviets treated the question of East German policies and the stability of the SED regime largely as an internal matter of the GDR and the Soviet Union. The Kremlin leaders hoped that a combination of moderate East German policies and Soviet aid would stem the refugee flow and solidify their German ally. During the Berlin Crisis, however, Khrushchev attempted to involve the West in the matter of the stabilization of the GDR. He anticipated that Western recognition of the SED regime and a reduced or eliminated Western presence in West Berlin would significantly alleviate the pressure on East Germany and put it on solid ground.

For key parts of this chapter, the West replaces Ulbricht as Khrushchev's key interlocutor, but Ulbricht returns in a key role in the next chapter. Unlike Chapters 1 and 2, there is very little about East German domestic politics in this chapter, because leadership struggles in the GDR largely ceased to exist after Ulbricht removed his most prominent critics from power in early 1958. Instead, this chapter and the next highlight top-level Soviet–East German interactions.

The evidentiary base for examining the Berlin Crisis is particularly strong. In addition to Western sources such as the Berlin Crisis volumes of the State Department's *Foreign Relations of the United States* series, there are numerous Russian and German documents detailing their high-level communications concerning Berlin and Germany between 1958 and 1961. These include records of conversations and letters between Khrushchev and Ulbricht and their senior colleagues, internal Soviet and East German deliberations, drafts of proposals, important memoir literature, and Warsaw Pact records. These materials allow the scholar to piece together a much more complete and nuanced picture of the Soviet and East German side of the Berlin Crisis than was previously possible. The Soviet and East German documents also yield a more personal picture of Khrushchev and Ulbricht and their interactions during the Berlin Crisis.

ULBRICHT AND KHRUSHCHEV IN THE FALL OF 1958

After Ulbricht consolidated his domestic power by ousting his opposition at the thirty-fifth plenum in February and the Fifth Congress in July, he turned his attention toward persuading Khrushchev to help him combat the challenges posed by West Berlin and West Germany and particularly their enticement of refugees. From 1953 to 1958, in the face of Soviet calls for moderation, Ulbricht had steadfastly refused to alleviate his domestic policies to deal with this problem. In the wake of the Hungarian revolution, he was even less inclined to do so. And he was more inclined to enact measures to shield his country, and his regime, from Western pressure.

Ulbricht knew that economic problems were central to the GDR's weakness. Accordingly, he resolved at the Fifth Congress that by 1961, East German per capita consumption would surpass that of West Germany.[1] It would be much easier for Ulbricht to achieve this if he could halt the depletion of his labor force by refugees.

Like Ulbricht, Khrushchev had also ousted his opposition, but not as comprehensively as Ulbricht had. While Khrushchev had removed the "anti-party group" from power, there were still many in the Soviet leadership who voiced their disapproval of Khrushchev's domestic and foreign policy reforms. Khrushchev had even pulled back from his de-Stalinization campaign and from his notion of "separate paths to socialism" in the wake of the events in Poland and Hungary and domestic criticism. Mao's increasingly public rebuke of Khrushchev's policies also put Khrushchev on the defensive. In addition, for all of Khrushchev's efforts at peaceful coexistence with the West, he had not signed any major agreements with the Western Powers; and in spite of his recognition of the FRG, he had still not obtained Western recognition of the GDR. Khrushchev made a bold attempt to simultaneously solve the GDR's problems and his own by commencing the Berlin Crisis.[2] Before charting Khrushchev's path to the November ultimatum, let us study the situation in Berlin which made it vulnerable to his pressure. West Berlin offered both a threat and an opportunity to Khrushchev.

Background on Berlin and Its Status after World War II

Agreements made among the Allies during and at the end of World War II stipulated that the capital, Berlin, would be treated separately from the rest of Germany.[3] Due to Berlin's special role as the center of the aggressive Nazi regime and the previous German imperial government from which they launched two World Wars, the Allies aimed to ensure that Berlin could not be the site for future war plans. Both Berlin and Germany were divided into four occupation zones to facilitate their take-over and stripping of power. According to the Potsdam Agreements of 1 August 1945, the occupying powers were to follow a policy of "complete disarmament and demilitarization," denazification, and democratization in Germany.[4]

In order for Americans, British, and French to move from their occupation zones of western Germany to their zones in western Berlin, they had to cross 177 kilometers of the Soviet occupation zone (see map 2). They reached only a vague agreement on guarantees of surface and air access to the western zones of Berlin at a conference with the Soviet commander Marshal Zhukov in June 1945. Zhukov's assertion "that possibly all points discussed at this conference may be changed" did not bode well for the future.[5] Indeed, when Stalin was faced with Western plans to create a West German state and institute a currency reform in the western zones of Germany and Berlin, he blockaded land and water access to West Berlin for a year in an effort to halt these Western plans.[6] Although Western access rights became somewhat clearer after the lifting of the Berlin blockade in May 1949, the West had few feasible means to ensure that these agreements would be fairly executed.[7]

With the creation of two German states in 1949, East and West Berlin remained under Four Power occupation and legally separate from each German state (although clearly connected in every other way).[8] And the Four Power agreements on Berlin remained in force. Only the Four Powers had control over access to West and East Berlin, not the Germans. Thus, it was the Soviet responsibility to provide for Western access rights to West Berlin. Yet, in September 1955, the Soviets transferred to the GDR supervision of civilian use of the Western access routes,[9] while Moscow retained oversight of Western military use of the access routes. As far as the Western Powers were concerned, this represented a unilateral Soviet abrogation of Four Power agreements on Berlin, and, worse, the Soviets transferred some of their responsibilities to a regime the West did not recognize, the GDR.[10] The United States reminded the Soviets that "these agreements can in no way be regarded as releasing the Soviet Government from its obligations under Four-Power Agreements, and in particular its responsibility for ensuring the normal functioning of communications between the different parts of Germany, including Berlin."[11] The Western Powers, however, acquiesced to this transfer of responsibility to the GDR for civilian movement between the FRG and West Berlin. Thus, after September 1955, GDR border officials checked the documents of everyone on the access routes except Western military representatives. Both the Soviets and the East Germans were now in a position to limit access to West Berlin if and when they wanted.

THE SITUATION IN WEST BERLIN AS SEEN BY THE EAST AND THE WEST

West Berlin's location 177 kilometers inside of GDR territory offered advantages and disadvantages to both East and West in a zero-sum way: Advantages for the East were disadvantages for the West and vice versa. Each side had different concerns over access to West Berlin. The West was particularly concerned with guaranteeing access in the direction from West Germany to West Berlin in order to supply the West Berliners with food and other goods and to provide the Western garrisons in West Berlin with equipment and troops. The East was particularly concerned with limiting access for refugees from East Berlin and East Germany to West Berlin and hindering the further escape of these refugees from West Berlin to West Germany.

The Eastern Perspective

From the perspective of the GDR and the Soviets, West Berlin posed a threefold threat. First, it was the only "loophole" through which citizens of the GDR could still escape, since the border between East and West Germany had been closed in 1952. Although the East German passport law of 11 December 1957 reduced the overall number of refugees leaving East Germany,[12] it drastically increased the proportion of refugees leaving through West Berlin, from 60 percent in 1957 to well over 90 percent by the end of 1958.[13] As a result, there was increasing pressure to close the escape hatch of West Berlin. As Mikhail Pervukhin, the Soviet ambassador to the GDR, observed, "The presence in Berlin of an open and essentially uncontrolled border between the socialist and capitalist worlds unwittingly prompts the population to make a comparison between both parts of the city, which, unfortunately, does not always turn out in favor of Democratic [East] Berlin."[14]

In the year prior to the crisis, the Soviets and East Germans met monthly on the refugee problem, and these meetings continued throughout the crisis. There were ongoing Soviet and East German analyses of the causes and trends of the refugee outflow. Their attention focused increasingly on the intelligentsia, the most educated sector of the population.[15] The CPSU CC Director on Relations with Communist and Workers' Parties of Socialist Countries, Yuri Andropov, wrote an urgent letter to the Central Committee on 28 August 1958 about the significant increase in the numbers of East German intelligentsia among the refugees (an increase of 50 percent from 1957). He reported that the GDR leadership maintained that the intelligentsia was leaving for the higher standard of living in West Germany, but that in fact testimony from the refugees indicated that their motives were more political than material. Andropov said that the SED officials did not know how to relate to the intelligentsia and needed help. "In view of the fact that the issue of the flight of the intelligentsia from the GDR has reached a particularly critical phase," Andropov wrote, "it would be expedient to discuss this with Comrade Ulbricht ... to explain to him our apprehensions on this issue."[16] The East German leadership had hoped that the resolutions of the Fifth SED Congress in July for strengthening the economy and stepping up plans to achieve "the conclusion of the construction of socialism in the GDR"[17] would decrease the refugee outflow, but they had the opposite effect.[18] In early October, Ulbricht reported to Ambassador Pervukhin on the continued difficult situation regarding the intelligentsia, stressing growing tensions between them and the SED regime.[19]

Ulbricht saw West Berlin as an economic threat to the GDR. The skilled, well-educated East Germans fleeing across the border to West Berlin constituted a "brain drain" on the East German economy.[20] So did the *Grenzgänger* problem—the roughly 50,000 East Berliners working in West Berlin.[21] These people had the advantage of the low cost of living in East Berlin, but contributed their labor to the West Berlin economy. In addition, Ulbricht was concerned about the West Berliners who came to East Berlin to buy goods and services for much cheaper prices than they had to pay in West Berlin. This depleted the number of goods and services available for the needier East Berliners and increased their incentive to go West.[22]

The final threat that West Berlin posed was its status as a base of espionage and subversion vis-à-vis East Berlin and East Germany. Khrushchev condemned Western use of West Berlin for "subversive activities" against East Germany and other countries of the Soviet bloc as an indication that "the very essence of the allied agreement on Berlin has vanished."[23] The location of West Berlin, "spy central," inside the GDR was perfect for American, British, French, and West German intelligence agencies to recruit East Germans and eavesdrop on East German and Soviet communications.[24] Ulbricht and Khrushchev wanted to put a stop to this, as well as to end hostile or critical radio and television transmissions from West Berlin, such as the RIAS broadcasts that had helped the demonstrators in the GDR in 1953.

Faced with these many perceived threats from the West, the East Germans and Soviets had a variety of options to help the East German regime counter these: They could (1) increase their influence in West Berlin and decrease Western influence there; (2) make it more difficult for East Germans to get to West Berlin and be tempted by it; and/or (3) inject more resources into the GDR economy to shore it up in the competition with the FRG. As the crisis progressed, there would be increasing differences between Khrushchev and Ulbricht over which of these strategies to follow, and how persistently.

What to do about the problem of West Berlin, and when, had been a subject of long-standing debate within East Germany, within the Soviet Union, between the East Germans and Soviets, and within the Warsaw Pact. There were differences of view on whether the West Berlin "problem"—its position as a refugee-enticing capitalist enclave housing Western espionage agencies—could be resolved separately from, and before, a German peace treaty. This debate was addressed at a May 1958 meeting between Peter Florin, then head of the International Department of the SED Central Committee, and O. Selianinov, a counselor at the Soviet embassy in East Berlin:

> Regarding the Berlin problem as a whole, Florin said that there are still big differences of opinion among the German comrades on how to approach its resolution. "We still do not have an agreed upon concept on this question, just as there is not a united, agreed upon position among us, the Soviet Union and the other countries of the socialist camp. In particular, some German comrades believe, for example, that the Berlin question cannot be resolved as long as Germany is not united. Others, on the other hand, believe that the Berlin question can be gradually resolved by starting now to carry out a determined line of political and economic conquest of West Berlin so as to create the preconditions for the unification of Berlin in the future." Florin noted that he is a proponent of the second point of view.[25]

Selianinov emphasized to Florin that although he agreed that they should start to resolve the West Berlin issue independently of a broader German settlement, this "demanded the preparation of a whole series of political and economic measures by the GDR *and other socialist countries* [emphasis added]."[26] In other words, the GDR should not act alone, but should coordinate its approach with other socialist countries, including most importantly, of course, the Soviet Union. As we shall see, the GDR did not always do this during the crisis.

Balanced against all of these disadvantages of having West Berlin in the middle of East Germany, there was one big advantage to the Soviets and East Germans: West Berlin with its 11,000 Western troops was surrounded by the 500,000 Soviet troops deployed in the GDR. The Soviets could play on this military imbalance to put pressure on the West.

The Western Perspective

From the perspective of the West, and especially the United States, West Berlin was a vulnerable outpost, difficult but essential to defend. Many American officials felt that the U.S. reputation as a great power and a reliable ally was riding on how well it protected West Berlin from East German and Soviet encroachment: If the United States did not defend the West Berliners, none of America's allies, beginning with West Germany, would trust its support. American policy makers thus perceived West Berlin as a "superdomino," in the words of William Burr; lose it to communism and other allies would fall too.[27] The British, however, had different views as to how important it was to hold on to West Berlin, and certainly never wanted to risk war to defend it.[28] The French and West Germans also had their own views on how they should respond to Soviet pressure on West Berlin. The Soviets and East Germans knew that if they pressed the West on Berlin, they would likely provoke conflicts within the Western camp.

For the Western Powers, occupation of West Berlin was also a huge coup: They had an outpost within the Soviet bloc and could utilize it to help undermine the socialist countries. They had a unique opportunity to establish listening posts, recruit spies, and construct a "show window" of capitalism. The flow of East German refugees was a boon to the West, demonstrating the greater attractiveness of capitalism and democracy compared to socialism. The West certainly did not want to give this up.

SOVIET AND EAST GERMAN PREPARATIONS FOR A NEW DIPLOMATIC INITIATIVE IN THE FALL OF 1958

In the midst of a new rather hopeless round of East-West proposals on a German peace treaty and reunification, the Soviets and East Germans were consulting closely on *Deutschlandpolitik* in the fall of 1958. Since the end of World War II, the Four Powers had failed to find a consensus on the terms of a peace treaty and reunification for Germany. Each side regularly made proposals that were rejected by the other side. The key disagreement between the two sides on reunification consisted of the West's insistence that free, all-German elections, monitored by the Four Powers, the UN, or some credible body, occur before unification. The Soviets, on the other hand, did not want to risk free elections and insisted that the present East and West German governments together formulate a plan for reunification. Given that a peace treaty would have to be signed by a German government, or German governments, the disagreements over the legitimacy of the two German governments and how to bring about a united German government prevented progress on a peace treaty.

In the context of these East-West proposals on Germany, in early September 1958, West Germany proposed a "four-power group (at least at the level of an ambassadors conference) with a mandate to prepare joint proposals for the solution of the German problem."[29] The East Germans insisted that a joint German commission also be involved.[30] On 30 September, the West responded, as usual, that free elections must precede the creation of any joint German commission.[31] The Soviets and East Germans then conferred on further tactics to engage the West on Germany. They held a series of high-level meetings (mostly among Ulbricht, Pervukhin, and A. A. Smirnov, the Soviet Ambassador to West Germany) on 26 September; on 2, 5, 10, 12, 15, 20 October; and on 17 November.

At Pervukhin's 2 October meeting with Ulbricht and Prime Minister Grotewohl to discuss preparing a response to the Western note on Germany of 30 September,[32] Pervukhin said that the Soviets "should answer the Western powers *with a special note*. In our note . . . we would again emphasize the position of the Soviet government on the German question and support the GDR proposal on the preparation of a peace treaty. In the note, we could formulate the basic parts of a peace treaty [emphasis added]." Ulbricht and Grotewohl agreed with this proposition and asked "that the Soviet note be publicized about a week or two before the GDR elections" in late November so that they could make use of the Soviet note in their propaganda work on the eve of the elections. Ulbricht further insisted that "we must speak to West Germany with a different language. We can't always be telling [West German leader Konrad] Adenauer that we propose negotiations, and he refuses them."[33] Ulbricht wanted the Soviet note to represent a toughening of *Deutschlandpolitik*. On 5 October, he counseled Pervukhin and Smirnov that "it would be good if the Soviet government would answer the latest letter from Adenauer such that West Germany could not sustain any illusions regarding the possibility of German reunification on Western terms."[34]

In the discussions between the East German leaders and the Soviet diplomats in Berlin, there was much talk of an imminent Western political and economic, and perhaps even military, offensive against East Germany that they must preempt.[35] They also expected a more general Western offensive regarding Germany once the West's attention turned away from the Far East, where communist Chinese shelling of the Nationalist-held offshore islands of Quemoy and Matsu had precipitated a crisis beginning on 23 August. Ulbricht and Grotewohl told Pervukhin in early October that they "had to keep in mind that as soon as the issue of the Chinese islands was shifted to the second burner, Germany would be next."[36] U.S. Secretary of State John Foster Dulles visited Taiwan in October and "drew clear parallels between the U.S. commitment to Quemoy and Matsu and to West Berlin."[37]

Ulbricht drew his own parallels between the offshore islands and West Berlin:

> Quemoy and West Berlin are not only misused as centers of provocation by those forces which currently exercise force over them, but are simultaneously developing as areas which are unjustifiably separated from their hinterland. Quemoy is located in the territorial waters of the PRC which also belong to the outer territorial waters of the national territory of the coastal state [Taiwan] for the time being. Berlin lies on the territory of the GDR. Just as the Chiang Kai-shek clique and its American backers and allies keep this source of provocation occupied in violation of human rights and use it against the PRC, so West Berlin must always find use in the view of its dictators as a trouble-maker against the GDR. Both positions have not only the same goals, but also the same weaknesses. Both are islands and have to carry all the consequences of an island location.[38]

Accordingly, just as Mao had shelled Quemoy and Matsu in August, Ulbricht wanted to go on the offensive against West Berlin, which the West could only defend with difficulty due to its "island" location deep inside GDR territory.

Indeed, it was Ulbricht who first publicly hinted at a harder line on West Berlin, probably in an effort to prod Khrushchev toward this tougher stand. In a late October 1958 speech and an article in *Neues Deutschland* directed to the West Berliners on the eve of elections there, Ulbricht declared: "All of Berlin lies on the territory of the [GDR]. . . . The Western powers have destroyed the legal basis for their presence in Berlin; they no longer have any legal, moral, or political justification for their continued occupation of West Berlin."[39] The year before, he had threatened the West Berliners even more clearly: "West Berliners know that West Berlin lies within the German Democratic Republic. The ties of the agents of imperialism and NATO propaganda extend into West Berlin. . . . Everyone understands that West Berlin's population may some day have to pay very dearly."[40]

Ulbricht did not just make these statements publicly. He also made similar arguments to the Soviets privately. In the year prior to Khrushchev's launching of the crisis, Ulbricht had argued repeatedly to the Soviets that the GDR, in order to exercise its full sovereignty, should have control over all of Berlin and all of the access routes to it, including the air corridors.[41] As A. James McAdams points out:

> Because of the attention Khrushchev's ultimatum received in late 1958, one may easily fail to notice that over an extended period between 1955 and 1957 Soviet officials barely mentioned the issue in their contacts with the West. Yet, over the same years, in contrast, the East German leader was actually pressing his allies on a routine basis to turn over the city to the GDR, including its western sectors, on the grounds that it was perfectly natural that Berlin in its entirety be steered down the path to socialism.[42]

Ulbricht had also been following a second track since 1952 to deal with the West Berlin problem: If the Soviets did not let him take over West Berlin and the access routes, he would try to get them to close the Berlin border.

On 5 November, the Soviets sent Ulbricht a draft of their next note to the United States on Germany and requested his response the same day. The note dealt with the status of Berlin and the need for a German peace treaty. Deputy Foreign Minister Winzer advised Ulbricht to make some objections to the draft: Instead of just stating that "Berlin does not belong to the territory of the Federal Republic, to say also that it belongs to the territory of the GDR, as you stated in your speech [of 27 October]," and to state in the note that "Berlin is the capital of the GDR."[43] Khrushchev acceded to these objections.

KHRUSHCHEV'S ULTIMATUM

While Soviet diplomats were preparing a note to the United States and discussing plans with the East Germans, Khrushchev himself was developing an initiative that would also reflect some of Ulbricht's aims. Khrushchev launched the Berlin Crisis with a speech in Moscow on 10 November and an ultimatum sent to the Western Powers on 27 November 1958. Speaking to a Soviet-Polish friendship meeting on 10 November, Khrushchev asserted that the Western Powers were using West Berlin as an outpost from which to launch aggressive maneuvers against the GDR and other countries of the socialist camp, including Poland. He accused the West of having broken all Four Power agreements concerning Germany, particularly the Potsdam provisions for the country's demilitarization. According to the Soviet leader, the only part of the Potsdam Agreements the West continued to honor was that stipulating Four Power occupation of Berlin, which the Americans, British, and French used for lording it [over] in West Berlin, turning that part of the city, which is the capital of the German Democratic Republic, into some kind of state within a state, and, profiting by this, conducting subversive activities from Western Berlin against the German Democratic Republic, against the Soviet Union and the other Warsaw Treaty countries. On top of all this, they have the right of unrestricted communication between Berlin and Western Germany through the air space, by the railways, highways and waterways of the German Democratic Republic, a state which they do not even want to recognize.[44]

This state of affairs could not go on any longer, Khrushchev intoned. The situation in Berlin, "the capital of the GDR, [must be] normalized."

In Khrushchev's view, this would entail abolishing the Potsdam occupation provisions, allowing the Soviets to "hand over to the sovereign German Democratic Republic the functions in Berlin that are still exercised by Soviet agencies," including the supervision of access between West Germany and West Berlin.[45] Controlling this access would allow Ulbricht to stem the refugee flow. For five years, Khrushchev had tried to get Ulbricht to find a way to make the GDR a more attractive place to live so people would not flee to the West. Now he would try a new approach, which he hoped would yield more benefits than just arresting the tide of refugees.

In an ultimatum to the Western Powers on 27 November, Khrushchev went even further in his demands on Berlin than he had on 10 November. He called for the West to transform West Berlin into a demilitarized "free city," which implied the withdrawal of Western forces. He also insisted on signing a World War II peace treaty with the two Germanys or with a united Germany.[46] He demanded that this all be done within six months. If the United States, Great Britain, and France did not agree, he would sign a separate peace treaty with the GDR and transfer to it control of the access routes between the FRG and West Berlin, with the clear implication that "the GDR would have been entitled to be less flexible in these matters than we had been."[47]

In calling for a demilitarized, "free city" in West Berlin (although not in East Berlin), Khrushchev declared that "[i]f this proposal is not acceptable to the U.S. government, there is no topic left for talks on the Berlin question by the former occupying powers." Furthermore, if the West did not recognize the Soviet right to transfer its rights and responsibilities of occupation in Berlin to the GDR and if it tried to hinder this transfer, perhaps by force, this would "result immediately in appropriate retaliation" by Warsaw Pact members.[48] The fact that Khrushchev sent the note at a time when he had been boasting about Soviet military strength due to its intercontinental ballistic missile (ICBM) capabilities hovered conspicuously in the background.[49]

How and why did Khrushchev decide on such a confrontational policy with the West? Presidium member Anastas Mikoian claims that Khrushchev made the speech "without prior discussion in the CC Presidium and the Council of Ministers."[50] Most of the evidence, however, belies this claim. At a minimum, Khrushchev probably had help preparing the speech from the German specialists at MID's Third European Department, as will be discussed below, and it is hard to imagine that he would have consulted them without any of his Kremlin colleagues finding out. In addition, the fact that Polish leader Wladyslaw Gomulka received an advance draft of Khrushchev's 10 November speech that made Gomulka believe that the Soviet leader wanted "to liquidate the western part of Berlin" indicates that Khrushchev's critique of Western policy in Berlin and of the Four Power status of Berlin was known to the Poles. Khrushchev also told Gomulka in their meeting on 10 November: "On the matters related to West Berlin, we consulted with the comrades from the GDR. They fully support these steps."[51] It is hard to believe that Khrushchev left his Kremlin colleagues in the dark when he gave both the Poles and East Germans advance information on his planned 10 November remarks on Berlin.

A report written by East German Ambassador Johannes König in Moscow, "Comments on the Preparation of the Steps of the Soviet Government Concerning a Change in the Status of West Berlin," details information König gleaned from the staff at MID's Third European Department regarding "preparations" for *both* the 10 November speech and the 27 November ultimatum. As König reported back to Berlin:

> Already several days before Comrade Khrushchev's appearance on 10 November on the occasion of the Soviet-Polish friendship meeting, comrades from MID let it drop on 6 November that Comrade Khrushchev's speech of 10 November would bring "something new" with regard to the German question. The Soviet comrades would not, however, hint a word about the substance of the "news."
>
> On 10 November, a few hours before Comrade Khrushchev's appearance, I was still at MID and had a conversation with Comrade [Ivan I.] Il'ichev, the head of the Third European Department. . . . He commented . . . that Comrade Khrushchev's speech would contain important statements regarding the German question. He told me nothing about what it would deal with. It was, however, obvious that the comrades of the Third European Department were informed excellently about the content of Comrade Khrushchev's speech.[52]

Mikoian describes how he raised objections after Khrushchev's speech of 10 November. He believed that Khrushchev had an "astonishing lack of understanding of the entire complex of issues" concerning Berlin, as was shown in his "readiness to repudiate the Potsdam Agreements" unilaterally. Indeed, Mikoian felt so strongly that Khrushchev was going down the wrong path on this issue that he considered resigning from the Presidium.[53] Soon after Khrushchev's speech, presumably at a Presidium meeting, Mikoian

> requested Gromyko's presence . . . to express the views of MID. Someone bellowed out something inarticulately. I repeated the question—someone again bellowed out: clearly the person did not have the courage to contradict Khrushchev, but also did not want to assume responsibility for such a step [of unilaterally renouncing the Potsdam Agreements]. I then spoke at length about the significance of the Agreements, enumerating the possible negative consequences for us of renouncing them [no doubt including the renunciation of the Soviet right to be in Berlin], based on the fact that we should not handle such issues in such haste. Finally, I proposed postponing the discussion for a week, commissioning MID to state its views in written form. Khrushchev had to accept this. The others just remained silent. When we were walking out, [Prime Minister Nikolai] Bulganin whispered to me: "You won!"[54]

Accounts by Aleksandrov-Agentov, Oleg Troyanovsky (assistant to Gromyko and Khrushchev), and König all corroborate Mikoian's account of the involvement of MID and the other members of the leadership at this stage.[55] No doubt in response to Mikoian's request that MID give its views on steps regarding the Berlin and German questions "in written form," as König reports "the entire Third European Department of MID was occupied exclusively with preparing the next steps. [They were] occupied for days with studying all agreements, arrangements, protocols, etc., which were concluded or made between the occupying powers with regard to West Berlin since 1945. . . . MID was essentially finished with this work on 19 November."[56]

Earlier, on 17 November, Pervukhin had met with Ulbricht and "informed him about the proposed measures of the Soviet government regarding the Four Power status of Berlin." This seems to indicate that the Soviets had at least a draft of the 27 November note on 17 November. Ulbricht expressed his support for the Soviet plan and Khrushchev's recent 10 November speech. He added that

> it would be helpful to publish the Soviet notes to the three Western powers, and also to the FRG and GDR governments, no later than 26 November, since this would provide the opportunity for us to use the principled position of these documents in the process of preparations for the elections in the West Berlin senate, which will take place on 7 December.[57]

The note was sent on 27 November.[58]

According to König, on 19 November, "Comrade Khrushchev personally received for a discussion several responsible officials of the Third European Department of MID who were occupied with the Berlin issue and spoke with them in great detail about the entire problem." Khrushchev gave them "several type-written pages which he had personally dictated containing his views on the entire problem and asked the comrades to observe this point of view in the composition of the documents and the determination of particular measures."[59] Clearly referring to this 19 November meeting, Aleksandrov-Agentov gives us a livelier, firsthand version of the meeting he "witnessed in the fall of 1958,"

> when Gromyko and two of his colleagues came to Khrushchev's office at the CC to give their ideas on our further demarches on the then-current issue of West Berlin. Andrei Andreevich [Gromyko] put on his glasses and began to read the prepared notes. But Khrushchev immediately interrupted him and declared: "This doesn't matter, listen to what I say—the stenographer is taking notes. If it coincides with what you have written there—good, and if not—throw your notes into the waste basket." And he began to dictate (as always in a confused and careless form, but sufficiently clear in concept) his idea on the transformation of West Berlin into a "free demilitarized city." . . . Clearly satisfied both with the idea itself and the fact that it came from him (who suggested it to him, I don't know, maybe Adzhubei, or maybe Nikita Sergeevich "gave birth" to it on his own), Khrushchev suddenly slapped his palm on his knee and happily said: "Ha [!], they will really be thrown in the West, they will say, Khrushchev, that son of a bitch, has now thought up a 'free city'!"[60]

Thus, the free city idea was apparently Khrushchev's. The record of his 1 December 1958 eight-hour conversation with Senator Hubert Humphrey also notes that Khrushchev "said he had given many months of thought to [the] Berlin situation and had finally come up with his proposal of a so-called free city."[61]

Ambassador König first heard on 22 November from I. Il'ichev that "it was planned to propose giving West Berlin the status of a free city [including its] demilitarization and neutralization."[62] While König learned about Khrushchev's free city idea indirectly, Ulbricht heard it directly from the horse's mouth. As Khrushchev later recounted:

> I proposed and forced work on this issue. I talked this over on the phone with Comrade Ulbricht. I laid out my proposal for him. . . . Comrade Ulbricht regarded it skeptically, especially the proposal on the free city. I answered that I myself considered the conditions very difficult, that perhaps it won't be accepted in peace talks, but that we don't have another proposal. We can't make any more concessions, giving up our gains and creating a unified Germany on a capitalist basis. The other side doesn't accept socialism. We must

discuss this realistically. . . . we must consider the existing situation together with the West. It would be smart for them to conclude a treaty with us, not creating an antagonistic conflict, not disturbing peaceful coexistence.

Comrade Ulbricht said [skeptically]:

—There was a precedent, Danzig was once a free city.[63] What came of that?

I answered:

—Something must come of it! So far not much has worked. Maybe we won't even get agreement from our former Western allies on our conditions. But we must search for an intelligent resolution. . . .

We thoroughly discussed this and came to an agreement. Comrade Ulbricht agreed with me.[64]

Khrushchev left Ulbricht in charge of drafting the agreements that East Germany would sign with the free city of West Berlin and the Western Powers about access, non-interference, electricity supplies, and other technical issues:[65] "We thought it would be better if the work on concrete proposals was undertaken by the German comrades. They have a better feel for the specifics."[66]

Ulbricht was "skeptical" about the free city idea in this phone conversation with Khrushchev, because it was significantly short of what Ulbricht really wanted: control over all of Berlin and the access routes or closure of the border to West Berlin. Indeed, in the 27 November ultimatum, Khrushchev himself said: "It should, of course, be borne in mind that the consent of the German Democratic Republic to the setting up of such an independent political organism as the free city of West Berlin within its territory would be a concession, a definite sacrifice by the German Democratic Republic." Khrushchev asserted that:

> The most correct and natural way to solve the problem would, of course, be for the western part of Berlin, which is virtually detached from the German Democratic Republic, to be reunited with its eastern part and for Berlin to become a single united city within the state on whose land it is situated.
>
> However, the Soviet government, taking into account the present unrealistic policy of the United States, and also of the United Kingdom and France, with regard to the German Democratic Republic, cannot fail to see the difficulties the [W]estern [P]owers have in contributing to such a solution of the Berlin problem.[67]

As A. James McAdams observes, Khrushchev "seemed to admit to the onlooking world that he and Ulbricht had not seen eye to eye" on the question of what to do about West Berlin.[68] The free city idea was no doubt Khrushchev's compromise between Ulbricht's entreaties for a more aggressive approach and his Kremlin colleagues' concerns (especially Mikoian's) that he not take undue risks.

It was probably around this time in mid-November, in response to the MID draft document as amended by Khrushchev with his free city idea, that the "CC Presidium discussed this issue several times," as Troyanovsky recounts:

> [In these discussions,] Khrushchev gave a persuasive set of arguments in support of the new course. He said that the Western Powers did not seem to appreciate moderation and refused to acknowledge the obvious truth that constructive steps by one side demanded a correspondingly positive reaction from the other. And he pointed out that our Western partners or opponents had not made a single substantial step to meet Soviet interests or those of their allies. On the contrary, they continue to pursue their beaten track of building up their military alliances, arming West Germany, surrounding the Soviet Union with military bases. Under these circumstances, there is no other possibility other than the one proposed, for the Soviet Union to seize the initiative in the "cold war." The Achilles heel of the West, Khrushchev was convinced, and it was also the general view, was West Berlin. Thus, he thought that if we wanted to seize the initiative, the pressure must be exerted precisely at this weak point.[69]

It is likely that some of the other Presidium members, including Mikoian, insisted that Khrushchev try to reach a settlement with the West over Berlin instead of unilaterally opting out of the Four Power agreements. As we have seen, Mikoian has maintained that he opposed a "unilateral" renunciation of these agreements, partly because he feared "negative consequences" for the Soviets. In Khrushchev's 10 November conversation with Gomulka, he seemed to be planning only to act unilaterally and not engage in any discussions with the West about Berlin. When Gomulka asked him: "Do you intend to address the three [Western] states about liquidating the status of Berlin," Khrushchev answered:

> No. My declaration today should be understood in such a fashion that we are unilaterally ceasing to observe the agreement on Berlin's status, that we are discontinuing to fulfill the functions deriving from our participation in the Control Commission. . . . Then the capitalist states will have to turn to the GDR on matters relating to Berlin, transit, and transport.[70]

Given that a little over two weeks later, after input from MID's Third European Department and from some of Khrushchev's colleagues in the Presidium, his ultimatum to the West did in fact call for negotiations, albeit with a six-month deadline, it may be that Khrushchev had to soften his stance to obtain Presidium approval for his new policy on Berlin.

Ambassador König's notes on this stage of the process also give evidence of increased Soviet caution, representing perhaps an effort by Khrushchev's associates to minimize risks. While on the one hand, the

Soviets were planning to "hold official negotiations with the GDR on transferring [Soviet quadripartite] functions to the competence of the GDR . . . [a]t the same time a hint was made that the Soviet Union would probably not be averse if it should prove to be expedient and necessary also to speak with the Western powers about this issue." Repeatedly in his report on Soviet policy making concerning Berlin, König relates that the Soviets spoke of the need to proceed "gradually, step by step. . . . Regarding the negotiations with the GDR or the transfer to the GDR of the functions which are still being exercised by the Sovet side, this will . . . probably proceed gradually." He reports that further Soviet policy on West Berlin "will probably not remain uninfluenced by the statements and responses by the Western powers and by developments within West Berlin itself." Indeed, the Soviets "will wait 2–3 weeks [after 27 November] so as to digest the reaction of the other side and then take a new step."[71] While perhaps Khrushchev's Kremlin colleagues initially had to force this caution on Khrushchev and this readiness to engage in negotiations with the West, as the Berlin Crisis progressed, Khrushchev would ultimately adopt this approach as his own, much to Ulbricht's chagrin.

In addition to agreeing to seek negotiations with the West and proceed "gradually" (although the six-month deadline hardly made the West feel Khrushchev's approach was gradual), Khrushchev may also have further reassured his worried Presidium colleagues in the same way he reassured Gomulka: "War will not result from it. . . . Five years ago—that was different. Then, we did not have the hydrogen bomb; now the balance of forces is different. Then, we could not reach the USA. The USA built its policies upon the bases surrounding us. Today, America has moved closer to us—our missiles can hit them directly."[72] Similarly, at his 31 July 1958 summit with Mao, Khrushchev had declared: "Now, that we have the transcontinental missile, we hold America by the throat as well. They thought America was beyond reach. But that is not true."[73] And in his 10 November speech, Khrushchev asserted:

> The fact that the balance of forces in the world today is in favo[r] of socialism makes hopeless the imperialist dream of restoring the old order of things in the socialist countries. . . . It is high time to reali[z]e that the times when the imperialists could act from "positions of strength" with impunity have gone never to return, and try as they may, the imperialists will not be able to change the balance of forces in their favo[r.] Nor should they forget the geographical position of Western Germany which—with military techniques as they are today—would not survive a single day of modern warfare.[74]

In response to König's view (expressed to a MID official) that "'The Western powers will not want to conduct a war for the sake of Berlin,' followed the answer: 'Our Presidium proceeds from the same assumption.'"[75] During the crisis, this would become a mantra of Khrushchev's: "[T]he West will not go to war over Berlin," because it would not want to risk a nuclear war.

Although Khrushchev's colleagues exerted a somewhat moderating influence, the Berlin ultimatum had all the hallmarks of a vintage Khrushchev approach: Catch the opponent by surprise with a bold new proposal or policy that tackled a problem in an unexpected way.[76] Faced with Ulbricht's pleas to close the border and gain control over the access routes, and given the refugee exodus and the Western refusal to recognize the GDR, Khrushchev devised a unique way of handling the situation. As Vladislav Zubok and Constantine Pleshakov observe, "Another autocratic ruler of the USSR, more pragmatic and cynical, like Beria and Malenkov, would have reacted to these developments in different ways: by removing Ulbricht or by closing down the border between [the] Western and Eastern sectors of Berlin before starting talks with the West. Khrushchev chose neither."[77] Instead, he sought a middle ground that would put him at the center of the solution, showcasing, he anticipated, his capacity for diplomacy, for dealing with the West. Khrushchev hoped that this would enable him personally to gain a victory over the West. He would also create more long-term stability for the GDR if the West agreed to what he demanded than if he had to act unilaterally without Western acceptance of the GDR.

Khrushchev's frustration in being outnumbered by the West in Four Power talks on Germany no doubt accounted in part for his decision to issue an ultimatum. He later observed to Adenauer that Four Power negotiations on Germany

> leave this question to be decided by a group of states where capitalist states have three voices, and the socialists have only one. But what would you say if it was proposed to submit the question of German reunification for decision by a group of states of a different composition, for example, composed of Poland, Czechoslovakia, China, and the Soviet Union. You, of course, would not be enthusiastic about this proposal, since you would know for sure that these states would support the socialist development of all of Germany.[78]

Khrushchev sought to tip the balance in his favor by taking the West by surprise on West Berlin.

KHRUSHCHEV'S MOTIVES IN LAUNCHING THE BERLIN CRISIS

Prior to the opening of former Soviet bloc archives, there was much speculation among scholars about what motivated Khrushchev to take a hard line on Berlin. The main hypotheses focused on Khrushchev's desire to get Western recognition of the GDR, prevent the nuclear arming of West Germany, undermine the Western alliance, and gain strength against his domestic and Chinese critics. All of these factors played a role in Khrushchev's thinking during the crisis, but the new archival evidence reveals that Khrushchev's concern about the GDR, combined with his desire to gain prestige by successful negotiations with the West, were the most consistent influences on him during the crisis.

Although the tactics Khrushchev chose were aggressive, his motivations were largely defensive. As he put it, he wanted to "strengthen the status quo" in Germany. Strengthening the status quo meant strengthening the GDR and defending it against hostile forces in West Berlin and West Germany. As Khrushchev had explained to his son: "We can't make any more concessions, giving up our gains and creating a unified Germany on a capitalist basis. The other side doesn't accept socialism. We must discuss this realistically. . . . we must consider together with the West the existing situation."[79] The status quo also was characterized by Soviet recognition of West Germany, but no Western recognition of East Germany. Khrushchev sought to obtain Western recognition of the GDR and its sovereignty.[80]

Khrushchev believed that the combination of Western recognition through the signing of a peace treaty with the GDR and the transformation of West Berlin into a "free city" would be enough to stabilize and strengthen the GDR with the most important result of stopping, or drastically reducing, the refugee exodus. Even getting the West to start talking about these issues and recognize that the situation in Berlin was "abnormal" and should be "normalized" would be advantageous to the GDR and the Soviet Union. By neutralizing West Berlin as a "free city," Khrushchev also intended that the hostile anti-socialist activities and agencies there would be shut down, leaving the GDR under much less pressure and West Berlin open to more influence from the East.

Khrushchev's number-one priority in making his 10 November speech and sending the 27 November ultimatum was to shore up the East German regime. A strong socialist regime in the GDR was important to Khrushchev for two reasons: military/strategic and reputational. By way of justifying his hard-nosed approach, Khrushchev told Gomulka on 10 November:

> There were some among us who [once] believed that we would have to withdraw from Berlin. Beria proposed this, and he was supported by "feeble" Malenkov. They believed that we should give up the GDR and Berlin. That was in 1953. What would we have accomplished after that? . . . Are we supposed to give up a population of 18 million in the GDR for nothing, without a fight? That's stupidity. We should fully support Ulbricht and Grotewohl.[81]

It was also the case that for Khrushchev, the reputation of the socialist system was on the line in Germany and Berlin. In order to demonstrate the superiority of socialism over capitalism in Germany, Khrushchev needed to couple his economic aid to the GDR with political efforts to achieve stability there. The refugee exodus to West Berlin, the hostile groups based in West Berlin, and the indications that West Germany might gain control over the nuclear weapons on its territory all led Khrushchev to believe that the GDR was being threatened and that he needed to take extraordinary measures to shore it up.[82]

Concern about West Germany acquiring nuclear weapons was a secondary factor for Khrushchev in the Berlin Crisis, mentioned much less frequently in his interactions with the East Germans and the Western Powers than his primary concern with shoring up the GDR.[83] In fact, Ulbricht tried to push Khrushchev to raise the issue more frequently in public, because he believed the German public would be much more supportive of a campaign against West German nuclear weapons than a campaign for a peace treaty.

As Marc Trachtenberg has recounted so thoroughly, the Eisenhower administration favored the idea of nuclear sharing with its West European allies so that U.S. troops could withdraw from Europe without leaving it vulnerable. Following the December 1957 NATO decision to deploy intermediate-range ballistic missiles (IRBMs) to Western Europe, the prospect of West Germany having control over the nuclear warheads stationed on its territory increased.[84] Khrushchev's colleague Anastas Mikoian raised Soviet concerns about this with Chancellor Adenauer in the spring of 1958.[85] And the matter was discussed several times between the Soviets and East Germans in the months leading up to the ultimatum.[86] At their 5 October meeting, Smirnov told Ulbricht, Pervukhin, and Yu. Astavin of the Soviet embassy in East Berlin that

> since April of this year, the situation in West Germany has become more much complicated for us. . . . In West Germany they are continuing the arming of the Bundeswehr with nuclear weapons, which are now legal. . . .
>
> In this connection, our general goal is to continue to exert a breaking influence on the arming of the Bundeswehr. If all countries of the socialist camp unite their forces in this direction, then the arming of the Bundeswehr could be delayed for 2–3 years, which would be a serious victory for our general cause.[87]

As the Soviet Ambassador to the FRG, Smirnov took a leading role in the protests against the possible nuclearization of the Bundeswehr.[88]

While the Soviets and East Germans were concerned in 1958 with the prospect of the FRG having nuclear weapons, this concern would diminish in importance in their communications during the Berlin Crisis and would assume more of a propagandistic, public relations role. At their 9 and 18 June 1959 meetings in Moscow, Ulbricht told Khrushchev: "[O]nly a part of the German people understands the slogans about a peace treaty. Thus we will put on the agenda those issues of the peace treaty which are more understood by all, such as for example, the liquidation of rocket bases and the prohibition of atomic arms in West Germany."[89] Ulbricht believed it would be easier to rally Germans around the Soviet and East German proposals if they focused on the dangers of the FRG acquiring nuclear weapons than if they focused on plans for a peace treaty and for transforming West Berlin into a free city. Ulbricht emphasized to Khrushchev: "[W]e are interested that the issue of nuclear disarmament remain on the agenda. We must constantly discuss this, since only by this path [as opposed to a path focusing on a peace treaty or the transformation of West Berlin into a free city] can we isolate Adenauer. Therefore we will put special stress on all issues which are understood by the majority of the German people."[90]

There were two other important, somewhat connected factors behind Khrushchev's launching of the Berlin Crisis, and these increased in significance as the crisis went on. First, for matters of personal and national prestige, Khrushchev wanted to participate in summit-level dialogue with the leaders of the Western Powers, especially those of the United States. He sought to force the West to negotiate on Germany and Berlin and ascertain what concessions his forceful personality could wrest from them. Second, Khrushchev aimed to demonstrate to his domestic[91] and foreign critics (in China,[92] the GDR,[93] and elsewhere) that he was not weak, that he was not appeasing the "paper tiger" West with peaceful coexistence, but was really exerting pressure on the West.

Khrushchev's goals were not always consistent, as we shall see. His priorities would change as he discerned the emergence of different threats (of GDR collapse or of conflict with the West) or opportunities (for resolving the problems in the GDR or for applying pressure on the West). His view as to whether West Berlin and its access routes constituted a prize that he would give Ulbricht or were a means to threaten the West, "a sword of Damocles," as he would say, shifted as the crisis developed. As Khrushchev's goals and tactics evolved during the crisis, they often conflicted with those of Ulbricht, greatly complicating the situation for both East and West.

THE CRISIS DEVELOPS

After sending the ultimatum to the Western Powers, Khrushchev waited anxiously for their response. In order to ease Mikoian's (as well as his own) worries about his aggressive move, Khrushchev sent Mikoian to the United States in January to propose a summit on Germany and Berlin.[94] While President Eisenhower agreed to meet with the Soviet deputy premier on 17 January 1959, the meeting did not yield any progress on Berlin or German issues.[95]

Khrushchev's twenty-three-year-old son, Sergei, asked his father what he would do if the Western Powers did not agree to his proposals. As Sergei recounts their discussion:

> I thought the Americans would never accept our proposed conditions. And what then? Father laughed at my fears. He said that no one would undertake war over Berlin. On the other hand, it was time to determine, to fix the existing post-war balance of forces. In his view, the West wouldn't try to stick to West Berlin. It was organically connected to the Eastern bloc independent of whether it had a capitalist order or a new socialist structure. On this issue, he completely left it to the inhabitants of the city.
>
> I asked for clarity on what we would do after 27 May of the next year [1959] if our proposals were rejected and the deadline for the ultimatum was up? Father didn't have a simple answer. He intended to act according to the circumstances, depending on the reaction of our partners. He hoped to scare them into agreeing to sit at the negotiating table.
>
> Father said that if he didn't give a final date, then the exchange of notes, messages, addresses and declarations would go on without end. A deadline prompts action on both sides, forcing them to find a compromise.
>
> —And if one isn't found?—I asked.
>
> —Then we will find a different way, something always turns up—my father answered with a displeased tone in his voice.[96]

The East German leaders counted on something "turning up," even more than Khrushchev. They took the Soviet ultimatum very seriously and looked forward to Khrushchev fulfilling his promises and his threats to sign a separate peace treaty with, and turn over to the GDR, control of the access routes to West Berlin when the West (as they anticipated) rejected his conditions.

The East Germans expected that Khrushchev would carry out his threats, especially after the Soviets sent a draft German peace treaty to the Western powers on 10 January 1959.[97] GDR officials quickly began to draw up draft proposals relating to a peace treaty, such as the document sent from Ulbricht to Gromyko on 4 February 1959, on "Problems in Connection with the Transfer of the Rights of the Soviet Representatives Concerning West Berlin to the GDR Government."[98] The East Germans also formulated detailed drafts of agreements that East Germany would sign with the new "free-city" of West Berlin and numerous proposals to the Soviets about how they should proceed with their *Deutschlandpolitik*.[99]

The Western Powers, meanwhile, were divided on how to respond to Khrushchev's ultimatum. The day before Khrushchev sent the ultimatum, U.S. Secretary of State John Foster Dulles hinted that U.S. and West German views differed on how to respond should the Soviets transfer their Four Power responsibilities in Berlin to East German officials. At a news conference on 26 November, Dulles agreed that "we might deal with [the East Germans] as agents of the Soviet Union."[100] The West Germans, however, opposed this Western policy of dealing with East German officials at border crossing points.[101] Adenauer did not want to give an inch to Khrushchev and Ulbricht in responding to the ultimatum. The reporters at Dulles's news conference surmised that Adenauer would not welcome Dulles's "agent theory" and pressed the secretary of state. Dulles ultimately conceded that "we would in these matters be largely guided by the views of the Federal Republic of Germany, which is primarily concerned, and which has a government with which we have the closest relations, and in which we have the greatest confidence."[102] Eager that Chancellor Adenauer not discern any wavering in the U.S. commitment to West Berlin and West Germany in the face of communist threats, the United States soon backed away from its "agents" idea.[103]

The French leader Charles de Gaulle also favored standing firm and not negotiating with the Soviets under pressure and was thus Adenauer's strongest ally during the crisis.[104] The British leader Harold Macmillan, on the other hand, was so eager to avoid war that he favored recognition of the GDR and a summit with the Soviets as soon as possible.[105] He even went to speak with Khrushchev in Moscow in February 1959 to see what sort of compromise on Germany and Berlin would be possible. All of these Allied differences were quite public and thus known to Khrushchev and Ulbricht.[106] The old communist strategy of exploiting "inter-imperialist contradictions" was easy under these circumstances and made Khrushchev optimistic of getting his way. This was especially the case when the Western Powers proposed (before Khrushchev's six-month deadline had expired) a Four Power Conference of Foreign Ministers in Geneva to begin negotiations on Germany and Berlin.

Already in February, the U.S. ambassador to Moscow, Llewellyn Thompson, cabled the State Department that "Khrushchev, merely by putting his Berlin proposal forward, appears to have succeeded in shaking our confidence in our position, and has gained at least a temporary advantage." Recognizing the clear military superiority of the Soviets in the area around Berlin, Thompson argued that "we should have ready a compromise solution for [the] Berlin question" short of nuclear war.[107] He also reminded Washington of the advantageous position the Soviets had in Berlin: "Since [Khrushchev] undoubtedly conceives of himself as being in [a] strategic situation vis-à-vis West which is much improved over that of recent years, and in [a] tactical position at Berlin which is almost ideal,"[108] the West was facing a real challenge and needed to respond carefully and firmly.

Proving that "Berlin has been [the] lever by which [the] Kremlin has pried loose Western resistance to top-level conferences,"[109] the United States, Great Britain, and France proposed to the Soviets on 16 February 1959 a Conference of Foreign Ministers to discuss "the problem of Germany in all its aspects and implications." Even better, the West "suggested that German advisers should be invited to the conference and consulted."[110] Thus, in less than three months, Khrushchev had succeeded through his ultimatum in getting the West to agree to high-level talks on Germany, which would clearly include Berlin, and to invite East and West German advisors to attend. Khrushchev, however, really wanted a summit meeting of the heads of state, not a CFM. In his response to the West on 2 March, he asserted that a summit would be a far more productive meeting, but that if the West would not agree, he would consent to a CFM of the Four Powers, the two Germanys, as well as Poland and Czechoslovakia (the West would veto the participation of the latter two). Khrushchev suggested that the CFM should meet for "not more than two or three months."[111] By late March, the Four Powers had settled on the opening of a CFM in Geneva on 11 May.

With Western acquiescence to Four Power talks, Khrushchev relaxed his six-month deadline and while visiting East Berlin in March told a disappointed Ulbricht: "Do not hurry. The wind does not blow in your face. . . . The conditions are not ripe as yet for a new scheme of things."[112] This was the first of several instances during the crisis when Khrushchev would counsel waiting for negotiations with the West and delaying the kinds of unilateral action Ulbricht favored to carry out his threats. Khrushchev had a broader agenda than Ulbricht did with the West and thus had more reasons to favor the gains that negotiations could bring. Ulbricht, conversely, feared that Khrushchev might strike a deal with the Western powers that would not take GDR interests sufficiently into account. Having his foreign minister, Lothar Bolz, at the CFM, however, would help dispel some of Ulbricht's worries.

In Western preparations for the Geneva CFM, there were many signs of willingness to make concessions to the Soviets and East Germans on Berlin and a sense that this was the only realistic option. Even Adenauer, who maintained a hard-line stance publicly, privately expressed worries to Secretary of State Dulles and the U.S. ambassador to the FRG, David Bruce, that if a Four Power "conference failed . . . the Berlin crisis was likely to become more acute. In consequence he thought there might be need for an interim or provisional solution of the problem of Berlin." In Adenauer's view, "the best provisional solution, which he was not sure we could get, would be an indefinite deferral of the May 27 date when the Soviets had promised they would turn over their rights to the GDR."[113]

Adenauer also told Dulles and Bruce that he was "concerned over the very real possibility of growing nervousness and even an exodus from West Berlin as the date approached."[114] Apprehension about the morale of the West Berliners under pressure from Khrushchev was a real issue for the Western Powers. Eisenhower considered "fundamental . . . that we have at stake 2.2 million free Germans who trust us and upon whom we may not turn our back."[115] Reports reaching Washington from the U.S. mission in Berlin were not reassuring. Assistant Mission Chief Bernard Gufler reported in March, there is "some corrosion [in] West Berlin in morale [which is] imperceptible in detail [but] is beginning [to] be discernible in cumulative effect. Apprehension re outcome [of] Berlin crisis has increasingly pervaded thinking of politically articulate segments of population." West Berliners viewed with distress the "apparent lack [of] Allied unity in dealing with Sov moves and inability (as reported in press) after three months' consultation [to] arrive at plan of action."[116] Not only did the 2.2 million inhabitants of West Berlin need to see U.S. resolve; with America's reputation on the line, Eisenhower and others believed it essential to demonstrate U.S. reliability as an ally and protector to Adenauer and other friends and foes. As Ambassador Bruce pointed out: "The abandonment by US of Berliners would destroy confidence in our engagements everywhere."[117] The United States must stand firm regarding West Berlin, "the superdomino."

The Western Powers were concerned not only with defending West Berliners against the Soviet and East German offensive, but also with guaranteeing their own access to West Berlin. And on the access routes, the United States, Great Britain, and France did not want their military forces to have to submit to inspections by East German officials, leading down "the slippery slope" to the recognition of the GDR, which Adenauer vehemently opposed.[118] How far the West was willing to go militarily to maintain its access to West Berlin and not deal with East German officials, was a matter of much dispute in the secret U.S.-British-French contingency planning arrangement conceived for dealing with the Berlin Crisis and code-named LIVE OAK.[119] Khrushchev had put the West in a very difficult position, as he no doubt had known he would, stepping on their "Achilles' heel."[120]

Indeed, a Western Four Power working group made up of U.S., British, French, and West German representatives started considering an interim Berlin settlement in March. Then at a Western Four Power foreign ministers meeting in Washington on 1 April, the British and French Ministers argued for making concessions. British Foreign Minister Selwyn Lloyd believed that acceding to the Soviet proposal to replace Western troops with those of the UN or some other more neutral countries was worth considering, since perhaps then "we could get more of an international presence in Berlin and get an international underwriting of the responsibility for keeping Berlin free." French Foreign Minister Couvé de Murville thought "[w]e should be prepared to consider some limitations on our position in Berlin, as for example, by a limitation on our forces in Berlin, and by restricting or eliminating some of our activities in Berlin (such as) the periodic meetings of the Bundestag in Berlin."[121] At the end of April, Herter persuaded the Western foreign ministers to stop discussing an interim solution on Berlin, fearing that this might leak and that the Soviets would know the West was starting to cave in.[122]

THE GENEVA CFM, MAY–AUGUST 1959

The Geneva CFM from 11 May–5 August 1959 yielded the Soviets and East Germans some significant gains.[123] First, it suggested that Khrushchev had been successful in compelling the West to negotiate with the Soviet Union on Germany and Berlin and within his six-month deadline. Second, he was able to persuade the Western Powers to agree, for the first time, to East and West German observers at the CFM, thus signaling a further step in Western recognition of the GDR and of the "existing situation" of two German states.[124] Third, the Soviets at the CFM, led by Gromyko, were able to convince the West, represented by Herter, Lloyd, and de Murville, to discuss the Berlin issue apart from a general German settlement, to consider an interim agreement on (West) Berlin, and to agree to the creation of an East German–West German committee before national elections. As Jack Schick points out, these Western concessions led the Soviets to the mistaken conclusion that they were getting somewhere in pushing the West out of West Berlin.[125] Finally, and most important, by the end of the CFM, Khrushchev had secured an invitation from Eisenhower to visit him in the United States in what would be the first such visit by a Soviet leader.

The East Germans and Soviets consulted closely on preparations for the CFM. The East Germans urged pursuing the following maximal goals: a peace conference, the signing of a peace treaty with both German states, and the creation of a demilitarized city in West Berlin. Soviet Deputy Foreign Minister Zorin responded that these goals were "very high" and "would be difficult to achieve."[126] Khrushchev himself hardly had high expectations about the likelihood of practical agreements being reached at Geneva. He told Ulbricht in June that the CFM "won't have any tangible results . . . since the situation itself still doesn't have a basis for positive resolutions. . . . Geneva—it's a test of strength, it's a sounding out of positions. Therefore, our proposals must be put in such a form that they will be attractive to the population." Khrushchev declared that it was "70 percent certain" that the West would not agree to his proposals and that it would "then . . . be even more necessary to have a summit meeting," which was what he really wanted all along.[127]

In addition, Khrushchev declared to Ulbricht that "not one self-respecting prime minister will allow his foreign minister, due to prestige considerations, to sign an agreement on concrete issues."[128] They would save this honor only for themselves. The Western Powers were in fact well aware that "there was little hope of real negotiation with Gromyko"[129] and that "[i]f any major settlement is to be reached Khrushchev will certainly wish [to] obtain full credit for it himself."[130] Thus, neither side thought much specific progress could be made at Geneva, but both hoped the meeting would reduce tensions over Berlin and Germany, perhaps with an interim agreement on (West) Berlin, although the nature of those hopes differed.

The West presented to the CFM its "package plan" on Berlin and Germany on 14 May. This was a four-stage plan that proceeded from free elections in Berlin leading to the unification of Berlin in the first stage, the creation of a mixed German committee to draft an electoral law for Germany in the second stage, free elections for an all-German government in the third stage, and the signing of a peace treaty with Germany in the fourth stage.[131] On 18 May Gromyko rejected this plan, arguing that the issues of West Berlin, German reunification, and a German peace treaty must be handled separately, not together as in the Western package, and that the issue of German reunification was up to the two Germanys to resolve, not the Four Powers.[132] Gromyko then asserted that only three possible solutions to the Berlin question existed: "(a) all Western troops leave and West Berlin becomes a free city, (b) Soviet troops join the Western forces in West Berlin, or (c) neutral troops replace Western troops in West Berlin."[133] The West rejected these, but agreed to uncouple discussion of Berlin from their package, which had they had planned in advance as a fallback option.[134]

Accordingly, the four foreign ministers discussed Berlin separately from a broader German settlement. The crucial differences, however, remained, with the West focusing on reuniting all of Berlin by free elections and the Soviets wanting to leave East Berlin as it was and transform West Berlin into a neutral, free city. The Soviets did get the Western foreign ministers to offer to place a limit on their troops in West Berlin. Lloyd spoke of reducing the troops from 11,000 to 8,500 or even 7,500. The West also proposed that a commission of the Four Powers and two Germanys manage the access routes, a step back from the Four Power agreements.[135]

Faced with continued Soviet intransigence in the face of Western concessions, U.S. Secretary of State Herter publicly criticized the Soviet negotiating strategy on 5 June. He announced that the "Western powers do not maintain that the present situation [in Berlin] is ideal. We do not say that it cannot be improved in some respects." In fact, he declared: "We recognize that Berlin, because of its unique situation, can be a source of friction. We are willing to search in good faith with the Soviet Union for some reciprocal improvement in the Berlin situation." Yet, Gromyko has made it clear that the Soviets' "preferred 'solution'" of the West Berlin problem would be its "annex[ation] to the so-called German Democratic Republic. Since the prime Soviet purpose is to remove the Allied presence from West Berlin, it is not surprising that the key part of the plan is the termination of Western occupation rights."[136]

Herter asserted that the West was not going to relinquish these rights: "West Berlin owes its viability to the Western military presence there and to its political, economic and social ties with West Germany. The entire thrust of the Soviet plan for West Berlin cuts into these ties and is clearly intended to establish a situation which will be but a 'way station' on the road to . . . the annexation of West Berlin by East Germany." Herter then laid down the Western conditions for an agreement on Berlin: "(a) respect for existing Western rights of presence and access to Berlin and existing agreements concerning such rights . . . ; (b) no recognition of the so-called GDR; [and] (c) maintenance of West Berlin's political and economic ties with the West."[137] These Western "essentials," however, were precisely what Khrushchev and Ulbricht wanted to change.

In spite of continued Western resistance to many of his demands, Khrushchev was quite optimistic about progress at the CFM. In early June, he told Ulbricht:

> Geneva has given good results. It has displayed the unrealistic policy of Dulles aimed at the so-called liberation of Eastern Europe. This policy, which is directed at a blockade of Eastern Europe, the subversion of these countries from within, etc., is completely bankrupt. And it was clearly shown that efforts to subvert Eastern Europe from the socialist path of development completely failed.
>
> Instead of this, they came to the conference in Geneva [and] agreed to the invitation of the GDR to the conference, which signifies de facto recognition of the GDR. Thus, the situation as a whole has turned out favorably for us.

Khrushchev went on to point out that it was not just on the issue of recognition of the GDR that progress had been made; the West had begun to make concessions on West Berlin also. "The USA recognizes that the situation in West Berlin is abnormal, and that it is necessary to normalize it. They are talking, for example, about reducing their troops from 10,000 to 7500. . . . They also proposed freezing the number of forces in West Berlin [and] agreeing that there won't be any rocket or atomic weapons there before unification."[138]

Given the movement in the Western positions that Khrushchev identified, he believed that more time would bring still more positive movement. Accordingly, he told Ulbricht that he was willing to pull back on his demands so as to buy more time in negotiations with the West. Khrushchev decided: "[I]t is necessary to allow time so that the Western powers can move away from their own position. And in a year or a year and half, they will be weaker and we will be stronger. . . . In 1961 the GDR will start to surpass the FRG in standard of living. This will have very great political significance. This will be a bomb for them. Therefore, our position is to gain time."[139] Ulbricht agreed that "[e]conomically we still cannot exert influence on the West; therefore, we must win time."[140]

Ulbricht, however, made it clear to Khrushchev that he needed significant Soviet help to improve the East German economy in its competition with the West. GDR Prime Minister Grotewohl emphasized that "in our conditions economic problems turn into political ones." Khrushchev understood this, but was unsure as to how much the Soviets were capable of helping economically: "We aren't tradesmen, we are friends. Therefore, we approach all issues politically. But before giving an answer, we must consider, we must look at our capabilities."[141]

The East Germans also had other causes for concern at this Moscow summit with Khrushchev. While the East Germans agreed with some of Khrushchev's arguments for easing pressure on the West, there were other aspects of the caution Khrushchev displayed at this summit that were not so welcome, in particular Khrushchev's comments on the issue of Western recognition of the GDR. Khrushchev told the East German leaders:

[We] don't think it's worth it now to push the West to the wall, so that we will not give the impression that we are seeking the recognition of the GDR.

The Americans don't want to recognize the GDR. They can't do this for prestige reasons. That, and we would be offended. They didn't recognize us for 16 years, and you want them to recognize you after 10 years. You need to wait at least 17 years. In any case, such a stating of the issue, such an intention from our side, would hinder the relaxation of tensions.

You know that there is a demagogic system in the USA, there are two parties, but both are charlatans. They have said so much against the socialist camp that they can't now recognize the GDR. And if Herter agreed to it, he would quickly be fired. So we have to reckon with such a situation.[142]

The historian really wishes for an audiotape of this conversation so as to hear Khrushchev's tone in telling Ulbricht he must wait seventeen years for U.S. recognition! Ulbricht did not respond to these comments, so we cannot judge how he understood Khrushchev's words. Whether or not Khrushchev was serious about making the GDR wait for one year longer than the Soviet Union had to wait for U.S. recognition (which would have meant until 1966), he certainly recognized that the United States was not then prepared to grant formal recognition to the GDR. Now that Khrushchev had tasted the satisfaction of forcing the West to the bargaining table to make some concessions, he did not want to deprive himself of the opportunity to make further gains by overplaying his hand.

Khrushchev also decided to pull back on his threat to sign a separate peace treaty with the GDR and turn over control of the access routes. He hoped that with more time, the Western Powers would come around to his way of thinking:

> Earlier we said that in the event of the Western Powers' refusal to sign a peace treaty with the two German governments, we would sign a peace treaty with the GDR. But now it is necessary to creaty a safety-valve. Therefore we are proposing the creation of an all-German committee [which Gromyko did at Geneva on 9 June]. Without us, but on our recommendation, the commitee would deal with the issue of the preparation of a peace treaty and the reunification of the country. We are proposing a concrete period of activity for this commiteee—for example, one to one and a half years, that is, until 1961. If the Germans don't come to an agreement among themselves in this period, we will be free from any obligations and we will look for the possibility of concluding a peace treaty with the two German governments or with one German government.
>
> But during this period, that is, until 1961, they must reduce their forces in West Berlin, stop subversive activity [and] propaganda, [and] liquidate espionage centers. This is the main thing. We agree to the temporary preservation of the occupation regime until 1961.[143]

Khrushchev wanted to make this proposal for three reasons: to show "pacifists" how intently the Soviets were seeking a peaceful resolution of the German and Berlin problems; to give the Western powers time to "move away from their old positions"; and to gain more time for economic and other strengthening of the GDR. Khrushchev felt time was on their side and that things had been going in their favor since his ultimatum and would continue this way: "Now already almost a year has gone by, but in this time we have already turned around the core of public opinion." Given how well things were going, Khrushchev told Ulbricht: "[I]f you have thrown the adversary to the ground, you don't need to then kneel on his chest."[144]

Grotewohl seemed to understand that Khrushchev's conciliatory tactics partly stemmed from the Soviets' broader perspective on East-West relations:

> Any time which we win for negotiations, any negotiations, is better than a "cold war." Precisely from this position, we must come to an appreciation of the world-wide historical scene, including the German question, which has subordinate significance.
>
> Sometimes among us Germans, it seems that for us only Germany exists. But as a whole in international politics, the German question must take up only as much space as it merits.

Ulbricht no doubt did not share Grotewohl's view of the "subordinate significance" of the German question and probably did not condone Grotewohl's expression of this view. They did, however, both agree that in their public campaign for a resolution of the German question, they should stress nuclear disarmament and a campaign against West Germany's acquiring nuclear weapons, since this was an issue "understood by the majority of the German people [and] only by this path can we isolate Adenauer."[145]

The day after this summit, on 10 June, Gromyko proposed to the CFM an extension of the occupation regime in Berlin for one more year during which time an East German–West German commission would develop plans for reunification and a peace treaty.[146] The Soviets had now made their first "concession," agreeing to "allow" the occupation regime to continue for another year. However, as usual, they maintained that if no agreement were reached by the German commission in this year, the Soviets would then sign a separate peace treaty with the GDR and give it control of the access routes. The Soviets also stipulated that in the one-year interim period, the forces in the Western garrisons in West Berlin must be reduced to "token contingents," hostile propaganda must cease, and there must be a ban on the deployment of nuclear weapons in West Berlin.[147]

The West rejected this proposal on 16 June and made a counterproposal for an interim agreement on all of Berlin, not just West Berlin. The Western Powers did, however, make several concessions in their proposal. They agreed to limit their forces in West Berlin to the then current level of approximately 11,000, and would "from time to time consider the possibility of reducing such forces if developments in the situation permit[ted]." They also pledged not to arm these forces with nuclear weapons. For the access routes between the FRG and West Berlin, they demanded "free and unrestricted access . . . for all persons, goods, and communications, including those of the [Western] forces stationed in West Berlin" (as well as "freedom of movement . . . between East and West Berlin"). However, they added that the "procedures applicable shall be those in effect in April 1959 [and that] without prejudice to existing basic responsibilities, these procedures may where it is not already the case be carried out by German personnel."[148] Thus, they were willing to formally agree to the September 1955 transfer of Soviet control over civilian access to the GDR and to a possible further expansion of an East German role on the access routes. Nonetheless, the Soviets rejected the Western proposal on 19 June, and the CFM recessed for three weeks.

The day before, Khrushchev and Ulbricht held another summit in Moscow. Khrushchev was gratified that the West had "made a series of concessions," but disappointed that the West "wants us to confirm their rights to maintain their occupation in West Berlin forever and to renounce signing a peace treaty." Once again, Khrushchev decided that the best strategy was to buy time in the expectation that the West would continue to make concessions: "Let's not give a time period. A year or a year-and-a-half—this isn't a key issue for us. We are agreed on different time periods, but we aren't agreed on endlessness. Let us act more flexibly on this issue, using a sliding scale of time periods. They are proposing two-and-a-half years, we [are proposing] one year. Maybe we will agree on something in between."[149] In fact, on 19 June Gromyko would offer to extend the time period again for a provisional agreement on West Berlin, this time from twelve to eighteen months.

At this 18 June meeting with Ulbricht, Khrushchev expressed most clearly his tactical approach to dealing with the West. He told Ulbricht: "I don't know whether we will bring this issue of the signing of a peace treaty with the GDR to realization; however, such a prospect acts in a sobering way on the Western Powers and West Germany. This, if you will, is pressure on them, Damocles' sword, which we must hold over them. Why? Because by the signing of a peace treay with the GDR they will lose all their rights to West Berlin."[150]

Both Khrushchev and Mikoian exuded confidence that this approach was working. Mikoian said:

When we proposed concluding a peace treaty with Germany, it was a correct and strong approach from our side. This proposal cut the ground out from under their feet. Before they didn't want to talk about Berlin at all, but now they are forced to carry out negotiations with us on it. . . . [I]f they are afraid that there will be a peace treaty signed with the GDR, which would deprive them of their occupation rights, then they will be forced to find a new path for agreement. The threat of signing a peace treaty will force them to carry out negotiations with us.

Khrushchev chimed in: "Look at how the situation has changed since 1956. They didn't want to shake hands with us. And now Macmillan himself came to us [in February]. And soon [U.S. Vice President R.] Nixon and [Averell] Harriman will come travel around our country. And it is because a difficult situation has been created for them, and it will become more difficult."[151]

Soviet pressure on the Western weak spot in Berlin had not only drawn the West to the bargaining table but had elicited Western concessions. Khrushchev said that such hard-line methods were the only way to deal with the Western powers: "They are bandits. If we were weak, they would long ago have resolved the Geman question to their advantage." Thus, Khrushchev also believed that "[t]he more the Western powers know that there is a balance in the area of atomic weapons and rockets, the better it is for us" and the more likely to deter them from risking war: "[I]t is clear that it would be unreasonable to threaten the lives of a hundred million people [merely] because of the two and half million inhabitants of West Berlin."[152] Khrushchev trusted that the combination of his advantageous position in Berlin and the nuclear balance would lead him to prevail in the Berlin Crisis; it was just a matter of time.

He may have also felt bolstered by the secret stationing of twelve SS-3 medium-range nuclear missiles in the GDR.[153] In December 1958 the Soviets deployed the missiles, and in April 1959 the atomic warheads arrived. Six were deployed in Fürstenberg an der Havel, 80 kilometers north of Berlin, and six were deployed south of that in Vogelsang. The East Germans, apparently, were not told about the deployment. It was administered by the Soviet 72nd Engineering Brigade which reported directly to the CPSU Central Committee. The deployment was done covertly, with the troops working on the bases only at night due to U.S. overflights of the area. Thus, three years before the Cuban Missile Crisis, Khrushchev deployed medium-range ballistic missiles (MRBMs) outside of the Soviet Union for the first time.

With a range of 1,200 kilometers, the missiles could reach Britain, France, and other U.S. bases in Europe, thus adding another threatening form of pressure to the one Khrushchev was placing on West Berlin. The United States had some knowledge, or at least inkling, of the new Soviet missiles in the GDR. At a meeting of the U.S. delegation to the Geneva CFM on 26 May,

> Herter asked whether there had been any confirmation of a report that atomic capable missiles were being taken into East Germany. Mr. [William] Bundy

[of the CIA] said that there had been no positive confirmation, although it was believed that other types of missiles had been introduced. Secretary [of Defense Neil] McElroy said that there had been no observation of sites of ground-to-ground missiles in the DDR. Mr. Bundy agreed but pointed out that there had been sightings of covered equipment on flat cars with profiles similar to those of missiles paraded in Moscow. It was therefore thought likely that such missiles are in the DDR.[154]

While this author is not aware of any records indicating that the United States confirmed the presence of Soviet medium-range nuclear missiles in the GDR in 1959, U.S. suspicions were enough to deepen U.S. apprehension over Khrushchev's attack on Western rights in Berlin.

Things did not go very well, however, for the Soviets with the deployment of the missiles. On 29 April there was a serious accident while moving the warheads. Lieutenant Colonel Nesterov, responsible for transportation, was fired as a result. There were other problems as well. The liquid oxygen in the missiles evaporated within thirty days. And "some of the soldiers replaced the blue-colored 92 percent ethanol, which was coveted by the troops as a drink under the name 'the Blue Danube,' with a typical yellow methanol."[155] In May, after resolving these problems, the chief of the Group of Soviet Forces in Germany, Marshall Zakharov, informed Khrushchev that the missiles were operational.

In the accessible records of the June Soviet–East German summits, there was no mention of the Soviet missiles. Khrushchev referred to the "balance in the area of atomic weapons and rockets," but otherwise focused on the need to release the pressure on the West to buy more time. He also emphasized to the East Germans on 18 June that "the main thing is to fulfill the resolution of the [SED's] 5th congress [of July 1958] to raise the standard of living. Then it will be clear to each German where there is freedom and where there isn't freedom."[156] As with the 9 June summit, this led to a detailed discussion of East German economic difficulties and ways the Soviets would help, although in some cases the Soviets agreed to give only half of what the East Germans were requesting.

While the East Germans agreed that they needed to buy more time with negotiations and to delay signing a peace treaty so as to strengthen their economy, Deputy Chairman of the Council of Ministers Paul Scholz expressed concern about the effect of this delay on "the domestic political situation in the GDR." He pointed out that due to Khrushchev's six-month 27 November 1958 ultimatum, "We already have experience with the date 27 May. As is well known, on that day everyone in the GDR expected that something would happen. Therefore, it is better not to decree a concrete date, but to preserve freedom of movement for oneself. It will aid our political work, although it may also seem that we are not consistent."[157] He did not want the GDR again to be in the embarrassing position of not carrying out their threats as a result of their own self-imposed deadline.

Ulbricht also agreed that there should be less public discussion of signing a peace treaty, because he doubted this was the best way to rally the German people, including the West Germans, around Soviet and East German proposals. As noted above, he believed a campaign against West German access to nuclear weapons would be more popular. Grotewohl added that if they signed a separate peace treaty, the West would "try to present [it] as deepening the division of the country," an impression the East Germans wanted to avoid.[158]

Two days after this Soviet–East German summit in Moscow, East German Deputy Foreign Minister Winzer cabled Berlin from Geneva with good news from Gromyko. Gromyko had met privately with Lloyd and learned that the British were much more flexible in dealing with such things as the all-German commitee than "Herter [who] showed no [such] elasticity in private talks. . . . Lloyd emphasized that [he was expressing his own views] which had not been coordinated with his colleagues." As Winzer reports:

> Gromyko thus judges the conference not bad, even good.
>
> 1.) The Western Powers feel that their position is weak and that they must ultimately leave West Berlin. The question is when and in what way. The USA clings to occupation rights, because it is afraid of losing all positions in Europe. The British want to negotiate and save face.
>
> 2.) The necessity of a change in the status of West Berlin is recognized. On several issues the West has already had to make concessions: the question of troops, agitation work, and German personnel. Lloyd and Murville have privately confessed to de-facto recognition of the GDR.[159]

In his meeting with Gromyko, Lloyd "alluded to differences of opinion among the Western allies [and said that] there was a common basis for negotiations between the British and Soviet delegations, but not with his allies." Gromyko thought that there were indications that "England and even the USA were not going to allow themselves to be tied by Adenauer's apron strings. It is not ruled out that they will seek agreement on several issues over Bonn's objections."[160] Thus, given the concessions the Western Powers had begun to make on their position in West Berlin and clear signs of disagreements among the Western Powers, the Soviets felt that they were going into the recess from Geneva in a strong position.

During the break from the CFM, New York Governor Averell Harriman met with Khrushchev in Sochi on 23 June and discussed the Berlin

Crisis. Harriman was so disturbed by his meeting with Khrushchev (as no doubt Khrushchev intended) that he entitled his description of their meeting, published in *Life* magazine, "My Alarming Interview with Khrushchev." Harriman quoted Khrushchev as blustering: "Your general talks of maintaining your position in Berlin with force. That is bluff. If you send in tanks, they will burn and make no mistake about it. If you want war, you can have it, but remember it will be your war. Our rockets will fly automatically."[161] The rockets Khrushchev had in mind were probably both the Soviet-based ICBMs and the GDR-based MRBMs. Khrushchev told Harriman: "What good does it do you to have 11 thousand troops in Berlin? If it came to war, we would swallow them in one gulp."[162]

In spite, or perhaps because of Khrushchev's continued aggressive approach and the lack of much progress from the Western perspective at Geneva, Eisenhower commissioned Deputy Under Secretary of State Robert Murphy to deliver an invitation to Khrushchev to visit the United States. Murphy apparently misunderstood Eisenhower's stipulation that the invitation was contingent on progress when the CFM re-convened in Geneva and issued an unqualified invitation.[163] According to Troyanovsky, Eisenhower's invitation to Khrushchev "was received in Moscow . . . as a kind of breakthrough, a concrete result of the pressure exerted on the Western powers on the issue of West Berlin."[164] Khrushchev agreed to the invitation on 22 July, and on 3 August it was announced that Khrushchev would visit the United States. Thus, when the CFM reassembled in Geneva from 13 July–3 August, it was not surprising that no progress was made. Khrushchev had already received his coveted invitation to a summit with the U.S. President and no longer had much interest in the CFM.

Whereas before the recess, the focus of discussions had been on an interim agreement on Berlin or West Berlin, now Gromyko returned to the issues of German unification and a peace treaty, over which there were even more disagreements. Gromyko did, however, announce on 22 July that "during [an] interim agreement on [West] Berlin . . . [the] Soviets would take no unilateral action if [the] Western powers observed [the] agreement."[165] Khrushchev would later refer to this repeatedly in his efforts to prevent Ulbricht from taking matters into his own hands. Even though there was no formal interim agreement, Khrushchev would tell Ulbricht that he had promised the West not to take "unilateral action" before a summit meeting with President Eisenhower.

Unable to reach agreement and with a Khrushchev-Eisenhower summit pending, the CFM ended on 4 August. The final communiqué noted that a "frank and comprehensive discussion took place on the Berlin question. The positions of both sides on certain points became closer.

The discussions which have taken place will be useful for the further negotiations which are necessary in order to reach an agreement."[166]

Perhaps to avoid the risk of wrecking the summit with Eisenhower, in August and September the Soviets suddenly removed all of the nuclear missiles from the GDR and transferred them to Kaliningrad, a Soviet territory on the Baltic coast, where they would supposedly be "more economical and more secure." In addition, by this time the Soviets had deployed new MRBMs in the Soviet Union with a range of 2,000 kilometers, enabling them to hit the same targets against which the SS-3s in the GDR were directed.[167]

KHRUSHCHEV TRAVELS TO THE UNITED STATES AND CHINA

The results of the Khrushchev-Eisenhower meetings in September 1959 at Camp David were similar to those of the CFM. Although they came to no specific agreements, Khrushchev achieved several gains. Most important, it was the first trip of a Soviet leader to the United States, thus bestowing much prestige upon Khrushchev personally, something that at moments seemed to supplant Khrushchev's goal of Western concessions on Berlin and Germany. Khrushchev's multifaceted twelve-day visit included Washington, New York, Los Angeles, Hollywood, Iowa, Pittsburgh, and points in between.[168] He met with such varied representatives of American life as politicians, Hollywood dancers and actors, farmers, and businessmen. As Khrushchev's advisor Troyanovsky relates, Khrushchev's "triumphal reception [in the United States] was seen as a second recognition of communist Russia by the top leader of the capitalist world [after the initial and long awaited recognition of 1933]. Given the insecurity complex which he retained, in Khrushchev's eyes this had great significance."[169] The invitation also indicated to Khrushchev that his strategy of compelling the West to negotiations was working.

In their talks at Camp David, Khrushchev obtained Eisenhower's admission that the situation in Berlin was "abnormal" and that negotiations over the city "should not be prolonged indefinitely."[170] But there were no detailed discussions on Berlin, their communiqué declaring only that regarding this issue "an understanding was reached, subject to the approval of the other parties directly concerned, that negotiations would be reopened with a view to achieving a solution which would be in accordance with the interests of all concerned."[171] They also agreed to a Four Power summit on Germany the following year (eventually planned for Paris in May 1960) and to a subsequent visit by Eisenhower to the Soviet Union. A tenuous "spirit of Camp David" prevailed.

Flying back to Moscow with Khrushchev, Troyanovsky shared his boss's "good mood." Khrushchev felt that his trip to the United States had been very successful and had "achieved real political results, [signaling the] beginning of a new era in Soviet-American relations [in which] the Western Powers would make concessions on the German problem."[172] The evaluation the Soviets gave to Ulbricht and Grotewohl of Khrushchev's talks with Eisenhower was similarly optimistic, although it contained a note of caution. On the one hand, the Soviets felt that "the talks showed that President Eisenhower and his close advisors are very upset about the dead end [to which] Dulles' cold war policy has led the USA." On the other hand, "it is clear that the USA-government attaches great significance to the Berlin question. In general Eisenhower maintains the earlier attitude of the USA regarding West Berlin, although he does this with a milder tone."[173]

Khrushchev's generally good mood after meeting with Eisenhower did not survive his October trip to Beijing for a summit with his increasingly difficult ally Mao Zedung. Before Khrushchev's trip to the United States, the Soviets had considered, according to a secret Soviet report, "having an exchange of views at a conference of the socialist camp." They decided against this, however, since "the convening of such a conference could give rise to various speculations about whether there were some sort of disagreements among the countries of the socialist camp about the issues to be discussed at the upcoming meeting."[174] The "disagreements" could very well have been China's critical attitude about Khrushchev's trip to the United States and his willingness to engage in negotiations with "the imperialists." Khrushchev probably decided it would be easier to meet with the Chinese after his trip to the United States than before.

The tension in Soviet-Chinese relations that had been increasing since the Soviet Twentieth Party Congress became stronger, broader, and more public in 1959 and 1960 and was also manifested in personal relations between Khrushchev and Mao.[175] Summits between the two leaders dissolved into severe disagreements and even shouting matches in 1958 and 1959.[176] Meeting Mao in Beijing on 2 October 1959, Khrushchev spoke of his visit with Eisenhower and then raised the question of the Chinese holding of five American "spies" in prison. As Khrushchev told Mao, "I only promised Eisenhower to raise this question in the form of friendly advice during my stay in the PRC." Not surprisingly, Mao took offense at the idea that Khrushchev came from Washington to Beijing to carry a U.S. message critical of Beijing. Khrushchev defensively responded: "I would like to emphasize that I am not a representative of the U.S. and not a middleman on behalf of Americans. I am a representative of my own Soviet socialist state, the Communist Party of the Soviet Union."[177] The summit was not off to a good start.

They went on to argue about Chinese policy regarding Taiwan, Tibet, and India and about the character of Soviet-Chinese relations. Ironically for someone who kept threatening the West about West Berlin but not carrying out these threats, Khrushchev was very critical of Mao's policy regarding the offshore islands of Quemoy and Matsu: "As for the firing at the off-shore islands, if you shoot, then you ought to capture these islands, and if you do not consider it necessary to capture these islands, then there is no use in firing. I do not understand this policy of yours."[178] Khrushchev also chided Mao for Chinese policy toward the Soviet Union. He felt the Chinese lectured and reproached the Soviets in a haughty way, but never accepted Soviet criticism. The summit deepened the growing rift between Khrushchev and Mao.

Khrushchev's view of Chinese treatment of the Soviets was mirrored by Mao's view of Soviet treatment of the Chinese. One of the key Chinese critiques of the Soviets since 1956 had been "great power chauvinism" in Moscow's relations with other socialist countries. The Yugoslavs had also spoken of Soviet "hegemonic" behavior. Putting the Soviets on the defensive about this issue helped the smaller countries of the bloc, including the GDR, express more independence. Chinese criticism of Khrushchev's willingness to negotiate with the West about Berlin and Germany was also viewed favorably by many in the East German leadership, including Ulbricht.

Shared interests continued to be an important part of East German–Chinese relations. In a letter to Mao for his sixty-fifth birthday on 18 December 1958, Ulbricht wrote that the GDR "sees in the victorious fight of the Chinese fraternal people against the intervention of America and its lackeys a luminous model for its own struggle against the criminal plans of German militarism and imperialism [and] for the creation of a united, peace-loving and democratic Germany."[179] Even if Mao had not actually seized Quemoy and Matsu, in Ulbricht's eyes Mao's aggressive moves against the islands constituted a more attractive model of foreign policy to him than Khrushchev's mere bluster with the West. During Grotewohl's trip to China in January 1959, the Chinese pledged in their joint declaration: "[T]he PRC treats any imperialist attack on the GDR as an attack on the entire socialist camp and will support the GDR with all means at its disposal."[180]

An important part of the Sino-Soviet rift was strong Chinese criticism of Khrushchev for pursuing peaceful coexistence with the West instead of realizing that the West was a "paper tiger" that should be dealt with more aggressively.[181] This line of thinking could only help Ulbricht's cause of persuading Khrushchev to turn over control of the borders and access routes to him.[182] As the U.S. State Department recognized, "There is considerable evidence that in 1959 and early 1960 the Chinese encouraged the East Germans in their desire for a stronger line on the Berlin question than the Soviets were willing to take. The Sino-Soviet controversy not yet having fully burst into the open, Ulbricht probably thought he could afford at least to flirt with Peking."[183]

THE PARIS SUMMIT AND THE U-2

Pressure from China added to the stakes for Khrushchev at the May 1960 Four Power summit on Germany.[184] While the Western Powers still disagreed on a joint approach to Khrushchev regarding Berlin and Germany as the Paris summit approached, they also were not willing to give up their occupation status in Berlin or to recognize the GDR. By pushing for a summit, Khrushchev had put a lot of pressure on himself to deliver, to show any domestic or foreign critics that he could get the West to make real concessions on Berlin and Germany without causing a war. Khrushchev's complicated and risky strategy of combining threats and deadlines with a willingess to negotiate and to keep postponing deadlines relied on his being able to develop and maintain a reputation as a strong leader. This strategy seemed to fall apart with the U.S. U-2 overflight of the Soviet Union on 1 May 1960.

After failing in previous attempts to shoot down U.S. high-altitude planes spying on the Soviets and especially their nuclear missile capability, the Soviets finally succeeded in downing the plane on 1 May and even captured the CIA pilot, Francis Gary Powers, alive.[185] Khrushchev then slowly leaked out information about a captured plane to see how the United States would respond. As Troyanovsky, who was involved in drafting Khrushchev's speeches on the incident, describes, "[W]e helped our boss lay a trap for the White House. I must say that Khrushchev did this with great pleasure." On 5 May Khrushchev announced that the Soviets had shot down a U-2, but said nothing about the pilot being alive. Initially the United States claimed that it was a NASA plane doing meteorological work that had accidentally gone astray. Khrushchev then announced on 7 May that the pilot was alive and on 11 May that he would be put on trial. In his public statements, Khrushchev vilified the United States, but did not criticize President Eisenhower directly, perhaps to offer him a chance to patch things up.[186]

On 14 May Khrushchev departed for Paris. Troyanovsky, who accompanied him, writes that the final decision about how to handle the U-2 incident was decided at the airport just before takeoff from Moscow. Khrushchev, Gromyko, Defense Minister Malinovsky, and other Presidium members stood talking outside the plane while the rest of the delegation waited on board. When Khrushchev boarded the plane, he told Troyanovsky and his other close advisors

> that he intended to demand of President Eisenhower that he promise absolutely to never again violate Soviet airspace, express regret for the violations

so far and punish those responsible. Khrushchev added that he thought it was practically inconceivable that Eisenhower would accept his demands. Thus, in his view it was quite certain that the summit would end in failure before it even began. "That is quite a pity," Khrushchev said, "but we have no choice. U-2 flights are not only cynical volations of international rights but also a serious insult to the Soviet Union."

Troyanovsky agreed that "[I]t wasn't just Khrushchev who was put in a difficult situation, but his country was also humiliated and insulted. There could be no doubt that if he didn't react strongly enough, hawks in Moscow and Peking would have used this incident—and not without foundation—as proof that at the head of the Soviet Union there was a leader who was ready to put up with any insult from Washington." Nonetheless, Troyanovsky notes that there was "an atmosphere of depression at the Soviet embassy in Paris" at the dashed hopes for the summit.[187]

In Paris, Eisenhower did not agree to Khrushchev's demands and in fact took personal responsibility for the U-2 flights, which he said were necessary for U.S. national security. In spite of de Gaulle's and Macmillan's attempts to keep the summit on track, Khrushchev refused to participate in the summit without Eisenhower's apology.[188] Instead, he walked out angrily and made it clear he would wait for the next U.S. administration to discuss Berlin and Germany.[189]

The insecurity in Khrushchev's personality, described by his former colleagues and advisors, combined with the critical attitude of the Chinese and others regarding Khrushchev's willingness to negotiate with the West help explain Khrushchev's decision to torpedo the Paris summit. After having felt that he and his country were receiving "a second recognition" by the United States during his trip in September 1959, the U-2 incident and Eisenhower's refusal to apologize was a long way to fall. Khrushchev's perhaps illusory expectations about Soviet-U.S. relations were dashed. Especially given growing Chinese criticism (perhaps shared by some of his Kremlin colleagues) of his policy toward the West, Khrushchev would not go forward with the summit under these circumstances.

This did not mean, however, that he was ready to carry out his threats to sign a separate peace treaty with the GDR and transfer to it control of the access routes. Khrushchev traveled home from Paris via East Berlin, where he announced on 20 May: "We are realists and we will never pursue a gambling policy. Under present conditions, it is worthwhile to wait a little longer and try to find a solution for the long-since ripe question of a peace treaty with the two German states. This will not escape our hands. We had better wait, and the matter will get more mature."[190] Ulbricht's patience, however, was beginning to wear thin with Khrushchev's strategy of delay.

CONCLUSION

Since Stalin's death, Khrushchev had grown increasingly cognizant of the challenges faced by the GDR. For the better part of five years, Khrushchev, together with other Soviet leaders, had urged Ulbricht to counter these challenges by a combination of alleviating socialism at home and developing more constructive ties with West Germans. Ulbricht, however, resisted Soviet advice and maintained his hard-line domestic and foreign policies. Accordingly, Khrushchev decided to take matters into his own hands and attempt to compel the West to relieve its pressure on the GDR. Khrushchev may very well have figured that he could kill more than one bird with the stone of his ultimatum to the West: In addition to forcing the West to accept the GDR, he would also prove to his domestic and other socialist critics that he was tough on the West.

Yet Khrushchev's focus shifted as the crisis he unleashed progressed. In preparing his ultimatum, Khrushchev intended to unilaterally relinquish to the GDR Soviet supervision of the access routes to West Berlin, without any talks with the West. Then, once his Kremlin colleagues persuaded him to engage in negotiations with the West on the matter, Khrushchev's plans changed further. Whereas forcing the West into negotiations on Germany and Berlin was initially a means to an end for Khrushchev, once he got a taste of high-level talks with Western leaders, he was wary of risking a rupture of these. Instead, his prime goal at times seemed to be to ensure that he could continue negotiating with the West. Khrushchev's initial impatience and insistence on a six-month deadline gave way to seemingly limitless (especially from Ulbricht's perspective) patience, as he let the deadline slip away for a year and then two.

In addition to seeking opportunities for meetings with Western leaders, Khrushchev's main strategy after launching the crisis was to play for time in negotiations, to get as much as possible in an interim agreement on Berlin, and to assume that by the time the interim agreement had expired (in 1961), the situation in West Berlin would be much more unstable, more advantageous to the East, the West would have caved in, and the GDR would be stronger economically and politically. This was the strategy Khrushchev laid out to Ulbricht at their summits in Moscow in June 1959. He forecast that if they could reach an interim agreement with the West for a year or year and a half, by the end of the interim period, the West would be weaker and the GDR and socialists stronger. In the meantime, Khrushchev told Ulbricht not to take unilateral actions, while he continued to pursue an agreement with the West.

Ulbricht, however, grew increasingly frustrated and worried about his regime as the refugees continued to leave, especially young, skilled workers. Time was running out for him. While Khrushchev's broad interest in negotiations with the West, in being received as an equal by the Western Powers, and being seen as an influential world statesman, sustained him in many ways during the crisis, Ulbricht had no such compensation. There were some growing signs of increasing Western willingness to recognize the GDR de facto, but not de jure, and it was not at all clear how long the process would take to achieve this. Ulbricht wanted more immediate, concrete help with his refugee problem. By the fall of 1960 he would decide to act on his own.

CHAPTER FOUR

1960–1961

Ulbricht, Khrushchev, and the Berlin Wall

KHRUSHCHEV'S PROCRASTINATION in transferring to the GDR control over the access routes to West Berlin was a source of great frustration for Ulbricht. After watching from the sidelines for almost two years as Khrushchev negotiated with the West, Ulbricht activated his own Berlin policy in the fall of 1960. Consequently, Khrushchev found himself with narrowing room to maneuver between Western intransigence and Ulbricht's unilateral moves to close the border in Berlin. In generating the Berlin Crisis, Khrushchev had unwittingly given his East German ally an instrument to exert pressure on Soviet policy. Khrushchev had served public notice that he would not tolerate the state of affairs in Berlin anymore; with increasingly daring persistence, Ulbricht pressed Khrushchev to follow his words with deeds. And if Khrushchev was reluctant to do this, Ulbricht would prepare to eliminate the threat from West Berlin on his own. Ulbricht's capacity to resist moderating Soviet policies in the early to mid-1950s was replaced by his capacity to compel forceful Soviet policies on Berlin. The tail boldly wagged the dog.

In this chapter, we witness the growing clash between the personalities, interests, and policies of Ulbricht and Khrushchev. As the East German economic situation worsened vis-à-vis West Germany, and the refugee exodus accelerated in 1960–61, the gap widened between Khrushchev's concern with avoiding war and Ulbricht's need to gain control over the borders and access routes through which refugees fled. The same lever Khrushchev sought to use against the West (access to Berlin) he found Ulbricht using without his approval during the final year of the Berlin Crisis. Soviet support for Ulbricht in 1953 and in 1956–58, combined with Khrushchev's initiation of the Berlin Crisis, gave Ulbricht the confidence to act provocatively and independently in the year leading up to the building of the Berlin Wall. Khrushchev struggled to put the East German genie he had created back into the bottle.

Ulbricht's tenacity in pursuing his goal of closing the refugees' escape hatch to West Berlin was like the recurring drum beat in the bass line of the Beethoven violin concerto: ominous, building in intensity, and not always under the conductor's control.[1] Ulbricht's pressure was "unabating" in the words of his former speechwriter and advisor Fedor Burlatsky.[2] Similarly, referring to the mid- to late 1950s, Khrushchev's foreign-policy advisor Oleg Troyanovsky observes in his memoirs:

> If we speak about East Germany, in the West the view has always prevailed that its leaders were no more than pawns, who moved on Moscow's chessboard. But really they were active players, constantly securing from Moscow more aggressive tactics against West Germany and West Berlin. Most often they used the argument that the German Democratic Republic was a kind of outpost of socialism and its open borders with West Berlin were used by the Western powers to undermine the position of the GDR, violating its financial system and enticing its population to the West. . . . There were periods when Moscow literally was bombarded by messages and phone calls[3] from East Berlin.[4]

As we shall see, the ten months preceding the building of the Berlin Wall constituted such a period.

Yuli Kvitsinsky, a diplomat at the Soviet embassy in East Berlin from 1958–62 and later a prominent nuclear arms control negotiator, writes even more specifically about Ulbricht's influence. As Kvitsinsky recounts it, when Ulbricht learned that a diplomat from the Soviet embassy did or said something he did not like, he was "merciless. The unlucky diplomat would be sent home immediately and often fired for attempted interference in the internal affairs of the GDR." This even extended to Soviet ambassadors. Kvitsinsky notes that no Soviet ambassador to the GDR who was liked by Ulbricht, or his successor, Honecker, was dismissed, but those who were not accepted by the East German leaders were removed.[5]

SOVIET–EAST GERMAN CONFLICTS DURING THE BERLIN CRISIS AND EAST GERMAN BARGAINING POWER

Some observers in the West have speculated that the divergent policies pursued by Khrushchev and Ulbricht during the Berlin Crisis were the result of a planned division of labor between them,[6] but the declassified documents reveal that these differences were real, not planned or staged, and that Khrushchev and Ulbricht never completely resolved these differences during the crisis or even in the aftermath of the Wall.[7] It was these differences that made the Berlin Crisis a Soviet–East German as well as an East-West crisis, and Ulbricht's behavior added to the intensity of the crisis.[8]

The Soviet and East German leaders differed over several issues: how and when to remedy the destabilizing influence on East Germany emanating from West Berlin; how much control the East Germans should have over the access routes between West Germany and West Berlin;

how to stop the East German refugee flow; the degree to which the Soviets and East Germans should risk a confrontation with the West over Berlin; whether the Soviet Union and other socialist countries should sign a separate peace treaty with East Germany in the event that the Western powers refused to sign a German peace treaty; the extent of relations the socialist countries should have with West Berlin; and the manner and extent to which the Western powers should be pressed to recognize formally the existence of the East German regime. In addition to these specific issues that were at the heart of the Berlin Crisis, there were also broader, ongoing tensions between the East Germans and Soviets regarding East German domestic policies, Soviet economic aid to East Germany, and relations with the PRC. These Soviet–East German differences escalated as did the stakes and tension during the Berlin Crisis. East German influence on Soviet policy actually increased as the stability of the East German regime weakened throughout the Crisis; from East Germany's weakness came bargaining strength.

Under the pressure of the crisis, the differing goals, priorities, and strategies of the East German and Soviet leaders came to the surface. Their different strategic positions as a superpower and small ally led Khrushchev and Ulbricht to have different policy preferences. While they both wanted to end the refugee exodus from East to West, obtain Western recognition of the GDR regime (in part by finally signing a peace treaty for World War II), uphold socialism in the GDR, and reduce or eliminate the Western presence in West Berlin, Khrushchev and Ulbricht had significant differences over how important these goals were and what they were willing to risk to achieve them.[9]

The main difference underlying Khrushchev's and Ulbricht's behavior during the Berlin Crisis was the fact that Khrushchev had larger, more global concerns and different issues at stake than just those directly connected to the Berlin Crisis and to the GDR.[10] As the leader of a superpower, Khrushchev had to contend with broader issues of war and peace between East and West, Soviet-U.S. relations, the Soviet status in the world, and his own status. Ulbricht's goals were narrower, focused on preserving his tight hold on power in the GDR and maintaining the GDR as a socialist state. Broader East-West concerns did not interest him.[11]

Khrushchev wanted to preside over the triumph of socialism over capitalism in Germany, "solve the West Berlin problem," and have good relations with the West. Ulbricht believed that only by achieving the second was the first possible. And as far as good relations with the West, Ulbricht gained more from tense than relaxed East-West relations. Accordingly, in their private communications about policy during the Berlin Crisis, Ulbricht was much more impatient and aggressive and Khrushchev was more patient and restrained about actually carrying out his threats vis-à-vis the West.

On issues where they differed, Ulbricht did his best to convert Khrushchev to his point of view. There were six factors that permitted Ulbricht to influence Khrushchev's policies during the crisis.[12] First, the strategic location of the GDR on the edge of the Soviet bloc in Europe made it of military importance to the Soviet Union. But that strategic location, next to West Berlin and West Germany, was also precisely what promoted the refugee exodus. Ulbricht turned this strategic vulnerability into a certain kind of bargaining asset with Khrushchev, a way of exerting pressure on him to do more and more to shore up the GDR. I do not argue that Ulbricht consciously attempted to make East Germany weaker so as to gain bargaining leverage over Khrushchev; rather, I maintain that Ulbricht became adept at transforming the weakness of his regime into bargaining leverage with Khrushchev on certain issues, especially economic aid and the regime on the Berlin sectoral border, as this chapter will illustrate.

Second, Ulbricht's geographic distance from Khrushchev gave him important control over local conditions, enabling him to follow different policies than Khrushchev wanted, just as he had in 1953 and 1956–58. There were limits to the Soviet capacity to project influence over GDR policy, as is generally the case with a "patron" and "client," the "imperial center" and the "periphery."[13] The approximately 500,000 Soviet troops in the GDR may have been able to deter domestic unrest after 1953, but they did not have much of an effect on Ulbricht's policies.[14]

Third, Ulbricht's tenacious, opportunistic, self-confident personality helped him to push events in the direction he wanted. Understanding the dynamics between the personalities and policies of Khrushchev and Ulbricht is essential to understanding the course of the Berlin Crisis. Another East German leader might not have had the gumption to push so hard for his wishes on Berlin as Ulbricht did. But, Ulbricht's hardline personality and policies would not have made the impact they did on the crisis if the Kremlin leader had not been open to influence. Thus, the fourth key factor allowing a meaningful East German role in the crisis was Khrushchev's commitment to a socialist GDR at virtually any cost. Keeping East Germany firmly in the Soviet communist camp was of great importance to Khrushchev personally, to the reputation of the Soviet Union, and to the communist cause. Due to its location as the westernmost socialist country, East Germany, and especially East Berlin, offered the first glimpse of socialism to most Westerners. Khrushchev wanted to do all he could to ensure that this glimpse would show the socialist system as superior to the capitalist. Khrushchev observed in 1956 that since the "conflict between socialism and capitalism proceeds in the German Democratic Republic as a country with open borders, particular attention by all forces in the peace camp must be directed towards GDR victory in the competition."[15] This was also why Khrushchev regularly told Ulbricht: "The GDR's needs are also our needs."[16] Ulbricht was able to exploit this strong dedication to the GDR to manipulate Khrushchev into making greater commitments to the GDR than would otherwise have been the case.

Ulbricht was fully aware of the importance of a strong, socialist GDR to Khrushchev. And it gave Ulbricht a certain sense of invincibility. Kvitsinsky observes that East German officials became "totally convinced that they could make any political mistake without fearing they would lose power. Moscow would always rush to help in decisive moments and use all their powers to preserve the GDR, since without it all Soviet positions in Europe would be lost."[17] Just as West Berlin was a "superdomino" to the United States, Ulbricht knew that East Berlin and East Germany represented a "superdomino," or "super-ally" to the Soviets: one Khrushchev felt the need to uphold no matter how taxing, even in the face of his colleagues' skepticism as expressed at the June 1957 "anti-party" plenum.

Fifth, Ulbricht knew he had the legacy of Beria and Malenkov's alleged willingness to "give up" the GDR in 1953 in his favor. Ongoing references especially to Beria as a traitor for allegedly proposing the abandonment of East Germany gave Ulbricht an instrument of pressure to extract Soviet support.

Finally, since the Berlin Crisis coincided with the burgeoning of the Sino-Soviet conflict, Ulbricht was able to use the latter to advance his aims in the former. Part of the reason Khrushchev would ultimately give in to Ulbricht's demands to close the Berlin border was to ensure that the East Germans and others continued to see the Soviet Union as the leader and greatest supporter of the socialist camp, as opposed to the Chinese. This factor was also present in Khrushchev's calculations the following year in deploying the missiles in Cuba.[18]

Just as Kathryn Weathersby has argued that the interaction of Kim Il Sung and Stalin was key in the origins of the Korean War, so the interaction of Ulbricht and Khrushchev was essential in leading to the construction of the Berlin Wall.[19] We must understand the perspectives and goals of both Ulbricht and Khrushchev in order to understand developments in the final year of the Berlin Crisis. Instead of conceiving of the Soviet Union and the GDR as a superpower and a weak ally in this period, it is much more productive to recognize their interdependence, their intersection as superpower and super-ally. Khrushchev wanted a strong socialist regime in the GDR just as Ulbricht needed Soviet help in shoring up this regime.

Ulbricht Moves to Force Khrushchev's Hand
by Unilateral Actions

In the face of Khrushchev's continued reluctance to carry out his threats to the West regarding a separate peace treaty and West Berlin, Ulbricht grew impatient. In late August and September 1960, he sought to carry out these threats unilaterally, while attempting to persuade Khrushchev to support him.

In early September 1960 Ulbricht took a stab at blocking movement on the West Berlin–East Berlin sectoral border. Due to concern about contagion from a rally of refugee organizations in West Berlin, from midnight on 31 August through midnight on 5 September, the East Germans forbade West Germans from entering East Berlin without a visitor's permit from the GDR Interior Ministry.[20] Given that West Germany did not recognize East Germany, it was highly unlikely that West Germans would submit themselves to this stipulation. The regulation was made permanent on 8 September. Since all of Berlin was still technically under Four Power control, the Western Powers protested the East German right to restrict travel into East Berlin, but the Soviets defended their right to do this.[21] On 13 September the GDR Interior Ministry began to issue new permits for West Germans and West Berliners desiring to visit East Berlin, with the new stipulation that West Berliners had to present their identity cards, not their West German passports, as identification, thus emphasizing that West Berlin was an entity separate from West Germany.[22] As Ann Tusa points out, "At one stroke residents of West Berlin had been turned into a separate category of citizen (even before the creation of a 'free city')."[23] In response to Western protests, the Soviets again publicly defended the East German decrees as a legitimate expression of their sovereign rights. Meanwhile, the Soviets and East Germans achieved another victory when the West German Bundestag decided on 20 September, in the face of Soviet and East German protests and threats, to postpone its planned session in West Berlin. On the same day, GDR Foreign Minister Bolz declared that the GDR would take steps to ban the "misuse" of GDR territory, including the access routes to West Berlin.[24]

Then, on 21 September, the East Germans announced in *Neues Deutschland* that Western diplomats accredited to embassies in Bonn had to obtain permission from the East German Foreign Ministry to enter East Germany and East Berlin. Since it was impossible to reach West Berlin without passing through GDR territory, this move represented a further effort to emphasize the separation of West Berlin from West Germany and a blatant disregard of Four Power agreement and practice. It was also an attempt to compel the West to deal with, and thus grant de facto recognition to the GDR. An article in the *New York Times* noted that this was "by far the strongest (measure) yet taken in the Communists' mounting campaign to undermine Greater Berlin's four-power status and isolate West Berlin." To test this, the U.S. ambassador in Bonn, Walter Dowling (who was also the chief of the U.S. Mission in Berlin), left Bonn for Berlin on 21 September.[25]

When Dowling tried to enter East Berlin on 22 September at the Brandenberg Gate, an East German border guard declared: "Diplomats accredited to Bonn cannot enter the democratic sector of Berlin. You must turn around and go back."[26] Dowling refused. The guard then asked him for some identification, in spite of the fact that Dowling was in his State Department limousine with the U.S. and ambassadorial flags on the front of the car and his official license plate. He showed his ID to the East German border guard, "thereby conceding the right of a guard to ask for it and surrendering his own right to unimpeded access" as part of Four Power occupation rights in Berlin, as Ann Tusa observes.[27] Dowling then drove around for a short time in East Berlin before returning to West Berlin. He left Berlin for Bonn on 23 September. On this date, the East Germans publicly "insisted on their right to inspect the documents of the Western Big Three ambassadors on their entry into East Berlin."[28]

Following the incident with Dowling, there were two meetings on 23 and 26 September between the GDR ambassador to Moscow, Johannes König, and Oleg Selianinov of the Soviet embassy in the GDR. These meetings indicated that the Soviets had not sanctioned or even known about the GDR measures announced on 21 September.[29] Selianinov expressed great concern that the East Germans were unilaterally changing their policy on the treatment of Western officials entering East Berlin. As König reported to Ulbricht after the first meeting:

> Selianinov wanted to talk about reports in the West Berlin press about the trip of the U.S. Ambassador to Bonn, Dowling, into the Democratic Sector [East Berlin] and ask some questions. Selianinov wanted to know whether there was an order for inspecting the documents of Western accredited diplomats in Bonn by our ministry or by other GDR organs. From his statements, I saw that he was astounded that such inspection was carried out vis-à-vis Western diplomats. He especially wanted to know whether it resulted in the conflicts with Dowling that were reported in the West Berlin press. Selianinov commented that the Ambassador and the diplomats of the Soviet embassy, as well as other ambassadors and diplomats of people's democracies in Berlin, who travel to West Berlin on occasion, were not asked for identification at the West Berlin checkpoints, especially when they drive with the flag, as was the case with the American Ambassador. . . .

Selianinov asked whether new measures in this regard were being carried out by our side.

I had the impression that Selianinov was very concerned that future measures by GDR officials against the ambassadors or diplomats of Western embassies could also be directed against the Soviet embassy personnel in their visits to West Berlin. It was clear that the Soviet embassy wanted to be informed in the future about measures of this kind.[30]

Selianinov was not satisfied with König's answers and returned three days later, which König also reported to Ulbricht:

[Selianinov] again brought up the question of future GDR measures concerning trips into Democratic Berlin by diplomats of Western embassies. He said that the USSR embassy had recently received a new directive from its government which foresaw stronger activity in relation to West Berlin, regarding trade, culture, etc. This would also result in more activity in West Berlin by the employees of the Soviet embassy. Selianinov said that Ulbricht and Grotewohl were being told about this new directive. He then requested that if new measures for inspection of the documents of Western diplomats entering Democratic Berlin were going to be taken, these measures must take into account the tasks connected with the new directives for the Soviet embassy. In his view, the new measures from our side and the tasks which arise for the Soviet embassy from the new directives must not conflict with each other.

I told him that I would report his opinion to the necessary people.

To Selianinov's question about what kind of measures we were planning, I said that I did not know.[31]

A confidential, unsigned report dated 17 August lays out the new Soviet directive to which Selianinov refers. The document is now located in Ulbricht's archival files, indicating that perhaps Ulbricht knew about the new Soviet policy concerning ties with West Berlin and instituted the new border measures in spite of it. The Soviet report asserts that "[i]n order to support the proposals for the formation of a free city of West Berlin, it is desirable to take further measures to loosen the dependence of West Berlin on the Federal Republic and to strengthen our influence in West Berlin." It then calls for developing more direct contacts between the Soviet Union and West Berlin in science, culture, tourism, the media, trade, and diplomacy.[32] This was precisely the kind of policy that Ulbricht consistently resisted, fearing that instead of increasing socialist influence in West Berlin, it would raise the prestige of West Berlin. Furthermore, he wanted to be the sole mediator between the socialist countries and West Berlin in order to be able to control these relations. He would feel left out and threatened if the Soviets expanded their own direct contacts with West Berlin. Ulbricht objected to similar Polish and Czechoslovak efforts to develop and expand such contacts.[33]

In Ambassador Pervukhin's annual report on the GDR for 1960, he referred to East German objections to the expansion of Soviet ties with West Berlin and to unilateral East German behavior regarding Berlin. Pervukhin noted that while the East German leaders initially agreed to the Soviet plans to expand contacts with West Berlin, they still

> do not fully understand the importance of the development of direct contacts between the Soviet Union and West Berlin. Thus, certain measures are adopted in the GDR that contradict the policy aimed at increasing the influence of socialist countries, including the GDR, in West Berlin. Some measures of the [East German] friends, on the contrary, lead to the isolation of West Berlin from the GDR and socialist countries [which is, of course, precisely what Ulbricht was aiming for], as well as to a deterioration of the situation and to complications in the resolution of the West Berlin issue. In particular, the German friends are rather jealous of the development of direct trade ties between the socialist countries and West Berlin. In the development of these ties, they see only one side, namely, that it would lead to the economic strengthening of West Berlin, forgetting that the development of economic ties between West Berlin and the countries of the socialist camp inevitably would lead to the elimination of the one-sided orientation of the West Berlin economy toward the West.
>
> To the same degree, there is a negative attitude of the GDR toward the development of direct cultural ties between the socialist countries and West Berlin.[34]

Pervukhin opined that "GDR policy concerning West Berlin must have a more flexible character and assist our general line of increasing the influence of socialist countries in West Berlin," but he did not seem particularly optimistic at being able to enforce this. Instead, he noted that GDR policies regarding West Berlin "are, as a rule, unilateral and have a primarily administrative character, which does not help in winning over the West German citizens to the GDR side. In general, these measures are mostly all kinds of limitations concerning movement between both parts of the city, job placement, etc." As an example of this and of "a certain inflexibility of the GDR leaders in practical activity concerning West Berlin," Pervukhin cited the September episode: "In September of the current year, the friends tried without prior consultation with us to establish a new order of control over crossing the sectoral border in Berlin for the citizens of West Germany, foreigners, and diplomatic and military representatives of the three Western Powers."[35] Pervukhin was very concerned about East German unilateral behavior in Berlin and blatant East German disregard for Soviet directives and policies.

Not to be deterred, Ulbricht himself took up the König-Selianinov discussions in a very self-assured letter to Khrushchev on 18 October

1960. Ulbricht forcefully defended the new treatment of Western diplomats by his border guards. He began the letter stating that "since the
prevention of the Paris summit by the Western Powers," the latter have
been trying to use the "former Four Power status" of Berlin as grounds
for their policies, which really are aimed at "the annexation of the capital of the GDR." The Western Powers had to be stopped, by deeds as
well as words. If Khrushchev would not act, Ulbricht would attempt
to usurp the right to change the regulations in Berlin. Complaining to
Khrushchev that "the USA demands uncontrolled entrance into the capital of the GDR in order to demonstrate that it does not recognize the
GDR," Ulbricht sought to put a stop to this. He concluded his discussion of the issue in his most lecturing tone:

> We do not believe that the work of the Soviet organs in West Berlin will be
> complicated by our inspection of documents. We cannot have a situation in
> which a four-power status is in principle not recognized, but in reality the
> representatives of the states which do not want to recognize the GDR govern-
> ment can come into the capital of the GDR without identifying themselves.[36]

Khrushchev responded tersely to Ulbricht on 24 October: "We would
find it useful to exchange views on all the issues raised in your letter
during your time in Moscow in November of this year. By this, we have
in mind that before the exchange of views in Moscow, no measures will
be carried out which would change the situation on the border of West
Berlin."[37] This would not be the last time that Khrushchev would tell
Ulbricht not to act in Berlin before they had conferred. Ulbricht was
going to Moscow in November to attend the Conference of Eighty-One
Communist and Workers Parties. At that time, he and Khrushchev and
their senior colleagues would also have a bilateral summit on 30 November for an "exchange of views."

Meanwhile, the refugee situation worsened significantly beginning in
the spring of 1960, with the numbers more than doubling from 9,803
in February to 20,285 in May.[38] In response, A. P. Kazennov, second
secretary at the Soviet embassy in the GDR, reported to Moscow on 17
October that

> our friends [the East Germans] are studying the possibility of taking measures
> directed towards forbidding and making it more difficult for GDR citizens to
> work in West Berlin, and also towards stopping the exodus of the population
> of the GDR through West Berlin. One of such measures by our friends could
> be the cessation of free movement through the sectoral border and the intro-
> duction of such a process for visiting West Berlin by GDR citizens as exists
> for visiting the FRG. Insofar as measures in this direction would have definite

consequences for the work of the embassy in West Berlin and for the development of direct Soviet contacts with West Berlin, it would be expedient to discuss with our friends at the appropriate level the question of the regime on the sectoral border in Berlin.[39]

On the same day, another Soviet report quoted a high-level GDR official in the Ministry of Internal Affairs as saying that "in the interests of a significant reduction of the exodus it was necessary to quickly resolve the question of West Berlin through which flow about 90 percent of all people leaving the Republic."[40] Reports like these would continue to stream into Moscow for the next ten months.

In the summer of 1960, the leaders in East Berlin had created the National Defense Council, with Ulbricht as the chairman. This body replaced the Politburo's Security Commission and was tasked with augmenting East Germany's defense capabilities. There are indications that the National Defense Council began considering measures related to sealing the Berlin border at its third meeting on 19 October 1960.[41] Soviet officials in Berlin no doubt learned of this.

On 22 November, to prime Khrushchev on the issues he wanted to discuss at their meeting in eight days, Ulbricht wrote him an eleven-page letter. The East German leader presented his views on the situation in Berlin, the GDR economy, and necessary East German security measures. He requested a thorough discussion of these matters at their meeting in the hopes that they could agree on basic strategy and then move forward tactically in specific areas.[42] After being criticized for acting without Soviet approval, Ulbricht was trying to show that he was prepared to consult on all matters of concern, although he also made it clear in his letter that he would continue pushing for the measures he deemed necessary, particularly regarding the Berlin borders and economic aid.

In his letter, Ulbricht complained at length about the situation in Berlin, which had developed to the disadvantage of the East since 1949. The FRG since then had steadily increased its ties to West Berlin, setting up branches of federal ministries there, giving West Berlin citizens West German passports, and using West Berlin for "the organization of 'flight from the Republic.'" Moreover, as Ulbricht implicitly criticized Khrushchev as one of the Four Powers, "the agreements between the Four Powers on transit to and from West Berlin were changed to the benefit of the Western Powers and the Bonn government (expanded train traffic, expanded air traffic) without any return benefits to the GDR." Ulbricht continued to complain that, "West Berlin factories are being used for West German armament production, [and] the capitalist world press is carrying out a campaign that West Berlin must be defended like New

York or Paris." To make matters worse, while the West was expanding its control over West Berlin, it was also insisting that East Berlin be held to a "no longer existing Four Power status." Thus, all sorts of people, including West German Bundestag deputies, spies, clergy, and members of the Western occupation forces could enter East Berlin uncontrolled and move around freely there. Ulbricht felt this was particularly unjust, since East German citizens could only travel in Western countries if they applied for permission at the appropriate West Berlin office.[43]

Ulbricht asserted that having "created a series of faits accompli" in Berlin, the Western Powers were trying to "get recognition of these."[44] "After years of tolerating an unclear situation" in Berlin, East Germany and the Soviet Union must change their behavior. Accordingly, Ulbricht remarked critically: "The public statement of Comrade Khrushchev that the existing situation must not be changed before a summit conference can be interpreted very differently, since the Bonn government and the Western Powers have appropriated rights in recent years which have never been established in treaties or protocols."[45] As far as Ulbricht was concerned, promising to preserve the current situation gave the benefit to the West, not the East.

Ulbricht also told Khrushchev that the economic gap between the GDR and FRG in the latter's favor was widening. West Germany was receiving economic help from the United States and the European Economic Community (EEC), and in some areas had even surpassed the United States in economic strength. In 1960 the rate of production growth in the FRG was 12–13 percent, whereas it was only 8 percent in the GDR. Unlike the East Germans, the West Germans had been able to reconstruct their main cities destroyed in the war and to increase workers' salaries while reducing their working hours.[46] Thus, especially in light of the West German announcement at the end of September that it would cancel the renewal of the "interzonal" trade agreement between the two countries at the end of the year, Ulbricht requested "large-scale help from the USSR." The GDR needed considerable supplies of raw materials, semi-finished goods, and basic foodstuffs, including meat and butter. This would help the GDR establish its "economic independence from the FRG [and] reduce the flight from the Republic [by] improving the living standards for a part of the intelligentsia, especially teachers and doctors." He assured Khrushchev: "We know that our proposals present difficult burdens and great sacrifices for the USSR" but he was certain Khrushchev understood how important it was to help the East German economy.[47]

Ulbricht's letters to Khrushchev of 18 October and 22 November, as well as a similar one on 10 October, mark the beginning of his intensive campaign to convince Khrushchev over the next nine months to act (instead of just threaten) to turn things around in Berlin.[48] He wanted to reduce Western influence and rights, seize East German control over the Berlin sectoral borders and access routes, and augment Soviet economic aid to the GDR.

THE 30 NOVEMBER 1960 ULBRICHT-KHRUSHCHEV MEETING

At the 30 November 1960 meeting between Ulbricht and Khrushchev and their top political and economic advisors, they discussed the issues Ulbricht had raised in his letter.[49] They focused on their tactics for 1961 regarding *Deutschland-* and *Berlinpolitik*, as well as Soviet economic aid to the GDR. The context of the meeting was very significant: The conflict between the Soviets and the Chinese had just escalated dramatically at the 10 November–1 December Conference of Eighty-One Communist and Workers' Parties in Moscow, and John F. Kennedy had been elected president of the United States three weeks earlier. As the reader will recall, Khrushchev had announced at the aborted Paris Summit of May 1960 that he would wait to continue negotiations on Germany and Berlin with the next U.S. administration. Now that a new U.S. administration had been elected, it was time to plan strategy.

Both Khrushchev and Ulbricht left the meeting believing that in the end they had gotten what they wanted. Ulbricht believed that the Soviets would give him all the economic aid he needed to compete with and surpass the West German economy. Khrushchev believed that Ulbricht would take no unilateral steps with regard to the regime on the Berlin sectoral border while he was trying to negotiate with the West.[50] Both were subsequently disappointed.

Ulbricht began the meeting laying out the difficulties with the economy and the challenges in Berlin:

> How will things develop in Berlin? We will maintain our tactics directed toward strengthening the position of the capital of the GDR and restricting interference by West Germany. However, the situation in Berlin has become complicated, not in our favor. West Berlin has strengthened economically. This is seen in the fact that about 50,000 workers from East Berlin now are still working in West Berlin [the *Grenzgänger*, or "border crossers"]. Thus, a part of the qualified working force goes to work in West Berlin, since there are higher salaries there. . . . [T]eachers in the West earn 200–300 marks more than in the East. Doctors also earn two times more there. In addition, by leaving for West Germany they receive large one-time grants there. . . . Why don't we raise our salaries for this category of people? First of all, we don't have the means. Secondly, even if we raised their salary, we could not satisfy their purchasing power with the goods that we have, and they would buy things with that money in West Berlin. But still, we will try to do this. . . .

Now we will try to protect ourselves from these unpleasant things, and the number of conflicts in Berlin will increase. We must do this, since we are obligated to protect the capital of the GDR, and we will not allow West Germany to do what it wants there. . . .

As a result, there will not be major conflict in Berlin, but there will be small conflicts.[51]

Ulbricht did not elaborate on how he planned to "try to protect ourselves from these unpleasant things." In view of his recent behavior, he probably had in mind tightening up the Berlin sectoral border and making it harder for East Berliners to work in West Berlin.

Ulbricht also sought to obtain more Soviet economic aid to help him equalize the economic situation in Berlin and in Germany. Ulbricht went out of his way in this meeting to give Khrushchev a clear picture of the challenges facing East Berlin and East Germany and the strong measures needed to meet these challenges. He was successful in many ways: Khrushchev seemed to understand for the first time the depth of the GDR's problems, remarking, "We didn't know that the GDR was so vulnerable to West Germany" economically.[52]

Khrushchev had two responses to Ulbricht's bleak portrayal of the situation, one much more positive than the other. First, Khrushchev vetoed Ulbricht's plans to change the border regime in Berlin or anything affecting the Western Powers in Berlin. He agreed with Ulbricht that "after the war, many of the conditions which violate GDR sovereignty remained," such as the presence of the Western Powers in Berlin and their use of the access routes independent of GDR control.

But all of this was already won de facto by the West. Now, when you want to liberate yourself from this, you will aggravate the situation. But this is not favorable to us now, since we gave our word that we would not change the existing situation until the summit meeting of the heads of government. And if we change something now, this will look as if we are violating our word. Since we already missed this opportunity, we cannot now correct the situation unilaterally. Let us wait until the moment before which we said we would not change the situation. There isn't much more [waiting] to endure now.[53]

Khrushchev's caution predominated. While he agreed with Ulbricht and kept complaining to the West that the existing situation in Berlin "violated GDR sovereignty," he remained unwilling, as he had been for two years, to carry out his threats to alter that situation unilaterally. As Pervukhin summarized the meeting later,

It was stipulated that the GDR government would not unilaterally take steps toward the liquidation of the remnants of the last war, although they run counter to GDR sovereignty, but their removal by unilateral acts could lead to an aggravation of the situation and hinder the negotiations of the USSR with the Western Powers on a peaceful settlement of the German question. This concerns, above all, the control regime for the crossing of the sectoral border in Berlin.[54]

While restraining Ulbricht from unilateral actions, Khrushchev hoped that the force of his personality and the justice of his proposals would persuade President Kennedy to make concessions, just as he had succeeded in getting the Eisenhower administration to offer concessions. At a minimum, Khrushchev looked forward to the positive effects on his international prestige of meeting with yet another U.S. president.

On the more positive side for Ulbricht at this 30 November encounter, Khrushchev agreed to grant substantial increased aid to the GDR. Indeed, much of the meeting focused on helping the East German economy. By the end of the meeting, Khrushchev had decided to take over the East German economy almost completely, with some help from other socialist countries, in order to enable it to prevail in competition with the FRG and thus, presumably, drastically reduce the refugee exodus. There was added pressure to aid the GDR if the FRG persisted in its September decision not to renew their trade agreement, which the GDR relied on for some important goods. Both Kosygin and Khrushchev believed, rightly, that the FRG would ultimately decide to renew the trade agreement. This was in part because of the "strong levers in your hands"—the access routes—and the West German knowledge that "by exacerbating this [trade] question, they subject Berlin to risk."[55]

Before promising major Soviet efforts to help the GDR economically, Khrushchev expressed his frustration at how things had evolved in the GDR:

> [I]t is both our and your fault that we did not think everything through sufficiently and did not work out economic measures. We should have examined the question of the liberation of the GDR from the FRG more closely. But we were taking life easy, for the time being Adenauer didn't give it to us on the nose. We will clear up who was more guilty, but we, the socialist camp as a whole, acted incorrectly here. We must create the conditions so that the GDR economy will not be vulnerable to our enemies. We didn't know that the GDR was so vulnerable to West Germany. This is not good; we must correct this now. . . .
>
> In this matter, you also are not without guilt, since you did not resist; you did not disentangle yourselves; you got used to thinking that Germany was one. . . .
>
> By old habit, you try to do everything through us. You should have learned how to walk on your own two feet, instead of leaning on us all the time.[56]

Once vetting his frustration at how things had developed, Khrushchev had a largely positive, although still somewhat mixed, response to Ulbricht's requests for significant economic aid. Khrushchev declared, "we must understand that the GDR's needs are also our needs. We can't permit it that they come to us in such a state that either they sink or we throw them a rope. Let's stop playing games about this question."[57] Reminiscent of Grotewohl's plea in June 1959 that East Germany's economic needs be viewed equally as political needs, Khrushchev declared: "We must give the GDR as much metal as it needs. We cannot be blind money-counters and every time construct our trade around whether to give or not to give them 1000 tons more. Malenkov and Beria wanted to liquidate the GDR, but we fired one and shot the other and said that we supported a socialist Germany."[58] Demonstrating that his commitment to helping East Germany was much more solid than that of Beria and Malenkov, Khrushchev declared: "We must create a special group in our Gosplan for [GDR economics chief Bruno] Leuschner which will acquire everything needed on his demand.[59] There is no other way. The GDR must develop and maintain the increase in standard of living of its populace."[60]

Khrushchev clearly believed that much was at stake in the economic competition in Germany. His references to the alleged desire of Malenkov and Beria to "liquidate" a socialist GDR may be illustrative of the pressure he felt regarding the connection between his policies on Germany and the future of his own political career. With his Berlin ultimatum, he had staked a lot on achieving a positive resolution of the situation in Germany and Berlin. Khrushchev's comments about the importance of helping the GDR also stemmed from his strategic and ideological commitment to a socialist GDR.

While Khrushchev pledged to help the GDR to whatever maximum was necessary, he hoped that the FRG would continue its trade agreement with the GDR so that he would only need to supply a more "minimum program" of economic aid. Khrushchev had concerns about his capacity to fulfill the Soviet Union's own economic needs while also supplying the GDR's needs. He told Ulbricht, "we don't want to kill the goose that lays the golden eggs," and "don't thrust your hands into our pockets." On the subject of the East German request for gold to pay off its debt to the West, Khrushchev sharply rebuffed Ulbricht: "[Y]ou ask for 68 tons of gold. This is inconceivable. We can't have a situation where you buy goods, and we must pay for them. We don't have much gold, and we must keep it for an emergency."[61] Thus, the question of whether the Soviet Union would really be able to fulfill the maximal needs of the GDR, especially if the FRG broke off trade relations, was not clear. On the one hand, Khrushchev said that he was committed to doing whatever was necessary to "liberate the GDR from economic dependence on the FRG," but on the other hand he made it plain that there were limits to the economic aid Moscow could offer the GDR.

At this meeting, Khrushchev and Ulbricht also continued to discuss their prospects and plans concerning a peace treaty. Both agreed that they risked their domestic and international reputations if they continued to threaten to sign a separate peace treaty without carrying out the threat. Ulbricht was the first to raise the subject:

> We would like to appeal to you with a question regarding what will happen in 1961. The thing is that we can't repeat our campaign in favor of a peace treaty as we did it before the Paris summit. We can only do this in the event that we actually achieve something. Otherwise, we would be forced to make changes that are too abrupt. . . . Therefore, for now we will be careful with propaganda about a peace treaty, since among our population there is already a mood developing where they say—you only talk about a peace treaty, but don't do anything about it. So we have to be careful.

Khrushchev agreed that "if we don't sign it in 1961, then our prestige will have been dealt a blow and the position of the West, and West Germany in particular, will be strengthened." Ulbricht, who understandably after two years did not trust Khrushchev's promises to carry out his threats, again warned: "If we don't succeed in concluding a peace treaty, and [instead] return to propaganda for a peace treaty, then we will have discredited our policy and will be able to recover our prestige only after one–two years. We cannot act the same way that we did in 1960."[62]

Khrushchev inferred from this that Ulbricht was being critical of the fact that they did not sign a separate peace treaty after the aborted Paris summit in May 1960:

> At that time we acted correctly, we took the right step, since otherwise we could have created the impression that we provoked the breakup of the summit in order to conclude a peace treaty. We showed that we did not want that, but that we were trying to create the maximum favorable opportunities for the conclusion of a peace treaty. If we look at what was said in the Western press also and at meetings which we had here with representatives of the Western Powers and even West Germany, then it is clear that this policy brought us a huge success. . . .
>
> Thus, we have not lost the two years which have passed since the time of the initiation our proposal, but have shaken up their position.[63]

For Ulbricht it was much less clear that the two years had not been "lost" since Khrushchev issued his ultimatum. Ulbricht's problems in the GDR had not been reduced at all; and in fact, the refugee exodus had increased under the pressure of the crisis. Ulbricht was skeptical the West would agree to a peace treaty and wanted to eliminate the threat from West Berlin even without a settlement with the West. He experienced the growing difficulties in the GDR much more directly than Khrushchev did and thus displayed less patience in waiting for the West to come around than Khrushchev.

As at their June 1959 meetings, Khrushchev expressed optimism that his strategy of pressure on the West was showing good effects and would ultimately be successful, at least with regard to the chances of concluding an interim agreement on West Berlin with the West. Khrushchev was confident that he could "work out with [Ulbricht] a plan for the gradual ouster of the Western powers from West Berlin, but without war. For this we will use the levers in the hands of the GDR,"—influence over the access routes and borders.[64]

He observed, however, that "it is less probable that there will be a peace treaty with the two German states." Ultimately, he feared that "we will not achieve anything with them [the West]" on a peace treaty. "Then we will have to exacerbate the situation and sign a peace treaty. When will we sign it, in 1961?" he asked Ulbricht. "No!" Ulbricht responded, "We don't have the heart." "Politically or economically?" Khrushchev asked. "Just economically. Politically I am in favor," Ulbricht answered.[65] Khrushchev then reassured Ulbricht that the West Germans probably would not institute an economic embargo against the GDR in the event of a separate treaty and that the Soviets would help create the economic preconditions in the GDR to prevail over the FRG with or without an economic embargo.

Khrushchev saw only one way of avoiding signing a separate peace treaty if he could not persuade President Kennedy to agree to a peace treaty: "We could get away with not signing a peace treaty if an interim agreement on West Berlin is concluded. If there is not an interim agreement, then we will sign a peace treaty with the GDR and let them see their defeat. They will not start a war. Of course, in signing a peace treaty, we will have to put our rockets on military alert. But, luckily, our adversaries still haven't gone crazy; they still think and their nerves aren't bad."[66]

The 30 November meeting ended with a strange, yet illustrative, disagreement about West Germany. Ulbricht, on the one hand, and Gromyko and Khrushchev, on the other, all stubbornly held their ground:

A. A. Gromyko: Propaganda is now being advanced in the GDR that the FRG is an illegal state. This doesn't correspond entirely with our position on two German states.

W. Ulbricht: We believe that two states exist in Germany, but the

West German state has not implemented the resolutions of the Potsdam Treaty and therefore is illegal. . . .

A. A. Gromyko: But do you know the FRG is a sovereign state?

W. Ulbricht: According to the Paris Treaties, the FRG gave up part of its rights. On this issue, the political and legal sides must be distinguished. Politically we can and must conclude a peace treaty with them. However, legally they do not represent us, and we do not represent them.

A. A. Gromyko: We can criticize the FRG as a militaristic state. But criticizing it as a non-sovereign state would be harmful for our tactics.

V. Ulbricht: Here the matter is in the consciousness of our people. Our people say that the GDR is a legal state which has fulfilled the Potsdam Treaty. But the Bonn state is illegal.

N. S. Khrushchev: How the GDR internally looks upon these issues is their internal affair. We will maintain our position on this matter. We are not obligated to repeat your position. We have diplomatic relations with both German states and believe that they are both sovereign.[67]

The fact that Khrushchev felt the need to say that he was "not obligated to repeat your position" demonstrates the increasing defensiveness he felt around Ulbricht and his bossy, dogmatic approach. The tense, unyielding tone of this conversation is that of one between equals: Ulbricht displayed confidence about his right to decide East German policy and push the Soviets in directions he deemed necessary; and the Soviets did not really put him in his place.

This interaction also portrays the different approaches of the Soviets and East Germans to West Germany. For Ulbricht, West Germany was only a threat, and he was frustrated that the Soviets were not doing more to counter that threat. The Soviets, however, saw both threat and opportunity in their relations with West Germany. Since Khrushchev had established relations with the FRG in 1955, he had tried to use these ties to make West German policy toward the Soviet bloc more accommodating and to pull the FRG away from its close ties with the West. Ulbricht had little confidence in this path.

THE BURGEONING REFUGEE EXODUS

The escalating pressure Ulbricht was feeling from the refugee exodus by early 1961 was an important factor in his aggressive tone with Khrushchev. The numbers of East Germans fleeing dropped significantly in 1958 and 1959 due to tighter East German regulations for travel to the West, but there was an increasingly overwhelming focus on West Berlin as the escape hatch. The overall numbers of refugees mounted dramatically in 1960 and 1961. According to East German and Soviet figures, refugee numbers rose from 120,230 in 1959 to 182,278 in 1960 and would continue to rise even more in 1961, as did the number of East German *Grenzgänger*.[68] Both the East Germans and Soviets were concerned about this. They continued to meet monthly to discuss the refugee exodus, its causes and possible remedies.[69]

On 1 December Politburo member Willi Stoph's personal advisor, Tzschorn, prepared a lengthy and detailed report on an "Analysis of Migration from 1 January through 30 September 1960." Tzschorn expressed concern that West Germany was succeeding in "drawing out of the GDR the most valuable part of the productive forces, [as was] demonstrated in the growing movement from the GDR of January through September 1960." Tzschorn stated that the "the largest part of the migration occurs via Berlin. The open border with West Berlin facilitates the crossing." In examining the reasons for the migration, Tzschorn listed many factors, including doubts and mistrust concerning the socialist regime and its policies, insufficient patriotism, reluctance to label refugees traitors, and the absence of any public campaign in the GDR against those leaving. He also pointed to economic difficulties, the cold, impersonal way many state officials treated "the people" and their concerns, and the sense that "over there one lives more peacefully."[70]

In a similar report several months earlier, Tzschorn had written of an "*underestimation* of flight from the Republic [among the people, since] its extent cannot be described in public [emphasis in original]." He complained that, "We have no *methodical struggle* against migration. This is a perceptible hole into which the enemy pushes. The causes of the migration are not individual phenomena, but in almost all cases stem from an entire *complex of sources* [emphasis in original]." A significant problem for the government was the fact that

> Flight from the Republic *is not seen as a crime* by the people—on the contrary! The passport law is perceived in its execution as arbitrary and hard, as an attack on family ties. The view is widely held that the prosecution of people who flee the Republic and their punishment contradicts the regulations on "freedom of movement" of our constitution [emphasis in original].[71]

Clearly not much had been done since 1953 to counter the refugee exodus.[72]

Drawing on Tzschorn's reports and others, in Ambassador Pervukhin's annual report on the GDR for 1960, he discussed the escalating refugee problem. He pointed out that in the first ten months of 1960, "152,000 people illegally left the GDR, which is 32,000 more than for all of 1959." Pervukhin asserted that the East Germans blamed the weak

GDR economy primarily for the large numbers of refugees. He, how-ever, blamed the SED's "administrative," "heartless" attitude toward many East Germans, the rapid implementation of collectivization, "measures against capitalist elements in cities," "inadequate ideological work with the population,"as well as "significant interruptions in supplying the population with commercial and food products." He concluded in a worried tone: "It is characteristic that the attempts of the friends to impede the exodus of the population to the West with the help of such measures as the activization of the passport law, the establishment of stricter methods for granting permission for temporary trips to the FRG, [and] the implementation of police measures for limited movement in Berlin have only led to the opposite results."[73] As the SED regime acted to diminish the refugee flow, the flow increased instead as people decided they better get out before the regime made it impossible to leave. *Torschlusspanik* spread—the fear of the door closing.

The year 1961 thus opened amid great concern over the GDR's refu-gee problem. In one of the first meetings of the new year, Ulbricht ad-dressed the issue at a 4 January 1961 Politburo session. He proposed that "a group of comrades be appointed to make a range of proposals on how flight from the Republic can be decisively blocked so that in international negotiations we don't have to deal with the argument 'the flight from the Republic is increasing.' It must be mostly stopped."[74] Six days later, the Politburo established a Working Group to formulate proposals to halt the refugee flow. Security chief Erich Honecker, Inte-rior Minister Karl Maron, and Stasi chief Erich Mielke comprised the Working Group.[75]

At the 4 January Politburo meeting, Ulbricht also discussed the GDR's economic difficulties, which were exacerbated by the open border to West Berlin. He declared that "the main battle in 1961 will be eco-nomic." The GDR, he insisted, must establish its economic indepen-dence from the FRG. The Berlin SED chief, Paul Verner, agreed that the economic repercussions of the loss of significant numbers of skilled workers to the West constituted a serious problem. He told the Polit-buro: "On [Western] recruitment [of our workers]: according to our survey, in the last year 8,000 workers from the Democratic Sector and 12–13,000 workers from the border areas have been recruited. This is the most serious problem." Leuschner agreed that "our problems are very big and cannot be resolved easily." He said that the GDR needed a one billion ruble credit from the Soviet Union to save them from even worse economic straits. He told his colleagues that when he recently went to Moscow to discuss the GDR's economic difficulties, "[W]e brought all the technical documents that we needed, packed them in suitcases, and needed an Il-14 just for transport alone."[76]

Heinrich Rau, the minister for Foreign and Intra-German Trade, declared that making the GDR economically independent from the FRG was "also a huge problem for the Soviet Union and the other socialist countries" from whom the GDR would need help. Despite concluding several economic agreements with the Soviets on his last visit to Moscow, he told the Politburo, "[N]ow it turns out that this is incredibly difficult for the Soviet Union and that they cannot supply us with many things." In the face of these economic difficulties, Rau concluded provocatively: "Regarding the West Berlin issue . . . [w]e cannot wait to deal with this until a summit conference."[77]

Ulbricht tried to focus his colleagues' attention on the gains they had made in their policies on Berlin. He proudly told them in his opening speech at the 4 January Politburo meeting, "We can say that our common view that a Four Power Agreement no longer exists since the establishment of the GDR, or really since the creation of a separate West German currency, that this view has prevailed." Ulbricht continued to rewrite history, pointing out, "In 1960, it was clear that a Four Power status did not exist and was not acknowledged by the GDR. . . ." Thus, not only did Ulbricht insist that a Four Power status did not currently exist in Berlin, but he asserted that in fact it had not existed since 1948 or 1949. "Regarding West Berlin," Ulbricht went on to say,

[I]n 1960 a number of uncertainties were eliminated which in the last ten years had been countenanced by an unnecessary tolerance regarding certain remnants of the war which had developed into customary rights. When I said for the first time here in Berlin [on 27 October 1958] that West Berlin belonged to the territory of the GDR, it was a sensation, including among our own comrades. . . . When the Soviet Union published its note [on 27 November 1958] in which it confirmed that West Berlin was located on the territory of the GDR and that there was not a question about Berlin but only about West Berlin and that West Berlin should be transformed into a free city[, w]ith this began the clarification of the issue which we did not have the strength to clarify in 1949/50. In 1960 . . . it was made clear and an understanding was reached between the Four Powers that there is an abnormal situation in West Berlin. . . . [I]n the two years since the proposal of the Soviet Union on the transformation of West Berlin into a free city . . . states and people have become accustomed to the fact that the West Berlin issue . . . cannot be resolved by measures against the capital of the GDR. This has been made clear in the meantime by us.[78]

These few sentences are among the best now available for understanding how Ulbricht thought about the past and the future. First, Ulbricht clearly believed that the Soviets had shown "unnecessary tolerance" regarding Western rights and behavior in West Berlin. Second, he pointed out that he was the one who for "for the first time [declared that] West Berlin belonged to the territory of the GDR" and that Khrushchev then confirmed this a month later. Ulbricht had pushed Khrushchev away from his "unnecessary tolerance" of the state of affairs concerning West Berlin. Third, Ulbricht stated that "in 1949/50 we did not have the strength" to deal with these issues, but did in 1960. Two weeks after this Politburo meeting, Ulbricht sent Khrushchev a letter that attempted further to break Khrushchev of his "unnecessary tolerance" of what Ulbricht viewed as nonexisting Western rights in West Berlin.

Ulbricht Continues to Push Khrushchev to Abandon His "Unnecessary Tolerance" of the West in Berlin

Ulbricht's fifteen-page letter of 18 January 1961 showed that he did not trust Khrushchev's resolve following their last meeting in November. Ulbricht believed Khrushchev needed stronger guidance.[79] In the letter, Ulbricht presented, as usual, his proposals on *Berlin-* and *Deutschland-politik* and on Soviet economic aid. Ignoring Khrushchev's assertion on 30 November 1960 that they must undertake no action on Berlin until he met with Kennedy, Ulbricht laid out a series of maximal demands, particularly those connected with "eliminating the remnants of the occupation regime in Berlin." In a confident tone, Ulbricht nearly demanded that Khrushchev must agree to his proposals.

After beginning with a snide comment implying that Khrushchev had retreated from his initial resolve regarding the West, Ulbricht noted that their hard-line policies had reaped some success and more could be expected:

> Since Comrade Khrushchev's statement on the West Berlin question in November 1958, two years have flowed by. In this time the Soviet Union and the GDR have succeeded in getting many countries to acknowledge that the remnants of the war in Germany and the abnormal situation in West Berlin must be eliminated.
>
> ... The governments of the NATO countries are ... aware that negotiations in 1961 over the elimination of the abnormal situation in West Berlin are unavoidable.
>
> The possibilities to eliminate at least a part of the remnants of the war in West Berlin and Germany in 1961 are thus favorable, since the Adenauer government is not interested in a worsening of the situation in the period of the Bundestag election campaign, and President Kennedy in the first year of his presidency also does not want any aggravation of the situation.[80]

Given the ripeness of the situation, as Ulbricht saw it, he urged the broadening of their public "campaign ... in the entire world on the necessity of eliminating the remnants of the war in Germany and especially the abnormal situation in West Berlin." He detailed precisely what measures must be taken to "eliminate the remnants of the war." He set forth his maximal demands:

> The elimination of the occupation regime in West Berlin, i.e., the dissolution of the Kommandantura and the abolition of the rights exercised on the basis of the occupation status.
>
> The abolition of the military missions in West Berlin and the transfer of their functions to regular consulates which the states in question manage in the West Berlin Senate.
>
> The removal of all military and other agencies of foreign powers and the Bonn government from West Berlin.
>
> The renunciation by foreign states as well as the Bonn government of radio stations and other state and quasi-state organs which aid in the struggle against the socialist states.
>
> The reduction of foreign troops in West Berlin with the goal of beginning their complete withdrawal.
>
> The abolition of the agreement between the USSR and the Western Powers on the military missions of the Western Powers on GDR territory.
>
> The transfer of functions still existing in Four- or Three-Power organs, for example, the Central Air Control Office, the Bureau for Mail and Telecommunications, [and] the Travel Boards (Travel Offices), to the appropriate organ of the GDR or a settlement of these issues by treaty arrangements with the GDR and the West Berlin Senate.
>
> The management of transit traffic to and from West Berlin on the connecting routes of the GDR through regular treaties with the GDR. . . .
>
> . . . The regulation agreed upon between the Soviet government and the Western Powers on air traffic concerns only military traffic. Since presently civilian air companies of the Western Powers use the air corridors in illegal ways [to fly refugees from West Berlin to West Germany], it is important that a contractual regulation be made for civilian air traffic between the GDR and the states concerned.[81]

The last two demands would have given Ulbricht control over the ground and air routes between West Germany and West Berlin, enabling him to stem the refugee flow. By giving Ulbricht this control, the general pressure on West Berlin would significantly increase. This would make Westerners more wary of living there, sapping the city of energy, another of Ulbricht's goals.

Ulbricht must have known that the Western Powers would not acquiesce to most of his demands. He certainly realized that Khrushchev had been reluctant to implement or force these policy changes unilaterally. Yet Ulbricht pushed forward, hoping to change Khrushchev's mind.

Ulbricht called for the Soviets to take three steps. First, the Kremlin should issue a public Soviet statement on its economic commitment to the GDR. This would serve notice that "economic blackmail against the GDR will have no chance of success." To further demonstrate Soviet support for the GDR, Ulbricht requested a publicly announced East German–Soviet summit in April. This would have "the goal of raising the authority of the GDR in future negotiations" with the West about West Berlin and Germany. Finally, Ulbricht sought a Warsaw Pact meeting, because "[t]hus far, most of the Warsaw Pact states have considered the peaceful resolution of the German and West Berlin questions as a matter which only involves the Soviet Union and the GDR. Although they report in the press about these problems, they basically feel uninvolved in this matter."[82] Ulbricht wanted increased economic and diplomatic engagement by his East European socialist brothers to help achieve his economic and diplomatic aims.

Khrushchev, however, had a different agenda. His agenda at the time of Ulbricht's letter focused primarily on a meeting with Kennedy. Although the Kremlin leader expressed agreement with Ulbricht's proposal for these meetings in a letter on 30 January, the publicly announced Soviet–East German summit in fact did not take place. The Warsaw Pact did convene in March and August to discuss the German and Berlin issues, as we shall see.

In Ulbricht's 18 January letter, he was very concerned about the East German economy and hoped Khrushchev could negotiate an interim agreement for West Berlin to give more time to improve the GDR economic situation. Ulbricht detailed "several problems of the 1961 national economic plan which have not yet been able to be clarified." Ulbricht's portrayal of the GDR's economic difficulties would be crucial to obtaining Khrushchev's agreement to close the border around West Berlin in the future. He told Khrushchev in the letter that the FRG economy had advanced even further ahead of the GDR's economy in 1960, and economic problems in East Germany had caused workers strikes. The GDR could not pay its debts to the West, could not fulfill its economic goals for 1961, and desperately needed Soviet credits to avert a crisis. "If it is not possible to give us this credit, then we cannot maintain the standard of living of the population at the level of 1960. We would enter into such a serious situation in supplies and production that we would be faced with serious crisis manifestations." Whereas in 1953 the Soviets had to force the East Germans to see that they were facing a crisis, now in 1961 Ulbricht was warning Khrushchev of an impending crisis in the GDR. Ulbricht declared that there must be "a merger with the USSR economy. There is no other way." He also asserted that "the economic stabilization of the GDR is the key task in 1961 to decrease flight from the Republic."[83]

Confessing that "it is unpleasant for us that every year we must direct such requests for help to the CPSU CC Presidium," Ulbricht asked rhetorically what the reasons for the East German economic problems were and gave three answers. First, he pointed out that the GDR "was created without having and still does not have a raw material base," since the main German raw materials were located in West Germany.[84] Second, the GDR "carries out the competition between both systems with open borders." This is the only reference Ulbricht made to the open borders in this letter, relying more on indirect references to the difficulties East Berlin experienced, which would be alleviated by closing the sectoral border.

Third, stressing the need for economic aid, Ulbricht not so subtly explained to Khrushchev that if East Germany had received the kind of aid from Moscow that West Germany had from Washington in the first postwar decade, it would not have such serious economic problems:

> While in the first ten postwar years we paid reparations by the withdrawal of existing plants and from current production, West Germany made no compensation from current production and instead received in addition large credits from the USA to save the monopoly capital system and German militarism. We devoted many resources in the first ten years to bring production on line at Wismut and to sustain it.[85] Of course, this was all necessary to reduce at least a portion of the destruction which the Soviet Union had suffered, and to strengthen the Soviet Union as the center of the socialist camp. These circumstances, however, brought us enormous difficulties in the competition with West Germany. West Germany could make large investments and achieve an extraordinary modernization of the production apparat at a very early point on the basis of the millions [of dollars] of aid from the USA. Until the [Soviet] pardoning of [East German] reparations in 1954 the per-capita investment in West Germany was twice as high as in the GDR. . . .
>
> This is the main reason that we have remained so far behind West Germany in labor productivity and standard of living. Due to this, a constant political pressure from West Germany could be exercised over us. The booming economy in West Germany, which is visible to every citizen of the GDR, is the main reason that in over ten years about two million people have left our Republic.[86]

In effect, Ulbricht was blaming the Soviets for the current crisis, including the refugee exodus, and implying that they owed it to the GDR to redress their previous economic wrongs.

Guilt was not the only form of leverage Ulbricht exerted to prod Khrushchev toward action in 1961. Ulbricht sought to reap some benefits from the Sino-Soviet rift and sent a delegation led by Politburo member Hermann Matern to Peking in January.[87] The trip was planned without Soviet advance knowledge. Ulbricht no doubt intended to enhance the pressure on Moscow to grant significant economic aid and sign a peace treaty. The East German delegation stopped at the airport in Moscow on the way to Beijing. In answer to the surprised Soviets' questions about the goals of the trip, Matern assured the Soviets that they would only discuss economic issues with the Chinese, not political issues.[88] At the meetings in Beijing, however, the Chinese and East Germans discussed more than just economics. They compared their analogous concerns about West Berlin and Taiwan, which Foreign Minister Chen Yi said had "much in common." Harboring "romantic images of imagining that the Americans would give up both positions," Chen Yi declared that Beijing completely supported GDR policy regarding West Berlin.[89]

The GDR and PRC leaders both resented the "imperialist occupation" of West Berlin and Taiwan. They also both felt that the Soviets were not doing enough to help them "recover" these territories and tried to assist each other in their similar efforts.[90] As Chinese Premier Zhou Enlai would tell GDR Ambassador Hegen in June 1961: "The socialist camp has . . . two fronts, one in the East and one in the West, whereby the strategic front is the one in the West. Thus, we understand very well that the GDR has a heavy load to carry. . . . The main problem is Germany. The struggles on all fronts have direct or indirect relation to the struggle in Germany. Accordingly, we support your fight in Germany."[91]

Horst Brie, a former East German diplomat at the GDR embassy in Peking in the 1950s and early 1960s, observed "a tendency on the part of the East German party leadership to use the relationship with the PRC in bargaining with the Soviet Union." There was always an underlying feeling "that one day, the Soviet Union, in [the interest of] improving relations with the United States, would sacrifice East Germany." Thus, even in the midst of the Sino-Soviet split, the East Germans were eager to maintain good relations with the PRC, especially in the hope that the Chinese would support their aims regarding West Berlin and a peace treaty.[92] In courting Beijing, Ulbricht sought increased leverage on Khrushchev to pursue a tougher policy on Berlin.

Feeling strain from his dispute with the Chinese, Khrushchev's efforts to show the GDR he was a more reliable ally than China played into Ulbricht's plans. At the 30 November 1960 Soviet-GDR summit in Moscow, in the midst of a discussion about giving the GDR more economic assistance, Khrushchev urged more coordination of the two nations' economies and proposed: "Let us create joint enterprises on our territory. It is true that when we proposed similar things to Poland or China, they were against it. But we aren't China; we are not afraid of giving the Germans a start."[93] He also intimated that he had a more realistic understanding of East German needs than the Chinese did, that he appreciated the connection between GDR economic needs and political needs: "We understand this well. For the Chinese the moral factor seems to decide everything. But our people also make demands for butter and other things." Thus, unlike the Chinese who, according to Khrushchev, were long on moral and ideological discussions and short on actual economic aid, Khrushchev would help the GDR with the economic aid they needed, telling the East Germans "the needs of the GDR are also our needs."[94] Ulbricht took advantage of this attitude of Khrushchev's as much as possible.

WAITING FOR AN ANSWER FROM KENNEDY

Khrushchev responded to Ulbricht's 18 January epistle on 30 January. Khrushchev's letter was formal and lacking in emotion compared to Ulbricht's urgent, accusatory letter. He told Ulbricht that the "CPSU CC has discussed your letter carefully" and agreed with the measures proposed regarding Berlin, economic cooperation, and meetings of the East Germans and Soviets and the Warsaw Pact. While politely agreeing with Ulbricht in theory, however, Khrushchev put him on hold:

> We know that you are . . . of the view that, due to the present situation with a new American president in office, it is necessary and important to try to resolve the issue of a peace treaty with Germany and the normalization of the situation in West Berlin on the basis of an understanding with the USA as well as with the other Western powers. Currently, we are beginning to initiate a detailed discussion of these questions with Kennedy. The probe which we carried out shows that we need a little time until Kennedy stakes out his position on the German question more clearly and until it is clear whether the USA government wants to achieve mutually acceptable resolutions. . . .
>
> . . . [I]t is desirable that the measures dealt with in your letter, which under certain circumstances will prove necessary, be coupled with the conclusion of a peace treaty. If we do not succeed in coming to an understanding with Kennedy, we will, as agreed, choose together with you the time for their implementation.[95]

In fact, from the time of Kennedy's election in November 1960, Khrushchev had gone out of his way to show his interest in an improvement in U.S.-Soviet relations and a summit meeting of the two leaders, at which Khrushchev would discuss West Berlin. In mid-November, Khrushchev made overtures to Kennedy through New York Governor Averell Harriman and the Soviet ambassador in the United States, Mikhail Menshikov. On 1 December, President-Elect Kennedy's brother, Robert F. Kennedy, met with a Mr. B., who allegedly worked for the Moscow newspaper *Izvestiia*, but was really a KGB agent. RFK told Mr. B. that his brother needed three or four months to develop his policies and would then welcome a summit to discuss various issues, including Berlin, if it was likely to yield positive results. Regarding Berlin, RFK added that "if in the next few months the Soviet Union applies pressure on this question, then Kennedy will certainly defend the position of the West."[96] In mid-December, Menshikov told Harrison Salisbury of the *New York Times*: "'Time is of the essence.' The two leaders must meet before those who would not like to see agreement have had a chance to act and prevent it." The allusion to opponents to an agreement probably referred to conservatives in the United States and the communist bloc. Meanwhile, Khrushchev had begun using another Mr. B., Georgi Bolshakov, an undercover Soviet intelligence agent in Washington, as his direct link to President Kennedy through RFK.[97]

On 22 February, without proposing anything on Berlin, President Kennedy wrote to Khrushchev expressing the hope "that 'before too long' they might meet personally for an informal exchange of views."[98] In March, the Kennedy administration announced that its position on Germany and Berlin would not include the Eisenhower administration concessions at the 1959 Geneva CFM but would start from scratch. Kennedy's interest in a summit may have been influenced in part by Thompson's cable of 16 March 1961, predicting that "in the absence of negotiations Khrushchev will sign a separate peace treaty with East Germany and precipitate a Berlin crisis this year. [At that point,] we must at least expect the East Germans to seal off the Sector boundary in order to stop what they must consider [an] intolerable continuation of [the] refugee flow through Berlin."[99]

In March Kennedy commissioned Thompson to convey an invitation to Khrushchev "to meet in a neutral city. On 1 April, Khrushchev told Thompson that he wanted to go ahead with Kennedy's suggestion of a summit meeting in late May, in either Vienna or Stockholm." Kennedy then chose 3–4 June in Vienna.[100] Khrushchev's final agreement came after Kennedy's failure at the Bay of Pigs in Cuba and the Soviet success in launching the first man into space.[101] Khrushchev probably believed both would give him an advantage at the summit meeting.[102]

THE MARCH WARSAW PACT MEETING

Having received Kennedy's invitation to a summit, Khrushchev again sought to ensure that Ulbricht do nothing to complicate matters in Berlin in the meantime. At the meeting of the Warsaw Pact's Political Consultative Commission (PCC) in Moscow on 28–29 March, Khrushchev reiterated that further action on Berlin was contingent on the outcome of his meeting with Kennedy. Indeed, in his speech on 28 March Khruschev notified the Warsaw Pact members that he intended to give the new

Kennedy administration a chance to come to terms on Berlin in a summit with him and that only if the summit was unsuccessful would the socialist countries then go ahead and act on their own and actually sign a separate peace treaty, with all the military and economic risks that would entail.[103] The main Soviet goal at the WTO meeting was to "strengthen the power and defense readiness of the entire socialist camp." Khrushchev told his allies that "the organizational structure of the troops, their arming with weapons and combat equipment, especially with rockets, tanks, modern planes and radios, do not correspond entirely to modern requirements. [He asserted the] need to take measures to arm the military forces with modern weapons and improve their technical outfitting. . . . The international situation does not allow us to postpone this for long."[104] Accordingly, the top-secret resolutions at the end of the WTO meeting called for enhancing military readiness, armaments, and military technology, and for the further specialization of military production.[105]

While Khrushchev's plan to upgrade the WTO with modern weapons stemmed from his belief that nuclear weapons had revolutionized international and military affairs, he clearly also sought to bolster his military capacity specifically to back up his campaign regarding West Berlin and a German peace treaty and to be ready to act alone if there was no agreement with Kennedy.[106] The final communiqué of the meeting, published on 31 March, called for a German peace treaty and West Berlin's transformation into a "free city."[107]

The accessible record of the August WTO meeting refers explicitly to the March discussions regarding Berlin and Germany. In the August protocols, Khrushchev made two references to the March session. In his opening speech on 3 August, Khrushchev reminded the WTO members: "At the last session of the Political Consultative Committee . . . we came to the unanimous opinion that if as a result of the meeting with Kennedy and other contacts, the Western powers did not show readiness to find a real path for the resolution of the question of a peace treaty with two German states, then our countries would start preparing to conclude a peace treaty with the GDR."[108] Khrushchev gave more detail the next day: "During our last meeting, we discussed how the preparation for the conclusion of a peace treaty would go and how those countries to whom we appeal would react[. W]e expected that they would exert opposition to us—they would intimidate us, calling all spirits against us so as to test our courage, our understanding, our will."[109] This expectation contributed to Khrushchev's decision to strengthen the WTO's armed forces, weaponry, and organization. In fact, the next month Soviet forces began to prepare for a military escalation of the Berlin Crisis, including increasing the number of Soviet troops in the GDR and updating their equipment.[110]

In their March WTO speeches, neither Khrushchev nor Ulbricht said anything about closing the border around West Berlin and building a wall. The only evidence we have of this being discussed at the March meeting comes from the testimony provided by Jan Sejna, who was the Czechoslovak minister of defense. According to Sejna, "Ulbricht put forward a proposal to make crossing the border from East to West Berlin impossible. . . . But none of the Warsaw Pact states agreed, [and] Romania opposed it especially vehemently."[111] Ulbricht reportedly declared that the refugee problem was becoming so great that the border controls had to be strengthened and supplemented by a barbed wire barrier on the sectoral border in Berlin. The Soviets and other Warsaw Pact allies, however, felt that this action would be too provocative, perhaps even leading to war with the West (in the words of Romanian leader Gheorghiu-Dej), and would "cause serious harm to the reputation of the entire communist movement" (in the words of Hungarian leader Kadar).[112] Instead, Khrushchev would continue to strive for negotiations with Kennedy, while monitoring the refugee crisis. In the meantime, Ulbricht was told that he could "prepare everything for a future contingency" under conditions of great secrecy. There is as yet no confirmation of this account in accessible archival documents.

Honoré M. Catudal claims that Ulbricht's plan for a wall had apparently "been drawn up in the 1950s by the SED Planning Commission and was known to American and West German intelligence agents as 'Operation Chinese Wall.'" The plan, which "provided for the eventual replacement of the fence of barbed wire with a concrete wall and palisades [had been] lying on ice for some time before the West obtained a copy in July 1958."[113] Curtis Cate maintains that the original plans for a wall were developed in 1952 by then Stasi chief, Wilhelm Zaisser, to retaliate against the expected formation of the (West) European Defense Community (EDC).[114] The border between the two parts of Germany, although not between the two parts of Berlin, was in fact closed in the summer of 1952.

In the available copy of Ulbricht's 29 March speech to the WTO, he spoke of West German economic and military pressure on the GDR, the urgency of signing a peace treaty and transforming West Berlin into a free city, and the need to make the GDR economy independent from the FRG. After describing hostile West German economic measures directed against the GDR such as limiting the supply of certain crucial goods and luring away its skilled workers, Ulbricht told the gathering: "In this economic and political struggle against our Republic, West Berlin plays the role of the channel with whose help this trade in people is practiced, and through which also food and other materials flow out of our Republic. West Berlin is therefore a big hole in the middle of our Republic, which costs us more than a billion marks each year."[115] Thus, while Ulbricht did not come right out and say that he wanted the West Berlin "hole" to be plugged, it was the clear implication of his remarks.[116]

Pressure from East Berlin before Vienna

In the two months between the WTO meeting and the Vienna summit, Khrushchev's attention was directed toward Kennedy, and Ulbricht's attention was focused on the refugee problem. Ulbricht's efforts to stem the refugee flow were not meeting with success. As a Soviet report in early April noted, "the efforts of our friends to impede the exodus of the populace to the West by introducing a passport law establishing a stricter process of granting permission for temporary departure to the FRG and introducing control over the railroads and highways leading to Berlin have not yielded the expected results."[117] In spite of Khrushchev's admonition not to take anymore aggressive measures to deal with the refugee exodus before Khrushchev met with Kennedy, Ulbricht felt increasing pressure to act. In fact, Ambassador Pervukhin wrote Foreign Minister Gromyko on 19 May that the East Germans wanted to close the Berlin sectoral border immediately and were not following Soviet policy:

> Our friends would like to establish now such control on the sectoral border between democratic and West Berlin which would allow them to, as they say, close "the door to the West" and reduce the exodus of the population from the Republic and weaken the influence of economic conspiracy against the GDR, which is carried out directly from West Berlin.
>
> Trying to liquidate the remnants of the occupation period as soon as possible, our German friends sometimes exercise impatience and a somewhat unilateral approach to this problem, not always studying the interests of the entire socialist camp or the international situation at the given moment. Evidence of this, for example, is their efforts to stop free movement between the GDR and West Berlin as soon as possible with any means, which in the present conditions would complicate carrying out the struggle for a peace treaty.[118]

This was precisely what Khrushchev sought to avoid, fearing that such East German behavior could cause President Kennedy to call off the summit. Pervukhin's assistant, Yuli Kvitsinsky, recollects efforts to restrain the East Germans:

> We in the embassy and in [MID's] Third European Department felt then and repeated again and again to the Germans since the spring of 1961 that we had

to show more restraint, that if we took measures to limit movement across the border, this would make our position on the creation of a free city in West Berlin less persuasive, that it would injure our initiatives regarding the conclusion of a peace treaty.[119]

Both Pervukhin and Kvitsinsky understood that East German efforts to limit movement across, or to close, the Berlin sectoral border would be incompatible with an effort to negotiate a Four Power peace treaty with Germany and agreement on West Berlin. The Soviet focus was on the latter issues, and the East German focus was on the former. Pervukhin noted that East German concerns were directed toward procuring "control of the sectoral border [and] full control over all GDR territory, including full control over the links between West Berlin and the FRG that go through the GDR," rather than on a peace treaty per se.[120]

On the specific issue of West Berlin, Pervukhin expressed frustration that the East Germans did not understand or support "the measures of the Soviet embassy, and also [of] the embassies of other socialist countries (Czechoslovakia and Poland) in the GDR on the development of direct contacts with West Berlin."[121] Instead, the East Germans displayed an "inconsistent" and clearly "restrained attitude" toward these measures. As noted above, these measures, initiated by the Soviets the previous summer, included more Soviet–West Berlin direct contacts in the areas of science, culture, tourism, the press, trade, and politics in an effort to replace Soviet for Western influence in West Berlin. No matter what the supposed goals of these expanded contacts were, the East Germans did not support them, fearing that the contacts would strengthen the position of West Berlin instead of undermining and isolating it.

In addition to East German–Soviet disagreements over contacts with West Berlin, Pervukhin also pointed to differences over the issue of a separate peace treaty. He asserted that East German attitudes toward a separate peace treaty "show a clear inconsistency" and "some vacillation." On the one hand, they "support the speedy conclusion of a peace treaty with the GDR" as the means to gain control over the access routes and enhance prestige. They believed that in the aftermath of this separate peace treaty, "the Western powers and the West Berlin Senate will be forced to enter negotiations with the GDR on resolving all issues of interest to them regarding West Berlin by concluding agreements with the GDR. The realization of these measures, as our friends believe, must lead in the end to de facto recognition of the GDR by the Western powers."[122]

On the other hand, the East Germans also had some important concerns about signing a separate peace treaty. First, "they fear[ed] that this act would present the GDR to the world public as the party responsible for the division of Germany." Signing a separate peace treaty might give the impression that they had given up on German unification and were willing to solidify the division legally in a peace treaty. Second, the separate peace treaty "would not resolve such an important national task of the German people as staving off West German militarism." The East Germans' most important concern with signing a separate treaty, however, was economic. They believed that "the GDR and even the Soviet Union [were] not ready economically for the conclusion of a peace treaty with the GDR," which the East Germans were certain would be answered by a West German economic boycott of the GDR and perhaps even a NATO-wide economic boycott of the Soviet bloc. Given that the "GDR industry at the present time is significantly dependent on the FRG supply of a variety of very scarce metals," the GDR economy would clearly suffer from such a boycott. Pervukhin agreed, with these East German reservations:

> Considering that neither in this year nor in 1962 will the Soviet Union and other socialist countries be in a position to completely satisfy all the declared needs of the GDR in these materials, and also considering the necessity of seriously reconstructing the mechanical engineering industry of the GDR so as to liberate it from economic dependence on the FRG, our friends have grounds for concern about possible difficulties in connection with concluding a peace treaty with the GDR.[123]

The best way to gain the necessary time for the economic and political situation in the GDR to improve was to come to an interim agreement with the West at the upcoming summit with President Kennedy. Pervukhin urged the Soviet government to fight for a provisional solution on West Berlin, "the preconditions of which were outlined already during the Geneva Conference of Foreign Ministers in 1959."[124] This provisional agreement would "allow" the Western powers to maintain their rights in Berlin for a certain limited period of time while an all-German commission made plans for reunification and a peace treaty.

The Soviets could understandably have concluded from Pervukhin's report that not much had changed in the GDR in the two and half years since Khrushchev had launched the Berlin Crisis, or even since the uprising of 1953: The GDR still needed more time to become stronger and more competitive with the FRG. The Soviets were continually trying to buy time to stabilize East Germany economically and politically, but time was running out, along with the refugees.

PREPARATIONS FOR VIENNA

Just before leaving Moscow for the Vienna Summit, Khrushchev bluntly told U.S. Ambassador Thompson that if he did not reach an agreement with Kennedy on Berlin, he would sign a separate peace treaty with the GDR after the West German elections in September and the Soviet Twenty-second Party Congress in October.[125] He said the same thing to Antonin Novotny and the other leaders of Czechoslovakia on 1 June when he stopped to meet with them at the Czechoslovak Communist Party resort in Smolenice, near Bratislava. Among other things, Khrushchev told the Czechs how he planned to raise the West Berlin and peace treaty issues with Kennedy at Vienna:

> What is our position at the current time? We think that we cannot further postpone the conclusion of a peace treaty with Germany, that all terms have already expired. If only from the point of view of the GDR, from the point of view of c[omrade] Ulbricht. You yourselves know very well what problems are created by the current situation, how West Germany disturbs economic construction in the GDR by means of enticing its specialists to the West. We can't tolerate this any more.[126]

Khrushchev made it clear that Ulbricht was putting pressure on him to act to protect the GDR economy. Khrushchev said he would propose to Kennedy that a peace treaty be signed within six months, but he did not expect Kennedy to agree.[127] Indeed, a profile of Kennedy prepared by the Soviet chargé d'affaires in Washington, Mikhail Smirnovski, noted that on "the Berlin question, Kennedy's position is outright bellicose; he openly announces that the USA should sooner start a nuclear war than leave Berlin."[128] Accordingly, Khrushchev expected he would have to sign a separate peace treaty with the GDR.

The next question was how the West would respond to this separate treaty. Khrushchev declared himself "95 percent" certain that the West would not go to war over West Berlin:

> Neither Macmillan, nor de Gaulle, nor even Adenauer will go to war. . . . As far as Kennedy is concerned, that's hard to say. The smartest politician in the USA in recent years was [John Foster] Dulles. We always knew what to expect with him. And Dulles wouldn't have gone to war. . . . There isn't such a politician now in the USA as Dulles was. We don't know Kennedy yet. The events in Cuba show that he isn't very clever. . . . [If we sign a peace treaty with the GDR, we don't think they will break off diplomatic or trade relations with us; rather] we think the US will limit itself to some sort of statement of protest and stop at that. Of course signing a peace treaty will cause a certain amount of exacerbation of the situation and will entail a certain risk. But such is life. Lenin also took a risk in carrying out the October Revolution in a semi-literate country, and that was a much greater risk. Today we are in a completely different position. We have missiles, we sent a man into space, and the general situation in the world is advantageous to us. What will happen if we don't

sign a peace treaty? We will lose a lot. They will say about us that we only talk, but don't do anything, thus that we are afraid. We cannot allow this. It is a tough nut, but we must crack it. . . . I'm sure things won't go as far as war. We aren't afraid and will sign a peace treaty.[129]

Two days before meeting with Kennedy, Khrushchev fully expected that the Vienna summit would not resolve the problems of Germany and Berlin. He was, therefore, prepared to sign a separate peace treaty with the GDR between October and December. He did, however, feel that he "didn't know Kennedy yet" and wanted to make sure that Kennedy would not respond militarily to the separate peace treaty. Accordingly, a key goal of Khrushchev's at Vienna was to determine how firmly Kennedy was prepared to defend Western rights in West Berlin, rights that Khrushchev planned to abolish with a separate peace treaty.

Kennedy and his advisors seemed to understand the need to demonstrate firmness with regard to West Berlin. Kennedy remarked to Macmillan on 6 April that "obviously the deterrent effect of our response keeps the Communists from engaging us in a major struggle on Berlin. It is necessary to keep the fact of the deterrent well forward."[130] A State Department position paper of 25 May observed: "Although Khrushchev is undoubtedly reluctant to risk a major war, the real danger is that he might risk just such a war without realizing he is doing so. He must, therefore, be warned in the firmest and most solemn manner that the US has no intention whatsoever of being forced out of Berlin and that in any attempt to do so he would be taking the gravest possible risk."[131] The deputy chief of the U.S. Mission in West Berlin, Edwin A. (Allan) Lightner, gave similar advice, showing great prescience regarding the mood and substance of the discussion that would occur at Vienna. He argued in customary cabelese that the

Vienna meeting provides opportunity, perhaps one of last opportunities, to convince Khrushchev of U.S. determination make good on Berlin pledges regardless of consequences.

Fact that Khrushchev will attempt convince President of his own determination solve Berlin along familiar Soviet-GDR lines only serves to emphasize importance this psychological duel at Vienna. I believe Soviet toughness re their Berlin intentions reflects serious desire change Berlin status, but also includes large element of bluff. I doubt Sov resolve is sufficient to risk thermonuclear war. Therefore, at this stage, U.S. must be even tougher if Khrushchev is to go away from Vienna convinced his threats are too risky to warrant carrying them out.

I realize President in first meeting with Khrushchev will not wish appear unreasonable; however, any indication President willing discuss "interim solutions," compromises, or modus vivendi if Sovs sign separate peace treaty, would reduce impact of warning Khrushchev of dire consequences of his miscalculating our resolve. . . .

In sum, Vienna will be psychological testing ground and U.S. position on Berlin in my view should be molded carefully to create strongest possible impression on Khrushchev of U.S. firmness of intention on Berlin in effort to deter him further from course of action he has been threatening since Nov 1958.[132]

Kennedy definitely understood the need to display firmness to Khrushchev, but was unsure about how to do this. On his way to Vienna, he met with de Gaulle on 31 May: "The President said the question was how to make the Western position believed by Mr. Khrushchev. There is a danger that he might not believe in our firmness." In his meetings with de Gaulle, Kennedy seemed at a loss regarding how to handle Khrushchev and the Berlin problem: "If Mr. Khrushchev signs a treaty with the GDR, this in itself is no reason for a military retaliation on our part. If the GDR starts stamping travel documents, this is not, per se, a cause for military action either. In what way, therefore, at what moment, shall we bring our pressure to bear?"[133] Kennedy found it hard enough to answer this question based on U.S. interests, but formulating a Western consensus on the response to Soviet and East German salami tactics was even more difficult, as Khrushchev and Ulbricht understood it would be.

THE VIENNA SUMMIT

Kennedy gave Khrushchev two strong messages at their summit of 3–4 June. First, the West would not under any circumstances relinquish its presence in West Berlin, its access to West Berlin, and its support for the democratic-capitalist system in West Berlin (the so-called three essentials). Second, anything beyond this, agreed to by the Soviets and East Germans in a separate peace treaty, was not a matter of concern to the United States. Kennedy drew a clear line in the sand for Khrushchev at Vienna, and Khrushchev saw it clearly. The stance taken on these issues by Kennedy at Vienna conveyed two things to Khrushchev: Signing a separate peace treaty and turning over control of the access routes to the GDR would be too risky; but closing the border around West Berlin to prevent East Berliners and East Germans from escaping would not be.

As Khrushchev and Ulbricht had agreed, and Pervukhin had advised, Khrushchev urged Kennedy several times at Vienna to agree to an interim arrangement on Berlin, similar to the one discussed in 1959.[134] However, as Lightner and others had counseled, Kennedy refused. Khrushchev repeated his demands that West Berlin be transformed into a demilitarized free city and that a Geman peace treaty be signed within six months or he would sign a separate peace treaty, turning over control of the access routes to the GDR. Kennedy firmly rebuffed this idea, reasoning: "If the U.S. were driven out of West Berlin by unilateral action, and if we were deprived of our contractual rights by East Germany, then no one would believe the US now or in the future. US commitments would be regarded as a mere scrap of paper." He went on to emphasize that "the US is committed to that area and it is so regarded by all the world. If we accepted Mr. Khrushchev's suggestion [for the withdrawal of Western troops from West Berlin,] the world would lose confidence in the US and would not regard it as a serious country. It is an important strategic matter that the world believe the US is a serious country." While Kennedy "recognized that the situation in Germany was abnormal," he did not believe that it was "the right time now to change the situation in Berlin and the balance in general."[135]

Insisting that his motives were defensive, not offensive as Kennedy seemed to believe, Khrushchev declared:

> The USSR does not wish any change; it merely wants to formalize the situation which has resulted from World War II. The fact is that West Germany is in the Western group of nations and the USSR recognizes this. East Germany is an ally of the socialist countries and this should be recognized as a fait accompli. East Germany has new demarcation lines and these lines should become borders. . . . The position of the GDR should be normalized and her sovereignty ensured. To do all this it is necessary to eliminate the occupation rights in West Berlin. No such rights should exist there.

Frustrated that Kennedy did not understand the logic of his position, the Soviet leader stated that "he was very sorry but he had to assure the President that no force in the world would prevent the USSR from signing a peace treaty . . . probably . . . at the end of the year, with all the ensuing consequences, i.e., all obligations will come to an end."[136] The United States and others would then have to come to agreements with the GDR on matters concerning West Berlin.

Several times in two separate meetings with Khrushchev on 4 June, Kennedy pressed Khrushchev about whether a separate Soviet-GDR peace treaty would affect Western rights in West Berlin and access to West Berlin, and Khrushchev repeatedly affirmed that it would. Kennedy underlined in their morning conversation: "The question is not that of a peace treaty with East Germany but rather of other aspects of this proposal which would affect our access to Berlin and our rights there." A little later in the conversation, Kennedy again stated that "the signing of a peace treaty is not a belligerent act. . . . However, a peace treaty denying us our contractual rights is a belligerent act. The matter of a peace treaty with East Germany is a matter for Mr. Khrushchev's judgment and is not a belligerent act. What is a belligerent act is transfer of our rights to East Germany."[137] That afternoon at a private meeting with only interpreters present, Kennedy pressed the point one final time and "stress[ed] the difference between a peace treaty and the rights of access to Berlin."[138]

Kennedy could not have said more to make it clear to Khrushchev that what he cared about was the Western presence in West Berlin and access to West Berlin and not about issues such as the situation in East Berlin and movement from East to West Berlin. And he definitely stated that the United States would view the transfer of its rights regarding West Berlin to the GDR as "a belligerent act," one that would necessitate the U.S. use of force, precisely what Khrushchev wanted to avoid.

Khrushchev bluffed his way through the end of the meeting, and in their final meeting told Kennedy: "It is up to the U.S. to decide whether there will be war or peace. The decision to sign a peace treaty is firm and irrevocable and the Soviet Union will sign it in December if the US refuses an interim agreement." He also declared that "if [Kennedy] insisted on US rights after the signing of a peace treaty and that if the borders of the GDR—land, air, or sea borders—were violated, they would be defended. . . . [F]orce would be met with force. . . . [I]f the US wanted war, that was its problem."[139] Kennedy responded: "Then, Mr. Chairman, there will be war. It will be a cold winter."[140] Khrushchev left Kennedy with an aide-memoire that repeated his ultimatum on West Berlin and Germany.

Moving toward Action

Now that Khrushchev's summit with Kennedy had failed on Berlin, it was time for the Soviet leader to move ahead with plans to sign a separate peace treaty with GDR, as he had indicated he would at the March Warsaw Pact meeting. Concerns about the GDR's economy and the economic repercussions of signing a separate peace treaty brought Soviet Vice Premier Anastas Mikoian to East Berlin for economic talks two days after the Vienna summit. Mikoian's remarks to the East Germans during these talks gave strong expression to the Soviet view of the special role of socialism in the GDR, which had been at the heart of Khrushchev's treatment of it for several years. In assuring the East Germans of more economic aid, Mikoian told Leuschner and his deputies that the GDR

is the western-most outpost of the socialist camp. Therefore, many, very many [people] look at the GDR. Our Marxist-Leninist theory must prove itself in the GDR. It must be demonstrated in the GDR that what the capitalists and renegades say is wrong.

The GDR, Germany, is the country in which it must be decided that Marxism-Leninism is correct, that communism is also the higher, better, social order for industrial states. And since this is so, the proving of socialism in Germany is, therefore, not just your affair. . . . Marxism was born in Germany and it must prove its correctness and value here in a highly developed industrial state. We must do everything so that your development constantly and steadily goes forward. You cannot do this alone. The Soviet Union must and will help with this. . . . We cannot and must not lose out to West Germany.

If socialism does not win in the GDR, if communism does not prove itself as superior and vital here, then we have not won. The issue is this fundamental to us. Therefore, we cannot proceed in such a way with any other country. And this is also the reason that the GDR occupies first place in negotiations or in credits.[141]

This ideological commitment enabled Ulbricht to extract additional aid from the Kremlin and avoid altering his own policies in order to persuade East German citizens not to flee to the West.

After the unsuccessful summit with Kennedy, it was even more important for the Soviets to shore up the GDR. The negative outcome of the summit stimulated the refugee flow. In addition to the other reasons for leaving, in the summer of 1961 East Germans were also fleeing to the West for fear that this option might soon be foreclosed. While 17,791 East Germans had fled in May, 19,198 fled in June, and 12,578 in the first two weeks of July.[142] A Soviet embassy report at the end of June observed that the public pressure on West Berlin since 1958 led many to "fear that this question will be resolved in the near future and that all paths for their exit to West Germany will be closed. Therefore some try to go to West Germany before it's too late."[143] This *Torschlusspanik* hastened the exodus of over 1,000 East Germans daily in July and the beginning of August.[144] Whereas one of the initial goals of Khrushchev and Ulbricht in the Berlin Crisis had been to change the situation in Berlin and Germany in order to stem the refugee exodus, their efforts to accomplish this instead helped accelerate and expand it. This effect of their policies was not lost on the Soviets and East Germans. Some observers have speculated that Ulbricht may have acted precisely to increase this exodus so that Khrushchev would be forced to agree to his firm measures.[145] While this author has found no documents even hinting at this, it would not have been out of character for Ulbricht to act in such a way.

Ulbricht was not the only East German official who sought to close the Berlin border to stop the refugees. On 10 June, Soviet attaché Yuli

Kvitsinski met with E. Hüttner of the GDR Foreign Ministry's Department on the Soviet Union. Hüttner described a recent meeting of lower level officials with senior SED leaders. Peter Florin, the director of the Central Committee's Department of International Relations, had told the group that "the further dragging out of the signing of a peace treaty is a crime." With a peace treaty, "the GDR is ready for just about any economic sacrifices" in facing the probable ensuing West German economic blockade. The meeting participants, however, were reassured that "the economic losses in connection with the conclusion of a peace treaty then will be compensated for by the . . . stopping of the exodus of the population to the West." Hüttner asked "whether this meant that as a result of the conclusion of a peace treaty with the GDR the sectoral border in Berlin would be closed." As he told Kvitsinsky, "People from the CC Department [of International Relations] said that if this did not occur immediately after the signing of a peace treaty, corresponding measures at the sectoral border would be taken sooner or later in one or another form."[146] Thus, in early June top SED officials spoke openly about their assumption that the Berlin sectoral border would be closed in the relatively near future. Kvitsinksi was concerned about this.

In another demonstration of Soviet–East German discord, Hermann Axen, a CC secretary and the chief editor of the party newspaper *Neues Deutschland*, told a Soviet Embassy official that

> . . . the Soviet Union declares, for example, that with the signature of a German peace treaty, the three Western Powers will lose all of their rights in regard to West Berlin. The GDR, however, has a somewhat different position on this issue. We declare that there are no existing rights of the three Western Powers regarding West Berlin in general, since the representatives of the GDR were not present at Teheran or in the Crimea or at Potsdam, and therefore it is in no way connected with the agreements achieved there. Comrade W. Ulbricht has repeatedly spoken on this issue in precisely the same spirit.[147]

Axen, Ulbricht, and others clearly were not intimidated from expressing their differences with Khrushchev and Soviet policy on Berlin.

Ulbricht's press conference of 15 June 1961—which, contrary to normal practice, East Berlin officials went out of their way to invite West Berlin-based correspondents to—may very well have been designed to prod Khrushchev toward sealing the border.[148] At the press conference, Ulbricht made it clear that a separate peace treaty with the GDR would give East German authorities control over the access routes to Berlin, which would presumably allow them to stop the West from flying East German refugees out of West Berlin to West Germany. With regard to Ulbricht's demand that West Berlin be transformed into a demilitarized free city, Annamarie Doherr of the *Frankfurter Rundschau* asked Ulbricht: "Does the formation of a Free City in your opinion mean that the state boundary will be erected at the Brandenburg Gate?" Ulbricht answered:

> I understand by your question that there are men in West Germany who wish that we [would] mobilize the construction workers of the GDR in order to build a wall. I don't know of any such intention. The construction workers of our country are principally occupied with home building and their strength is completely consumed by this task. No one has the intention of building a wall.[149]

This is the first known mention of building a wall in Berlin and implies that it was at least an option under discussion by the East Germans and Soviets if not yet settled on. In light of the fact that a wall was built two months later, there are a variety of ways to read Ulbricht's statement. First, Ulbricht could have been telling the truth. It may be that there was no agreement at the time to build a wall, just plans to sign a separate peace treaty and turn over control of the access routes to the GDR, coupled with tighter controls over or even a closing of the Berlin sectoral border, although without a wall.[150] Second, Ulbricht may have been nervous and slipped. In light of later evidence on the extreme secrecy surrounding the decision to close the border around West Berlin and build the Berlin Wall, it is unlikely that Ulbricht would have deliberately mentioned anything about it in public. After lobbying so long and hard for permission from Khrushchev to close the border, Ulbricht would not have wanted to do anything that might make Khrushchev less likely to agree. A third possibility is that Ulbricht deliberately made the comments about the wall knowing that this would stimulate panic in the GDR and accelerate the exodus. Khrushchev would then feel compelled to finally acquiesce in closing the border and signing a separate peace treaty. In light of the archival evidence, Norman Gelb's argument is convincing:

> At that stage, despite his ultimatum to Kennedy [at Vienna], Nikita Khrushchev wasn't sure he wanted to risk a showdown by handing control of the western access routes to Berlin over to Ulbricht, with the implied backing of Soviet forces in East Germany. Nor had he yet decided, as an alternative, to let the East Germans take action to stop the refugees. . . .
>
> Now, to the great annoyance of the Soviets, Ulbricht . . . was trying to force the pace and thus preclude another Khrushchevian climb-down. . . .
>
> Ulbricht could not act against the wishes of the Kremlin. But he could influence events and attitudes. His presence at the press conference and his comments implying that West Berlin would soon be his to do with as he pleased

were calculated to raise the level of tension already building in the city, and they did.[151]

The number of refugees rose dramatically the next day, "as the East German leader must have known it would." Ulbricht was seeking to shape events. Although he "could not act against the wishes of the Kremlin, . . . he could influence events and attitudes."[152]

Not long after the press conference, Pervukhin told him that Ulbricht "wanted a consultation of the first secretaries of the communist and workers' parties of the countries of the Warsaw Pact as soon as possible" for the preparation of separate peace treaty with the GDR.[153] This was precisely the kind of meeting Ulbricht originally had requested five months earlier. After speaking with Pervukhin, Ulbricht wrote Khrushchev on 24 June, saying that he would contact the East European leaders about having consultations on preparations for a peace treaty.[154] Ulbricht proposed having the meeting in Moscow on 20–21 July. He also attached for Khrushchev's response the SED's proposed "Measures against *Grenzgänger*" to be taken *before* the signing of a peace treaty.[155]

The CPSU CC Presidium met on 29 June to consider Ulbricht's request for the Warsaw Pact meeting.[156] In a resolution on 30 June, the Presidium members commissioned Pervukhin to inform Ulbricht that they had accepted his proposal for a meeting "on the exchange of views on issues connected with the preparation and conclusion of a peace treaty." They set the date for 3 August. Pervukhin was told to inform Ulbricht that the other issues in his letter, such as the measures concerning *Grenzgänger*, could be discussed when he came to Moscow in August.[157]

Florin had been in Moscow just before the 29 June Soviet Presidium meeting.[158] Florin noted that there were unofficial reports indicating that the Chinese felt that the Soviets were moving too quickly on the peace treaty issue and that compromises should be explored more thoroughly.[159] According to diplomatic reports reaching East Berlin later, the Chinese were not happy with Khrushchev's renewed deadline to Kennedy at Vienna:

> The Chinese were very worried when the Soviet Union made the proposal to resolve the issue of a peace treaty with Germany absolutely in this year, since it was clear to them that due to the complicated situation in Europe and the expected resistance of the Western powers, especially the USA, military conflicts could occur which could lead to a great war. Due to their concern about this, the Chinese comrades were very restrained for a period on this issue.[160]

Contrary to the usual assumption that the Chinese were pushing Khrushchev to be hard-line in the crisis, this evidence suggests a different Chinese role.[161] A Soviet MID report in the summer of 1961 cited statements by top Chinese officials urging the Soviets to exercise extreme care and find a compromise with the West on Berlin, since "small wars are possible now in Laos, Algeria, [and] Taiwan, but not in Berlin," where a conflict would lead to large-scale warfare. The Chinese felt that "on the German question one should not act in such a categorical way as the USSR is."[162] Thus, while the Chinese were publicly (as well as in meetings with the Soviets) accusing the Soviets of yielding too much to the West, in private they feared that Khrushchev's policies on Germany and Berlin might embroil them in a world war.[163]

In his speech to the thirteenth SED plenum on 3 July 1961, Ulbricht was convinced that a German peace treaty would be signed in the next few months, transferring to the GDR control over all transit routes on GDR territory to West Berlin by land, sea, and air.[164] Ulbricht told the CC members that Khrushchev had warned Kennedy that they would not wait until West Germany finished its atomic armament to sign a peace treaty and resolve the West Berlin situation.[165] He also spoke of measures to be taken against the *Grenzgänger*. Ulbricht's "Peace Plan of the German People" spoke of the need for all East German officials and citizens to be firm in carrying out their duties in the preparation for a peace treaty over the next few months.

Whether to Seal the Border with West Berlin or Take Control of the Western Access Routes

On 4 July Pervukhin sent a detailed sixteen-page report to Gromyko analyzing "practical measures which will arise from the forthcoming conclusion of a peace treaty with the GDR, which could be used in the preparation of materials for the negotiations with our German friends."[166] Pervukhin did not doubt that a peace treaty with the GDR would be signed soon. In the wake of the peace treaty, Pervukhin was concerned about how East Germany would stop the refugee flow. More than 100,000 refugees fled the GDR in the first half of 1961, and the *Torschlusspanik* grew worse over the summer.[167] Western airplanes from West Berlin to the FRG were filled with East German refugees.[168]

Pervukhin told Gromyko that to halt the refugee exodus, there were "two paths—we can either introduce effective control over the movement of the German population between West Berlin and the FRG on all means of transportation, including air, or close the sectoral border in Berlin." The question was at which stage of escape they would stop the refugees—in their initial attempt to leave the GDR/East Berlin and enter West Berlin, or in their onward journey from West Berlin to the FRG. Pervukhin argued for attempting the latter first, while leaving "the regime on the sectoral border in Berlin without fundamental changes."[169]

To do this, he called for designating the one Berlin-area airport lo-

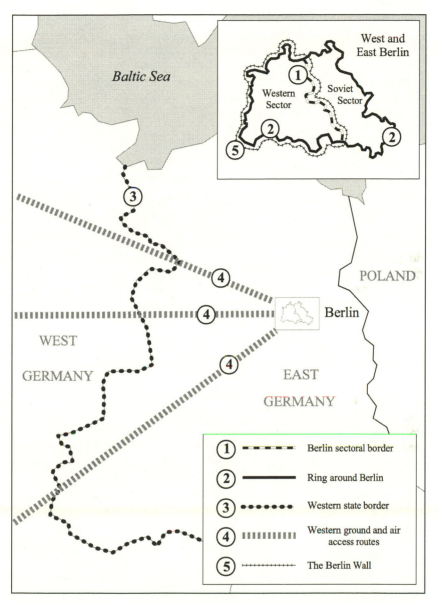

Map 3. Five Places to Stop the Refugees

cated in the GDR, Schönefeld, the main airport for Berlin, instead of the two airports located in the West, Tempelhof and Gatow. He also advocated closing down the Four Power Berlin Center for Air Security and replacing it with a GDR authority. Pervukhin assumed that by making it much more difficult for refugees to fly from West Berlin to West Germany, they would be less likely to flee from the GDR. Pervukhin noted, though, that it was unlikely that the West would acquiesce to GDR control of the air corridors and that accordingly "the GDR must have at its disposal at the moment of the signing of the peace treaty all technical means for detecting planes violating its air space and also the airports and the necessary number of military planes for the forced landing of violating planes."[170] This image of the GDR forcing Western planes to land probably ensured that Khrushchev, seeking to avoid war, would not turn over control of the air corridors to the GDR.

Pervukhin also argued that in addition to gaining control over air traffic between West Berlin and the FRG, if the Berlin sectoral border remained open, "our friends should examine the question of the possible introduction of a visa regime" on the automobile and train transit routes between West Berlin and the FRG. He was worried about this, however, forecasting that

> a visa system would lead to great inconveniences for Germans and would cause displeasure both in the FRG and West Berlin. Therefore, at first we should keep the transit order unchanged. If GDR control over the transit routes through the checking of documents by the border police does not lead to a reduction of the exodus of the GDR population through West Berlin, then we will have to introduce a visa regime on the transit routes . . . and in the extreme case close the sectoral border in Berlin. It is obvious that in both cases we would have to expect political difficulties.[171]

Pervukhin reported that "[a]bout 250,000 people now cross the sectoral border in Berlin every day, mainly on the S-bahn [the city train], the Ü-bahn [the subway], by foot and also in cars. The GDR police carry out selective checking of people crossing the sectoral border into West Berlin, but in practice cannot really arrest citizens illegally leaving the GDR." In order to deal directly with the problem of East Germans getting to West Berlin, Pervukhin put forward three options: first, "introducing restrictive measures" for East Germans to enter both East Berlin and West Berlin; second, "strengthening the guarding of the border around Berlin"; and third, "stopping free movement" between East and West Berlin. Again, Pervukhin continued to be wary of closing the sectoral border, pointing out that it would make all Berliners and Germans resentful of the Soviet and East German regimes (just as the Soviets had argued in March 1953, rebuffing the GDR proposal to close the border).[172]

Pervukhin also cautioned that closing the sectoral border would be a technical challenge: "We must . . . keep in mind the serious technical difficulties in connection with closing the sectoral border. This would necessitate building obstructive structures for the whole expanse of the border within the city (46 km) and adding a large number of police posts, establishing permanent police control at the points where the S-bahn and Ü-bahn cross the border." However, he concluded, "it would be incorrect to exclude in general the possibility of closing the sectoral border in Berlin in one or another way, since with the exacerbation of the political situation, closed borders could be necessary. Therefore, it is necessary to also prepare a plan of measures in the event of the introduction of a state border regime on the sectoral border."[173]

Pervukhin warned that the issues he discussed "demand serious preliminary preparation and agreement with the GDR." He urged the Soviet leaders to decide which approach they would sanction so that he and others at the Soviet embassy in Berlin could make the preparations with the East Germans for "the agreed upon measures in a timely fashion." Pervukhin surmised that West Germany would probably institute an economic embargo against the GDR in the event of a separate peace treaty and that therefore the Soviet Union must be ready to extend any necessary economic help to the GDR. He pointed out that raising the fees the GDR charged for use of the transit routes across its territory would be one way to provide East Germany with more income in the wake of the embargo.[174]

Pervukhin's letter laid out for Gromyko and the Soviet leaders the prime options for dealing with the refugee exodus. As the envoy had noted on 19 May, the East German leaders wanted to "close the 'door to the West'" and "stop free movement between the GDR and West Berlin as soon as possible by any means," an option he supported only as the last resort. Whereas Pervukhin had presented plans to gain control over the West Berlin–West German transit routes and the Berlin sectoral border largely as either/or options, the SED regime sought to accomplish both. The East Germans also favored going forward on both tracks of a separate peace treaty *and* closing the West Berlin border instead of choosing one or the other.

Kvitsinsky writes in his memoirs that at the end of June or the beginning of July Ulbricht invited Pervukhin (Kvitsinsky accompanied him as translator) to his country house for an important meeting. He told Pervukhin that "the situation in the GDR was growing visibly worse. The growing flood of refugees was increasingly disorganizing the entire life of the Republic. Soon it must lead to an explosion." Ulbricht asked Pervukhin to tell Khrushchev that "if the present situation of open borders remains, collapse is inevitable. [Ulbricht] refuse[d] all responsibility for what would then happen. He could not guarantee that he could keep the situation under control this time."[175] This was the first time Kvitsinsky heard Ulbricht speak of closing the border.[176] Khrushchev's advisors Troyanovsky and Burlatsky also attest that the idea for sealing the border came from Ulbricht.[177]

According to Khrushchev's son, Sergei, in early July, the Soviet leader had asked his military commander in Berlin, chief of the GSFG, Ivan Yakubovski, to give his military assessment of the possibility of completely closing the border in Berlin. Khrushchev also requested that a detailed map of the border in Berlin be sent to him at his residence in the Crimea. After considering Yakuboski's information on the possibility of completely barricading the border through the city, as well as consulting with Gromyko and Semenov, Khrushchev agreed to close the West Berlin border.[178] Khrushchev later told the West German ambassador to Moscow, Hans Kroll: "I don't want to conceal from you that it was I who finally gave the order for this. Ulbricht indeed had pushed me for a long time and more vehemently in the last months, but I don't want to hide behind Ulbricht's back." In sum, "The wall was ordered by me due to Ulbricht's pressing wish."[179] Defending Khrushchev's decision to sanction "this hateful thing," the Soviet leader told Kroll:

> What should I have done? More than 30,000 people, in fact the best and most qualified people from the GDR, left the country in July. You can easily calculate when the East German economy would have collapsed if we hadn't done something soon against the mass flight. There were, though, only two kinds of countermeasures: cutting off air traffic or the Wall. The former would have brought us to a serious conflict with the United States which possibly could have led to war. I could not and did not want to risk that. So the Wall was the only remaining option.[180]

Once Khrushchev had decided to grant Ulbricht's request to close the border in Berlin, he transmitted his decision to East Berlin. As Kvitsinsky remembers it, "one day" (as he wrote in his 1993 memoirs),[181] "6 July" 1961 (as he testified in a *Spiegel* interview forty years later), Pervukhin told him "We have a yes from Moscow": find Ulbricht immediately.[182] Ulbricht was at the parliament, the *Volkskammer*, just a few blocks from the Embassy.[183] Pervukhin and Kvitsinsky rushed over and "conveyed to him a short message from Khrushchev. This gave his agreement to close the border to West Berlin and to begin the practical preparations for this under the greatest secrecy. The action must be carried out quickly and unexpectedly for the West."[184] Khrushchev's tactical approach of acting quickly and catching the West by surprise would be repeated the following year, although much less successfully, in the Cuban Missile Crisis.

When Pervukhin communicated Khrushchev's approval to Ulbricht, the East German leader immediately went into great detail about what must be done. He said that the only way to close the entire border quickly was to use barbed wire and fencing, a huge amount of it, all brought secretly to Berlin. He also said that the Ü-bahn and S-bahn to West Berlin must be stopped and that a glass wall should be put up at the main Friedrichstrasse train station so that East Berliners could not change over to the train to West Berlin. When Ulbricht saw "the look of surprise on Pervukhin's face" in response to the depth of his command of these details, he cautioned that they should not underestimate how difficult the border closing would be and that timing would be essential. Ulbricht said they should do it (early) on a Sunday, when most Berliners would be out of the city in the forests nearby. When the Berliners returned Sunday night, they would have finished sealing the border.[185]

Due to Ulbricht's fear of West German agents in the GDR's party and state organs, he insisted the preparations be carried out by a very small number of his most trusted top leaders. These included Stasi chief Erich Mielke, Interior Minister Karl Maron, Defense Minister Heinz Hoffman, and Transportation Minister Erwin Kramer. Erich Honecker would oversee the plans.[186] Ulbricht designated one person, initially his chief bodyguard, to hand-deliver documents on the border closure operation between his office and Kvitsinsky or Pervukhin at the Soviet embassy.[187]

On 7 July, at a meeting of high-ranking Stasi officials, Mielke ordered immediate preparations "so that operational measures can be carried out at a certain time according to a united plan [and ordered a] strengthening of security of the western state border and the ring around Berlin."[188] Soviet–East German military cooperation intensified shortly after this. On 15 July, the WTO commander Marshal Grechko transferred control of the East German military forces to the GSFG. The World War II military hero Marshal Konev would take over command of the GSFG in August. Representatives of the East German Interior Ministry and the GSFG met on 25 and 27 July to formulate a joint plan to secure the sectoral border in Berlin, the ring around Berlin, and the GDR-FRG border. The plan was for only the East German Interior Ministry and Border Police to have forces at the front lines of the borders. The GSFG and the East German National People's Army would be stationed one to two kilometers behind them to step in if needed.[189] Throughout the summer, the Soviets sent more troops, especially tank troops and air reconnaissance units, to the GDR and upgraded the weapons and equipment of the GSFG.[190]

On 24 July Bruno Wansierski, Deputy Director of the SED CC's Department for Security Issues, sent Ulbricht a report updating him on preparations to close the border. In his "Overview of the Scope of the

Engineering Operations on the Western Outer Ring of Berlin" (the border between West Berlin and East Germany), he informed Ulbricht about the troop units that would implement the border closure. He also reported that "so far 54.1 kilometers of the border length have been wired with barriers. Still to close off are 92.2 kilometers." The problem, as Wansierski told Ulbricht, was that even if they "use all available materials from the rest of the borders for the strengthening of the ring around Berlin, we will still be short 303 tons of barbed wire, 31.9 tons of mesh wire, 1700 kgs of connecting wire, 1100 kgs of cramps, 95 fms of timber, and 2100 concrete pillars."[191] Nonetheless, they obtained the materials they needed not only to seal off the outer ring of West Berlin, but also the border of West Berlin with East Berlin. The border length Wansierski refers to totals 146.3 km, the length of the whole border around West Berlin, including the border with East Berlin. On 31 July the Interior Ministry issued a top secret order to the border troops "to prepare the intensification of the engineering construction" of the border to West Berlin. Additional concrete posts were produced to be stored in and around Berlin.[192]

As the East Germans prepared to clamp down on all movement across the Berlin sectoral border, they finally succeeded in obtaining Soviet approval in late July to move against one kind of such movement: that of the *Grenzgänger* who lived in East Berlin but worked in West Berlin. The East Germans had been preparing these measures since March.[193] The East German actions against these 65,000 people, 15 percent of East Berlin's work force, aimed to make it no longer profitable for them to work in West Berlin. They would have to pay their rent and other necessities in West German marks and exchange 40 percent of their salary at a 1 : 1 rate for East German marks (instead of the prevailing exchange of 1 : 4, 4.5 or 5). They also would have to register their employment location with the East German authorities and get permission from them to travel to their place of employment in West Berlin. If the *Grenzgänger* did not comply, they would be fined 10,000 marks or imprisoned.

On 24 June Ulbricht informed Khrushchev of the measures the SED proposed to take against the *Grenzgänger* and requested Khrushchev's approval.[194] The Soviets were in no rush and responded that the plans to deal with the *Grenzgänger* could be discussed in August at the WTO meeting in Moscow.[195] The East Germans, however, believed that "measures against the *Grenzgänger* should be implemented as soon as possible."[196] They probably persuaded Pervukhin to make their case again to the Kremlin. Pervukhin did this in a letter to Gromyko on 29 June. Pervukhin declared that the *Grenzgänger* problem "has recently become particularly acute [and the numbers of *Grenzgänger*] have increased sharply in the past half year [to] a level of 70,000 people. . . . *Grenz-*

gänger are essentially one form of the exodus of the work-capable population of the GDR to the West. This phenomenon is reflected in an unhealthy way on the work of the industrial and trade enterprises in Democratic Berlin, where in comparison with the other areas of the GDR the shortage of work forces is especially severe. . . . Considering the great economic difficulties the GDR is going through, especially with the shortage of workers, the Soviet embassy thinks it possible to agree with the intended measures of our friends regarding the *Grenzgänger*." While he cautioned that implementing these measures could cause some of the *Grenzgänger* to move to West Berlin, he still argued for sanctioning the move against the *Grenzgänger*. Pervukhin supported the SED Politburo's desire to enact the measures "before the conclusion of a peace treaty." Finally, he reassured Gromyko: "Measures against *Grenzgänger* are an internal matter of the GDR and do not affect the interests of the Western Powers."[197]

On 19 July, Gromyko recommended to the CPSU CC that they agree to Pervukhin's advice. Gromyko repeated the economic arguments in favor of moving against the *Grenzgänger*, but cautioned that "the corresponding measures should be carried out gradually, not initially resorting to severe measures of administrative coercion, so as not to give the chance to exacerbate the situation and for counter-measures by the Western Powers."[198] The CPSU CC Presidium accepted precisely this advice, and on 20 July commissioned Pervukhin to inform Ulbricht of the decision.[199]

The East Germans then proceeded to implement measures against the *Grenzgänger* in the face of Western protests.[200] The SED also announced that only East Germans living in the country could buy apartments, cars, televisions, and other such desirable goods. Accordingly, in July, six times more *Grenzgänger* moved to West Berlin than usual.[201] The refugee exodus, which the East Germans were trying to reduce, expanded, sharpening the need to close the border.

In late July, as the East Germans moved against the *Grenzgänger* and undertook preparations to be ready to close the Berlin border when the political leaders gave the order, Ulbricht drafted the speech he would give at the early August Warsaw Pact meeting in Moscow. Ulbricht had learned from one of his colleagues returning from Moscow in mid-July that the East Germans might not get approval at the meeting for everything they wanted, that is, anything beyond the border closure. The Soviets advised the East Germans to be well prepared to discuss political, economic, and military issues related to West Berlin and a peace treaty.[202] Accordingly, Ulbricht's draft speech, approved by the SED Politburo at a special meeting on 24 July, made a strong and detailed case for the need to close the Berlin border and conclude a peace treaty.[203]

Between 25 and 27 July Ulbricht's draft speech and appended documents on the border closure were sent to Pervukhin and on to the Kremlin. In Ulbricht's cover letter, clearly in an effort to maintain secrecy, he told Khrushchev: "With regard to control over the movement of GDR citizens to Berlin and the movement of people from the capital of the GDR to West Berlin on roads and streets, we have prepared all the necessary measures so that written information is not necessary."[204] Expressing a similar concern to keep details of the border closure plan tightly held, Gromyko and Andropov reminded the Soviet Central Committee on 28 July that any information given to the East Europeans at the WTO meeting "could become known to the Western Powers."[205] Kvitsinsky later explained: "We didn't then have great faith that our friends, especially those in Poland and Hungary, were 'water-tight.' "[206] In fact, Ulbricht specifically asked Khrushchev to not supply the communist allies before or during the WTO meeting with any materials that would not be made public. Accordingly, when the Warsaw Pact allies were invited to the early August meeting in Moscow, they were not given any specific information about the agenda of the meeting. In response to a complaint from Polish leader Wladislaw Gomulka, the Soviets told him cryptically that the agenda would "be determined by the participants at the meeting. But of course we are expecting discussion on the issue of Germany, on the conclusion of a peace treaty and also other things connected with these questions in light of Kennedy's recent speech."[207]

Following the plan of maintaining secrecy, in Ulbricht's draft speech he did not speak of "closing" the border, only of increasing "control" of it, although closure was the clear implication of his words and had long been his goal.[208] The Soviet embassy's summary of Ulbricht's draft, however, threw caution aside and stated: "There is now a large exodus of the GDR population through West Berlin. This situation gives rise to the necessity at a suitable time of closing the sectoral border in Berlin, creating on it the regime of a state border."[209]

In addition to his draft speech, Ulbricht forwarded to the Kremlin several documents on other preparations the East Germans were making and steps they recommended be made concerning the preparation for a peace treaty and the situation in Berlin. These included detailed information on exactly how to stop the movement of trains, subways, trams, boats, cars, planes, and people from East Germany and East Berlin into West Berlin. One of these documents dealt with "Measures for securing the control of movement between the GDR, including its capital, and West Berlin." Others described "Measures for the securing of the control of movement with the conclusion of a peace treaty" and "Measures for the securing of control of air traffic with the conclusion of a peace treaty." While these latter two documents detailed measures to be undertaken with the conclusion of a peace treaty, the measures of the first document were not discussed with reference to a peace treaty. This suggests that the plans to close the border to West Berlin were intended to be carried out separate from a peace treaty with the GDR.[210] Pervukhin informed Khrushchev that the East Germans estimated they needed eight days to prepare the new regime on the Berlin sectoral border and the ring around Berlin, and they needed four to five weeks to prepare changes to the Ü-bahn and S-bahn in Berlin.[211]

While preparing these measures, the Soviets and East Germans monitored Western actions and policies concerning Berlin and Germany. On 20 July, the KGB chief Shelepin informed Khrushchev that Soviet intelligence had picked up indications of Western preparations for military conflict with the Soviet Union in Germany. Shelepin reported in particular that if the Soviets signed a separate peace treaty with the GDR that closed off Western access to West Berlin, the Western Powers were prepared to use force to maintain that access. The KGB chief warned Khrushchev that the planned Western military measures "could pose a real danger to the security of the Soviet Union."[212] The only relief his report provided was his conclusion that the Western Powers had not yet agreed on a unified plan. East German reports a week later similarly noted the lack of Western unity in responding to Soviet and East German proposals on Berlin and Germany.[213]

Lending credence to Shelepin's report of Western military preparations to defend their rights in Berlin, President Kennedy gave a forceful radio and television address on 25 July emphasizing his commitment to West Berlin. Kennedy called West Berlin "the great testing place of Western courage and will." He insisted: "We cannot and will not permit the Communists to drive us out of Berlin, either gradually or by force. . . . We must meet our oft-stated pledge to the free peoples of West Berlin—and maintain our rights and their safety, even in the face of force—in order to maintain the confidence of other free peoples in our word and our resolve."[214] To back up his words with deeds, Kennedy raised the U.S. defense budget by $3.5 billion, announced a call-up of reserves, and pledged to increase U.S. naval and air power. He asked Congress for $207 million for civilian defense, including fallout shelters, and pledged to meet the Soviet challenge.[215] While Kennedy declared that "[w]e do not want to fight, but we have fought before" and would again if necessary, he also made it clear he was willing to negotiate with the Soviets on reasonable proposals.[216]

If Khrushchev examined Kennedy's speech closely, he would have noticed that Kennedy's focus was on West Berlin, not on East Berlin or the freedom of movement between East and West Berlin.[217] Regarding the latter, a few days after his speech, Kennedy privately and presciently told Walt Rostow: "Khrushchev is losing East Germany. He cannot let that happen. . . . He will have to do something to stop the flow of refugees—perhaps a wall. And we won't be able to prevent it."[218] Indeed, in a public statement on 30 July, U.S. Senator William Fulbright, the influential chairman of the Committee on Foreign Relations, expressed the same sentiment. Fulbright declared that he did not understand why the East Germans were not closing their border to stop the refugee exodus, something he believed they had a right to do.[219] Perhaps the Soviet ambassador to West Germany, A. A. Smirnov, was referring to Fulbright's remarks when he told Chancellor Adenauer: "By the way, to a certain degree the measures taken in Berlin were suggested to us by political actors in the USA."[220] In Khrushchev's 3 August meeting in Moscow with the Italian premier, Amintore Fanfani, Khrushchev observed: "Fulbright is a smart man, he does not want war."[221]

The August Warsaw Pact Meeting

Until recently, scholars assumed that the decision to close the Berlin border was made at the 3–5 August meeting in Moscow of the leaders of the Warsaw Pact states. We now know, as described above, that this decision was reached in early July. The Soviets, however, still viewed a WTO meeting as necessary. Kvitsinky gives the most elucidating account of the Soviet motivation for convening the meeting before closing the borders. En route to Moscow, probably on 1 August, Pervukhin discussed the upcoming Warsaw Pact meeting with Kvitsinsky. He said the meeting was being held for two reasons: first, to inform the other members of the decision to close the borders and get their agreement; and second, to present the border closure to the West as an act of the entire Warsaw Pact, thus deterring the West from stopping it. Pervukhin told Kvitsinsky: "We cannot let the GDR's action [i.e., closing the border] be seen as only its plan; this could provoke the Federal Republic and its allies to an intervention. The Soviet Union and the entire Warsaw Pact must stand in front of the GDR so it will be clear to all that there is no way back."[222] In addition to deterring a Western response, the meeting was also necessary to plan future economic policies regarding the GDR and to discuss the question of a separate peace treaty.

Ulbricht and sixty other East German military, economic, and political officials flew to Moscow on 1 August for the Warsaw Pact meeting.[223] As Ulbricht's translator Werner Eberlein remembers, Ulbricht kept the delegation strictly separated so that he was the only one with a complete overview of the plans.[224] Ulbricht had requested that he meet with Khrushchev separately before the opening of the WTO conference.[225]

This meeting occurred on the morning of 3 August, and the conference opened in the afternoon.[226]

Khrushchev and Ulbricht spoke of the large numbers of refugees and the need to close the borders. They discussed the process and timing of closing the Berlin sectoral border and the ring around Berlin, for which the Soviet and East German military forces had been preparing for over a month. Khrushchev declared that they must "encircle Berlin with an iron ring. . . . Our forces must create such a ring, but your troops must control it."[227] During the very days of the WTO meeting, in fact, the Soviets sent over 4,000 soldiers to Berlin.[228] Khrushchev said Soviet forces were concealing tanks on the border with West Germany, behind the positions of the soldiers.[229] This was precisely how the planning had been developing over the summer since Khrushchev's approval to go forward with the preparations: The Soviet military took the lead, but it was clear that the East German forces would be the only ones on the front lines when the time came.

The key part of this meeting was the discussion of the timing to carry out the border closure. Khrushchev said that "it must be done before the conclusion of a peace treaty." He argued that it would add pressure on the West to sign a peace treaty and that it would help stop the refugee exodus. Thus, Khrushchev, it seemed, was still not giving up on compelling the West to sign a peace treaty on Germany. Ulbricht, as usual, did not have much faith in obtaining Western agreement to a peace treaty and had long wanted control over access to West Berlin to stop the refugees. Ulbricht told Khrushchev it would take two weeks to be ready to stop free movement between East and West. Khrushchev asked: "When would it be best for you to do this? Do it when you want, we can do it at any time."[230] As Ulbricht had told Pervukhin in early July, the most propitious time to maximize the level of surprise was during the night between Saturday and Sunday. Ulbricht and Khrushchev agreed on the night of 12–13 August.[231] Khrushchev recollected in his memoirs: "The date for the beginning of border control was to be August 13, 1961. We kidded among ourselves that in the West the thirteenth is supposed to be an unlucky day. I joked that for us and for the whole socialist camp it would be a very lucky day indeed."[232]

Khrushchev asked Ulbricht how he planned to close the border on streets where one side was located in East Berlin and the other in West Berlin. Ulbricht described the plan: "In those homes which have an exit to West Berlin, we will brick up the exit. In other places, we will erect barriers of barbed wire. The wire has already been assembled. All of this can be done very quickly."[233]

The two leaders also discussed new regulations for the movement of citizens of East and West Berlin, East and West Germany, and the Western allies after the border closure.[234] These new regulations largely followed the East German proposals of the previous year. As far back as October 1960, the East German interior minister, Karl Maron, had formulated new rules for the movement of different categories of people across the Berlin sectoral border. These had been rebuffed by Khrushchev, who wanted to wait to meet President Kennedy before changing anything in Berlin.[235] But Khrushchev now agreed to make it almost impossible for East German citizens to enter East or West Berlin and for East Berliners to go to West Berlin.

As always, Ulbricht was concerned about the economic repercussions of their plans and requested that an economic conference take place before the border closure. Ulbricht expected such a conference would provide an explanation to the East German people of how their economic needs would be met if faced with a West German economic blockade. Khrushchev rejected this proposal, saying it might hint to people that something was about to happen, resulting in an even larger flood of refugees. He told Ulbricht to do his best to prepare the economy over the next week or two before the border closure.[236]

Thus, by the time the WTO conference opened in the afternoon of 3 August, Khrushchev and Ulbricht had made all the key decisions about the border closure. And the Soviet Presidium had passed all the resolutions that would be agreed to at the WTO meeting, including the public declaration to be made on the morning of 13 August.[237] Now Khrushchev and Ulbricht needed to inform their other allies of their plans and create a united socialist front behind them. If the FRG really did respond to the border closure with an economic blockade, the allies would need to be prepared for this and might need to help the GDR. With regard to a peace treaty, Khrushchev hoped the border closure would push the West into accepting a peace treaty with both Germanys. But his backup plan remained a separate peace treaty, and he wanted to discuss that and its ramifications with the Warsaw Pact leaders. While there was much discussion of a separate peace treaty with the GDR at the WTO conference, Khrushchev probably intended to wait to see the West's response to the border closure before moving ahead with a separate peace treaty.

Prior to the accessibility in Moscow and Berlin of transcripts of the August WTO meeting, the only source available on the meeting was the account by the Czechoslovakian defense minister, Jan Sejna, whose recollection of the March 1961 WTO PCC meeting was cited earlier.[238] According to Sejna, upon Ulbricht's arrival in Moscow, Khrushchev agreed that he could close the border around West Berlin, but that a peace treaty would not be concluded at the time. Khrushchev wanted to continue exploring options in negotiations with the West. Ulbricht also wanted to close the air corridors between West Berlin and the FRG. Khrushchev refused this risky move, however, and Ulbricht had to be content with putting a wall around West Berlin on East German territory. Telling Ulbricht to use barbed wire first and watch the Western response, Khrushchev gave Ulbricht the go-ahead to close the border, but told him, "not one millimeter farther." This probably meant that the barbed wire should not stray onto West Berlin territory and that Ulbricht should not provoke the West. These aspects of Sejna's account hold up well in light of the documentary evidence.

In his opening remarks at the WTO meeting on 3 August, Khrushchev told the socialist leaders that the goals of the conference were "to have a detailed discussion of the question of concluding a German peace treaty, to consult about practical measures which must be taken in the near future [i.e., the Berlin border closure], and to work out united tactics." He then referred to Kennedy's 25 July television address in which Kennedy "essentially threatened us with war if we implement measures for liquidating the occupation regime in West Berlin. Under these conditions, we must work out a detailed plan of agreed upon action in all areas—foreign, economic, and military policy."[239] Given Khrushchev's proven aversion to undue risks of war during the Berlin Crisis, opening the conference with this reference to Kennedy's threat can be seen as his way of signaling that he was going to look for a way to resolve the "West Berlin problem" without violating the rights of the Western Powers there.

In the extensive but incomplete record of the August WTO conference in the Moscow and Berlin archives, three main points stand out, two concerning economics and one the Sino-Soviet split.[240] First, Ulbricht made it abundantly clear in his 4 August speech (as well as in a letter the same day to Khrushchev)[241] on the situation in the GDR and East Berlin that the main reason he needed to "control" (or close) the "open border" in Berlin was economic. In particular, he needed to stop the loss of skilled workers to West Berlin and West Germany. Second, Khrushchev pressed strongly for all of the other socialist countries to help the GDR economically. To his evident frustration and even anger, however, the East European socialist leaders presented a wall of polite yet firm and detailed protest, citing their own economic problems. This of course made it even more urgent to close the border in Berlin. Third, the Sino-Soviet split hovered conspicuously over the meeting, as both the opening session on the afternoon of 3 August and the closing session on the afternoon of 5 August focused not on West Berlin and Germany but on criticism of Albania as China's surrogate.

In Ulbricht's lengthy speech to the conference, he reiterated the points he had made for years, sometimes verbatim. He spoke of the need to sign a German peace treaty, transform West Berlin into a free city, and obtain control of the borders and access routes on GDR territory. Ulbricht declared that with the conclusion of a separate peace treaty, he would gain the capacity to control his borders and his territory the way any sovereign state should. After describing the "revanchist," "militaristic," and threatening economic, military, political, cultural, and generally subversive policies of West Germany, he asserted that the main factor allowing the FRG to threaten the GDR, especially economically, was the open border in Berlin:

> The enemy is trying with all means to exploit the open border between the GDR and West Berlin to undermine our government and its economy, primarily by means of recruiting and trading people. It is necessary to say openly: the aggressive forces of West Germany and the Western powers have already succeeded in causing serious harm to the GDR by these means. . . . In the interests of the existence and the development of the GDR, active measures for ending the recruitment of people from our Republic are necessary.
>
> The open border with West Berlin has brought enormous damages to the GDR economy for many years. To a great extent, the burden of the consequences of the struggle between the two systems lies on our shoulders.[242]

In a letter on 24 June, Ulbricht had told Gomulka that "West Berlin is a hole through which one million marks flow out every year" due to the loss of the workers.[243] In his speech of 4 August, he accused West Germany of "the plunder of the GDR," which has been helped by West Berlin, through which the "West German imperialists want to annex the human and economic potential of the German Democratic Republic so as thereby to be supported by increased military and economic power."[244]

In an economic report delivered to Khrushchev on the same day, Ulbricht referred to the open border in Berlin eight times. In the conclusion to his report, Ulbricht listed nine factors as the "most important grounds for" the GDR's economic problems, and number one was "the repercussions of the open borders." Ulbricht told Khrushchev that the loss of the work force to West Germany in 1961

> led to an absolute reduction for the first time of the overall numbers of those employed in the GDR economy and especially in many crucial industrial factories. This shortage of workers intensified in the first half of 1961 and led to a failure to fulfill the plan in many key industries. This problem is particularly great in Berlin, the center of electro-technical industry.
>
> According to rough calculations, the loss of the working force by this recruitment led to a drop in production in 1960 and 1961 in industry alone of 2.5–3 billion DM.[245]

Ulbricht also pointed out that the "open borders forced us to raise the standard of living faster than corresponded to our national economic means,"[246] which meant buying many goods from the West that the GDR could not pay for and thus going into debt with the West. Ulbricht reminded Khrushchev of the uniqueness of the GDR's situation: "Under the conditions of their *closed borders*, all the peoples' democracies can tackle the resolution of such political-economic questions differently than is possible under our political conditions [emphasis added]."[247]

> Similarly, in his speech to the WTO conference, Ulbricht concluded pessimistically: As long as West Germany surpasses the German Democratic Republic in its economic strength and its standard of living of the population, we cannot reduce the organizational and financial enticement by great means of people from our Republic. It is precisely these economic facts which make the subversive work of the espionage and sabotage centers in West Berlin so dangerous. But the continuation of the strong economy in West Germany as well as the economic development in the socialist camp does not permit us to expect that the German Democratic Republic will catch up with West Germany in standard of living of the population in the near future.

In light of "these economic facts," Ulbricht announced to his socialist allies: "This situation necessitates the introduction of a regulation stipulating that at a certain time the government border of the GDR (going through Berlin) *be closed and* could be crossed by citizens of the GDR only in the presence of the corresponding permission for exit or, in so far as it concerns visiting West Berlin by citizens of the capital of the GDR, with a special pass [emphasis added]."[248] Ulbricht used the italicized words above about actually closing the Berlin sectoral border only when he spoke at the conference; they were omitted from the version of his speech given to the Soviets, and they were not in the final, corrected protocol of the conference, presumably due to an effort to preserve secrecy.[249]

After proposing to close the Berlin sectoral border to GDR citizens, Ulbricht went on to propose some limitations on movement from West to East:

> Visitation of the capital of the GDR by citizens of West Berlin would be possible on the basis of a West Berlin identity card (but not on the basis of a West German passport). The previous agreements on transit from West Berlin to West Germany would not be affected by these measures. The current regulations would also remain for the transit of foreigners. . . . In the interests of the peaceful and constructive work by the citizens of the German Democratic Republic and of the peoples of the other Warsaw Pact states, it is necessary

to stop the wooing away [of refugees] and other hostile activities. On these grounds, we propose that the Warsaw Pact states agree, in the interests of the cessation of the subversive activity, to implement control along the GDR borders, including the borders in Berlin, comparable to that existing along the state borders of the Western Powers.[250]

The Polish leader Wladislaw Gomulka was the first to respond to Ulbricht's proposal for closing and creating a state border around West Berlin. Gomulka understood that Ulbricht intended that this should be done together with or after the signing of a peace treaty and the abolition of the occupation status of West Berlin. Gomulka, however, proposed that the border be closed beforehand, something he had apparently been arguing for some time:

> In our view, the question arises as to whether we should wait for all the difficult months which remain before the conclusion of a peace treaty for the implementation of the measures whose goal is to close off access to West Berlin from the territory of the German Democratic Republic.
>
> We are of the opinion that from a legal standpoint, the regulation of this question already now falls under the competence of the German Democratic Republic. We think that we should consider whether we should not already today take decisive measures in this area. I propose that we discuss this question.[251]

In the available records of the conference, however, there is no extensive discussion of the possibility of closing the Berlin border "today." Probably this was discussed outside of the full sessions, such as in the bilateral meetings of the afternoon of 4 August or during the morning of 5 August. The main discussion, as we shall see, during the formal group sessions revolved around the question of helping the GDR economically.

Indicating that the border closure was a given and that the question was backing it up with economic aid, the main part of the discussion after Ulbricht's speech focused on his request for significant economic aid from his socialist allies to help him if faced with a West German economic embargo. Ulbricht presumed that in response to a separate peace treaty, "it is very probable that the Bonn government could unilaterally denounce the trade agreement between the [GDR] and the [FRG] and that NATO could enact an economic embargo against the [GDR]." Ulbricht described what high economic standards the GDR had to have, how dependent it was economically on the FRG, how neccesary and difficult it would be to break off this dependence, and how important it was that the socialist countries step in to replace the FRG in supplying the GDR with the goods it needed to keep its people satisfied. He pointed out that while the Soviet Union had helped the GDR significantly, and would continue to, even the Soviet Union "cannot give us help in all areas. It is necessary, therefore, to reach concrete agreements quickly with the Czechoslovak Socialist Republic, the Polish People's Republic, and other socialist governments regarding the additional supplies." He declared: "The most important step which we must take now is an agreement on supplies from the Soviet Union and the people's democracies with the goal of making the GDR economy independent from West Germany." In case his socialist comrades had any doubt about why it was in their economic interest to help the GDR, Ulbricht reminded them: "With regard to the volume of production, our Republic is the second industrial state in the socialist camp. Safe-guarding its industrial production from all interference is therefore in the interests of the whole socialist camp."[252]

While Ulbricht's East European allies expressed their solidarity with the GDR against the hostile machinations of the FRG, they also explained that they had their own economic problems and doubted they had the capacity to step in to supply the GDR with all it needed. The Polish and Czechoslovak leaders Wladislaw Gomulka and Antonin Novotny spoke in the morning after Ulbricht's speech, and the Hungarian leader Janos Kadar spoke that evening. They were all worried about the chance of a West German and maybe even NATO economic boycott of the GDR and perhaps the whole socialist bloc. Khrushchev, on the other hand, forecast only a 50 percent chance that this economic boycott would occur, even the more limited one of an FRG boycott of the GDR. But then, the Soviets were far less dependent on trade with the West than the East Europeans were and thus had less cause for concern.[253]

Gomulka may have begun his comments supporting the immediate closure of the Berlin border so as to reduce the GDR's need for economic help from its allies. He pointed out that an embargo by the FRG and possibly all the NATO countries would affect them all, not just the GDR, and he proposed that the Council for Mutual Economic Assistance (COMECON), the socialist economic bloc, meet to discuss this. He told the conference delegates that Poland had shortages also, relied on trade with the West, and was in debt to the West. In fact, he even suggested that in the case of an FRG boycott, the GDR should export the goods to Eastern Europe that it usually exported to the FRG. He concluded that "these aren't easy issues, and they demand a thorough and precise examination of all the details . . . so that the plans of the other socialist countries will be affected as little as possible."[254]

Novotny was even more pessimistic than Gomulka. He expected that the West would respond to a separate peace treaty not just with an economic embargo, but perhaps also with a rupture or freezing of diplomatic relations, an interruption of land and air communications, and a curtailment of the movement of socialist ships at sea. Novotny conceded that the GDR would bear the brunt of the Western response and that the other socialists must help the GDR, but, as with Gomulka, he spoke of his own economic problems limiting his capacity to help Ulbricht. Agricultural difficulties in Czechoslovakia meant that he could not supply the GDR with agricultural products: "[W]e have to undertake all efforts to guarantee the supply of our [own] population [with food.] We will have a poor harvest of potatoes. For many years already our plan has been far from fulfilled." Furthermore, Novotny pointed out that "we have relatively the most significant [economic] relations with the capitalist states of all the socialist countries and consequently would obviously suffer the most in the case of the imposition of an embargo against the socialist countries."[255]

That evening Kadar continued in this vein, in spite of Khrushchev's intervening speech demanding that the socialist allies help the GDR, discussed below. Kadar agreed with Gomulka that the economic issues concerning a likely NATO economic blockade should have been addressed earlier: "it was a mistake not to discuss this issue in all its larger contexts." The larger context for Hungary was the fact that "30 percent of its foreign trade is with the capitalist West and a quarter of this is with the FRG." In the one hint in the available conference proceedings of a date around the time of the subsequent border closure, Kadar said he expected that "the economic attack against" the GDR would "according to all appearances begin on 15 August" and that "the GDR must be given the greatest possible support."[256]

Ulbricht's Russian interpreter, Werner Eberlein, recalls that during the breaks between sessions at the conference, there was a "certain reserve regarding Ulbricht" on the part of the other delegates and that "they interpreted his statements regarding supplies from the socialist countries as a certain threat." Kadar in particular asked Ulbricht, "Is [the situation] really so serious, or have you just played it up here?"[257]

Kadar expressed his support for signing a separate peace treaty and transforming West Berlin into a free city, but warned: "It is obvious that in the preparation for the resolution of such a complicated issue, we must do everything possible to achieve a resolution through negotiations and with peaceful means. This also means that an acceptable compromise must be possible." While he believed economic countermeasures much more likely than military countermeasures in the event of a separate treaty, Kadar still recommended "on the basis of our conference to give an order to the Commander-in-Chief of the joint forces, Marshal Comrade Grechko, to carry out the appropriate coordinated preparations for the joint armed forces" in case there is a Western military response.[258] Clearly, he was worried and recommended that they continue to discuss their coordinated plans in October during the celebrations of the anniversary of the Russian revolution and at the Twenty-second Congress in Moscow.

The North Korean and Bulgarian representatives at the conference shared Kadar's apprehension. The North Korean delegate, Li Che-Sun, agreed with the need for "great vigilance."[259] The Bulgarian leader Todor Zhivkov similarly noted that with the signing of a separate peace treaty, "[w]e must assume that the international situation will be temporarily complicated. . . . We don't believe . . . that the imperialists will resort to military conflict. But we must also be prepared for this."[260]

Khrushchev doubted that the West would respond militarily and start a war over the signing of a separate peace treaty with the GDR, although, like the others, he declared that they must be prepared for that possibility. Khrushchev was very proud that in April he had sent the first human being, Yuri Gagarin, into space, orbiting the earth in a spacecraft, before the Americans achieved this. He boasted about Soviet space superiority: "Our space ships fly above the earth, and the much-vaunted Americans hop like frogs. This is also moral satisfaction. They aren't flying but jumping into space right now."[261]

Khrushchev probably believed that it was these advantages that were deterring the West from the stronger reactions against Soviet pressure on West Berlin and Germany he had expected at the March WTO meeting. He admitted: The West "proved to be less tough than we assumed. You could say that there is still no peace treaty, and the adversary has still to show himself. It is true, he could show himself, but we can already say now that we expected more pressure, but so far the strongest intimidation has been Kennedy's [25 July] speech." Accordingly, Khrushchev declared that "our CC and government think that so far the preparation [for a peace treaty] is going better than we expected[. I]t will still heat up, but the main thing is the cooling down. Therefore we must be prepared for these temperature changes and make our policy have an influence on them. We can do this."[262]

On the other hand, Khrushchev warned that "no one can give a guarantee that there will be no war" and that it was always safer to "prepare for the worst." Accordingly, he announced that they must "strengthen our defense, strengthen our military forces. . . . We must, comrades, show them our will and decisiveness, [or they] "will say that we are . . . bluffing and consequently will strengthen the pressure against us. Therefore I think we must commission the ministers of defense to make provisions for everything possible." More specifically, Khrushchev announced: "Our military forces are now taking several measures in agreement with the GDR. We are thinking of putting tanks in defense of the entire border. We must close it strongly everywhere, so that the adversary can search for a weak spot [and not find it]. We must also prepare other measures for reinforcement."[263] The Soviet troops sent to Berlin in early August were part of this reinforcement.

In addition to making military preparations for the border closure, Khrushchev also sought to get the WTO allies lined up to help the GDR weather a potential West German economic blockade. He was very frustrated with the hand wringing by some of the conference participants about giving the GDR economic aid. He spoke passionately of the necessity of helping the GDR. Khrushchev emphasized the strategic, political, and economic reasons for "treating seriously the needs of the German Democratic Republic . . . as our own needs":

> I think that we must help the GDR. Let us, comrades, perceive this better, deeper and more keenly. . . .
>
> Now, comrades, we will all help the GDR. I will not say who of you will help most. All must help and must help more. Let us look at it this way: if we do not now turn our attention to the needs of the GDR and we do not make sacrifices, they cannot endure; they do not have enough internal strength.

He went on, referring specifically to Poland and Czechoslovakia, probably because of the excuses Gomulka and Novotny had made about their difficulties with giving the GDR economic help:

> What would it mean if the GDR was liquidated? It would mean that the Bundeswehr would approach the Polish borders, it would come up to the border with Czechoslovakia; it would mean the Bundeswehr would come closer to our Soviet border and to the borders of other countries. I think that if this happened as a result of our lack of understanding, it would cost us more, and significantly more, not only in the political but also in the material regard, than it is now necessary to do to help the GDR and strengthen it. By strengthening its position, we strengthen our position. Therefore, comrades, this would be help, I would say, not only to Comrade Walter [Ulbricht] and to the Germans of the GDR, but also to us ourselves.[264]

Khrushchev was angry, going out of his way to persuade the reluctant Poles, Czechoslovaks, and others to agree to help East Germany, going so far, as quoted above, to essentially order them to help: "Now, comrades, we will all help the GDR. I will not say who of you will help most. All must help and must help more." In response to Ulbricht's request for 50,000 workers to replace those who had fled to the West, Khrushchev declared that he "could give 50 thousand or 100 thousand" from Moscow, Leningrad, and Kiev and that he would send "married and unmarried people, they will marry Germans, and this will enable the strengthening of mutual understanding and so on."[265] While Khrushchev agreed to help replace the brain drain the GDR had suffered, he was much less sympathetic about helping East Germany with unskilled workers. As he recollected in his memoirs: "Walter Ulbricht even asked us to help by providing a labor force. We didn't want to give them unskilled workers. Why? Because we didn't want our workers to clean their toilets. I had to tell Comrade Ulbricht: 'Imagine how a Soviet worker would feel. He won the war and now he has to clean your toilets. It will not only be humiliating—it will produce an explosive reaction in our people. We cannot do this. Find a way out yourself.'"[266]

Khrushchev's energetic defense of helping the GDR was directed not just to the East Europeans, but also to his Kremlin colleagues. Referring to the cost of maintaining Soviet troops in the GDR and how "each division costs many times more there than it would if it were deployed at home, [Khrushchev declared:] People could say to us: what is the GDR to us, we are strong, we have weapons, etc., we will remain at our borders. This would really be national narrow-mindedness, but not a communist understanding of the tasks which stand before us, communists."[267] This echoed the angry defensiveness expressed by Mikoian in June 1957. Khrushchev and Mikoian felt it was their communist duty to defend the GDR.

In addition to the emphasis on the East German economic need to close the border around West Berlin and the reluctance of the East Europeans to commit themselves to significant economic aid to the GDR, the third issue that stands out from the WTO meeting is the shadow of the Sino-Soviet dispute. At two of the four conference sessions recorded in the protocols, the afternoons of 3 and 5 August, the conference delegates directed their attention to a critique of Albania whose leaders had been siding with China in the Sino-Soviet dispute since mid-1960. On 3 August, Ulbricht presented to the conference delegates for their approval and signature a letter he had drafted to the Albanians. The letter sharply criticized the Albanians for sending a representative to the conference who was not "competent" enough to participate in the discussions. The Albanian representative, Ramiz Alia, CC secretary in Tirana, was the only East European representative who was not the leader of his party. He was effectively shut out of the conference and left. Upon departing, Alia delivered a note of protest to Khrushchev at not being permitted to give his speech at the conference and gave Khrushchev a copy of the speech.[268]

In the speech, he echoed the contradictory Chinese criticisms of Khrushchev for, on the one hand, engaging in negotiations for too long with the West and without sufficient results, and, on the other hand, risking war with the West. However, Alia concluded, and "in spite of ideological differences which exist between some of our parties, our party, our government, our people, we have, we do and we will stand together with the Soviet Union and the other fraternal states."[269]

As Bonwetsch and Filitov point out in their examination of the conference sessions, "with the exception of . . . Mongolia, the Asian representatives at the conference demonstratively did not join in the accusatory campaign against Albania. [In addition,] with the exception of the Vietnamese representative . . . relatively insignificant delegates from the Asian countries attended the conference." Criticism against Albania was so heavy that at one point on 5 August Zhivkov proposed they discuss whether Albania should remain a member of the WTO.[270] The disagreements about Albania are probably behind the decision to change the title of the conference in the final, corrected protocol: "The Conference of First Secretaries of Central Committees of Communist and Workers' Parties of Socialist Countries for the Exchange of Views on Questions Concerning the Preparation and Conclusion of a German Peace Treaty" became "The Conference of . . . Member-States of the Warsaw Pact."[271] Calling it a Warsaw Pact conference, instead of a conference of socialists made it easier to shut out the views of the Chinese, Mongolian, North Korean, and North Vietnamese delegates, although they were listed as observers.

Bonwetsch and Filitov ascribe some of the passion of Khrushchev's attempts to get everyone on board helping the GDR to his "tendency to make the Berlin and German issues into an instrument of internal bloc disciplining."[272] "One can infer that the Soviet leadership depended on using the decision about Berlin . . . as a lever to either reestablish the lost unanimity of the socialist camp or to mobilize unanimity against the 'deviationist' Albania and in this way also to challenge the Communist Party of China."[273] Ulbricht no doubt hoped that by taking a leading role in the criticism of Albania at the conference, he would obtain more support from Khrushchev.[274] In the years of the Berlin Crisis and the widening of the Sino-Soviet split, Ulbricht alternated between methods of using the split to push Khrushchev into action on Berlin and Germany: Initially he gave indications of siding with China on many issues concerning domestic and foreign policy; and then he increasingly returned to the Soviet side expecting that his loyalty would be rewarded by Khrushchev.

According to evidence from the conference protocols and other related documents, the delegates left the conference with the understanding that the border around West Berlin would be closed, and that relatively soon, probably by the end of the year, they would sign a separate peace treaty with the GDR that would turn over to East Germany control of the access routes to Berlin. All the concerns voiced at the conference, however, about the likely Western economic and possibly military response to a separate peace treaty may have led some of the delegates, including Khrushchev, to the conclusion that it might be better not to sign the treaty. At the conference, Khrushchev asserted that they must sign a peace treaty but counseled moving toward "this in a well thought out way, without impulsiveness."[275]

The Concrete "Rose"

Back in Berlin Ulbricht reported on the Moscow talks to the Politburo on 7 August. He announced that "the beginning of the planned measures for control will occur in the night from Saturday to Sunday [12–13 August] on the basis of a resolution of the Council of Ministers."[276] On 11 August, Mielke informed high-level Stasi officials: "Measures will be taken against flight from the Republic, whereby especially the ring around Berlin will be the focus. . . . Since in the next days, decisive measures will be decided, any hostile activity must be hindered. . . . All preparatory work is to be carried out under the protection of conspiracy and under the strictest secrecy. The entire operation has the code name 'Rose.'"[277]

Soviet Embassy officials had a final pre-border closure meeting with the East German leaders twenty-four hours before commencement of the operation. The Soviets still did not trust Ulbricht not to go too far. Referring to the less than friendly personal relations between them and Ulbricht's propensity for unilateral behavior, Ambassador Pervukhin told Ulbricht:

> "[Y]ou can have whatever view of me you want, but now the situation is critical." Pervukhin thus asked him to move ahead on all issues only together and not to conceal anything from one another. "This is also in your own interest," Pervukhin observed. "If something goes wrong, we'll both lose our heads."
>
> Ulbricht nodded and said that Pervukhin did not need to have any doubt of his complete loyalty.[278]

Honecker headed the operation in great secrecy from Berlin police headquarters with a very small staff. At 4 P.M. on 12 August, Ulbricht signed the orders to close the border, and at midnight on 12–13 August, the alert was given and the border closure operation began.[279] The Warsaw Pact Declaration, carried at 1 A.M. on 13 August by the GDR press agency ADN, announced that the border closure was being carried out at the request of the Warsaw Pact member states so as to "securely block the way to subversive activity against the countries of the socialist camp." The Western Powers had "used the order now existing on the border of West Berlin for their own perfidious, subversive aims. An end must be put to the present abnormal situation through stronger protection and control on the border with West Berlin."[280] The weight of the Warsaw Pact stood behind the East German border closure.

Parents and children, friends, lovers, colleagues, and schoolmates were suddenly divided. All the bluster of the three years of the Berlin Crisis did not diminish the shock to the Berliners and Germans of the closing of the border. The East Germans started by securing the border with barbed wire, but then added concrete blocks, guard towers, mine strips, dogs, and a shoot-to-kill order. Free movement on foot, by car, truck, train, and boat from East to West Berlin was terminated. The Ü-bahn, S-bahn, trams, and buses were all stopped from crossing the border, and their old crossing points were blocked. Citizens of the GDR and East Berlin needed a (very-hard-to-obtain) visa from the East German People's Police, the VoPos, to visit West Berlin and could no longer work in West Berlin.

For movement from West Berlin to East Berlin, thirteen border-crossing points initially remained open, but on 23 August these were reduced to seven: one for foreigners (Checkpoint Charlie), one for West Berliners (Invalidenstrasse), and five for West Germans. West Berliners could visit East Berlin using their identity card, and West Germans could get a one-day pass to visit East Berlin using their passport. On the night of 14–15 August, the East Germans announced a new regulation—that West Berlin cars could only enter East Berlin with a special permit.[281] For foreigners and representatives of Western occupation forces entering East Berlin, the regulations initially remained the same, although soon the East Germans would demand that Western civilian representatives show IDs at the border.

Four days after the barbed wire was put up, concrete blocks began to be added to the barrier in some places.[282] According to Kvitsinsky, about two weeks after 13 August, Ulbricht called Pervukhin for a meeting:

> Ulbricht explained to us that the hot phase of the operation was over; now we must consolidate the situation and tighten up the border. The barbed wire can't stay in the city forever, it entices the people and provokes them constantly to make new attempts to break through the border. "We will build a concrete wall instead of the barbed wire," Ulbricht said, "and even plaster it. To do this we will have to reduce our construction program somewhat. But we have no other choice."[283]

The Soviets agreed, but the East German leaders had been divided on the decision to build a wall. Several of the top SED officials argued that a wall would "cast shadows at night and provide favorable opportunities for the enemy to approach it." Mielke preferred barbed wire, saying: "it is more durable and more suitable for countering breakthroughs in the border." Defense Minister Heinz Hoffmann called for "a wire fence with concrete posts and trenches." Ulbricht's plan for a wall, however, prevailed.[284] He was never one for half-measures.

THE AFTERMATH OF THE WALL

Not only the Berliners and Germans, but the Western Powers were caught by surprise when the East Germans started to close the border around West Berlin in the early morning hours of 13 August. There was no official Western response at first. It took forty-eight hours for an Allied protest to the Soviet military commander in Karlshorst and seventy-two hours for an Allied complaint to Moscow.[285] Since the West did not recognize the GDR, they did not address any protests to East Berlin. West Berlin mayor Willy Brandt was deeply disappointed with and indignant at the passive Western response. He felt abandoned and warned his Western allies publicly that by allowing the East Germans and Soviets to get away with closing the border, they risked a "second Munich" of appeasement.[286] Brandt angrily approached the barbed wire at Potsdamer Platz and the Brandenberg Gate, with television crews following him, but he wanted Western military might behind him, not television crews.[287]

U.S. silence about 13 August did not stem just from surprise and Kennedy's summer sail off Hyannisport. It also came from relief and a sense that perhaps the crisis would die down now that the East Germans had control of their population. In fact, Kennedy privately told his advisors: "It's not a very nice solution, but a wall is a hell of a lot better than a war." He correctly saw Khrushchev's move as defensive: "Why would Khrushchev put up a wall if he really intended to seize West Berlin? There wouldn't be any need of a wall if he occupied the whole city. This is his way out of his predicament."[288]

It was clear to Kennedy and others that the border closure had been carried out carefully so that the barbed wire was erected inside GDR territory and did not impinge on the territory of West Berlin. The move was obviously taken against the East Germans and did not initially affect Allied rights in Berlin.

The Soviet and East German leaders were very self-congratulatory and relieved about the success of the operation to close the border and the lack of any serious Western countermeasures (or demonstrations by the East German people à la June 1953).[289] In reporting to Khrushchev on 15 September, Ulbricht wrote:

The carrying out of the resolution for the closing of the border to West Berlin went according to plan. The tactic of carrying out the measures gradually made it more difficult for the enemy to orient himself with regard to the extent of our measures and made it easier for us to find the weak places in the border. I must say that the enemy undertook fewer counter-measures than was expected.[290]

Khrushchev agreed: "You carried it all out beautifully—quickly and under conditions of secrecy."[291]

Chinese Foreign Minister Chen Yi was impressed on 31 August by "[t]he fact that the West has still not taken any serious countermeasures."[292] Similarly, Honecker reported on 18 September to representatives of socialist countries accredited to the GDR: "One can say that as a whole the GDR's measures of 13 August 1961 occurred with better results than we expected during their preparation. The implementation of these measures did not entail any serious complications." As the supervisor of operation "Rose," Honecker patted himself on the back, telling the socialist diplomats: "The events of 13 August were unexpected for the West. In spite of the fact that the measures taken for strengthening the GDR's borders with [the] West demanded much preparatory work, the adversary did not anticipate the carrying out of such measures. This is, without question, a defeat for Western intelligence. Many in the GDR were [also] astounded by the precise and rapid implementation of the measures of 13 August."[293]

Honecker attributed the weak Western response to "the new correlation of forces in the world. As in the GDR, so also in West Germany it was understood that behind the GDR's measures stood the forces of all the countries of the socialist camp."[294] Thus, just as Pervukhin had told Kvitsinsky that the border closure would be requested by the whole Warsaw Pact to ensure that the West would be deterred from a military response, Honecker was announcing that this strategy had been successful.

The fact that the East Germans and Soviets were relieved and surprised at the lack of serious Western countermeasures to the border closure raises the issue of whether the West could have stopped the wall by tearing down the barbed wire.[295] Clearly the Soviets and East Germans expected the West to do more, but it is unclear what they would have done if the West had responded more forcefully. Thus far, there are no accessible documents relating to East German and Soviet contingency plans for this. Given Khrushchev's desire to avoid war, perhaps he would have instructed Ulbricht to stop closing the border in the face of Western resistance, but one cannot be certain. Khrushchev and Ulbricht never had to face this scenario, however, since President Kennedy would have had to support the move to tear down the barbed wire, and he did not.

Kennedy wanted to avoid war over Berlin and in fact was eager to resume negotiations with the Soviets on Berlin and Germany to reduce the tensions in the center of Europe. Khrushchev had told Ulbricht on 3 August that he hoped the border closure would make the West take the idea of a German peace treaty more seriously and compel them to return to the negotiating table. Meeting with the North Vietnamese leader, Ho Chi Minh, at Pitsunda just four days after sealing the Berlin border, Khrushchev said that the West "had given the impression that it is ready for negotiations [on the German question]. . . . Undoubtedly there will be negotiations. We have prepared the Western powers for this using all means—both logic and a club."[296]

On 14 August, in fact, Kennedy had given instructions to George Kennan, ambassador in Belgrade, to let the Soviets know he wanted "a peaceful solution to the Berlin crisis . . . which takes account of the interests of all the various parties involved." A week later, Kennedy directed Secretary of State Rusk that it was "time to talk" with the Soviets. He told Rusk that by 1 September he wanted to propose negotiations with the Soviets, and by 1 October he expected preliminary talks to be under way. Accordingly, Rusk approached the Soviet chargé d'affaires in Washington on 31 August, and Ambassador Thompson in Moscow spoke with Gromyko on 7 September. Rusk and Gromyko then held talks on Germany and Berlin in New York beginning on 21 September.[297] Gleefully reporting to the Central Committee on the talks, Gromyko observed: "[T]he Western Powers are not even raising in the talks the question of eliminating the control on the borders of West Berlin. Even more, representatives of the USA recognized in talks that the measures of 13 August 1961 correspond to the vital interests of the GDR and the other socialist states."[298] Just as with the Western call for negotiations of foreign ministers soon after Khrushchev's 27 November 1958 ultimatum, Khrushchev must have felt that his actions, this time in closing the border, prodded the West to the negotiating table.

Skeptical about an agreement with the West, Ulbricht continued to press Khrushchev for a separate peace treaty. Letters from Ulbricht to Khrushchev after 13 August indicate that Ulbricht viewed the border closure as only "the first part of the task of the preparation for the [separate] peace treaty."[299] Khrushchev, however, was still—or again—holding out hope for a peace treaty with the Western Powers, especially once talks between Gromyko and Rusk got under way. To supplement their formal channels of communication, Khrushchev proposed to Kennedy in early September that they exchange off-the-record correspondence on Germany and West Berlin. Khrushchev began this "pen pal" exchange with a letter on 29 September.[300]

Once talks on Germany resumed between Gromyko and Rusk (and

between the two leaders), Khrushchev gave priority to the chance of coming to an agreement with the West over Ulbricht's pressure for a separate treaty. A report from Gromyko to the Central Committee on 17 August is indicative of the Soviet decision not to rush into a peace treaty with the GDR, as of course had been their policy for almost three years. In informing the CC of MID's progress preparing documents on a peace treaty and West Berlin, Gromyko said that "[c]onsidering the developing international situation, this work is being done simultaneously on two tracks, [the first being the] preparation of drafts of documents for possible talks with the Western Powers [and the second being] the preparation of drafts of documents for the conclusion of a peace treaty with the GDR." The first set of documents would be ready at the beginning of September, and the second set of documents would be ready at the beginning of October. The former was clearly a higher priority for Gromyko than the latter.[301]

Khrushchev himself told Ulbricht that the priority in the fall was in talks with the West. In response to Ulbricht's entreaties for a separate treaty, Khrushchev cautioned him on 28 September (in the midst of the Gromyko-Rusk talks):

Under the present conditions, since the measures for the securing and control of the borders of the GDR with West Berlin were carried out successfully, and since the Western Powers are tending towards negotiations and there have already been contacts established between the USSR and the USA in New York, such steps which could exacerbate the situation, especially in Berlin, should be avoided. In this connection it is especially appropriate to abstain from new measures which would change the control order set up by the GDR government on the border with West Berlin.[302]

A high-level Soviet delegation attending the GDR's twelfth anniversary ceremonies from 5–8 October may have warned the East Germans that Khrushchev would announce at the Twenty-second Congress a rescinding of his ultimatum on a peace treaty.[303] On 17 October, the opening day of the Congress, Khrushchev announced that a peace treaty would not have to be signed with the West necessarily by the end of 1961.[304]

By way of explaining the Soviet approach to a separate treaty after the building of the Wall, Kvitsinsky has explained:

The Wall itself was the way with a lot of fuss and ceremony to bury the idea of a German peace treaty, in the sense of a separate treaty with the GDR. After the building of the Wall, the signing of a separate treaty with the GDR was not necessary. All issues that needed to be resolved were resolved. Ulbricht saw in a peace treaty a way to receive international recognition. For us, international recognition of the GDR was important, but not the most important. We saw that this would happen no matter what; it was a question of time. After the borders were closed, there would be no other choice than for the West to recognize the GDR. And that is what happened.[305]

In his memoirs, Khrushchev seems to agree that a peace treaty was not necessary: "I would say that we didn't quite achieve the same sort of moral victory that a peace treaty would have represented, but on the other hand we probably received more material gains without a peace treaty. If the West had agreed to sign a peace treaty, it would have meant concessions on our part, particularly with regard to the movement of people across the border . . . the gates would have remained open."[306]

Another reason for the Soviet decision not to sign a separate peace treaty may have been their intelligence about General Lucius D. Clay, sent by Kennedy to boost morale in West Berlin, and the mock Berlin Wall he had built to practice knocking it down.[307] In addition, Khrushchev must have known that his claims of nuclear superiority were just a myth. The public dispelling of that myth on 21 October in a speech by U.S. Deputy Secretary of Defense Roswell Gilpatric with his announcement that "the missile gap" actually favored the United States presumably restrained Khrushchev. The Checkpoint Charlie standoff a week later would have further lessened Khrushchev's desire to provoke the West.

Frustrated with Khrushchev's 17 October announcement that a peace treaty must not necessarily be signed by the end of the year, Ulbricht wrote him a thirteen-page letter on 30 October, insisting that the Soviets push ahead with measures for the preparation of a peace treaty, including increased emphasis on GDR sovereignty. The imperious tone of the letter is indicated in the following passage:

[I]t is necessary first of all to establish in reality the sovereignty of the GDR and its capital.

We request in this connection that the representatives of the USSR categorically demand in talks with representatives of the Western powers that the . . . US military patrol runs be immediately stopped on the Helmstedt-Berlin stretch [of the transit route]. The present situation in which jeeps with US supervisory officers are accompanied by a Soviet vehicle does not improve the situation. This actually gives the impression of a legalization of this patrol route on the highway. This issue is so important to us, because the Western powers want to create through these regular . . . trips a fait accompli directed towards the creation of an extraterritorial corridor between West Germany and West Berlin, demanded by West German militarists.[308]

Ulbricht was very frustrated by Soviet support for these U.S. rights. He also disapproved of the dual functions of Pervukhin as both Soviet ambassador to the GDR and as "representative of the Four-Power status" of Berlin. When Ulbricht raised this later in Moscow, Vladimir Semenov told him: "[W]e all play in one communist orchestra. In this, comrade Ulbricht plays the first violin for the party, and the Soviet Ambassador only the oboe for the party."[309] Not surprisingly, this did not placate Ulbricht, who always preferred to play solo or be the conductor.

While Ulbricht could not force Khrushchev to sign a separate peace treaty with him, he could increase further the obstacles East Germans faced in trying to flee to West Berlin. While the measures of 13 August had made it much harder to escape to West Berlin, people still did escape. By 20 September, 417 East Germans had made it to freedom in West Berlin. Honecker told top officials that "all attempts to break through [the border] must be made impossible."[310] As early as 15 August GDR border guards fired at and missed a couple who swam across the Teltow Canal to West Berlin.[311] And on 29 August they did shoot and kill a man trying to swim across the canal.[312] On 31 August the Chinese foreign minister, Chen Yi, "expressed his satisfaction" to the East Germans that they were "shooting at border violators."[313] In the twenty-eight years until the dismantling of the Berlin Wall, hundreds of East Germans were killed or injured by border guards trying to stop them from escaping.[314] After German unification, the GDR's infamous "shoot-to-kill" Order 101 was never found by German state lawyers looking into the issue of responsibility for the deaths of people shot trying to escape, yet it clearly existed. In the post-unification federal trials of former East German border guards and leaders, some of the accused, Egon Krenz in particular, defended their actions at the border by blaming the Soviets and the general cold war atmosphere.[315] The overwhelming preponderance of evidence examined in this book, however, indicates that the GDR leaders were intimately involved with the decisions on the border regime in Berlin.

Ulbricht's provocative behavior on the Berlin border was probably a significant reason Khrushchev decided not to sign a separate treaty and turn over to him control of the access routes. In fact, the American scholar Bruce W. Menning, who has consulted the Soviet General Staff archives' files on Berlin for 31 August–31 December 1961, has found continued Soviet frustration and concern over East German unilateral and dangerous behavior in Berlin even after the border closure. The files, based on daily reports of events at the border in Berlin, contain multiple complaints by the Soviets about two issues. The East Germans were shooting too readily and frequently at people trying illegally to cross the border; and they were too restrictive of Western Allied access to East Berlin. Both of these actions, the Soviets feared, could lead to "undesirable serious consequences" and threaten U.S.-Soviet relations.[316]

Marshal Konev and others complained in vain to Ulbricht and Honecker several times in August and September about "disorderly firing" along the border, East German unilateral policies against Western Allied officials, and the need for East German restraint. Foreign Minister Gromyko and Defense Minister Rodion Malinovsky advised Khrushchev on 19 October "that Ulbricht be counseled against taking any new measures without prior discussion with the Soviets." Again on 25 October, they told Khrushchev: "We consider it necessary to review the situation created in the GDR and request that comrade Ulbricht take measures to halt such actions of the police and GDR authorities which create tensions not corresponding with the requirements of the given moment." As Menning summarizes, Soviet reports about the situation on the border in Berlin "indicate both growing apprehensions about the ability to contain incidents and growing impatience with the East German penchant for violence. They also reveal a willingness to seek compromise [with the West] on issues likely to provoke additional confrontations, especially at Checkpoint Charlie."[317]

Drawing on Menning's evidence of Soviet complaints about East German unilateral policies on the border and Soviet concern that East German border guards were demanding identification of Allied personnel, W. R. Smyser asserts that the Checkpoint Charlie crisis was a result of this unilateral East German policy.[318] The Checkpoint Charlie crisis began on 22 October when East German border guards requested the identification papers of Allan Lightner, the deputy chief of the U.S. Mission in Berlin. Two months earlier, Foreign Minister Otto Winzer had recommended to Ulbricht, Stoph, and Maron that all Western diplomats, even with official license plates, show identification at the border. This precaution was necessary, Winzer said, since otherwise the Western officials might smuggle East Germans out in their cars.[319]

Lightner was crossing into East Berlin at Checkpoint Charlie to go to the opera with his wife. They were riding in his official car with a U.S. Mission license plate and should have been just waved through, as usual. When they were not, Lightner called General Clay. Clay sought to demonstrate the continued right of officials of the Allied powers to enter East Berlin after 13 August. Thus (after Lightner's wife left the car), at Clay's orders, U.S. military forces escorted Lightner across the checkpoint and into East Berlin. Lightner then repeated the whole thing with a stronger military escort, and four U.S. tanks approached the checkpoint.

The Soviets assured the Americans that the incident had been a mistake, but on the next day the GDR announced that Allied personnel dressed in civilian clothes had to show identification to cross the border into East Berlin. Clay sent more American officials, backed up with military force, to test their right to enter East Berlin. The process escalated with both the Americans and the Soviets sending tanks to Checkpoint Charlie, until on the afternoon of 27 October there were ten tanks on each side. And they remained there for sixteen hours. This was the first and only direct face-to-face U.S.-Soviet military confrontation of the cold war. Since some of the American tanks were equipped with bulldozer shovels and were the very tanks Clay had been using to practice bringing down the Berlin Wall, the Soviets believed that the United States was going to attempt to remove the Wall.[320]

Kennedy, however, had no such plans. He activated his secret back channel connection to Khrushchev through R.F.K. and Georgi Bolshakov. Kennedy requested that Khrushchev withdraw the tanks and promised that he would immediately thereafter withdraw the American tanks. Khrushchev agreed. On the morning of 28 October, Soviet tanks pulled back about ten yards from the checkpoint, followed by a similar American pullback. The Soviets then pulled back more, and the Americans followed. After several rounds of this, the Soviet and American tanks left the area of Checkpoint Charlie.[321]

Michael Lemke's research in archives of the former GDR led him to agree with Smyser that the Checkpoint Charlie crisis was indeed brought on by unilateral East German policies aimed at torpedoeing Soviet-American talks. As Lemke points out, while the Soviets and Americans withdrew their tanks in relief from Checkpoint Charlie, "Ulbricht decorated the VoPos and others who were based at the Friedrichstrasse [Checkpoint Charlie] crossing."[322]

Conclusive evidence on Ulbricht's role in the crisis, however, is still lacking. During the whole Checkpoint Charlie incident, Ulbricht was in Moscow attending the CPSU's Twenty-second Congress. On the sidelines of the Congress, he and Khrushchev must have been consulting about the events in Berlin. On 27 October, at the height of the crisis, Ulbricht sent a top-secret, urgent telegram to the Politburo in Berlin instructing them to continue demanding that Western Allied personnel in civilian clothes show their identification to the VoPos. He also instructed Mielke "to prepare a steel barrier for the entire width of Friedrichstrasse within three days. A special order will follow on the timing of installing this barrier."[323] One must assume that Ulbricht was waiting for this "special order" from Khrushchev. Two days later, Ulbricht sent more instructions to the Politburo. Clearly in the wake of the tank standoff at Checkpoint Charlie, Ulbricht was angry that "the anti-tank barriers that were supposed to have been installed on the border long ago" by the Defense Ministry had not been. Perhaps Ulbricht was passing on Khrushchev's irritation about this. Ulbricht demanded that anti-tank obstacles be installed at "the most important political border points" such as the Brandenburg Gate and Potsdamer Platz. He also directed the Defense Ministry and Stasi to prepare anti-tank barriers for Friedrichstrasse and the other six checkpoints.[324] Ulbricht and Khrushchev wanted to deter a repeat appearance of U.S. tanks at the border.

Partly to avoid precisely just such confrontations with the Americans, Khrushchev had not concluded a separate peace treaty with the GDR or given it control of the access routes. Meeting with Gomulka at the end of October in Moscow, Khrushchev underlined his desire to avoid confrontation with the Americans. Khrushchev practically stumbled over his words in expressing his concern about war, while trying to pretend he was not concerned: "There will not be a war, but signing a peace treaty with the GDR might exacerbate the situation. . . . Although there will be no war, we should not exacerbate the situation. We must continue our game. We are not afraid, but we do not want war." He then gave Gomulka an economic argument against signing the treaty: "What will we gain and what will we lose by concluding a peace treaty with the GDR[?] We will lose: The Americans, the English, [and] the French might declare an economic blockade against the USSR and the socialist countries. Regarding the USSR, these are empty platitudes, but the other countries—the GDR, Poland, Hungary, and to a lesser extent, Romania—might suffer if they do that. . . . We should not force the conclusion of a peace treaty with Germany, but continue to move forward."[325] Ulbricht's stress on the GDR's economic difficulties and the need for help from the other socialist countries thus appears to have partially backfired on him in contributing to Khrushchev's decision not to sign a separate treaty. The description by other socialist leaders of their economic woes at the Moscow WTO meeting also no doubt contributed.

Exceeding all bounds of logic, Ulbricht would not stop pushing Khrushchev to sign a separate treaty. Meeting with Khrushchev after the conclusion of the Twenty-second Congress, Ulbricht was so persistent that Khrushchev grew angry: "I do not agree that the more the conclusion of a peace treaty is postponed, the worse the GDR economy will be. We are having an old conversation with you." Khrushchev declared that a separate peace treaty would not change the GDR's internal or external circumstances. He was very critical of the GDR's economic dependence on others and the demands for Soviet help. Khrushchev advised that Ulbricht's top priority must be to establish more economic independence.[326]

In January 1962 Khrushchev announced to his Presidium colleagues that they no longer needed a German peace treaty. The West was not going to agree, he said, and besides (reminiscent of Mao's strategy of threatening but not seizing the offshore islands), he wanted to hold on to the levers over Berlin to keep pressure on the West: It is "better to have Berlin for aggravating the West than to make concessions." Khrushchev also felt much less pressure after sealing the border around West Berlin. He said that before 13 August West Berlin was a bone stuck in their throat, but that since building the Wall it became a bone stuck in the West's throat. "Now we can live with this bone. Let them live [with it]."[327]

In late February 1962 Ulbricht came once again to Moscow to plead his case for a peace treaty. Khrushchev did his best to end the conversation telling the East German leader: "On 13 August, we achieved the maximum of what was possible. . . . What is pushing us to a peace treaty? Nothing. Until 13 August, we were racking our brains over how to move forward. Now, the borders are closed."[328] Not only did Khrushchev believe that the Berlin Wall solved the key problems for the GDR, but he also continued to fear that a separate peace treaty could result in war or an economic blockade, neither of which he wanted to risk. Khrushchev rhetorically asked Ulbricht if risking war was "worth it because of Berlin? No. We would be idiots to do this."[329] And as in their last meeting in October, on 26 February Khrushchev expressed his resentment of Ulbricht's constant requests for economic aid. Referring to the separate peace treaty, Khrushchev said: "You want to [just] give a signature, and we are supposed to give economically" to save the GDR when West Germany responded with an economic boycott. "The main question, [Khrushchev asserted,] is not the peace treaty, but a consolidation of the economic situation. That is what we have to concentrate on." But the military risk was clearly nagging at Khrushchev just as much, and he added immediately: "I say once again with regard to a peace treaty, that I believe there would be no war, but who can guarantee that?"[330]

In sum, there were at least five reasons that Khrushchev never concluded a separate peace treaty with the GDR: fear of a military conflict with the West; fear of a Western economic boycott; the success of the wall in stemming the refugee exodus; Kennedy's resumption of negotiations with the Soviets via talks between Rusk and Gromyko; and fear of Ulbricht's aggressive and unilateral methods in Berlin. Khrushchev did not want to give Ulbricht further encouragement by turning over control of the access routes to him in a separate peace treaty.

Regarding the last factor, Khrushchev even spoke to Ulbricht about Kennedy's concerns: "In one interview, [Kennedy] posed the question himself of what one can do and to whom one can turn if, for example, Ulbricht infringes upon the [existing] order regarding access routes to Berlin."[331] Khrushchev was probably almost as concerned as Kennedy about Ulbricht's potential to exacerbate the situation in Berlin and embroil him in a military conflict with the West. A comment in Pervukhin's annual report on the GDR in 1961 would have backed up Khrushchev's reluctance on this issue. Pervukhin wrote that in the months after the border closure, the East German regime was "very upset with the lack of clarity regarding a concrete date for the conclusion of a peace treaty with the GDR" through which they expected to gain "control over the communications of the GDR which ran from West Berlin to the FRG." Pervukhin noted in a worried tone "that the GDR leadership gives insufficiently deep consideration to questions regarding how to accomplish [this] without causing a military conflict."[332] Kennedy similarly wrote to Khrushchev on 16 October 1961 about the dangers that would be connected with augmenting Ulbricht's control over Berlin:

> This area would . . . be rendered less peaceful if the maintenance of the West's vital interests were to become dependent on the whims of the East German regime. Some of Mr. Ulbricht's statements on this subject have not been consistent with your reassurances or even his own—and I do not believe that either of us wants a constant state of doubt, tension and emergency in this area, which would require an even larger military build-up on both sides.[333]

After battling to restrain Ulbricht for several years, Khrushchev agreed with Kennedy's desire not to give Ulbricht the capacity to have such control over U.S.-Soviet relations.

If Khrushchev had given up on whatever intention he may once have had to sign a separate peace treaty, believed the wall was "the maximum possible," and wanted to avoid military conflict with the West, why did he continue his public campaign for a peace treaty in 1962 and initiate harrassment of Western flights in the air corridors? Part of the answer may have been Khrushchev's desire to keep pressure on Berlin as a distraction from his secret deployment of nuclear missiles in Cuba.[334] While President Kennedy was convinced that the Cuban Missile Crisis of October 1962 constituted Khrushchev's continuation of the Berlin Crisis by other, even more threatening, means, there is so far no indication in Soviet documents of this.[335] Instead, Khrushchev's goals in sending nuclear missiles to Cuba were centered around defending Castro's socialist regime from an American attack and bolstering the Soviet side of the strategic nuclear balance (which, indirectly, would have added weight to Soviet diplomacy). There is also evidence that Khrushchev used the missile deployment to persuade wavering Cuban leaders to remain on the Soviet side of the Sino-Soviet split.[336]

There was another reason for Khrushchev's continued pressure on Berlin. After such a long and vocal campaign for a peace treaty, which provoked Chinese and Albanian criticism that this campaign yielded no success, Khrushchev did not want people to think that after the Wall, he had just given up and pulled back with his tail between his legs.[337]

Khrushchev and Ulbricht agreed that "for propaganda reasons," they needed to keep up the campaign—to show the Germans and the rest of the world that they were not "giving up."[338]

In addition, Khrushchev sought to keep the West on the defensive about West Berlin and push the West into further concessions in negotiations, especially since the Western Powers continued to be divided about how to handle Khrushchev's demands.[339] Khrushchev told Gomulka in October 1961:

> We think we should continue with our [current] line, should keep applying pressure and exploit the weaknesses of the enemy. We should strive to remove the official representatives from West Berlin and liquidate Adenauer's pretentions to West Berlin. . . . The game continues, we should keep applying pressure. We should coordinate our position with Comrade Ulbricht. We should carry on salami tactics with regard to the rights of Western countries. . . . We have to pick our way through, divide them, exploit all the possibilities.[340]

In February 1962 Khrushchev assured Ulbricht he would continue talking about a peace treaty: "We will continue the campaign aggressively, for the signing of a peace treaty. We will exploit all possibilities for talks on this, but we will decide the time when it will be concluded."[341] Khrushchev, however, would never decide that the time was right for a separate peace treaty with the GDR and for turning over more control to his aggressive, self-assured, narrow-minded ally. It was the same persistent pressure from Ulbricht that led, on the one hand, to Khrushchev's acquiescence to sealing the border around West Berlin and, on the other hand, to Khrushchev's ultimate refusal to give Ulbricht any more of what he wanted.

CONCLUSION

In the months leading up to and throughout the crisis, it became increasingly clear that Ulbricht intended to deal with the West Berlin issue separately and soon, instead of waiting for a peace treaty. Khrushchev, on the other hand, wanted to wait as long as possible to see if he could come to some sort of agreement, at least a provisional one, with the Western Powers on West Berlin and Germany as a whole. After Khrushchev sent the first ultimatum to the West on 27 November 1958, and then did not follow through on signing a separate treaty with the GDR and handing over to the GDR control of the West Berlin access routes within six months, Ulbricht did not believe that Khrushchev would do this in the near future either. Thus, Ulbricht moved to take matters into his own hands, in particular by trying to usurp control of the Berlin sectoral border. As the crisis dragged on, the numbers of East German refugees increased, the state of the East German economy plunged, and Ulbricht grew more desperate. This led him to work harder to convince Khrushchev that East German economic and political collapse was imminent unless the Soviets and other socialist countries helped soon and that the demise of East Germany would undermine the prestige of Khrushchev and the entire socialist camp.

The strength of Ulbricht's influence over Khrushchev actually grew as the East German domestic situation became more precarious. The Ulbricht who sent an East German delegation to China without giving the Soviets any notice, acted against Soviet wishes regarding the control regime on the Berlin sectoral border, and instructed Khrushchev on how to handle negotiations with the West in 1961 was hardly a weak, passive ally. Ulbricht's influence proved strong enough to persuade Khrushchev to allow him to seal the border around West Berlin, but not strong enough to force the Soviet leader to sign a separate peace treaty or turn over control of the access routes.

Ulbricht's maximal aim was the absorption of West Berlin into the GDR. He saw West Berlin much more as a "prize" than as the "lever" that it represented for Khrushchev. For both Ulbricht and Khrushchev, a separate peace treaty signed between them was really an option of last resort. Much more desirable was a Four Power peace treaty with both Germanies that would legitimate East Germany's right to exist and give the East German populace the confidence to stay instead of fleeing to the West. While waiting skeptically for this peace treaty or for a provisional settlement with the West, Ulbricht lost patience. As the refugee numbers mounted, the safest option Ulbricht saw for protecting his state from collapse was a series of unilateral steps to increase East German control over the Berlin sectoral border, which would serve both to stem the flow of refugees and to force the Western powers to recognize the East German regime.

Ulbricht did finally force Khrushchev to act. After initially resisting Ulbricht's pleas, Khrushchev came to see Ulbricht's concrete "Rose" not only as a way to save the GDR by stemming the refugee exodus, but also as a way to wall in Ulbricht in East Berlin so that he could not enact measures on the inter-Berlin border that would risk provoking an East-West military conflict. Thus, as Henry Krisch points out, the "de facto acceptance of the existing European interstate relations [implied in the building of the wall] came at the expense of the GDR. The GDR's ability to exert pressure on Berlin and the Federal Republic was reduced, and its prior conditions for an East-West accommodation (such as formal recognition) were pushed aside."[342]

In his memoirs, former Stasi chief Ernst Wollweber agrees that under the circumstances the Wall had to be built, but believes that it could have been avoided and the situation improved earlier if there had been a collective leadership in the GDR, instead of Ulbricht's dictatorship.[343] Wollweber's point is well taken: Ulbricht did prevent the Soviets' preferred course of a change in leadership and policy. Khrushchev felt that the "best and most logical way to fight [Western influence] was to try to win the minds of the people by using culture and policies to create better living conditions," [recalling:] "It was my dream to create such conditions in Germany that the GDR would become a showcase of moral, political, and material achievement—all attractively displayed for the Western world to see and admire."[344] While dangling this dream in front of Khrushchev's face, however, Ulbricht's leadership made it impossible for this ever to be realized. Indeed, the end result of Ulbricht's policies was the Wall, followed by the collapse of the GDR in 1989.

Khrushchev believed that "[i]f the GDR had fully tapped the moral and material potential [of its citizens] . . . there could be unrestricted passage back and forth between East and West Berlin." What Khrushchev may never have realized, however, was that it was not just the vast difference he identified in the economic foundations of East and West Germany that worked against him, but also Ulbricht himself, who probably would always view "unrestricted passsage back and forth between East and West Berlin" as one of his worst nightmares. While Khrushchev "spent a great deal of time trying to think of a way . . . [to] introduce incentives in the GDR to counteract the force behind the exodus of East German youths to West Germany," Ulbricht devoted himself instead to giving the Soviets further incentives to continue their massive aid to the GDR and to support sealing the West Berlin border.[345]

The combination of Ulbricht's pressure and the West's unwillingness to compromise led Khrushchev to keep adopting delaying tactics in the crisis. Searching for policies that would be acceptable to both Ulbricht and the West, Khrushchev kept switching approaches during the crisis. The same was true of the U.S. relationship with West Germany, as so thoroughly described by William Burr and Marc Trachtenberg.[346] Each superpower was constrained by its German ally in the policies it would adopt and the proposals it would put forward, and thus the crisis dragged on for three years.

The role of the weak East German economic situation looms quite large in the documents as a key factor for the Soviets and the East Germans during the crisis, just as it had been in the 1953–58 period. As Ulbricht pointed out in his 15 September 1961 letter to Khrushchev:

> The experiences of the last years have proven that it is not possible that a socialist country such as the GDR can carry out a peaceful competition with

an imperialist country such as West Germany with open borders. Such opportunities appear first when the socialist world system has surpassed the capitalist countries in per-capita production.[347]

The Wall was in part meant to protect and support the East German economy from competition with West Germany. At a time when the Soviets had essentially agreed to do whatever was necessary to support and improve the East German economy, Moscow saw the Wall as a way to help do this without putting overwhelming pressure on the Soviet or other socialist economies. As Kvitsinsky put it, "the scale of Soviet economic aid to the GDR was unprecedented. The GDR was like a sick child. We had to feed it, cure it, help it as much as we could."[348] The Wall was a way to limit this.

Thus, from Khrushchev's perspective, the Berlin Wall accomplished four main things, or at least he hoped it would. First, it saved the GDR regime (for the time being). Second, it eased the economic pressure on the Soviet Union and the other socialist countries to help the GDR. Third, the Wall allowed Khrushchev to wrest more control of events away from Ulbricht. Even with the Wall, however, Khrushchev still feared Ulbricht's unilateral behavior, which could harm Soviet relations with the West, as his letter of 28 September to Ulbricht urging him to "avoid . . . such steps which could exacerbate the situation, especially in Berlin" attested.[349] If Khrushchev felt he had sufficient control over Ulbricht, he would not have needed to write such a letter. Finally, Khrushchev no doubt hoped that the border closure in Berlin would show the Chinese, the Albanians, and other critics that he *could* stand up to the West and carry out his threats without embroiling them in a war. The Chinese, however, viewed Khrushchev's long-awaited agreement to build the Berlin Wall and the lack of "any serious Western countermeasures" as indication of the righteousness of their views of the West as a "paper tiger."[350] Like the Chinese, some of Khrushchev's colleagues who would oust him three years later were critical of his behavior in the "notorious Berlin Crisis," both for bringing them to the "brink of war" with the West over Berlin and for retreating from his several ultimatums.[351]

Khrushchev had started the Berlin Crisis far more optimistic about his capacity to pressure the West and the potential of the GDR to compete with the FRG than he concluded it. Khrushchev's views of what was achievable narrowed during the crisis. In 1958 he felt a military confidence from Sputnik, an economic confidence in the capacity of the Soviet Union to surpass the United States and the GDR to surpass the FRG, and he did not foresee the coming breach with China.[352] In 1961 he was faced with an open break with his most powerful ally, the PRC, a clear nuclear inferiority vis-à-vis the West, a GDR on the verge of collapse, and continued resistance at home to many of his domestic and foreign policies. He scaled back his goals accordingly.[353]

From Ulbricht's perspective, in August 1961 he finally achieved his goal of sealing the border to West Berlin. This had long been his minimal demand for stabilizing the situation in the GDR consolidating his own rule and solving the "West Berlin problem." He also got his wishes for more Soviet economic aid and Soviet pressure on the other East European countries to increase their aid to the GDR. Ulbricht, however, did not get a peace treaty or control of the access routes.

With regard to the differences in East German and Soviet goals, priorities, and strategies during the Berlin Crisis, for the most part the side with the greater motivation on a particular issue prevailed on that issue.[354] Thus, Ulbricht got his way on issues of GDR domestic politics, economic aid from the Soviets, and border closure; and Khrushchev got his way on issues directly involving the West, such as a peace treaty (not signing one), the status of West Berlin (not changing it), and the access routes for the Western Powers (not turning over their control to the GDR).

The process and the outcome of the Berlin Crisis cannot be understood without taking into account the role of the GDR. By examining the goals and strategies of both Ulbricht and Khrushchev, one gains a fuller understanding of the crisis than by concentrating solely on its East-West dimension. While the GDR leaders could not, or would not, close the Berlin border without Soviet approval, they had significant means for persuading the Soviets to approve that action. Their persistent and highly motivated appeals to the Soviets, lack of implementation of New Course–type domestic policies, and unilateral actions at the Berlin border were crucial. They also took advantage of the Sino-Soviet dispute, the legacy of Beria's and Malenkov's alleged desire to abandon the GDR, Western unwillingess to back down, and Khrushchev's commitment to the triumph of socialism over capitalism in Germany. Khrushchev's frequent assertion that "East German needs are our needs" illustrated the intense identification between this superpower and "super-ally."

These factors allowed Ulbricht to turn around the earlier Soviet refusal to close the Berlin border. On 13 August 1961, the Soviet protestations of March 1953 and July 1961 that closing the border was "unacceptable and grossly simplistic [and would entail] serious technical difficulties [and] political problems" were distant memories. The problems necessitating the border closure, however, were never completely resolved and played an essential role in the revolution of 1989 in the GDR.[355]

While the new archival evidence has revealed multiple instances of the importance of allies in the cold war, there are also some unique factors in this particular case of the Berlin Crisis. First, the crisis occurred during the period of the expansion of the Sino-Soviet rift, but before the rift became irrevocable. Thus, it was a time when it was possible for a country such as the GDR to experiment with utilizing the rift for its own purposes. Once the rift crystalized, it would be more difficult to do this. Second, the role of Khrushchev himself as the Soviet leader was important. Khrushchev was really a "true believer" in socialism and had a personal commitment to socialism in the GDR that Stalin before him and Brezhnev after him did not share in quite the same way. Stalin's commitment to the GDR wavered,[356] and Brezhnev did not allow himself to be manipulated by the GDR leader as much as Khrushchev had.[357] Third, the history of Malenkov and Beria "wanting to give up the GDR" with one of them as a result being "fired and the other shot" certainly would have inspired any Soviet leader to stand by the GDR. Fourth, East Germany's strategic location was essential for the defense of the Warsaw Pact, and the Soviets could not afford to lose it. In addition, the very fact of the open border and the challenge from West Germany and West Berlin next door compelled Khrushchev to pay special attention to developments in the GDR. Finally, just as Khrushchev's personality played a specific role in the crisis, so did Ulbricht's. His forceful, haughty, and aggressive personality annoyed and somewhat intimidated Khrushchev. It was probably a combination of a desire to get Ulbricht off his back with his constant requests for more aid and for the closure of the border, and his fear of Ulbricht's undertaking anymore unilateral actions that finally pushed Khrushchev to cave in to his pleas. Ulbricht simply drove Khrushchev up the wall.

Conclusion

THIS BOOK HAS examined an important and insufficiently studied aspect of the cold war: Moscow's complicated alliance relations, focusing on East Berlin. It was not just Washington that experienced difficulties controlling its allies; Moscow did as well. This work has portrayed three cases of the East German leadership resisting, hindering, and changing Soviet policies. In 1953 Ulbricht resisted the Soviet *New Course* and ousted its East German proponents Zaisser and Herrnstadt. In 1956 and 1957 Ulbricht countered the more liberal view of the implications of the Soviet Twentieth Congress and the Hungarian uprising for the GDR, and he removed from power those who favored the liberal approach, including Schirdewan and Wollweber. During the Berlin Crisis of 1958–61, Ulbricht increasingly acted on his own, ignoring Khrushchev's pleas not to take any unilateral action in Berlin while the Soviet leader sought an agreement with the West. To a large degree, the policies carried out in the GDR and in Berlin, the front line of the cold war, were formulated by the East Germans, not the Soviets, and were often carried out against Soviet wishes.

The conflicts between the Soviet and East German leaders were in part the inevitable result of their different geostrategic positions: As a global superpower, the Soviets had broader interests, needs, and goals than did the East Germans. While both sought to preserve and strengthen socialism in the GDR and ideally expand it to the FRG, they each had another interest that was at times of competing importance: for Ulbricht it was the maintenance of his own personal power as leader, and for Khrushchev it was maintaining or improving, or at least not unduly exacerbating, relations with the West. Ulbricht's goals, as those of any smaller power, were narrower than Khrushchev's and thus able to be more consistently pursued. Khrushchev had to juggle constantly between the conflicting preferences of his German ally and those of the West, while also looking over his shoulder at the Chinese.

From the winter of 1952–53 through the summer of 1961, the Soviets consistently rebuffed East German proddings to close the border in Berlin on several grounds. First, the Kremlin leaders argued that closing the border would make Berliners and Germans on both sides hostile toward the East German and Soviet leaders. Second, the West might respond militarily or with harmful economic sanctions. Third, the Soviets anticipated it would be technically very difficult to close the border. In March 1953 the Soviet leaders judged East German proposals to close the border "politically unacceptable and grossly simplistic," and in July 1961 they still feared the "political and technical difficulties." While the Soviets worried that the costs of closing the border might be too high, for Ulbricht the costs of the open border were already too high and getting higher in terms of the negative economic and political effects on his regime. The dilemma of whether to close the border around West Berlin or not highlighted the different perspectives and interests of the East German and Soviet leaders.

Khrushchev wanted to be able to achieve multiple objectives simultaneously: stabilization of the situation in the GDR; improvement in East-West relations; formal Western recognition of the Soviet sphere of influence in Eastern Europe, including the GDR; increased prestige for the Soviet Union and Khrushchev himself in the world; the maintenance of Soviet leadership of the international communist movement in the face of Chinese challenges; and an invigoration of the Soviet economy so that it could catch up and surpass that of the United States. As any leader, he wanted to maximize his gains and minimize his losses. Thus, a policy that would allow him, for example, both to stabilize the situation in the GDR and to improve, or at least not worsen, relations with the West was preferable to one that would improve the situation in the GDR at the expense of relations with the West. Ulbricht was not sensitive to this trade-off, since tense East-West relations actually helped bolster his arguments about the need to close the border to protect the GDR from hostile Western influences. Even when Khrushchev himself strained East-West relations by his threats to the West during the Berlin Crisis, he wanted to be able to control the level of pressure or accommodation in these relations instead of transferring this control to Ulbricht. The SED leader, however, naturally wanted to steer things in a direction more conducive to his own interests, which meant acting unilaterally to assume more control over the Berlin border, even if, or especially if, that would exacerbate Soviet-Western relations.

With great persistence and determination, Ulbricht followed the same clear path from 1953–61, that of consolidating his control over the GDR and its borders and of resisting any challenges to this. He was much more concerned with his firm command of life in the GDR than with the legitimacy of his regime in the eyes of the people. Ulbricht did not have much patience for persuasion; he was much more comfortable imposing socialism and assuming that people would ultimately realize they had no choice but to accept it. As he asserted in 1957, "the struggle for the protection of the workers' and peasants' state and of socialism must be carried out not only with means of persuasion but also with the means of state power."[1] Ulbricht said this in the context of criticizing those, such as Schirdewan, who believed that, in the wake of the Hungarian uprising and given the open border in Berlin, persuasive means would be sufficient or permissible in the GDR. Ulbricht, on the other hand, always felt that the only reliable way to "protect" socialism in the GDR from hostile forces within and without was by harsh measures, by punishing people who did not prove themselves to be reliable socialists, by wielding the stick, not the carrot.

While the Soviets also utilized "state power" in their own country and in others, they, perhaps unrealistically or idealistically, felt it was important that Ulbricht make efforts to rely more on attraction than coercion in the GDR. Although hardly paragons themselves, the Soviets repeatedly told the East Germans between 1953 and 1961 to treat their citizens less "bureaucratically" and "heartlessly" so that they would not flee to the West. Precisely because the Soviets hoped, at times more than the East Germans did, that the socialist system in the GDR would be strong enough not only to attract East German citizens but also to be a magnet for West Germans, they felt that under conditions of the open border in Berlin, it was even *more* imperative, not less, as Ulbricht thought, to rely on persuasion instead of diktat. Khrushchev in particular, who was so critical of Stalin's methods and the effects of these, probably felt that Ulbricht's methods were having the same negative effects on the system and its legitimacy in the eyes of the people. Especially because of Khrushchev's optimistic personality and his strong conviction in the superiority of socialism over capitalism, he had great faith, at least until some time in late 1960 or 1961, that a socialist GDR could prosper and surpass the capitalist FRG. He did not want to allow Ulbricht's methods to ruin this chance, yet he could find no way to prevent Ulbricht from doing just this.

How was Ulbricht able to successfully resist Soviet efforts to get him to implement a more accommodating form of socialism and to obtain Soviet sanctioning of the closure of the border around West Berlin? First, as described above, Ulbricht was much more intently focused on these issues than the Soviets were, since these issues were at the center of his attention, but had to share attention with other issues on the Soviet agenda. Ulbricht lobbied the Soviets relentlessly for more aid and for closing the border. As Khrushchev's former advisor Troyanovsky attests, "There were periods when Moscow was literally bombarded by messages and phone calls from East Berlin."[2]

Second, Ulbricht's capacity to control the situation on the ground in the GDR and Berlin was essential. For the Soviets, it was the old problem of how to project power from the center to the periphery of an empire. Even with all the Soviet political, military, economic, intelligence, and other advisors, to say nothing of troops stationed in the GDR, Ulbricht still had the capacity to take actions unilaterally and without

Soviet support. Ulbricht was rarely intimidated from expressing disagreement with the Soviet leaders in person and in letters; he certainly was not going to be shy about doing this when he was at home in East Berlin. Soviet intelligence was not always able to learn of East German decisions in advance, to say nothing of develop the capability to prevent them from being implemented. David Murphy, former chief of the CIA's Berlin base; Sergei Kondrashev, a former leading KGB expert on Germany; and George Bailey, former director of Radio Liberty observe that in the mid- to late 1950s, the "KGB officers were often impatient with the growing reluctance of German officials, particularly those in the [Stasi] to follow orders 'without question'."[3] As they point out, Ulbricht dominated the Stasi, and this complicated the KGB's relations with their East German counterpart. The GDR leader was eager to preserve as much independence as he could from his superpower patron, including its intelligence services.

While the location of the GDR at the front line of the cold war, with its open border in Berlin, made East Germany dependent on Soviet support, this dependence was mutual, especially as interpreted by Khrushchev. For military-strategic and prestige considerations, Khrushchev increasingly felt the importance of the GDR to the Soviet side of the cold war in the 1950s. The uprising in the GDR in 1953, followed by the uprisings in Poland and Hungary in 1956, made crystal clear the possibility of the collapse of the SED regime and the likelihood of its absorption into the FRG. In the military-strategic sense, Khrushchev did not want the 18 million East Germans to be added to the power of Adenauer's West Germany and NATO,[4] nor did he want to see the Bundeswehr and NATO take over the GDR and thus move closer to the Polish, Czech, and Soviet borders.[5] Khrushchev said again and again that the Soviets must "treat seriously the needs of the German Democratic Republic . . . as our own needs."[6] In fact, at the prospect of not giving the GDR sufficient economic assistance to survive and flourish, Khrushchev "exploded" at his colleagues.[7] He felt so strongly about this also because he wanted to make the GDR and East Berlin into a "showcase of the moral, political and material achievement" of socialism.[8]

Given their location at the westernmost point of the Soviet bloc, Khrushchev knew that many people would first see and judge socialism in East Berlin and the GDR. He wanted to make sure that the model of socialism on display there was an attractive one. Mikoian was particularly forthright in telling the East Germans how absolutely essential the success of socialism in the GDR was to the Soviet, communist cause: "If socialism does not win in the GDR, if communism does not prove itself as superior and vital there, then we have not won."[9] East Germany's status as a super-ally was in the eye of the Soviet beholder. Khrushchev felt that the reputation of the whole Soviet bloc was riding on the GDR's success or failure. This often put him at the mercy of Ulbricht's portrayal of the situation in the GDR and what Ulbricht deemed necessary to strengthen socialism in the GDR.

Khrushchev's eagerness to not be accused, as Beria and Malenkov were, of pursuing policies that would result in the liquidation of the socialist GDR put additional pressure on him to support East Berlin. In November 1958 Khrushchev recounted to Gomulka the history of Beria and Malenkov's plans to give up East Germany in 1953: "Are we supposed to give up a population of 18 million in the GDR for nothing, without a fight? That's stupidity. We should fully support Ulbricht and Grotewohl."[10] Similarly, Khrushchev reminded Ulbricht in 1961 that "Malenkov and Beria wanted to liquidate the GDR, but we fired one and shot the other and said that we supported a socialist Germany."[11] Thus, Ulbricht knew full well Khrushchev's eagerness to set himself apart from Beria and Malenkov and the room this could give him, Ulbricht, to press Moscow for increasing amounts of economic and other support.

Ulbricht also exploited the Sino-Soviet split. To cajole Khrushchev into sanctioning East German aims and tactics, Ulbricht initially sought to use the closeness of East German–Chinese relations due to the similarity of their national situations (each part of a divided country with "imperialists" occupying the other part) and their critical views of Khrushchev's reforms in domestic and foreign policy. Then he switched to openly siding with Khrushchev against the Chinese and Albanians, especially at the WTO meeting of early August 1961, to show what a loyal Soviet ally he was and how he deserved to be rewarded with augmented aid. Ulbricht and the other East bloc leaders had witnessed the open and vehement arguments between the Soviets and Chinese and between the Soviets and Albanians at various communist bloc meetings and knew the pressure Khrushchev was under. At their 30 November 1960 bilateral meeting in Moscow, Ulbricht had also seen Khrushchev eager to show himself more supportive of the GDR than China was: "[W]e aren't China; we aren't afraid of giving the Germans a start" with economic help.[12] As with the legacy of Beria and Malenkov, so the effects of the Sino-Soviet split helped Ulbricht obtain more aid from Khrushchev, who needed to avoid being seen as anything less than fully supportive of a socialist GDR.

All the factors described above led to a situation in which, as Yuli Kvitsinsky has observed, East German officials, including Ulbricht, "were totally convinced that they could make any political mistake[, including resisting Soviet policy initiatives and advice, I would argue,] without fearing they would lose power. Moscow would always rush to help in decisive moments and use all its powers to preserve the GDR."[13] Indeed,

Khrushchev's equation of East German with Soviet needs also had the effect of turning East German weakness into strength. The weaker the SED regime was, the greater its needs and requests (which increasingly seemed like demands), the higher the stakes were for the Soviets. Ulbricht was particularly adept at emphasizing the vulnerability of the GDR and East Berlin to the FRG and West Berlin and the corresponding need for greater and greater amounts of Soviet support—in the form of economic aid and border closure—to offset the negative effects of the FRG and West Berlin. The weaker the GDR became as the refugees streamed out, the stronger was Ulbricht's argument about the necessity of Soviet help.

This trend began with the June 1953 uprising in the GDR that laid bare the GDR's weakness. Once the Berlin Wall was built, however, Ulbricht's leverage diminished for two reasons. First, once the Wall solved the refugee problem, the Soviets and other East Europeans did not have the same concern that the GDR was so fragile and had to be treated so gingerly and preferentially. There was no longer a sense that the GDR was on the verge of collapse, so there was less need to cave in to all of Ulbricht's requests or demands. Second, the very strength Ulbricht exerted in relations with Khrushchev to persuade him to agree to close the border led Khrushchev to resent Ulbricht, to be fed up with his requests and demands, and to be wary of giving him the opportunity to exert such strength or influence in the future, such as by having control over the access routes to West Berlin.

It is difficult to construct as clear a picture of Khrushchev's goals regarding the GDR and Germany as of Ulbricht's goals. There are several reasons for this. First, we still do not have access to many high-level Soviet documents for this period, such as Presidium member V. Malin's notes or minutes of Presidium meetings at which policy toward Germany was discussed. The problem is compounded by Khrushchev's unpredictable, emotional way of thinking. One gets the distinct feeling that Khrushchev was not always sure what he wanted, that he frequently improvised and changed his mind, and said things for public consumption that he did not really mean or believe. Trying to follow the logic of Khrushchev's thinking, one frequently finds oneself going around in circles, as on his ever-changing views of whether to conclude a separate peace treaty with the GDR or not.

While Khrushchev was often uncertain about what he could get from the West and how hard he wanted to push, he enjoyed trying to pressure the West into concessions. Khrushchev loved to bluster. He seemed to take glee in regularly warning the West: "We will most definitely sign a separate peace treaty and soon"; and "five of our missiles would be enough to destroy your country." He proudly confessed in his memoirs that on his trip to the United States in 1959, he staged a fit of anger in his hotel room in Los Angeles: "I ranted on about how I wouldn't tolerate being treated like this, and so on."[14] He wanted to get the attention of Ambassador Henry Cabot Lodge and others Khrushchev assumed were listening to the hidden microphones in his room.

As he monitored the Western response to his "rantings," Khrushchev would alter his expectations and goals accordingly. This was often exasperating for Ulbricht. A prime example was Khrushchev's telling Ulbricht in June 1959 that since it had taken the United States sixteen years to recognize the Soviet Union, Ulbricht should be prepared "to wait at least seventeen years" for Western recognition.[15]

While Khrushchev had been the one to heat up tensions by launching the Berlin Crisis in November 1958, he also wanted to be able to control the level of tension and reduce it when the Western Powers seemed to be making concessions, as they did at the Geneva CFM in the summer of 1959. Precisely because Khrushchev's policies, expectations, and intentions with the West changed with some frequency, Ulbricht's consistent, hard, demanding line in Berlin and the GDR mattered a great deal. While Khrushchev was trying to keep his options open with the West for some sort of agreement on West Berlin in which the West could be induced to make further concessions, Ulbricht's interventionist, unilateral actions at the Berlin border gave the Western Powers additional doubts about the trustworthiness of Khrushchev's guarantees of free access between West Berlin and the FRG and caused Khrushchev concern about his capacity to avoid military conflict with the West.

Khrushchev and Ulbricht both had very strong personalities, and they frequently clashed even as Khrushchev gave his support to Ulbricht's regime. In the communist "workers' and peasants' state," Ulbricht was the worker from the city, and Khrushchev was, at least to a significant degree, the peasant from the country. Ulbricht clearly thought Khrushchev was an unsophisticated country bumpkin who did not understand the measures necessary in a city like Berlin. With his cold, controlled demeanor, Ulbricht was probably shocked by Khrushchev's emotional outbursts and his unpredictability. For his part, the earthy Khrushchev did not appreciate Ulbricht's bossiness and his frequent demands. Yet he tolerated Ulbricht because of Khrushchev's view of the importance of a stable and socialist GDR.

Whereas the Soviets geared part of their *Deutschlandpolitik* toward German unification in the *New Course* of 1953, by the late 1950s, they had given up on this, except as propaganda. In March 1953, Stalin's successors told the East Germans that their calls to close the sectoral border in Berlin "would place in doubt the sincerity of the policy of the

Soviet government and the GDR government, which are actively and consistently supporting the unification of Germany and the conclusion of a peace treaty with Germany."[16] And in the *New Course* directive given to the East Germans on 2 June 1953, the Soviets declared that "at present the main task is the struggle for the unification of Germany on a democratic and peace-loving basis."[17] However much the Soviets may have held out hope for an acceptable form of German unification emerging from agreement with the West, in the wake of the East German uprising in 1953 and the integration of a rearmed West Germany into NATO in 1955, Khrushchev focused his attention more realistically on the existence of two German states not likely to reunite anytime soon.

Accordingly, he recognized West Germany in 1955 and set about trying to influence the FRG in favorable ways, while also increasing his support for the GDR. At meetings with Ulbricht during the Berlin Crisis, Khrushchev declared that it was clear that the French, British, West German, and American leaders were not in support of German unification and that therefore it was not a realistic item on the international agenda.[18] Due to the Western commitment to the FRG and the communist inability to make any headway there, Khrushchev increasingly devoted his energy to his German ally and not to German unification. No longer was East Germany just war booty to be plundered; now it was to be supported with all possible means and held up as a symbol of the communist system.

This book has attempted to demonstrate that the traditional approach of studying the cold war by focusing on the superpowers and security issues is wholly insufficient for understanding some of its events and key dynamics. Factors that the traditional, realist account of international relations reject as unimportant, such as the nongreat powers, personality, ideology, and domestic politics, were actually essential factors in the development of the cold war.[19] It is not possible to really grasp how the cold war evolved in Germany and why the Berlin Wall came to be built without understanding the personalities, policies, and preferences of both Ulbricht and Khrushchev.

Both Khrushchev and Ulbricht were ousted in part because of their strong personalities and policies. Khrushchev was removed from power just three years after the erection of the Berlin Wall. His opponents complained about his threatening behavior toward both his socialist colleagues and his adversaries in the West. At the October 1964 Presidium meeting marking Khrushchev's ouster, he was told that on the "Berlin question—your position brought damage [to us]." Khrushchev stood his ground, arguing: "On Berlin—we carried out policy well."[20] His colleagues disagreed. D. S. Polianskii's draft of Mikhail Suslov's keynote speech for the plenum declared:

[O]n mistakes in foreign policy activity[—]don't resort to a policy of black-mail and threats. Our country kept finding itself pulled into this and that situation in which the danger of war was very close. Take the Suez crisis [of 1956 in which Khrushchev threatened Britain and France with nuclear weapons[21]]. . . . And the notorious "Berlin question"! . . . . Comrade Khru-shchev presented an ultimatum: either in a certain time Berlin will become a free city, or we won't stop short of even war. It's not clear what his calcula-tion was. You know, we don't have such idiots who would think that we should fight "for the free city of Berlin." In this time, more than one deadline passed, and Berlin still didn't become a free city. It's true, we built the wall, but we didn't need to put forth an ultimative demand for this. . . . Khrushchev wanted to scare the Americans, but they weren't scared, and we had to retreat, experiencing a palpable blow to the authority and prestige of the country, our policy, and our armed forces.[22]

The "retreat" no doubt referred to both the Checkpoint Charlie episode and the fact that the West had not caved in to demands to leave West Berlin. It may also have signified recognition that building the Wall rep-resented a defeat for the communist system, as Khrushchev himself un-derstood.

Referring to Khrushchev's policies concerning Suez, Berlin, and Cuba, Polianskii asserted: "As you see, over the past seven years, the Soviet state without any serious reason and basis has been on the brink of war three times. This was not accidental, but a system, a special 'help' of conducting our foreign policy by means of threatening the imperialists with war. Of course, when there is no other way, we can and must threaten the imperialists with the use of force to sober them up. But you can't do that systematically."[23] Khrushchev's aggressive behavior, his proclivity to act without his colleagues' backing, and his volatile person-ality cost him his job.

Similar factors led to Ulbricht's ouster. In particular, Khrushchev's successor, Leonid Brezhnev, was not willing to tolerate Ulbricht's holier-than-thou attitude the way Khrushchev had. As Brezhnev said in 1970 to Erich Honecker, who would replace Ulbricht:

[T]here is a certain superiority of [the East Germans] with regard to the other socialist countries, your experiences, methods of leadership, etc. This is also directed towards us. This also upsets us, this must be changed[;] the SED PB [Politburo], you, must change this. . . . I know myself how Walter [Ulbricht] deals with these questions—from my own experience. . . . But actually it is not he who does anything—in reality—we are there—our power—we account for the concrete situation. It is this way in many areas. So, the superiority in the GDR must be eliminated.[24]

Indeed, in the year following this conversation, Brezhnev and Honecker engineered Ulbricht's ouster.

Ulbricht's haughtiness was not the only reason for his removal. His proven penchant for acting without Soviet approval was also very important. In the midst of long-sought Soviet and East German negotiations on bilateral treaties with West Germany and on a Quadripartite Agreement on Berlin in 1970 and 1971, "Ulbricht seemed unreliable" because of his previous behavior. Brezhnev believed "Honecker seemed less likely to take risks on his own."[25] Hence, Brezhnev promoted Ulbricht's replacement by Honecker.

The leaders changed, yet the Wall remained as a legacy of the unique interaction of Ulbricht and Khrushchev. Ulbricht's preference for hardline solutions and Khrushchev's commitment to propping up the GDR at all costs created the Wall. That Wall, however, solidified an East German state that could not survive in the long run and was in fact an indication of the further crumbling of the regime's legitimacy. In November 1989 it came tumbling down. Soviet leader Mikhail Gorbachev refused to send in tanks to prop up the socialist regime in East Berlin as his predecessors had. Gorbachev's aversion to the use of force outside of Soviet territory, his conviction that he had more to gain from relations with West Germany and other Western powers than from the GDR, and his diminished sense of a cold war threat stayed his hand.

As I write, the Israelis are constructing a fence to separate themselves from the Palestinians. The circumstances are vastly different from those surrounding the building of the Berlin Wall, but the effort to solve, or at least manage, problems by creating a physical divide is the same. Just as the Berlin Wall did not erase the fundamental problems that led to its erection, so this Israeli fence is unlikely to be a long-term solution to the challenges involved in Israelis and Palestinians living side by side.

The lessons of the Soviet–East German relationship described in this book also present a cautionary tale for present and future great-power efforts at crisis management that rely on the conduct of an important junior partner. This seems particularly relevant at a time when the United States is relying on countries like Pakistan and Uzbekistan in its war on terrorism in Afghanistan.

I hope that this book will inspire scholars to examine other instances of important allies affecting the cold war and superpower policy, especially on the communist side of the cold war, since there is so much new evidence available. Kathryn Weathersby's work on Soviet–North Korean relations and the Korean War, Pjero Gleijeses study of the Cuban role in Africa, Chen Jian's work on China, and Ilya Gaiduk's investigation of North Vietnamese relations with the Soviets and Chinese are valuable contributions to this effort that others can build on.[26]

It would be worth investigating whether there were allies other than the GDR that got such special Soviet attention and whom the Soviets felt compelled to accommodate to such a great extent.

There is also much room for future research on the effects of the Sino-Soviet schism on Soviet and Chinese foreign policy and on Soviet–East European relations and Soviet–Third World relations. If initial tensions and then the split between the two communist giants affected the Korean War, the Berlin Crisis, the Cuban Missile Crisis, and the Vietnam War, there are probably still more and important consequences to be uncovered.

With regard to the development of Soviet–East German relations after the construction of the Berlin Wall, Mary Sarotte has written a compelling study of the 1969–73 détente period, but there is still a need for a close examination of the relationship following this period and encompassing the tumultuous events of 1989–90.[27] Just as Ulbricht, Honecker also acted independently from the Soviets at some key moments, such as during the "second cold war" of the early 1980s, when he maintained friendlier relations with the West than the Soviets did, and during the Gorbachev period when he resisted the Soviet leader's calls for domestic reforms. In both instances, his actions ultimately contributed to the collapse of the GDR.

Another fruitful line of inquiry raised by this book would be an investigation of the impact of Ulbricht and Honecker's hard-line policies, including the Berlin Wall and its consequences, on the events of 1989–90 and German unification. The coming together of East and West Germany in 1990 and afterward no doubt would have been more harmonious and not have entailed such a stark break with East Germany's past without these policies and without the Wall. Ulbricht's damage to developments in Germany has lasted far beyond his time in power.

Given that there are many still inaccessible Soviet documents relating to this book, it is possible that some future release of documents could affect its findings. These documents could in particular fill in some of the details regarding high-level Soviet decision-making in the summer of 1953, in the winter of 1957–58, and in the summer of 1961. They could shed light on Beria's policies and the decision to put down the East German uprising with tanks, the decision to back Ulbricht against Zaisser and Herrnstadt and then against Schirdewan, and the decision to build the Berlin Wall. The vast number of documents consulted for this book, however, yields such a clear picture of the relationship between Khrushchev and Ulbricht that it is hard to imagine that other documents could change the image of an aggressively insistent Ulbricht and a cautious, foot-dragging Khrushchev, especially during the Berlin Crisis. The policies of this determined super-ally directly and indirectly affected the policies of the Soviet superpower in this important place and time of the cold war.

Notes

Unless otherwise noted, all translations throughout the text are mine.

Preface

1. John Tagliabue, "15,000 East Germans Cross Two Borders to New Lives," *New York Times* (6 November 1989), A1.

2. Serge Schmemann, "East Germany's Cabinet Resigns, Bowing to Protest and Mass Flight," *New York Times* (8 November 1989), A1.

3. For a newspaper article that gives a good feel for what the mood was like, see Ian Johnson, "Hero's Welcome in Berlin for Willy Brandt," *Seattle Times* (11 November 1989), A2.

4. Schneider, *The Wall Jumper*, 119.

5. Klingemann and Hofferbert, "Germany: A New 'Wall in the Mind'?" 30–43; and Kapferer, "'Nostalgia' in Germany's New Federal States as a Political and Cultural Phenomenon of the Transformation Process," 28–40.

Introduction

The Dynamics of Soviet–East German Relations in the Early Cold War

1. Schwartz, *America's Germany*; Hanrieder, *Germany, America, Europe*; Ninkovich, *Germany and the United States*; Burr, "Avoiding the Slippery Slope," 21–24, 32; and Trachtenberg, *A Constructed Peace*.

2. Two exceptions are Childs, *The GDR: Moscow's German Ally* and Phillips, *Soviet Policy toward East Germany Reconsidered*.

3. Naimark, *The Russians in Germany*, esp. chaps 2–3.

4. "Zapis' besedy tovarishcha N. S. Khrushcheva s tovarishchem V. Ul'brikhtom, 30 noiabria 1960 goda," Arkhiv Vneshnei Politiki Russkoi Federatsii (AVPRF), Fond (F.) 0742, Opis' (Op.) 6, Papka (Pap.) 43, Portfel' (Por.) 4, 14. See also the English translation, "Memorandum of Conversation of Comrade N. S. Khrushchev with Comrade W. Ulbricht, 30 November 1960," Appendix A in Harrison, "Ulbricht and the Concrete 'Rose.'" This book follows the Library of Congress Russian transliteration system, except in names where the more common "y" is used instead of "i," as in Yuri and Malinovsky. In citations to Russian and German documents in this book, the page number of the document is used, as opposed to the leaf (*List* or *Blatt*) number.

5. Smith, "New Bottles for New Wine," 567–91. Smith emphasizes the roles of countries other than the superpowers in expanding, intensifying, and prolonging the cold war. See also Leffler, "Inside Enemy Archives," 122, 128–31; and Westad, "Russian Archives and Cold War History," esp. 268–70.

6. Hershberg, "The Crisis Years, 1958–1963," in Westad, ed., *Reviewing the Cold War*, 304.

7. Smith, "New Bottles for New Wine," 570–71, 588, 591; and Leffler, "Inside Enemy Archives," 128–31.

8. Ben-Zvi, *The United States and Israel*, 8.

9. Farquharson, "The 'Essential Division': Britain and the Partition of Germany, 1945–49," 23–45.

10. Lundestad, *The American "Empire."*

11. Wriggins, *Dynamics of Regional Politics: Four Systems on the Indian Ocean Rim*; McMahon, *The Cold War on the Periphery: The United States, India and Pakistan*; Lundestad, *The American "Empire,"* 78, 81, 123; and Ben-Zvi, *The United States and Israel*.

12. McMahon, "United States Cold War Strategy in South Asia: Making a Military Commitment to Pakistan, 1947–1954," 815, 840.

13. Park, "The Influence of Small States upon the Superpowers, 97–117. In a rare instance of an examination of the dynamics of superpower–small state alliances in both the United States and the Soviet bloc, see Suhrke, "Gratuity or Tyranny: The Korean Alliances," 508–32.

14. Risse-Kappen, *Cooperation among Democracies*, Chap. 4.

15. Burr, "Avoiding the Slippery Slope," 21–24, 32; and Trachtenberg, *A Constructed Peace*, Chap. 7.

16. Glenn H. Snyder, "The Security Dilemma in Alliance Politics," 461–95; Hoffmann, *Gulliver's Troubles*; and Osgood, *NATO: The Entangling Alliance*.

17. Keohane, "The Big Influence of Small Allies," 161–82; Lundestad, *The American "Empire,"* 77–78; Risse-Kappen, *Cooperation among Democracies*, 4–5, 209–11; and Bar-Siman-Tov, "Alliance Strategy: U.S.–Small Allies Relationships," 205–206.

18. Risse-Kappen, *Cooperation among Democracies*.

19. Gaddis, *We Now Know*, 151. On the connection between U.S. perceptions of credibility and the domino theory, see Bar-Siman-Tov, "Alliance Strategy: U.S.–Small Allies Relationships," 204.

20. On the strength of a weaker ally in bargaining coming in part from weaknesses in superpower capacity to exert power, see Ben-Zvi, *The United States and Israel*, 9.

21. Weathersby, "Soviet Aims in Korea and the Origins of the Korean War, 1945–1950: New Evidence from Russian Archives," 23.

22. Naimark, *The Russians in Germany*, 470.

23. For a good example of this, see Randall Stone's account of how in the 1960s–1980s Poland, Hungary, and Czechoslovakia "ran roughshod over any [economic] treaty obligations [to the Soviets] they preferred to ignore [and succeeded in] manipulating and outmaneuvering" the Soviets due to the Soviets' lack of enforcement and monitoring of these treaties. The Soviets could not compel the local powers to implement the agreements. Stone, *Satellites and Commissars: Strategy and Conflict in the Politics of Soviet-Bloc Trade*, 3–5, 21.

24. As David Baldwin observes, "What functions as a power resource in one policy-contingency framework may be irrelevant in another." Baldwin, "Power Analysis and World Politics," 166. Similarly, Abraham Ben-Zvi points out that power resources are not so easily transferrable: "the existence of an *overall*

asymmetry in power resources between nominally strong and weak powers cannot in itself guarantee the compliance of the weak in any *specific* policy-contingency framework." Ben-Zvi, *The United States and Israel*, 8.

25. On the distinction between "fate control" and "behavior control," see Hughes, "On Bargaining," in Triska, ed., *Dominant Powers and Subordinate States*, 175.

26. Glenn Snyder terms this phenomenon "indirect dependence." The Soviets were indirectly dependent on the GDR not to fall into the Western camp with its territorial, human, and other resources. Snyder, "The Security Dilemma in Alliance Politics," 472. On the importance of the weak state's control of strategic assets, like territory, see Handel, "Does the Dog Wag the Tail or Vice Versa? Patron-Client Relations," 31–32.

27. Nikita Khrushchev, *Khrushchev Remembers*, 456.

28. On the role of ideology in the cold war, see Westad, Bernath Lecture, "The New International History of the Cold War: Three (Possible) Paradigms," 552–56; idem., "Secrets of the Second World," 263–68; Zubok and Pleshakov, *Inside the Kremlin's Cold War*, 3–6, 178–79, 275–76; and Gould-Davies, "Rethinking the Role of Ideology in International Politics During the Cold War," 90–109.

29. Gaddis, *We Now Know*, 150.

30. On the concept of strength through weakness, see Schelling, *The Strategy of Conflict* 17, 22; idem, *Arms and Influence*, 37–39; and Glenn Snyder, *Alliance Politics*, 170. On East German economic weakness giving it leverage in negotiations with the Soviets, see Richter, *Khrushchev's Double Bind*, 116. On both Germanys being able to parlay their weakness (the possibility of them falling under the control of the other side) into strength in bargaining with their superpower allies, see Gaddis, *We Now Know*, 150. For an examination of Austria's use of the "leverage of the weak" in the cold war, see Bischof, *Austria in the First Cold War, 1945–55*.

31. On the positive effects on bargaining power of "weaker" states, see Bacharach and Lawler, *Bargaining: Power, Tactics, and Outcomes*, 186, 190; Snyder and Diesing, *Conflict among Nations*, 29–30, 443; Keohane, "The Big Influence of Small Allies"; Park, "The Influence of Small States upon the Superpowers"; Fox, *The Power of Small States: Diplomacy in World War II*; and Handel, *Weak States in the International System*.

32. Glenn H. Snyder, "The Security Dilemma in Alliance Politics," 461–95; and idem, *Alliance Politics*.

33. Burr, "Avoiding the Slippery Slope," 180. On the notion of a "superdomino," see also Dower, "The Superdomino in Postwar Asia: Japan in and out of the Pentagon Papers," 101–142.

34. On the Sino-Soviet rift, see Westad, ed., *Brothers in Arms*.

35. Weathersby, "Soviet Aims in Korea and the Origins of the Korean War, 1945–1950," 29.

36. Bonwetsch and Filitov, "Chruschtschow und der Mauerbau: Die Gipfelkonferenz der Warschauer-Pakt-Staaten vom 3.–5. August 1961," 164–66, 168.

37. Fursenko and Naftali, *"One Hell of a Gamble,"* 167–70. See also Zubok, "Stalin's Plans and Russian Archives," 304.

38. Gaiduk, "The Vietnam War and Soviet-American Relations, 1964–1973: New Russian Evidence," 251.

39. For works that encompass the subject of this book and were completed, or largely completed, without the benefit of archival documents from the former Soviet bloc, see the following still very useful books: Ulam, *Expansion and Coexistence*; Adomeit, *Soviet Risk-Taking and Crisis Behavior*; Slusser, *The Berlin Crisis of 1961*; Phillips, *Soviet Policy toward East Germany Reconsidered*; McAdams, *Germany Divided*; and Richter, *Khrushchev's Double Bind*. Of the final two sources, McAdams's work makes use of his extensive interviews with former East and West German officials conducted mostly in 1990 and 1991; and Richter was able to integrate a few of the documents from the newly opened Russian archives into his work as he was finishing it.

40. Books making use of these archival sources and addressing topics related to Soviet–East German relations in the 1950s and 1960s include Lemke, *Die Berlinkrise 1958 bis 1963*; Wettig, *Bereitschaft zu Einheit in Freiheit?*, Filitov, *Germanskii Vopros: ot raskola k ob'edineniiu*; Karl-Heinz Schmidt, *Dialog über Deutschland*; and Zubok and Pleshakov, *Inside the Kremlin's Cold War*. Two books which make use of the new archival sources and examine Soviet–East German relations in the period just preceeding that of this book and thus give very useful background are Naimark, *The Russians in Germany*, and Loth, *Stalin's Unwanted Child*.

41. On the new international cold war history, see the description by Hershberg in the "Series Preface," in Westad, ed., *Brothers in Arms*, x–xi.

Chapter One
1953

1. This section on Ulbricht's personality and background is drawn from the following sources: Stern, *Ulbricht*, 28, 41–45, 69–70, 125; Podewin, *Walter Ulbricht*, 47–48, 96, 298–99; Leonhard, *Child of the Revolution*, 360–61, 430; Loth, *Stalin's Unwanted Child*, 95; and Naimark, *The Russians in Germany*, 42, 287.

2. Stern, *Ulbricht*, 3–12; and Podewin, *Walter Ulbricht*, 19–29.

3. Stern, *Ulbricht*, 5.

4. Ibid., 10; and Podewin, *Walter Ulbricht*, 32–33.

5. Podewin, *Walter Ulbricht*, 38–41.

6. Stern, *Ulbricht*, 21–35; Podewin, *Walter Ulbricht*, 41–86.

7. Podewin, *Walter Ulbricht*, 59.

8. Ibid., 71–73.

9. Stern, *Ulbricht*, 31–33.

10. Leonhard, *Child of the Revolution*, 360, 430.

11. Podewin, *Walter Ulbricht*, 67, 75–77; Stern, *Ulbricht*, 34.

12. Podewin, *Walter Ulbricht*, 77–86.

13. Stern, *Ulbricht*, 36–37, 47.

14. Ibid., 55, 69–70; Podewin, *Walter Ulbricht*, 105–118.

15. Stern, *Ulbricht*, 95.

16. Podewin, *Walter Ulbricht*, 129–49; Stern, *Ulbricht*, 76–87; Leonhard, *Child of the Revolution*, 179, 201–203.

17. Stern, *Ulbricht*, 87–91, Podewin, *Walter Ulbricht*, 151.

18. Leonhard, *Child of the Revolution*, 350–53; Stern, *Ulbricht*, 91–92.

19. Leonhard, *Child of the Revolution*, 355–60; Podewin, *Walter Ulbricht*, 167; Stern, *Ulbricht*, 97; and Naimark, *The Russians in Germany*, 252–53.

20. Leonhard, *Child of the Revolution*, 352.

21. Stern, *Ulbricht*, 104. Thirteen of the sixteen signatories of the KPD manifesto had been in the Soviet Union during the Nazi period. Leonhard, *Child of the Revolution*, 419.

22. Stern, *Ulbricht*, 101–105. See also Podewin, *Walter Ulbricht*, 168, 172; Leonhard, *Child of the Revolution*, 418–20; and Naimark, *The Russians in Germany*, 254.

23. As the British historian, Peter Grieder, points out, however, the distinction between "native" and "Muscovite" German communists did not always result in policy differences. Grieder, *The East German Leadership, 1946–1973*, 213–14.

24. Leonhard, *Child of the Revolution*, 397–98.

25. Stern, *Ulbricht*, 119–20.

26. Podewin, *Walter Ulbricht*, 159; and Leonhard, *Child of the Revolution*, 374–77.

27. Leonhard, *Child of the Revolution*, 351–52; and Podewin, *Walter Ulbricht*, 168.

28. Leonhard, *Child of the Revolution*, 390. See also Naimark, *The Russians in Germany*, chap. 2, "Soviet Soldiers, German Women, and the Problem of Rape," 69–140.

29. Leonhard, *Child of the Revolution*, 391.

30. Podewin, *Walter Ulbricht*, 96, 160.

31. Ibid., 189; Stern, *Ulbricht*, 107.

32. Naimark, *The Russians in Germany*, 275–84, 308–13.

33. Ibid., 302–303.

34. Loth, *Stalin's Unwanted Child*, 181.

35. Naimark, *The Russians in Germany*, chap. 5, "The Tiul'panov Question and Soviet Policy-Making in the Zone," 318–52.

36. Loth, *Stalin's Unwanted Child*, 100.

37. Podewin, *Walter Ulbricht*, 199–200; Stern, *Ulbricht*, 109–115; and Naimark, *The Russians in Germany*, 303–304.

38. Loth, *Stalin's Unwanted Child*, 108.

39. Soviet "Record of Conversation of Leaders of the Socialist Unity Party of Germany W. Pieck, W. Ulbricht, and O. Grotewohl with J. V. Stalin," 7 April 1952, reprinted in Ostermann, *Uprising in East Germany, 1953*, 38.

40. Loth, *Stalin's Unwanted Child*, 100–170. For a discussion of the controversy over Loth's thesis, represented in the title of his book, see Ihme-Tuchel, *Die DDR*, 15–17. On the need not to overestimate Ulbricht's influence on Soviet policies and to recognize the fundamental contradictions in Stalin's policies in this period, see van Dijk, "The Apparatchik in 'Power': Walter Ulbricht and the German Question, 1948–1951."

41. In April 1952, Stalin told the East German leaders: "In reality, an independent state is being created in [West] Germany [by the Americans]. And you

too need to organize an independent state. The demarcation line between East and West Germany should be considered a border—and not just any border, but a dangerous one. . . . The Germans will guard the first line of defense, and we will put Russian troops on the second line." Soviet "Record of Conversation of Leaders of the Socialist Unity Party W. Pieck, W. Ulbricht, and O. Grotewohl with J. V. Stalin," 7 April 1952, reprinted in Ostermann, *Uprising in East Germany*, 34–35.

42. As the Soviet ambassador to the GDR, Mikhail Pervukhin, would later observe: "The presence in Berlin of an open and, to speak to the point, uncontrolled border between the socialist and capitalist worlds unwittingly prompts the population to make a comparison between both parts of the city, which, unfortunately, does not always turn out in favor of Democratic Berlin." "O nekotorykh voprosakh ekonomicheskogo i politicheskogo polozheniia v demokraticheskom Berline (politicheskoe pis'mo)," 10 December 1959, AVPRF, F.: Referentura po GDR, Op. 4, Pap. 27, Por. 3, 1.

43. AVPRF, F. 0742, Op. 41, Por. 92, cited in Loth, *Stalin's Unwanted Child*, 43.

44. Interestingly, it was Molotov who proposed in a meeting of the East German leaders with Stalin on 1 April 1952 that they "introduce a system of passes for visits of West Berlin residents to the territory of East Berlin [so as to stop] free movement of Western agents" in the GDR. Stalin agreed that the situation was "intolerable" and that the East Germans needed to build up their border defenses. Soviet "Record of Conversation of Leaders of the Socialist Unity Party of Germany W. Pieck, W. Ulbricht, and O. Grotewohl with J.V. Stalin," 1 April 1952, reprinted in Ostermann, *Uprising in East Germany*, 33.

45. The document is dated 18 March 1953, AVPRF, F. 06, Op. 12, Pap. 18, Por. 283 and was Molotov's recommendation to the Council of Ministers of the Presidium, which presumably approved it, since the Berlin sectoral border was not closed. On 13 March, the Presidium of the Council of Ministers asked the Foreign Ministry to draft a negative response to the SKK telegram of 4 December 1952 requesting the border closure. On 16 March, Marshal Sokolovsky (chief of the Soviet General Staff) and Deputy Foreign Minister Pushkin submitted the draft to Molotov, who forwarded it to the Presidium of the Council of Ministers on 18 March. The document cited is also reprinted in Ostermann, *Uprising in East Germany*, 50–51.

46. See the report to the Foreign Ministry written up by two diplomats in the Soviet embassy in the GDR, O. Selianinov, adviser, and A. Kazennov, second secretary, "O polozhenii v zapadnom Berline," 24 February 1958, TsKhSD, Rolik (R.) 8875, F. 5, Op. 49, Delo (D.) 82, 22–23.

47. For the best account of the high-level SED (and Soviet) opposition to Ulbricht in 1953, see Stulz-Herrnstadt, *Das Herrnstadt-Dokument*.

48. Nikita Khrushchev, *Khrushchev Remembers: The Glasnost Tapes*, 163.

49. Schenk, *Im Vorzimmer der Diktatur*, 182–83, 185, 188–99; and Jänicke, *Der Dritte Weg*, 25.

50. "Reshenie Sovetskogo pravitel'stva ob okazanii ekonomicheskoi pomoshchi germanskoi demokraticheskoi respublike," 18 April 1953, AVPRF, F. 06, Op. 12a, Pap. 52, Por. 214.

51. Karl Schirdewan, then first secretary of the SED in Sachsen, emphasizes that the Politburo resolution for the *Aufbau des Sozialismus* was a "complete surprise" to everyone and that he, Ernst Wollweber (then state secretary in the Ministry of Transport, and later Stasi chief), and others felt it was a grave mistake that this policy was announced without any preparatory discussion in the party. They also believed that it was premature to introduce full-scale socialism in the GDR at the time. See "Die Führung lag in Moskau," Michael Schumann und Wolfgang Dressen im Gespräch mit Karl Schirdewan, *Niemandsland. Tugendterror* 4 (October/November 1992), 305–7.

52. On the "Construction of Socialism" program and the severe economic difficulties it caused, see Baring, *Uprising in East Germany*, 3–20; and Stasi chief Ernst Wollweber's memoirs, Otto, "Ernst Wollweber: Aus Erinnerungen," 357.

53. Heidemeyer, *Flucht und Zuwanderung aus der SBZ/DDR*, 338.

54. Zubok, " 'Unacceptably Rude and Blatant on the German Question," 2, 5; and Ostermann, intro. and annot., " 'This Is Not A Politburo, But A Madhouse,' Soviet *Deutschlandpolitik* and the SED: New Evidence from Russian, German, and Hungarian Archives," 62.

55. For these memoranda, see "Zapiska po germanskomu voprosu," 21 April, AVPRF, F.: Referentura po Germanii, Op. 41, Pap. 271, Por. 18; "Predlozheniie po germanskomu voprosu," 24 April, AVPRF, F.: Referentura po Germanii, Op. 41, Pap. 271, Por. 19; and "O nashikh dal'neishikh meropriiatiiakh po germanskomu voprosu," 28 April, AVPRF, F.: Referentura po Germanii, Op. 41, Pap. 271, Por. 18. The 28 April document is also located in AVPRF, F. 06, Op. 12, Pap. 16, D. 259, and published in English in CWIHP, *Bulletin* 10 (March 1998): 72–74.

56. Semjonow, *Von Stalin bis Gorbatschow: Ein halbes Jahrhundert in diplomatischer Mission 1939–1991*, 290.

57. "Zapiska po germanskomu voprosu," AVPRF, F.: Referentura po Germanii, Op. 41, Pap. 271, Por. 18, 6.

58. Ibid., 6–7.

59. Lippmann, *Honecker and the New Politics of Europe*, 153–54.

60. This report is cited (with a reproduction of the first and third pages) in Murphy, Kondrashev, and Bailey, *Battleground Berlin*, 156–58, 476, as Report, no. 44/B, to the Presidium of the CC CPSU, signed by L. Beria, 6 May 1953, SVRA (Archives of the *Sluzhba Vneshnei Razvedki*, Foreign Intelligence Service, Moscow) file 3581, vol. 7; and in Kramer, "The Early Post-Stalin Succession Struggle" (Part 1), 23, as "V Prezidium TsK KPSS," Memorandum No. 33/B (Top Secret), 6 May 1953, from L. Beria to the CPSU Presidium, in SVRA, F. 2589, T. 7, D. 3581, 326–28.

61. L. Beria, Report, no. 44/B, to the Presidium of the CC CPSU, 6 May 1953, SVRA file 3581, vol. 7, 2.

62. Ibid., 2–3.

63. On the 14 May Presidium meeting, see "Protokol No. 8 zasedaniia Prezidiuma TsK KPSS ot 14 maia 1953 goda," 14 May 1953, TsKhSD, F. 3, Op. 10, D. 23, 41–42, cited in Kramer, "The Early Post-Stalin Succession Struggle" (Part 1), 24–25.

64. On the 13th plenum, see Baring, *Uprising in East Germany*, 21–22; Lippmann, *Honecker and the New Politics of Europe*, 153; and Jänicke, *Der Dritte Weg*, 25–28.

65. "Protokol No. 8 Zasedaniia Prezidiuma TsK KPSS ot 14 maia 1953 goda," cited in Kramer, "The Early Post-Stalin Succession Struggle" (Part 1), 24.

66. "K voprosu o predotvrashchenii begstva naseleniia iz GDR v zapadnuiu germaniiu," 15 May 1953, AVPRF, F. 0742, Op. 41, Pap. 280, Por. 92.

67. This document, "On the reasons for the flight from the German Democratic Republic by the population to West Germany and also proposals for stopping this flight," from the Presidential Archives, APRF, F. 3, Op. 64, D. 802, 12–44, has been translated in CWIHP, *Bulletin* 10: 74–78.

68. Knight, *Beria: Stalin's First Lieutenant*, 192.

69. Kramer, "The Early Post-Stalin Succession Struggle" (Part 1), 12–22.

70. Ibid., 7; Tompson, *Khrushchev*, 117; Zubok and Pleshakov, *Inside the Kremlin's Cold War*, 154–55; and *Khrushchev Remembers*, 324–25.

71. Tompson, *Khrushchev: A Political Life* 114; and Kramer, "The Early Post-Stalin Succession Struggle" (Part 2), 27.

72. Malenkov, Khrushchev, Beria, Molotov, Kliment Voroshilov, Nikolai Bulganin, Lazar Kaganovich, Anastas Mikoian, Maxim Saburov, and Mikhail Pervukhin were the full members of the CPSU Presidium. Initially Malenkov was made head of both the party and the state, but on 14 March he was relieved of his party leadership position. Until September, no one was then appointed to replace Stalin as General (or First) Secretary, head of the CPSU Presidium, although Khrushchev remained in charge of the CPSU Central Commitee Secretariat. Khrushchev would only become First Secretary in September. At the Council of Ministers, Malenkov was the Chairman, and Beria, Molotov, Bulganin, and Kaganovich were first deputy chairmen.

73. Thus far, Vladislav Zubok and Mark Kramer have located documentary evidence of CPSU Presidium meetings on 14 and 20 May and CM Presidium meetings on 22 April, 5 and 27 May, and 2 June dealing with the situation in the GDR. Zubok, "Unacceptably Rude and Blatant on the German Question," 5–7; Kramer, "The Early Post-Stalin Succession Struggle" (Part 1), 24–29. It was the CPSU Presidium that had requested, at Beria's urging, on 14 May an SKK memo of analysis and recommendations concerning the refugee exodus, and it was to Malenkov at the CPSU Presidium that the SKK sent their memo on 18 May. Yet it was an expanded meeting of the CM Presidium that convened on 27 May to consider the SKK and MID proposals and then delivered to the GDR leaders on 2 June their *New Course* directive for the GDR. Later it was at a session of the CPSU Presidium (although originally scheduled as a CM Presidium meeting) that Beria would be arrested on 26 June, and his letter from prison on 1 July to Malenkov was addressed to him at the CPSU Central Committee. APRF, F. 3, Op. 24, D. 463. For an English translation of Beria's letter to Malenkov, see Document No. 23 in Ostermann, ed., *Uprising in East Germany*, 155–57.

74. On Khrushchev's presence at most CM Presidium meetings in the spring of 1953, see Kramer, "The Early Post-Stalin Succession Struggle" (Part 2), 27.

75. For evidence on the important role of Molotov, see Chuev, *Sto sorok besed s Molotovym*, 332–33; Richter, "Reexamining Soviet Policy," 15, 17; Harrison, "The Bargaining Power of Weaker Allies in Bipolarity and Crisis: The Dynamics of Soviet–East German Relations, 1953–1961," chap. 2; Zubok, "Unacceptably Rude and Blatant on the German Question," 4–7; and Kramer, "The Early Post-Stalin Succession Struggle" (Part 1), 4.

76. Kramer refers to the 2 June *New Course* document as "the Molotov-Beria document." "The Early Post-Stalin Succession Struggle" (Part 1), 30.

77. Malenkov's opening speech at the proceedings against Beria, top secret stenographic protocol of the CPSU CC special plenum from 2–7 July 1953, "Delo Beriia, Plenum TsK KPSS Iiuli 1953 goda, Stenograficheskii Otchet," 144. See also Molotov's speech making similar remarks, ibid., 162.

78. Editor's note 12, ibid., 144.

79. Chuev, *Sto sorok besed*, 332–33.

80. Ibid., 333; Richter, "Reexamining Soviet Policy," 15, 17; and Molotov's mention of the proposal submitted by him at the 27 May meeting in his speech at the 2–7 July 1953 plenum on Beria, "Delo Beriia," 163.

81. Nikita S. Khrushchev, "Aktsii," in V. F. Nekrasov, ed., *Beria: Konets kar'eru*, 262; Chuev, *Sto sorok besed*, 333; Molotov's speech on 2 July at the plenum on Beria, "Delo Beriia," 162–63; and Malenkov's speech on 2 July, ibid., 144.

82. At the January 1955 CPSU CC plenum, Malenkov (clearly under pressure) confessed: "Today I admit that I essentially took a wrong position on the German question . . . in April or May" 1953. Stenographic report of the plenum, 31 January 1955, TsKhSD, F. 2, Op. 1, D. 129; and English translation, CWIHP, *Bulletin* 10: 35.

83. Gromyko, *Memories*, 316.

84. Chuev, *Sto sorok besed*, 333. See also Molotov's speech at the 2 July plenum, "Delo Beriia," 163; Khrushchev's speech on 2 July, ibid., 157; and Bulganin's speech on 3 July, ibid., 173.

85. Ibid. See also Khrushchev, "Aktsii," 262; and Gromyko, *Memories*, 316.

86. Khrushchev's speech at the 2 July plenum, "Delo Beriia," 157.

87. For information on the Kremlin applying the *New Course* to Hungary and Albania, see Document 22 in Ostermann, ed., *Uprising in East Germany*, 144–54; Kramer, "The Early Post-Stalin Succession Struggle" (Part 1), 37–39; and János Rainer, "The New Course in Hungary in 1953."

88. For sources on these meetings, see Grotewohl's handwritten notes on the meetings, SAPMO-BArch, DY 30 J IV 2/2/286, and the English translation in CWIHP, *Bulletin* 10: 81; SAPMO-BArch, J NL 2/32; Przybylski, *Tatort Politbüro*, 240; Stulz-Herrnstadt, *Das Herrnstadt Dokument*, 57–61; Khrushchev's speech on 2 July, "Delo Beriia," 157–58; Malenkov's speech on 2 July, ibid., 143; and Stöckigt, "Ein Dokument von grosser historischer Bedeutung vom Mai 1953, 648–54.

89. For the final two drafts of the document on 31 May and 1 June, see AVPRF, F. 06, Op. 12, Pap. 16, D. 236. For the German version of the final document, see Stöckigt, "Ein Dokument von grosser historischer Bedeutung vom Mai 1953," 648–54. For the Soviet version of the 2 June document, see APRF,

F. 3, Op. 64, D. 802 and the English translation, "USSR Council of Ministers Order 'On Measures to Improve the Health of the Political Situation in the GDR,'" Document No. 18 in Ostermann, ed., *Uprising in East Germany*, 133–36. Citations to this *New Course* document will refer to this English translation, in Ostermann, "On Measures to Improve the Health of the Political Situation in the GDR." The quotes are from ibid., 134, 133.

90. Ostermann, "On Measures to Improve the Health of the Political Situation in the GDR," 133.

91. Ibid, 134. For a summary of the reasons for the resolution, see also the speeches by Malenkov and Molotov on 2 July at the Beria plenum, "Delo Beriia," 143, 162.

92. "On Measures to Improve the Health of the Political Situation in the GDR," 134–36.

93. Stulz-Herrnstadt, *Das Herrnstadt-Dokument*, 57–59. Record of the East German written response has not been found. See also Khrushchev's 2 July speech at the Beria plenum, "Delo Beriia," 157–58.

94. Stulz-Herrnstadt, *Das Herrnstadt-Dokument*, 58–59; and Khrushchev's 2 July speech, "Delo Beriia," 157–58. Beria's lieutenant, Pavel Sudoplatov, claims that Beria, Malenkov, and Khrushchev were so frustrated by Ulbricht's response in their meetings that they decided to oust him. Sudoplatov and Sudoplatov, *Special Tasks*, 365.

95. Grotewohl's handwritten notes of the 3 June meeting, CWIHP, *Bulletin* 10: 81.

96. Stulz-Herrnstadt, *Das Herrnstadt-Dokument,* 58–59; and Elke Scherstjanoi, "'Wollen wir den Sozialismus?' Dokumente aus der Sitzung des Politbüros des ZK der SED am 6. Juni 1953," 662. Grotewohl's handwritten notes of the 3 June meeting indicate that this quote was from Beria. CWIHP, *Bulletin* 10: 81.

97. Stöckigt, "Ein Dokument von grosser historischer Bedeutung," 649.

98. "On Measures to Improve the Health of the Political Situation in the GDR," 135. See also Richter, "Reexamining Soviet Policy;" and Kramer, "The Early Post-Stalin Succession Struggle" (Part 1), 30. Kramer argues that "the clear implication was that the fate of socialism in the GDR must be subordinated to the larger goal of German unity."

99. "On Measures to Improve the Health of the Political Situation in the GDR," 136.

100. "Central Committee Plenum of the CPSU, Ninth Session, Morning, 31 January 1955," CWIHP, *Bulletin* 10: 35.

101. Scherstjanoi, "'Wollen wir den Sozialismus?' Dokumente aus der Sitzung des Politbüros des ZK der SED am 6. Juni 1953," 648–54.

102. Stöckigt, "Ein Dokument von grosser historicher Bedeutung vom Mai 1953," 649.

103. Stulz-Herrnstadt, *Das Herrnstadt-Dokument,* 60–61. In an interview by the author with Karl Schirdewan on 21 September 1992, Schirdewan stated that Pieck was the only figure in the East German leadership who could really challenge Ulbricht in Politburo meetings and that whenever the Soviets were concerned with Ulbricht, they went to Pieck. See also "Die Führung lag in

Moskau," Michael Schumann und Wolfgang Dressen im Gespräch mit Karl Schirdewan, 311. Pieck had lived in the Soviet Union from 1934 to 1945. See also Wollweber's memoirs, Otto., ed., "Ernst Wollweber. Aus Erinnerungen," 360.

104. Kramer, "The Early Post-Stalin Succession Struggle" (Part 3), 4–8; and Wettig, *Bereitschaft zu Einheit in Freiheit? Die sowjetische Deutschland-Politik 1945–1955*, 247–56. The only evidence we have of Beria's intentions, other than from his accusers, is from one of his lieutenants, Pavel Sudoplatov, in charge of the KGB Administration for Special Tasks. Sudoplatov maintains that his boss told him he favored a neutral, united Germany, with the GDR regime an autonomous province therein. But many of Sudoplatov's claims do not correspond with other evidence regarding the events he describes and thus seem dubious. Sudoplatov and Sudoplatov, *Special Tasks*, 363–66.

105. APRF, F. 3, Op. 24, D. 463; English translation, "Letter from Lavrentii Beria to Georgii Malenkov Reflecting on the Events of Spring 1953," 1 July 1953, Document No. 23 in Ostermann, ed., *Uprising in East Germany*, 156.

106. The Politburo members were W. Ulbricht, O. Grotewohl, W. Pieck, F. Ebert, H. Matern, F. Oelssner, H. Rau, and W. Zaisser. The candidate members were A. Ackermann, R. Herrnstadt, E. Honecker, H. Jendretsky, E. Mückenberger, and E. Schmidt.

107. Stulz-Herrnstadt, *Das Herrnstadt-Dokument*.

108. SAPMO-BArch, ZPA, J IV 2/2–286, cited in Scherstjanoi, "'Wollen wir den Sozialismus?'" 661.

109. Several records of this meeting on 6 June exist in the SED archives and have been published, including the protocol, Grotewohl's notes, Herrnstadt's statement, and Ebert's statement. Scherstjanoi, "Wollen wir den Sozialismus?" 658–80. She found the documents in SAPMO-BArch, ZPA, J IV 2/2–278 and SAPMO-BArch, ZPA, NL 90/699. All Politburo members and candidates were at the meeting, except for Pieck, Matern, and Ackermann.

110. Stöckigt, "Über die Massnahmen zur Gesundung," 653.

111. Zaisser had made most of the criticisms regarding leadership style that were raised at this meeting already more than a year earlier at a Politburo meeting in March 1952. See "Bericht des Genossen Willi Zaisser vor dem Politbüro der SED im März 1952 über die Rolle des Politbüros und das Verhältnis von Politbüro und Sekretariat," in Otto, "Dokumente zur Auseinandersetzung in der SED 1953," 667–70.

112. See the records of the meeting in Scherstjanoi, "Wollen wir den Sozialismus?" 669–80.

113. For Semenov's comments at the 6 June Politburo meeting, see Grotewohl's notes, SAPMO-BArch, ZPA, NL 90/699, cited in Scherstjanoi, "Wollen wir den Sozialismus?" 670; and Jendretzky's report to a meeting of the Berlin SED district administration on 7 June, cited in Brandt, *The Search for a Third Way*, 191.

114. "Protokol Nr. 33/35 der ausserordentlichen Sitzung des Politbüros des Zentralkomitees am 6. Juni 1953," SAPMO-BArch, ZPA, J IV 2/2–287, cited in Scherstjanoi, "Wollen wir den Sozialismus?" 668.

115. Brandt, *The Search for a Third Way*, 186, 191.

116. Herrnstadt's "Notizen aus der Sitzung am 6. Juni 1953," in Scherstja-noi, "Wollen wir den Sozialismus?" 671.

117. The existing available record of this meeting comes from Herrnstadt's notes. Stulz-Herrnstadt, *Das Herrnstadt-Dokument*, 62–66. The following three paragraphs are based on this. Pieck and Matern were the only Politburo members not present at the meeting.

118. Stern, *Ulbricht*, 122.

119. Stulz-Herrnstadt, *Das Herrnstadt-Dokument*, 72–73, 74.

120. For another view of the publication decision, see Brandt, *The Search for a Third Way*, 198. He believed that Ulbricht's success in publishing the 9 June communiqué on 11 June without a meeting of the Central Committee or Secretariat, which might have removed him from power, must have been due to "support in Moscow at the last moment. Surely he must have threatened that his overthrow at this time would lead to a collapse of the whole regime." Brandt assumes that Ulbricht received support from Molotov and Kaganovich in the Kremlin.

121. Brandt, *The Search for a Third Way*, 193–94.

122. "The Report to the Soviet Leadership," "On the Events of 17–19 June 1953 in Berlin and the GDR and Certain Conclusions from These Events," by Sokolovsky, Semenov, and Yudin, CWIHP, *Bulletin* 5 (Spring 1995): 17.

123. Baring, *Uprising in East Germany*, 32, 33; and Brandt *The Search for a Third Way*, 203. Arnulf Baring points out that the main reason the increased work norms were not rescinded was that this was the only way the government saw to increase production in the face of decreasing state revenue, especially when the Soviets had not yet promised any massive aid to help the East Germans implement the *New Course*. Baring, *Uprising in East Germany*, 12–14, 31.

124. Schenk, *Im Vorzimmer der Diktatur*, 207.

125. Brandt, *The Search for a Third Way*, 212; and Schenk, *Im Vorzimmer der Diktatur*, 203–204.

126. Schenk, *Im Vorzimmer der Diktatur*, 155, 157; and Brandt, *The Search for a Third Way*, 210.

127. Lippmann, *Honecker and the New Politics of Europe*, 157.

128. Ostermann, ed., *Uprising in East Germany*, 165.

129. Schenk, *Im Vorzimmer der Diktatur*, 207–208. See also the Telefono-gramma po V Ch (secure, high-frequency telephoned telegram) at 18:30, 17 June from Semenov and Grechko in Berlin to Molotov, Bulganin, Malenkov, Beria, Voroshilov, Khrushchev, Kaganovich, Mikoian, Savurov, Pervukhin, Vyshinksy, Gromyko, Pushkin, and Grigoriev with the text of the state of emergency announcement, AVPRF, F.: Sektretariata t. V.M. Molotova, Op. 12a, Por. 200, Pap. 51, secret; and the Telefonogramma po V Ch from Semenov in Berlin at 14:00, 17 June to Moscow, which reports in detail on the day's events, ibid.

130. Stulz-Herrnstadt, *Das Herrnstadt-Dokument*, 82–83.

131. Ibid., 84. In spite of the harsh criticism leveled against Zaisser for the failures of the Stasi to gain advance knowledge of, and prevent the unrest on, 16 and 17 June, and in spite of his clear opposition to Ulbricht, he received the traditional big greeting in *Neues Deutschland* on his birthday on 20 June and an award, and Ulbricht attended his birthday celebration at Stasi headquarters.

See Baras, "Beria's Fall and Ulbricht's Survival," 391; and Wollweber's memoirs, Otto, ed., "Ernst Wollweber: Aus Erinnerungen," 358–59.

132. A "telefonogramma po V Ch" with a translation of this, "Zaiavlenie pravitel'stva GDR k polozheniiu v Berline," was sent from Semenov to Molotov on 17 June. AVPRF, F.: Sektretariata t. V.M. Molotova, Op. 12a, Por. 200, Pap, 51, secret.

133. See also the account of the events from 17–19 June given to the Soviet leaders by Sokolovsky, Semenov, and Yudin on 24 June, "The Report to the Soviet Leadership," "On the Events of 17–19 June 1953 in Berlin and the GDR and Certain Conclusions from These Events," CWIHP, *Bulletin 5* (Spring 1995): 10, 17–20.

134. Most of these can be found in AVPRF, F.: Sekretariata t. V.M. Molotova, Op. 12a, Por. 200, Pap. 51, secret; AVPRF, F.: Referentura po Germanii, Op. 41, Por. 93, Pap. 280; and AVPRF, F.: Sekretariata t. V.M. Molotova, Op. 12a, Por. 314, Pap. 52, secret. Some of them are also reprinted in Ostermann, ed., *Uprising in East Germany*.

135. Telefonogramma po V Ch, 23:00, 17 June, from Grechko and Semenov to Molotov and Bulganin, AVPRF, F.: Sekretariata t. V.M. Molotova, Op. 12a, Por. 200, Pap. 51, secret.

136. Telefonogramma po V Ch, 23:00, 17 June, from Sokolovsky and Semenov to Molotov and Bulganin, ibid. See also Semenov's urgent Telefonogramma po V Ch to Molotov, 18 June, ibid., that GDR Deputy Prime Minister Otto Nuschke had been abducted by West Berliners at 3 P.M. on 17 June and was in the hands of American authorities. Semenov reported that Nuschke's health was not good and that the Soviets "should take ugent measures to liberate" him. Semenov and Sokolovsky later reported that Nuschke was returned by American officers to the Soviets at 11:30 A.M., 19 June. Telefonogramma po V Ch, 19 June, from Sokolovsky and Semenov to Molotov and Bulganin, ibid.

137. On the night between 17 and 18 June, the Soviet forces made 3,361 arrests and the East German Interior Ministry officials made 909 arrests, 521 in Berlin. Telefonogramma po V Ch, 18 June from Sokolovsky and Semenov to Molotov and Bulganin, ibid. A total of 21 people were killed in all of the GDR on 17 June, and there were 300,000–372,000 people involved in the demonstrations, thus 5.5–6.8 percent of the population; Baring *Uprising in East Germany*, 52, 80. According to Soviet figures, a total of 1,240 people were later convicted: 468 were sentenced to up to one year in prison, 619 for one to five years, 87 for five to ten years, 14 for more than ten, 4 for life, 2 received the death penalty, and 46 were sentenced to "other punishment," "Otchet o politicheskom i ekonomicheskom polozhenii GDR v tret'em kvartale 1953g," report sent by A. Orlov to Semenov on 19 November 1953, AVPRF, F.: Referentura po Germanii, Op. 41, Por. 12, Pap. 270. See also the "Otchet o rabote Predstavitel'stva Verkhovnogo Komissara v g. Berline za 1953 god," by S. Den'gin, Deputy Soviet High Commissioner in Berlin and sent by Zhiliakov, senior advisor to the high commissioner, to Gribanov, head of the Third European Department of the Soviet Foreign Ministry, on 8 May 1954, AVPRF, F.: Referentura po Germanii, Op. 42, Por. 10, Pap. 284. This report states that about 80,000 people partici-

pated in the uprising in Berlin, of which about 30,000 were workers and employees of national enterprises, and 10,000 from West Berlin. The report concludes that the uprising was put down thanks to Soviet troops, the German police, the declaration of a state of emergency in the Soviet sector, and the closing of the Berlin sectoral border. The report also states that after the events of June, a new regime for guarding the sectoral border was introduced in 1954. Round-the-clock posts were established on eighty-one of the eighty-six streets leading into West Berlin, and all of the metro and railway stops on the border; 1192 policemen were stationed at the border.

138. Stulz-Herrnstadt, *Das Herrnstadt-Dokument*, 85.

139. Schenk, *Im Vorzimmer der Diktatur*, 225–26. It can be implied from Schenk's account that this meeting that he described took place at this time, but it may have been a little later.

140. Stulz-Herrnstadt, *Das Herrnstadt-Dokument*, 85–86. Jendretzky told Brandt that "the 'friends' demanded the 'X-Day' story," Brandt, *The Search for a Third Way*, 222.

141. See the following in AVPRF, F.: Sekretariata t. V.M. Molotova, Op. 12a, Por. 200, Pap, 51, secret: Urgent telefonogramma po V Ch, 18 June from Sokolovsky and Semenov to Molotov and Bulganin reporting on the situation in Berlin and the GDR as of 9:00 Berlin time; Telefonogramma po V CH, 18 June, from Sokolovsky and Semenov to Molotov and Bulganin reporting on the situation in Berlin and the GDR as of 14:00 Berlin time; Telefonogramma po V Ch, 19 June, from Sokolovsky and Semenov to Molotov and Bulganin reporting on the situation on 18 June at 21:00 Berlin time; Telefonogramma po V Ch, 19 June, from Sokolovsky and Semenov to Molotov and Bulganin reporting on the situation on 19 June at 11:00; Telefonogramma po V Ch, 19 June, 19:50, from Sokolovsky and Semenov to Molotov and Bulganin reporting on the situation at 17:00 Berlin time; Telefonogramma po V Ch, 19 June, 24:00, from Sokolovsky and Semenov to Molotov and Bulganin on the situation at 21:00; Telefonogramma po V Ch, 20 June, from Semenov to Molotov and Bulganin on the situation at 8:00; Telefonogramma po V Ch, 20 June, from Sokolovsky and Semenov to Molotov and Bulganin on the situation at 12:00; Telefonogramma po V Ch, 20 June, from Sokolovsky and Semnov to Molotov and Bulganin on the situation at 17:00; and the Telefonogramma po V Ch, 20 June, from Sokolovsky and Semenov to Molotov and Bulganin on the situation at 21:00.

142. In subsequent analyses of the uprising and its causes, however, the Soviets were much more open than the East Germans were about the role of domestic problems. See the contrasting accounts in Ostermann, intro. and comment., "Report to the Soviet Leadership," and "The Report to the SED Central Committee," CWIHP, *Bulletin 5* (Spring 1995): 10–21.

143. Telefonogramma po V Ch, 19 June, from Sokolovsky and Semnov to Molotov and Bulganin, reporting on the situation at 11:00, AVPRF, F.: Sekretariata t. V.M. Molotova, Op. 12a, Por. 200, Pap. 51, secret. For more information on the role of the United States in covert operations in the GDR in 1953, see Marchio, "From Revolution to Evolution: The Eisenhower Administration and Eastern Europe"; and Ostermann, "The United States and the 'Other' Germany: The GDR in U.S. Perception and Policy, 1949–1953." For Western denial

of participation in and provocation of the demonstrations, see the letters from the three Western commandants in Berlin to Dibrova on 23 June, copies of which were sent by Semenov to Molotov on 27 June, Telefonogramma po V Ch, AVPRF, F.: Sekretariata t. V.M. Molotova, Op. 12a, Por. 200, Pap, 51, secret; the letters from the three Western commandants in Berlin to Dibrova on 6 July, copies of which were sent by Lun'kov to Pushkin on 7 July by Telefonogramma, ibid.; the letters from the three Western commandants to Dibrova on 10 July, copies of which were sent from Yudin to Pushkin on 11 July by telefonogramma, ibid.; and the "Letter from President Eisenhower to Chancellor Adenauer on the Implications of the East German Uprising, 23 July 1953," U.S. Department of State, ed. *Documents on Germany, 1944–1985*, 402–404.

144. Telefonogramma po V Ch, 23:00, 17 June, from Sokolovsky and Semenov to Molotov and Bulganin, AVPRF, F. Sekretariata t. V.M. Molotova, Op. 12a, Por. 200, Pap. 51.

145. "Minutes of Discussion at the 150th Meeting of the National Security Council on 18 June 1953," 19 June 1953, reprinted in Ostermann, ed., *Uprising in East Germany*, 227.

146. Beate Ihme-Tuchel, *Die DDR*, 36–39.

147. "Minutes of Discussion at the 150th Meeting of the National Security Council on 18 June 1953," 19 June 1953, reprinted in Ostermann, ed., *Uprising in East Germany*, 228.

148. Cited in Hershberg, *James B. Conant: Harvard to Hiroshima and the Making of the Nuclear Age*, 660. See also Ostermann, "The United States, the East German Uprising of 1953, and the Limits of Rollback."

149. Ostermann, ed., *Uprising in East Germany*, 177–78. See also Larres, "Neutralisierung oder Westintegration: Churchill, Adenauer, die USA und der 17. Juni 1953," 568–83.

150. They had to resort to writing him, because Semenov told Dibrova to refuse to meet with them. Telefonogramma po V Ch, 19 June, from Semenov to Molotov, AVPRF, F.: Sekretariata t. V.M. Molotova, Op. 12a, Por. 200, Papka 51, secret.

151. A copy of the letter was sent by Semenov to Molotov, Telefonogramma po V Ch, 27 June, AVPRF, F.: Sekretariata t. V.M. Molotova, Op. 12, Por. 200, Pap. 51, secret.

152. "The Report to the Soviet Leadership" by Sokolovsky, Semenov and Yudin on 24 June, "On the Events of 17–19 June 1953 in Berlin and the GDR and Certain Conclusions from These Events," CWIHP, *Bulletin* 5 (Spring 1995): 21.

153. For the draft, see Telefonogramma from Semenov and Yudin to Molotov, 26 June, AVPRF, F.: Sekretariata t. V.M. Molotova, Op. 12, Por. 200, Pap. 51, secret. See also the draft sent by Vyshinsky and Pushkin to Molotov on 27 June, ibid. For the text of the final letter, see Telefonogramma po V Ch, 30 June, from Pushkin to Semenov, ibid.

154. Telefonogramma po V Ch, 7 July, from Lunk'ov to Pushkin, AVPRF, F.: Sekretariata t. V.M. Molotova, Op. 12a, Por. 200, Pap. 51, secret.

155. Top secret letter from Pushkin to Vyshinsky, 6 July, AVPRF, F.: Referentura po Germanii, Op. 41, Por. 93, Pap. 280. The letter also mentioned that measures would be taken to strength the People's Police (the VoPos). On Soviet

and East German plans to take steps toward reopening the sectoral border, see: Telefonogramma, from Miroshnichenko and Lun'kov in Berlin, received by Semenov on 4 July in Moscow, proposing, with Ulbricht's support, the partial easing of movement across the sectoral border, AVPRF, F.: Sekretariata t. V.M. Molotova, Op. 12a, Por. 200, Pap. 51, secret; and the letter sent to Dibrova by the three Western commandants demanding the resumption of free movement in Berlin, sent by Telefonogramma po V Ch, 7 July, from Lun'kov in Berlin to Pushkin in Moscow, AVPRF, F.: Sekretariata t. V.M. Molotova, Op. 12a, Por. 200, Pap. 51, secret.

156. "Memorandum from Vladimir Semyonov and Pavel Yudin to Vyacheslav Molotov Regarding Inter-Zonal Movements in Berlin," 4 July 1953, Document No 66, in Ostermann, ed., *Uprising in East Germany*, 295–96.

157. Schirdewan recounts that in a meeting with Semenov, Yudin, and about twenty other Soviet functionaries and two marshals in Karlshorst on 19 June, Schirdewan replied to Semenov's question of his view of the political situation, asking him, in turn: "Where is the political leadership? We have an extremely precarious situation and the party leadership has disappeared." Thus, Schirdewan urged the immediate convening of the fourteenth plenum. "Die Führung lag in Moskau," 316–17.

158. Stulz-Herrnstadt, *Das Herrnstadt-Dokument*, 88–92.

159. Ibid., 104.

160. Letter sent by V Ch from Molotov to Semenov, 24 June, 23:00, secret, AVPRF, F.: Sekretariata t. V.M. Molotova, Op. 12a, Por. 314, Pap. 52.

161. See the top-secret accounting sent from Mikoian to Malenkov and Khrushchev on 11 August, AVPRF, F.: Sekretariata t. V.M. Molotova, Op. 12a, Por. 215, Pap. 52.

162. On U.S. policy toward the GDR in 1953, see Ostermann, "'Keeping the Pot Simmering': The United States and the East German Uprising of 1953," 61–89.

163. Schenk, *Im Vorzimmer der Diktatur*, 226–31.

164. See Stulz-Herrnstadt's proposed resolutions, in Wilfriede Otto, "Dokumente zur Auseinandersetzung in der SED 1953," 658–59; and Stulz-Herrnstadt, *Das Herrnstadt-Dokument*, 105–106.

165. Jänicke, *Der Dritte Weg*, 33.

166. Schirdewan had been a Central Committee member and the secretary in charge of the construction and control of the department of "Leading Organs of the Party and the Mass Organizations" since December 1952. Schirdewan himself believed that Semenov supported his Politburo membership; Schumann and Dressen, eds., "Die Führung lag in Moskau," 316.

167. This account of the meeting is taken from Stulz-Herrnstadt, *Das Herrnstadt-Dokument*, 111–18.

168. Semenov and Yudin must have been at the CPSU Central Committee plenum on Beria from 2–7 July.

169. This account of the meeting comes from Stulz-Herrnstadt, *Das Herrnstadt-Dokument*, 126–30.

170. "Postanovlenie plenuma TsK KPSS o prestupnykh antipartiinykh i antigosudarstvennykh deistviiakh Beriia," in "Delo Beriia. Plenum TsK KPSS Iiuli

1953 goda. Stenograficheskii Otchet," 203, 204. Khrushchev notes in his memoirs that Malenkov was afraid that he might be attacked also, since he had shared some of Beria's views on Germany. As Khrushchev writes, the leadership assured Malenkov then that the problem with Beria was much deeper than just his views on Germany. See Khrushchev, "Aktsii," 279.

171. "Postanovlenie plenuma TsK KPSS o prestupnykh antipartiinykh i antigosudarstvennykh deistviiakh Beriia," in "Delo Beriia," 203, 205–206, 208.

172. "The Report to the Soviet Leadership," by Sokolovsky, Semenov, and Yudin, "On the Events of 17–19 June 1953 in Berlin and the GDR and Certain Conclusions from These Events," CWIHP, *Bulletin 5* (Spring 1995): 10, 17–21.

173. Stulz-Herrnstadt, *Das Herrnstadt-Dokument*, 130.

174. Ibid., 159.

175. See Ulbricht's speech of 24 July, SAPMO-BArch, ZPA, IV 2/1/247, 110. The entire stenographic protocol of the stormy plenum can be found in the SED archives, ibid. See also Stulz-Herrnstadt, *Das Herrnstadt-Dokument*,158–83.

176. Grotewohl emphasized in his opening speech on 24 July, however, that the methods of implementation of the East German *New Course* must be based upon the existing conditions in the GDR, not upon the conditions existing in Russia at the start of the New Economic Policy (NEP) in 1921. Soviet experience should be learned from but not always imitated. SAPMO-BArch, ZPA, IV 2/1/247, 29–31.

177. Kramer, "The Early Post-Stalin Succession Struggle" (Part 3), 7.

178. On the economic situation in the GDR in July and August, U.S. efforts to sell food to the East German population inexpensively, and the economic actions taken by the Soviets to aid the East Germans prior to the arrival of the GDR delegation in Moscow on 20 August, see Telefonogramma po V Ch, from West Berlin to Pushkin, 16 July, "O Prodazhe fruktov i moloka v amerikanskom sektore dlia zhitelei Vostochnogo Berlina," AVPRF, F.: Referentura po Germanii, Op. 35, Por. 37, Pap. 125; Telefonogramma po V Ch, from Semenov and Yudin in Berlin to Pushkin in Moscow, AVPRF, F.: Sekretariata t. V. M. Molotova, Op. 12a, Por. 314, Pap. 52; Telefonogramma po V Ch, from Matynov in Berlin to Mikoian, "Chlenam Prezidiuma TsK KPSS," ibid; letter from Pushkin to Molotov, 25 July, "Spravka," AVPRF, F.: Sekretariata t. V.M. Molotova, Op. 12a, Por. 320, Pap. 54; "Mitteilung des Ministerrates der DDR über zusätzliche Lebensmittellieferungen aus der UdSSR," 21 July 1953, in Ministerium für Auswärtige Angelegenheiten der DDR and Ministerium für Auswärtige Angelegenheiten der UdSSR, eds., *Beziehungen DDR-UdSSR, 1949–1955*, 1, 440–41; "Mitteilung des Ministeriums für Aussenhandel und inner-deutschen Handel der DDR über sowjetische Lebensmittel- und Rohstofflierferungen an die DDR im Jahre 1953," 21 July 1953, in ibid.; "Schreiben des Hohen Kommissars der UdSSR in Deutschland an den Hohen Kommissar der USA in Deutschland, M.B. Conant, zum Beschluss der USA-Regierung über die sogenannte Lieferung von Lebensmitteln nach Berlin," 21 July 1953, in ibid.; and "Aus der Erklärung der DDR zur Versorgung der DDR mit Lebensmitteln," 29 July 1953, in ibid.

179. See the top-secret note, 30 July to Molotov from Gromyko and Pushkin sending him the draft CPSU CC resolution and corresponding memorandum on

the German question, "V Prezidium TsK KPSS," AVPRF, F.: Sekretariata t. V. M. Molotova, Op. 12, Por. 264, Pap. 16, top secret; and "O meropriiatiiakh zapadnykh derzhav v sviazi s predstoiashchimi parlamentskimi vyborami v Zapadnoi Germanii i o meropriiatiiakh Sovetskogo Soiuza, napravlennykh na povyshenie avtoriteta GDR," sent "V Prezidium TsK KPSS. tovarishchu G. M. Malenkovu, tovarishchu N.S. Khrushchevu." The document is dated only "August 1953," but the text makes it clear that it was sent from the Foreign Ministry to the Presidium by 3 August.

180. "O meropriiatiiakh zapadnykh derzhav v sviazi s predstoiashchimi parlamentskimi vyborami v zapadnoi germanii i o meropriiatiiakh sovetskogo soiuza napravlennykh na povyshenie avtoriteta GDR," August 1953, AVPRF, F.: Referentura po germanii, Op. 41, Por. 15, Pap. 270, Inv. 101, t. 2.

181. See the "Eight-Power Declaration Issued at the End of the Moscow Conference of East European Countries, December 2, 1954," in *Documents on Germany*, 441–42.

182. Telegram received by Grotewohl on 15 August from the chief of the East German diplomatic mission in Moscow, Rudolf Appelt, reporting on the delivery of a letter from Molotov at 13:30, SAPMO-BArch, ZPA, 90/471. By Semenov's account, he gave it to Pieck, Ulbricht, and Grotewohl on 16 August. Telefonogramma po V Ch from Semenov in Berlin to Molotov, AVPRF, F.: Referentura po Germanii, Op. 41, Por. 19, Pap. 27.

183. Schenk, *Im Vorzimmer der Diktatur*, 231.

184. Schenk notes wryly that the East Germans were a bit surprised by Semenov's upgrading, since this had supposedly just happened on 28 May with the liquidation of the Soviet Control Commission in the GDR. Thus, Schenk recounts that Ulbricht "pretended that the Soviet note of 28 May was just a Soviet proposal that was put into effect on 22 August"; Ibid., 231–32. The East Germans no doubt felt the same way when they "received sovereignty" again on 25 March 1954 and 20 September 1955. For the German record of the opening session, see "Eröffnungssitzung vom 20. August 1953 im Kreml," SAPMO-BArch, ZPA, NL 90/471.

185. See ibid and also "Protokoll über den Erlass der deutschen Reparationsleistungen und über andere Massnahmen zur Erleichterung der finanziellen und wirtschaftlichen Verpflichtungen der Deutschen Demokratischen Republik, die mit den Folgen des Krieges verbunden sind," 22 August, in Ministerium für Auswärtige Angelegenheiten der DDR and Ministerium für Auswärtige Angelegenheiten der UdSSR, eds., *Beziehungen DDR-UdSSR, 1949-1955*, 1, 462–64; "Aus dem gemeinsamen Kommuniqué über die Verhandlungen zwischen der Regierung der Union der Sozialistischen Sowjetunion und einer Regierungsdelegation der Deutschen Demokratischen Republik," 22 August, ibid., 465–67; and the "Communiqué Announcing the Soviet Economic Relief for the German Democratic Republic and the Exchange of Ambassadors, Moscow, August 22, 1953," in *Documents on Germany, 1944–1985*, 406–408. Schenk writes that the economic agreements had been prepared by Semenov and his deputies in Karlshorst. *Im Vorzimmer der Diktatur*, 231. Mikoian stated in his speech on 20 August that the Soviets had come to agreements on what credits and what additional supplies the GDR needed with the GDR economics delegation in

Moscow led by Leuschner. SAPMO-BArch, ZPA, NL 90/471. In addition, Molotov, Gromyko, Pushkin, and others had been working on the economic and other details of the agreements.

186. "Eröffnungssitzung vom 20. August 1953 im Kreml," SAPMO-BArch, ZPA, NL 90/471, 10–11; 14–16.

187. See the 24 June report on the uprising by Sokolovsky, Semenov, and Yudin, "The Report to the Soviet leadership," CWIHP, *Bulletin* 5 (Spring 1995): 19.

188. This is seen most clearly in ibid., especially in the section of the report containing their recommendations, which included abolishing Ulbricht's position as general secretary and narrowing his responsibilities, 20.

189. See chapters 3 and 4.

190. Wettig, *Bereitschaft zu Einheit in Freiheit?* 268–74.

191. In the terminology of Glenn Snyder, Khrushchev's fears of being "abandoned" by the GDR via its collapse and absorption into the FRG (the lesson of the uprising) combined with his fears of being accused of abandoning the GDR (the lesson of Beria's ouster) would come to "entrap" him into supporting Ulbricht and some of his more undesirable policies. Glenn Snyder, *Alliance Politics* and idem., "The Security Dilemma in Alliance Politics," 461–95.

Chapter Two
1956–1958

1. SAPMO-BArch, ZPA, IV 2/1/249, Ulbricht's speech on 17 September, 34. Khrushchev would declare two German states two years later.

2. For the Politburo resolutions of 12 January 1954 on Herrnstadt, Zaisser, Ackermann, Jendretzky, and Schmidt, see SAPMO-BArch, ZPA, NL 90/292.

3. "Aus der Ansprache des Mitgliedes des Präsidiums des ZK der KPdSU, A.I. Mikojan, an den IV. Parteitag der SED, 1. April 1954," in Ministerium für Auswärtige Angelegenheiten der DDR and Ministerium für Auswärtige Angelegenheiten der UdSSR, eds., *Beziehungen DDR-UdSSR, 1949–1955*, 2, 644–57.

4. Cited in Stern, *Ulbricht*, 151. See also Brandt, *The Search for a Third Way*, 240.

5. For example, see the following MID report, "Politicheskoe polozhenie v GDR i deiatel'nost' politicheskikh partii i massovykh organizatsii v pervom polugodii 1954 goda," secret, AVPRF, F.: Referentura po Germanii, Op. 42, Por. 10, Pap. 284.

6. Schirdewan, *Aufstand gegen Ulbricht*, 71–72.

7. TsKhSD, R. 5147, Op. 28, D. 325. "Ob ukhode chasti grazhdan Germanskoi Demokraticheskoi Respubliki v Zapadnuiu Germaniiu," top secret, prepared by I. Tugarinov, 28 December 1955, and sent by Gromyko to Suslov on 28 December 1955. See also the "Spravka o perekhode grazhdan GDR na Zapad i pribytii nemtsev iz Zapadnoi Germanii na postoiannoe mestozhitel'stvo v GDR," secret, 21 January 1955, by P. Nazarov, director of the department of political questions of the GDR at the USSR embassy in the GDR, TsKhSD, R. 5149, F. 5, Op. 28, D. 329. For East German analyses of the refugee problem,

see NL 90/448, 3 August 1955 letter from General Major Last to Grotewohl; and 5 August 1955 letter from Minister Macher to Grotewohl. See also Ambassador Pushkin's 27 March 1956 report on the situation in the GDR in 1955, including the numbers of refugees. AVPRF, F.: Referentura po GDR, Op. 1, Por. 1, Pap. 1.

8. Ibid.

9. "Zapis' besedy s pervym sekretarem GK SEPG Berlina A. Noimanom," 30 January 1956, from the diary of A. L. Orlov, advisor to the USSR embassy in the GDR, 11 February 1956 secret, TsKhSD, R. 5181, F. 5, Op. 28, D. 427, 3.

10. Otto, intro. and annot. , "Ernst Wollweber: Aus Erinnerungen," 361.

11. Zubok and Harrison, "The Nuclear Education of Nikita Khrushchev," 141–68.

12. Weathersby, "On the Korean War, 1950–53, and the Armistice Negotiations," 17; and Zubok and Pleshakov, *Inside the Kremlin's Cold War*, 70–72, 155.

13. *Khrushchev Remembers*, 374–91.

14. Aleksander-Agentov, *Ot Kollontai do Gorbacheva*, 95.

15. On the Austrian path to unification and neutrality, see Bischof, *Austria in the First Cold War, 1945–55*. A. M. Aleksander-Agentov, director of the section on Austria at MID's Third European Department, writes that MID's proposals for Austrian neutrality "were connected with a final withdrawal of foreign troops with the resolution of the German question." *Ot Kollontai do Gorbacheva*, 95.

16. On the Geneva summit, see Bischof and Dockrill, eds., *Cold War Respite: The Geneva Summit of 1955*. For Khrushchev's recollections, see *Khrushchev Remembers*, 392–400. For Soviet documents on the Geneva summit, see TsKhSD, R. 5672, F. 5, Op. 30, D. 114 and 116.

17. For the text of the announcement, see Ministerium für Auswärtige Angelegenheiten der DDR and Ministerium für Auswärtige Angelegenheiten der UdSSR, eds., *Beziehungen DDR-UdSSR, 1949–1955*, 2, 639–40.

18. "Mitteilung der Regierung der UdSSR über die Aufhebung von Befehlen und Anordnungen der SMAD und der SKK in Deutschland," 6 August 1954, ibid., 703–704.

19. "Erlass des Präsidiums des Obersten Sowjets der UdSSR über die Beendigung des Kriegszustandes zwischen der Sowjetunion und Deutschland," Moscow, Kremlin, 25 January 1955, ibid., 825–27.

20. Aleksandrov-Agentov, *Ot Kollontai do Gorbacheva*, 100.

21. On the Soviets waiting six years after the founding of NATO to form a counterpart in response to their sense of threat from a rearmed West Germany in NATO, see Ulam, *Expansion and Coexistence*, 504–506, 557–58. On the December 1954 and March 1955 preparatory meetings in Moscow for the formation of the WTO, see "Deklaration der Moskauer Konferenz europäischer Länder zur Gewährleistung des Friedens und der Sicherheit in Europa," 2 December 1954, in Ministerium für Auswärtige Angelegenheiten der DDR und Ministerium für Auswärtige Angelegenheiten der UdSSR, eds., *Beziehungen DDR-UdSSR*, 2, 768–82; "Mitteilung des Allgemeinen Deutschen Nachrichtendienstes (ADN) über Beratungen über den Abschluss eines Vertrages über Freund-

schaft, Zusammenarbeit und gegenseitigen Beistand zwischen den Teilnehmer-ländern der Moskauer Konferenz europäischer Länder zur Gewährleistung des Friedens und der Sicherheit in Europa," 21 March 1955, ibid., 845–46; SAPMO-BArch, ZPA, NL 90/196; and SAPMO-BArch, ZPA, NL 90/460. On the preparations for and carrying out of the 11–14 May Warsaw Pact founding meeting, see SAPMO-BArch, ZPA, NL 90/461.

22. Aleksandrov-Agentov, *Ot Kollontai do Gorbacheva*, 101–102.

23. The other members were the Soviet Union, Poland, Hungary, Czechoslo-vakia, Bulgaria, Romania, and Albania.

24. Wettig, *Bereitschaft zu Einheit in Freiheit?* 282–86.

25. For Khrushchev's account of this meeting, see his memoirs, *Khrushchev Remembers: The Last Testament*, 357–60. For Soviet preparations for the meet-ing, see the documents in AVPRF, F.: Referentura po Germanii, Op. 43, Por. 14, Pap. 303; AVPRF, F.: Referentura po Germanii, Op. 42, Por. 12, Pap. 284; and AVPRF, F.: Referentura po Germanii, Op. 43, Por. 15, Pap. 303. For Soviet documents regarding the meetings, see AVPRF, F.: Referentura po Germanii, Op. 43, Por. 16, Pap. 303; and AVPRF, F.: Referentura po Germanii, Op. 43, Por. 15, Pap. 303. For a Soviet report on the East German response to the Soviet establishment of relations with the FRG, see the secret report by A. Zheltov, 7 October 1955, "O politicheskikh nastroeniiakh naseleniia GDR v sviazi s sostoi-avshimsia v Moskve peregovorami mezhdu pravitel'stvennymi delegatsiiami SSSR i GFR," TsKhSD, R. 4574, F. 5, Op. 30, D. 122. For Adenauer's account of the meeting, see his memoirs, Adenauer, *Erinnerungen, 1955–1959*, 447–50, 487–556.

26. See SAPMO-BArch, ZPA, J IV 2/202/125. For East German analyses of the talks, see SAPMO-BArch, ZPA, IV 2/20/226.

27. Khrushchev notes in his memoirs that he was very concerned on his first trip as leader to Germany that he would get a hostile reception from the Ger-mans due to World War II and the Soviet victory. He was relieved when this did not occur. *Khrushchev Remembers*, 400; and *Khrushchev Remembers: The Glasnost Tapes*, 161.

28. "Aus dem Kommuniqué über den Aufenthalt der Regierungsdelegation der UdSSR in der DDR," 27 July 1955, in *Beziehungen DDR-UdSSR*, 2, 948–50. See also "Rede des Genossen N.S. Chruschtschows auf der Kundgebung der Werktätigen Berlins am 26. Juli 1955," SAPMO-BArch, ZPA, NL 90/204; and Schirdewan, *Aufstand gegen Ulbricht*, 70.

29. Schenk, *Im Vorzimmer der Diktatur*, 280. "Vertrag über die Beziehungen zwischen der Deutschen Demokratischen Republik und der Union der Sozialis-tischen Sowjetrepubliken," 20 September 1955, in, *Beziehungen DDR-UdSSR*, 2, 992–95. For Soviet preparations of the treaty with the GDR, and the broader character of Article 4 of the treaty than in Soviet treaties with other socialist countries, see "Poiasnitel'naia zapiska k stat'e 4 proekta Dogovora o druzhbe i vzaimnoi pomoshchi mezhdu Sovetskim Soiuzom i GDR," by Pushkin and Se-menov, top secret, 19 January 1955, AVPRF, F.: Referentura po Germanii, Op. 43, Por. 31, Pap. 305. For the speeches given at the meeting, see SAPMO-BArch, ZPA, NL 90/471. Soviet sources stress a significant activization of East Germa-ny's foreign policy after this and Michael Lemke asserts that this treaty "opened

up a certain room for maneuver in GDR foreign policy." Michael Lemke, "Die deutschlandpolitischen Handlungsspielräume der SED innerhalb der sowjetischen Deutschlandpolitik der Jahre 1949–1955," in Gustav Schmidt, ed., *Ost-West Beziehungen: Konfrontation und Détente, 1945–1989*, II, 325–26, 329.

30. "Beschluss des Ministerrates der UdSSR über die Abschaffung des Amtes des Hohen Kommissars der UdSSR in Deutschland," 20 September 1955, in MfAA der DDR, MfAA der UdSSR, eds., *Beziehungen DDR-UdSSR, 1949 bis 1955*, 2, 1001.

31. "Briefwechsel zwischen dem Stellvertreter des Ministers für Auswärtige Angelegenheiten der Union der Sozialistischen Sowjetrepubliken und dem Minister für Auswärtige Angelegenheiten der Deutschen Demokratischen Republik zur Frage des Schutzes und der Kontrolle an den Grenzen der DDR," 20 September 1955, ibid., 996–98.

32. For the debate over the seriousness of the 10 March 1952 "Stalin Note," see Wettig, "Die Stalin-Note vom 10 März 1952 als geschichtswissenschaftliches Problem," 157–67; idem, "Die Stalin-Note vom 10 März 1952—Antwort auf Elke Scherstjanoi," 862–65; Scherstjanoi, "Zu Gerhard Wettig, 'Die Stalin-Note vom 10 März 1952 als geschichtswissenschaftliches Problem," ibid., 858–62; and van Dijk, "The 1952 Stalin Note Debate: Myth or Missed Opportunity for German Unification?"

33. *Khrushchev Remembers: The Glasnost Tapes*, 69–70; and Zubok, trans., "First Conversation of N. S. Khrushchev with Mao Zedong, 31 July 1958, Hall of Huaizhentan," CWIHP, *Bulletin* 12/13 (Fall/Winter 2001): 260. Not surprisingly, Molotov does not mention this disagreement in his memoirs in the form of his published conversations with Felix Chuev, in which he recounts his policy toward Beria of defending the GDR and arguing for its importance and for the necessity of supporting socialism there. Chuev, *Sto sorok besed s Molotovym*, 333–35.

34. For a wonderful example of Khrushchev's optimism about communism, see his "kitchen debate" with Vice President Richard Nixon in Moscow in July 1959 in CNN, *Cold War*, Episode 8, "Sputnik."

35. This section on Khrushchev is drawn from the following sources: Burlatsky, *Khrushchev and the First Russian Spring*; Aleksandrov-Agentov, *Ot Kollontai do Gorbacheva*; Mikoian, *Tak Bylo*; N. Khrushchev, *Khrushchev Remembers*; Zubok and Pleshakov, *Inside the Kremlin's Cold War*; Tompson, *Khrushchev: A Political Life*; Taubman, "Khrushchev vs. Mao: A Preliminary Sketch of the Role of Personality in the Sino-Soviet Split"; idem., "Khrushchev and Sino-Soviet Relations"; "Takovy, tovarishchi, fakty," and "Zapisi V. Malina na zasedanii Prezidiuma TsK KPSS," 13–14 October 1964 in *Vestnik Arkhiva Prezidenta Rossiiskoi Federatsii* 2 (1998): 101–143; and Mel'chin, Sigachev, and Stepanov, "Kak Snimali N. S. Khrushcheva: Materialy plenuma TsK KPSS. Oktiabr' 1964g." See also William Taubman's biography, *Khrushchev: The Man and His Era*.

36. Burlatsky, *Khrushchev and the First Russian Spring*, 46, 59, 61, 63.

37. Troyanovsky, *Cherez Gody i Rasstoiania*, 206–207.

38. Mikoian, *Tak Bylo*, 597–98, 601–602, 607.

39. Troyanovsky, *Cherez Gody i Rasstoiania*, 206.

40. Taubman, "Khrushchev and Sino-Soviet Relations," 1, 3, 17.

41. Mikoian also characterizes Khrushchev as disloyal. *Tak Bylo*, 600.

42. Mel'chin, Sigachev, and Stepanov, "Kak Snimali N. S. Khrushcheva: Materialy Plenuma TsK KPSS. Oktiabr' 1964g," 10.

43. "Takovy, tovarishchi, fakty," 103; 114. In addition, see Aleksandrov-Agentov's account of Khrushchev "indelicately teasing Gromyko, including in the presence of foreigners." *Ot Kollontai do Gorbacheva*, 71. Troyanovsky also writes of Khrushchev's sharp and crude behavior, *Cherez Gody i Rasstoianiia*, 208.

44. "Takovy, tovarishchi, fakty," 116, 103, 117.

45. Ibid., 112–13.

46. Mikoian, *Tak Bylo*, 616.

47. Podewin, *Walter Ulbricht*, 48.

48. Leonhard, *Child of the Revolution*, 360.

49. Podewin, *Walter Ulbricht*, 148–49.

50. *Khrushchev Remembers*, 206.

51. Zubok and Pleshakov, *Inside the Kremlin's Cold War*, 175; Burlatsky, *Khrushchev and the First Russian Spring*, 44, 49.

52. Tompson, *Khrushchev: A Political Life*, 5–7.

53. Burlatsky, *Khrushchev and the First Russian Spring*, 45.

54. *Khrushchev Remembers*, 23.

55. Zubok and Pleshakov, *Inside the Kremlin's Cold War*, 178–79.

56. *Khrushchev Remembers*, 22.

57. Tompson, *Khrushchev: A Political Life*, 8.

58. Zubok and Pleshakov, *Inside the Kremlin's Cold War*, 178, 179. The CNN 24-part documentary series, *Cold War*, is especially useful for being able to "look" at Khrushchev in this way, such as Episode 9, "Mousetrap," containing footage of Khrushchev's furious response to the 1 May 1960 U.S. U-2 overflight of the Soviet Union.

59. Tompson, *Khrushchev: A Political Life*, 10–12; Burlatsky, *Khrushchev and the First Russian Spring*, 50–51.

60. Tompson, *Khrushchev: A Political Life*, 20–26; Burlatsky, *Khrushchev and the First Russian Spring*, 51–52.

61. *Khrushchev Remembers*, 36–44.

62. Troyanovsky, *Cherez Gody i Rasstoianiia*, 207.

63. Burlatsky, *Khrushchev and the First Russian Spring*, 45.

64. Troyanovsky, *Cherez Gody i Rasstoianiia*, 207.

65. Tompson, *Khrushchev: A Political Life*, 28–57; Burlatsky, *Khrushchev and the First Russian Spring*, 52–57.

66. Tompson, *Khrushchev: A Political Life*, 70–81.

67. Cited in Podewin, *Walter Ulbricht*, 148. For Khrushchev's recollection of this gathering, see *Khrushchev Remembers*, 206–207.

68. Tompson, *Khrushchev: A Political Life*, 81–82, 86–109.

69. On Khrushchev's key role in Beria's ouster, see *Khrushchev Remembers*, 321–41; Mikoian, *Tak Bylo*, 586–88; and Kramer, "The Early Post-Stalin Succession Struggle: Internal-External Linkages in Soviet Policy Making (Part 2)," 9–38.

70. Aleksandrov-Agentov, *Ot Kollontai do Gorbacheva*, 56; 70–71.

71. Ibid., 59, 61–62; and Troyanovsky, *Cherez Gody i Rasstoianiia*, 206. Mikoian claims that it was his own idea to establish a commission to investigate the Stalin period before the Twentieth Congress. *Tak Bylo*, 589–96.

72. For the text of the secret speech, see the appendix to *Khrushchev Remembers*, 559–618.

73. For the text of this report, see *XX C"ezd Kommunisticheskoi Partii Sovetskogo Soiuza, Stenograficheskii Otchet, 14–25 fevralia 1956 goda*, 31–32.

74. Stalin, himself, at times displayed an understanding of the need for separate paths to socialism. Meeting with the East German leaders in Moscow in April 1952, in response to Ulbricht's request for some advice on "methods of work of the Central Committee and the state apparatus," Stalin replied: "We have nothing to hide from you, but you simply have somewhat different circumstances." Ulbricht in turn assured him that the East Germans "would be able to decide how to apply the Soviet experience to the GDR's conditions." "Record of Conversation of Leaders of the Socialist Unity Party of Germany W. Pieck, W. Ulbricht, and O. Grotewohl with J.V. Stalin," 1 April 1952, Document No. 1 in Ostermann, ed., *Uprising in East Germany*, 33–34.

75. The Soviets had called for the East Germans to expand ties with the SPD in the *New Course* of June 1953 also.

76. TsKhSD, R. 5182, F. 5, Op. 28, D. 430.

77. See, for example, Khrushchev's comments to this effect at his summit with Ulbricht on 9 July 1959. Harrison, intro., annot., trans., "The Berlin Crisis and the Khrushchev-Ulbricht Summits in Moscow, 9 and 18 June 1959," 207.

78. W. Erfurt, *Moscow's Policy in Germany: A Study in Contemporary History*, 68, cited in Grieder, *The East German Leadership, 1946–1973*, 124.

79. Although he does note in his memoirs : "Russia's relations with Germany have not always been so bad. Before the Revolution—and before Hitler's rise to power—we used to have close economic ties with Germany." *Khrushchev Remembers: The Last Testament*, 189–90.

80. Khrushchev's 23 June 1959 conversation with Governor Averell Harriman, *Foreign Relations of the United States, 1958–1960, Vol. VIII, Berlin Crisis, 1958–1959*, 942.

81. For Schirdewan's description of the atmosphere and disagreements within the SED Politburo after the Twentieth Congress, see Schirdewan, *Aufstand gegen Ulbricht*, 76–91.

82. Schumann and Dressen, interview with Karl Schirdewan, "Die Führung lag in Moskau," 318. See also Karl Schirdewan's "Stellungnahme" of 1 January 1958, in Bretschneider, Libera, and Wilhelm, eds., "Karl Schirdewan: Fraktionsmacherei oder gegen Ulbrichts Diktat? Eine Stellungnahme vom 1. Januar 1958," 512.

83. Schirdewan, *Aufstand gegen Ulbricht*, 77.

84. When Schirdewan asked Ulbricht over breakfast the next morning, 26 February, what he should say about Khrushchev's secret speech in his address to the East Germans studying at the CPSU party school in Moscow, Ulbricht flippantly remarked, "You can safely say that Stalin isn't a classic." Schirdewan felt that this was an overly simplistic way of dealing with such a profound issue.

Ibid., 79. In an article on 4 March in *Neues Deutschland*, Ulbricht did indeed say that due to the way in which Stalin's cult of personality caused harm to the CPSU and the Soviet people, "One cannot count Stalin among the classics of Marxism." See the text of Ulbricht's article in Gabert et al., eds., *SED und Stalinismus*, 93–115. Quote from 113. In Schirdewan's "Statement" of 1 January 1958, he said that Ulbricht's assertion "unleashed great unrest and confusion in the party [and] put the leaders of the communist parties of Poland, Hungary, and Czechoslovakia, who obviously wanted to proceed more slowly on this issue, in a new situation." See Schirdewan's "Statement," "Stellungnahme," 502. At the twenty-sixth plenum on 22 March 1956, Hanna Wolf, director of the SED high school, also criticized Ulbricht for making such an extreme statement so quickly after Stalin had been propagated as a hero for so long in the GDR. She felt that the Stalin period in the Soviet Union and the GDR should be analyzed in detail by all, instead of suddenly announcing that Stalin was no longer a classic. Each person needed to go through a personal re-education process, as did the country as a whole, in her view. See her speech at the plenum, SAPMO-BArch, ZPA, DY 30/IV 2/1/79, 97–98, 100–101.

85. Recalling Carola Stern's discussion of differences between the "native" and "Muscovite" German communists in terms of where they spent the Nazi years, Schirdewan compares his reaction to the speech to the different reaction by the "Moscow cadres," Ulbricht and Neumann. Schirdewan, *Ein Jahrhundert Leben: Erinnerungen und Visionen*, 253.

86. Schirdewan, *Aufstand gegen Ulbricht*, 81, 82.

87. SAPMO-BArch, ZPA, DY 30/J IV 2/2/J-181.

88. "Über den XX. Parteitag der Kommunistischen Partei der Sowjetunion. Artikel von Walter Ulbricht vom 4. März 1956," in Gabert et. al. eds., *SED und Stalinismus*, 93–115.

89. SAPMO-BArch, ZPA, DY 30/IV 2/1/79, 134. It is not clear how honest Ulbricht was being here about his delay. He said that the Politburo "had to ask the CPSU CC Presidium to allow them to inform the CC about the closed session of the Twentieth Party Congress. I was only able to give the text which was necessary for this to Comrade Schirdewan yesterday evening. We could not inform the Central Committee on the basis of some key words taken down by two comrades who did not take part in the session. [He says that he] and Grotewohl were not present, were not there. Okay, fine, couldn't Comrade Schirdewan have spoken [since he was the one who received the briefing from the Soviet CC official on the secret speech]? But what situation would he have been in? He could have informed you just on the basis of several key words. What would have happened in this CC session?" Ibid. According to Schirdewan's later account, however, he was able to take word-for-word notes of the briefing on Khrushchev's secret speech, much more than just writing down a few key words. Schirdewan, *Aufstand gegen Ulbricht*, 77.

90. Schirdewan, *Aufstand gegen Ulbricht*, 77. For some of Ulbricht's comments to a conference of Berlin district delegates, see "Antworten auf Fragen auf der Berliner Bezirksdelegiertenkonferenz der SED. Aus der Diskussionsrede Walter Ulbricht am 17. März 1956," in Gabert et al., eds., *SED und Stalinismus*, 116–30. At the Berlin conference, Ulbricht did discuss Stalin's cult of per-

sonality and mistakes made because of it and also said that the SED had to eliminate mistakes made due to the cult of personality in the GDR. Ibid., 122. See also Ulbricht's speech to the twenty-sixth plenum. SAPMO-BArch, ZPA, DY 30/IV 2/1/79, 134–36.

91. Ibid., 134.

92. SAPMO-BArch, ZPA, DY 30/J IV 2/2A/482. See also Schirdewan's speech to the twenty-sixth plenum, SAPMO-BArch, ZPA, DY 30/IV 2/1/79, 32.

93. "Informatsionnaia zapiska," undated, but received at the CPSU CC on 10 May 1956. The report was written by E. Gusev, advisor in the CPSU CC Department on Relations with Communist Parties of Socialist Countries. TsKhSD, R. 5181, F. 5, Op. 28, D. 425.

94. As reported by A. L. Orlov, a Soviet adviser in the embassy in East Berlin, "Zapis besedy s sekretarem Tsentral'nogo Komiteta SEPG t. Shirdevanom," 9 April 1956, from Orlov's diary, secret. TsKhSD, R. 5181, F. 5, Op. 28, D. 425.

95. "Politicheskoe pis'mo o nekotorykh voprosakh ideologicheskoi raboty SEPG v sviazi s itogami XX-go s"ezda KPSS i 3 konferentsii SEPG," TsKhSD, R. 5181, F. 5, Op. 28, D. 426, 18–19.

96. "Politicheskoe Pis'mo/1. kvartal 1956 goda," secret report on hostile propaganda against the GDR written by Pushkin, 27 April 1956. AVPRF, F.: Referentura po GDR, Op. 1, Por. 1, Pap. 1, 20.

97. SAPMO-BArch, ZPA, DY 30/IV 2/1/161, 27 July 1956, 25.

98. SAPMO-BArch, ZPA, DY 30/ 2/1/162, 28 July 1956, 147–48.

99. "Zapis' besedy s kandidatom v chleny PB TsK SEPG, pervym sekretarem Berlinskogo Tsk SEPG A. Noimanom," 13 July 1956, TsKhSD, R. 5182, F. 5, Op. 28, D. 430, 3–5.

100. "Zapis' besedy s sekretarem Tsentral'nogo Komiteta SEPG t. Shirdevanom," 9 April 1956, TsKhSD, R. 5181, F. 5, Op. 28, D. 425.

101. See Kiefert's speech to the plenum on 29 July, SAPMO-BArch, DY 30/ IV 2/1/163, 267–68.

102. See the record of Rakosi's meeting with Soviet President Klement Voroshilov on 26 June 1956. TsKhSD, F. 89, Perechen' (list) 45, Document 2, 2–4. For more on the events in Hungary in the summer and fall of 1956, see Csaba Bekes, "The 1956 Hungarian Revolution and World Politics"; and Bekes, Byrne, and Ostermann, eds. and comps., *The Hidden History of Hungary 1956: A Compendium of Declassified Documents*.

103. Schirdewan, *Aufstand gegen Ulbricht*, 108–109.

104. SAPMO-BArch, DY 30/IV 2/1/163, 24. For other references to Western attacks on Ulbricht and the SED, see Ulbricht's report at the third party conference, SAPMO-BArch, ZPA, DY 30/IV 1/3/1, 128–29; Schirdewan's report on the Twentieth Congress at the SED third party conference, ibid., DY 30/IV 1/3/ 2, 279, 283; Wollweber's remarks, ibid., DY 30/J IV 1/3/7, 1020/1021; and Ulbricht's "Schlusswort" at the twenty-eighth plenum, 29 July 1956, ibid., DY 30/IV 2/1/163, 386.

105. Schirdewan, *Aufstand gegen Ulbricht*, 81, 82.

106. Wittkowski was First Deputy Chairman of the State Planning Commission.

107. SAPMO-BArch, ZPA, DY 30/IV 2/1/79, 83; 85–86.

108. See Ulbricht's speech at the plenum, ibid., 140.

109. SAPMO-BArch, ZPA, DY 30/IV 1/3/1, "Stenografische Niederschrift der 3. Parteikonferenz 24.–30. März 1956."

110. Bredel had been with Ulbricht in Moscow during World War II and was one of the founders of the National Committee for a Free Germany there. In 1956 he was a CC member and chief editor of one of the SED's literary publications.

111. SAPMO-BArch, ZPA, DY 30/IV 1/3/4, 27 March 1956, 538.

112. SAPMO-BArch, ZPA, DY 30 J IV 2/2/472, "Anlage Nr. 1 zum Protokoll Nr. 18 vom 17. April 1956."

113. SAPMO-BArch, ZPA, DY 30/J IV 2/2/480.

114. SAPMO-BArch, ZPA, DY 30/J IV 2/2/483.

115. On the events in Poland and Hungary, see Nowak, "Poles and Hungarians in 1956"; and Bekes, "The 1956 Hungarian Revolution and World Politics."

116. See SAPMO-BArch, ZPA, NL 90/471 and Ulbricht's speech at the twenty-eighth plenum on 27 July 1956, in SAPMO-BArch, ZPA, DY 30/IV 2/1/161, 5–6.

117. SAPMO-BArch, ZPA, J IV 2/202/315, *Brief des ZKs der KPdSU an die ZKs der Komm. Parteien der Unionsrepubliken, an die Bezirkskomitees, Gebietskomitees, Stadtkomitees, Kreiskomitees der Partei, an alle Grundorganisationen der KPdSU.*

118. TsKhSD, R. 8979, F. 5, Op. 49, D. 381. Addendum #1, "Ukhod naseleniia iz GDR v Zapadnuiu Germaniiu v 1950–1960gg," to the report by Ambassador Pervukhin to the CPSU CC on 7 April 1961, "K voprosu ob ukhode naseleniia GDR v Zapadnuiu Germaniiu (kratkaia spravka)"; and SAPMO-BArch, ZPA, DY 30/J IV 2/2/483, "Anlage zur Vorlage über die Republikflucht," from the *Protokoll Nr. 29/56 der Sitzung des Politbüros des Zentralkomitees am 19. Juni 1956 im Zentralhaus der Einheit, Grosser Sitzungssaal.*

119. SAPMO-BArch, ZPA, DY 30/J IV 2/2/472, "Protokoll Nr. 18/56 der Sitzung des Politbüros des Zentralkomitees am 17. April 1956 im Zentralhaus der Einheit, Grosser Sitzungssaal," and letter from CC Secretary Albert Norden "An alle Mitglieder des Politbüros," 17 April 1956, ibid., DY 30/J IV 2/2A/491.

120. "Protokoll Nr. 29/56 der Sitzung des PBs des ZKs am 19. Juni 1956 im Zentralhaus der Einheit, Grosser Sitzungssaal," "Anlage zur Vorlage über die Republikflucht," SAPMO-BArch, ZPA, DY 30/J IV 2/2/483.

121. Ibid.

122. *Anlage Nr. 4 zum Protokoll Nr. 29/56 vom 19.6.1956*, "Bericht der Kommission zu Fragen der Republikflucht," ibid.

123. "Vorschlag für okonomische Massnahmen zur Einschränkung und Überwindung der Fluktuation an Arbeitskraften," ibid.

124. "Vorschlag an die Kommission des PBs zur Aufhebung und Veränderung bestehender Gesetze und Anweisungen der Staatsorgane der DDR, die sich nachteilig auf die Stimmung und Haltung der Bevölkerung ausgewirkt haben," 9 May 1956, ibid.

125. Oelssner was a Politburo member, deputy chairman of the Council of Ministers, and the chairman of the Commission for Issues of Consumer Goods Production and the Supply of the Population.

126. SAPMO-BArch, ZPA, DY 30/IV 2/1/162, 203; 202.

127. See Grotewohl's notes on Khrushchev's comments, SAPMO-BArch, ZPA, NL 90/471, cited in Lemke, "Die deutschlandpolitischen Handlungsspielräume der SED innerhalb der sowjetischen Deutschlandpolitik der Jahre 1949–1955," 26.

128. Letter from SED CC and GDR government to Khrushchev and Bulganin, 19 May 1956, J IV 2/202/39, 1, cited in Lemke, "Die deutschlandpolitischen Handlungsspielräume der SED innerhalb der sowjetischen Deutschlandpolitik der Jahre 1949–1955," 329. See also the documents on the plenum in SAPMO-BArch, ZPA, IV 2/1/161.

129. Lemke, "Die deutschlandpolitischen Handlungsspielräume der SED innerhalb der sowjetischen Deutschlandpolitik der Jahre 1949–1955," 25–26.

130. Ackermann had been in Moscow for most of World War II and was the leader of the one of the three German communist groups sent back to Germany as the war was ending. In 1946 he published an article "Is There a Separate German Road to Socialism?" but was forced to recant his positive answer to this in 1948 after the ousting of Tito from the Cominform. Ackermann himself was ousted from his positions along with Herrnstadt and Zaisser in 1953–54, but then was rehabilitated after the Twentieth Congress, in July 1956. Barth et al., eds., *Wer war Wer in der DDR*, 14; Leonhard, *Child of the Revolution*, 439–42, 498–99; and Podewin, *Walter Ulbricht*, 200.

131. SAPMO-BArch, ZPA, DY 30/IV 2/1/79, 27.

132. SAPMO-BArch, ZPA, DY 30/IV 1/3/1, 15.

133. "Zapis' besedy s kandidatom v chleny PB TsK SEPG, pervym sekretarem Berlinskogo Tsk SEPG A. Noimanom," 13 July 1956, TsKhSD, R. 5182, F. 5, Op. 28, D. 430, 3–5.

134. Steinitz was a professor of philology at Humboldt University in Berlin and vice president of the Historical Studies Department of the German Academy of Sciences in Berlin.

135. Nowak, "Poles and Hungarians in 1956."

136. Bekes, "The 1956 Hungarian Revolution and World Politics."

137. For documents in East German archives on the connection between East German intellectuals, especially Harich, and the Petöfi circle in Hungary, see SAPMO-BArch, ZPA, DY 30/J IV 2/202/307; and Ulbricht's speech to the 30th SED plenum on 30 January 1957, SAPMO-BArch, ZPA, DY 30/IV 2/1/170, 117–119.

138. It is this plan that is probably what is contained in the mistakenly labeled file in SAPMO-BArch, ZPA, NL 182/893, *Materialen K. Schirdewan in Vorbereitung auf die 30. [sic] Tagung des ZK der SED. November 1956.* Harich was not secretive about this and went to talk to Ulbricht personally about it on 7 November. Staritz, *Geschichte der DDR, 1949–1985*, 113–14. See also Schirdewan, *Aufstand gegen Ulbricht*, 105, 115–19.

139. "Aktennotiz aus dem Staatssekretariat für Hochschulwesen über einen geplanten Einsatz von Kampfgruppen der SED an der Berliner Humboldt-Universität, 1.11.1956," from SAPMO-BArch, ZPA, DY 30/IV 2/9.04/432, 62, cited in Hoffmann, Schmidt and Skyba, *Die DDR vor dem Mauerbau: Dokumente zur Geschichte des anderen deutschen Staates 1949–1961*, 260–61. See

also Schirdewan, *Aufstand gegen Ulbricht*, 116; and Kurt Hager's speech to the twenty-ninth plenum, SAPMO-BArch, ZPA, DY 30/IV 2/1/166, 57.

140. SAPMO-BArch, ZPA, DY 30/IV 2/1/163, 29 July 1956, 389–91.

141. See the preparatory material for the twenty-eighth plenum, "*Informa-tion I. Die ideologischen Unklarheiten in der Partei und bei der Bevölkerung. Aus den Berichten der Sekretäre für Agitation und Propaganda der 14 Bezirkslei-tungen zusammengestellt.*" SAPMO-BArch, ZPA, DY 30/IV 2/1/160, 12.

142. SAPMO-BArch, ZPA, DY 30/IV 2/1/163, 291. See also Schirdewan, *Aufstand gegen Ulbricht*, p. 109.

143. See the preparatory material for the twenty-eighth plenum, "*Informa-tion I. Die ideologischen Unklarheiten in der Partei und bei der Bevölkerung. Aus den Berichten der Sekretäre für Agitation und Propaganda der 14 Bezirkslei-tungen zusammengestellt.*" SAPMO-BArch, ZPA, DY 30/IV 2/1/160, 13.

144. SAPMO-BArch, ZPA, DY 30/IV 2/1/161, 9.

145. SAPMO-BArch, ZPA, DY 30/IV 2/1/163, 387.

146. Author's interview with Horst Brie, Pankow Nieder-Schönhausen, 1 June 1992. Brie was a diplomat at the GDR Embassy in Beijing for most of the time between 1958 and 1964, with intervening periods based at the GDR For-eign Ministry in Berlin at the First Non-European Department, responsible for China.

147. J. König, "Bermerkungen über die Vorbereitung der Schritte der Sowje-tregierung betreffend Änderung des Status von Westberlin," 4 December 1958, MfAA, Staatssekretär, A17723.

148. Author's interview with Horst Brie, Pankow Nieder-Schönhausen, 1 June 1992. This is abundantly clear in comparing the quality of the reports written by diplomats at the GDR Embassy in Beijing versus at the GDR embassy in Moscow, with the former being far more substantive and insightful and so-phisticated than the latter.

149. MfAA, A9493, Sektion China, "Bericht über die Entwicklung der Bezie-hungen zwischen der DDR und der VR China im Jahre 1954," 1.

150. Ray, "Peking und Pankow—Anziehung der Gegensätze," 623.

151. SAPMO-BArch, ZPA, IV 2/20/115, FBS 339/13412, "Vorläge für das Sekretariat," by the SED CC's Department of Foreign Policy and International Relations, 29 January 1960, 2.

152. MfAA, 6520, Sektion China, "Aktenvermerk über eine Besprechung zwischen dem 1. Sekretär der Botschaft der VR China, Herrn Li und Herrn Jaeschke und Frau Spenke vom MfAA am 11.6.1957 in der Zeit von 15.00–16.00 Uhr." And, see the notes at the bottom of "Auszug aus AV über Besprech-ung Shü/Grüttner/ Jaeschke/Lockhuff am 5. September 1957." I, unfortunately, never located an East German response to the Chinese questions about the refu-gee exodus. It may be that Soviet criticism of the East Germans for not taking the refugee exodus seriously enough was correct, and the East Germans were too embarrassed about their insufficient and unsuccessful policies to reduce the refugee exodus to discuss these policies with the Chinese.

153. SAPMO-BArch, ZPA, NL 90/477, letter from Zhou Enlai to Grotewohl, 11 August 1953.

154. MfAA A6661, Sektion China, "Bericht über die Beziehungen zwischen

der DDR und der VR China im Jahre 1956," 1–8. Horst Brie also emphasized the importance of economic ties with China and GDR imports of foodstuffs and minerals from China. Author's interview, 1 June 1992.

155. Ray, "Peking und Pankow—Anziehung der Gegensätze," 625.

156. See Ulbricht's speeches to the twenty-ninth plenum, SAPMO-BArch, ZPA, DY 30/IV 2/1/167, 3 and the thirtieth plenum, ibid., DY 30/IV 2/1/170, 110–112. See also Stern, "Relations Between the DDR and the Chinese People's Republic, 1949–1965," in Griffith, ed., *Communism in Europe*, 101.

157. Ray, "Die ideologische Achse Peking-Pankow," 823; and Esslin, "East Germany: Peking-Pankow Axis?" 87.

158. Stern, "Relations Between the DDR and the Chinese People's Republic, 1949–1965," 103–104; 103 n. 22; and author's interview with Schirdewan, 11 March 1992.

159. In an interview with the author, Horst Brie observed that Mao's ideological and policy innovations in China invited emulation in the GDR. Interview, 1 June 1992. See also Ray, "Die ideologische Achse Peking-Pankow," 819–20, 821.

160. Troyanovsky, *Cherez Gody i Rasstoianiia*, 232.

161. On the events in Poland and Hungary and the Soviet response to them, see Bekes, "The 1956 Hungarian Revolution and World Politics;" Kramer, intro., trans. and annot., "Hungary and Poland, 1956. Khrushchev's CPSU CC Presidium Meeting on East European Crises, 24 October 1956," 1, 50–56; idem, "New Evidence on Soviet Decision-Making and the 1956 Poland and Hungarian Crises"; idem., trans. and annot., "The 'Malin Notes' on the Crises in Hungary and Poland, 1956," 358–410; and idem., "New Light Shed on 1956 Soviet Decision to Invade Hungary," 35–40.

162. Jian, "Beijing and the Polish and Hungarian Crises of 1956," in Jian, *Mao's China and the Cold War*, 145–62.

163. SAPMO-BArch, ZPA, DY 30/J IV 2/2/511 and DY 30/J IV 2/2A/511. The Politburo resolution is also published in Hoffmann et. al., *Die DDR vor dem Mauerbau*, "Politbürobeschluss über 'Massnahmen zur Unterdrückung konterrevolutionärer Aktionen', 8.11.56," 263–67.

164. See Schirdewan's Politburo report to the twenty-ninth plenum, 12 November 1956, SAPMO-BArch, ZPA, DY 30/IV 2/1/165, 38; and Honecker's report to the thirtieth plenum, 30 January 1957, SAPMO-BArch, ZPA, DY 30/IV 2/1/170, 49.

165. See Honecker's Politburo report to the thirty-fifth plenum on 3 February 1958, SAPMO-BArch, ZPA, DY 30/IV 2/1/191, 69–73; and Schirdewan, *Aufstand gegen Ulbricht*, 108–112.

166. Schirdewan, *Aufstand gegen Ulbricht*, 109. Stasi chief Wollweber later wrote that it was clear to him from this time on that it would ultimately be Schirdewan who was ousted from the SED leadership. Otto, ed., "Ernst Wollweber: Aus Erinnerungen," 370.

167. Matern was a Politburo member and Chairman of the Central Party Control Commission.

168. "Kurze Information über die PB Sitzung am 11. Januar 1958," (BStU), 10993. See also "Ernst Wollweber: Aus Erinnerungen. Ein Porträt Walter Ulbrichts," 374; and Schirdewan, *Aufstand gegen Ulbricht*, 122–23.

169. See Schirdewan's Politburo report to the plenum on 12 November, SAPMO-BArch, ZPA, DY 30/IV 2/1/165, 4–58.

170. See Florin's speech in ibid., 64–65.

171. 13 November 1956, SAPMO-BArch, ZPA, DY 30/IV 2/1/166, 204; 209.

172. Leuschner was the chairman of the State Planning Commission, candidate Politburo member and deputy minister president of the GDR.

173. Wandel was the Central Committee Secretary for Culture and Education.

174. Otto, ed,. "Ernst Wollweber: Aus Erinnerungen," 371.

175. *Khrushchev Remembers: The Glasnost Tapes*, 165; and *Khrushchev Remembers*, 456.

176. November 12, 1956, SAPMO-BArch, ZPA, DY 30/IV 2/1/165, 84–85. See also Rakosi's comments to Voroshilov, TsKhSD, F. 89, Per. 45, Dok. 2, 1, report from Voroshilov "V Prezidium TsK KPSS," 26 June 1956.

177. 12 November 1956, SAPMO-BArch, ZPA, DY 30/IV 2/1/165, 87–88.

178. 13 November 1956, SAPMO-BArch, ZPA, DY 30/IV 2/1/166, 167–68; 175.

179. Ibid., 128–29.

180. Ibid., 249.

181. Jan Foitzik, "Die parteiinterne Behandlung der Geheimrede Chruschtschows auf dem XX. Parteitag der KPdSU durch die SED, die PVAP und die KPTsch," in Kircheisen, ed., *Tauwetter ohne Frühling*, 80.

182. Barth et al., eds., *Wer war Wer in der DDR*, 273, 337.

183. "Bericht der Zentralen Parteikontrollkommission der SED über die Entstehung und Ziele der 'Gruppe Harich', 26.3.1957," in Hoffmann et al., *Die DDR vor dem Mauerbau*, 268–274. See also Barth et al., eds., *Wer war Wer in der DDR*, 273, 338. Harich was amnestied and set free at the end of 1964. Janke was set free in 1960.

184. In view of the GDR's desire to get control over its air space, including the Western air corridors between West Berlin and the FRG, it is interesting to note that in their January 1957 meetings, the Soviets and East Germans "agreed that the existing Four Power agreements on the use of the air corridors by airplanes of the USA, England and France between Berlin and West Germany have a temporary character and do not affect the principle of the recognition of the GDR's air sovereignty." Thus, as the Soviets wanted, the GDR could not stop the Western Powers from using the air corridors, and, as the East Germans wanted, their "air sovereignty" was recognized. See Grotewohl's "Gedenken für eine gemeinsame Erklärung zu den Verhandlungen zwischen den Regierungsdelegationen der Deutschen Demokratistchen Republik und der UdSSR," SAPMO-BArch, ZPA, Nl 90/472, 14–15.

185. "Einige offene Fragen in den Beziehungen der DDR und der UdSSR," report and cover letter sent from Winzer to Grotewohl, 19 December 1956, SAMPO-BArch, ZPA, NL 90/471.

186. SAPMO-BArch, ZPA, NL 90/472. Verner was the chairman of the Central Committee Department for All-German Issues. Rau was a Politburo member and minister for Foreign and Inner-German Trade.

187. Author's interview with Schirdewan on 2 October 1993; and Schirdewan, *Aufstand gegen Ulbricht*, 124–25.

188. Micunovic, *Moscow Diary*, 21, 36–37, 58, 76–77, 123–24, 159, 180, 187–88, 210, 277; and Lippmann, *Honecker and the New Politics of Europe*, 178.

189. In the author's interview with Schirdewan on 2 October 1993, Schirdewan said that he believed that the uprisings in Poland and Hungary ultimately doomed Khrushchev's support for him.

190. See SAPMO-BArch, ZPA, DY 30/IV 2/1/170–173.

191. Otto, ed., "Ernst Wollweber: Aus Erinnerungen," 371.

192. Przybylski, *Tatort Politbüro*, 273.

193. SAPMO-BArch, ZPA, DY 30/IV 2/1/170, 9; 49–51. Interestingly, Honecker added that the party functionaries receiving the pistols needed to become more responsible, since there had already been a few cases of the misuse of these weapons.

194. Ibid., 77; 96–98.

195. Ibid., 11, 103.

196. SAPMO-BArch, ZPA, DY 30/IV 2/1/171, 103.

197. First Deputy Chairman of the Council of Ministers. Kaganovich, of course, had been Khrushchev's main mentor in his early career.

198. "Posledniaia 'Antipartiinaia' Gruppa," third session, evening, 24 June, *Istoricheskii Arkhiv* 4 (1993): 28–29.

199. For Khrushchev's 4 August 1961 speech to the Warsaw Pact meeting in Moscow, see the German translation in Bonwetsch and Filitov, "Kak prinimalos' reshenie o vozvedenii Berlinskoi steny," 72. See also *Khrushchev Remembers: The Last Testament*, 358 for a similar explanation.

200. *Khrushchev Remembers*, 456.

201. "Anlage 2 zum [Politbüro] Protokoll Nr. 24 vom 6.6.1961. Niederschrift über die wichtigsten Gedanken, die Genosse Mikojan in einem Gespräch mit dem Genossen Leuschner in kleinstem Kreis . . . ausserte," SAPMO-BArch, ZPA, J IV 2/2/766, 1–3. On the subject of Soviet economic support for the GDR, Stalin also had moments where he wanted to give the GDR everything he possibly could, such as in his April 1952 meeting with the East German leaders. In the face of Mikoian's doubts about giving up precious Soviet resources, Stalin agreed to everything the East Germans requested and added: "we will give as much as possible [and] we would give you twice as much if only we could." "Record of Conversation of Leaders of the Socialist Unity Party of Germany W. Pieck, W. Ulbricht, and O. Grotewohl with J. V. Stalin," 1 April 1952, Document No. 1 in Ostermann, ed., *Uprising in East Germany, 1953*, 30, 32.

202. SAPMO-BArch, ZPA, DY 30/IV 2/1/171, 19, 31.

203. See Ulbricht's speech at the thirty-second SED plenum of 10–12 July 1957, SAPMO-BArch, ZPA, DY 30/IV 2/1/177, 86–106.

204. SAPMO-BArch, ZPA, NL 90/472.

205. See "Aktenvermerk," Moscow, 18 June 1957, written up by Rossmeisl, SAPMO-BArch, ZPA, NL 90/474. For later analyses of Adenauer's CDU victory in the elections, see "Zapis' besedy s chlemon Politburo TsK SEPG G. Maternom," 17 September 1957, secret, from the diary of S. T. Astavin, temporary chargé d'affaires at USSR embassy in the GDR, 24 September 1957, TsKhSD,

R. 8853, F. 5, Op. 49, D. 17; Grotewohl's speech of 17 October at the 33rd plenum, SAPMO-BArch, ZPA, IV 2/1/256, 219; and Micunovic, *Moscow Diary*, 274. The joint statement at the end of the Soviets' visit to East Berlin criticized West Germany's militaristic policy, and maintained that it was the main obstacle to German reunification. SAPMO-BArch, ZPA, J IV 2/201/475.

206. See Ulbricht's comments and "Zwischenrede" at the thirty-third plenum, SAPMO-BArch, ZPA, DY 30/IV 2/1/184 and 186.

207. SAPMO-BArch, ZPA, DY 30/IV 2/1/186, 556. Schirdewan and others had opposed Ulbricht's use of force against the protestors at Humboldt University, and this was Ulbricht's defense. Schirdewan, *Aufstand gegen Ulbricht*, 116.

208. The information on this meeting in this paragraph is from "Ernst Wollweber: Aus Erinnerungen," 373–74. In addition to Pushkin's support, Schirdewan also believed he had the support of the officials in MID's Third European Department dealing with Germany. Author's interview with Schirdewan, 2 October 1993.

209. "Aus dem Bericht des Politbüros an das ZK (35. Tagung) am 3. Februar 1958, erstattet von Erich Honecker," in Przybylski, *Tatort Politbüro*, 261.

210. Przybylski, *Tatort Politbüro*, 263; 94–95.

211. Ibid., 81.

212. As cited previously, this statement, "Stellungnahme," has been published in *Beiträge zur Geschichte der Arbeiterbewegung* (Berlin) 32, no. 4 (1990): 499–512.

213. See Honecker's 3 February 1958 speech to the thirty-fifth plenum, Przybylski, *Tatort Politbüro*, 275.

214. Schirdewan, "Stellungname," 504; and the author's interviews with Schirdewan on 22 April and 21 September 1992. Leuschner and Matern both asserted at the 11 January Politbüro meeting that they had heard Schirdewan criticize Ulbricht for asking for too much economic aid from the Soviets. "Kurze Information über die PB Sitzung am 11. Januar 1958," BStU, 10993.

215. Schirdewan, "Stellungnahme," 510–11.

216. "Kurze Information über die PB Sitzung am 11. Januar 1958," BStU, 10993.

217. See Andropov's report, "V Tsentral'ny Komitet KPSS," 30 January 1958, TsKhSD, R. 8873, F. 5, Op. 49, D. 76. The author shared a German translation (done by Dr. Beate Ihme-Tuchel) of this document with Karl Schirdewan, who then gave a copy to Peter Grieder. Schirdewan published the translation in *Ein Jahrhundert*, 321.

218. Grotewohl's handwritten notes from the 29 January 1958 meeting with Khrushchev in the Kremlin, SAPMO-BArch, ZPA NL 90/699, cited in Grieder, *The East German Leadership, 1946–1973*, 130.

219. He did this partly because he assumed Schirdewan would remain a Central Committee secretary, since Khrushchev did not want Schirdewan ousted entirely. This, however, was not to be. Interview with Schirdewan on 21 September 1992.

220. SAPMO-BArch, ZPA, J IV 2/2A-610, "*Protokoll Nr. 5/58* der ausserordentlichen Sitzung des Politbüros des Zentralkomitees am Freitag, dem 31. Januar 1958 im Zentralhaus der Einheit, Grosser Sitzungssaal."

221. SAPMO-BArch, ZPA, NL 182/895. For Honecker's speech, see Przybylski, *Tatort Politbüro*, 261–79. Ulbricht and Honecker were so heartened by the progress of the thirty-fifth plenum that they raised the punishments against Schirdewan and Wollweber in a Politburo meeting on 5 February. Now in addition to removing Schirdewan from the Politburo and the Secretariat, he was to be removed from the CC also; and Wollweber was not just to be expelled from the CC, but also to receive a strong reprimand; ibid., 100.

222. "Ernst Wollweber: Aus Erinnerungen," 376.

223. Hager was CC Secretary for Science, National Education and Culture.

224. SAPMO-BArch, ZPA, DY 30/IV 2/1/166, 65.

225. Grieder concludes that "Ulbricht's success in averting a 'second Hungary' in East Germany was the decisive factor persuading Khrushchev to back him." *The East German Leadership, 1946–1973*, 130. The Chinese also were impressed that the GDR did not erupt in 1956 as Poland and Hungary did. MfAA A6661, Sektion China, "Bericht über die Beziehungen zwischen der DDR und der VR China im Jahre 1956," 2.

226. See ibid., 373, 376–77 and Schirdewan's "Stellungnahme," 510–11.

227. On this kind of internal-external linkage, see Kramer, "The Early Post-Stalin Succession Struggle and Upheavals in East-Central Europe: Internal-External Linkages in Soviet Policy Making," Parts 1–3.

CHAPTER THREE
1958–1960

1. See the "political letter" written by V. Kochemasov, temporary chargé d'affaires at the Soviet embassy in the GDR, "O khode vypolneniia postavlennoi V s'ezdom SEPG glavnoi ekonomicheskoi zadachi GDR (politicheskoe pis'mo)," secret AVPRF, Ref. po GDR, Op. 4, Por. 3, Pap. 27. Just before the Congress, Ulbricht was in Moscow consulting with the Soviets on the plans for the Congress. "Zapis' besedy s. V. Ul'brikhtom," 23 June 1958, from the diary of M. G. Pervukhin on 27 June 1958, TsKhSD, R. 8873, F. 5, Op. 49, D. 76.

2. On the combination of domestic and foreign pressures on Khrushchev, see Richter, *Khrushchev's Double Bind*.

3. "Protocol on Zones of Occupation in Germany and Administration of the 'Greater Berlin' Area, Approved by the European Advisory Commission, 12 September 1944," in United States Department of State, *Documents on Germany, 1944–1985*, 1–3; "Allied Statement on Zones of Occupation in Germany and the Occupation of 'Greater Berlin,' 5 June 1945," in ibid., 38; "Allied Agreement on the Quadripartite Administration of Berlin, 7 July 1945," in ibid., 43–44; and "Agreement Further Amending the Protocol of 12 September 1944 To Include France in the Occupation of Germany and Administration of 'Greater Berlin,' Approved by the European Advisory Commission, 26 July 1945," ibid., 44–48.

4. "Protocol of the Proceedings of the Berlin (Potsdam) Conference, 1 August 1945," in *Documents on Germany*, 56. The Potsdam Conference of the leaders of the United States, Great Britain, and the Soviet Union took place from 17 July–2 August, 1945.

5. "Notes of a Conference among Marshal Zhukov, General Clay, and General Weeks on Surface and Air Access to Berlin, 29 June 1945," ibid., 42–43.

6. On the Berlin blockade and airlift, see Adomeit, *Soviet Risk-Taking and Crisis Behavior*, 67–182; Laufer; "Die UdSSR und die Ursprunge der Berlin-Blockade, 1944–1948," 564–79; and Offner, *Another Such Victory: President Truman and the Cold War, 1945–1953*, 244–73.

7. "Recommendations of the Transport Directorate Concerning Rail Traffic Between the Western Zones of Germany and Berlin, Approved by the Allied Control Council, 10 September 1945," *Documents on Germany*, 65–68; "Recommendations of the Air Directorate Respecting Air Corridors in the Zones of Occupation in Germany, Transmitted to the Control Council, 28 November 1945," ibid., 69–72; and "Order Number 56 of the Soviet Military Administration in Germany Lifting the Berlin Blockade Effective May 12, Issued 9 May 1949," ibid., 258–60.

8. "Statement of Principles Governing the Relationship Between the Allied Kommandatura and Greater Berlin, Signed by the Three Western Commandants, Berlin, 14 May 1949," ibid., 262–64.

9. "Letter from Foreign Minister Bolz of the German Democratic Republic to Deputy Foreign Minister Zorin of the Soviet Union on Control of Access to West Berlin, 20 September 1955," ibid., 460–61.

10. "Statement by the Foreign Ministers of France, the United Kingdom, and the United States Reaffirming Four-Power Responsibility for Germany and Berlin, 28 September 1955"; and "Note from the United States to the Soviet Union Reaffiming Four-Power Responsibility for Germany and Berlin, 3 October 1955," ibid., 461–62.

11. "Note From the United States to the Soviet Union Reasserting Soviet Responsibility for Insuring 'the Normal Functioning of Communications Between the Different Parts of Germany, Including Berlin,' 27 October 1955," ibid., 464.

12. This law proclaimed a three-year prison sentence for unauthorized exit from the country or for the preparation or attempt to leave the country without permission. See Heidemeyer, *Flucht und Zuwanderung aus der SBZ/DDR*, 61.

13. "Zapis' besedy s Ministrom vnutrennykh del GDR Maronom," 27 January 1958, from the diary of N. R. Shelekh, adviser at the Soviet embassy in the GDR, 6 February 1958, TsKhSD, R. 8875, F. 5, Op. 49, D. 82; "Zapis' besedy s zaveduiushchim otdelom vnutrennykh del MVD GDR Bergmanom," 27 February 1958, from the diary of P. G. Bushman, First Secretary of the USSR embassy in the GDR, 11 March 1958, TsKhSD, ibid.; and "Zapis' besedy s zaveduiushchim otdelom vnutrennykh del MVD GDR Bergmanom," 26 April 1958, from the diary of P. G. Bushman, First Secretary of the USSR embassy in the GDR, 28 April 1958, TsKhSD, ibid.

14. "O nekotorykh voprosakh ekonomicheskogo i politicheskogo polozheniia v demokraticheskom Berline (politicheskoe pis'mo)," AVPRF, Referentura po GDR, Op. 4, Por. 3, Pap. 27, p. 1. For other references to the "open border" in Berlin, implying that it could be closed, "Zapis' besedy s Ministrom vnutrennykh del GDR Maronom," 27 January 1958, from the diary of Shelekh, adviser to the Soviet embassy in the GDR, TsKhSD, R. 8875, F. 5, Op. 49, D. 82, 1; "O polozhenii v Zapadnom Berline," 24 February 1958, by Selianinov and

Kazennov of the Soviet embassy in the GDR, TsKhSD, ibid; and Pervukhin's report "O nekotorykh Voprosakh ekonomicheskogo i politicheskogo Polozhen-iia v demokraticheskom Berline," 10 December 1959, AVPRF, Referentura po GDR, Op. 4, Por. 3, Pap. 27.

15. See for example "Zapis' besedy s zaveduiushchim otdelom vnutrennykh del MVD GDR Bergmanom," 18 June 1958 from the diary of the First Secretary of the Soviet embassy in the GDR, P. G. Bushman on 21 June 1958, TsKhSD, R. 8875, F. 5, Op. 49, D. 82; "Zapis' besedy s nachal'nikom otdela vnutrennykh del MVD GDR Bergmanom," 8 August 1958, from the diary of the First Secre-tary of the Soviet embassy in the GDR, P. G. Bergman on 14 August 1958, TsKhSD, R. 8875, F. 5, Op. 49, D. 82; report on the East German intelligentsia fleeing, by Yuri Andropov, "K Tsentral'nyi Komitet KPSS," 28 August 1958, TsKhSD, R. 8875, F. 5, Op. 49, D. 82; "Zapis' besedy s zamestitelem Ministra vnutrennykh del GDR Griunshtainom," 2 September 1958, from the diary of First Secretary of the Soviet embassy in the GDR, P. G. Bushman on 8 Septem-ber 1958, TsKhSD, R. 8875, F. 5, Op. 49, D. 82; and "Zapis' besedy s nachal'-nikom otdela vnutrennykh del MVD GDR Bergmanom," from the diary of Bus-hman, first secretary of the Soviet embassy in the GDR, 13 December 1958, TsKhSD, R. 8875, F. 5, Op. 49, D. 82.

16. Letter from Yu. Andropov, "K Tsentral'nyi Komitet KPSS," 28 August 1958, TsKhSD, R. 8875, F. 5, Op. 49, D. 82, 1–3.

17. See Ambassador Smirnov's comments to Ulbricht on 11 October, "Zapis' besedy s t. V. Ul'brikhtom 5 oktiabria 1958 goda," from the diary of M. G. Pervukhin on 11 October 1958, TsKhSD, R. 8875, F. 5, Op. 49, D. 82, 9.

18. As GDR Deputy Interior Minister H. Grünstein told P. G. Bushman, First Secretary in the Soviet embassy, "Zapis' besedy s zamestitelem Ministra vnutren-nykh del GDR Griunshtainom," 2 September 1958, from the diary of Bushman, 8 September 1958, TsKhSD, R. 8875, F. 5, Op. 49, D. 82.

19. "Zapis' besedy s t.t. V. Ul'brikhtom i O. Grotevolem 2 oktiabria 1958g.", from the diary of M. G. Pervukhin, 12 October 1958, and "Zapis' besedy s t. V. Ul'brikhtom 5 oktiabria 1958 goda," from the diary of M. G. Pervukhin, 11 October 1958, TsKhSD, R. 8875, F. 5, Op. 49, D. 82.

20. Khrushchev, *Khrushchev Remembers*, 454.

21. See Pervukhin's comments on this in his report, "O nekotorykh vopro-sakh ekonomicheksogo i politicheskogo polozheniia v demokraticheskom Ber-line (politicheskikh pis'mo)," 10 December 1959, AVPRF, Fond: Referentura po GDR, Op. 4, Por. 3, Pap. 27, Inv. 022, 18–21.

22. After closing the border in August 1961, Ulbricht wrote to Khrushchev in September 1961 telling him that one of the many positive effects of this was the availability of more food and goods in shops in East Berlin. Letter from Ulbricht to Khrushchev 15 September 1961, SAPMO BArch, ZPA, J IV 2/202/ 130, 6. For an English translation, see Appendix I in Hope M. Harrison, "Ul-bricht and the Concrete 'Rose.'"

23. "Soviet Note to the United States on the Berlin Question (27 November 1985)," in Embree, ed., *The Soviet Union and the German Question*, 33.

24. Murphy, Kondrashev, and Bailey, *Battleground Berlin*. It was not, how-ever, just the Western Powers using Berlin as an espionage base. The East Ger-

mans and Soviets did also. Secretary of State Herter went into great detail at the Geneva Conference of Foreign Ministers in June 1959 about the "highly objectionable" activities of the East German Stasi directed at "subverting the existing constitutional and social order in West Berlin and West Germany." "Statement by Secretary Herter Regarding Berlin, Geneva, 5 June 1959," *Documents on Germany*, 656–58.

25. "Zapis' besedy s zav. mezhdunarodnym otdelom TsK SEPG P. Florinom," 12 May 1958, from the diary of O. P. Selianinov, adviser to the USSR embassy in the GDR, 16 May 1958, TsKhSD, R. 8873, F. 5, Op. 49, D. 76, 1. See also "O polozhenii v Zapadnom Berline," 24 February 1958, report by O. Selianinov, adviser, and A. Kazennov, Second Secretary, TsKhSD, R. 8875, F. 5, Op. 49, D. 82, 22–23.

26. "Zapis' besedy s zav. mezhdunarodnym otdelom TsK SEPG P. Florinom," 12 May 1958, from the diary of O. P. Selianinov, adviser to the USSR embassy in the GDR, 16 May 1958, TsKhSD, R. 8873, F. 5, Op. 49, D. 76, 2.

27. Burr "Avoiding the Slippery Slope," 180. See also idem., "Dwight D. Eisenhower and American Policy During the Berlin Crisis, 1958–1960." For the original use of the term "superdomino," see Dower, "The Superdomino in Postwar Asia: Japan in and out of the Pentagon Papers," 101–42.

28. On the British approach to the Berlin Crisis, see Gearson, *Harold Macmillan and the Berlin Wall Crisis*.

29. See the "Aide-Memoire From the Federal Republic of Germany to the United States Proposing Establishment of a Four-Power Ambassadorial Group To Make Preliminary Recommendations on German Reunification, 8 September 1958" in *Documents on Germany*, 536–37.

30. For the text of the version of the East German note to the Four Powers that was sent to the Soviets, see "German Democratic Republic's Note to the Soviet Union Outlining Proposals for a Peace Treaty (5 September 1958)," in Embree, ed., *The Soviet Union and the German Question*, 3–5. For Soviet involvement in the process, see 13 August 1958 letter to the CPSU CC from N. Patolichev, AVPRF, Referentura po FRG, Op. 3, Por. 14, Pap. 18; "Aktenvermerk über die Unterredung des Stellv. Ministers Winzer mit Geschäftsträger Astawin am 27.8.58," Berlin 28 August 1958, MfAA, Bestand: M. B. König, A16427; Report to the CPSU CC from V. Kuznetsov, 12 September 1958, AVPRF, F. 0742, Op. 3, Por. 33, Pap. 21; and Letter from Otto Winzer to Hermann Axen on 23 August 1958, SAPMO-BArch, ZPA, J IV 2/202/125. See also the "Note From the Soviet Union to the United States Supporting an East German Proposal To Establish a Four-Power Commission and a West German–East German Commission to Prepare a Peace Treaty with Germany, 18 September 1958," which includes a detailed description of the East German note of 4 September, in *Documents on Germany*, 537–39.

31. "Note From the United States to the Soviet Union Insisting on Creation of an All-German Government Through Free Elections Prior to Negotiation of a German Peace Treaty, 30 September 1958," in ibid., 540.

32. The Soviets asked the East Germans more than once and urgently for speedy input into the Soviet drafting of a response to the West. See "*Auszug aus einem Aktenvermerk über ein Gespräch des Kollegen Thun mit den Genossen*

Shiljakow und Bykow in MID am 10.10.58," SAPMO-BArch, ZPA, J IV 2/202/125; and the letter from Deputy Foreign Minister Winzer to Ulbricht on 5 November 1958 in ibid.

33. "Zapis' besedy s t.t. V. Ul'brikhtom i O. Grotevolem 2 oktiabria 1958g.," from the diary of M. G. Pervukhin on 12 October 1958, TsKhSD, R. 8875, F. 5, Op. 49, D. 82.

34. "Zapis' besedy s. t. V. Ul'brikhtom 5 oktiabria 1958 goda," from the diary of M. G. Pervukhin on 11 October 1958, TsKhSD, ibid. At a reception at the East German embassy in Moscow celebrating the anniversary of the founding of the GDR on 7 October, Rossmeisl of the embassy learned from Soviet MID officials that they were finalizing their proposals for "a sharper policy toward West Germany" to be taken by the Soviets and the other socialist countries, including Czechoslovakia and Poland. "Aktenvermerk über einige persönliche Gespräche mit leitenden Mitarbeitern des sowjetischen MID während des Empfangs in unserer Botschaft aus Anlass des Nationalfeiertages, am 7. Oktober 1958," by Rossmeisl. MfAA, Bestand: M. B. König, A16427.

35. "Zapis' besedy s tov. V. Ul'brikhtom 26.9.58g.," from the diary of the USSR Ambassador to the GDR M. G. Pervukhin on 30 September 1958, TsKhSD, R. 8873, F. 5, Op. 49, D. 76, 1; "Zapis' besedy s t.t. V. Ul'brikhtom i O. Grotewolem 2 oktiabria 1958g.," from the diary of M. G. Pervukhin on 12 October 1958, TsKhSD, R. 8875, F. 5, Op. 49, D. 82, 1; and "Zapis' besedy s t. V. Ul'brikhtom 5 oktiabria 1958 goda," from the diary of M. G. Pervukhin on 11 October 1958, TsKhSD, R. 8875, F. 5, Op. 49, D. 82, 1.

36. "Zapis' besedy s t. V. Ul'brikhtom 5 oktiabria 1958 goda," from the diary of M. G. Pervukhin on 11 October 1958, TsKhSD, R. 8875, F. 5, Op. 49, D. 82, 4.

37. Vladislav Zubok, "Khrushchev and the Berlin Crisis," 7. Zubok hypothesizes that since the Americans seemed to be moving toward recognition of two Chinas by restraining Chiang Kai-Shek in his response to the mainland's bombardment of the islands, Khrushchev thought the Americans might be pressured to recognize two Germanys as well. For background on this Taiwan Straits crisis, see Chen Jian, *Mao's China and the Cold War*, 163–204.

38. "Zum Status Berlin," SAPMO-Arch, ZPA, J IV 2/202/125, 2–3.

39. "An die Arbeiterschaft und alle friedliebenden Bürger Westberlins!" Ulbricht's speech of 27 October, published in *Neues Deutschland*, 28 October 1958, cited in Stern, *Walter Ulbricht*, 187. See also Ulbricht's draft, "Zum Status Berlin," SAPMO-BArch, ZPA, J IV 2/202/125; McAdams, *Germany Divided*, 29; and Adomeit, *Soviet Risk-Taking and Crisis Behavior*, 271–72. Deputy Foreign Minister Otto Winzer urged Ulbricht to think very seriously before he made this new statement. Winzer questioned "whether it is expedient that Comrade Ulbricht say this now. When someone from the [Foreign] Ministry says it, that is one thing, when Walter says it, the issue has a completely different weight, since there is something in it about the role of the Four Powers in Berlin. Comrade Walter himself must decide." "Bemerkung von Genossen Otto Winzer," 21 October 1958, SAPMO-BArch, ZPA, J IV 2/202/125. Ulbricht decided to go ahead.

40. Ulbricht, "Macht Berlin zur Hauptstadt des Friedens!" speech at a meet-

ing of Berlin Party activists, 21 May 1957, *Neues Deutschland*, 23 May 1957, cited in Stern, *Walter Ulbricht*, 187.

41. Lemke, "Sowjetische Interessen und ostdeutscher Wille: Divergenzen zwischen den Berlinkonzepten von SED und UdSSR in der Expositionsphase der zweiten Berlinkrise," in Ciesla, Lemke, and Lindenberger, eds., *Sterben für Berlin?*, 204–209.

42. McAdams, *Germany Divided*, 29, 41.

43. Letter from Winzer to Ulbricht with attachments, 5 November 1958, SAPMO-BArch, ZPA, J IV 2/202/125.

44. "N. S. Khrushchov's [*sic*] Speech at the Soviet-Polish Friendship Meeting (10 November 1958)," in Embree, ed., *The Soviet Union and the German Question*, 18.

45. Ibid., 19.

46. For the text of the note, see "Soviet Note to the United States on the Berlin Question (27 November 1958)," in Embree, ed., *The Soviet Union and the German Question*, 23–40.

47. *Khrushchev Remembers: The Last Testament*, 503. See also *Khrushchev Remembers*, 454.

48. "Soviet Note to the United States on the Berlin Question (27 November 1958)," in Embree, ed., *The Soviet Union and the German Question*, 38, 39.

49. For analyses on the connection between Khrushchev's policies during the Berlin Crisis and the development of Soviet nuclear weapons capabilities, see Horelick and Rush, *Strategic Power and Soviet Foreign Policy*; Schelling, *Arms and Influence*; Bundy, *Danger and Survival*; and Zubok and Harrison, "The Nuclear Education of Nikita Khrushchev," 141–68.

50. Mikoian, *Tak Bylo*, 604.

51. See Selvage, intro., trans., and annot., "Minutes from the Discussion Between the Delegation of the PRL [People's Republic of Poland] and the Government of the USSR," 25 October–10 November 1958, excerpt from session on 10 November 1958, in CWIHP, *Bulletin* 11 (Winter 1998): 200–203. Khrushchev referred to advance consultations with the East Germans in his ultimatum also. See the "Soviet Note to the United States on the Berlin Question (27 November 1958)," in Embree, ed., *The Soviet Union and the German Question*, 37–38.

52. "Bemerkungen über die Vorbereitung der Schritte der Sowjetregierung betreffend Änderung des Status von Westberlin," J. König, Moscow, 4 December 1958, MfAA, Staatssekretär, A17723. See the English trans, annot., and commentary by Harrison, "New Evidence on Khrushchev's 1958 Berlin Ultimatum," 35–39.

53. Mikoian, *Tak Bylo*, 604; 598. His opposition to Khrushchev's course on Berlin is confirmed in Malin's notes from the 13–14 October 1964 Presidium meeting on ousting Khrushchev. "Zapisi V. Malina na zasedanii Presidiuma TsK KPSS," *Vestnik Arkhiva Prezidenta Rossiiskoi Federatsii* 2 (1998): 132.

54. Mikoian, *Tak Bylo*, 605.

55. Troyanovsky, *Cherez gody i rasstoianiia*, 212.

56. Harrison, trans. of König, 4 December 1958, "Comments on the Preparation of the Steps of the Soviet Government Concerning a Change in the Status of West Berlin," in CWIHP, *Bulletin* 4: 37.

57. "Zapis' besedy s tovarishchem V. Ul'brikhtom 17.11.58g.," from the diary of M. G. Pervukhin on 24 November 1958, TsKhSD, R. 8873 F. 5, Op. 49, D. 77.

58. At 9 A.M. on 27 November, Pervukhin gave GDR Foreign Minister Bolz the Soviet note to the GDR on the Berlin question and a copy of the Soviet note to the United States, which Pervukhin informed him would be published the following day. "Aktenvermerk Unterredung Botschafter Perwuchin mit Minister Dr. L. Bolz am 27.11.1958 um 9 Uhr," MfAA, Bestand: Staatssekretär, A17723.

59. Harrison, trans. of König, 4 December 1958, "Comments on the Preparation of the Steps of the Soviet Government Concerning a Change in the Status of West Berlin," in CWIHP, *Bulletin* 4: 37. Unfortunately, Khrushchev's typed suggestions have not yet surfaced.

60. Aleksandrov-Agentov, *Ot Kollontai do Gorbacheva*, 71; 103. See also Grineveskij, *Tauwetter: Entspannung, Krisen und neue Eiszeit*, 20–21.

61. "Telegram From the Embassy in the Soviet Union to the Department of State, Moscow, 3 December 1958, 2 P.M.," from Ambassador Thompson, *Foreign Relations of the United States, 1958–1960, Volume VIII, Berlin Crisis 1958–1959*, 149. Valentin Falin, who was then at the Department of Information of the CPSU's Central Committee, has also stated that the free-city idea was Khrushchev's. Falin, *Politische Erinnerungen*, 225, 336.

62. Harrison, trans. of König, 4 December 1959, "Comments on the Preparation of the Steps of the Soviet Government Concerning a Change in the Status of West Berlin," in CWIHP, *Bulletin* 4: 37.

63. Danzig was a "free city" established by the Western Powers after World War I. German access to the city on the Baltic coast was provided by a corridor across Poland. Hitler took Danzig by force when he seized Poland (with the Soviets) in September 1939 at the beginning of World War II. Ulbricht's point was: Danzig did not last long as a free city.

64. See Sergei Khrushchev, *Krizisy i Rakety*, tom 1, 414.

65. See, e.g., the letter from Foreign Minister Winzer to Ambassador König on 8 December 1958, MfAA, Bestand: Staatssekretär, A17723.

66. Sergei Khrushchev, *Krizisy i Rakety*, tom 1, 415.

67. "Soviet Note to the United States on the Berlin Question (27 November 1958)," in Embree, ed., *The Soviet Union and the German Question*, 38; 36.

68. McAdams, *Germany Divided*, 30.

69. Troyanovsky, *Cherez gody i rasstoianiia*, 212–13.

70. See Selvage, trans., "Minutes from the Discussion Between the Delegation of the PRL [People's Republic of Poland] and the Government of the USSR," CWIHP, *Bulletin* 11: 202.

71. Harrison, trans. of König, 4 December 1958, "Comments on the Preparation of the Steps of the Soviet Government Concerning a Change in the Status of West Berlin," in CWIHP, *Bulletin* 4: 37–38.

72. Selvage, trans., "Minutes from the Discussion between the Delegation of the PRL [People's Republic of Poland] and the Government of the USSR," CWIHP *Bulletin* 11: 202.

73. Zubok, trans., "First Conversation of N. S. Khrushchev with Mao Zedong, 31 July 1958, Hall of Huaizhentan," CWIHP, *Bulletin* 12/13: 256.

74. "N. S. Khrushchov's [sic] Speech at the Soviet-Polish Friendship Meeting (10 November 1958)," in Embree, ed., *The Soviet Union and the German Question*, 14–15.

75. Harrison, trans. of König, 4 December 1958, "Comments on the Preparation of the Steps of the Soviet Government Concerning a Change in the Status of West Berlin," in CWIHP, *Bulletin* 4: 37.

76. Aleksandrov-Agentov, *Ot Kolontai do Gorbacheva*, 100–101. On Khrushchev's development of a domestic strategy of coercive surprises vis-à-vis his colleagues and opponents, which he then applied to his foreign policy, see Goldgeier, *Leadership Style and Soviet Foreign Policy: Stalin, Khrushchev, Brezhnev, Gorbachev*, 21–25.

77. Zubok and Pleshakov, *Inside the Kremlin's Cold War*, 196.

78. AVPRF, F. Referentura po FRG, Op. 4, Por. 9, Pap. 22, 18 August 1959 letter from Khrushchev to Adenauer, 7–8.

79. As quoted in Sergei Khrushchev, *Krizisy i Rakety*, 414.

80. See the discussion of Soviet goals in the annual report of the Soviet embassy in the GDR: "Otchet Posol'stva SSSR v GDR o vnutrennei i vneshnei politike GDR i deiatel'nosti Posol'stva za 1958 god," 28 February 1959, AVPRF, Referentura po GDR, Op. 4, Por. 26, Pap. 30, 86b.

81. See Selvage, trans., "Minutes from the Discussion Between the Delegation of the PRL [People's Republic of Poland] and the Government of the USSR," in CWIHP, *Bulletin* 11: 202.

82. For scholars who have stressed Khrushchev's fears of West German nuclear weapons as a motivation for his launching of the Berlin Crisis, see Trachtenberg, "The Berlin Crisis," 169–234; idem., *A Constructed Peace*; Schick, *The Berlin Crisis*; and Ulam, *Expansion and Coexistence*, 610, 619–620, 639.

83. For his reference to West German access to nuclear weapons in the ultimatum, see "Soviet Note to the United States on the Berlin Question (27 November 1958)," in Embree, ed., *The Soviet Union and the German Question*, 27.

84. Trachtenberg, *A Constructed Peace*, 146–240. Trachtenberg's thesis that Khrushchev's primary motivation in the Berlin Crisis was to prevent West German access to nuclear weapons is based solely on his own deductions from Western policy, not on any Soviet evidence, as he notes in the preface to his book, ix–x.

85. One particularly important example of Soviet protests against West German acquisition of nuclear weapons is Mikoian's trip to Bonn, where he met with Adenauer twice on 26 April 1958, both times emphasizing at length Soviet opposition to West German nuclear weapons and the potential dangers and risks of West German acquisition of them. "Zapis' besedy A. I. Mikoiana s Adenauerom v ego Rezidentsii 26 aprelia 1958 goda," secret, and "Zapis' besedy A. I. Mikoiana s federal'nym kantslerom FRG K. Adenauerom na prieme v Bonne 26 aprelia 1958 goda," secret, AVPRF, Fond: Referentura po FRG, Op. 3, Por. 3, Pap. 17.

86. "Zapis' besedy s tov. V. Ul'brikhtom 26.9.58," from the diary of USSR Ambassador to the GDR M. G. Pervukhin on 30 September 1958, TsKhSD, R. 8873, F. 5, Op. 49, D. 76; "Zapis' besedy s t.t. V. Ul'brikhtom i O. Grotevolem

2 oktiabria 1958g," from the diary of M. G. Pervukhin on 12 October 1958, TsKhSD, R. 8875, F. 5, Op. 49, D. 82; and "Zapis' besedy s t. V. Ul'brikhtom 5 oktiabria 1958 goda," from the diary of M. G. Pervukhin on 11 October 1958, TsKhSD, R. 8875, F. 5, Op. 49, D. 82.

87. "Zapis' besedy s t. V. Ul'brikhtom 5 oktiabria 1958 goda," from the diary of M. G. Pervukhin on 11 October 1958, TsKhSD, R. 8875, F. 5, Op. 49, D. 82, 7–8. It is interesting that Smirnov mentions delaying the nuclear arming of the Bundeswehr by two years here, because during Mikoian's April 1958 meetings with Adenauer in Bonn, Adenauer and others kept responding to Mikoian's protests regarding West German nuclear weapons by saying that "the decision of the Bundestag is of preliminary character and is not a law which absolutely must come into being. . . . for the realization of the Bundestag's decision we need at least two years and if there is an agreement on disarmament in that period, then the atomic arming of the FRG will not be carried out." See the Foreign Ministry report written up on 13 May 1958, "Ob itogakh poezdki A. I. Mikoiana v FRG (25–28 aprelia 1958 goda)," AVPRF, Referentura po FRG, Op. 3, Por. 16, Pap. 18, 4.

88. "Zapis' besedy s tov. V. Ul'brikhtom 20 oktiabria, 1958 goda," from the diary of M. G. Pervukhin on 23 October 1958, secret, TsKhSD, R. 8875, F. 5, Op. 49, D. 82, 1. In light of concerns about a nuclear attack, the East German army planned their first maneuvers under simulated conditions of a nuclear strike for 20–25 October 1958. "Zapis' besedy s tov. V. Ul'brikhtom 15 oktiabria 1958 goda," from the diary of M. G. Pervukhin on 18 October 1958, TsKhSD, R. 8875, F. 5, Op. 49, D. 82, 1–2.

89. Harrison, trans., "Summary of the Talks with the GDR Party–Governmental Delegation on 18 June," in CWIHP, *Bulletin* 11: 214.

90. Harrison, trans., "Short Summary of the Talks with the GDR Party–Governmental Delegation on 9 June 1959," in CWIHP, *Bulletin* 11: 210–11.

91. On the role of domestic politics, see Richter, *Khrushchev's Double Bind*; Jack Snyder, *Myths of Empire: Domestic Politics and International Ambition*; Breslauer, *Khrushchev and Brezhnev as Leaders*; Linden, *Khrushchev and the Soviet Leadership, 1957–1964*; and Slusser, *The Berlin Crisis of 1961*.

92. Ulam, *Expansion and Coexistence*, 621, 655; and Zagoria, *The Sino-Soviet Conflict, 1956–61*.

93. For works that recognize significant East German influence on Soviet policy, see Lemke, *Die Berlinkrise 1958 bis 1963*; Tusa, *The Last Division*; Manfred-Hartmut Prowe, "City Between Crises: The International Relations of West Berlin from the End of the Berlin Blockade in 1949 to the Khrushchev Ultimatum of 1958"; and Steele, *Socialism with a German Face: The State That Came in from the Cold*. For a very good summary of the argument for East German influence on Soviet policy, see Adomeit, *Soviet Risk-Taking and Crisis Behavior*, 271–74.

94. Mikoian, *Tak Bylo*, 605; and Sergei Khrushchev, *Nikita Khrushchev and the Creation of a Superpower*, 307. Khrushchev erroneously notes the date of Mikoian's meeting with Eisenhower as 19 January instead of 17 January 1959.

95. "Memorandum of Conversation," Washington, 17 January 1959, 9 A.M., *FRUS, 1958–1960, Vol. VIII, Berlin Crisis, 1958–1959*, 276–81.

96. Sergei Khrushchev, *Krizisy i Rakety*, 416.

97. For the text of the Soviet draft treaty, see "Soviet Draft Peace Treaty for Germany and the Accompanying Note to the United States (10 January 1959)," in Embree, ed., *The Soviet Union and the German Question*, 81–100. Rossmeisl of the GDR Embassy in Moscow learned from MID officials on 30 December 1958 about the Soviet draft peace treaty for Germany. See the telegram from Rossmeisl in Moscow to Foreign Minister Winzer in Berlin. 30 December 1958, MfAA, Bestand: Staatssekretär, A17723.

98. SAPMO-BArch, ZPA, J IV 2/202/127.

99. See SAPMO-BArch, ZPA files J IV 2/202/127, J IV 2/202/128, J IV 2/202/129, and J IV 2/202/130.

100. "News Conference Remarks by Secretary of State Dulles Reasserting the 'Explicit Obligation' of the Soviet Union to Assure 'Normal Access to and Egress from Berlin,' 26 November 1958," extracts, in *Documents on Germany*, 547–48.

101. The British scholar Ann Tusa writes very critically of this tendency, which she argues allowed the Soviets and East Germans to "sharpen the salami knife" to whittle away at Western rights concerning Berlin. Tusa, *The Last Division*, 60. See also 48, 51, 53, 59–60, 71–72, 174–75, 218–19, 253, 304, 316. In addition, on the use of salami tactics regarding Berlin, see George and Smoke, "The Berlin Deadline Crisis, 1958–1959," and "The Berlin *Aide-Memoire* Crisis, 1961," chaps. in *Deterrence in American Foreign Policy*.

102. "News Conference Remarks by Secretary of State Dulles Reasserting the 'Explicit Obligation' of the Soviet Union to Assure 'Normal Access to and Egress from Berlin,' 26 November 1958," extracts, in *Documents on Germany*, 548; 549.

103. Burr, "Dwight D. Eisenhower and American Policy During the Berlin Crisis, 1958–1960." On Adenauer's veto over U.S. policy, see also McAdams, *Germany Divided*, 18–20. On West German policy during the crisis, see also Trachtenberg, *A Constructed Peace*, 274–82.

104. On the French willingness, on the other hand, to consider concessions out of the public eye, see Trachtenberg, *A Constructed Peace*, 267–4.

105. Gearson, *Harold Macmillan and the Berlin Wall Crisis*, 36–43, 56–78; and Trachtenberg, *A Constructed Peace*, 263–67.

106. On the conflicts between Washington and Bonn over how to respond to Khrushchev's pressure on Berlin, see the report from the Soviet embassy in the FRG on Bonn's reactions to Khrushchev's summit with Eisenhower at Camp David in September 1959, "Otsenka v Bonne itogov poezdki N. S. Khrushcheva v SShA," sent to Zorin on 10 October 1959, AVPRF, Fond: Referentura po FRG, Op. 4, Por. 9, Pap. 22. On the differences between Washington and London, between British Foreign Minister Lloyd and U.S. Secretary of State Herter, at the Geneva Conference of Foreign Ministers, see Winzer's "Telegramm von 20.6.1959 aus Genf—Eingang 20.6.59, 21.15 Uhr," SAPMO-BArch, NL 90/464.

107. "Telegram From the Embassy in the Soviet Union to the Department of State," Moscow, 19 February 1959, 5 p.m., *FRUS, 1958–1960. Vol. VIII, Berlin Crisis, 1958–1959*, 381.

108. "Telegram From the Embassy in the Soviet Union to the Department of State," Moscow, 9 April 1959, 7 P.M., ibid., 596.

109. Ibid.

110. "Note from the United States to the Soviet Union Proposing a Foreign Ministers Meeting on Germany, 16 February 1959," *Documents on Germany*, 608.

111. "Note From the Soviet Union to the United States Agreeing to a Foreign Ministers Meeting Preparatory to a Summit Meeting on Germany, 2 March 1959," ibid., 609–11.

112. Cited in McAdams, *Germany Divided*, 45.

113. "Memorandum of Conversation," Bonn, 8 February 1959, 10:30 A.M., *FRUS 1958–1960, Vol. VIII, Berlin Crisis, 1958–1959*, 347.

114. Ibid.

115. "Memorandum of Conference With President Eisenhower [and Congressional Leaders]," Washington, 6 March 1959, 10:30 A.M., ibid., 432.

116. "Telegram From the Mission at Berlin to the Embassy in Germany," Berlin, 9 March 1959, 9 P.M., ibid., 444. See also "Telegram From the Mission at Berlin to the Department of State," 10 April 1959, 5 P.M., ibid., 600.

117. "Telegram From the Embassy in Germany to the Department of State," Bonn, 2 March 1959, 1 P.M., ibid., 406. See also Burr, "Avoiding the Slippery Slope," 180.

118. Burr, "Avoiding the Slippery Slope."

119. On LIVE OAK, see Pedlow, "Allied Crisis Management for Berlin: The LIVE OAK Organization, 1959–1963," 87–116.

120. Khrushchev also referred to West Berlin in the following way: "[T]he American foot in Europe had a sore blister on it. That was West Berlin. Any time we wanted to step on the Americans' foot and make them feel the pain, all we had to do was obstruct Western communications with the city across the territory of the German Democratic Republic." *Khrushchev Remembers: The Last Testament*, 501.

121. "Memorandum of Conversation," Washington, 1 April 1959, *FRUS, 1958–1960, Vol. VIII, Berlin Crisis, 1958–1959*, 568–69.

122. "Telegram From the Delegation to the Western Foreign Ministers Meeting to the Deptartment of State," Paris, 29 April 1959, 11 P.M., ibid., 668.

123. For a good summary of the course of the Geneva CFM, see Schick, *The Berlin Crisis*, 77–96; and Tusa, *The Last Division*, 163–78. For internal GDR views on the Geneva CFM, see SAPMO-BArch, ZPA, NL 90/464.

124. However, the West rebuffed the Soviet request for Polish and Czechoslovak participation in the CFM, thus denying the socialists an equal number of representatives with the capitalists.

125. Schick, *The Berlin Crisis*, 91.

126. "Durch Konsultation mit der Sowjetunion zu klärende Fragen," and "Telegramm von Botschafter König aus Moskau vom 13.4.1959," SAPMO-BArch, ZPA, NL 90/464, 27–35.

127. Harrison, trans., "Short Summary of the Talks with the GDR Party–Governmental Delegation on 9 June 1959," in CWIHP, *Bulletin* 11: 208, 209.

128. Ibid., 208.

129. President Eisenhower's comment, "Memorandum of Conference With President Eisenhower [and Congressional Leaders]," Washington, 6 March 1959, 10:30 A.M., *FRUS, 1958–1960, Vol. VIII, Berlin Crisis, 1958–1959*, 431.

130. Thompson, "Telegram From the Embassy in the Soviet Union to the Department of State," Moscow, 19 February 1959, 5 P.M., ibid., 378.

131. "Western Peace Plan for Germany Submitted to the Foreign Ministers Meeting, Geneva, May 14, 1959," *Documents on Germany*, 624–29.

132. "Telegram From the Delegation to the Foreign Ministers Meeting to the Department of State," Geneva, 18 May 1959, midnight, *FRUS, 1958–1960, Vol. VIII, Berlin Crisis, 1958–1959*, 717.

133. "Memorandum of Conversation," Geneva, 18 May 1959, noon, "Lloyd's Report of May 18 Talk with Gromyko and General Discussion of Tactics," ibid., 714.

134. "Memorandum of Conference With President Eisenhower," Washington, 27 May 1959, ibid., 770.

135. Schick, *The Berlin Crisis*, 82–84.

136. "Statement by Secretary of State Herter Regarding Berlin, Geneva, 5 June 1959," *Documents on Germany*, 654; 655; 652.

137. Ibid., 653; 655.

138. Harrison, trans., "Short Summary of the Talks with the GDR Party–Governmental Delegation on 9 June 1959," in CWIHP, *Bulletin* 11: 207; 208.

139. Ibid., 208–209. The Soviet leaders also shared this view about the importance of improving the GDR's economy with their American interlocuters. Thompson cabled Washington in February: "As indicated by Mikoyan in US [in January] and by Kosygin to me yesterday, Soviets apparently believe that by raising standard of living in East Germany they can consolidate hold of Communist regime there in next few years particularly if Berlin problem can somehow be resolved." "Telegram From the Embassy in the Soviet Union to the Department of State," Moscow, 25 February 1959, 6 P.M., *FRUS, 1958–1960, Vol. VIII, Berlin Crisis, 1958–1959*, 391. Thompson also wrote: "Mikoyan indicated Soviet belief that in two or three years they could raise living standards in East Germany to something approaching those of West Germany." "Telegram From the Embassy in the Soviet Union to the Department of State," Moscow, 19 February 1959, 5 P.M., ibid., 379.

140. Harrison, trans., "Short Summary of the Talks with the GDR Party–Governmental Delegation on 9 June 1959," in CWIHP, *Bulletin* 11: 210.

141. Ibid., 211; 212.

142. Ibid., 208.

143. Ibid.

144. Ibid., 209.

145. Ibid., 209–10.

146. Tusa, *The Last Division*, 170–72.

147. Schick, *The Berlin Crisis*, 85–86.

148. "Western Draft Proposal on Berlin Handed to Foreign Minister Gromyko at Geneva, 16 June 1959," *Documents on Germany*, 665–66. For Tusa's critical view of these proposals, see *The Last Division*, 174.

149. Harrison, trans., "Summary of the Talks with the GDR Party–Governmental Delegation on 18 June 1959," in CWIHP *Bulletin*, 11: 213.

150. Ibid., 215.

151. Ibid., 215–216.

152. Ibid., 216; 213.

153. The following information on the Soviet deployment of MRBM's to the GDR comes from Uhl and Ivkin, "'Operation Atom': The Soviet Union's Stationing of Nuclear Missiles in the German Democratic Republic, 1959," 299–307. See also Bayer, "Geheimoperation Fürstenberg," 42–46.

154. "Delegation Record of Meeting," Geneva 26 May 1959, 9:30 A.M., *FRUS, 1958–1960, Vol. VIII, Berlin Crisis, 1958–1959,* 764.

155. Bayer, "Geheimoperation Fürstenberg," 44.

156. Harrison, trans., "Summary of the Talks with the GDR Party–Governmental Delegation on 18 June 1959," in CWIHP, *Bulletin* 11: 214. See also their final communiqué, *Pravda,* 20 June 1959, 1.

157. Harrison, trans., "Summary of the Talks with the GDR Party–Governmental Delegation on 18 June 1959," CWIHP, *Bulletin* 11: 215.

158. Ibid., 214.

159. Winzer, "Telegramm von 20.6.1959 aus Genf—Eingang 20.6.1959, 21.15 Uhr," SAPMO- BArch ZPA, NL 90/464.

160. "Telegramm Nr. 4 aus Genf vom 16. Juli," from Winzer to Ulbricht, Grotewohl and König, SAPMO-BArch, ZPA, DY 30/3380.

161. W. Averell Harriman, "My Alarming Interview with Khrushchev," *Life* (13 July 1959): 33. See also the conversation between Harriman and Khrushchev recounted in "Telegram From the Embassy in the Soviet Union to the Department of State," Moscow, 25 June 1959, 2 P.M., in *FRUS, 1958–1960, Vol. VIII, Berlin Crisis, 1958–1959,* 941–43.

162. "Telegram From the Embassy in the Soviet Union to the Department of State," Moscow, 25 June 1959, 2 P.M., in *FRUS, 1958–1960, Vol. VIII, Berlin Crisis, 1958–1959,* 941.

163. Schick, *The Berlin Crisis,* 88. See also Dwight D. Eisenhower, *The White House Years: Waging Peace, 1956–1960,* 405–408, 411–12.

164. Troyanovsky, *Cherez Gody i Rasstoianiia,* 217–18.

165. "Telegram From the Delegation to the Foreign Ministers Meeting to the Department of State," Geneva, 22 July 1959, 9 P.M.," *FRUS, 1958–1960, Vol. VIII, Berlin Crisis, 1958–1959,* 1029.

166. See the 5 August 1959 final communiqué in ibid., 1116.

167. Bayer, "Geheimoperation Fürstenberg," 46.

168. On Khrushchev's trip to the United States, see *Khrushchev Remembers,* 368–416; Tompson, *Khrushchev: A Political Life,* 207–11; and Nikita S. Khrushchev, *Khrushchev in America.*

169. Troyanovsky, *Cherez Gody i Rasstoianiia,* 218.

170. Tusa, *The Last Division,* 184. Ulbricht was in Moscow just prior to Khrushchev's departure for the United States and presumably urged Khrushchev to push hard on Berlin.

171. Schick, *The Berlin Crisis,* 99.

172. Troyanovsky, *Cherez Gody i Rasstoianiia,* 219.

173. Secret report, unsigned, sent from the Soviets to Ulbricht and Grotewohl, 13 October 1959, copies in German and Russian, SAPMO-BArch, ZPA J IV 2/202/330, 2, 6.

174. Secret report, unsigned, 14 August 1959, SAPMO-BArch, ZPA, J IV 2/202/330.

175. See Kramer, "The USSR Foreign Ministry's Appraisal of Sino-Soviet Relations on the Eve of the Split, September 1959," CWIHP, *Bulletin* 6–7 (Winter 1995/1996): 170–85; and the following three articles in CWIHP, *Bulletin* 8–9 (Winter 1996/1997): Taubman, "Khrushchev vs. Mao: A Preliminary Sketch of the Role of Personality in the Sino-Soviet Split," 243–48; "A New 'Cult of Personality': Suslov's Secret Report on Mao, Khrushchev, and Sino-Soviet Tensions, December 1959," 244, 248; and Jian, "A Crucial Step Toward the Sino-Soviet Schism: The Withdrawal of Soviet Experts from China, July 1960," 246, 249–50. See also Troyanovsky, *Cherez Gody i Rasstoianiia*, 232; and Jian, *Mao's China and the Cold War*, 64–84.

176. See Zubok, intro., annot., trans., "The Mao-Khrushchev Conversations, 13 July–3 August 1958 and 2 October 1959," 244–72.

177. "Memorandum of Conversation of N. S. Khrushchev with Mao Zedong, Beijing, 2 October 1959," ibid., 264.

178. Ibid.

179. SAPMO-BArch, ZPA, IV 2/20/114.

180. MfAA, A6661, Sektion China, "*Kurzbericht* über die Entwicklung der Beziehung zwischen der DDR und der Volksrepublik China im Jahre 1959," 7.

181. Thus, Chinese Premier Chou En-lai in June 1961 pointed out to GDR Ambassador Hegen in Beijing: "When Khrushchev raised the West Berlin issue [with his 1958 ultimatum] the USA didn't shoot, it withdrew and declared itself ready for negotiations," clearly indicating that one can easily pressure this "paper tiger." "Vermerk über den Antrittsbesuch Botschafter Hegens beim Ministerpräsident der VR China, Genossen Tschou En-lai am 9.6.1961," written by Hegen, 12 June 1961, Staatssekretär Winzer, MfAA A17879, 4.

182. Among previous authors who have argued the importance of GDR and Chinese common interests and even an "axis" in this period, see Ray, "Die Ideologische Achse Peking-Pankow," 819–25; Esslin, "East Germany: Peking-Pankow Axis?" 85–88; Zagoria, *The Sino-Soviet Conflict*, 396; Schick, *The Berlin Crisis*, 25–27; and Meissner with Feege, eds., *Die DDR und China 1949 bis 1990*, 13–14, 66–67, 102–105, 181–83.

183. Unsigned document, 27 March 1961, "Re: The Sino-Soviet Dispute and the Berlin Situation," in United States Department of State *The Declassified Documents Quarterly Catalogue and Microfiche*. Beth Lester provided the author with a copy of this document. Horst Brie, a cultural attaché at the GDR embassy in Beijing during the Berlin Crisis, told the author that there was a group of officials around Chairman Mao who felt that the East Germans should not "put up" with the West Berlin situation and should start a crisis to lead to their seizure of West Berlin. They kept accusing the East Germans of giving in to Soviet pressure on the Berlin issue and not looking out for their own interests. Interview with the author, Pankow, Niederschönhausen, 1 June 1992.

184. Tusa, *The Last Division*, 200.

185. For a detailed, if now somewhat dated, account of the U-2 affair, see Beschloss, *Mayday: The U-2 Affair. The Untold Story of the US-USSR Spy Scandal.* For Khrushchev's account, see *Khrushchev Remembers: The Last Testament*, 443–49.

186. Troyanovsky, *Cherez Gody i Rasstoianiia*, 223; 224. See also the live footage of Khrushchev venting his fury about the U-2 overflights on CNN, *Cold War*, Episode 9, "Mousetrap."

187. Troyanovsky, *Cherez Gody i Rasstoianiia*, 226; 225; 226.

188. De Gaulle pointed out, among other things, that Soviet spy satellites flew over France every day and that he did not make a fuss about it. Khrushchev was not affected by this line of argumentation. Ibid., 227.

189. For Khrushchev's account of the events in Paris, see *Khrushchev Remembers: The Last Testament*, 449–61.

190. Schick, *The Berlin Crisis*, 121–22.

CHAPTER FOUR
1960–1961

1. Thanks to Richie Freedman and Carlo Rotella for discussing with me the musical expression of this idea.

2. Burlatsky, *Khrushchev and the First Russian Spring*, 157.

3. Unfortunately, there are thus far no accessible archival records of phone calls between Khrushchev and Ulbricht.

4. Troyanovsky, *Cherez Gody i Rasstoianiia*, 209.

5. Kwizinskij, *Vor dem Sturm*, 169; 170.

6. Adomeit, *Soviet Risk-Taking and Crisis Behavior*, 272. Adomeit opines that while there may have been a good-cop-bad-cop division of labor between Khrushchev and Ulbricht, there were also "genuine differences of interest" between them during the crisis.

7. A. James McAdams wrote about these differences even before the opening of the archives; *Germany Divided*, 24–30, 44–57.

8. On countries other than the superpowers affecting the intensity of the cold war, see Smith, "New Bottles for New Wine," 568, 582–88.

9. On regional powers' greater willingness to risk war than the superpowers', see Ben-Zvi, *The United States and Israel*, 53.

10. Adomeit, *Soviet Risk-Taking and Crisis Behavior*, 272; and McAdams, *Germany Divided*, 24–30, 44–57.

11. On the broad interests of great powers and the narrow interests of small powers, see Fox, *The Power of Small States: Diplomacy in World War II*, 181.

12. See Kenneth N. Waltz's observation that "[w]hen great powers are in a stalemate, lesser states acquire an increased freedom of movement," *Theory of International Politics*, 184. See also Snyder and Diesing, *Conflict among Nations*, 442, 445; and Rothstein, *Alliances and Small Powers*, 249.

13. On the limits of a great power's capacity to project influence over weaker powers, see the discussion on the difference between "fate control" and day-to-day "behavior control" in Hughes, "On Bargaining," chap. 7 in Triska, ed.,

Dominant Powers and Subordinate States, 175. See also Handel, "Does the Dog Wag the Tail or Vice Versa? Patron-Client Relations," 24–35; and Bar-Siman-Tov, "Alliance Strategy: U.S.–Small Allies Relationships," 202–16.

14. On the discrepancy between power capabilities and real influence and the nontransferability of power resources from one framework to another, see Ben-Zvi, *The United States and Israel*, 8; Baldwin, "Interdependence and Power; A Conceptual Analysis," 502; and idem, "Power Analysis and World Politics: New Trends versus Old Tendencies," 163–67.

15. Reported by GDR Deputy Foreign Minister Peter Florin at the GDR conference of its ambassadors in 1956, SAPMO-BArch, ZPA, J IV 2/201–429, Bd. 2, 187.

16. For example, their conversation on 30 November 1960. "Zapis' besedy tovarishcha N. S. Khrushcheva s tovarishchem V. Ul'brikhtom, 30 noiabria 1960 goda," AVPRF, F. 0742, Op. 6, Por. 4, Pap. 43, 14. English translation in Appendix A of Harrison, "Ulbricht and the 'Concrete Rose.'"

17. Kwizinskij, *Vor dem Sturm*, 170.

18. On Soviet concern about members of the Cuban leadership turning toward China in the spring of 1962 at the time Khrushchev made the decision to deploy the missiles, see Fursenko and Naftali, *"One Hell of a Gamble"*, 167–70.

19. Weathersby, "Soviet Aims in Korea and the Origins of the Korean War, 1945–1950," 23.

20. "Decree of the German Democratic Republic Imposing a Five-Day Restriction on Entry of West German Citizens Into East Berlin, 29 August 1960," in *Documents on Germany, 1944–1985*, 715–16. Many of the measures listed in this paragraph are described in Adomeit, *Soviet Risk-Taking and Crisis Behavior*, 200–201. See also Tusa, *The Last Division*, 217–18.

21. "Note from the United States to the Soviet Union Protesting the Extension of East German Travel Restrictions on Entry Into East Berlin, 12 September 1960"; and "Note From the Soviet Union to the United States Asserting the Right of the German Democratic Republic to Regulate Travel Into East Berlin, 26 September 1960," in *Documents on Germany*, 719, 720–21.

22. In August the East Germans had finally succeeded in getting the Soviets to stop giving visas to West Berliners on West German passports to visit the Soviet Union, and only to give them visas on the basis of their West Berlin identity card. See the Soviet note to East Germany of 17 August 1960 (in response to the East German note of 30 January 1960), SAPMO-BArch, ZPA, J IV 2/202/128, Bd. 4.

23. Tusa, *The Last Division*, 218.

24. Sydney Gruson, "Bonn to Put Off Parley in Berlin" and "German Reds Renew Threats," 21 September 1960, *New York Times*, 8.

25. Sydney Gruson, "Red German Curb Perplexes West. New Berlin Squeeze Feared as Entry of Envoys Posted to Bonn is Restricted," *New York Times*, 22 September 1960, 8.

26. Sydney Gruson, "German Reds Fail in Bid to Bar Envoy of U.S. From East Berlin: Police Order Dowling Back to Western Sector, Then Yield As He Stands Firm," *New York Times*, 23 September 1960, 2.

27. Tusa, *The Last Division*, 218.

28. "German Reds Retreat on Issue of Envoys' Entry in East Berlin," *New York Times*, 24 September 1960, 4.

29. On Soviet–East German disagreements about this, see also Karl-Heinz Schmidt, *Dialog über Deutschland*, 31.

30. Letter from König to Ulbricht, 23 September 1960, SAPMO-BArch, ZPA, J IV 2/202/128, 1–2.

31. Letter from König to Ulbricht, 27 September 1960, ibid., 1–2.

32. DY 30/J IV 2/202/333. See also Gromyko's 31 January 1960 letter to the CPSU CC proposing more direct Soviet ties with West Berlin so as to separate it from the FRG, AVPRF, F. 0742, Op. 5, Pap. 39, D. 38; Pervukhin's nineteen-page report on this to Gromyko on 11 July 1960, "K voprosu ob usilenii vliianiia Sovetskogo Soiuza i GDR v zapadnom Berline," ibid; and Gromyko's 7 August 1960 proposal to the CPSU CC on expanding ties with West Berlin, ibid. Pervukhin had begun the compaign to expand Soviet ties with West Berlin so as to pull it away from the FRG with a top-secret report to Gromyko, "K voprosu o Zapadnom Berline," 21 November 1959, AVPRF, F.: Referentura po GDR, Op. 4, Pap. 34, Por. 60, inv. 620, t. 2.

33. "Zapis' besedy s zav. mezhdunarodnym otdelom TsK SEPG P. Florinom," 12 May 1958, from the diary of O.P. Selianinov, 16 May 1958, TsKhSD, R. 8873, F. 5, Op. 49, D. 76, 2–5; "Zapis' besedy s t. Val'terom Ul'brikhtom, 11.6.58," from the diary of M. G. Pervukhin, 12 June 1958, TsKhSD, R. 8875, F. 5, Op. 49, D. 81, 1–3; Note from Deputy Foreign Minister Zorin to Pervukhin on 6 April 1959, AVPRF, Referentura po GDR, Op. 5, Por. 26, Pap. 30; "Zapis' besedy s zamestitelem ministra inostrannykh del GDR I. Kënigom," from the diary of O. P. Selianinov, 4 December 1959, TsKhSD, R. 8911, F. 5, Op. 49, D. 189; and letter from Ambassador Pervukhin to the Minister of Foreign Affairs of the USSR, Comrade A. A. Gromyko, 19 May 1961, AVPRF, Referentura po GDR, Op. 6, Por. 34, Pap. 46, 4–5.

34. "Otchet o rabote Posol'stva SSSR v GDR za 1960 god," 15.12.60, Pervukhin, TsKhSD, R. 8948, F. 5, Op. 49, D. 287, 85.

35. Ibid., 87; 86; 77. See also Pervukhin's 19 October 1960 report to Gromyko, "K voprosu o razryve zapadnoi Germaniei soglasheniia o vnutrigermanskoi torgovle s GDR," AVPRF, F. 5, Pap. 40, D. 40, 3.

36. SAPMO-BArch, ZPA, J IV 2/202/128, Bd. 4; 1; 4–5.

37. 24 October 1960 letter from Khrushchev to Ulbricht, SAPMO-BArch, ZPA, DY 30/J IV 2/202/66.

38. Heidemeyer, *Flucht und Zuwanderung aus der SBZ/DDR*, 339.

39. "Zapis' besedy s sekretarem Berlinskogo okruzhkoma SEPG G. Daneliisom," 17 October 1960, from the diary of A. P. Kazennov, Second Secretary of the USSR embassy in the GDR, 24 October 1960, TsKhSD, R. 8948, F. 5, Op. 49, D. 288, 5.

40. "Zapis' besedy s nachal'nikom otdela vnutrennykh del MVD GDR tov. Bergmanom, 17 October, 1960," from Sul'din's diary, 25 October 1960, TsKhSD, R. 8946, F. 5, Op. 49, D. 281, 2.

41. See the work of Armin Wagner, based on the military archive of the former GDR. Wagner, *Walter Ulbricht und die geheime Sicherheitspolitik der SED*; and Uhl and Wagner, "Another Brick in the Wall."

42. Letter from Ulbricht and the SED delegation in Moscow to the First Secretary of the CC of the CPSU, Comrade Khrushchev, Moscow, 22 November 1960, SAPMO-BArch, ZPA, DY 30/ J IV 2/202/336, Bd. 2, 1; 11.

43. Ibid., 4.

44. Of course, the West had the same sense of Soviet and East German actions.

45. Letter from Ulbricht to Khrushchev, 22 November 1960, Moscow, SAPMO-BArch, ZPA, DY 30/ J IV 2/202/336, Bd. 2, 5.

46. Ibid., 2–3. For a detailed description of the various ways the FRG was actively seeking to undermine the GDR economy and recruit the best workers, see the report of the Soviet embassy in the FRG, "Agressivnyi kurs politiki FRG v otnoshenii GDR," 29 October 1960, written by Second Secretary I. Kuz'michev and Third Secretary L. Usichenko, AVPRF, F. 0757, Op. 5, Por. 10, Pap. 25, 6–12.

47. Ulbricht requested that the Soviets send 20,000 more tons of meat in December and then at least 75,000 tons of meat and 47,000 tons of butter in 1961. Letter from Ulbricht and the SED delegation in Moscow to the First Secretary of the CC of the CPSU, Comrade Khrushchev, Moscow, 22 November 1960, SAPMO-BArch, ZPA, DY 30/ J IV 2/202/336, Bd. 2, 8–9.

48. 10 October 1960 letter from Ulbricht to Khrushchev, SAPMO-BArch, ZPA, J IV 2/202–29. In this letter, Ulbricht had described the very difficult GDR economic situation, which he said could be saved only by significant help from the Soviets and other socialists: "[W]e are in such a situation where we currently don't know how under the current conditions we can go on at all . . . ." See also Ulbricht's letter to Khrushchev on the economic situation in the GDR in 1960, 23 July 1960, ibid.

49. "Zapis' besedy tovarishcha N. S. Khrushcheva s tovarishchem V. Ul'brikhtom, 30 noiabria 1960 goda," AVPRF, F. 0742, Op. 6, Por. 4, Pap. 43. For a full English translation, see Appendix A in Harrison, "Ulbricht and the Concrete 'Rose.'" See also Pervukhin's summary of the meeting in his annual "Otchet o rabote Posol'stva SSSR v GDR za 1960 god," TsKhSD, R. 8948, F. 5, Op. 49, D. 287, 88–90; and the East German summary, "Aktenvermerk über die Unterredung des Genossen Walter Ulbricht mit Genossen N. S. Chruscev," SAPMO-BArch, ZPA, J IV 2/202/30.

50. Pervukhin, "Otchet o rabote Posol'stva SSSR v GDR za 1960 god," sent to Andropov on 15 December 1960, TsKhSD, R. 8948, F. 5, Op. 49, D. 287, 88–90.

51. "Zapis' besedy tovarishcha N. S. Khrushcheva s tovarishchem V. Ul'brikhtom, 30 noiabria 1960 goda," AVPRF, F. 0742, Op. 6, Por. 4, Pap. 43, 3–4.

52. Ibid., 9.

53. Ibid., 9–10.

54. "Otchet o rabote Posol'stva SSSR v GDR za 1960 god," 15.12.1960, Pervukhin, TsKhSD, R. 8948, F. 5, Op. 5, D. 287, 88.

55. "Zapis' besedy tovarishcha N. S. Khrushcheva s tovarishchem V. Ul'brikhtom, 30 noiabria 1960 goda," AVPRF, F. 0742, Op. 6, Por. 4, Pap. 43, 11, 19.

56. Ibid., 9; 12–14.

57. Ibid.

58. Ibid., 13.

59. This did occur soon afterward, as Leuschner reported to Ulbricht by letter from Moscow on 5 December 1960 regarding a meeting with his Soviet counterpart, Novikov, on 2 December. The Soviets set up a special group at Gosplan to focus on supplying the GDR. They also agreed to establish a group of Soviet economic advisors in Berlin to keep direct contact between the GDR and Soviet State Planning Commissions. Leuschner told Ulbricht, however, that the Soviets were finding it a challenge to come up with as much economic aid for the GDR in a short time as requested. SAPMO-BArch, ZPA, J IV 2/202–29.

60. "Zapis' besedy tovarishcha N. S. Khrushcheva s tovarishchem V. Ul'brikhtom, 30 noiabria 1960 goda," AVPRF, F. 0742, Op. 6, Por. 4, Pap. 43, 13.

61. Ibid., 12, 13, 19.

62. Ibid., 7–8; 11; 15.

63. Ibid., 9.

64. Ibid., 15–16.

65. Ibid., 10–11.

66. Ibid., 11–12; 15.

67. Ibid., 21–22.

68. On 7 April 1961, Pevukhin sent to the CPSU CC a report written up by V. Sul'din of the Soviet embassy in the GDR, "K voprosu ob ukhode naseleniia GDR v Zapadnuiu Germaniiu (kratkaia spravka)," TsKhSD, R. 8979, F. 5, Op. 49, D. 381, Attachment No. 1, "Ukhod naseleniia iz GDR v ZG v 1950–1960gg." West German figures for the same years show a comparable but slightly less dramatic rise in refugee numbers, going from 137,437 in 1959 to 186,640 in 1960 and then 133,574 from January–July 1961 and 208,332 for all of 1961. Heidemeyer, *Flucht und Zuwanderung aus der SBZ/DDR*, 339, 47. On *Grenzgänger*, see "Zapis' besedy s Predsedatelem Gosplana GDR B. Leuschnerom," 15 May 1961, from Pervukhin's diary, 19 May. TsKhSD, R. 8980, F. 5, Op. 49, D. 383, 4.

69. For records of these meetings in 1960, see TsKhSD, R. 8946, F. 5, Op. 49, D. 281, and in 1961, see TsKhSD, R. 8979, F. 5, Op. 49, D. 381. The discussants were usually V. A. Sul'din, First Secretary of the Soviet embassy, and Bergman, head of the Department of Internal Affairs at the GDR Ministry of Internal Affairs.

70. 1 December 1960 letter from Tzschorn to Stoph, "Analyse der Abwanderung vom 1.1. bis 30.9.1960," SAPMO-BArch, ZPA, NL 90/448, 1–30.

71. "Zu den Ursachen des Wegzugs aus der DDR," 5./7.60, SAPMO-BArch, ZPA, NL 90/448, 2–4. Interestingly, in the post-unification Wall trials, the prosecution lawyers asserted that the GDR had in fact violated its own constitution and laws by shooting people attempting to flee the country. McAdams, *Judging the Past in Unified Germany*, 29–34.

72. See also the eleventh plenum's Politburo report on refugees among the intelligentsia, "Zur Lage in der Intelligenz," SAPMO-BArch, IV 2/1/259, materials for eleventh plenum of 1–3 December 1960.

73. "Otchet o rabote Posol'stva SSSR v GDR za 1960 god," 15.12.60, Pervukhin, TsKhSD, R. 8948, F. 5, Op. 49, D. 287, 63–65.

74. Politburo "Reinschriftenprotokoll Nr. 1 vom 4.1. 1961," SAPMO-BArch, ZPA, J IV 2/2/743, 7 of "Schlussbemerkungen des Genossen Ulbricht."

75. Politburo "Reinschriftenprotokoll Nr. 2 vom 10.1.1961," "Anlage Nr. 1 zum Protokoll Nr. 2 vom 10.1.1961," 2. There were indications of another group also dealing with stopping the refugee flow. This group included chief of the State Planning Commission Bruno Leuschner, Minister of Transportation Erwin Kramer, and Construction Minister Ernst Scholz. See the memoirs of the GDR minister of culture, Hans Bentzien, cited in Uhl and Wagner. "Another Brick in the Wall." Thus far, researchers have not found documentary records of the work of these groups. On the absence of some key documents in the archives regarding plans to halt the refugee flow and close the Berlin border and the possibility of the destruction of these documents, see Schmidt, *Dialogue über Deutschland*, 71–72.

76. "Stichwort-Protokoll der Beratung des Politbüros am 4. Januar 1961 über *Die gegenwärtige Lage und die Hauptaufgaben 1961*," Politburo "Reinschriftenprotokoll Nr. 1 vom 4.1.1961," SAPMO-BArch, ZPA, J IV 2/2/743, 3, 9–12, 14; 42; and "Continuation of the Politburo Discussion," 8–9.

77. Ibid., 13; 15.

78. "Stichwort-Protokoll der Beratung des Politbüros am 4. Januar 1961 über *Die gegenwärtige Lage und die Hauptaufgaben 1961*," ibid., 2; 8–9.

79. For preparatory materials for this letter, see the top-secret materials sent by First Deputy Foreign Minister Otto Winzer to Ulbricht on 10 January 1961, "Möglichkeiten des taktischen Vorgehens in der Frage Friedensvertrag und Westberlin," and *Massnahmeplan* zu organisatorischen Fragen im Zusammenhang mit der Vorbereitung des Abschlusses eines Friedensvertrages mit der DDR und der Einberufung einer Friedenskonferenz," SAPMO-BArch, ZPA, J IV 2/202/129. For the letter, see ibid., and the English translation in Appendix B of Harrison, "Ulbricht and the Concrete 'Rose.'"

80. SAPMO-BArch, ZPA, J IV 2/202/129, 1–2.

81. Ibid., 3–6.

82. Ibid., 6.

83. Ibid., 9–15; 7.

84. While Ulbricht blamed the Soviets for the poor state of the East German economy, on his January 1959 visit to Washington, Anastas Mikoian implicitly blamed the post-war U.S. reparations policy, which did not give the Soviets anywhere near as much as they sought from the Western zones of Germany. Mikoian told Secretary Dulles that the Soviets "had had to take reparations from East Germany because they did not get them from West Germany. Thus the economic situation had been bad in 1953," contributing to the June 1953 uprising. "Memorandum of Conversation" between Mikoian, Dulles, and others, 16 January 1959, 10:30 A.M.–12:45 P.M., Washington, FRUS, *1958–1960, Vol. VIII, Berlin Crisis, 1958–1959*, 273.

85. Wismut was the East German–Soviet joint industrial enterprise mining uranium, from which mainly the Soviets reaped the benefits. For details, see Norman Naimark, *The Russians in Germany*, 238–50.

86. SAPMO-BArch, ZPA, J IV 2/202/129, 13–14. Mikoian openly recognized in a meeting with East Germans on 6 June 1961 the reality of the negative

effects on the GDR economy of Soviet reparations policy. "Anlage 2 zum Proto-koll Nr. 24 vom 6.6.1961," SAPMO-BArch, ZPA, J IV 2/2/766.

87. On the Sino-Soviet rift, see Westad, ed., *Brothers in Arms*; Zagoria, *The Sino-Soviet Conflict, 1956–61*; Jian, *Mao's China and the Cold War*; Zubok, "'Look What Chaos in the Beautiful Socialist Camp!': Deng Xiaoping and the Sino-Soviet Split, 1956–1963," 152–62; Jian, "Deng Xiaoping, Mao's 'Continuous Revolution,' and the Path Toward the Sino-Soviet Split: A Rejoinder," in ibid., 162–64; and the related documents in ibid., 165–82. Just as the East Germans tried to use the Sino-Soviet rift to their own advantage, so the Chinese tried to use the GDR for its own purposes to put more pressure on Khrushchev and to make gains in the Sino-Soviet dispute. Ray, "Die ideologische Achse Peking-Pankow," 822; and Krüger, "Die Volksrepublik China in der Aussenpoli-tischen Strategie der DDR (1949–1989)," 49.

88. See the one-page report that was sent by Yuri Andropov to the Central Committee on 18 January 1961, and written by I. Kabin, chairman of the German section in the CPSU CC Department on Relations with Communist and Workers' Parties of Socialist Countries, TsKhSD, R. 8978, F. 5, Op. 49, D. 377. The SED Politburo met on 17 January to discuss Matern's trip to Peking. Unfortunately, the Reinschriftenprotokoll of the meeting supplies no information on the discussion. SAPMO-BArch, ZPA, J IV 2/2/745.

89. "*Aktenvermerk* über den Abschiedsbesuch beim Stellv. Ministerpräsiden-ten und Minister für Auswärtige Angelegenheiten der VR China, Genossen Tschen I, am Montag, den 30. Januar 1961, 10:00 bis 11:00 Uhr," written up by GDR Ambassador to Peking Paul Wandel, 30 January 1961, SAPMO-BArch, ZPA, IV 2/20/123.

90. Thus, for example, the East Germans publicly supported the Chinese shelling of the offshore islands of Quemoy and Matsu in 1958 more than Mos-cow did, as well as the Chinese side in its border dispute with India in 1959. Richter, *Khrushchev's Double Bind*, 198. See also "Bericht über die Ent-wicklung der Beziehungen zwischen der DDR und der VR China im Jahre 1954," Sektion China, MfAA A9493, 1–2. In the GDR-PRC 1955 Treaty on Friendship and Cooperation, the two countries promised "mutual support in the fight for peace and socialism, [and] the Chinese people granted every imaginable help [to the GDR] in its struggle against German imperialism and militarism as well as for the conclusion of a peace treaty with Germany and the resolution of the West Berlin issue." See the reference to this in the GDR plans for the Ger-man-Chinese friendship week in the GDR from May 29–June 4, 1960, "Vorläge für das Sekretariat," by the SED CC's Department of Foreign Policy and Inter-national Relations, 29 January 1960, SAPMO-BArch, ZPA, IV 2/20/115, 2.

91. "Vermerk über den Antrittsbesuch Botschafter Hegens beim Ministerprä-sident der VR China, Genossen Tschou En-lai am 9.6.1961," written by Hegen, 12 June 1961, Staatssekretär Winzer, MfAA A17879, 2–3, 6.

92. Author's interview with Horst Brie, Pankow, 1 June 1992. Yuli Kvitsin-ski, who was a Soviet diplomat in the embassy in the GDR at the time, made similar comments in an interview with the author in Moscow on 26 October 1992. Brie also emphasized the importance of old German-Chinese communist ties and East German–PRC economic ties and said that many East German com-

munists who became disillusioned with the results of socialism in the Soviet Union were more inspired by the PRC model of socialism.

93. "Zapis' besedy tovarischcha N. S. Khrushcheva s tovarishchem V. Ul'-brikhtom, 30 noiabria 1960 goda," AVPRF, F. 0742, Op. 6, Por. 4, Pap. 43, 14. For Mao's angry, suspicious rebuff of Khrushchev's proposal for any joint undertakings in China, see Zubok, trans., "First Conversation of N. S. Khrushchev with Mao Zedong[,] Hall of Huaizhentan [Beijing], 31 July 1958," CWIHP, *Bulletin* 12/13 (Fall/Winter 2001): 250–57.

94. "Zapis' besedy tovarischcha N. S. Khrushcheva s tovarishchem V. Ul'-brikhtom, 30 noiabria 1960 goda," AVPRF, F. 0742, Op. 6, Por. 4, Pap. 43, 16; 14.

95. German unofficial translation of Khrushchev's 30 January 1961 letter to Ulbricht, SAPMO-BArch, ZPA, J IV 2/202/129, 1–2. This is translated in Appendix C of Harrison, "Ulbricht and the Concrete 'Rose.'" See also the Soviet draft letter, 25 January 1961, in AVPRF, F. 0742, Op. 6, Por. 34, Pap. 46. Six sentences from the 25 January Soviet draft of Khrushchev's 30 January letter are missing in the letter received by the Germans. The most important missing sentence is the following at the end of the second paragraph after "acceptable resolutions" in the quote above: "Open unilateral action from our side could be used in such a situation by certain circles in the USA to exacerbate the situation so as to push Kennedy into a position not differing essentially from Eisenhower's position on the German question, which would be advantageous to the FRG and reactionary circles in the West." Although it is possible that the person doing the unofficial German translation of the letter left out this and the other five sentences by mistake, the more likely and interesting possibility is that the Soviets decided not to include this and the other sentences and thus be more subtle in urging Ulbricht not to act unilaterally.

96. Fursenko and Naftali, *"One Hell of a Gamble,"* 80–82.

97. Salisbury memo, 15 December 1960, John F. Kennedy Library (hereafter JFKL), cited in Beschloss, *The Crisis Years,* 42; 152–57. On the Bolshakov back channel, see Fursenko and Naftali, *"One Hell of a Gamble,"* 109–28.

98. Tusa, *The Last Division,* 231.

99. "Telegram From the Embassy in the Soviet Union to the Department of State," Moscow, 16 March 1961, 7 P.M., *FRUS, 1961–1963, Vol. XIV, Berlin Crisis, 1961–1962,* 32.

100. Fursenko and Naftali, *"One Hell of a Gamble,"* 88.

101. Tusa, *The Last Division,* 236; and Fursenko and Naftali, *"One Hell of a Gamble,"* 116.

102. Fursenko and Naftali, *"One Hell of a Gamble,"* 102.

103. The accessible record of the March Warsaw Pact meeting is much smaller than that of the August 1961 meeting. Files on the March meeting can be found at SAPMO-BArch, ZPA, J IV 2/202–251, Bd. 3 and DY 30/J IV 2/202/244 and at MfAA A14659. Until recently, the only direct evidence we had of the March meeting were references to it by Khrushchev at the August meeting, Ulbricht's speech to the March meeting, invitation letters from Khrushchev announcing the meeting, the three top-secret resolutions made at the meeting, and the published communiqué from the meeting. In addition, Jan Sejna, the

Czechoslovak then–Deputy Defense Minister who was at the meeting and later defected to the West, has given an oft-cited account of the meeting, claiming that Ulbricht called for closing the border and was refused, a claim thus far not corroborated by the documents. On Sejna's account, see Catudal, *Kennedy and the Berlin Wall Crisis*, 48–51; Gelb, *The Berlin Wall*, 71–72; Zolling and Bahnsen, *Kalter Winter im August*, 102–104; and "Kennedy: 'Vielleicht eine Mauer,'" *Der Spiegel* (16 August 1976): 16. We can now add to the available record Khrushchev's 28 March speech to the Warsaw Pact meeting. Oldrich Tuma has located this document (in Czech, and helpfully provided this author with a translation) at the Czech Central State Archive, the Archive of the Central Committee of the Communist Party of Czechoslovakia, Vol. 303, Sign. 387, "Speech of Comrade N. S. Khrushchev at the Meeting of the Political Consultative Committee of the Warsaw Pact."

104. See Khrushchev's 24 January 1961 letter of invitation to the leaders of the WTO member-states, SAPMO-BArch, ZPA, J IV 2/202–245; 1–2.

105. The other top secret resolution at the end of the meeting warned Albania, which had been siding with China against the Soviet Union, that the WTO "would have to think seriously about removing WTO naval ships from Albanian waters if the Albanians did not abandon their hostile attitude to the Soviet Union in alliance with the PRC." See the three top-secret "Reshenie Politicheskogo Konsul'tativnogo Komiteta gosudarstv-uchastnikov Varshavksogo dogovora," in Russian, SAPMO-BArch, ZPA, J IV 2/202–251, Bd. 3. This final Russian text of the resolutions was sent to Ulbricht from Winzer on 5 April 1961.

106. Zubok and Harrison, "The Nuclear Education of Nikita Khrushchev," 141–68. See also Khrushchev's discussion with Mao about the nature of modern warfare, Zubok, trans., "First Conversation of N. S. Khrushchev with Mao Zedong[,] Hall of Huaizhentan [Beijing], 31 July 1958," 250–56, 260.

107. "KOMMIUNIKE o zasedanii PCC gosudarstv-uchastnikov Varshavskogo dogovora o druzhbe, sotrudnichestve i vzaimnoi pomoshchi," SAPMO-BArch, ZPA, J IV 2/202–251, Bd. 3, 1–5.

108. 3 August 1961, Khrushchev's opening speech, SAPMO-BArch, ZPA, J IV 2/202/130, and the English translation, Appendix G in Harrison, "Ulbricht and the Concrete 'Rose.'"

109. Khrushchev's speech published by Bonwetsch and Filitov, "Iz stenogrammy soveshaniia pervykh sekretarei TsK kommunisticheskikh i rabochikh partii stran-uchastnits varshavskogo dogovora po voprosam, sviazannym s podgotovkoi k zakliucheniiu germanskogo mirnogo dogovora," Moscow, 4 August 1961, morning session, 63–64.

110. Uhl and Wagner, "Another Brick in the Wall."

111. "Kennedy: 'Vielleicht eine Mauer,'" *Der Spiegel* (16 August 1976): 16.

112. Lemke, *Die Berlinkrise 1958 bis 1963*, 157–58. See also Catudal, *Kennedy and the Berlin Wall Crisis*, 48–51.

113. Catudal, *Kennedy and the Berlin Wall Crisis*, 50; 210.

114. Cate, *The Ides of August*, 143–44, 517.

115. SAPMO-BArch, ZPA, DY 30/J IV 2/202/251, 7. References to Ulbricht's

speech are from the copy sent by Deputy Foreign Minister Winzer to Mr. Herpold in Ulbricht's office on 7 April, 6.

116. For the "vague memories" of Ulbricht's interpreter at the meeting, Werner Eberlein, see "Wortlaut eines Gesprächs von Wilfriede Otto mit Werner Eberlein am 5. September 1996 über die Beratung der Ersten Sekretäre des ZK der kommunistischen und Arbeiterparteien der Staaten des Warschauer Vertrages vom 3. bis 5. August 1961 in Moskau," *Beiträge zur Geschichte der Arbeiterbewegung* 2 (1997): 88–89.

117. Sul'din, "K voprosu ob ukhode naseleniia GDR v Zapadnuiu Germaniiu (kratkaia spravka)," report sent from Pervukhin to the CPSU on 7 April 1961, TsKhSD, R. 8979, F. 5, Op. 49, D. 381, 3.

118. Report from Ambassador Pervukhin to Foreign Minister Gromyko, 19 May 1961, AVPRF, Fond: Referentura po GDR, Op. 6, Por. 34, Pap. 46, 2–3. For an English translation, see Appendix C in Harrison, "Ulbricht and the Concrete 'Rose.'"

119. Author's interview with Yuli Kvitsinsky, Moscow, 26 October 1992.

120. Report from Ambassador Pervukhin to Foreign Minister Gromyko, 19 May 1961, AVPRF, Fond: Referentura po GDR, Op. 6, Por. 34, Pap. 46, 2.

121. Ibid., 4.

122. Report from Ambassador Pervukhin to Foreign Minister Gromyko, 19 May 1961, AVPRF, Fond: Referentura po GDR, Op. 6, Por. 34, Pap. 46, 2–4.

123. Ibid., 4–5.

124. Ibid., 6–7.

125. Thompson to Rusk, 24 and 30 May 1961, JFKL, and The *New York Times*, 25 May 1961, cited in Beschloss, *The Crisis Years*, 180.

126. Luniak and Reiman, intro. and annot., trans. Reiman, "1961, 1 iiunia, Praga. Zapis' besedy N. S. Khrushcheva s rukovodiashchimi deiateliami TsK KPCH i pravitel'stva Chekhoslovakii v Smolenitse pod Bratislavoi i tost Khrushcheva vo vremia obeda," 86–87.

127. Ibid., 88.

128. TsKhSD, F. 5, Op. 30, D. 335, 92–108; and English trans. by Benjamin Aldrich-Moody, "'A Typical Pragmatist': The Soviet Embassy Profiles John F. Kennedy, 1960," CWIHP, *Bulletin* 4 (Fall 1994): 66. Georgi Kornienko, on the other hand, argues that before Vienna, Ambassador Menshikov misled Khrushchev into believing that JFK would back down on Berlin. G. M. Kornienko, "'Upushchennaia Vozmozhnost': Vstrecha N. S. Khrushcheva i Dj. Kennedi v Vene v 1961g," 102.

129. Luniak and Reiman, "'Lenin tozhe riskoval.' Nakanune vstrechi Khrushcheva i Kennedi v Vene v iiune 1961g," 89.

130. "Memorandum of Conversation: The President's Meetings with Prime Minister Macmillan," Washington, 6 April 1961, 3:45 P.M., *FRUS, 1961–1963, Vol. XIV, Berlin Crisis, 1961–1962*, 44.

131. "Position Paper Prepared in the Department of State: Berlin and Germany," Washington, 25 May 1961, ibid., 74.

132. "Telegram From the Mission at Berlin to the Department of State," Berlin, 25 May 1961, 7 P.M., Lightner, ibid., 76.

133. "Memorandum of Conversation: President's Visit," Paris, 31 May 1961, 12:30 P.M., ibid., 81; 83.

134. Beschloss, *The Crisis Years*, 217–23. The Soviets sent the East Germans all the records of the Khrushchev-Kennedy conversations at Vienna. For these, see SAPMO-BArch, ZPA, J IV 2/202/331.

135. "Memorandum of Conversation, Meeting Between the President and Chairman Khrushchev in Vienna," Vienna, 4 June 1961, 10:15 A.M., *FRUS, 1961–1963, Vol. XIV: The Berlin Crisis, 1961–1962*, 91; 94; 89.

136. Ibid., 90–93.

137. Ibid., 90; 94.

138. "Memorandum of Conversation, Vienna Meeting Between The President and Chairman Khrushchev," Vienna, 4 June 1961, 3:15 P.M., ibid., 97.

139. Ibid., 98; 97–98.

140. Reeves, *President Kennedy: Profile of Power*, 171.

141. "Anlage 2 zum [Politbüro] Protokoll Nr. 24 vom 6.6.1961. Niederschrift über die wichtigsten Gedanken, die Genosse Mikojan in einem Gespräch mit dem Genossen Leuschner in kleinstem Kreis . . . äusserte," SAPMO-BArch, ZPA, J IV 2/2/766, 1–3.

142. Tusa, *The Last Division*, 252.

143. 30 June 1961, Iu. Ruibakov, "O politicheskikh nastroeniiakh srednikh sloev naseleniia GDR (spravka)," sent by Pervukhin to CPSU CC, TsKhSD, R. 8979, F. 5, Op. 49, D. 381, 25. See also "K voprosu ob ukhode naseleniia GDR v Zapadnuiu Germaniiu (kratkaia spravka)", 7 April 1961, V. Sul'din, TsKhSD, R. 8979, F. 5, Op. 49, D. 381, 3.

144. Slusser, *The Berlin Crisis of 1961*, 94; Gelb, *The Berlin Wall*, 121–22; Smyser, *From Yalta to Berlin*, 157; and Major, "Torschlusspanik und Mauerbau. 'Republikflucht' als Symptom der zweiten Berlinkrise," in Ciesla, Lemke, Lindenberger, eds., *Sterben für Berlin?*, 221–43.

145. Gelb, *The Berlin Wall*, 99–100.

146. "Zapis' besedy so starshim referentom otdela Sovetskogo Soiuza MID GDR E. Hiuttnerom," 10 June 1961, from the diary of Yu. A. Kvitsinski, attaché at the USSR embassy in the GDR, 14 June 1961, TsKhSD, R. 8980, F. 5, Op. 49, D. 384, 1–2.

147. "Zapis' besedy s glavnym redaktorom gazety *Neues Deuschland* tov. G. Aksenom, 30.7.61g," [the correct date is 30 June, not July], from the diary of first secretary of the USSR Embassy in the GDR, A. Ia. Bogomolov, secret, 8 July 1961, TsKhSD, R. 8981, F. 5, Op. 49, D. 385, p. 2.

148. Gelb, *The Berlin Wall*, 97.

149. Catudal, *Kennedy and the Berlin Wall Crisis*, 125. See also "News Conference Remarks by Chairman Ulbricht Spelling Out the Consequences of Creating a 'Free City' of West Berlin, 15 June 1961," *Documents on Germany*, 737.

150. Uhl and Wagner, "Another Brick in the Wall."

151. Gelb, *The Berlin Wall*, 99–100. See also the account of the press conference in Cate, *The Ides of August*, 58–65.

152. Gelb, *The Berlin Wall*, 100. Adomeit makes a similar argument, *Soviet Risk-Taking and Crisis Behavior*, 273.

153. See the reference to this in Ulbricht's June 1961 letter (no exact date

given, but other evidence indicates it was dated 24 June) to Khrushchev, SAPMO-BArch, ZPA, J IV 2/202/129.

154. After receiving Soviet approval on 30 June for the WTO meeting, Ulbricht wrote the WTO members, as well as China and Albania, on 5 July inviting them to a meeting to discuss "political, diplomatic, economic and organizational measures connected with the conclusion of a peace treaty on 3 August 1961 in Moscow." The other leaders were to give their "opinion on this proposal directly to Khrushchev." SAPMO-BArch, ZPA, J IV 2/202/130. See the copy of his letter to Kadar as well as Kadar's 10 July response and the 15 July Chinese response in ibid.

155. The letter in the German archives, SAPMO-BArch, ZPA, J IV 2/202/129 is dated only "June 1961" (and see the English translation in Harrison, "Ulbricht and the Concrete 'Rose,'" Appendix E), but the Soviet Presidium resolution of 30 June agreeing to Ulbricht's request for a WTO meeting to coordinate preparations for the peace treaty makes it clear that Ulbricht's letter was dated 24 June. "Postanovlenie Prezidiuma TsK KPSS o sozyve soveshchaniia pervykh sekretarei kommunisticheskikh i rabochikh partii stran Varshavskogo dogovora po germanskomu voprosu," 30 June 1961, "O pis'me t. V. Ul'brikhta ot 24 iiuniia 1961 g," TsKhSD, F. 3, Op. 13, D. 488, l. 5, cited in "Okazat' nezamedlitel'nuiu pomoshch,'" documents prepared by Vodop'ianova and Zubok, *Istoricheskii Arkhiv* 1 (1998): 38.

156 As reported by Florin, who had returned from Moscow the previous day, to Ulbricht on 29 June in a handwritten note. SAPMO-BArch, ZPA, J IV 2/202/129, 1.

157. "Postanovlenie Prezidiuma TsK KPSS o sozyve soveshchaniia pervykh sekretarei kommunisticheskikh i rabochikh partii stran Varshavskogo dogovora po germanskomu voprosu," 30 June 1961, "O pis'me t. V. Ul'brikhta ot 24 iiuniia 1961 g," TsKhSD, F. 3, Op. 13, D. 488, l. 5, cited in "Okazat' nezamedlitel'nuiu pomoshch,'" documents prepared by Vodop'ianova and Zubok, *Istoricheskii Arkhiv*, 38.

158. Handwritten note from Florin to Ulbricht, SAPMO-BArch, ZPA, J IV 2/202/129.

159. On 5 July, Ulbricht sent Mao an urgent note, which was delivered by the GDR ambassador in Beijing, Wenning, to CC member Wu Siu-tuan on 6 July. Wenning delivered the note concerning a German peace treaty and West Berlin "with the appropriate references to the significance and confidentiality" of the note, requesting that it be delivered to Mao "as soon as possible." "Aktenvermerk über eine Besprechung mit Genossen Wu Sjiu-tjuan, Mitglied des ZK und Stellv. leiter der Abt. Intern. Verbindungen beim ZK, am 6.7.1971 anlässlich der Übergabe des Briefes des Genossen Walter Ulbricht an Genossen Mao Tse-tung," written up by Wenning, 12 July 1961, MfAA A17879. On 15 July Wenning received Mao's response to Ulbricht and sent it on to Winzer on 17 July, but was unable to learn who "would be in the Chinese delegation." See the letter from Wenning to Winzer, 17 July 1961, ibid. Clearly the letters concern Ulbricht's invitation to Mao to attend the meeting in Moscow in early August.

160. "*Aktenvermerk* über eine Besprechung mit dem Genossen Flato, Minis-

terrat der polnischen Botschaft, am 1.12.61," written up by the East German Ambassador to Peking, [Josef] Hegen, and [Werner] Wenning, counselor at the embassy on 6 December 1961, SAPMO-BArch, ZPA, IV 2/20/123, 1–2. Flato was reporting on his conversation "with a leading PRC comrade in the Central Committee," whom he did not name.

161. For additional such evidence, see the secret report prepared by the First Non-European Department of the East German Foreign Ministry, 13 July 1961, "*Bemerkungen* zur Einschätzung der Rede des Genossen Liu Schau-tji auf der Festveranstaltung zum 40. Jahrestag der Gründung der Kommunistischen Partei Chinas, am 30.6.1961," SAPMO-BArch, ZPA, IV 2/20/123; "2. Information zur Berichterstattung der chinesischen Press über Fragen des Abschlusses eines Friedensvertrages und die Lösung des Westberlinproblems in der Zeit vom 6. bis 18. Juli 1961," compiled by Hähnel, section leader (of the First Non-European Department of the East German Foreign Ministry), Berlin, 24 July 1961, SAPMO-BArch, ZPA, IV 2/20/115; top secret report by [Helmut] Liebermann, the senior counselor of the First Non-European Department, China Section, of the East German Foreign Ministry, 23 October 1961, "Haltung der VR Ch zu den Fragen des Abshlusses eines deutschen Friedensvertrages, der Lösung des Westberlinproblems sowie zu den von der Regierung der DDR getroffenen Schutzmassnahmen," ibid.; top-secret report by Liebermann, 3 November 1961, "Ergänzung zur Einschätzung der Haltung der VR Ch zu den Fragen des Absch-lusses eines deutschen Friedensvertrages, der Lösung des Westberlinproblems sowie zu den von der Regierung der DDR getroffenen Schutzmassnahmen," ibid; "*Aktenvermerk* über eine Beprechung mit dem Genossen Flato, Ministerrat der polnischen Botschaft, am 1.12.61," written up by the East German Ambassador to Peking, Hegen, and Wenning, counselor at the embassy on 6 December 1961, SAPMO-BArch, ZPA, IV 2/20/123; and the secret report by [Fritz] Stude, sec-tion leader of the First Non-European Department of the East German Foreign Ministry, 1 March 1962, "Zur Haltung der VR China zu den Fragen des deut-schen Friedensvertrages und des Westberlin-Problems," SAPMO-BArch, ZPA, IV 2/20/115. For another view of the role of the Chinese in the Berlin Crisis, see Zubok, "Khrushchev and the Berlin Crisis."

162. "O meropriiatiiakh prav-a KNR po voprosu zakliucheniia germanskogo mirnogo dogovora i normalizatsii polozheniia v zapadnom berline (fakticheskaia spravka)," 27 July 1961, from the attaché of the Far Eastern Dept. of MID, O. Perskov. AVPRF, F. 0742, Op. 6, Por. 4, Pap. 43, Inv. 193/3, t. 1.

163. The Chinese did not really come around to supporting a peace treaty with the GDR in 1961 or 1962. They told GDR representatives in the fall of 1961 that they could not legally sign a German peace treaty, since they did not see themselves as the legal successors to the Chinese Kuomintang regime, which had fought against Germany in World War II. See the top secret *Abschrift* sent from Stude in the First Non-European Department of the East German Foreign Ministry to East German Ambassador Hegen in Peking on 13 September 1961, SAPMO-BArch, ZPA, IV 2/20/123; and the top-secret letter from section leader Hähnel at the East German Foreign Ministry to [Norbert] Jeschke in Rangoon on 14 September 1961, ibid. Perhaps this was the Chinese excuse to avoid the conflict with the West that they feared in the wake of the conclusion of a sepa-

rate peace treaty with the GDR. It also could be that since Beijing's attitude toward the GDR was increasingly governed by the worsening of Chinese relations with the Soviet Union, the Chinese for this reason refrained from supporting the Soviet public campaign for a separate peace treaty with the GDR in 1961 and 1962. "*Aktenvermerk* über eine Besprechung mit dem Genossen Flato, Ministerrat der polnischen Botschaft, am 1.12.61," SAPMO-BArch, ZPA, IV 2/20/123, 5.

164. "Stenografische Niederschrift der 13. Tagung des ZK der SED im Plenarsaaal des Hauses des ZKs am 3. und 4. Juli 1961," p. 4 of Ulbricht's speech on 3 July, SAPMO-BArch, ZPA, IV 2/1/257. For the Russian translation of Ulbricht's speech, see TsKhSD, R. 8978, F. 5, Op. 49, D. 377.

165. "Stenografische Niederschrift der 13. Tagung des ZK der SED im Plenarsaaal des Hauses des ZKs am 3. und 4. Juli 1961," p. 4 of Ulbricht's speech on 3 July, SAPMO-BArch, ZPA, IV 2/1/257. With Ulbricht's reference to the prospect of West German nuclear weapons, one is reminded of his comments to Khrushchev in June 1959 that the most effective way to get support for the campaign against Adenauer and West Germany was to focus on nuclear weapons.

166. Letter from Ambassador Pervukhin to Minister of Foreign Affairs of the USSR, Comrade A. A. Gromyko, 4 July 1961, AVPRF, Referentura po GDR, Op. 6, Por. 34, Pap. 46, Inv. 193/3, t. 1, 1. For an English transl., see Appendix F in Harrison, "Ulbricht and the Concrete 'Rose.'"

167. Heidemeyer, *Flucht und Zuwanderung aus der SBZ/DDR*, 339.

168. Catudal, *Kennedy and the Berlin Wall Crisis*, 164, 184.

169. Letter from Ambassador Pervukhin to Minister of Foreign Affairs of the USSR, Comrade A. A. Gromyko, 4 July 1961, AVPRF, Referentura po GDR, Op. 6, Por. 34, Pap. 46, Inv. 193/3, t. 1, 1–2; 7.

170. Ibid., 2–5.

171. Ibid., 8–9.

172. Ibid., 6.

173. Ibid., 6–7.

174. Ibid., 9–16.

175. Kwizinskij, *Vor dem Sturm*, 179; 175.

176. Ibid., 216. See also Kvitsinsky's statement to the Berlin district court in the trial against former members of the GDR Defense Council for the order to shoot "border violators," "Kwizinski: Anstoss zum Bau der Mauer kam von Ulbricht: Früherer Sowjetbotschafter sagt als Zeuge vor Berliner Landgericht aus," *Der Tagesspiegel*, 23 July 1993; and "Mauerbau mit Genehmigung Moskaus. Kwizinski als Zeuge im Kessler-Prozess," *Frankfurter Allgemeine Zeitung*, 23 July 1993.

177. Troyanovsky, *Cherez gody i Rasstoianiia*, 235–36; and Burlatsky, *Khrushchev and the First Russian Spring*, 165. See also Brandt, *The Search for a Third Way*, 294. For a contrary view, see "Falin: Die Frage des Regimes an der Grenze war eine innere Angelegenheit der DDR. Die Aussage des sowjetischen Diplomaten und Deutschland-Fachmanns vor dem Berliner Landgericht," *Frankfurter Allgemeine Zeitung*, 30 July 1993.

178. For an account of this with important errors, including the notion that

it was the Soviet leader's idea initially to close the border, see Sergei Khrushchev, *Nikita Khrushchev: Krizisy i Rakety*, tom 2, 129–30; and the English version, Sergei Khrushchev, *Nikita Khrushchev and the Creation of a Superpower*, 454.

179. November 9 meeting between Khrushchev and Kroll in Moscow, described in Kroll, *Lebenserinnerungen eines Botschafters*, 512; 526. In contrast, in his memoirs, Khrushchev asserts: "I had been the one who thought up the solution to the problem which faced us as a consequence of our unsatisfactory negotiations with Kennedy in Vienna." *Khrushchev Remembers: The Last Testament*, 508; and *Khrushchev Remembers: The Glasnost Tapes*, 169.

180. Kroll, *Lebenserinnerungen eines Botschafters*, 512.

181. Kwitzinskij, *Vor dem Sturm*, 179.

182. Klaus Wiegrefe, "Die Schandmauer," 71.

183. The fact that the only meeting of the *Volkskammer* around this time was on 6 July lends credence to Kvitsinsky's belated recollection of 6 July as the date of Khrushchev's crucial message to Ulbricht. I am grateful to Armin Wagner for pointing this out to me.

184. Kwitzinskij, *Vor dem Sturm*, 179–80.

185. Ibid., 180.

186. No doubt to coordinate plans with the Soviets, Honecker was in Moscow in mid-July. See the unsigned report to Ulbricht, 15 July 1961, "Besondere Informationen an Genossen Walter Ulbricht," SAPMO-BArch, ZPA, J IV 2/202/130, Bd. 6.

187. Kwitzinskij, *Vor dem Sturm*, 180–81.

188. "Protokoll über die Dienstbesprechung am 7.7.1961," top secret, Central Analysis and Information Group of the Ministry for State Security (ZAIG) MfS 4899, 9.

189. Uhl and Wagner, "Another Brick in the Wall"; and Wiegrefe, "Die Schandmauer," 71.

190. Uhl and Wagner, "Another Brick in the Wall."

191. "Übersicht über den Umfang der Pioniermassnahmen am westlichen Aussenring von Berlin," 24.7.61, report written by Wansierski and sent to Ulbricht on the same day. SAPMO-Barch ZPA J IV 2/202/65. See also Uhl and Wagner, "Another Brick in the Wall."

192. Major, "Torschlusspanik und Mauerbau," 239.

193. See Pervukhin's conversation with Ulbricht on 20 March 1961, "Zapis' besedy s pervym sekretarem TsK SEPG V. Ul'brikhtom," from Pervukhin's diary, 22 March 1961, TsKhSD, R. 8978, F. 5, Op. 49, D. 377; "Vorschläge zur weitgehenden Eindämmung der Grenzgänger-Bewegung aus der Hauptstadt und den Grenzkreisen um Berlin nach Westberlin," SAPMO-BArch, ZPA, J IV 2/202/65; the 6 June 1961 SED Politburo meeting, "Anlage 4 zum Protokoll Nr. 24 vom 6.6.61," top secret, letter from Verner to all PB members and candidate members with attachment, "Vorlage zur weitgehenden Eindämmung der Grenzgängerbewegung nach Westberlin aus der Hauptstadt der DDR," SAPMO-BArch, ZPA, J IV 2/2/766; and "Massnahmen zur weitgehenden Eindämmung der Grenzgänger-Bewegung aus dem demokratischen Berlin und den Grenzkreisen um Berlin nach Westberlin," SAPMO-BArch, ZPA, J IV 2/202/65.

194. The letter is dated only "June 1961," but it it clear from other documents that it was sent on 24 June. SAPMO-BArch, ZPA, J IV 2/202/129.

195. "Postanovlenie Prezidiuma TsK KPSS o sozyve soveshchaniia pervykh sekretarei kommunisticheskikh i rabochikh partii stran Varshavskogo dogovora po germanskomu voprosu," 30 June 1961, in "'Okazat' nezamedlitel'nuiu pomoshch'," documents collected and introduced by Vodop'ianova and Zubok, 38.

196. 6 June 1961 Politburo report, "Massnahmen zur weitgehenden Eindämmung der Grenzgänger-Bewegung aus dem demokratischen Berlin und den Grenzkreisen um Berlin nach Westberlin," SAPMO-BArch, ZPA, J IV 2/202/65, 3.

197. 29 June 1961 letter from Pervukhin to Gromyko, AVPRF, F. 0742, Op. 6., Por. 51, Pap. 48, 1–3.

198. Recommendation from Gromyko to the CPSU CC, 19 July, AVPRF, F. 0742, Op. 6, Pap. 45, D. 25.

199. "Postanovlenie Prezidiuma TsK KPSS ob otvete na pis'mo V. Ul'brikhta o provedenii mer po sokrashcheniiu chisla grazhdan GDR, rabotaiushchikh v Zapadnom Berline," 20 July 1961, TsKhSD, F. 3, Op. 14, D. 491, l. 21, cited in *Istoricheskii Arkhiv* 1 (1998): 45.

200. "Letter from the Western Commandants in Berlin to the Soviet Commandant Protesting East German Discrimination Against East Berliners Employed in the Western Sectors, 3 August 1961," in *Documents on Gemany*, 765–66.

201. Tusa, *The Last Division*, 253.

202. Unsigned report to Ulbricht, 15 July 1961, "Besondere Informationen an Genossen Walter Ulbricht," SAPMO-BArch, ZPA, J IV 2/202/130, Bd. 6.

203. "Reinschriftenprotokoll Nr. 36 vom 24.7.1961. Protokoll Nr. 36/61 der ausserordentlichen Sitzung des PBs am Montag, dem 24. Juli 1961 im Sitzungssaal des PBs," SAPMO-BArch, ZPA, J IV 2/2/778. Honecker was absent from the meeting, probably because he was still in Moscow coordinating plans for the border closure.

204. July 1961 letter from Ulbricht to Khrushchev, copies in Russian and German, with the Russian probably the final version, SAPMO-BArch, ZPA, DY 30/J IV 2/202/129.

205. "TsK KPSS," 28 July 1961 letter from Gromyko and Andropov, AVPRF, F. 0742, Op. 6, Por. 34, Pap. 46, t. 1, 1.

206. Kwizinskij, *Vor dem Sturm*, 182.

207. Fursenko, "Kak Byla Postroena Berlinskaia Stena," 77. This article has many factual and interpretive errors and must be used only in combination with other more reliable sources.

208. For Ulbricht's draft speech for the 3–5 August WTO meeting in Moscow, see the Russian version, SAPMO-BArch, ZPA, 2/202/129, and the English translation, Appendix H, in Harrison, "Ulbricht and the Concrete 'Rose.'" The German version can be found in SAPMO-BArch, ZPA J IV 2/201/1216 and has been published by Otto, "13. August 1961—eine Zäsur in der europäischen Nachkriegsgeschichte," 55–92.

209. G. Zhiliakov, "Kratkoe soderzhanie proekta rechi t. V. Ul'brikhta na

soveshchanii gosudarstv-uchastnikov Varshavskogo dogovora 3–4 avgusta c.g. v Moskve," sent from Pervukhin to Gromyko on 26 July 1961, AVPRF, F. 0742, Op. 6, Por. 4, Pap. 43, Inv. 193/3, t. 1, 7. See also "Perechen' voprosov zatronutykh v proekte rechi tov. V. Ul'brikhta na predstoiashchem soveshchanii 3–4 avgusta v Moskve," ibid. Without providing any explanatory background, the Russian historian Aleksandr Fursenko attests that on 27 July, Pervukhin reported to Khrushchev: "Ulbricht completely agrees with your views regarding the implementation of a new stricter regime on the sectoral border in Berlin than was expressed in his draft speech for the conference at the Kremlin." Fursenko, "Kak Byla Postroena Berlinskaia Stena," 77. Of course, the tighter the border, the better as far as Ulbricht was concerned.

210. SAPMO-BArch, ZPA, J IV 2/202/130, Bd. 6; and ibid., DY 30/J IV 2/202-333-334. See also Fursenko, "Kak Byla Postroena Berlinskaia Stena," 76–77.

211. Fursenko, "Kak Byla Postroena Berlinskaia Stena," 77.

212. Ibid., 75. It seems that Shelepin had learned of LIVEOAK, the secret U.S., British and French military plans to secure access to West Berlin if the Soviets and East Germans blocked it. See Pedlow, "Allied Crisis Management for Berlin: The LIVE OAK Organization, 1959–1963," 87–116.

213. J IV 2/202/130, Bd. 6. "Analyse der Antwortnotes der drei Westmächte vom 17. Juli 1961 auf das sowjetische Deutschland-Memorandum vom 4. June 1961," 27 July 1961; and "*Materialien* zu Widersprüchen in den Stellungnahmen von Staatsmännern, massgeblichen Politikern und Kommentatoren der USA, Grossbritanniens, Frankreichs und Westdeutschlands zum Deutschland-problem," 28 July 1961, ibid.

214. "Report by President Kennedy to the Nation on the Berlin Crisis, 25 July 1961," *Documents on Germany*, 764.

215. Tusa, *The Last Division*, 254–55; and Beschloss, *The Crisis Years*, 256–61.

216. "Report by President Kennedy to the Nation on the Berlin Crisis, 25 July 1961," *Documents on Germany*, 764–65.

217. McGeorge Bundy asserts that Kennedy's focus on West Berlin and neglect of East Berlin in his 25 July speech was deliberate and was intended to show Khrushchev and the American people what the West would and would not fight for. Bundy, *Danger and Survival*, 368–69.

218. Rostow, *The Diffusion of Power: An Essay in Recent History*, 231, cited in Gaddis, *We Now Know*, 148.

219. *New York Times*, 3 August 1961, cited in Catudal, *Kennedy and the Berlin Wall Crisis*, 201.

220. "Zapis' besedy posla SSSR v FRG A. A. Smirnova s kantslerom Adenauerom, 16 avgusta, 1961 goda," AVPRF, F.: Referentura po FRG, Op. 6, Pap. 28, Por. 4.

221. "Niederschrift der Unterredung des Vorsitzenden des Ministerrats der UdSSR, N. S. Chruschtschow mit dem Vorsitzenden des Ministerrates Italiens," A. Fanfani am 3 August 1961 (2. Unterredung), SAPMO-BArch, ZPA, DY 30/J IV 2/202/329, 19.

222. Kwizinskij, *Vor dem Sturm*, 181–82.

223. Wiegrefe, "Die Schandmauer," 72; and 31 July 1961 letter from the SED CC General Department to A. Gorchakov of the Soviet Embassy informing him of the composition of the delegation leaving on 1 August, SAPMO-BArch, ZPA, DY 30/J IV 2/202/336, Bd. 2.

224. Wiegrefe, "Die Schandmauer," 72.

225. See the German version of Ulbricht's letter to Khrushchev, dated "July 1961," and delivered between 25 and 27 July. SAPMO-BArch, ZPA, DY 30/J/ IV 2/202/129 and "Vorschläge zur Durchführung der Beratungen," 31.7.1961, SAPMO-BArch, ZPA, DY 30/J IV 2/202/333.

226. Ulbricht's handwritten notes on his meeting with Khrushchev on the morning of 3 August can be found at SAPMO-BArch, ZPA, DY 30/3682 and in English translation in Uhl and Wagner, "Another Brick in the Wall." Information from Soviet notes on the meeting can be found in Fursenko, "Kak Byla Postroena Berlinskaia Stena," 78–79.

227. Fursenko, "Kak Byla Postroena Berlinskaia Stena," 78.

228. Uhl and Wagner, "Another Brick in the Wall."

229. Fursenko, "Kak Byla Postroena Berlinskaia Stena," 78.

230. Ibid.

231. The available records of this meeting do not record the date, but Ulbricht's report to the SED Politburo on 7 August announced that in Moscow they had set the date for 12–13 August. SAPMO-BArch, ZPA, J IV, 2/2/781, 1–2, "Protokoll Nr. 39/61 der ausserordentlichen Sitzung des Politbüros des Zentralkomitees am Montag, dem 7. August 1961 im Sitzungssaal des Politbüros." See also the English translation appended to Uhl and Wagner, "Another Brick in the Wall."

232. Khrushchev Remembers: The Last Testament, 506.

233. Fursenko, "Kak Byla Postroena Berlinskaia Stena," 79.

234. See Ulbricht's handwritten notes of the meeting, SAPMO-BArch, ZPA, DY 30/3682.

235. Maron's proposals accompanied Ulbricht's 18 October 1960 letter to Khrushchev and were rebuffed in Khrushchev's letter to Ulbricht of 24 October. SAPMO-BArch, ZPA, DY 30/J IV 2/202/66. See also the East German materials sent to Khrushchev in late July 1961 on the details of stopping movement across the border, SAPMO-BArch, ZPA, J IV 2/202/130, Bd. 6.

236. Fursenko, "Kak Byla Postroena Berlinskaia Stena," 79.

237. Uhl and Wagner, "Another Brick in the Wall."

238. The following account is based on Wyden, Wall, 132, 139–45, 154–61; and Beschloss, The Crisis Years, 266–68.

239. Khrushchev's 3 August speech opening the WTO meeting, SAPMO-BArch, ZPA, J IV 2/202/130; and the English translation, Appendix G, in Harrison, "Ulbricht and the Concrete 'Rose.'"

240. In Moscow, the author was shown the uncorrected protocol of this meeting, "Soveshchanie sekretarei TsK kommunisticheskikh i rabochikh partii sotsialisticheskikh stran dlia obmena mneniiami po voprosam, sviazannym s podgotovkoi i zakliucheniem germanskogo mirnogo dogovora" ("Conference of CC Secretaries of Communist and Workers Parties of the Socialist Countries for the Exchange of Views on Questions Connected with the Preparation and

Conclusion of a German Peace Treaty"), at TsKhSD before it had been given any further citation information. Bernd Bonwetsch and Alexei Filitov have published in German much of the final, corrected protocol of this meeting from TsKhSD files with notes referring to differences between this final version, the first, uncorrected version, and the second, authors' version with the authors' markings, "*Dokumentation*. Chruschtschow und der Mauerbau. Die Gipfelkonferenz der Warschauer-Pakt-Staaten vom 3.–5. August 1961," 155–98. They published Khrushchev's full speech of 4 August, but only a summary of Ulbricht's speech of 4 August, since Ulbricht's speech was published in German, following an introduction by Otto, "Dokumente und Materialien. 13. August 1961—eine Zäsur in der europäischen Nachkriegsgeschichte. Dokument 1. Rede Walter Ulbrichts am 3. [*sic*] August 1961," 55–84. For the uncorrected original of Ulbricht's 4 August speech translated into Russian, see SAPMO-BArch, ZPA, J IV 2/202/129, and the English translation, Appendix H, in Harrison, "Ulbricht and the Concrete 'Rose.'" Bowetsch and Filitov have also published the final, corrected version of Khrushchev's 4 August speech with their introduction and analysis in Russian, "Kak prinimalos' reshenie o vozvedenii berlinskoi steny," 53–75.

241. August 4, 1961, letter from Ulbricht to the First Secretary of the Central Committee of the CPSU, Comrade N. S. Khrushchev, "*Information* über die Ursachen die wirtschaftlichen Schwierigkeiten der DDR," SAPMO-BArch, ZPA, DY 30/J IV 2/202/30.

242. In the German archives, the speech is actually labeled "Brief vom ZK der SED an das ZK der KPdSU über Friedensvertrag Deutschland, März 1961" ("Letter from the SED CC to the CPSU CC on a German Peace Treaty, March 1961"), but it is obvious from the text that it was Ulbricht's speech at the 3–5 August 1961 WTO PCC conference, and this is confirmed by the record of the conference in the archives of the TsKhSD. The speech in the German archive is in Russian, SAPMO-BArch, ZPA, DY 30/J IV 2/202/129, 25–26; 32–33.

243. Ulbricht's 24 June 1961 letter to Gomulka, SAPMO-BArch, ZPA, DY 30/J IV 2/202/369, 2.

244. Ulbricht's 4 August speech, SAPMO-BArch, ZPA, J IV 2/202/129, 16; 7.

245. "*Information* über die Ursachen der wirtschaftlichen Schwierigkeiten der DDR," with cover letter from Ulbricht to Khrushchev, 4 August 1961, SAPMO-BArch, ZPA, DY 30/J IV 2/202/30, 17; 4–5.

246. Ibid., 12.

247. Ibid., 6–7; 12.

248. Ulbricht 4 August speech, SAPMO-BArch, ZPA, DY 30/J IV 2/202/129, 26; 28–28a. In his memoirs, Honecker writes that at this meeting, "[i]n agreement with the CPSU, the SED proposed that the borders of the GDR with Berlin-West and the FRG should be controlled in the way customary between sovereign states" and that Ulbricht gave Honecker the task of preparing and implementing the plan. Honecker, *From My Life*, 210.

249. Bonwetsch and Filitow, "Dokumentation. Chruschtschow und der Mauerbau," 169, 172.

250. Ulbricht's 4 August speech, SAPMO-BArch, ZPA, DY 30/J IV 2/202/129, 28a.

251. Bonwetsch and Filitow, "Dokumentation. Chruschtschow und der Mauerbau," 174. At a meeting of the Polish and East German leaders in 1969, Premier Cyrankiewicz told Ulbricht, "I would like to remind you of how many times the Poles proposed that [the border to West Berlin] be closed." Gomulka added, "And how much earlier!" Ulbricht responded: "We know about this and have not forgotten. We were always of the same opinion as you. . . . " Gomulka declared: "I would have shut it far earlier. How many times I told Khrushchev about it!" See "Document No. 1 (Excerpt). Transcript of a Meeting between the Delegations of the PZPR and the SED in Moscow, 2 December 1969," trans., annot., intro., Douglas Selvage, CWIHP, *Bulletin* 11 (Winter 1998): 222. Three months after the wall was built, Gomulka also told his Central Committee, on 22 November, "we were saying among ourselves here long before the Moscow [WTO] meeting . . . why not put an end to it [hostile Western policies toward the GDR from West Berlin]? Close off, wall off Berlin. And later we made such a decision in Moscow." See Selvage, "The End of the Berlin Crisis, 1961–62: New Evidence from the Polish and East German Archives," ibid., 219.

252. Ulbricht's 4 August speech to the WTO conference, SAPMO-BArch, ZPA, J IV 2/202/129, 33. Ulbricht's 4 August speech to the WTO conference, SAPMO-BArch, ZPA, J IV 2/202/129, 29–32. On 21 June, Ulbricht had told the Gosplan representative in the GDR, T. P. Bobuirev, that while the East Europeans understood the need to conclude a peace treaty, "they close their eyes to the economic side of the question." "Zapis' besedy s pervym sekretarem TsK SEPG tov. V. Ul'brikhtom," 21.6.61, from the diary of the counselor of the embassy of the USSR in the GDR, T. P. Bobyrev, 27.6.61, TsKhSD, R. 8978, F. 5, Op. 49, D. 376, 4.

253. See Khrushchev's 4 August speech, morning session, in Bonwetsch and Filitov, "Iz stenogrammy soveshaniia," 70.

254. Gomulka's comments, morning session of 4 August, in Bonwetsch and Filitov, "Chruschtschow und der Mauerbau," 175; 176.

255. Novotny's comments, morning session, 4 August, in ibid., 177; 178.

256. Kadar's speech, evening of 4 August, in ibid., 196.

257. Otto, "Worlaut eines Gesprächs von Wilfriede Otto mit Werner Eberlein am 5. September 1996 über die Beratung der Ersten Sekretäre des ZK der kommunistischen und Arbeiterparteien der Staaten des Warschauer Vertrages vom 3. bis 5. August 1961 in Moskau," 86.

258. Kadar's speech, evening of 4 August, Bonwetsch and Filitov, "Chruschtschow und der Mauerbau," 195–196.

259. Comments of Li Che-Sun at the evening session, 4 August, ibid., 197.

260. Comments of Tidor Zhivkov at the morning session, 4 August, ibid., 180.

261. Khrushchev's 4 August 1961 speech, Bonwetsch and Filitov, "Iz stenogrammy soveshaniia," 67, 74.

262. Ibid., 63–64; 75.

263. Ibid., 68–70.

264. Ibid., 71–72. Khrushchev had also urged the socialist countries at the March WTO meeting to be prepared to give economic aid to the GDR in the event of a hostile Western economic response to a separate peace treaty. See

also *Khrushchev Remembers: The Last Testament*, 358, for a similar explanation.

265. Khrushchev's 4 August speech, Bonwetsch and Filitov, "Iz stenogrammy soveshaniia," 73.

266. *Khrushchev Remembers: The Glasnost Tapes*, 169.

267. Khrushchev's 4 August speech, Bonwetsch and Filitov, "Iz stenogrammy soveshaniia," 72.

268. Alia's 3 August speech as given to Khrushchev in Russian, SAPMO-BArch, ZPA, J IV 2/202/130. For excerpts from and discussion of the speech, see also Slusser, *The Berlin Crisis of 1961*, 101–104.

269. SAPMO-BArch, ZPA, J IV 2/202/130, 8–9. Meeting with North Vietnamese leader Ho Chi Minh on 17 August, Khrushchev again complained about the Albanians: "The current Albanian leadership criticized us because we have been threatening to conclude a German peace treaty and decide the West Berlin question for three years now, but have not undertaken anything practical in that direction. But that's how people who don't know anything about politics talk. . . . It was, however, necessary to force the Western powers to consider the question of a German peace treaty and to establish the necessary preconditions for it. That took about three years. Now such conditions are there and nothing is to stop us from resolving the issue." See the transcript of this meeting, "Zapis' besed Pervogo sekretaria TsK KPSS tov. N. S. Khrushcheva s predsedatelem TsK PTV tov. Ho Shi Minom, Pitsunda, 17.8.1961g," in "'Ia veriu v velichie starshego brata.' Besedy N. S. Khrushcheva s Kho Shi Minom," *Istochnik* 2 (1998): 84.

270. Bonwetsch and Filitow, "Chruschtschow und der Mauerbau," 164–65; 198.

271. Ibid., 165.

272. Ibid., 171. Even before the records of this meeting were made accessible, Hannes Adomeit speculated that "Soviet policies towards West Berlin and West Germany (and the Western allies as guarantee powers) are influenced to a high degree by requirements of intra-bloc cohesion." *Soviet Risk-Taking and Crisis Behavior*, 190.

273. Bonwetsch and Filitow, "Chruschtschow und der Mauerbau," 164.

274. Zagoria, *The Sino-Soviet Conflict*, 396.

275. Khrushchev's 4 August speech, Bonwetsch and Filitov, "Iz stenogrammy soveshaniia," 74.

276. "*Protokoll Nr. 39/61* der ausserordentlichen Sitzung des Politbüros des Zentralkomitees am Montag, dem 7. August 1961 im Sitzungssaal des Politbüros," SAPMO-BArch, ZPA, J IV, 2/2/781, 1–2.

277. "Protokoll über die Dienstbesprechung am 11.8.1961," top secret, ZAIG 4900, BStU, 1, 3, 6.

278. Kwizinskij, *Vor dem Sturm*, 182; 184.

279. Honecker, *From My Life*, 210–11.

280. "Declaration by the Warsaw Pact Powers Urging Establishment of 'Reliable Safeguards and Effective Control . . . Around the Whole Territory of West Berlin.' 13 August 1961," *Documents on Germany, 1944–1985*, 774. See also Tusa, *The Last Division*, 271.

281. Tusa, *The Last Division*, 294.

282. Gelb, *The Berlin Wall*, 222.

283. Kwizinskij, *Vor dem Sturm*, 186–87.

284. Bundesarchiv-Militärarchiv, DVW-1/39573, cited in Uhl and Wagner, "Another Brick in the Wall." See also the late October/early November 1961 discussion between Khrushchev and Ulbricht about tightening up the border beyond barbed wire in Fursenko, "Kak Byla Postroena Berlinskaia Stena," 86.

285. Wiegrefe, "Die Schandmauer," 76; Steininger, *Der Mauerbau*, 271.

286. Willy Brandt, *People and Politics: The Years 1960–1975*, 20, 31; and Steininger, *Der Mauerbau*, 271–72.

287. Tusa, *The Last Division*, 280; and Steininger, *Der Mauerbau*, 263.

288. Cited in Beschloss, *The Crisis Years*, 278.

289. Due to fears of a repeat of June 1953 in response to the sealing of the border, the Soviets sent troops to several East German cities "to keep order if necessary," as Defense Minister Malinovsky put it. TsKhSD, 5/30/367, Report of the Soviet Defense Ministry to the CPSU CC on the Situation in Berlin and the GDR, 22 August 1961, cited in Uhl and Wagner, "Another Brick in the Wall."

290. Ulbricht's 15 September 1961 letter to Khrushchev, SAPMO-BArch, ZPA, J IV 2/202/130, 1. See also the English translation, Appendix I in Harrison, "Ulbricht and the Concrete 'Rose.'" Khrushchev had also remarked at the WTO PCC meeting on 4 August that he and his colleagues felt that the West had been reacting less severely to Soviet proposals about Berlin than they had expected. He said that they had "expected more force," but the strongest intimidation was Kennedy's speech. Bonwetsch and Filitov, "Soveshchanie sekretarei TsK," 141.

291. Fursenko, "Kak Byla Postroena Berlinskaia Stena," 81.

292. "Aktenvermerk über ein Gespräch des Botschafters mit dem Mitglied des Pbs und Aussenministers der VR China, Genossen Tschen Ji, mit anschliessendem Mittagessen am 31.8.61 in der Zeit vom 11.00 bis 12.45 Uhr," written up by Ambassador Hegen, 5 September 1961. MfAA A17879, Staatssekretär. Chen Yi may have been responding to Khrushchev's "Note from the Soviet Union to the United States Stressing the Temporary Nature of the Travel Restrictions Imposed by the East Germans in Berlin, 18 August 1961," *Documents on Germany*, 780–81. In his note, Khrushchev said that the "temporary travel restrictions," i.e., the closing of the border around West Berlin, would last only until the conclusion of a German peace treaty and resolution of the situation in West Berlin through the peace treaty.

293. "Zapis' informatsii chlena PB, sekretkaria TsK SEPG, c. Honnecker dlia glav diplomaticheskikh predstavitel'stv sotsialisticheskikh stran v GDR," secret, written up by G. Zhiliakov, advisor at Soviet embassy, 18 September 1961. TsKhSD, R. 8981, F. 5, Op. 49, D. 385, 2–3. With a cover letter from Pervukhin to Andropov on 23 September 1961, this was sent on to the CPSU CC. On the West being caught off guard, see also Murphy, Kondrashev, and Bailey, *Battleground Berlin*, 376–79; Wyden, *Wall*, 133–36, 142–43, 239–42; Gelb, *The Berlin Wall*, 183, 189–96; and Cate, *The Ides of August*, 255–61, 301, 306–307.

294. "Zapis' informatsii chlena PB, sekretkaria TsK SEPG, c. Honnecker dlia

glav diplomaticheskikh predstavitel'stv sotsialisticheskikh stran v GDR," secret, written up by G. Zhiliakov, advisor at Soviet embassy, 18 September 1961. TsKhSD, R. 8981, F. 5, Op. 49, D. 385, 1.

295. Tusa, *The Last Division*, 301–306; and Beschloss, *The Crisis Years*, 282.

296. "Zapis' besed Pervogo sekretaria TsK KPSS tov. N. S. Khrushcheva s predsedatelem TsK PTV tov. Ho Shi Minom, Pitsunda, 17.8.1961g," in "'Ia veriu v velichie starshego brata.' Besedy N. S. Khrushcheva s Kho Shi Minom," *Istochnik*, 77.

297. Steininger, *Der Mauerbau*, 266–68; 280; 285–88. For Russian notes on the Gromyko-Rusk talks, see "Zapis' besedy tov. Gromyko A. A. c gosudarstvennym sekretarem CShA Raskom 21 sentiabria 1961 goda v N'iu-Iorke," AVPRF, F. 029, Op. 5, Pap. 3, Por. 25.

298. "Proekt materiala po voprosu o germanskom mirnom dogovore dlia obsuzhdeniia i soglasovaniia s druz'iami," sent from Gromyko to the CPSU CC on 22 October 1961, AVPRF, F. 0742, Op. 6, Por. 36, Pap, 46, 10.

299. See Ulbricht's 15 September 1961 letter to Khrushchev, SAPMO-BArch, ZPA, J IV 2/202/130.

300. Letter from Khrushchev to Kennedy, 29 September 1961, *FRUS, 1961–1963, Vol. 6, Kennedy-Khrushchev Exchanges*, 26–31. See also ibid., 24–5 and Steininger, *Der Mauerbau*, 286–87. Khrushchev hoped that his differences with Kennedy over Germany and West Berlin could be overcome by their personal correspondence, but this was not to be the case.

301. "TsK KPSS," 17 August 1961 report from Gromyko. AVPRF, F. 0742, Op. 6, Por. 35, Pap. 46.

302. Letter from Khrushchev to Ulbricht, 28 September 1961, SAPMO-BArch, ZPA, J IV 2/202/130, 2. For an English translation, see Appendix J in Harrison, "Ulbricht and the Concrete 'Rose.'"

303. Slusser, *The Berlin Crisis of 1961*, 293.

304. For Khrushchev's speech on 17 October 1961 rescinding the ultimatum, see *Materialy XXII C"ezda KPSS*, 31–32.

305. Author's interview with Kvitsinsky, Moscow, 26 October 1992.

306. *Khrushchev Remembers: The Last Testament*, 507–508; and *Khrushchev Remembers*, 455.

307. See Catudal, *Kennedy and the Berlin Wall Crisis*, 133; Beschloss, *The Crisis Years*, 335; Garthoff, "Berlin 1961," 142–56; Steininger, *Der Mauerbau*, 308–309; Fursenko, "Kak Byla Postroena Berlinskaia Stena," 81–82; *Khrushchev Remembers*, 457, 459; and *Khrushchev Remembers: The Last Testament*, 506–507.

308. SAPMO-BArch, ZPA, NL 182/1206, 3. For an English translation of the letter from Ulbricht to Khrushchev on 30 October 1961, see Appendix K in Harrison, "Ulbricht and the Concrete 'Rose.'"

309. "Zapis' besedy s predsedalem gosudarstvennogo soveta GDR tov. V. Ul'brikhtom," 27 February 1962, from the diary of V. S. Semenov, 6 April 1962, AVPRF, F.: Referentura po GDR, Op. 7, Pap. 51, Por. 4, inv. 030/031, top secret.

310. Uhl and Wagner, "Another Brick in the Wall."

311. Gelb, *The Berlin Wall*, 216.

312. Tusa, *The Last Division*, 325.

313. "Aktenvermerk über ein Gespräch des Botschafters mit dem Mitglied des Pbs und Aussenministers der VR China, Genossen Tschen Ji, mit anschliessendem Mittagessen am 31.8.61 in der Zeit vom 11.00 bis 12.45 Uhr," written up by Ambassador Hegen, 5 September 1961. MfAA A17879, Staatssekretär.

314. My thanks to Armin Wagner for looking into this for me. Schultke, *"Keiner kommt durch": Die Geschichte der innerdeutschen Grenze, 1945–1990*, 194; Lapp, *Gefechtsdienst im Frieden: Das Grenzregime der DDR, 1945–1990*, 194; and Wagner, *Walter Ulbricht und die geheime Sicherheitspolitik der SED*, 2.

315. Among the voluminous reporting on these trials, see Ian Traynor, "Justice day for the master of the Wall," *The Guardian* (25 August 1997), 9; Roger Boyes, "Six years' jail for last East German boss," *The Times* (London) (26 August 1997), 8; Roger Boyes, "Last Iron Curtain despot faces trial," *The Times* (London) (9 November 1999), 18; Edmund L. Andrews, "Long After the Wall, Questions About Punishment," *New York Times* (26 December 1999), 3; and Wiessala, "Political Justice in Post-Unification Germany: The Legal Legacy of the GDR," 52–57. "As a main plank in his defense, Krenz noted that when President Ronald Reagan visited the Berlin Wall in 1987, he proclaimed to the Soviet President Mikhail S. Gorbachev, 'Mr. Gorbachev, tear down this wall!' He did not cry, 'Honecker, or Krenz, tear down the wall!'" AP, "Ex-E. German leader jailed for Berlin Wall deaths," the *Baltimore Sun* (26 August 1997), 1A. On the trials and other methods of coming to terms with the GDR's past, see McAdams, *Judging the Past in Unified Germany*, 23–54. For the process of dealing with the past in Germany, Poland, and Czechoslovakia, see Rosenberg, *The Haunted Land: Facing Europe's Ghosts after Communism*.

316. Menning, "The Berlin Crisis from the Perspective of the Soviet General Staff," 49–62.

317. Ibid., 59, 60.

318. Smyser, *From Yalta to Berlin*, 172–76.

319. Letter from Winzer to Ulbricht, Stoph and Maron, 21 August 1961, SAPMO-BArch, ZPA, DY 30/J IV 2/202/336, Bd. 2.

320. Garthoff, "Berlin 1961," 146–48; Steininger, *Der Mauerbau*, 309; and Fursenko, "Kak Byla Postroena Berlinskaia Stena," 81. See also the secret report on 25 October from Colonel-General S. P. Ivanov in Berlin to Defense Minister Malinovsky about the appearance of U.S. tanks armed with bulldozers, "Marshalu Sovetskogo Soiuza Tovarishu Malinovskomu P.Ia.," TsKhSD, R. 4632, F. 5, Op. 30, D. 367. For reporting throughout the crisis from the Soviet military in Berlin to Malinovsky and from Malinovsky to the Soviet Central Committee, see the secret reports in ibid.

321. Smyser, *From Yalta to Berlin*, 173–76; Steininger, *Der Mauerbau*, 306–13; Garthoff, "Berlin 1961," 145, 152–53; *Khrushchev Remembers*, 459–60; and *Khrushchev Remembers: The Last Testament*, 507.

322. Lemke, *Die Berlinkrise 1958 bis 1963*, 175.

323. Top-secret, urgent telegram from Ulbricht in Moscow to the SED Politburo and Hermann Matern, 27 October 1961, DY 30/J NL 2/29.

324. Letter from Ulbricht in Moscow to Politburo members and Matern, 29 October 1961, ibid.

325. "Document No. 2. Rough Notes from a Conversation (Gromyko, Khrushchev, and Gomulka) on the International Situation, n.d. [October 1961]," intro., trans., annot. Selvage, CWIHP, *Bulletin* 11 (Winter 1998): 223–24.

326. Fursenko, "Kak Byla Postroena Berlinskaia Stena," 84–86.

327. Ibid., 87.

328. See the report on the meeting written up by the GDR Ambassador to Moscow, Dölling on 7 March 1962, "Vermerk über die Besprechung am 26.2.1962," MfAA, G-A476, Ministerbüro (Winzer), 4–5. For the English translation, see Selvage, "The End of the Berlin Crisis, 1961–62: New Evidence from the Polish and East German Archives, Document No. 3, Note on the Discussion Between Khrushchev and Ulbricht in Moscow, 26 February 1962 (Excerpts)," CWHIP *Bulletin* 11 (Winter 1998): 224–26. Quote from p. 225. See also Fursenko, "Kak Byla Postroena Berlinskaia Stena," 88.

329. Fursenko, "Kak Byla Postroena Berlinskaia Stena," 87.

330. Selvage, trans., "Note on the Discussion Between Khrushchev and Ulbricht in Moscow, 26 February 1962 (Excerpts)," 225.

331. Ibid.

332. "Otchet o rabote Posol'stva SSSR v GDR za 1961 god," 22 February 1962, written by Pervukhin and sent to Andropov, TsKhSD, R. 8980, F. 5, Op. 49, D. 382, 72–73.

333. Letter from President Kennedy to Chairman Khrushchev, Hyannis Port, 16 October 1961, *FRUS, 1961–63, Vol. VI: Kennedy-Khrushchev Exchanges*, 41.

334. Fursenko, "Kak Byla Postroena Berlinskaia Stena," 89.

335. May and Zelikow, *The Kennedy Tapes: Inside the White House During the Cuban Missile Crisis*, 176–77, 256–57, 280, 281, 284–86, 691. See also Allison and Zelikow, *Essence of Decision: Explaining the Cuban Missile Crisis*, 2nd ed., 99–108; and Risse-Kappen, "A 'Strike on Cuba Which May Lose Berlin': The Europeans and the 1962 Cuban Missile Crisis," Chap. 6 in *Cooperation among Democracies*, 146–82.

336. Fursenko and Naftali, "*One Hell of a Gamble*,'" 167–69.

337. See his remark to Ulbricht on 26 February 1962: "The Albanians and Chinese criticize us with regard to the peace treaty and West Berlin. [Yet w]hat are they doing themselves?" Selvage, trans., "Note on the Discussion Between Khrushchev and Ulbricht in Moscow, 26 February 1962 (Excerpts)," 225.

338. See the conversation between Khrushchev, Gromyko, and Ulbricht in late October or early November 1961, described in Fursenko, "Kak Byla Postroena Berlinskaia Stena," 85.

339. Khrushchev told Ulbricht in late February 1962 that the peace treaty was "a means of pressure on West Berlin." Ibid., 88.

340. Selvage, trans., "Document No. 2. Rough Notes from a Conversation (Gromyko, Khrushchev, and Gomulka) on the International Situation, n.d. [October 1961]," 223–24.

341. Selvage, trans., "Note on the Discussion Between Khrushchev and Ul-

bricht in Moscow, 27 February 1962 (Excerpts)," CWHIP, *Bulletin* 11 (winter 1998): 227.

342. Krisch, *The German Democratic Republic*, 15.

343. Otto, "Ernst Wollweber: Aus Erinnerungen," 372, 377–78.

344. *Khrushchev Remembers: The Glasnost Tapes*, 163; 456.

345. Ibid., 456; 454.

346. Burr, "Avoiding the Slippery Slope," 177–205; idem., "Dwight D. Eisenhower and American Policy During the Berlin Crisis, 1958–1960," 2, 43, 55, 56; and Trachtenberg, *A Constructed Peace*, 251–343.

347. Ulbricht's 15 September 1961 letter to Khrushchev, SAPMO-BArch, ZPA, J IV 2/202/130.

348. Author's interview with Kvitsinsky, Moscow, 26 October 1992. Kvitsinsky also told the author that as far as he knew, Ulbricht's pressure on Khrushchev to act, especially between March and 13 August 1961, explained "90 percent of the Soviet decision to sanction the building of the Wall."

349. SAPMO-BArch, ZPA, J IV 2/202/130, 2.

350. "Haltung der VR China zu den Fragen des Abshlusses eines deutschen Friedensvertrages, der Lösung des Westberlinproblems sowie zu den von der Regierung der DDR getroffenen Schutzmassnahmen," written up by Liebermann and others from the First External European Department, the China section, 23 October 1961, SAPMO-BArch, ZPA, IV 2/20/115, 2; and "Aktenvermerk über ein Gespräch des Botschafters mit dem Mitglied des PBs und Aussenministers der VR China, Genossen Tschen Ji, mit anschliessendem Mittagessen am 31.8.61 in der Zeit von 11;00 bis 12.45 Uhr," written up by Hegen, 5 September 1961, MfAA A17879, Staatssekretär, 2. The Chinese were also critical of Khrushchev's rescinding of the peace treaty deadline again in October 1961, which they thought made him look weak and like a "bluffer" whose threats would no longer be "credible." "*Aktenvermerk* über eine Besprechung mit des Genossen Flato, Ministerrat der polnischen Botschaft, am 1.12.61," SAPMO-BArch, ZPA, IV 2/2-/123, 2.

351. See the report prepared by D. Poliianskii on 14 October 1962 for the CPSU CC plenum on Khrushchev's ouster, "'Takovy, tovarishchi, fakti,'" *Vestnik* 2 (1998): 112–13.

352. Thus, at their 9 June 1959 summit, Khrushchev confidently told Ulbricht that their main strategy regarding Berlin and a peace treaty should be to gain time, perhaps one and a half to two years, because by the end of that time, East Germany would start to surpass West Germany in standard of living. "*Kratkaia zapis' peregovorov* s partiino-pravitel'stvennoi delegatsiei GDR 9 iunia 1959 g," 6–7.

353. Adomeit, *Imperial Overstretch: Germany in Soviet Policy from Stalin to Gorbachev*, 100–109; and Selvage, "The End of the Berlin Crisis," 218.

354. I am grateful to Robert Jervis for discussing this with me. Glenn H. Snyder observes that one "major determinant of alliance bargaining power is the parties' interest in the specific issue about which they are bargaining," *Alliance Politics*, 170. See also Snyder and Diesing, *Conflict Among Nations*, 31.

355. On the events that led to the collapse of the Berlin Wall and the GDR, see Ash, *The Magic Lantern: The Revolution of '89 Witnessed in Warsaw, Bu-*

dapest, Berlin and Prague, 61–77; Pond, *Beyond the Wall: Germany's Road to Unification,* 1–139; Hertle, "The Fall of the Wall: The Unintended Self-Dissolution of East Germany's Ruling Regime," 131–64; and idem., *Chronik des Mauerfalls: Die dramatischen Ereignisse um den 9. November 1989.*

356. Naimark, *The Russians in Germany* and Loth, *Stalin's Unwanted Child.*

357. See his comments to Honecker in July 1970, "Protokoll einer Unterredung zwischen L. I. Breschnew und Erich Honecker am 28. Juli 1970," SAPMO, BArch, ZPA, J NL 2/32. Also published in Przybylski, *Tatort Politbüro,* 284–85. See also Sarotte, *Dealing with the Devil,* 80–83.

Conclusion

1. Ulbricht's "Zwischenrede" to the thirty-third plenum, 19 October 1957, SAPMO-BArch, ZPA, DY 30/IV 2/1/186, 556.

2. Troyanovsky, *Cherez Gody i Rasstoianiia,* 209.

3. Murphy, Kondrashev, and Bailey, *Battleground Berlin,* 291.

4. See Khrushchev's comments to Gomulka on 10 November, 1958, "Minutes from the Discussion Between the Delegation of the PRL [People's Republic of Poland] and the Government of the USSR," trans., annot., intro. Douglas Selvage, CWIHP, *Bulletin* 11 (winter 1998): 202.

5. Khrushchev's 4 August 1961 speech to the WTO PCC conference in Moscow, as published by Bonwetsch and Filitov, "Iz stenogrammy soveshaniia . . . " 72.

6. Khrushchev's 4 August 1961 speech, in ibid., 72.

7. As recounted by Mikoian at the June 1957 "anti-party" plenum in Moscow. "Poslednaia 'Antipartiinaia' Gruppa," third session, evening, 24 June 1957, *Istoricheskii Arkhiv* 4 (1993): 29.

8. *Khrushchev Remembers,* 456.

9. "Anlage 2 zum [Politbüro] Protokoll Nr. 24 vom 6.6.1961. Niederschift über die wichtigsten Gedanken, die Genosse Mikojan in einem Gespräch mit dem Genossen Leuschner in kleinstem Kreis . . . äusserte," SAPMO-BArch, ZPA, J IV 2/2/766, 1–3.

10. See Selvage's translation of the Polish minutes of the 10 November 1958 meeting, CWIHP *Bulletin,* 11 (winter 1998): 202.

11. Khrushchev's comments to Ulbricht, 30 November 1960, "Zapis' besedy tovarishcha N. S. Khrushcheva s tovarishchem V. Ul'brikhtom, 30 noiabria 1960 goda," AVPRF, F. 0742, Op. 6, Por. 4, Pap. 43, 13, English translation in Appendix A of Harrison, "Ulbricht and the Concrete 'Rose.'"

12. Ibid., 14, 16.

13. Kwizinskij, *Vor dem Sturm,* 170.

14. *Khrushchev Remembers: The Last Testament,* 389.

15. "Short Summary of the Talks with the GDR Party–Governmental Delegation on 9 June 1959," from AVPRF, F. 0742, Op. 4, Por. 33, Pap. 31, trans., annot., intro. Harrison, CWIHP, *Bulletin* 11 (Winter 1998): 208.

16. AVPRF, F. 06, Op. 12, Pap. 18, Por. 283.

17. USSR Council of Ministers Order "On Measures to Improve the Health of the Political Situation in the GDR," CWIHP, *Bulletin* 10 (March 1998): 81.

18. "Short Summary of the Talks with the GDR Party–Governmental Delegation on 9 June 1959," trans., annot., intro. Harrison, CWIHP, *Bulletin* 11 (Winter 1998): 207.

19. Such as Waltz, *Theory of International Politics*.

20. October 13–14, 1964, "Zapisi V. Malina na zasedanii Prezidiuma TsK KPSS," *Vestnik Arkhiva Prezidenta Rossiiskoi Federatsii* 2 (1998): 128; 135.

21. For Khrushchev's recollections of the Suez crisis and his role, see *Khrushchev Remembers: The Last Testament*, 430–37.

22. Polianskii's draft was subsequently toned down before Suslov delivered his speech, since Khrushchev was generally contrite in response to his colleagues' criticisms. "Doklad Prezidiuma TsK KPSS na oktiabr'skom Plenume TsK KPSS (variant)," *Vestnik Arkhiva Prezidenta Rossiiskoi Federatsii* 2 (1998): 112–13. The date of the document is noted as "no later than 14 October 1964."

23. Ibid., 113.

24. "Protokoll einer Unterredung zwischen L. I. Breschnew und Erich Honecker am 28. Juli 1970," SAPMO-BArch, ZPA, J NL 2/32; also published in Przybylski, *Tatort Politburo*, 284–85.

25. Sarotte, *Dealing with the Devil*, 168.

26. Weathersby, "Soviet Aims in Korea and the Origins of the Korean War, 1945–1950: New Evidence from Russian Archives"; idem, "'Should We Fear This?': Stalin and the Danger of War with America"; idem, her contributions in the CWIHP *Bulletin*; Gleijeses, *Conflicting Missions: Havana, Washington, and Africa, 1959–1976*; Jian, *Mao's China and the Cold War*; and Gaiduk, *The Soviet Union and the Vietnam War*.

27. A good beginning has been made by Adomeit, *Imperial Overstretch*; and McAdams, *Germany Divided*.

Note on Sources

The most important sources for this book are documentary records from former East German and Soviet archives. In Berlin I worked in the archives of the former East German ruling Socialist Unity Party at the *Stiftung Archive der Parteien und Massenorganisationen im Bundesarchiv, Zentrales Parteiarchiv* (SAPMO-BArch, ZPA) (see Harrison, "Inside the SED Archives"); the archives of the former East German Foreign Ministry, *Politisches Archiv des Auswärtigen Amtes, Aussenstelle Berlin, Ministerium für Auswärtige Angelegenheiten*; and the archives of the former East German secret police, the *Bundesbeauftragte für die Unterlagen des Staatssicherheitsdienstes der ehemaligen Deutschen Demokratische Republik* (BStU). In Moscow I consulted the Russian Foreign Ministry Archives, *Arkhiv Vneshnei Politiki Russkoi Federatsii* (AVPRF), and the post-1952 Central Committee Archives, the *Tsentr Khraneniia Sovremmenoi Dokumentatsii* (TsKhSD, recently renamed *Rossiiskii Gosudarstvennyi Arkhiv Noveishei Istorii*, [RGANI], the Russian State Archive of Contemporary History). These archives contain a treasure trove of documents about relations between the Soviet Union and East Germany at all levels and on all subjects. Working in two countries and five archives allowed me to check and compare sources.

Archival documents I have examined include letters and records of meetings between Nikita Khrushchev and Walter Ulbricht and other high ranking officials; Soviet and East German reports on and analyses of the political, economic, military, and social conditions in Germany and Berlin; Soviet and East German analyses of Soviet–East German relations; recommendations by Soviet officials for Soviet policy toward Germany; recommendations by East German officals for relations with the Soviets; preparatory materials by the Soviets and East Germans for their meetings; records from East German Politburo and Plenum meetings; telegrams from Ulbricht while in Moscow to his office and the Politburo in Berlin; some Soviet Plenum records and notes on Politburo meetings; some records of speeches at Warsaw Pact meetings; records of meetings between East German and Chinese officials; Soviet and East German analyses of Soviet-U.S. relations; Soviet Interior Ministry analyses of the East German refugee exodus; and detailed East German plans for stopping the refugee exodus.

Since the end of the cold war, access to the former GDR archives relevant to this book has become easier, while access to the former Soviet archives has become steadily more difficult after an initial "golden age" in 1992–93. The East German archives were integrated into the new united Germany's federal archival system over the course of several years. By the late 1990s, SAPMO-BArch, in particular, had computerized its finding aids and its system for requesting documents. The already excellent catalogue system there became even better and easier to use. The archivists there, however, were still streamlining the file identification system when I completed my work in SAPMO. Thus, some of the files I refer to in this book will have new numbers. When I started my work in the archives in Berlin in 1991–92, archivists in all three of the archives I used were still going through documents that had not been read or classified in a long time. In the MfAA archives, for example, the archivist told me he had to look through documents stuffed into big burlap bags in the basement to find things for me. It was not a speedy or easy process.

SAPMO-BArch is the most thoroughly acccessible archive that I have worked in. Justifiably, many people refer to it as a "gold mine" of information on the GDR and the cold war. Every aspect of East German domestic and foreign policy is covered there in depth, and the archive also contains copies of many documents from elsewhere, such as Moscow and Beijing, that are not accessible in Moscow or Beijing. Thus, in addition to being a fantastic source in its own right, SAPMO is also a "back door" to other archives. The stenographic protocols of the East German Politburo and Central Committee meetings, Ulbricht's personal files, and correspondence with the Soviets are among the many elucidating documents at SAPMO.

While there are some jewels to be found in the archive of the former East German Foreign Ministry, generally this archive does not have as interesting and high-level documents as SAPMO does, because the officials at the top of the party were making the key decisions, not the foreign ministry officials. The documents at MfAA are also generally less sophisticated than those at SAPMO, because the MfAA officials had much less training. Especially in the 1950s, the Foreign Ministry was still being formed, and the diplomats often sought detailed advice from the Soviets on how to set up and run it.

The Stasi files I used included protocols of internal Stasi meetings held by director Erich Mielke and others, files examining the views and mood of the GDR population, and regular reports on the state of affairs in various regions of the GDR. Particularly useful were reports from the Stasi's Central Analysis and Information Group (ZAIG) on topics including "Working Meetings of the Minister for State Security in 1961," "Collegium Meetings of the MfS in 1961," "Problems in Controlling the Sectoral Borders in Berlin," and "Report on the Carrying out of Measures for Securing the State Border, August 1961."

Archival work in Moscow has been more complicated than in Berlin. I first gained access to the Central Committee archive (then called TsKhSD) in the winter of 1992–93 as part of an agreement reached between the archive and the Washington-based Cold War International History Project (CWIHP). Financial help from CWIHP to the archive granted access to several scholars, including myself, who would present the results of their work at a conference in Moscow in January 1993 on the history of the cold war. These presentations were published in I. V. Gaiduk et al., *Kholodnaia Voina*, and several of the papers were also published in revised, expanded form as working papers with CWIHP. For a wonderful year before and after the conference, we basked in the glow of the open archival doors at TsKhSD. Most important for my research, I was able to work in the files of the General Department (*Obshchii Otdel'*) and the International Department, including their sections on Relations with Foreign Communist Parties (including East and West Germany), Relations with Communist Parties of Capitalist Countries (Sector on the FRG), and Relations with Communist Parties of Socialist Countries (Sector on the GDR). These files contained crucial correspondence and meetings between the Soviet and East German leaders.

In the summer of 1993, however, the doors to TsKhSD slammed shut. The main cause was an Australian scholar's finding and the publication of a document from TsKhSD indicating that the Soviets knew of many more American prisoners of war in North Vietnam in 1972 than they had let on (Kramer, "Archival Research."). This increased Russian-U.S. tensions and, combined with growing nationalism in Russia and anger with the West for its "shock therapy" advice on the Russian economy, made it much harder for Western scholars to gain access to interesting documents at TsKhSD. When they reopened the doors, the best files I had seen were now off limits to most people, including myself, as a sheepish archivist told me in the summer of 1996. Thus, I was not allowed to see documents I had already seen and taken extensive notes on.

Access to the former Soviet Foreign Ministry archives has been more consistent if less exciting. Although not everyone I know shared this experience, I gained access to the MID archives by a simple letter to the director. Within weeks of sending the letter, miraculously, I received a positive response from the director, V. Sokolov, in March 1992. I began working there in the summer of 1992. Combining MID documents with TsKhSD documents is very useful, since MID files contain many recommendations made to the Central Committee, drafts of important documents, and preparations for international negotiations, and TsKhSD documents show the outcome of the MID proposals and preparations. At MID I focused on the file groups on Germany (*Fond* 082), the GDR (*Fond* 0742), the FRG (*Fond* 0757), and Foreign Minister Molotov's office (*Fond* 06). Initially, I had access to MID's quarterly and yearly "surveys" (*otcheti*) on relations with the GDR and FRG, but then these were "reclassified." The ciphered cables between embassies and Moscow, unfortunately, remain classified. Documents in the Russian archives are categorized by collection or record group (*Fond* [F.] or *Referentura*), microfilm reel (*Rolik* [R.]), record series (*Opis'* [Op.]), folder (*Papka* [Pap]), file (*Portfel'* [Por.] or *Delo* [D.]), and volume (*Tom* [T.]).

Some of the key archives in Moscow never opened in a general way and remain closed for all but a handful of researchers, including the Presidential/Kremlin, KGB, and Military archives. The Russian archival situation is described by Patricia Grimsted ("Archives of Russia") and David Wolff ("Coming in from the Cold"). We have very little direct information, of the sort likely stored in the Kremlin's Presidential Archives, on relations among the top leaders and the kinds of policy disagreements they had. Only by gaining access to all of these files can we hope for a definitive account of the cold war. Yet even then, we would only have what was put down on paper *and* kept in the files. Some decisions were arrived at verbally, either in person or on the telephone. There are occasional references to these, especially to phone conversations, in the memoir literature and in some documents. These references help the researcher, but also make the researcher wonder just how many decisions or parts of decisions are not recorded in the accessible archives.

I have supplemented archival documents with interviews of former Soviet and East German officials and the memoir accounts of some of these officials, the most important of which are Aleksandrov-Agentov, Burlatsky, Chuev, Herrnstadt, Khrushchev, Kwizinskij, Mikoian, Schirdewan, Schenk, and Troyanovsky. In addition, I have drawn on books and articles published over the past decade on the basis of new archival evidence and the publication of documents by other researchers in journals. The main journals, particularly in Russia and Germany, which publish such documents are *Istochnik, Istoricheskii Arkhiv, Vestnik Arkhiva Prezidenta Rossiiskoi Federatsii, Novaia i Noveishaia Istoriia, Deutschland Archiv, Beiträge zur Geschichte der Arbeiterbewegung,* and *Vierteljahrsheft für Zeitgeschichte,* as well as the Working Papers and *Bulletins* of the American CWIHP. Many of these sources have not appeared in English until now. Combining these sources with English-language sources, such as the three volumes of the *Foreign Relations of the United States* series on the Berlin Crisis, has provided a very rich evidentiary base for this book.

Bibliography

ARCHIVES

Arkhiv Vneshnei Politiki Russkoi Federatsii (AVPRF, Archive of Foreign Policy of the Russian Federation), Moscow, 1952–1962: Fond 082, Germany; Fond 0742, the German Democratic Republic; Fond 0757, the Federal Republic of Germany; Fond 06, Foreign Minister Viacheslav Molotov's secretariat.

Der Bundesbeauftragte für die Unterlagen des Staatssicherheitsdienstes der ehemaligen Deutschen Demokratischen Republik (BStU, the Federal Commission for the Files of the State Security Service [the Stasi] of the former German Democratic Republic), Berlin, 1953–1961: ZAIG, Central Analysis and Information Group.

Ministerium für Auswärtige Angelegenheiten (MfAA, Ministry for Foreign Affairs), *Politisches Archive des Auswärtigen Amtes, Aussenstelle Berlin* (Political Archive of the Foreign Office, Berlin Branch [of records from the former GDR]), 1953–1962: Beijing Embassy; Budapest Embassy; Cadre Department; Conferences and Negotiations with GDR Participation; Department of General Issues; Department on West Germany; Department on the Soviet Union; First European Department; Main Department/I Secretariat; Moscow Embassy; Office of the Minister (Lothar Bolz, Johannes König, Sepp Schwab, Otto Winzer); Political Department (Sections on China, Hungary, Poland); State Secretary (Anton Ackermann, Otto Winzer); Warsaw Embassy.

Stiftung Archive der Parteien und Massenorganisationen im Bundesarchiv, Zentrales Parteiarchiv (SAPMO-BArch, ZPA, Foundation of the Archives of the Parties and Mass Organizations [of the former GDR] at the Federal Archive, Central Party Archive), Berlin, 1952–1962: Hermann Axen's Office; Central Committee (CC) Department of International Relations (Internal Party Archive)—Relations with the People's Republic of China, Relations with the Soviet Union; CC Department on Agriculture; CC Department on Party Organs; CC Department on Propaganda; CC Department of Security Issues; CC Plenum protocols (working and corrected); CC West Commission; Erich Honecker's Office; Hermann Matern's Office; Politburo Foreign Policy Commission; Politburo session protocols (working and corrected); Politburo resolutions (Internal Party Archive); Walter Ulbricht's office (Internal Party Archive); Personal files of Otto Grotewohl, Georg Handke, Wilhelm Pieck, Heinrich Rau, Otto Schön, Walter Ulbricht, Wilhelm Zaisser.

Tsentr Khraneniia Sovremmenoi Dokumentatsii (TsKhSD, Center for the Preservation of Contemporary Documentation [the former Soviet Central Committee Archive]) *Rossiiskii Gosudarstvennyi Arkhiv Noveishei Istorii*, [RGANI], the Russian State Archive of Contemporary History, Moscow, 1953–1962: Fond 5, Opis 28 (March 1953–February 1957), General Department, CPSU CC Department on Relations with Foreign Communist Parties, Sector on Relations with Germany, Austria and the Scandinavian Countries; Fond 5, Opis 50 (21 February 1958–1961), General Department, International Department of CPSU CC, Relations with Communist Parties of Capitalist Countries, and (after 14 February 1961) Sector on the Countries of Western Europe (FRG, Austria, Greece, Holland, and Luxemburg); Fond 5, Opis 30 (1954–1961), International Department, CPSU CC Secretariat; Fond 5, Opis 49 (21 February 1957–1961), CPSU CC Department on Relations with Communist Parties of Socialist Countries, Sector on the GDR; Fond 89, miscellaneous files.

Published Documents, Documentary Collections, and Other Primary Sources

Bekes, Csaba, Malcolm Byrne, and Christian F. Ostermann, eds. *The Hidden History of Hungary 1956: A Compendium of Declassified Documents.* Reader prepared for "Hungary and the World, 1956: The New Archival Evidence, An International Conference, Budapest, 26–29 September 1996."

Bonwetsch, Bernd, and A. M. Filitov, intro. and annot. "Iz stenogrammy soveshchaniia pervykh sekretarei TsK kommunisticheskikh i rabochikh partii stranychastnits Varshavskogo Dogovora po voprosam, sviazannym s podgotovkoi k zakliucheniiu Germanskogo mirnogo dogovora," Moskva, 4 avgusta 1961 g, Utrennee zasedanie, Vystuplenie tov. N. S. Khrushcheva. In "Kak primalos' reshenie o vozvedenii Berlinskoi steny." *Novaia i Noveishaia Istoriia* 2 (March–April 1999): 33–75.

———, introduction, annotation, and translation. "Beratung der Ersten Sekretäre der Zentralkomitees der kommunistischen und Arbeiterparteien der Teilnehmerländer des Warschauer Vertrages zu Fragen, die im Zusammenhang mit der Vorbereitung des Abschlusses eines Friedensvertrages mit Deutschland stehen." In "Chruschtschow und der Mauerbau: Die Gipfelkonferenz der Warschauer-Pakt-Staaten vom 3.–5. August 1961." *Vierteljahrshefte für Zeitgeschichte* 1 (2000): 155–98.

Bretschneider, Günther, Kurt Libera, and Rena Wilhelm. "Karl Schirdewan: Fraktionsmacherei oder gegen Ulbrichts Diktat? Eine Stellungnahme vom 1. Januar 1958." *Beiträge zur Geschichte der Arbeiterbewegung* 32, no. 4 (March 1990): 498–512.

Cold War International History Project (CWIHP) *Bulletin* and Working Papers. Washington, D.C.: The Woodrow Wilson International Center for Scholars.

"Delo Beriia: Plenum TsK KPSS Iiuli 1953 goda. Stenograficheskii Otchet." *Izvestiia TsK KPSS* 1, 2 (January and February 1991): 140–214, 147–208.

Embree, George D., ed. *The Soviet Union and the German Question: September 1958–June 1961.* The Hague: Martinus Nijhoff, 1963.

Gabert, Josef, et al., eds. *SED und Stalinismus: Dokumente aus dem Jahre 1956.* Berlin: Dietz Verlag, 1990.

Harrison, Hope M., introduction, annotation, and translation. "New Evidence on Khrushchev's 1958 Berlin Ultimatum," CWIHP, *Bulletin* 4 (Fall 1994): 35–39.

———, introduction, annotation, and translation. "The Berlin Crisis and the

Khrushchev-Ulbricht Summits in Moscow 9 and 18 June 1959," CWIHP, *Bulletin* 11 (Winter 1998): 204–17.

Hoffmann, Dierk, Karl-Heinz Schmidt, and Peter Skyba, eds. *Die DDR vor dem Mauerbau: Dokumente zur geschichte des anderen deutschen Staates, 1949– 1961*. Munich: R. Piper GmbH & Co. KG, 1993.

Institut für Internationale Beziehungen, Potsdam-Babelsberg, ed. *Geschichte der Aussenpolitik der DDR. Abriss*. Berlin: Staatsverlag der Deutschen Demokratischen Republik, 1984.

Izvestiia.

Khrushchev, Nikita S. *Khrushchev in America: Full texts of the speeches made by N. S. Khrushchev, Chairman of the Council of Ministers of the USSR, on his tour of the United States, September 15–27, 1958*. N.Y.: Crosscurrents Press, 1960.

———. *Khrushchev in New York: A documentary record of Nikita S. Khrushchev's trip to New York, September 19 to October 13, 1960, including all his speeches and proposals to the United Nations and major addresses and news conferences*. N.Y.: Crosscurrents Press, 1960.

———. *The Soviet Stand on Germany: 9 Documents Including Diplomatic Papers and Major Speeches by N. S. Khrushchev, Proposals for a German Peace Treaty*. N.Y.: Crosscurrents Press, 1961.

Kramer, Mark, introduction, translation and annotation. "The 'Malin Notes' on the Crises in Hungary and Poland, 1956." CWIHP, *Bulletin*, 8–9 (Winter 1996/1997): 385–410.

———. introduction, translation, and annotation. "Hungary and Poland, 1956. Khrushchev's CPSU CC Presidium Meeting on East European Crises, 24 October 1956." CWIHP, *Bulletin* 5 (Spring 1995): 1, 50–56.

Luniak, Petr, and Mikhal Reiman, introduction and annotation. Translation by Tamara Reiman. "1961, 1 iiunia, Praga. Zapis' besedy N. S. Khrushcheva s rukovodiashchimi deiateliami TsK KPCH i pravitel'stva Chekhoslovakii v Smolenitse pod Bratislavoi i tost Khrushcheva vo vremia obeda." In "'Lenin tozhe riskoval,' Nakanune vstrechi Khrushcheva i Kennedy v Vene v iiune 1961 g." *Istochnik* 3 (1998): 85–97.

Materialy XXII C"ezda KPSS. Moscow: State Publisher of Political Literature, 1961.

Mel'chin, S., Yu. V. Sigachev, and A. S. Stepanov. "Kak Snimali N. S. Khrushcheva: Materialy plenuma TsK KPSS. Oktiabr' 1964g." *Istoricheskii Arkhiv* 1 (1993): 3–19.

Ministerium für Auswärtige Angelegenheiten der DDR and Ministerium für Auswärtige Angelegenheiten der UdSSR, eds., *Beziehungen DDR-UdSSR, 1949–1955*. 2 Volumes. Berlin: Staatsverlag der Deutschen Demokratischen Republik, 1975.

Neues Deutschland.

New York Times.

Ostermann, Christian F., introduction and annotation. "'This Is Not A Politburo, But A Madhouse,' Soviet *Deutschlandpolitik* and the SED: New Evidence from Russian, German, and Hungarian Archives." CWIHP, *Bulletin* 10 (March 1998): 61–110.

———, editor and compiler. *Uprising in East Germany, 1953: The Cold War, the German Question, and the First Major Upheaval Behind the Iron Curtain.* Budapest and NY: Central European University Press, 2001.

Otto, Wilfriede. "Dokumente zur Auseinandersetzung in der SED 1953." *Beiträge zur Geschichte der Arbeiterbewegung* 32, no. 5 (1990): 655–72.

———. "Sowjetische Deutschlandnote 1952. Stalin und die DDR. Bisher unveröffentlichte handschriftliche Notizen Wilhelm Piecks." *Beiträge zur Geschichte der Arbeiterbewegung* 33, no. 3 (1991): 374–89.

———. "13. August 1961—eine Zäsur in der europäischen Nachkriegsgeschichte." *Beiträge zur Geschichte der Arbeiterbewegung* 1 (1997): 40–74 and 2 (1997): 55–92.

"Posledniaia 'Antipartiinaia' Gruppa." *Istoricheskii Arkhiv* 4 (1993): 4–82.

Pravda.

Scherstjanoi, Elke. "'Wollen wir den Sozialismus?' Dokumente aus der Sitzung des Politbüros des ZK der SED am 6. Juni 1953." *Beiträge zur Geschichte der Arbeiterbewegung* 33, no. 5 (1991): 658–80.

Schirdewan, Karl. "Eine Stellungnahme vom 1. Januar 1958." *Beiträge zur Geschichte der Arbeiterbewegung* 32, no. 4 (March 1990): 498–512. Edited by Günther Bretschneider, Kurt Libera, and Rena Wilhelm.

Seattle Times.

Selvage, Douglas, introduction, translation, and annotation. "Khrushchev's November 1958 Berlin Ultimatum: New Evidence from the Polish Archives." CWIHP, *Bulletin* 11 (Winter 1998): 200–203.

———, introduction, translation, and annotation. "The End of the Berlin Crisis, 1961–62: New Evidence from the Polish and East German Archives." CWIHP, *Bulletin* 11 (Winter 1998): 218–29.

Steury, Donald P. *On the Front Lines of the Cold War: Documents on the Intelligence War in Berlin, 1946 to 1961.* Washington, D.C.: CIA History Staff, Center for the Study of Intelligence, 1999.

Stöckigt, Rolf. "Ein Dokument von grosser historischer Bedeutung vom Mai 1953." *Beiträge zur Geschichte der Arbeiterbewegung* 32, no. 5 (1990): 648–54.

"Takovy, tovarishchi, fakty," and "Zapisi V. Malina na zasedanii Prezidiuma TsK KPSS," 13–14 October 1964. *Vestnik Arkhiva Prezidenta Rossiiskoi Federatsii* 2 (1998): 101–43.

United States Department of State. *Documents on Germany, 1944–1985.* Publication 9446. Washington, D.C.: Government Printing Office (GPO).

———. *Foreign Relations of the United States, 1958–1960. Vol. VIII. Berlin Crisis, 1958–1959.* Washington, D.C.: GPO, 1993.

———. *Foreign Relations of the United States, 1958–1960. Vol. IX. Berlin Crisis, 1959–1960.* Washington, D.C.: GPO, 1993.

———. *Foreign Relations of the United States, 1961–1963. Vol. XIV. Berlin Crisis, 1961–1962.* Washington, D.C.: GPO, 1993.

———. *Foreign Relations of the United States, 1961–1963. Vol. VI. Kennedy-Khrushchev Exchanges.* Washington, D.C.: GPO, 1996.

———. *The Declassified Documents Catalogue and Microfiche.* Woodbridge, Conn.: 1978.

Vodop'ianova, Z. K., and V. M. Zubok. "'Okazat' nezamedlitel'nuiu pomoshch.' Postanovleniia Prezidiuma TsK KPSS ob ekonomicheskikh sviaziakh s GDR 1961 g." *Istoricheskii Arkhiv* 1 (1998): 36–62.

XX C"ezd kommunisticheskoi partii sovetskogo soiuza: stenographicheskii otchet, 14–25 fevralia 1956 goda. Moscow: State Publisher of Political Literature, 1956.

"Zapis' besed pervogo sekretaria TsK KPSS tov. N. S. Khrushcheva s predsedatelem TsK PTV tov. Ho Shi Minom, Pitsunda, 17.8.1961g." In "'Ia veriu v velichie starshego brata.' Besedy N. S. Khrushcheva s Kho Shi Minom." *Istochnik* 2, (1998): 76–85.

INTERVIEWS

Bezymensky, Lev, Russian expert on Germany and journalist (interview by author, 25 October 1990, Moscow).

Brie, Horst, former counselor in East German embassy in Peking (interview by author, 1 June 1992, Pankow Nieder-Schönhausen).

Dachishev, Vyacheslav, Russian expert on Germany (interview by author, 9 November 1990, Berlin).

Eberlein, Werner, Ulbricht's Russian interpreter (interview by Wilfriede Otto). "Wortlaut eines Gesprächs von Wilfriede Otto mit Werner Eberlein am 5. September 1996 über die Beratung der Ersten Sekretäre des ZK der kommunistischen und Arbeiterparteien der Staaten des Warschauer Vertrages vom 3. bis 5. August 1961 in Moskau." *Beiträge zur Geschichte der Arbeiterbewegung* 2 (1997): 85–89.

Falin, Valentin, former Soviet ambassador to West Germany (interview by author, 22 September 1993, Bochum, Germany).

Galkin, Alexander A., Russian expert on Germany (interview by author, 23 October 1990, Moscow).

Kremer, Ilya, Russian expert on Germany (interviews by author, 8 and 29 October 1990, Moscow).

Krüger, Wolfgang, former East German expert on China (interview by author, 6 March 1992, Berlin).

Kvitsinky, Yuli, former attaché in Soviet embassy in East Berlin (interview by author, 26 October 1992, Moscow).

Malenkov, Andrei, son of Georgi Malenkov (interview by Dmitrii Varskii), "Skhvatka." *Vostochnii Ekspress* 16 (1991): 8–9.

Melnikov, David, Russian expert on Germany (interviews by author, 15 and 26 October 1990, Moscow).

Schirdewan, Karl, former East German Politburo member (interviews by author, 11 March, 22 April, and 21 September 1992, and 2 October 1993, Potsdam, Germany). "Die Führung lag in Moskau." Michael Schumann und Wolfgang Dressen im Gespräch mit Karl Schirdewan. *Niemandsland. Tugendterror* 4 (October/November 1992): 305–26.

Semenov, Vladimir, former Soviet ambassador to East Germany (interviews by author, 14 September 1992, by phone, and 30 September 1992, in person, Cologne).

Sukhanov, Dmitri, former aid to Georgi Malenkov (interview by Lev Bezymen-sky), *New Times* 48 (1991): 32–34.

Memoirs, Books, Articles, and Unpublished Papers

Adenauer, Konrad. *Erinnerungen, 1955–1959*. Stuttgart: Deutsche Verlagsan-stalt, 1967.

———. *Erinnerungen, 1959–1963*. Stuttgart: Deutsche Verlagsanstalt, 1968.

Adomeit, Hannes. *Soviet Risk-Taking and Crisis Behavior: A Theoretical and Empirical Analysis*. Boston: George Allen and Unwin, 1982.

———. *Imperial Overstretch: Germany in Soviet Policy from Stalin to Gorba-chev*. Baden-Baden: Nomos Verlagsgesellschaft, 1998.

Aleksandrov-Agentov, A. M. *Ot Kollontai do Gorbacheva*. Moscow: Interna-tional Relations, 1994.

Allison, Graham, and Philip Zelikow. *Essence of Decision: Explaining the Cuban Missile Crisis*, 2nd ed. N.Y.: Addison-Wesley Educational Publishers, 1999.

Ash, Timothy Garton. *In Europe's Name: Germany and the Divided Continent*. N.Y.: Random House, 1993.

———. *The Magic Lantern: The Revolution of '89 Witnessed in Warsaw, Buda-pest, Berlin and Prague*. N.Y.: Vintage Books, 1993.

Axen, Hermann. *Ich War ein Diener der Partei*. Berlin: edition ost, 1996.

Bachrach, Peter, and Morton S. Baratz. "Two Faces of Power." *American Politi-cal Science Review* LVI, no. 4 (December 1962): 947–52.

———. "Decisions and Nondecisions: An Analytical Framework." *American Political Science Review* LVII, no. 3 (September 1963): 632–42.

Bacharach, Samuel B., and Edward J. Lawler. *Bargaining: Power, Tactics, and Outcomes*. Washington, D.C.: Jossey-Bass Publishers, 1981.

Badstübner, Rolf. "Zum Problem der historischen Alternativen im ersten Nach-kriegsjahrzehnt. Neue Quellen zur Deutschlandpolitik von KPdSU und SED." *Beiträge zur Geschichte der Arbeiterbewegung* 33, no. 5 (1991): 579–92.

Baldwin, David. "Power Analysis and World Politics." *World Politics* 31, no. 2 (January 1979): 161–94.

———. "Interdependence and Power. A Conceptual Analysis." *International Organization* 34, no. 4 (Autumn 1980): 471–506.

Bar-Siman-Tov, Yaacov. "Alliance Strategy: U.S.–Small Allies Relationships." *Journal of Strategic Studies* 3, no. 2 (September 1980): 202–16.

Baras, Victor. "Beria's Fall and Ulbricht's Survival." *Soviet Studies* XXVII, no. 3 (July 1975): 381–95.

Baring, Arnulf. *Uprising in East Germany: June 17, 1953*. Translated by Gerald Onn, with introduction by David Schoenbaum, and foreword by Richard Lo-wenthal. Ithaca: Cornell University Press, 1972.

Barth, Berndt-Rainer, Christoph Links, Helmut Müller-Enbergs, and Jan Wiel-gohs, eds. *Wer war Wer in der DDR.: Ein biographisches Handbuch*. Berlin: Fischer Taschenbuch Verlag, 1995.

Bayer, Wolfgang. "Geheimoperation Fürstenberg." *Der Spiegel* 3 (17 January 2000): 42–46.

Bekes, Csaba. "The 1956 Hungarian Revolution and World Politics." CWIHP, Working Paper No. 16 (September 1996).

———— and Janos Rainer. "The 1956 Hungarian Revolution." *Fact Sheets on Hungary* 6 (1996). Budapest: Ministry of Foreign Affairs.

Ben-Zvi, Abraham. *The United States and Israel: The Limits of the Special Relationship*. N.Y.: Columbia University Press, 1993.

Bernd-Rainer, Barth, et. al., eds. *Wer war Wer in der DDR: Ein biographisches Handbuch*. Berlin: Fischer Taschenbuch Verlag, 1996.

Beschloss, Michael R. *Mayday: The U-2 Affair: The Untold Story of the Greatest US-USSR Spy Scandal*. N.Y.: Harper & Row, Publishers, 1986.

————. *The Crisis Years: Kennedy and Khrushchev 1960–1963*. N.Y.: Harper-Collins Publishers, 1991.

Betts, Richard. *Nuclear Blackmail and Nuclear Balance*. Washington, D.C.: The Brookings Institution, 1987.

Bischof, Günter. *Austria in the First Cold War, 1945–55: The Leverage of the Weak*. N.Y.: St. Martin's Press, 1999.

Bischof, Günter, and Saki Dockrill, eds. *Cold War Respite: The Geneva Summit of 1955*. Baton Rouge: Louisiana University Press, 2000.

Bonwetsch, Bernd, and A. M. Filitov, "Kak prinimalos' reshenie o vozvedennii Berlinskoi steny," *Novaia i Noveishaia Istoriia* 2 (March–April 1999): 53–75.

————. "Chruschtschow und der Mauerbau: Die Gipfelkonferenz der Warschauer-Pakt-Staaten vom 2.–5. August 1961." *Vierteljahrshefte für Zeitgeschichte* 1 (2000): 155–98.

Brandt, Heinz. *The Search for a Third Way: My Path Between East and West*. Translated by Salvator Attanasio. Garden City, N.Y.: Doubleday & Company, 1970.

Brandt, Willy. *People and Politics: The Years 1960–1975*. Translated by J. Maxwell Brownjohn. Boston: Little Brown and Company, 1978.

Breslauer, George. *Khrushchev and Brezhnev As Leaders: Building Authority in Soviet Politics*. Boston: George Allen and Unwin, 1982.

Bundesministerium für Gesamtdeutsche Fragen, ed. *SBZ von A bis Z: Ein Taschen- und Nachschlagebuch über die Sowjetische Besatzungszone Deutschlands*. Bonn: Deutscher Bundesverlag, 1963.

Bundy, McGeorge. *Danger and Survival: Choices about the Bomb in the First Fifty Years*. N.Y.: Random House, 1988.

Burlatsky, Fedor. *Khrushchev and the First Russian Spring: The Era of Khrushchev Through the Eyes of His Advisor*. Translated by Daphne Skillen. N.Y.: Charles Scribner's Sons, 1991.

Burr, William. "New Sources on the Berlin Crisis, 1958–1962." CWIHP, *Bulletin* 2 (Fall 1992): 21–24, 32.

————. "Dwight D. Eisenhower and American Policy During the Berlin Crisis, 1958–1960." Unpublished paper presented to the Nuclear History Program's authors' conference, for the book project "New Perspectives on the Berlin Crisis." Woodrow Wilson Center, Washington, D.C. (20–21 May 1993).

————. "Avoiding the Slippery Slope: The Eisenhower Administration and the Berlin Crisis, November 1958–January 1959." *Diplomatic History* 18, no. 2 (Spring 1994): 177–205.

Cate, Curtis. *The Ides of August: The Berlin Crisis, 1961*. N.Y.: M. Evans and Company, 1978.

Catudal, Honoré M. *Kennedy and the Berlin Wall Crisis: A Case Study in U.S. Decision-Making*. Berlin: Berlin Verlag, 1980.

Childs, David. *The GDR: Moscow's German Ally*. Boston: George Allen and Unwin, 1983.

Chuev, Feliks. *Sto sorok besed s Molotovym*. Moscow: Terra, 1991.

Ciesla, Burghard, Michael Lemke, and Thomas Lindenberger. *Sterben für Berlin? Die Berliner Krisen 1948:1958*. Berlin: Metropol, 2000.

Deutscher Bundestag. Protokoll der 46. Sitzung der Enquete-Kommission "Aufarbeitung von Geschichte und Folgen der SED-Diktatur in Deutschland." Public hearing on "Internationale Rahmenbedingungen der Deutschlandpolitik 1949–1989," 12 October 1993.

Diedrich, Torsten. *Der 17. Juni 1953 in der DDR: Bewaffnete Gewalt gegen das Volk*. Berlin: Dietz Verlag GmbH, 1991.

Dower, John W. "The Superdomino in Postwar Asia: Japan in and out of the Pentagon Papers." Chap. 8 in The Senator Gravel Edition of *The Pentagon Papers: Critical Essays Edited by Noam Chomsky and Howard Zinn and an Index to Volumes One–Four. Volume V*. Boston: Beacon Press, 1972, 101–142.

Eisenberg, Carolyn. *Drawing the Line: The American Decision to Divide Germany, 1944–1947*. N.Y.: Cambridge University Press, 1996.

Eisenhower, Dwight D. *The White House Years: Waging Peace*. N.Y.: Doubleday and Company, 1965.

Epley, William W., ed., *International Cold War Military Records and History: Proceedings of the International Conference on Cold War Military Records and History Held in Washington, D.C., 21–26 March 1994*. Office of the Secretary of Defense: Washington, D.C. 1996.

Esslin, M. J. "East Germany: Peking-Pankow Axis?" *The China Quarterly* 3 (July–Sept. 1960): 85–88.

Fabritzek, Uwe G. "Die DDR und der Konflikt zwischen Moskau und Peking." *Deutschland Archiv* 8 (August 1972): 828–36.

Falin, Valentin. *Politische Erinnerungen*. Translated by Heddy Pross-Weerth. Munich: Droemer Knaur, 1993.

Farquharson, John. "The 'Essential Division': Britain and the Partition of Germany, 1945–1949," *German History* IX (February 1991): 23–45.

Filitov, A. M. *Germanskii Vopros: ot raskola k ob'edineniiu*. Moscow: International Relations, 1993.

Flocken, Jan v., and Michael F. Scholz, *Ernst Wollweber: Saboteur-Minister-Unperson*. Berlin: Aufbau Verlag, 1994.

Fodor, Neil. *The Warsaw Treaty Organization: A Political and Organizational Analysis*. London: The Macmillan Press Ltd, 1990.

Fox, Annette Baker. *The Power of Small States: Diplomacy in World War II*. Chicago: University of Chicago Press, 1959.

Frank, Mario. *Walter Ulbricht: Eine Deutsche Biographie*. Berlin: Siedler Verlag, 2001.

Frei, Otto. "Die Beziehungen zwischen Pankow und Peking." *Osteuropa* 7–8 (1961): 541–44.

Fursenko, Aleksandr. "Kak Byla Postroena Berlinskaia Stena." *Istoricheskie Zapiski* (Moscow) 4 (2001): 73–90.

Fursenko, Aleksandr, and Timothy Naftali. *"One Hell of a Gamble:" Khrushchev, Castro, and Kennedy, 1958–1964*. N.Y.: W.W. Norton & Company, 1997.

Gaddis, John Lewis. "The Tragedy of Cold War History: Reflections on Revisionism." *Foreign Affairs* 73, no. 1 (January/February 1994): 142–54.

———. *We Now Know: Rethinking Cold War History*. Oxford, England: Clarendon Press, 1997.

Gaiduk, Ilya V. "The Vietnam War and Soviet-American Relations, 1964–1973: New Russian Evidence." CWIHP, *Bulletin* 6/7 (Winter 1995/1996): 232, 250–58.

———. *The Soviet Union and the Vietnam War*. Chicago: Ivan R. Dee, 1996.

Gaiduk, Ilya V., M. K. Korobochkin, M. M. Narinsky, and A. O. Chubarian, eds., *Kholodnaia Voina: Novye Podkhody, Novye Dokumenty*. Moscow: Russian Academy of Sciences, Institute of Universal History, 1995.

Garthoff, Raymond. "Berlin 1961: The Record Corrected." *Foreign Policy* 84 (Fall 1991): 142–56.

———. "Some Observations on Using the Soviet Archives." *Diplomatic History* 2, no. 2 (Spring 1997): 243–57.

Gearson, John P. S. *Harold Macmillan and the Berlin Wall Crisis, 1958–62: The Limits of Interests and Force*. N.Y.: St. Martin's Press, Inc., 1998.

Gearson, John P. S., and Kori Schake, eds. *The Berlin Wall Crisis: Perspectives on Cold War Alliances*. London: Palgrave, 2002.

Gelb, Norman. *The Berlin Wall: Kennedy, Khrushchev, and a Showdown in the Heart of Europe*. N.Y.: Dorset Press, 1986.

George, Alexander L. *Avoiding War: Problems of Crisis Management*. Boulder, Colo.: Westview Press, 1991.

George, Alexander L., and Richard Smoke. "The Berlin Deadline Crisis, 1958–1959" and "The Berlin Aide-Mémoire Crisis, 1961." Chaps. in *Deterrence in American Foreign Policy*. N.Y.: Columbia University Press, 1974.

Gleijeses, Piero. *Conflicting Missions: Havana, Washington, and Africa, 1959–1976*. Chapel Hill: University of North Carolina Press, 2002.

Goldgeier, James M. *Leadership Style and Soviet Foreign Policy: Stalin, Khrushchev, Brezhnev, Gorbachev*. Baltimore: Johns Hopkins University Press, 1994.

Gould-Davies, Nigel. "Rethinking the Role of Ideology in International Politics During the Cold War," *Journal of Cold War Studies* 1, no. 1 (Winter 1999): 90–109.

Grieder, Peter. *The East German Leadership, 1946–1973*. N.Y.: Manchester University Press, 1999.

Grimsted, Patricia Kennedy. "Archives of Russia Seven Years After: 'Purveyors of Sensations' or 'Shadows Cast to the Past'?" CWIHP, Working Paper No. 20 (September 1998).

Grinevskij, Oleg. *Tauwetter: Entspannung, Krisen und neue Eiszeit*. Translated by Konrad Fuhrmann. Berlin: Siedler Verlag, 1996.

Gromyko, Andrei. *Memories*. Translated by Harold Shukman. London: Hutchinson, 1989.

Handel, Michael I. "Does the Dog Wag the Tail or Vice Versa? Patron-Client Relations." *The Jerusalem Journal of International Relations* 6, no. 2 (Winter 1982): 24–35.

———. *Weak States in the International System*. London: Frank Cass, 1990.

Hanreider, Wolfram F. *Germany, America, Europe: Forty Years of German Foreign Policy*. New Haven: Yale University Press, 1989.

Harrison, Hope M. "Inside the SED Archives: A Researcher's Diary." CWIHP, *Bulletin* 2 (Fall 1992): 20, 28–32.

———. "Ulbricht and the Concrete 'Rose': New Archival Evidence on the Dynamics of Soviet–East German Relations and the Berlin Crisis, 1958–1961." CWIHP, Working Paper No. 5. (May 1993).

———. "The Bargaining Power of Weaker Allies in Bipolarity and Crisis: The Dynamics of Soviet–East German Relations, 1953–1961." Ph.D. diss. Ann Arbor: University Microfilms International, 1994.

———. "Soviet–East German Relations after World War II." *Problems of Post-Communism* no. 5 (September–October 1995): 9–17.

———. "Driving the Soviets Up the Wall: A Super-Ally, a Superpower, and the Building of the Berlin Wall, 1958–61." *Cold War History* 1, no. 1 (August 2000): 53–74.

Haslam, Jonathan. "Russian Archival Revelations and Our Understanding of the Cold War," *Diplomatic History* 21, no. 2 (Spring 1997): 217–28.

Heidemeyer, Helge. *Flucht und Zuwanderung aus der SBZ/DDR, 1945/1940–1961: Die Flüchtlingspolitik der Bundesrepublik Deutschland bis zum Bau der Berliner Mauer*. Dusseldorf: Droste Verlag, 1994.

Hershberg, James. *James B. Conant: Harvard to Hiroshima and the Making of the Nuclear Age*. N.Y.: Knopf, 1993.

——— in Odd Arne Westad, ed., *Reviewing the Cold War: Approaches, Interpretations, Theory*. London: Frank Cass Publishers, 2000, 303–325.

Hertle, Hans-Hermann. *Chronik des Mauerfalls: Die dramatischen Ereignisse um den 9. November 1989*. Berlin: Christoph Links Verlag, 1996.

———. "The Fall of the Wall: The Unintended Self-Dissolution of East Germany's Ruling Regime." CWIHP, *Bulletin* 12/13 (Fall/Winter 2001): 131–64.

Hertle, Hans-Hermann, Konrad H. Jarausch, and Christoph Klessmann. *Mauerbau und Mauerfall: Ursaschen—Verlauf—Auswirkungen*. Berlin: Christoph Links Verlag, 2002.

Hoffman, Stanley. *Gulliver's Troubles, or the Setting of American Foreign Policy*. N.Y.: McGraw-Hill Book Company, 1968.

Holden, Gerard. *The Warsaw Pact: Soviet Security and Bloc Politics*. N.Y.: Basil Blackwell Ltd., 1989.

Holloway, David. *The Soviet Union and the Arms Race*. 2nd ed. New Haven: Yale University Press, 1984.

Holsti, Ole R., P. Terrence Hopmann, and John D. Sullivan. *Unity and Disinte-*

gration in International Alliances: Comparative Studies. N.Y.: John Wiley & Sons, 1973.

Honecker, Erich. *From My Life.* N.Y.: Pergamon Press, 1981.

Horelick, Arnold L., and Myron Rush. *Strategic Power and Soviet Foreign Policy.* Chicago: University of Chicago Press, 1965, 1966.

Ihme-Tuchel, Beate. *Das "nördliche Dreieck." Die Beziehungen zwischen der DDR, der Tschechoslowakei und Polen in den Jahren 1954 bis 1962.* Cologne: Verlag Wissenschaft und Politik, 1994.

———. *Die DDR.* Darmstadt, Germany: Wissenschaftliche Buchgesellschaft, 2002.

Iklé, Fred Charles. *How Nations Negotiate.* N.Y.: Harper & Row Publishers, 1964.

Jänicke, Martin. *Der Dritte Weg: Die antistalinistische Opposition gegen Ulbricht seit 1953.* Cologne: Neuer Deutscher Verlag, 1964.

Jervis, Robert. "Hypotheses on Misperception." *World Politics* 20 (April 1968): 454–79.

———. *Perceptions and Misperceptions in International Politics.* Princeton: Princeton University Press, 1976.

———. "Cooperation under the Security Dilemma." *World Politics* 30 (January 1978): 167–214.

Jian, Chen. "Deng Xiaoping, Mao's 'Continuous Revolution,' and the Path toward the Sino-Soviet Split: A Rejoinder." CWIHP, *Bulletin* 10 (March 1998): 162–82.

———. *Mao's China and the Cold War.* Chapel Hill: University of North Carolina Press, 2001.

Kapferer, Norbert. "'Nostalgia' in Germany's New Federal States As a Political and Cultural Phenomenon of the Transformation Process." In Howard Williams, Colin Wight, and Norbert Kapferer, *Political Thought and German Reunification: The New German Ideology?* N.Y.: Palgrave, 2000, 28–40.

Keohane, Robert O. "The Big Influence of Small Allies." *Foreign Policy* 2 (Spring 1971): 161–82.

Khrushchev, Nikita S. *Khrushchev Remembers.* With an introduction, commentary, and notes by Edward Crankshaw. Translated and edited by Strobe Talbott. Boston: Little, Brown, 1970.

———. *Khrushchev Remembers: The Last Testament.* With a foreword by Edward Crankshaw and an introduction by Jerrold L. Schecter. Translated and edited by Strobe Talbott. Boston: Little, Brown, 1974.

———. *Khrushchev Remembers: The Glasnost Tapes.* With a foreword by Strobe Talbott. Translated and edited by Jerrold L. Schecter with Vyacheslav V. Luchkov. Boston: Little, Brown and Company, 1990.

———. "Aktsii." In V. F. Nekrasov, ed. *Beria: Konets kar'eru.* Moscow: Politizdat, 1991: 262–81.

Khrushchev, Sergei. *Nikita Khrushchev: Krizisy i Rakety. Vzgliad iznutri*, Tom. 1–2. Moscow: Novosti, 1994.

———. *Nikita Khrushchev and the Creation of a Superpower.* Translated by Shirley Benson. University Park: Pennsylvania State University Press, 2000.

Kircheisen, Inge, ed. *Tauwetter ohne Frühling: Das Jahr 1956 im Spiegel blockinterner Wandlungen und internationaler Krisen.* Berlin: Berliner Debatte, 1995.

Klein, Thomas, Wilfriede Otto, and Peter Grieder. *Visionen: Repression und Opposition in der SED (1949–1989),* Teil 1–2. Frankfurt/Oder: Frankfurter Oder Editionen, 1996.

Klingemann, Hans-Dieter, and Richard I. Hofferbert, "Germany: A New 'Wall in the Mind'?" *Journal of Democracy 75,* no. 1 (January 1994): 30–43.

Knight, Amy. *Beria: Stalin's First Lieutenant.* Princeton: Princeton University Press, 1993.

Kopstein, Jeffrey. *The Politics of Economic Decline in East Germany, 1945–1989.* Chapel Hill: University of North Carolina Press, 1997.

Kornienko, G. M. "'Upushchennaia Vozmozhnost': Vstrecha N. S. Khrushcheva i Dj. Kennedi v Vene v 1961g." *Novaia i Noveishaia Istoriia* 2 (1992): 97–106.

Kramer, Mark. "Archival Research in Moscow: Progress and Pitfalls." CWIHP, *Bulletin* 3 (Fall 1993): 1, 18–39.

———. "New Light Shed on 1956 Soviet Decision to Invade Hungary." *Transition* 2, no. 23 (15 November 1996): 35–40.

———. "New Evidence on Soviet Decision-Making and the 1956 Polish and Hungarian Crises." CWIHP, *Bulletin* 8–9 (Winter 1996/1997): 358–84.

———. "The Early Post-Stalin Succession Struggle and Upheavals in East-Central Europe: Internal-External Linkages in Soviet Policy Making," Parts 1–3. *Journal of Cold War Studies* I, nos. 1–3 (Winter, Spring, Fall 1999): 3–66.

Krisch, Henry. *The German Democratic Republic: The Search for Identity.* Boulder: Westview Press, 1985.

Kroll, Hans. *Lebenerinnerungen eines Botschafters.* Cologne and Berlin: Kiepenheuer & Witsch, 1967.

Krüger, Joachim. "Die Volksrepublik China in der Aussenpolitischen Strategie der DDR (1949–1989)." In Heng-yue Kuo, Leutner, Mechthild, eds., *Deutschland und China: Beiträge des 2. Internationalen Symposiums zur Geschichte der deutsch-chinesischen Beziehungen.* Munich: Minerva Press, 1994, 43–58.

Kwizinskij, Julij A. *Vor dem Sturm: Erinnerungen eines Diplomaten.* Berlin: Siedler Verlag, 1993.

Lapp, Peter Joachim. *Gefechtsdienst im Frieden: Das Grenzregime der DDR, 1945–1990.* Bonn: Gernard & Gräfe Verlag, 1999.

Larres, Klaus. "Neutralisierung oder Westintegration; Churchill, Adenauer, die USA und der 17. Juni 1953," *Deutschland Archiv* 45, no. 6 (1993): 568–83.

Larres, Klaus, and Kenneth A. Osgood, eds. *An Early End to the Cold War? The East-West Conflict in the Aftermath of Stalin's Death.* Lanham, Md.: Rowman and Littlefield, 2003.

Laufer, Jochen. "Die UdSSR und die Ursprunge der Berlin-Blockade, 1944–1948." *Deutschland Archiv* 31, no. 4 (1998): 564–79.

Lebow, Richard Ned. *Between Peace and War: The Nature of International Crisis.* Baltimore: Johns Hopkins University Press, 1981.

Leffler, Melvyn P. "Inside Enemy Archives: The Cold War Reopened." *Foreign Affairs* 75, no. 4 (July/Aug. 1996): 120–35.

———. "The Cold War: What Do 'We Now Know'?" *American Historical Review* 104, no. 2 (April 1999): 501–24.

Lemke, Michael. "Die deutschlandpolitischen Handlungsspielräume der SED innerhalb der sowjetischen Deutschlandpolitik der Jahre 1949–1955." In Gustav Schmidt, ed., *Ost-West Beziehungen: Konfrontation und Détente, 1945–1989*, II. Bochum: Universitätsverlag Dr. N. Brockmeyer, 1993, 305–332.

———. *Die Berlinkrise 1958 bis 1963: Interessen und Handlungsspielräume im Ost-West-Konflikt*. Berlin: Akademie Verlag, 1995.

———. "Sowjetische Interessen und ostdeutscher Wille: divergenzen zwischen den Berlinkonzepten von SED und UdSSR in der Expositionsphase der zweiten Berlinkrise." In Burghard Ciesla, Michael Lemke, and Thomas Lindenberger, *Sterben für Berlin? Die Berliner Krisen 1948: 1958*. Berlin: Metropol Verlag, 2000, 203–219.

———. *Einheit oder Sozialismus?: Die Deutschlandpolitik der SED 1949–1961*. Cologne: Böhlau Verlag, 2001.

Leonhard, Wolfgang. *Child of the Revolution*. Translated by C. M. Woodhouse. Chicago: Henry Regnery Company, 1958.

Linden, Carl A. *Khrushchev and the Soviet Leadership, 1957–1964*. Baltimore: Johns Hopkins University Press, 1966.

Lippmann, Heinz. *Honecker and the New Politics of Europe*. Translated by Helen Sebba. N.Y.: The Macmillan Company, 1972.

Liska, George. *Nations in Alliance*. Baltimore: Johns Hopkins University Press, 1968.

Lockhart, Charles. *Bargaining in International Conflicts*. N.Y.: Columbia University Press, 1979.

Loth, Wilfried. *Stalin's Unwanted Child: The Soviet Union, the German Question, and the Founding of the GDR*. Translated by Robert F. Hogg. N.Y.: St. Martin's Press, Inc., 1998.

Lundestad, Geir. "Empire by Invitation? The United States and Western Europe, 1945–1952." *Journal of Peace Research* 23, no. 3 (1986): 263–77.

———. *The American "Empire."* Oxford and Oslo: Oxford University Press and Norwegian University Press, 1990.

Mackintosh, J. M. *Strategy and Tactics of the Soviet Union*. London: Oxford University Press, 1963.

Major, Patrick. "Torschlusspanik und Mauerbau: 'Republikflucht' als Symptom der zweiten Berlinkrise." In Burghard Ciesla, Michael Lemke, and Thomas Lindenberger, *Sterben für Berlin? Die Berliner Krisen 1948: 1958*. Berlin: Metropol Verlag, 2000, 221–43.

Malenkov, Andrei. "Protivoborstvo." *Zhurnalist* 2 (February 1991): 60–66.

Marchio, Jim. "From Revolution to Evolution: The Eisenhower Administration and Eastern Europe." Unpublished paper presented to the Annual conference of the Society of Historians of American Foreign Relations (SHAFR) at the University of Virginia, Charlottesville, V.A, (17–20 June 1993).

Mastny, Vojtech. *The Cold War and Soviet Insecurity: The Stalin Years*. N.Y.: Oxford University Press, 1996.

Mauer, Victor. "Macmillan und die Berlin-Krise 1958/59." *Vierteljahrshefte für Zeitgeschichte* 2 (April 1996): 229–56.

May, Ernest R., and Philip Zelikow. *The Kennedy Tapes: Inside the White House During the Cuban Missile Crisis.* Cambridge: Harvard University Press, 1997.

McAdams, A. James. *Germany Divided: From the Wall to Reunification.* Princeton: Princeton University Press, 1993.

———. *Judging the Past in Unified Germany.* Princeton: Princeton University Press, 2001.

McMahon, Robert J. "United States Cold War Strategy in South Asia: Making a Military Commitment to Pakistan, 1947–1954." *Journal of American History* 75, no. 3 (1988): 812–40.

———. *The Cold War on the Periphery: The United States, India and Pakistan.* N.Y.: Columbia University Press, 1994.

Meissner, Werner, with Anja Feege, eds. *Die DDR und China 1949 bis 1990.* Berlin: Akademie Verlag, 1995.

Menning, Bruce W. "The Berlin Crisis from the Perspective of the Soviet General Staff." In William W. Epley, ed., *International Cold War Military Records and History: Proceedings of the International Conference on Cold War Military Records and History Held in Washington, D.C., 21–26 March 1994.* Washington, D.C.: Office of the Secretary of Defense, 1996, 49–62.

Micunovic, Veljko. *Moscow Diary.* Translated by David Floyd. NY: Doubleday & Co., 1980.

Mikoian, Anastas. *Tak Bylo: Razmyshleniia o Minuvshem.* Moscow: Vagrius, 1999.

Moreton, N. Edwina. *East Germany and the Warsaw Alliance: The Politics of Détente.* Boulder, Co.: Westview Press, 1978.

Morgenthau, Hans J. "Alliances in Theory and Practice." In Arnold Wolfers, *Alliance Policy in the Cold War.* Baltimore: Johns Hopkins University Press, 1959, 184–212.

Müller-Enbergs, Helmut. *Der Fall Rudolf Herrnstadt: Tauwetterpolitik vor dem 17. Juni.* Berlin: LinksDruck Verlags-GmbH, 1991.

Murphy, David E., Sergei A. Kondrashev, and George Bailey. *Battleground Berlin: CIA vs. KGB in the Cold War.* New Haven: Yale University Press, 1997.

Muth, Ingrid. *Die DDR-Aussenpolitik, 1949–1972: Inhalte, Strukturen, Mechanismen.* Berlin: Christoph Links Verlag, 2001.

Naimark, Norman. *The Russians in Germany: A History of the Soviet Zone of Occupation, 1945–1949.* Cambridge, Mass.: The Belknap Press of Harvard University Press, 1995.

Neustadt, Richard. *Alliance Politics.* N.Y.: Columbia University Press, 1970.

Ninkovich, Frank A. *Germany and the United States: The Transformation of the German Question since 1945.* N.Y.: Twayne Publishers, 1994.

Nowak, Jan. "Poles and Hungarians in 1956," unpublished paper presented to the international conference, "Hungary and the World, 1956: The New Archival Evidence," Budapest, 26–29 September 1996.

Offner, Arnold A. *Another Such Victory: President Truman and the Cold War, 1945–1953.* Stanford: Stanford University Press, 2002.

Osten, Walter. "Moskau-Peking und die SED." *Osteuropa* 4 (1964): 447–56.

Ostermann, Christian F. "The United States and the 'Other' Germany: The GDR in U.S. Perception and Policy, 1949–1953." Unpublished paper presented to the annual conference of SHAFR at the University of Virginia, Charlottesville, Va. (17–20 June 1993).

———. "The United States, the East German Uprising of 1953, and the Limits of Rollback." CWIHP, Working Paper No. 11 (December 1994).

———. "'Keeping the Pot Simmering': The United States and the East German Uprising of 1953." *German Studies Review* XIX, no. 1 (February 1996): 61–89.

———. "Das Ende der 'Rollback'-Politik. Eisenhower, die amerikanische Osteuropapolitik und der Ungarn-Aufstand von 1956." In Winfried Heinemann and Norbert Wiggershaus, *Das internationale Krisenjahr 1956: Polen, Ungarn, Suez*. Munich: J. R. Oldenbourg Verlag, 1999, 515–32.

———. "'Die beste Chance für ein Rollback'? Amerikanische Politik und der 17. Juni 1953." In Christoph Klessmann and Bernd Stöver, eds., *1953: Krisenjahr des Kalten Krieges in Europa*. Cologne: Böhlau Verlag, 1999, 115–39.

Otto, Wilfriede, introduction and annotation. "Ernst Wollweber: Aus Erinnerungen. Ein Porträt Walter Ulbrichts." *Beiträge zur Geschichte der Arbeiterbewegung* 32, no. 3 (1990): 350–78.

Park, Chang Jin. "The Influence of Small States upon the Superpowers: United States–South Korean Relations As a Case Study, 1950–1953." *World Politics* XXVIII, no. 1 (October 1975): 97–117.

Pedlow, Gregory W. "Allied Crisis Management for Berlin: The LIVE OAK Organization, 1959–1963." In William W. Epley, ed., *International Cold War Military Records and History: Proceedings of the International Conference on Cold War Military Records and History Held in Washington, D.C., 21–26 March 1994*. Washington, D.C.: Office of the Secretary of Defense, 1996, 87–116.

Penkovsky, Oleg. *The Penkovsky Papers*. Introduction and commentary by Frank Gibny, foreword by Edward Crankshaw, translated by P. Deriabin. London: Collins, 1965.

Phillips, Ann L. *Soviet Policy Toward East Germany Reconsidered: The Postwar Decade*. N.Y.: Greenwood Press, 1986.

Podewin, Norbert. *Walter Ulbricht: Eine neue Biographie*. Berlin: Dietz Verlag, 1995.

Pond, Elizabeth. *Beyond the Wall: Germany's Road to Unification*. Washington, D.C.: The Brookings Institution, 1993.

Prowe, Diethelm Manfred-Hartmut. "City Between Crises: The International Relations of West Berlin from the End of the Berlin Blockade in 1949 to the Khrushchev Ultimatum of 1958." Ph.D. diss., Stanford University, 1967.

Pruitt, Dean G., and Steven A. Lewis. "The Psychology of Integrative Bargaining." In *Negotiations: Social-Psychological Perspectives*, ed. by Daniel Druckman. Beverly Hills: Sage Publications, Inc., 1977, 161–92.

Przybylski, Peter. *Tatort Politbüro: Die Akte Honecker*. Berlin: Rowohlt Verlag GmbH, 1991.

Putnam, Robert. "Diplomacy and Domestic Politics: The Logic of Two-Level Games." *International Organization* 42, no. 3 (Summer 1988): 427–60.

Rainer, János. "The New Course in Hungary in 1953." *CWIHP*, Working Paper No. 38 (June 2002).

Ray, Hemen. "Die ideologische Achse Peking-Pankow." *Aussenpolitik* 11 (1960): 819–25.

———. "Peking und Pankow—Anziehung der Gegensätze: Chinas Engagement in Osteuropa und das Verhältnis zur DDR." *Europa-Archiv* 16 (1963): 621–28.

Reeves, Richard. *President Kennedy: Profile of Power*. N.Y.: Simon and Schuster, 1993.

Richardson, James L. *Germany and the Atlantic Alliance*. Cambridge: Harvard University Press, 1966.

Richter, James. "Reexamining Soviet Policy Towards Germany During the Beria Interregnum." CWIHP, Working Paper No. 3 (June 1992).

———. *Khrushchev's Double Bind: International Pressure and Domestic Coalition Politics*. Baltimore: Johns Hopkins University Press, 1994.

Risse-Kappen, Thomas. *Cooperation among Democracies: The European Influence on U.S. Foreign Policy*. Princeton: Princeton University Press, 1995.

Roesler, Jörg. "Der Handlungsspielraum der DDR-Führung gegenüber der UdSSR. Zu einem Schlüsselproblem des Verständnisses der DDR-Geschichte." *Zeitschrift für Geschichtswissenschaft* 40, no. 4 (1993): 293–304.

Rosenberg, Tina. *The Haunted Land: Facing Europe's Ghosts after Communism*. N.Y.: Vintage Books, 1996.

Rostow, W. W. *The Diffusion of Power: An Essay in Recent History*. N.Y.: Macmillan 1972.

Rothstein, Robert L. *Alliances and Small Powers*. N.Y.: Columbia University Press, 1968.

———. *The Weak in the World of the Strong*. N.Y.: Columbia University Press, 1977.

Sarotte, M. E. *Dealing with the Devil: East Germany, Détente, and Ostpolitik, 1969–1973*. Chapel Hill: University of North Carolina Press, 2001.

Schecter, Jerrold L., and Peter S. Deriabin. *The Spy Who Saved the World: How a Soviet Colonel Changed the Course of the Cold War*. N.Y.: Charles Scribner's Sons, 1992.

Schelling, Thomas. *The Strategy of Conflict*. Cambridge, Mass.: Harvard University Press, 1960.

———. *Arms and Influence*. New Haven: Yale University Press, 1966.

Schenk, Fritz. *Im Vorzimmer der Diktatur: 12 Jahre Pankow*. Cologne: Kiepenheuer und Witsch, 1962.

Scherstjanoi, Elke. "Offener Brief an Monika Kaiser." *Beiträge zur Geschichte der Arbeiterbewegung* 33, no. 5 (1991): 654–56.

———. "Zu Gerhard Wettig, 'Die Stalin-Note' vom 10 März als geschichtswissenschaftliches Problem." *Deutschland Archiv* 25 (August 1992): 858–62.

Schick, Jack. *The Berlin Crisis, 1958–1962*. Philadelphia: University of Pennsylvania Press, 1971.

Schirdewan, Karl. *Aufstand gegen Ulbricht: Im Kampf um politische Kurskorrektur, gegen stalinistische, dogmatische Politik*. Berlin: Aufbau Taschenbuch Verlag, 1994.

———. *Ein Jahrhundert Leben: Erinnerungen und Visionen.* Berlin: edition ost, 1998.

Schmidt, Gustav. *Ost-West Beziehungen: Konfrontation und Détente, 1945– 1989,* 2 volumes. Bochum: Universitätsverlag Dr. N. Brockmeyer, 1993.

Schmidt, Karl-Heinz. *Dialog über Deutschland: Studien zur Deutschlandpolitik von KPdSU und SED, 1960–1979.* Baden-Baden: Nomos Verlagsgesellschaft, 1998.

Schneider, Peter. *The Wall Jumper: A Berlin Story.* Translated by Leigh Hafrey. Chicago: University of Chicago Press, 1983.

Schultke, Dietmar. *"Keiner kommt durch:" Die Geschichte der innerdeutschen Grenze, 1945–1990.* Berlin: Aufbau, 1999.

Schwartz, Thomas A. *America's Germany: John J. McCloy and the Federal Republic of Germany.* Cambridge: Harvard University Press, 1991.

Semjonow, Wladimir S. *Von Stalin bis Gorbatschow: Ein halbes Jahrhundert in diplomatischer Mission, 1939–1991.* Translated by Hilde and Helmut Ettinger. Berlin: Nicolaische Verlagsbuchhandlung Beuermann GmbH, 1995.

Slusser, Robert. *The Berlin Crisis of 1961: Soviet-American Relations and the Struggle for Power in the Kremlin.* Baltimore: Johns Hopkins University Press, 1973.

Smith, Tony. "New Bottles for New Wine: A Pericentric Framework for the Study of the Cold War." *Diplomatic History* 24, no. 4 (Fall 2000): 567–91.

Smyser, W. R. *From Yalta to Berlin: The Cold War Struggle over Germany.* N.Y.: St. Martin's Press, 1999.

Snyder, Glenn H. "The Security Dilemma in Alliance Politics." *World Politics* XXXVI (July 1984): 461–95.

———. *Alliance Politics.* Ithaca: Cornell University Press, 1997.

Snyder, Glenn H., and Paul Diesing. *Conflict among Nations: Bargaining, Decision Making, and System Structure in International Crises.* Princeton: Princeton University Press, 1977.

Snyder, Jack. *Myths of Empire: Domestic Politics and International Ambition.* Ithaca, N.Y.: Cornell University Press, 1991.

Sodaro, Michael. *Moscow, Germany, and the West: From Khrushchev to Gorbachev.* Ithaca, N.Y.: Cornell University Press, 1991.

Sokolov, Vladimir V,. and Sven G. Holtsmark. "Note on the Foreign Policy Archive of the Russian Federation." CWIHP, *Bulletin* 3 (Fall 1993): 26, 52.

Spittmann, Ilse. "Ulbricht zwischen Stalin und Chruschtschow." *SBZ-Archiv* 23 (1 December 1961): 361–64.

Staritz, Dietrich. *Geschichte der DDR, 1949–1985.* Frankfurt am Main: Suhrkamp Verlag, 1985.

Steele, Jonathan. *Socialism with a German Face: The State That Came in from the Cold.* London: Jonathan Cape, 1977.

Steininger, Rolf. *Der Mauerbau: Die Westmächte und Adenauer in der Berlinkrise 1958–1963.* Munich: Olzog, 2001.

Stern, Carola. *Ulbricht: A Political Biography.* N.Y.: Praeger, 1965.

———. "Relations Between the DDR and the Chinese People's Republic, 1949–1965." In William E. Griffith, ed., *Communism in Europe: Continuity, Change, and the Sino-Soviet Dispute,* Vol. 2. Cambridge: MIT Press, 1996, 97–119.

Stone, Randall W. *Satellites and Commissars: Strategy and Conflict in the Politics of Soviet-Bloc Trade*. Princeton: Princeton University Press, 1996.

Stulz-Herrnstadt, Nadja, ed. *Das Herrnstadt-Dokument: Das Politbüro der SED und die Geschichte des 17. Juni 1953*. Hamburg: Rowohlt Taschenbuch Verlag GmbH, 1990.

Sudoplatov, Pavel and Anatoli Sudoplatov, with Jerrold L. and Leona P. Schechter. *Special Tasks: The Memoirs of an Unwanted Witness—A Soviet Spymaster*. Boston: Little, Brown and Company, 1994, 1995.

Suhrke, Astri. "Gratuity or Tyranny: The Korean Alliances." *World Politics* 25, no. 4 (July 1973): 508–32.

Sykhodrev, V. M. *Iazyk Moi—Drug Moi: Ot Khrushcheva do Gorbacheva*. Moscow: AST Press, 1999.

Taubman, William. "Khrushchev vs. Mao: A Preliminary Sketch of the Role of Personality in the Sino-Soviet Split." CWIHP, *Bulletin* 8–9 (Winter 1996/1997): 243–48.

———. "Khrushchev and Sino-Soviet Relations." Unpublished paper presented to the International Symposium on Sino-Soviet Relations and the Cold War, Beijing, China, 22–25 October 1997.

———. *Khrushchev: The Man and His Era*. N.Y.: W. W. Norton, 2003.

Taubman, William, Sergei Khrushchev, and Abbott Gleason, eds. *Nikita Khrushchev*. New Haven: Yale University Press, 2000.

Tompson, William J. *Khrushchev: A Political Life*. N.Y.: St. Martin's Griffin, 1995, 1997.

Trachtenberg, Marc. "The Berlin Crisis." Chap. 5 in *History and Strategy*. Princeton: Princeton University Press, 1991, 169–234.

———. *A Constructed Peace: The Making of the European Settlement, 1945–1963*. Princeton: Princeton University Press, 1999.

Triska, Jan F., ed. *Dominant Powers and Subordinate States: The United States in Latin America and the Soviet Union in Eastern Europe*. Durham: Duke University Press, 1986.

Troyanovsky, Oleg. *Cherez Gody i Rasstoianiia: Istoriia Odnoi Sem'i*. Moscow: Vagrius, 1997.

Turner, Henry Ashby Jr. *Germany from Partition to Reunification*. New Haven: Yale University Press, 1992.

Tusa, Ann. *The Last Division: A History of Berlin, 1945–1989*. Reading, Mass.: Addison-Wesley Publishing Company, 1997.

Uhl, Matthias, and Vladimir I. Ivkin. "'Operation Atom': The Soviet Union's Stationing of Nuclear Missiles in the German Democratic Republic, 1959." CWIHP, *Bulletin* 12/13 (Fall/Winter 2001): 299–307.

Uhl, Matthias, and Armin Wagner. "Another Brick in the Wall: Reexamining Soviet and East German Policy During the 1961 Berlin Crisis: New Evidence, New Documents." CWIHP Working Paper, forthcoming.

Ulam, Adam B. *Expansion and Coexistence: Soviet Foreign Policy, 1917–73*, 2nd ed. N.Y.: Holt, Rinehart and Winston, Inc., 1974.

van Dijk, Ruud. "The 1952 Stalin Note Debate: Myth or Missed Opportunity for German Unification?" CWIHP, Working Paper No. 14 (1996).

———. "The Apparatchik in 'Power': Walter Ulbricht and the German Question, 1948–1951." Unpublished paper presented to the annual conference of SHAFR at the University of Georgia at Athens, Ga. (21–23 June 2002).

Wagner, Armin. *Walter Ulbricht und die geheime Sicherheitspolitik der SED: Der Nationale Verteidigungsrat der DDR und seine Vorgeschichte, 1953–1971.* Berlin: Christoph Links Verlag, 2002.

Wagner, R. Harrison. "What Was Bipolarity?" *International Organization* 47, no. 1 (Winter 1993): 77–106.

Waltz, Kenneth N. *Theory of International Politics.* N.Y.: Random House, 1979.

Weathersby, Kathryn. "Soviet Aims in Korea and the Origins of the Korean War, 1945–1950: New Evidence from Russian Archives." CWIHP, Working Paper No. 8 (November 1993).

———, introduction, annotation, translation. "On the Korean War, 1950–53, and the Armistice Negotiations," CWIHP, *Bulletin* 3 (Fall 1993): 15–18.

———. " 'Should We Fear This?': Stalin and the Danger of War with America." CWIHP, Working Paper No. 39 (July 2002).

Weber, Hermann. *Geschichte der DDR.* Munich: Deutscher Taschenbuch Verlag GmbH & Co. KG, 1985.

———. *DDR: Dokumente zur Geschichte der Deutschen Demokratischen Republik, 1945–1985.* Munich: Deutscher Taschenbuch Verlag GmbH & Co. KG, 1986.

———. "Immer noch Probleme mit Archiven." *Deutschland Archiv* 6 (Juni 1992): 580–87.

Wendler, Gürgen. "Zur Deutschlandpolitik der Sozialistischen Einheitspartei Deutschlands (SED) in den Jahren 1952 bis 1958." In Gustav Schmidt, ed., *Ost-West Beziehungen: Konfrontation und Détente, 1945–1989,* II. Bochum: Universitätsverlag Dr. N. Brockmeyer, 1993, 349–65.

Westad, Odd Arne. "Secrets of the Second World: The Russian Archives and the Reinterpretation of Cold War History. "*Diplomatic History* 21, no. 2 (Spring 1997): 259–71.

———, ed. *Brothers in Arms: The Rise and Fall of the Sino-Soviet Alliance, 1945–1963.* Washington, D.C., and Stanford, Calif.: Woodrow Wilson Center Press and Stanford University Press, 1998.

———. Bernath Lecture, "The New International History of the Cold War: Three (Possible) Paradigms." *Diplomatic History* 24, no. 4 (Fall 2000): 551–65.

Wettig, Gerhard. "Die Stalin-Note vom 10 März 1952-Antwort auf Elke Scherstjanoi," *Deutschland Archiv* 25 (August 1992): 862–65.

———, ed. *Die sowjetische Deutschland-Politik in der Ära Adenauer.* Rhöndorfer Gespräche, Band 16, Stiftung Bundeskanzler-Adenauer-Haus. Bonn: Bouvier Verlag, 1997.

———. "Die sowjetische Politik während der Berlinkrise 1958 bis 1962. Der Stand der Forschungen." *Deutschland Archiv* 30 (1997): 383–98.

———. *Bereitschaft zu Einheit in Freiheit? Die sowjetische Deutschland-Politik 1945–1955.* Munich: Günter Olzog Verlag GmbH, 1999.

———. "Die UdSSR und die Krise um Berlin. Ultimatum 1958—Mauerbau 1961—Modus vivendi 1971." *Deutschland Archiv* 34 (2001): 592–613.

Whitney, Craig R. *Spy Trader: Germany's Devil's Advocate and the Darkest Secrets of the Cold War.* N.Y.: Times Books, 1993.

Wiegrefe, Klaus. "Die Schandmauer." *Der Spiegel* (6 August 2001): 64–77.

Wiessala, Georg. "Political Justice in Post-Unification Germany: The Legal Legacy of the GDR." *Debatte* 1 (1996): 49–71.

Willging, Paul. "Soviet Foreign Policy and the German Question, 1950–1955." Ph.D. diss., Columbia University, 1971.

Wohlforth, William C. "New Evidence on Moscow's Cold War: Ambiguity in Search of Theory." *Diplomatic History* 21, no. 2 (Spring 1997), 229–42.

Wolfe, Thomas W. *Soviet Power and Europe, 1945–1970.* Baltimore: Johns Hopkins University Press, 1970.

Wolfers, Arnold. "Power and Influence: The Means of Foreign Policy." In *Discord and Collaboration. Essays on International Politics.* With a foreword by Reinhold Niebuhr. Baltimore: Johns Hopkins University Press, 1962.

Wolff, David. "Coming in from the Cold." *Perspectives,* the American Historial Association Newsletter 37, no. 7 (October 1999): 1, 15–20.

Wollweber, Ernst. "Aus Erinnerungen. Ein Porträt Walter Ulbrichts." *Beiträge zur Geschichte der Arbeiterbewegung* 32, no. 3 (1990): 350–78.

Wriggins, W. Howard, with F. Gregory Gause, III, Terrence P. Lyons, and Evelyn Colbert. *Dynamics of Regional Politics: Four Systems on the Indian Ocean Rim.* N.Y.: Columbia University Press, 1992.

Wyden, Peter. *Wall: The Inside Story of Divided Berlin.* N.Y.: Simon and Schuster, 1989.

Zagoria, Donald S. *The Sino-Soviet Conflict, 1956–61.* N.Y.: Atheneum, 1964.

Zimmerman, William. *Soviet Perspectives on International Relations, 1956–1967.* Princeton: Princeton University Press, 1969.

Zolling, Hermann, and Uwe Bahnsen, *Kalter Winter im August.* Oldenburg: Gerhard Stalling Verlag, 1967.

Zubok, Vladislav M. "Khrushchev and the Berlin Crisis (1958–1962)." CWIHP, Working Paper No. 6 (May 1993).

———. "'Unacceptably Rude and Blatant on the German Question . . .' The Succession Struggle after Stalin's Death, Beria and the Significance of the Debate on the GDR in Moscow in April–May 1953. " Unpublished paper prepared for the conference "Das Krisenjahr 1953 und der Kalte Krieg in Europa." Potsdam, Germany, 10–12 November 1996.

———. "Stalin's Plans and Russian Archives." *Diplomatic History* 21, no. 2 (Spring 1997): 295–306.

———. "CPSU Plenums, Leadership Struggles, and Soviet Cold War Politics." CWIHP, *Bulletin* 10 (Winter 1998): 28–43, 50–60.

———. "'Look What Chaos in the Beautiful Socialist Camp!': Deng Xiaoping and the Sino-Soviet Split, 1956–1963." CWIHP, *Bulletin* 10 (March 1998): 152–62.

———, introduction, annotation, and translation. "The Mao-Khrushchev Conversations, 13 July–3 August 1958 and 2 October 1959." CWIHP, *Bulletin* 12/13 (Fall/Winter 2001): 244–72.

Zubok, Vladislav, and Constantine Pleshakov. *Inside the Kremlin's Cold War: From Stalin to Khrushchev*. Cambridge, Mass.: Harvard University Press, 1996.

Zubok, Vladislav, and Hope M. Harrison. "The Nuclear Education of Nikita Khrushchev." In John Lewis Gaddis, Philip H. Gordon, Ernest R. May, and Jon Rosenberg, eds., *Cold War Statesmen Confront the Bomb: Nuclear Diplomacy since 1945*. N.Y.: Oxford University Press, 1999, 141–168.

Index

Abel, Rudolf, xii
Ackermann, Anton, 18, 74, 75, 262n. 130
Adenauer, Konrad, 3, 54, 65, 90, 103, 113, 115, 116, 118, 119–20, 126, 130, 153, 161, 173, 192, 218; meeting with Mikoian (1958), 275n. 85, 276n. 87
Adomeit, Hannes, 282n. 6, 302n. 272
Adzhubei, Aleksei, 109
Afghanistan, 233
Albania, 28, 44, 56, 195, 203–4, 217, 302n. 269; warning from the WTO to, 290n. 105
Aleksandrov-Agentov, A. M., 63, 108, 109, 254n. 15
Alia, Ramiz, 203–4
"alliance security dilemma," 5, 7, 253n. 191
Alliluyeva, Nadezhda, 61
Andropov, Yuri, 92, 100, 190
Astavin, S., 75
Aufbau des Sozialismus (*Construction of Socialism*), 19, 21–22, 24, 26, 27, 28, 34, 46, 50, 241n. 51
Aufbau Press, 76
Austrian State Treaty, 53
Axen, Hermann, 179

Bailey, George, 227
Baring, Arnulf, 246n. 123
Bay of Pigs (Cuba), 167, 173
Bentzien, Hans, 287n. 75
Ben-Zvi, Abraham, 2, 236–37n. 24
Beria, Lavrenty, 9, 19, 24, 26, 27–28, 29, 42, 43, 53, 56, 62, 86, 89, 92, 113, 114, 234; alleged desire to abandon the GDR, 47, 89, 143, 154, 222–23, 228, 245n. 104; and the Beria question, 31–32; execution of, 154; ouster of, 40–41, 46, 47
Berlin, 98–99, 126, 130, 303n. 290; Berlin blockade, 98; developments in after the worker uprising, 38–40, 248n. 142; economic problems of the open border, 196–97; as espionage base, 100–101, 270–71n. 24; Four Power occupation of, 98–99, 105–6, 135, 144, 265n. 184; and the *Grenzgänger*, 73, 100, 151,

158, 181–82, 188–89; interim solution/ agreement on Berlin, 120–21, 122, 126, 131, 137, 156, 163, 172, 174, 175, 177; Soviet troops in, 193, 201–2; specifics of border closure, 193–95, 205–7. *See also* Berlin Crisis; Berlin sectoral border/inter-Berlin border; Berlin Wall; West Berlin
Berlin Crisis (1958–1961), 7–8, 9–10, 96–97, 140–43, 168–69, 182, 184–92, 218–23, 230; background, 19–21, 98–99; and Chinese criticism of Soviet approach, 181–82, 203, 217, 221, 307n. 350; development of, 116–21; and different approaches of Khrushchev and Ulbricht, 140–43, 150, 156, 157, 171, 212, 218, 219, 222, 224–25; Eastern perspectives on, 99–102; Khrushchev's motives, 97–98, 113–16, 137, 221, 275n. 84; and Khrushchev's threats, 104–5; and Khrushchev's ultimatum, 105–13, 273n. 51; and sources of GDR bargaining power during, 142–43, 222–23, 226–29; and unilateral East German policies, 101–2, 138, 139–40, 144–51, 152, 170–71, 205, 210, 212–14, 216, 218, 219, 221, 223, 224, 225, 233, 289n. 95; Western perspectives on, 102; Western response to Khrushchev's ultimatum, 118–21. *See also* Berlin sectoral border/inter-Berlin border; Berlin Wall; Khrushchev, Nikita S.; peace treaty with Germany; Soviet–German Democratic Republic relations; Ulbricht, Walter; Vienna Summit; West Berlin
Berlin sectoral border/inter-Berlin border, movement across and potential for closure, 19–21, 24, 35, 36, 37, 38, 47, 52, 83, 99, 110, 113, 143, 144–45, 147–49, 152, 153, 157–61, 164, 167, 169, 170, 179, 182–95, 206, 248n. 137. See also *Torschlusspanik*
Berlin Wall, 7, 10, 48, 94, 139–40, 169, 180, 186–87, 192, 210–11, 206, 214, 216, 221, 229, 233, 286n. 71, 301n. 251, 305n. 315, 307n. 348; and communist relief at absence of Western at-

Berlin Wall (*cont.*)
tempts to stop it, 207–8; as the "concrete" Rose (Stasi codename for),
205–7; and East German disagreement
over cement or barbed wire construction, 206–7; fall of, xi–xiii, 233, 234;
GDR economic need for, 169–70, 196–
99; preparations for, 186–88, 190–95,
201–2, 205; and "shoot to kill" order,
212; "Wall trials," xiii–xiv, 212; West-
ern reaction to, 207–9
Bierut, Boleslaw, 75
Bolshakov, Georgi, 167, 214
Bolz, Lothar, 55, 119, 144, 274n. 58
Bonwetsch, Bernd, 204
Brandenburg Gate, xii, 145, 180, 207,
214
Brandt, Heinz, 35
Brandt, Willy, xii, 207
Bredel, Willi, 70
Brezhnev, Leonid, 58, 223, 232
Brie, Horst, 165, 263n. 146, 263–64n.
154, 264n. 159, 281n. 183, 288–89n.
92
Bruce, David, 119–20
Bulganin, N. A., 31, 44–45, 108
Bulgaria, 26, 27, 44
Bundeswehr, 89, 115, 202, 227, 276n. 87
Bundy, William, 128–29
Burlatsky, Fedor, 59, 139–40, 186
Burr, William, 102, 220

Camp David Summit (1959), 132
capitalism, 83, 84, 142–43, 226
Cate, Curtis, 169
Catudal, Honoré M., 169
Checkpoint Charlie, 206; and Checkpoint
Charlie crisis, 211, 213–14, 232; Ul-
bricht's role in, 214–15
Chen Jian, 233
Chen Yi, 165, 208, 212
Chiang Kai-Shek, 104, 272n. 37
China. *See* People's Republic of China
Chou En-Lai, 281n. 181
Chuev, Felix, 256n. 33
Chuikov, V. I., 19, 25, 31
Churchill, Winston, 16
Clay, Lucius, 211, 213, 214
Communist Party of China (CCP), Eighth
Congress, 80
Communist Party of Germany (KPD), 13–
14, 16–17

Communist Party of the Soviet Union
(CPSU), 8, 23, 24, 26–27, 33, 79–80,
87–88, 128, 258–69n. 84, 259n. 89;
anti-party group (1957), 88, 97, 143;
Comintern, 14–15; and Khruschev's
role in Moscow party politics, 61–62;
Presidium meeting dates, 242n. 73; Pre-
sidium membership list, 242n. 72. *See
also* Communist Party of the Soviet
Union, Twentieth Congress; Communist
Party of the Soviet Union, Twenty-
Second Congress
Communist Party of the Soviet Union,
Twentieth Congress, 49–50, 63–66, 86,
87, 90, 133, 201; and discussion of Sta-
lin's mistakes, 69–71; effects of on East
German leadership, 66–78; and party
plenums, 70, 90
Communist Party of the Soviet Union,
Twenty-Second Congress, 210, 214, 215
Conant, James, 38
Conference of Foreign Ministers (CFM),
53–54, 118, 119–20, 121–32, 167,
172, 230, 278n. 124
Council for Mutual Economic Assistance
(COMECON), 199
Cuban Missile Crisis, 8, 81, 128, 143,
186, 217, 234
Czechoslovakia, 26, 27, 44, 85, 89, 113,
146, 171, 173, 199, 202, 236n. 23; ag-
ricultural problems in, 200

Dahlem, Franz, 24
Danzig, free city of, 110, 274n. 63
de Gaulle, Charles, 118, 136, 173, 282n.
188; meeting with Kennedy, 175
Deng Xiaoping, 81
Deutschlandpolitik. See Soviet *Deutsch-
landpolitik*
Dibrova, Commandant, 35, 38
Doherr, Annamarie, 180
domino theory, 3
Dowling, Walter, 145
Dulles, Allen, 37–38
Dulles, John Foster, 104, 118, 119, 120,
123, 133, 173, 287n. 84

East Berlin, 144–45, 170–72, 206; creation of National Defense Council, 149.
See also Berlin Crisis; Berlin sectoral bor-
der/inter-Berlin border; Berlin Wall;
Torschlusspanik

East German National People's Army (NVA), 54

East German People's Police (VoPos), 28, 39, 206

East Germany. *See* German Democratic Republic

Eberlein, Werner, 192, 200

Ebert, F., 92

Eisenhower, Dwight D., 7, 37, 115, 117, 120, 121, 133; invitation to Khrushchev to visit the United States (1959), 131; and the U-2 incident, 135–36

European Defense Community (EDC), 169

European Economic Community (EEC), 150

Fadeikin, Ivan, 24

Fanfani, Amintore, 192

Federal Republic of Germany (FRG), 5, 18, 30, 54–55, 64–65, 153, 156–57, 171–72, 198–99, 227, 231; and economic relations with Eastern Europe, 199–200; and GDR refugee problem, 72–73, 157–61; and nuclear weapons, 114, 115–16, 126, 130, 275nn. 84, 85, 276nn. 87, 88; as threat to the Soviet Union, 89–90. *See also* Adenauer, Konrad; Berlin Crisis; Berlin Wall; German Democratic Republic

Filitov, A. M., 204

Florin, Peter, 83, 101, 179, 181

Four Power(s), 53, 103, 113, 119–21, 147, 149, 160, 265n. 184, 272n. 39. *See also* Berlin, Four Power occupation of

France, 3, 38, 59, 110, 119, 120

free city of West Berlin. *See* West Berlin, free city of

Fulbright, William, 192

Fursenko, Aleksandr, 298n. 209

Gaddis, John Lewis, 3–4, 5

Gagarin, Yuri, 201

Gaiduk, Ilya, 233

Gelb, Norman, 180

Genscher, Hans-Dietrich, xii

German Democratic Republic (GDR) 1, 9, 219–23, 229, 287n. 84; and control of its air space, 265n. 184; and economic problems, 84–85, 159, 163, 195–97; and economic relations with the FDR, 150, 153, 154–55, 159–60, 169, 172,

173, 185, 197, 198; 1953 uprising, 7, 23, 34–38, 52, 68, 69, 73, 82, 247–48n. 137, 303n. 289; number of Soviet troops in, 4, 303n. 289; reaction to the Hungarian revolution, 81–85; refugee exodus (*Republikflucht*) problem, xi, 5, 7, 8, 10, 12, 19–21, 22, 23, 24, 25, 27, 28, 46, 47, 50–52, 71–74, 77, 79, 82, 90, 91, 94, 97, 99–100, 102, 106, 114, 137, 139, 141, 148, 149, 153, 155–56, 157–61, 164, 167, 170, 178–81, 182, 183, 184–86, 189, 193, 195, 219, 229, 287n. 75; and relations with the FRG, 74, 76–78, 93, 156–57; relations with the PRC, 50, 78–80, 134, 164–65, 263–64n. 154, 281n. 183; relations with West Berlin, 75; and socialism, 16–19, 24–25, 49, 65, 74–76, 84, 89, 90, 142–43, 220–21, 226, 227–28; sovereignty of, 152–53, 211; and strength through weakness, 1, 5, 50, 141, 142, 219, 229. *See also* Berlin; Berlin Crisis; Berlin Wall; East Berlin; Soviet–German Democratic Republic relations; *Torschlusspanik*; Ulbricht, Walter; West Berlin

German reunification, 30, 33–34, 47, 53, 65, 78, 90, 92, 102–3, 122, 172, 230, 231, 234, 266–67n. 205; initiatives for, 102–5

Germinal (Zola), 59–60

Gerö, Ernö, 75

Gilpatric, Roswell, 211

Gleijeses, Piero, 233

Glienecker Brücke, xii

Gomulka, Wladislaw, 58, 75, 81, 82, 107, 111, 112, 114, 190, 196, 198, 199, 202, 215, 218, 301n. 251; and sealing the border around West Berlin, 198

Gorbachev, Mikhail, 55–56, 233, 305n. 315

Great Britain. *See* United Kingdom

Grechko, Andrei, 31, 36, 187, 200

Grenzgänger. See Berlin, and the *Grenzgänger*

Gribanov, M., 22

Grieder, Peter, 239n. 23, 268n. 225

Gromyko, Andrei, 27, 63, 108, 109, 121–23, 125–27, 130, 170, 182, 185, 186, 190, 209–10, 213, 216; dialogue with Ulbricht, 156–57

Grotewohl, O., 18, 28, 29, 32, 33, 35–36, 39–40, 45, 51, 66, 68, 72, 78, 84–86, 90–92, 103, 105, 114, 124, 126, 130, 133, 154, 176; on the *New Course* policy, 251n. 176; trips to China, 78–79, 134
Group of Soviet Forces in Germany (GSFG), 36, 187
Gufler, Bernard, 120

Hager, Kurt, 92–93
Harich, Wolfgang, 76, 85, 265n. 183
Harriman, Averell, 65, 128, 166; interview with Khrushchev, 130–31
Herrnstadt, Rudolf, 21, 23, 33, 34, 35–37, 39–43, 86, 93, 224, 234; expulsion from the SED, 50
Hershberg, James G., 2
Herter, Christian, 121, 123, 124, 128–29, 130
Hitler, Adolf, 15, 16, 17, 18, 274n. 63
Ho Chi Minh, 209, 302n. 269
Hoffman, Heinz, 187, 207
Honecker, Erich, 77, 86–87, 92, 140, 159, 187, 205–6, 208, 212–13, 215, 232–33, 234, 266n. 193, 268n. 221, 296n. 186; on closing of West Berlin/ GDR borders, 300n. 248
Humphrey, Hubert, 109
Hungarian revolution, 49, 81; effects on the GDR, 75, 81–95; effects on the Soviet Union, 88–93, 266n. 189; reaction to in the GDR, 81–85; Soviet military suppression of, 9
Hungary, 28, 44, 70, 73, 74, 75–76, 81, 93, 190, 236n. 23; economy of, 84; and trade with the West, 200
Hüttner, E., 179

Il'ichev, I., 24, 25, 107, 109
inter-German border, closure of (1952), 19, 73, 99, 169
Israel, 2, 233

Janka, Walter, 76, 85, 265n. 183
Jendretzky, Hans, 33, 35, 245n. 106

Kabin, I., 31, 42
Kadar, Janos, 75, 81, 87, 169, 199–201
Kaganovich, Lazar, 29, 60, 88, 266n. 197
Kaliningrad, 132

Kazennov, A. P., 148
Kennan, George, 209
Kennedy, John F., xii, 4, 7, 96, 151, 153, 156, 161, 163, 166–67, 168, 170, 172, 173, 174, 175–77, 190, 191–92, 194, 195, 201, 216, 217, 304n. 300; reaction to the Berlin Wall, 207–11. *See also* Vienna Summit
Kennedy, Robert F., 166–67, 214
Khrushchev, Nikita S., 1, 4, 5, 7–10, 19, 21, 26, 28, 29, 31, 42, 55, 58, 86, 88–89, 97–98, 109, 140–43, 225, 231–33, 253n. 191, 255n. 27, 258n. 79, 289n. 95, 304n. 300; and agreement to close the Berlin border, 186; and anti-party group, 88–90; boasting of transcontinental missile capability, 106, 113; commitment to socialism in the GDR, 65–66, 142–43, 154, 203, 222, 223, 226, 227–28; complaints against Albania, 302n. 269; and deployment of medium-range ballistic missiles (MRBMs) in the GDR, 128–29, 132; deployment of missiles in Cuba, 128–29, 132, 143, 283n. 18; de-Stalinization policies, 49, 66, 93; five primary reasons for opposition to separate peace treaty with the GDR, 216–17; on the GDR refugee exodus, 51, 64, 65, 66; and German reunification, 65, 109–10; goals achieved with the Berlin Wall, 221; goals in Germany, 55–57, 64–66, 93–94; and lessons from GDR's 1953 worker uprising, 46–47; and Marxism, 60, 80, 84; meeting with Eisenhower (1959), 131, 132–33; meeting with Kennedy (1961), 166–67; meeting with Mao Zedong (1959), 133–35; meeting with Ulbricht (1959), 307n. 352; meeting with Ulbricht (1960), 151–57; on nuclear weapons, 64, 128, 129, 131; at the Paris Summit (1960), 135–36; personality of, 57–59, 229–32; political career, 60–63; on relations with the FRG, 76–78; and the U-2 incident, 135–36, 257n. 58; and Warsaw Pact meetings (1961), 167–70, 192–205, 289–90n. 103, 301–2n. 264. *See also* Berlin Crisis; Communist Party of the Soviet Union, Twentieth Congress; Conference of Foreign Ministers; Sino-Soviet rift; Soviet–German Democratic relations; Ulbricht, Walter; Vienna Summit

Khrushchev, Sergei, 117, 186
Kiefert, Hans, 69
Kim Il Sung, 143
Knorr, Klaus, 2
Kohl, Helmut, xii
Kondrashev, Sergei, 227
Konev, Ivan, 187, 213
König, Johannes, 78, 107, 108–9, 111–12, 145
Korean War, 8, 53, 81, 143, 234
Kornienko, Georgi, 291n. 128
Kosygin, Aleksei, 153
Kramer, Erwin, 187, 287n. 75
Kramer, Mark, 43
Krenz, Egon, xiv, 212, 305n. 315
Krisch, Henry, 219
Kroll, Hans, 186
Kvitsinsky, Yuli, 140, 143, 170–71, 178–79, 185–86, 190, 192, 206, 208, 210–11, 221, 228, 288–89n. 92, 295n. 176, 307n. 348

Lemke, Michael, 74, 214
Lenin, V. I., xiv, 14, 18, 173
Leonhard, Wolfgang, 14, 17, 58
Leuschner, Bruno, 83–84, 86, 154, 159, 177, 265n. 172, 267n. 214, 286n. 59, 287n. 75
Li Che-Sun, 201
Lightner, Edwin A., 174–75, 213
Liu Shaoqui, 81
LIVE OAK plan, 120, 298n. 212
Lloyd, Selwyn, 121, 122, 130
Lodge, Henry Cabot, 230

Macmillan, Harold, 118, 128, 136, 173, 174
Malenkov, Georgi, 19, 23, 26, 28, 29–30, 42, 44–45, 47, 52–53, 62, 88, 113, 114, 243n. 82; 250–51n. 170; alleged desire to abandon the GDR, 143, 154, 222–23, 228; ouster of as head of state, 52–53
Malik, Ya., 22
Malin, V., 229
Malinovsky, Rodion, 213
Mao Zedong, 50, 78, 80, 97, 104, 112, 133–34, 215, 264n. 159, 281n. 183, 293n. 159; and Khrushchev, 133–35; relations with the GDR, 50, 164–65, 263–64n. 154; and Ulbricht, 80. See also People's Republic of China; Sino-Soviet rift

Maron, Karl, 72, 159, 187, 194, 213, 299n. 235
Matern, Hermann, 68, 82, 164–65, 264n. 167, 267n. 214
Matsu, 104, 134, 288n. 90
Mauer im Kopf ("wall in the mind"), xiv
McAdams, James, 105, 110
McElroy, Neil, 129
medium-range ballistic missiles (MRBMs) deployed in GDR. See Khrushchev, Nikita S., and deployment of medium-range ballistic missiles (MRBMs) in the GDR
Menning, Bruce W., 212, 213
Menshikov, Mikhail, 166–67, 291n. 128
Mielke, Erich, 159, 187, 205, 207, 214, 312
Mikoian, Anastas, 57, 58, 81, 86, 88–89, 90, 107, 108, 110, 111, 115, 177–78, 203, 227, 252–53n. 185, 275n. 86, 279n. 139, 287n. 84; meeting with Adenauer (1958), 275n. 85, 276n. 87; on peace treaty with the GDR, 127–28; trip to the United States (1959), 116–17; on U.S. reparations policy, 287–88n. 86
Miroschnichenko, V., 40
Mollet, Guy, 65
Molotov, Viacheslav, 19–21, 22, 24, 27, 28, 39, 42, 44–45, 53, 54, 56, 62–63, 69, 88, 89, 240nn. 44, 45, 256n. 33
Momper, Walter, xii
Mongolia, 204
Murphy, David, 227
Murphy, Robert, 131
Murville, Couvé de, 121

Nagy, Imre, 75, 81
Naimark, Norman, 4
National Committee for Free Germany (NKFD), 16
Nazism, 16, 17, 87
Neues Deutschland, 21, 67, 144
Neumann, Alfred, 52, 66, 69, 75, 83, 85, 86
New Course. See Soviet–German Democratic Republic relations, and the New Course policy
Nikitin, P. V., 21
Nixon, Richard M., 128
North American Treaty Organization (NATO), 2, 54, 172, 198–99, 227, 231; deployment of intermediate-range ballistic missiles (IRBMs), 115

North Korea, 143, 204, 233
North Vietnam, 204, 209, 233, 313
Novotny, Antonin, 173, 199–200, 202
Nuschke, Otto, 247n. 136

Oelssner, Fred, 28, 29, 31, 32, 33–34, 73, 83–85, 91, 93, 261n. 125; on the GDR refugee problem, 73
"On Measures for the Recovery of the Political Situation in the German Democratic Republic," 28. *See also* Soviet–German Democratic relations, and the *New Course* policy
Orlov, A., 52, 69

Pakistan, 2, 233
Palestinians, 233
Paris Summit (1960), 135–36, 151, 155
peace treaty with Germany, 44, 53, 102–3, 105, 106, 114, 117, 122, 136, 155, 156, 157, 166, 168, 170, 173, 193, 209, 211, 215, 218
People's Republic of China (PRC), 78–80, 81, 263–64n. 154; on Chinese/GDR peace treaty, 294–95n. 163; refugee problem, 79; shelling of Quemoy and Matsu islands, 104, 134, 272n. 37, 288n. 90; view of proposed Soviet–GDR peace treaty, 181–82, 294–95n. 163, 307n. 348. *See also* Berlin crisis; German Democratic Republic, relations with the PRC; Mao Zedong; Sino-Soviet rift; Ulbricht, and exploitation of the Sino-Soviet rift
Pervukhin, Mikhail, 99, 100, 103, 108, 147, 152, 158–59, 170–72, 181, 182, 184–87, 191, 192, 205–6, 208, 211, 216–17, 240n. 42, 274n. 58, 297–98n. 209
Petöfi circle (Hungary), 75, 76
Pieck, Wilhelm, 31, 244–45n. 103
Pleshakov, Constantine, 60, 113
Podewin, Norbert, 58
Poland, 69–70, 73, 74, 75–76, 81, 88, 89, 93, 105, 113, 146, 171, 190, 199, 202, 215, 236n. 23, 266n. 189; annexation of Eastern Poland into the USSR, 62
Polianskii, D. S., 57–58, 231–32, 309n. 22
Potsdam Agreements, 98, 105, 108
Potsdamer Platz, xii, 207, 214, 264

Powers, Francis Gary, xii, 135
Poznan (Poland), riots in, 75
Presidium of the Council of Ministers (CM), 26–27
Pushkin, G., 22, 68, 82, 86, 91, 92

Quemoy, 104, 134, 188n. 90

Radio in the American Sector (RIAS), 25, 35–36, 37
Rakosi, Mátyás, 69, 72, 75, 82
Rau, Heinrich, 39, 86, 160
Reagan, Ronald, 305n. 315
refugee exodus. *See* German Democratic Republic, refugee exodus (*Republikflucht*) problem
reparations, Soviet, taken from GDR, 22, 31, 44–45, 164, 287–88n. 86
Rhee, Syngman, 3
Risse-Kappen, Thomas, 3
Romania, 44, 169, 215
Roosevelt, Franklin D., 16
Rostow, Walt, 192
Rusk, Dean, 209–10, 216

Salisbury, Harrison, 167
Sarotte, Mary, 234
Schick, Jack, 121
Schirdewan, Karl, 40, 66, 69, 77, 82, 86, 90–94, 224, 225, 234, 241n. 51, 244–45n. 103, 250nn. 157, 166, 258–59n. 84, 259n. 89, 266n. 189, 267n. 208; criticism of Ulbricht, 267nn. 207, 214; ouster from SED leadership, 264n. 166, 267n. 219, 268n. 221; report on Hungarian revolution, 82–84
Schloss Charlottenburg, xiv
Schmidt, Waldemar, 35
Schneider, Peter, xiv
Scholz, Ernst, 287n. 75
Scholz, Paul, 129–30
Sejna, Jan, 169, 194–95, 289–90n. 103
Selbmann, Fritz, 83–84, 91
Selianinov, O., 101, 145–46
Semenov, Vladimir, 18, 19, 23, 28, 31, 33, 34, 35–40, 186, 212, 250n. 157, 252n. 184
separate peace treaty between USSR and GDR. *See* Soviet–German Democratic Republic relations, and separate peace treaty

17 June (1953) syndrome, 74, 95
Shelepin, Aleksandr, 191
"shoot to kill" Order 101, 212
Shu Ming, 79
Sino-Soviet rift, 7, 8, 50, 56, 78, 86, 133–35, 143, 151, 164, 195, 203, 204, 217, 222–23, 234; exploitation of by GDR, 78–80, 164–66, 204, 219, 228. *See also* Mao Zedong; Ulbricht, Walter
Smirnov, A. A., 103, 192
Smirnovski, Mikhail, 173
Smith, Tony, 2
Smyser, W. R., 213, 214
Snyder, Glenn, 5, 7, 237n. 26, 253n. 191
Social Democratic Party (SPD), 13, 64, 77
socialism, 83, 84, 142–43. *See also* German Democratic Republic, and socialism; Khrushchev, Nikita S., commitment to socialism in the GDR
Socialist Unity Party (SED), 5, 7, 18, 23–24, 29, 35, 41, 46, 65, 73–74, 90, 169; and the Hungarian revolution, 82–83
Sokolovsky, V. D., 36, 37, 38, 42, 240n. 45
Soviet Control Commission (SKK), 19, 24–25, 26, 27, 29
Soviet *Deutschlandpolitik*, 10, 22, 27–28, 50, 53, 54, 102, 103, 230
Soviet–Federal Republic of Germany relations, 54, 74, 94, 157
Soviet–German Democratic Republic relations (general), 1–4, 27–28, 55–56, 140, 224–25; importance of to the Soviets, 7–8; and separate peace treaty, 8, 106, 155–56, 171–72, 173, 174, 177–80, 181, 182, 190–91, 194, 196, 201, 204–5, 209–12, 210–12, 215–18, 219, 229; and Stalin's immediate successors, 19–25, 52. *See also* Berlin Crisis; German Democratic Republic, and strength through weakness; Soviet–German Democratic Republic relations, and the *New Course* policy; Soviet–German Democratic Republic relations (1953); Soviet–German Democratic Republic relations (1956–1958); Soviet–German Democratic Republic relations (1958–1960); Soviet–German Democratic relations (1960–1961); Soviet–German Democratic Republic relations, and economic aid policies; super-ally; superpower-ally relations

Soviet–German Democratic Republic relations (1953), 13, 45–48; developments in Berlin after the worker uprising, 38–40; economic aid policies, 44–45; and the worker uprising, 34–38, 247–48n. 137, 248n. 142
Soviet–German Democratic Republic relations (1955–1956), 49–50; background, 50–52; and Soviet foreign policy, 52–57. *See also* Communist Party of the Soviet Union, Twentieth Congress
Soviet–German Democratic Republic relations (1958–1960), 96–99, 102–5, 137–38, 271–72n. 32. *See also* Berlin Crisis
Soviet–German Democratic Republic relations (1960–1961), 171–72; conflicts during the Berlin Crisis, 140–43; GDR–Soviet summit (1960), 151–57, 165–66
Soviet–German Democratic Republic relations, and economic aid policies, 44–45, 71, 74, 88–89, 90, 94–95, 124, 129, 150, 151, 152, 153–55, 160, 163–66, 177–78, 198–99, 202–3, 216, 221, 246n. 123, 252–53n. 185, 279n. 139, 285nn. 47, 48, 286n. 59, 287n. 84
Soviet–German Democratic Republic relations, and the *New Course* policy, 9, 24, 25–28, 41, 46, 47, 49, 50–51, 66, 89, 230–31, 251n. 176; backtracking from, 40–43; Chinese response to, 78–80; East German deliberations about, 32–34; East German response, 78–80; presentation of to East Germans, 28–33
Soviet Interior Ministry (MVD), 23–24, 27
Soviet Union, 87; Politburo members, 245n. 106; relationship with allies, 3, 227–28. *See also* Soviet–German Democratic Republic relations
Soviet–West Berlin relations, 75, 146–47, 148–49, 171, 284n. 32
Soviet Zone of Occupation (SBZ), 17, 18
Stalin, Joseph, 1, 9, 16, 18–19, 53, 56, 62, 72, 98, 143, 223, 239n. 40, 240n. 44; and his cult of personality, 64, 66, 258–59n. 84, 259–60n. 90; on economic support for the GDR, 266n. 201; on the formation of East Germany, 239–40n. 41; on socialism in the GDR, 258n. 74. *See also* Communist Party of

Stalin, Joseph (*cont.*)
  the Soviet Union, Twentieth Congress, discussion of Stalin's mistakes; Khrushchev, Nikita S., de-Stalinization policies; Ulbricht, on Stalin
Stalinism. *See* Stalin, Joseph
Stasi, 79, 187, 227, 246n. 131
Steinitz, Wolfgang, 75, 76, 262n. 134
Stoph, Willi, 85, 92, 158, 213
Sudoplatov, Pavel, 245n. 104
Suez Crisis (1956), 3, 81, 232
Sul'din, V. A., 286n. 69
super-ally, 7, 12, 143, 227–28, 234
superdomino, 7, 102, 120, 143. *See also* West Berlin
superpower-ally relations, 3–4, 236–37n. 24, 237n. 30; importance of strategic location, 4–5; and "indirect dependence," 237n. 26; and interdependence, 2; symbolic functions, 5; in the Western alliance system, 2–3
Suslov, Mikhail, 31, 57, 81, 231–32, 309n. 22

Taiwan, 2, 78, 133, 165, 182
Taubman, William, 57
Third European Department of the Soviet Foreign Ministry (MID), 22–23, 25, 27, 29, 43–44, 107–9, 210
Thompson, Llewellyn, 118–19, 167, 172, 209
Tito, Josip, 18, 53
Tiul'panov, Sergei, 18
Tompson, William, 60
Torschlusspanik, 159, 178, 182. *See also* Berlin sectoral border/inter-Berlin border; German Democratic Republic, refugee exodus (*Republikflucht*) problem
Trachtenberg, Marc, 115, 220, 275n. 84
Troyanovsky, Oleg, 57, 61, 80, 108, 111, 131, 132, 140, 186, 226; at the Paris Summit, 135–36
Truman, Harry S., 3
Tugarinov, I., 51–52
Tusa, Ann, 144, 145, 277n. 101

Ukraine, 62, 65
Ulbricht, Ernst, 13
Ulbricht, Pauline, 13
Ulbricht, Walter, 1, 4, 5, 7–10, 12–19, 28, 29, 31, 35–37, 39–43, 45, 46, 58–

59, 69–70, 90, 96, 97–98, 103, 104, 109–10, 137–38, 139, 140–43, 155–56, 218–19, 231–34, 246n. 120, 267n. 207, 268nn. 221, 225, 270n. 22, 272n. 39; biographical data, 13–15; and "blackmail" of Khrushchev, 74; closing the border of West Berlin, 185–86, 197–98, 207–8, 211–12, 297–98n. 209; consolidation of control over the GDR, 41–43, 90, 93, 225–27; on contacts with the SPD, 77–78; criticism of, 33–34, 82; and his cult of personality of, 34, 68–69; demands on Khrushchev concerning West Berlin, 161–66; dialogue with Gromyko (1960), 156–57; disapproval of Pervukhin, 210–11; and East European suspicion of his motives, 200; effect of Hungarian revolution on his policies, 82, 85–88, 93–95; and exploitation of the Sino-Soviet split, 78–80, 164–66, 204, 219, 228; fear of Western economic embargo, 198–200; and "Gruppe Ulbricht," 16; meeting with Khrushchev (1960), 151–57; and nuclear weapons, 295n. 165; personality of, 9, 13, 18, 33–34, 41, 42, 58–59, 223, 230, 232–33; and presentation of the *New Course*, 32–33; resentment toward "native" communists, 17; on socialism, 225–26; Soviet support for, 43–45; speech at Warsaw pact meeting (August 1961), 195–98; on Stalin, 258–59n. 84, 259–60n. 90; and the war years in Moscow, 15–16. *See also* Berlin; Berlin Crisis; Berlin Wall; Conference of Foreign Ministers, the; German Democratic Republic; Khrushchev, Nikita S.; Vienna Summit; Warsaw Pact, Ulbricht's role in
United Kingdom, 3, 38, 110, 119, 120, 130
United States, 99, 102, 110, 119, 120, 125, 130, 133, 150, 225; as a "paper tiger," 281n. 181; on recognition of the two Chinas, 272n. 37; troop reductions in West Berlin, 123–24. *See also* Eisenhower, Dwight D.; Kennedy, John F.; superpower-ally relations, in the Western alliance system; Vienna Summit
uprising, 1953. *See* German Democratic Republic, 1953 uprising
Uzbekistan, 233

Verner, Paul, 86, 159
Vienna Summit, 175–77; failure of, 177–78; and Kennedy's "three essentials" concerning West Berlin, 175; preparations for, 172–75; and search for interim agreement on West Berlin, 175–76
Vietnam War, 8, 234

Waltz, Kenneth N., 282n. 12
Wandel, Paul, 83, 159
Wansierski, Bruno, 187–88
Warsaw Pact, 3, 54, 56, 81, 89, 106, 163, 166, 181, 190, 289–90n. 103; and the "concrete rose," 205–7, 293n. 155; Khrushchev's speech (March 1961), 290–91n. 103; meeting of August 1961, 168, 192–205, 228; meeting of March 1961, 167–70; Ulbricht's role in, 293nn. 154, 155; and Ulbricht's speech (August 1961) and request to seal the border around West Berlin, 195–99
Warsaw Pact Declaration on closing the border around West Berlin, 205–6
Warsaw Treaty Organization (WTO). See Warsaw Pact
Weathersby, Kathryn, 4, 143, 233
West Berlin, 99, 104, 106, 111, 123–24, 149–50, 161–66, 169–70, 218–19, 278n. 120, 283n. 22, 303n. 292; and capitalism, 102; and conflicting communist approaches to, 75, 101–2, 146–48, 171, 176, 179; as economic threat to the GDR, 100; free city of, 146, 160, 168, 171, 180; GDR policies concerning, 146–50; refugee problem in, xi, 99, 157–61; sealing of border by Soviet–GDR agreement, 182, 184–90; and status as a "free city," 10, 106, 109–11, 114, 116, 117–18, 122; as subversive

threat to the GDR, 100–101; as "super-domino" to the West, 102, 120, 143; Western access/transit routes between West Berlin and West Germany, 8, 55, 98–99, 105, 106, 110, 116, 117, 120, 123, 126–27, 134, 136, 144, 147, 153, 156, 162, 171, 175–76, 179, 182, 191, 197, 216, 217, 265n. 184, 278n. 120; Western troops in, 122. See also Berlin Crisis; Berlin sectoral border/inter-Berlin border
West Germany. See Federal Republic of Germany
Wilhelm, Claudia, xii, xiv
Winzer, Otto, 69, 105, 130, 213, 272n. 39
Wismut, 45, 164, 287n. 85
Wittkowski, Greta, 70
Wolf, Hanna, 258–59n. 84
Wollweber, Ernst, 52, 84, 86, 90–91, 92, 93, 264n. 166, 224, 268n. 221; on the Berlin Wall, 219–20
WTO. See Warsaw Pact

Yakubovski, Ivan, 186
Yalta Conference (1945), 16
Yudin, P., 24, 25, 26, 31, 38, 42, 250n. 157

Zaisser, Wilhelm, 21, 23, 32, 35–36, 38, 39–43, 86, 93, 169, 224, 234, 245n. 111, 246–47n. 131; expulsion of from the SED, 50
Zakharov, M. V., 129
Zhivkov, Todor, 201, 204
Zhou Enlai, 165
Zhukov, Marshal, 98
Ziller, Gerhart, 91, 92
Zola, Emile, 59
Zorin, V., 55, 65, 121
Zubok, Vladislav, 60, 113, 272n. 37